The Evolving Structure of South Africa's Economy: Faultlines and Futures

EDITED BY

Seeraj Mohamed, Amuzweni Ngoma and Basani Baloyi

MAPUNGUBWE
INSTITUTE FOR STRATEGIC REFLECTION (MISTRA)

First published by the Mapungubwe Institute for Strategic Reflection (MISTRA) in 2023

142 Western Service Road
Woodmead
Johannesburg

ISBN 978-1-920690-39-7

Production and design by Jacana Media, 2023
Cover design: HotHouse South Africa
Text editor: Ali Parry
Copy editor: Megan Mance
Proofreader: Ali Parry
Indexer: Ali Parry
Designer: Sam van Straaten
Set in Stempel Garamond 10.5/15pt

Please cite this publication as follows:
MISTRA. 2023. *The Evolving Structure of South Africa's Economy: Faultlines and Futures.* Seeraj Mohamed, Amuzweni Ngoma and Basani Baloyi (eds). Johannesburg: Mapungubwe Institute for Strategic Reflection

Contents

PART 3: GOVERNANCE, LABOUR AND LIVELIHOODS

Acknowledgements

The Mapungubwe Institute for Strategic Reflection (MISTRA) would like to express its sincere gratitude to the editors of this volume: Seeraj Mohamed, Amuzweni Ngoma and Basani Baloyi. Thanks are also extended to Wandile Ngcaweni, the project coordinator. MISTRA is honoured to have worked with the authors who contributed to this volume, and extends its profound thanks to them too. Gratitude also goes to the peer reviewers whose assistance was invaluable in ensuring the quality of this publication.

Thanks are also due to the MISTRA staff who contributed to the successful outcome of this project: Prof Susan Booysen for her efforts to ensure that the publication meets the highest standards; Dr Khwezi Mabasa who helped with project conceptualisation and initiation; Lorraine Pillay for financial management with support from Magati Nindi-Galenge; and Terry Shakinovsky for overseeing the publication process. Deepest gratitude also goes to Joel Netshitenzhe for his thorough reading of the manuscript.

MISTRA extends its appreciation to the production team: Ali Parry who edited the text and Jacana Media who was responsible for the design and layout of the book.

MISTRA funders

Intellectual endeavours of this magnitude are not possible without financial resources. MISTRA thanks the donors who support the Institute and make its work possible. They include:

Anglo American Platinum
Anglo American Head Office

Batho Batho Trust
Department of Science and Innovation
Discovery Central Services
Friedrich-Ebert-Stiftung (FES)
Harith Partners General
National Institute for Humanities and Social Sciences (NIHSS)
Oppenheimer Memorial Trust (OMT)
Royal Bafokeng Holdings
Shell South Africa
Simeka Capital Holdings
Standard Bank
Transnet
Yellowwoods

Acronyms and abbreviations

4IR	Fourth Industrial Revolution
ACSA	Airports Company South Africa
ADRS	Applied Development Research Solutions
AERS	Accelerated Economic Recovery Strategy
AfCFTA	African Continental Free Trade Area
AFOLU	agriculture, forestry and other land use
AgriBEE	agricultural black economic empowerment
AI	artificial intelligence
ANC	African National Congress
APDP	Automotive Production and Development Programme
APSS	Agro-Processing Support Scheme
ARDL	autoregressive distributed lag
AsgiSA	Accelerated and Shared Growth Initiative for South Africa
AU	African Union
AUKUS	Australia, United Kingdom and United States
B4SA	Business for South Africa
B-BBEE	broad-based black economic empowerment
BBC	Black Business Council
BEE	black economic empowerment
BLSA	Business Leadership South Africa
BRICS	Brazil, Russia, India, China, South Africa
BUSA	Business Unity South Africa
CAGR	compound annual growth rate
CBAM	carbon border adjustment mechanism
CCRED	Centre for Competition, Regulation and Economic Development
CCSA	Competition Commission South Africa
CDE	Centre for Development and Enterprise

CEF	Central Energy Fund
CEO	chief executive officer
CGE	computable general equilibrium
CGE	Commission for Gender Equality
CIP	Competitive Industrial Performance (Index)
CIPC	Companies and Intellectual Property Commission
CoGTA	Department of Cooperative Governance and Traditional Affairs
COMESA	Common Market for Eastern and Southern Africa
COP	Conference of the Parties
COSATU	Congress of South African Trade Unions
CPI	consumer price index
CSI	corporate social investment
CSIR	Council for Scientific and Industrial Research
CSP	community, social and personal services
CTL	coal-to-liquid
CWAO	Casual Workers Advice Office
DALRRD	Department of Agriculture, Land Reform and Rural Development
DBE	Department of Basic Education
DBSA	Development Bank of Southern Africa
DCDT	Department of Communications and Digital Technologies
DEL	Department of Employment and Labour
DFFE	Department of Forestry, Fisheries and the Environment
DFI	development finance institution
DG	director-general
DHA	Department of Home Affairs
DHET	Department of Higher Education and Training
DHS	Department of Human Settlements
DIMMSIM	Dynamically Integrated Macro–Micro Simulation Model
DIRCO	Department of International Relations and Cooperation
DMRE	Department of Mineral Resources and Energy
DMV	Department of Military Veterans
DoH	Department of Health
DoT	Department of Transport
DPE	Department of Public Enterprises
DPME	Department of Planning, Monitoring and Evaluation

DPSA	Department of Public Service and Administration
DPWI	Department of Public Works and Infrastructure
DSAC	Department of Sport, Arts and Culture
DSBD	Department of Small Business Development
DSD	Department of Social Development
DSI	Department of Science and Innovation
DSP	developmental state paradigm
DT	Department of Tourism
DTI	Department of Trade and Industry
DTIC	Department of Trade, Industry and Competition
DWS	Department of Water and Sanitation
DWYPD	Department of Women, Youth and Persons with Disabilities
EAC	East African Community
EAM	East Asian Miracle
ECB	European Central Bank
ECM	error correction model
EDD	Economic Development Department
EIUG	Energy Intensive Users Group
EPA	Economic Partnership Agreement
EPC	engineering, procurement and construction
ERRP	Economic Reconstruction and Recovery Plan
Esops	employee share-ownership plans
ETIGC	economic transformation, inclusive growth and competitiveness
ETS	Emissions Trading Scheme
EU	European Union
EVI	Economic Vulnerability Index
FDI	foreign direct investment
FI	financial institution
FIREBS	finance, insurance, real estate and business services
FMCG	fast-moving consumer goods
FOLU	forestry and other land use
FOSAD	Forum of South African Directors-General
FSSC	Food Safety System Certification
FTA	free trade agreement
FTSS	full-time shop steward

GCIS	Government Communication and Information System
GDP	gross domestic product
GEAR	Growth, Employment and Redistribution
GEM	Global Entrepreneurship Monitor
GEPF	Government Employees Pension Fund
GFC	global financial crisis
GFCF	gross fixed capital formation
GGT	Growing Gauteng Together
GHG	greenhouse gas
GNP	gross national product
GPG	Gauteng Provincial Government
GVC	global value chain
GW	gigawatt
HACCP	Hazard Analysis Critical Control Point
HCW	healthcare worker
HoD	head of department
ICT	information and communication technology
IDC	Industrial Development Corporation
IDMS	infrastructure development management system
IIO	Infrastructure and Investment Office
ILO	International Labour Organization
IMC	Inter-Ministerial Committee
IMF	International Monetary Fund
IoT	Internet of Things
IP	intellectual property
IPAP	Industrial Policy Action Plan
IP–ERR	Implementation Plan for Economic Reconstruction and Recovery
IPP	independent power producer
IPPU	industrial processes and product use
IRP	Integrated Resource Plan
ISDP	Indicative Strategic Development Plan
ISI	import-substitution industrialisation
ISO	International Organization for Standardization
IT	information technology
ITAC	International Trade Administration Commission
ITC	information and communication technology

JCS	Justice and Correctional Services
JETP	Just Energy Transition Partnership
JSE	Johannesburg Stock Exchange
KPI	key performance indicator
KW	kilowatt
LDC	least-developed country
LDHV	low density, high value
LPI	Logistics Performance Index
MCSA	Minerals Council South Africa
MDDA	Media Development and Diversity Agency
MDG	Millennium Development Goals
MEC	minerals–energy complex
MEFC	minerals–energy–finance complex
MERG	Macroeconomic Research Group
MERS	Microeconomic Reform Strategy
MIDP	Motor Industry Development Programme
MISTRA	Mapungubwe Institute for Strategic Reflection
MNC	multinational corporation
MNE	multinational enterprise
MSA	Moving South Africa
MTBPS	Medium-Term Budget Policy Statement
MTEF	Medium-Term Expenditure Framework
MW	megawatt
NAACAM	National Association of Automotive Component and Allied Manufacturers
NBI	National Business Initiative
NDC	Nationally Determined Contribution
NDP	National Development Plan
Nedlac	National Economic Development and Labour Council
NEET	not in employment, education or training
NEF	National Empowerment Fund
NGO	non-governmental organisation
NGP	New Growth Path
NHFC	National Housing Finance Corporation
NIBUS	National Informal Business Upliftment Strategy
NIC	newly industrialised country
NIDS	National Income Dynamics Study

NIP 2050	National Infrastructure Plan 2050
NPC	National Planning Commission
NPM	New Public Management
NT	National Treasury
NUMSA	National Union of Metal Workers of South Africa
NYC	National Youth Commission
NYDA	National Youth Development Agency
OECD	Organisation for Economic Cooperation and Development
OEM	original equipment manufacturer
OPEC	Organization of the Petroleum Exporting Countries
OSH	occupational safety and health
QGIS	Quantum Geographic Information System
PARI	Public Affairs Research Institute
PCAS	Policy Coordination and Advisory Services
PCC	Presidential Climate Commission
PCSOE	Presidential Commission on State-Owned Enterprises
PEAC	Presidential Economic Advisory Council
PERSAL	Personnel and Salaries Management System
PFI	public financial institution
PFMA	Public Finance Management Act
PGM	platinum group metal
PIC	Public Investment Corporation
PICC	Presidential Infrastructure Coordinating Commission
PPA	power purchase agreement
PPGI	Public–Private Growth Initiative
PPI	producer price index
PPI	Port Performance Index
PPP	public–private partnership
PPPFA	Preferential Procurement Policy Framework Act
Prasa	Passenger Rail Agency of South Africa
PSEC	Presidential SOE Council
PV	photovoltaic
PWC	Presidential Working Committee
PWC	post-Washington Consensus
PWV	Pretoria, Witwatersrand, Vereeniging
QLFS	Quarterly Labour Force Survey

R&D	research and development
RBCT	Richards Bay Coal Terminal
RDP	Reconstruction and Development Programme
REC	regional economic community
REER	real effective exchange rate
REIPPPP	Renewable Energy Independent Power Producer Procurement Programme
RET	radical economic transformation
RISDP	Regional Indicative Strategic Development Plan
ROI	return on investment
RSA	Republic of South Africa
RTG	Ready to Govern
RVC	regional value chain
SAA	South African Airways
SAB	South African Breweries
SABC	South African Broadcasting Corporation
SACP	South African Communist Party
SACU	Southern African Customs Union
SADC	Southern African Development Community
SADCC	Southern African Development Coordination Conference
SAFCOL	South African Forestry Company Limited
SAHHA	South African Heavy Hauls Association
SAIRR	South African Institute of Race Relations
Saita	South African Informal Traders' Alliance
SANRAL	South African National Roads Agency
SAP	structural adjustment policy/programme
SAPO	South African Post Office
SAR&H	South African Railways & Harbours
SARB	South African Reserve Bank
SARS	South African Revenue Service
SASBO	South African Society of Bank Officials
SCIS	Southern Centre for Inequality Studies
SCP	social compacting paradigm
SDGs	Sustainable Development Goals
SEDA	Small Enterprise Development Agency
SEFA	Small Enterprise Finance Agency
SEZ	special economic zone

SIDs	small island developing states
SIP	Strategic Integrated Project
SME	small and medium enterprise
SMME	small, medium and micro enterprise
SOE	state-owned enterprise
SoNA	State of the Nation
SSA	State Security Agency
SSA	sub-Saharan Africa
StatsSA	Statistics South Africa
TEU	twenty-foot equivalent unit
TIPS	Trade and Industrial Policy Strategies
TMF	Thabo Mbeki Foundation
UID	Unity in Diversity
UIF	Unemployment Insurance Fund
UK	United Kingdom
UN	United Nations
UNCTAD	United Nations Conference on Trade and Development
UNDP	United Nations Development Programme
UNFCCC	United Nations Framework Convention on Climate Change
UNIDO	United Nations Industrial Development Organization
UNRISD	United Nations Research Institute for Social Development
US	United States
US Fed	US Federal Reserve
USB IFR	University of Stellenbosch Business School Institute for Futures Research
USSR	Union of Soviet Socialist Republics
VAT	value-added tax
VC	value chain
WC	Washington Consensus
WEF	World Economic Forum
WMC	white monopoly capital
WRI	World Resources Institute
WTG	wind turbine generator
WTO	World Trade Organization

Contributors

Alan Hirsch is Professor of Development Policy and Practice at The Nelson Mandela School of Public Governance at the University of Cape Town (UCT) and its founding director from 2011 to 2019. Born in Cape Town, he studied economics and history at UCT, the University of the Witwatersrand (Wits) and Columbia University and has also taught at UCT.

Amuzweni Ngoma is a political economy researcher at the Mapungubwe Institute for Strategic Reflection (MISTRA). She has an honours degree in Development Studies and an MA in Sociology from the University of the Witwatersrand (Wits). With over 15 years of research experience, she has managed and overseen the publication of multiple research and evaluation reports. Her areas of development expertise cover economic development, entrepreneurship and skills development. She has also initiated and implemented research and development projects on topics ranging from HIV/AIDS, race, the economy and politics, to class, gender and youth.

Andrew Mukandila holds an MCom in Development Theory and Policy, a postgraduate degree in Mathematical Statistics and a master's degree in Demography and Population Studies from the University of the Witwatersrand (Wits). Andrew's main research interests are numerical and data analysis and industrialisation and policy development in a South African context.

Asghar Adelzadeh is the Director and Chief Economic Modeller at Applied Development Research Solutions (ADRS) in the US. With over 20 years of experience in economic modelling, he has built large-scale economic models with user-friendly web interfaces to enable policymakers and analysts to design and assess the impact of policy choices and make future projections.

Ayabonga Cawe is a development economist, columnist, radio presenter, photographer and activist. He is Managing Director of Xesibe Holdings (Pty) Ltd, a platform offering advisory, facilitation and content development services across a wide range of fields. He hosts #MetroFMTalk on Metro FM and writes a regular column for the *Daily Maverick* and *Business Day*. He is also a co-founder of Rethink Africa NPC, a youth-led policy research, advocacy and advisory organisation. His professional experience spans economic research, policy and supply chain analysis, advocacy, development programme design, and monitoring and evaluation (M&R). He has taken part in a wide range of research, advisory and policy engagements on development issues surrounding agriculture, rail, urban design and labour market policy.

Basani Baloyi is the Climate, Energy and Infrastructure Programme Lead at the Institute for Economic Justice (IEJ). She is a development economist, feminist and activist. She acquired her research experience while in academia, working on industrial policy issues at the Centre for Competition, Regulation and Economic Development (CCRED) at the University of Johannesburg (UJ) and the Corporate Strategy and Industrial Development (CSID) Unit at the University of the Witwatersrand (Wits). She is the former Inequality Programme Lead at Oxfam South Africa, where she used her research and management experience to advocate, drive and coordinate economic and social justice, in partnership with social movements. She holds a PhD in Economics from the University of London, and an MA in Public Policy and an MCom in Economics, both from Wits.

Ben Fine is Professor of Economics in the School of Oriental and African Studies at the University of London. He has (co)authored or edited over 30 books and published over 250 articles covering economic theory, economic and social policy, development economics, political economy and the history of economic thought. He also has a strong intellectual commitment to interdisciplinarity.

Busani Ngcaweni is the principal of the National School of Government, having previously served as Deputy Director-General in The Presidency. Prior to that, he was Senior Policy Analyst in the Presidency's Policy Unit, following his tenure as a senior manager and director at the Umsobomvu Youth Fund. He has also worked as a researcher for various academic and private-sector institutions.

Eddie Rakabe is the Senior Researcher for Political Economy at the Mapungubwe Institute for Strategic Reflection (MISTRA). Prior to joining MISTRA, he worked at the Financial and Fiscal Commission focusing on public education and health finance, housing, public expenditure management and intergovernmental fiscal relations. He has also worked as an economist at the National Treasury and in the South African Square Kilometre Array (SKA) bid at the National Research Foundation (NRF). He holds a master's degree in Economic Development from the University of Johannesburg (UJ).

Irvindra Naidoo is an independent strategy, infrastructure and transport analyst and advisor. He spent more than 15 years at Transnet as Lead Strategy Analyst to the Transnet Executive Committee and Board and has extensive experience in the planning and rollout of large-scale infrastructure projects. He is currently Chairman of the BRICS Business Council's Infrastructure Working Group whose role is to crowd in private investment in infrastructure for the purpose of improving intra-regional and intra-BRICS trade connectivity. He holds a BSc degree in Electronic Engineering from the University of Natal and a Master of Business Leadership (MBL) from the University of South Africa (UNISA).

Jason Bell is an economist and researcher at the Centre for Competition, Regulation and Economic Development (CCRED) at the University of Johannesburg (UJ) and part of the latter's Industrial Development

Think Tank (IDTT) focusing on issues related to industrial policy, political economy, and regional and global value chains in South Africa and the wider SADC region. He holds a BCom with majors in economic science, corporate finance and investment from the University of the Witwatersrand (Wits). He also holds an honours in Economic Sciences (Cum Laude) and an MCom in Economics.

Jesse Burton is a researcher in the Energy Systems Research Group at the University of Cape Town (UCT) and a senior associate at global think tank E3G, where she provides analysis and policy advice on coal transitions globally. She is a specialist in coal and electricity markets and energy and climate change policy in South Africa. Her research focuses on the challenges and opportunities associated with the energy transition in coal-dependent countries, including just transition strategies.

Joel Netshitenzhe is the Executive Director of the Mapungubwe Institute for Strategic Reflection (MISTRA). He has an MSc in Financial Economics, a Postgraduate Diploma in Economic Principles from the University of London and a Diploma in Political Science from the Institute of Social Sciences in Moscow. He is currently a visiting professor at the University of the Witwatersrand (Wits) School of Governance.

Lucy Baker works in the Science Policy Research Unit at the University of Sussex and is Associate Professor, DST/NRF/Newton Fund Trilateral Chair in Transformative Innovation, the Fourth Industrial Revolution and Sustainable Development in the College of Business and Economics at the University of Johannesburg (UJ). She has theoretical expertise in development studies, political economy, economic geography and transitions to sustainability. Her three main research focus areas are: ownership, finance and renewable energy; electricity governance in a time of technological disruption; and technological capabilities and global production networks in renewable energy.

Mark Swilling is the programme coordinator of the Sustainable Development Programme in the School of Public Leadership at Stellenbosch University, the Academic Director of the Sustainability Institute and the co-director of the Stellenbosch Centre for Complex Systems in Transition at Stellenbosch University. During his career, his primary research interest has been 'societal transitions' within the wider discipline of sustainability science and governance, with a particular contextual focus on urban sustainability.

Miriam Di Paola is an activist and independent researcher focusing on labour and gender, public health and development. She has worked with trade unions in South Africa (National Union of Metalworkers of South Africa (NUMSA) and South African Federation of Trade Unions (SAFTU), amongst others) and internationally (European Federation of Public Service Unions (EPSU) and Public Services International (PSI)) and has authored numerous reports (for the International Labour Organization (ILO), Friedrich-Ebert-Stiftung (FES) and Oxfam South Africa) and academic publications on subjects relating to her areas of interest. She is a PhD candidate at the Centre for Researching Education and Labour (REAL) at the University of the Witwatersrand (Wits).

Monde Gqoli is the Executive Manager of Commercial Strategy Design in the Group Strategy and Planning function at Transnet, having previously worked as a management consultant. Monde has 13 years of experience working in industry and the professional services sector, with the last two years having been spent in the Economics Strategy function at Transnet. He holds a BA from the University of the Witwatersrand (Wits) and a Postgraduate Diploma in Business Administration (PDM) and MBA from the Wits Business School and has also obtained certificates in Infrastructure Financing and Investment.

Musawenkosi H. Malabela is a researcher at the Chris Hani Institute (CHI). Prior to joining the CHI, he was an assistant lecturer in Sociology at the University of Johannesburg (UJ). He has also worked as a researcher at the National Labour and Economic Development Institute (NALEDI) and an assistant researcher in the Society, Work and Politics Institute (SWOP) at the University of the Witwatersrand (Wits). His research interests include trade union democracy, local government politics, the ANC at the sub-national level, and broad issues around social cohesion and justice and the world of work. He holds a master's degree in Political Sociology and a BA (Honours) in Industrial Sociology from Wits. He is currently pursuing a PhD in Industrial Sociology at Wits.

Nina Callaghan is a master's student at Stellenbosch University, with a keen interest in formulating better questions around, and enhancing research techniques in, the areas of development, politics, family relations and human interactions. Her research on governance focuses specifically on state capture and geopolitics and how to better influence these narratives in the public domain. Previously she was a director of Children's Radio Foundation (an NGO), a broadcast journalist and a theatre performer.

Nkululeko Gobhozi is a railway engineer with 20 years of experience in the development and deployment of condition-assessment systems, data-communication interfaces and integration, digital systems integration and systems engineering. He is currently Chief Engineer at Transnet Freight Rail leading the multi-disciplinary engineering team of Technology Management. He holds a BSc in Electrical Engineering from the University of Cape Town (UCT), and a GDE in Industrial Engineering and an MEng in Systems Engineering from the University of the Witwatersrand (Wits).

Reena Das Nair is a senior researcher at the Centre for Competition, Regulation and Economic Development (CCRED) and Associate Professor and Programme Coordinator in the Master of Commerce in Competition and Economic Regulation programme at the University of Johannesburg (UJ). Prior to joining CCRED, she was Programme Manager: Industrial Policy at Trade and Industrial Policy Strategies (TIPS). She has also worked for specialist economic consultancy, Acacia Economics, where she advised on competition and regulatory economics.

Ruth Castel-Branco is the research manager on the Future of Work Project. Previously, Ruth worked at the International Labour Office in Mozambique focusing on social and maternity protection. She first became interested in questions surrounding labour as a student activist, eventually becoming a labour organiser at DC Jobs with Justice in the US. Ruth is an alumna of the International Center for Development and Decent Work and a fellow of the Open Society Foundations' Inequality Fellowship Program. Her research interests include agrarian transformation and the changing nature of work, (informal) workers' rights and organisation, the redistributive role of the state and social protection. She has a BA in Geography and African Studies from the University of Wisconsin-Madison, an MA in Development Studies from the University of KwaZulu-Natal (UKZN) and a PhD in Sociology from the University of the Witwatersrand (Wits).

Samantha Ashman is Associate Professor of Economics in the School of Economics at the University of Johannesburg (UJ). She acts as the director of the university's MPhil programme in Industrial Policy, run jointly with the Senegal-based UN-IDEP (African Institute for Economic Development and Planning), which is aimed at enhancing the knowledge and capacity of African policymakers in the field of industrial development. She is currently visiting the African Studies Centre at the University of Oxford where she is working on a research monograph on the South African economy, exploring how and why it remains dominated by many economic, social and environmental extremes.

Seeraj Mohamed has worked in the field of economic policy and development since the early 1990s. He is the Deputy Director for Economics in the South African Parliamentary Budget Office. Previously, he was Associate Professor of Economics at the University of the Western Cape (UWC) and Director of the Corporate Strategy and Industrial Development research programme at the University of the Witwatersrand (Wits).

Teboho Bosiu is a researcher at the Centre for Competition, Regulation and Economic Development (CCRED) at the University of Johannesburg (UJ). His research work has largely focused on industrial development, competition policy, development finance, black economic empowerment (BEE), value chain analysis, and the role of large and lead firms. He holds a master's degree in Economics from the University of the Witwatersrand (Wits).

Thabang Sefalafala is a lecturer in the Department of Sociology and a research fellow in the Southern Centre for Inequality Studies (SCIS) at the University of the Witwatersrand (Wits). Previously, he worked for the Gauteng Department of Economic Development (GDED) as Deputy Director for Sector and Industry Development. He is also a former research fellow in the Society, Work and Development Institute (SWOP) at Wits. His current research focuses on the psychosocial impact of unemployment, the changing nature of work, livelihoods, inequality and masculinity in South Africa. He holds a PhD in Sociology from Wits.

Thando Vilakazi is the executive Director of the Centre for Competition, Regulation and Economic Development (CCRED) and a senior lecturer in the School of Economics at the University of Johannesburg (UJ). His research focuses on competition policy, economic regulation, and industrial development in Africa.

Vukani Nkasa has formal training both in commerce and science, with 15 years of experience in the fields of economic research and business analytics. He is currently Chief Economist at Transnet National Ports Authority. He holds an MCom in Maritime Economics from the University of KwaZulu-Natal (UKZN) and various certificates in econometrics and financial modelling.

Wendy McCallum, a development economist, is a researcher at the Centre for Sustainability Transitions (CST) at Stellenbosch University, focusing on how to leverage development finance to improve the economic and social situation in developing regions. In this regard, she brings together financiers, government, business, academia and communities to shape innovative, socially just approaches to energy transition and other development initiatives. She premises this work on the combination of her practical experience, including working for the Development Bank of Southern Africa (DBSA), and academic qualifications in economics, futures studies and development finance.

Yacoob Abba Omar is the Director for Operations at the Mapungubwe Institute for Strategic Reflection (MISTRA). Previously he was Head of Strategy and Communications at the Banking Association South Africa (BASA). He has also served as South African Ambassador to Oman and the United Arab Emirates respectively and as Deputy Director-General of South Africa's Government Communication Information System (GCIS).

Preface

There are serious questions regarding the extent to which the South African economy has evolved to be developmental, resilient and inclusive. In the wake of the global financial crisis and now the COVID-19 pandemic, South Africa is grappling with low economic growth and high unemployment, rendering poverty and inequality persistent societal challenges. These obstacles exert pressure on South Africa to foster structural transformation so that it may achieve its developmental goals. Informed by this urgent intent, this book examines the evolving structure of the South African economy over time.

The imperative for structural transformation in South Africa comes at a historically significant moment for humanity. More than ever, the nation is confronted by a polycrisis of colliding transitions – ranging from a maladjusted political economy to geopolitical tensions, declining state legitimacy, natural disasters and violent crime. The COVID-19 pandemic aggravated many of these challenges.

The Evolving Structure of South Africa's Economy was written against this backdrop. The authors have been alive to how South Africa's structural transformation agenda is affected by the global context, including rising inflation and interest rates. This context brings important nuances to their perspectives on structural transformation.

South Africa's economy is characterised by uneven outcomes. In the first 15 years of democracy, the country experienced periods of high economic growth, but the last decade-and-a-half has been characterised by low growth. The authors of this book offer technical and analytical insights on the overlapping structural faultlines that have produced this uneven performance. Bound by an analytical thread that centres on power relations and political settlements, the authors explain the changes and continuities of South Africa's economic structure. They take cognisance of spatial disparities and capital intensity within the context of low skills, uneven power relations and low investment alongside a trust deficit in state–business and labour–business relations, as well as inadequate attention given to environmental challenges and social reproduction.

Other structural constraints discussed in this volume include macroeconomic policy and its effect on the real economy, state–capital relations, state capabilities, labour and the changing nature of work, investments and technology, and integration into regional and global value chains. The authors show how poor governance and corruption have slowed down structural reform. This has been further exacerbated by the inconsistent availability of energy and the deterioration of logistics and transport. These structural faultlines have also slowed down the economic rebound of wholesale and retail trade and the construction sector – areas in which many low- and medium-skilled workers earn their livelihood.

Over recent decades, the financial and services sector has grown to dominate the economy, especially in its employment intensity. Notwithstanding this, South Africa's economy has not diversified out of its minerals–energy core, and manufacturing has been declining. It is in this context that this book discusses deindustrialisation and deagrarianisation as significant shifts within a financialised minerals–energy complex (MEC).

Authors adopt multiple theoretical and empirical perspectives to take stock of the historical and contemporary structure of the South African economy, its evolving nature and possible future pathways. Their analyses take forward the debate on the extreme social impacts of globalised and financialised economic structures, which are dominated by large corporations.

The book details the structural reforms and policy regimes necessary for increasing productive capacity in South Africa's agriculture, manufacturing, agro-processing, retail and services, energy and mining sectors. It also reflects on the role that micro and informal enterprises can play if afforded the necessary support.

The technical detail and analyses in the book point to the need for a radical review of macroeconomic policy to facilitate reindustrialisation and to leverage interlinkages that will reduce the country's chronic vulnerability to unemployment, poverty and inequality.

Critically, the transition to a low carbon economy, with associated opportunities in the hydrogen economy, can help to further change the structure of the South African economy. A 'green' MEC can open up new opportunities across value chains and help empower blacks, women and youth.

Given the magnitude of the challenges, political settlements and compacts amongst social actors are urgently required.

The Mapungubwe Institute for Strategic Reflection (MISTRA) expresses its deep appreciation to the contributors to this volume, whose insights will, we hope, generate important reflections amongst policymakers, industry leaders and broader society. We are also grateful to MISTRA's donors who made the publication of this research possible.

Prof. Sibusiso Vil-Nkomo
Chairperson: MISTRA Board of Governors

ONE

Introduction

Seeraj Mohamed, Amuzweni Ngoma
and Basani Baloyi

This book explores important aspects of the structural transformation of the South African economy over time, providing a policy vision and discussion centred on progressive, developmental transformation. This vision of structural transformation is closely associated with improving conditions for households, and the reproduction thereof, within a broader framework of social and economic development. The transformation of the economy is focused on reconfiguring the supply side and economic infrastructure, not only to support economic growth but also to ensure that such growth induces generally improved wellbeing.

The negative impacts of neoliberal globalisation and the adoption of neoliberal policies have manifested across the globe, and in South Africa they have manifested as greater macroeconomic instability and heightened insecurity at the household level. The ongoing cycle of poverty, inequality and unemployment, low levels of fixed investment in productive activities and an increase in the financialisation of the economy have led to declining economic resilience, heightened risks of extreme weather events induced by climate change, geopolitical conflicts, and strong prospects of future epidemics and pandemics as well as financial crises and contagion. As a result, this book includes but also extends beyond the common characterisation of structural transformation as a shift from low- to high-productivity economic activities within a country. Rather, the structural transformation of the economy is regarded as one side of the coin, while societal resilience, household reproduction and the overarching goal of improved wellbeing in an inclusive society constitute the other side.

Structural transformation is typically regarded as changes in the contribution and size of different sectors in the economy, with primary sectors (such as mining and agriculture) accounting for a smaller share of economic activity, and higher value-adding sectors (such as manufacturing and associated productive services sectors) accounting for a larger share of economic activity.

Lewis (1954) developed a two-sector model showing how productivity shifts would spur economic growth and development when more labour moved from the traditional agricultural sector to the modern industrial sector. Studies such as those by Kuznets (1973) on developed countries and Chenery and Syrquin (1975) on developing countries (after the Second World War) identified patterns of structural change, including the growth of industrialisation, the accumulation of more physical and human capital, expanding urbanisation, and shifts in demand for food and basic necessities to a wider array of manufactured goods and services. Kuznets argues that structural transformation leads to the modernisation of an economy. He mentions changes in education and shifting class positions as well as changes in belief systems and customs as being a result of urbanisation and work experiences. He portrays structural transformation as requiring a 'controlled revolution' because of the widespread changes that must be introduced within a society (Kuznets, 1973: 52).

Importantly, the interrelationship between improved wellbeing and social welfare with structural transformation was present in the early literature on development economics and patterns of change in economies.

An updated definition of structural transformation, less encumbered by outdated perspectives on modernisation and anchored in the widespread view that industrialisation is important for structural transformation, is provided by Andreoni et al. (2021: 1):

> By structural transformation, we refer to changes in the structure of the economy towards activities with the scope for sustained high growth in productivity, in particular through cumulative improvements. This has a strong sectoral dimension, and specifically recognizes the central importance of industrialization to a path of sustained economic growth and catching up.

Andreoni et al. (2021: 1) make the important point that causality between industrial development and structural transformation runs in both directions. They assert:

> [I]ndustrialization both drives and is sustained by broader social, institutional, and political economy changes. And these changes are crucial for delivering sustainable and inclusive outcomes along countries' development journeys.

Structural transformation includes the diversification and deepening of the industrial base. Accordingly, innovation and technological change are important aspects of structural transformation. Innovation and technology have stimulated greater linkages and interactions between sectors. In some cases, such as the agricultural and agro-processing or automotive sectors (evidenced in the linkages between retailing, services and manufacturing), it is technology-driven change that has strengthened interactions and integration.

The approach to structural transformation discussed here is that, ultimately, structural transformation requires disruption and a shift in the power relations within the economy and in the relationship between the state and vested interests. Chapters in this book, particularly in Parts 1 and 2, provide important insights that help to expand on the common definition of structural transformation.

In Chapter 13, Baloyi, Di Paola and Mukandila provide an important feminist political economy analysis, showing the inadequacy of definitions of structural transformation that separate economic, ecological and social dynamics. In Chapter 2, Fine and Mohamed explain that neoliberal ideology and discourse have undermined and eroded the concepts of transformation and development. They propose that local economies should be viewed as national systems of accumulation within a global context. Their chapter draws on the concept of a minerals–energy complex (MEC) as the South African system of accumulation developed in Fine and Rustomjee (1996). Furthermore, they argue that with the incorporation of the MEC into globalised, financialised neoliberalism, the term minerals–energy–finance complex (MEFC) is more apposite.

Ashman, in Chapter 3, makes a case that even though the MEC has been degraded, the MEFC is the best framework for understanding the South African economy today. This view is supported in Chapter 6 by Vilakazi and Bosiu in their analysis of key trends amongst the top 100 firms on the Johannesburg Stock Exchange (JSE). Therefore, structural transformation in South Africa should consider reversing gender discrimination and addressing the inadequate economic structure associated with the MEFC, including reversing the financialisation of the economy.

In Chapter 7, Cawe considers broad-based black economic empowerment (B-BBEE) and the important additional requirement that the transformation of the economy should address the ongoing racially determined concentration of ownership and wealth in South Africa. Cawe reflects on the important role that the state can play in supporting B-BBEE in renewable energy and the just transition. In Chapter 8, Das Nair and Bell highlight the need to address current ownership patterns and power structures in, and the control of, value chains. Then, in Chapter 9, Baker and Burton discuss the issue of the just transition as a consideration in structural transformation.

Justice and equality were intrinsic to the vision of a new democratic South African society during the struggle against apartheid. For many, the Freedom Charter (adopted in Kliptown in 1955) is a manifestation of that alternative vision. People wanted land, liberty and peace. They wished to live in 'brotherhood', with 'equal rights and opportunities for everyone, regardless of colour, race, sex or belief' (Freedom Charter, 1955). The struggle against racial oppression was aimed at achieving the just transformation of society, where wealth would be shared by all. To this end, it was envisaged that a transformed, post-apartheid, democratic state would drive a programme of structural economic transformation to ensure inclusivity in the provision of social and economic services related to housing, employment, education, nutrition and healthcare (Freedom Charter, 1955). South Africans had witnessed the defeat of fascism and were influenced by the liberation struggle for independence from colonialism and self-determination after the Second World War. They drew lessons from developed countries' post-war reconstruction efforts and recovery. The Keynesian economic policies and the building of democratic welfare states in all the (then) developed countries undoubtedly had a strong influence on those struggling against apartheid and their vision of the future.

According to Van Niekerk (2013: 116–117), this post-war conceptualisation of the democratic welfare state '... was the inspiration for generations of thinkers within the ANC [African National Congress] who saw its value for a post-segregation post-apartheid South Africa'. This was a vision of a capitalist South Africa with a deeply embedded state that would regulate finance and its allocation in the economy to promote investment and employment. The embedded state would own banks, mines and industrial enterprises. State-owned enterprises (SOEs) and agencies would build houses and infrastructure and provide important services – the latter, in particular, being the responsibility of large-scale utilities, such as electricity and water service providers. As Naidoo, Gqoli, Nkasa and Gobhozi point out in Chapter 10, underinvestment in the rail network (including the underutilisation of closed lines), reduced port efficiency and limited integration across the various modes of transport have hampered the development of efficient logistics systems. Their chapter traces the main driving forces behind the modal shift from rail to road and illustrates how this has adversely affected the agricultural, mining, beneficiation and consumption supply chains, thus eroding the efficiency and competitiveness of these sectors.

The above-mentioned notion of an embedded state was both acknowledged and prevalent, albeit at different levels of intensity, in all the Western, developed-country, welfare capitalist states during the post-Second World War period until the rise of neoliberalism (Glyn, 2007; Helleiner, 1994). It also influenced the future leaders of liberation movements struggling against colonialism (Amsden, 2008). Social democratic and welfare capitalist ideology coexisted uneasily with that of strongly embedded states, alongside visions (within many nationalist movements and struggles) of future socialist states. However, neoliberalism would ultimately gain hegemony over embedded welfare capitalism in Zimbabwe, Namibia and South Africa as well as in countries that had been part of the Soviet Bloc before it eventually crumbled. The false dichotomy between the state and the market, which took hold with the advent of neoliberalism, was reinforced during the Cold War. The anti-welfare, neoliberal ideas popularised by the likes of Margaret Thatcher and Ronald Reagan (Prime Minister of the United Kingdom (UK) and President of the United States (US), respectively), aided by the Washington Consensus, were advocated in developing countries through the World Bank and International Monetary Fund (IMF). This process led to the imposition of a dominant ideological perspective that capitalism should have laissez-faire policies and markets should be deregulated, and that welfare created an unhealthy dependence. The triumphalism of neoliberals after the collapse of the Soviet Union and the end of the Cold War reinforced this neoliberal perspective of capitalism, including in developing countries.

The history of structural transformation efforts in developed and developing countries has shown that structural transformation that diversifies and deepens manufacturing and productive services, while also enhancing societal wellbeing, requires macroeconomic stability and containment of the disruptive effects of inadequately regulated finance (Chang et al., 2014). People's understanding of macroeconomic stability in the period following the Second World War, when Keynesian macroeconomic views were dominant, was very different from the neoliberal macroeconomic perspectives adopted in the late 1970s. The main goal of macroeconomic policy in most developed and many developing countries after the war was to achieve full employment, with the state managing aggregate demand to attain and maintain full employment (Chang et al., 2014). Fiscal policy was dominant and monetary policy supported fiscal policy choices within this full employment-focused macroeconomic regime.

Agreements in terms of the use of capital controls and managed currencies were part and parcel of the Bretton Woods arrangements. Central banks were not independent, and many played a developmental role during the post-war recovery efforts (Epstein, 2009). This approach to macroeconomic and financial policymaking provided late industrialising countries, such as the Asian Tigers, with an economic environment in which high levels of domestic aggregate demand and macroeconomic and financial stability were ensured. Trade regulations, capital controls and a financial regulatory regime all nurtured and protected countries' industrialisation and developmental programmes, while constraining harmful financial speculation and capital flight.

The impact of neoliberalism on developing countries has been particularly severe, with the challenges of laissez-faire policies in increasingly integrated global trade and financial markets contributing significantly to the 1980s international debt crisis. The structural adjustment programmes of the 1980s reversed social and industrial development gains made in many African and Latin American countries during the post-independence era (Hujo, 2021; Mkandawire and Soludo, 1998). Even the East Asian countries that were less inclined to adopt laissez-faire policies suffered large setbacks in the wake of the Asian financial crisis as a result of financial liberalisation (Crotty and Lee, 2009; Palma, 2003).

Changes in global corporate structures from the late 1990s onwards and the reorganisation of global value chains have contributed significantly to increased concentration of global markets (Nolan, 2003). Today, most global value chains are dominated by lead corporations based in countries of the Global North (Lee and Gereffi, 2015).[1] The financialisation of corporations and economies of the North had a marked influence on the governance and functioning of most global value chains. The end of the Cold War was expected to reduce geopolitical conflicts. However, these have continued unabated since the collapse of the Soviet Union and the fall of the Berlin Wall. World peace seems increasingly unlikely due to various interrelated challenges, such as the continued reliance on fossil fuels; the growth in demand for raw materials to support fast-growing technology sectors in an increasingly interconnected world; growing inequality within and between countries and regions; ongoing political and social conflict within countries (which is heavily linked to high levels of inequality); the increasing likelihood of debt and financial crises; disasters and widespread displacement caused by global climate change (evidenced in droughts, floods and fires); and the increasing likelihood of pandemics (UNCTAD, 2020). These are some of the key risks to livelihoods and democracy (where it exists) across the globe.

The way in which these events have impacted South Africa have to be examined against the backdrop of South Africa's history and the political, socioeconomic events and policy choices that have shaped outcomes at the national, regional and local scales. In Chapter 4, Adelzadeh painstakingly describes the impact at the national scale of the South African government's shift to neoliberal economic choices over the past few decades. He argues that unless heterodox economic views are embraced, the chronic crises of low economic growth and high levels of unemployment, poverty and inequality will persist in South Africa. Low resilience to serious risks in the global economy and South Africa, which has long wrestled with extraordinarily high levels of unemployment, poverty and inequality, threaten the vitality and viability of democratic institutions and democracy itself. The discontent within impoverished communities, particularly amongst the millions of unemployed young people, exacerbates these risks.

In Chapter 13, Baloyi, Di Paola and Mukandila discuss the impact of uneven development on the crisis of social reproduction in two ways. First, they argue that private accumulation in pre- and post-apartheid South Africa is associated with private-sector corporations shirking their reproductive role, which has been thrust upon an under-resourced public sector and impoverished communities and households. Second, they argue that the exploitation of workers involved in care (including paid and unpaid work) is fundamental to the continuation of capitalist development and that the damaging effects of austerity and financialisation, which have occurred in the health sector, have resulted in work restructuring and casualisation. They point out that workers' (including health workers') livelihoods and lives have been put under severe strain by the very processes of accumulation that they sustain.

Moreover, despite great expectations that the end of apartheid would bring about improved working conditions for the majority, these have largely not materialised, as argued by Sefalafala, Castel-Branco and Malabela in Chapter 14. They use the labour process theory to illustrate how capital has leveraged technological innovation to achieve surplus value, enforce managerial control and weaken the social basis of trade unions. They argue that declining investment in productive sectors as well as outsourcing and automation are some of the dominant drivers of structural unemployment. They also point to emerging forms of worker power in response to changes in the labour process, which they say challenges Braverman's (1975) theory of deskilling and declining worker power in the face of technological innovation. They add that whether the trade union movement can leverage these forms of worker power to shape how technology is used, and for whom, remains to be seen.

High levels of wealth and market concentration not only constrain the growth of new enterprises, employment and B-BBEE, they also exacerbate the parallel streams of lived economic experiences within the South African economy at the spatial scale, which Netshitenzhe, in Chapter 11, labels 'the colony' and 'the metropolis'. His chapter examines key intersecting trends (equity and exclusion) evident in the labour market, disaggregated according to race, gender, age, education and skills, to illustrate the dual development tracks of the South African economy. This duality is also illustrated by the income and asset inequality trends. The chapter envisions a complementary process of facilitating inclusivity by combining the lifting of 'the colony' in terms of developmental outcomes with the continued improvement of 'the metropolis'. Pegged to the three areas of special economic zone (SEZ), agriculture and microenterprise development, Netshitenzhe's proposals point to the need for system-wide institutional initiatives to drive the gradual convergence of the respective development outcomes of the metropolis and the colony.

Importantly, regional integration has contributed to structural transformation in South Africa, providing export markets for South

African manufactures and skill-intensive services, as argued by Hirsch in Chapter 12. However, Hirsch asserts that while the government has committed itself to the deepening of African integration, it has actually weakened the process of integration by adopting a protectionist stance in respect of some imports from other African countries, by moving too slowly in the building of regional value chains, and by being ultra-cautious in affording Africans the freedom to move across borders on the continent. These constraints to entrepreneurship and market access facing a large proportion of the population have paved the way for corruption amongst those able to take advantage of access to state power. Corruption, in turn, has helped to undermine democratic institutions and political stability (Von Holdt, 2019). It has hollowed out and weakened key SOEs and reduced the capacity of the state to deliver basic services in South Africa. It has also eroded society's trust in and opinion of the state and its capabilities.

In Chapter 5, Rakabe characterises South Africa's macroeconomic vulnerabilities as exposure to economic shocks arising from economic openness, import concentration and a lack of export diversification, and describes how macro management strategies adopted since 1994 have been able to address these. Taking a multi-year view, his analysis delves into the origins of, and assesses continuities in, both the vulnerability indicators and the corresponding policy responses and, critically, determines whether these provided a foundation resilient 'enough' to sustain the economy through subsequent episodes of economic shock.

In Chapter 17, Swilling, Callaghan and McCallum contend that the recent emergence of political settlements literature provides insights into the persistent challenge of building effective state capabilities to drive economic development, particularly in the African context. Using the political settlements approach, the authors zero in on the microdynamics of intra-state relations which can help in the rebuilding of SOEs and other state institutions. The authors advance the core argument that building capable and effective state institutions, notably SOEs, requires the establishment of politically protected spaces in which competent groups of people initiate, lead and operationalise purposeful, impactful mandates in ways that simultaneously create agile, goal-driven and efficient institutional capabilities. They argue that the latter process involves more than just 'fixing them' or 'selling them off', but rather engaging in incremental institutional rebuilding.

In Chapter 15, Abba Omar highlights the importance of successful policy implementation through state–society relations. He offers a conceptual and historical analysis of the relationship between developmental states and social compacting in South Africa. Abba Omar employs Ben Fine's (2016) conceptual framing of the developmental state paradigm (DSP) and the social compacting paradigm (SCP) to highlight two formulaic tensions in economic policy positions. The first tension is that South Africa's economic plans identify the need for a capable and developmental state, one that is also 'ethical' and capable of competently driving transformative social compacts. Abba Omar argues that the ethical, capable and developmental state would also be able to coax and incentivise the private sector to participate in the transformation of the economy. The second tension, he claims, inverts the first. In this regard, he advocates discussions amongst social partners with a view to nurturing a robust social compact to build state capacity and set the South African economy on an inclusive growth path.

This book aims to contribute to the literature on the structural transformation of the South African economy by examining not only the economic structure, in terms of the contributions of different sectors to gross domestic product (GDP), but also the broader dynamics within the economy. The aim of this book is not to debate and critique recent literature on the South African economy, but rather to contribute to an important, dynamic discussion on the nature of the South African economy and its transformation over time. The fundamental premise of this book is that understanding the structure of the South African economy involves more than plotting data to reveal relative contributions to GDP, employment, investment and capital stock over time. It also involves more than determining South Africa's relative export success and integration into global value chains. What is equally important is South Africa's economic transformation and the contributions that have been made recently to this conversation.

The book is structured into thematic parts which are explained in the next section.

PART 1: EVOLVING STRUCTURE OF THE SOUTH AFRICAN ECONOMY

Part 1 of this book showcases a collection of chapters that examine, in different ways, the evolving structure of the South African economy. The MEFC, set within a neoliberal capitalist context, illuminates a persistently uneven pattern of development, which is associated with multiple intersecting crises related to climate, unemployment, social reproduction, deindustrialisation and deagrarianisation.

In Chapter 3, Ashman contends that, while some corporations – particularly those with ties to the old MEC which benefited from the racist cheap labour system under colonialism and apartheid – have had some successes, the MEC has fragmented overall. She examines the biggest companies in the economy and how 'the winners' from the transition have directed their strategies at the globalised, financialised world. Ashman's view is that the deep crisis in the economy reflects the fragmentation of the MEC and that no one is capable of driving a reindustrialisation strategy in South Africa.

In Chapter 4, Adelzadeh argues that the country's uneven development can be attributed to the post-apartheid government embracing mainstream economic policies. Adelzadeh indicates that, during the National Development Plan (NDP) period (2010–2019), the country's fiscal and monetary policy measures gradually became tighter and more austere. He argues that the consequences of this austerity and tightening during the 10-year period following the global financial crisis were lower average growth and lower public- and private-sector investment. He warns that since 2019, the South African government has been following an even more austere version of its post-1996 fiscal policy, despite the fact that neither the fiscal nor monetary authorities have presented any evidence that the present combination of fiscal austerity, a restrictive monetary policy and a suite of supply-side measures would improve economic and development outcomes.

In Chapter 6, Vilakazi and Bosiu examine how South Africa's large corporations have changed and describe South Africa's evolving economic structure through a system-of-accumulation lens. This is complemented by a rich empirical analysis of data on company structures, investment and profitability over the period 1990–2020. Vilakazi and Bosiu illustrate how large conglomerates that dominate most market segments have had a significant influence over the country's industrial structure. Their analysis shows that the orientation and evolving strategies of South Africa's lead firms listed in the top tiers of the JSE are important for understanding patterns of accumulation and structural transformation in an economy.

In Chapter 7, Cawe considers B-BBEE within the context of South Africa's energy transition. He considers the role of the state and its use of rents and policy instruments, such as preferential procurement and designation for local production, to foster the adoption of new technologies, enhance the sophistication of local industrial value chains and broaden ownership opportunities and economic participation amongst historically disadvantaged persons, groups and communities.

PART 2: STRUCTURAL CHANGE AND SECTOR BALANCES

Part 2 of this book contains a collection of chapters that examine how structural change has taken place at the sectoral and spatial scales and the implications thereof for sustainable economic development. At the sectoral scale, the dynamics within the manufacturing, retail, agricultural and energy sectors are unpacked through an examination of the power dynamics underpinning structural change. At the spatial scale, efficient logistics, SEZs and regional integration initiatives are identified as mechanisms to drive inclusive development.

In Chapter 8, Das Nair and Bell use a value chain framework, capturing the power dynamics that have affected participation and upgrading in the manufacturing and retail sectors since South Africa's economic liberalisation. They argue that to understand the downward trends in the selected manufacturing sub-sectors and the evolution of the grocery retail landscape, one needs to grasp the power imbalances in value chains and the implications thereof for participation, upgrading and structural transformation.

In Chapter 9, Baker and Burton analyse the evolving structure of the MEC within the context of the just transition, which is increasingly finding its way into South Africa's climate policies and industrial and economic policies. The authors focus on coal and electricity, in particular, and uncover a host of unresolved issues and tensions that emerged in the light of increased pressure and commitments to pursue climate change mitigation strategies and an energy transition.

In Chapter 10, Naidoo, Gqoli, Nkasa and Gobhozi examine the role of efficient logistics in achieving competitive supply chains in South Africa and reflect on the immediate tasks of Transnet, the state rail monopoly. The authors advise that the enhancement of rail capacity and improved provision of services will require a collaborative effort by the various stakeholders involved in the logistics industry, including policymakers, logistics service providers and Transnet.

In Chapter 11, Netshitenzhe offers a forthright account of how to put the South African economy on a path towards greater inclusion through informed policies, programmes and resource allocation. He envisions a complementary process of facilitating inclusivity by combining the lifting of 'the colony' in terms of developmental outcomes with the continued improvement of 'the metropolis', pegged to the three areas of SEZ, agriculture and microenterprise development.

In Chapter 12, Hirsch examines the role of regional integration in structural transformation. He provides a much-needed overview of the different forums and agreements across the southern African region and the continent, including Southern African Development Community (SADC) agreements and the much-vaunted African Continental Free Trade Area (AfCFTA). He arrives at the conclusion that to accelerate the implementation of regional integration commitments and to advance integration, South Africa needs to devote considerably more resources to the development of both public- and private-sector capabilities and, furthermore, to educate citizens about the advantages of African integration.

PART 3: GOVERNANCE, LABOUR AND LIVELIHOODS

Part 3 of this book contains a collection of chapters that pushes the definition of structural transformation beyond the tight confines of sectoral composition, highlighting the implications of South Africa's particular form of structural transformation for social reproduction, structural unemployment, worker livelihoods and solidarity. In addition, the chapters evaluate how social compacts have helped to build bridges between business, the state, labour and the community; how to restore social reproduction through investments in public services; how to restore worker power through new forms of organising; and how to build a developmental state through renewed political settlements.

In Chapter 13, Baloyi, Di Paola and Mukandila argue that instead of pursuing structural transformation through the deepening of industrialisation, which in itself is an insufficient measure of development, post-apartheid South Africa has perpetuated an unhealthy pattern of uneven development, which has contributed to the ongoing crisis of social reproduction. They explain that the MEFC shapes the pattern of uneven development which defines the South African industrial development landscape and is associated with the crisis of economic reproduction. They contend that the crisis of economic reproduction has been forced on and absorbed by an undervalued and unrecognised social reproductive sphere, which is intertwined with and invisibilised by the economic reproductive sphere that it sustains. They point out that workers' livelihoods and lives in the productive sphere (using mining as a case study) and the reproductive sphere (using care work as a case study) have been put under severe strain by the very processes of accumulation that they sustain.

In Chapter 14, Sefalafala, Castel-Branco and Malabela use labour process theory to illustrate how capital has leveraged technological innovation to achieve surplus value, enforce managerial control and weaken the social basis of trade unions. They identify several critical actions that pre-emptive and proactive trade unions could take in response to the impact of technology on the labour market. As such, they call upon trade unions to identify strategic points of organisation and recruit workers in emerging sectors, including young and casual workers; to invest in research, worker education and the upskilling of shop stewards; and to collaborate with worker organisations outside the trade union movement.

In Chapter 15, Abba Omar offers a conceptual and historical analysis of the relationship between developmental states and social compacting in South Africa. His analysis draws on the review of the process to formulate the South African government's October 2020 Economic Reconstruction and Recovery Plan (ERRP). He proposes that, in addition to the National Economic Development and Labour Council (Nedlac) (which should continue to act as an ERRP social dialogue forum), a new institutional arrangement should be developed, aimed at coordinating the social partners in the implementation and assessment of the ERRP. This 'stitching' action would, in the short to medium terms, form the basis of social compacting in the economic reconstruction and recovery drive.

In Chapter 16, Ngoma and Ngcaweni draw on Mazzucatto's important work on the entrepreneurial state and the use of state-led missions to address key social and economic challenges in society. The authors assert that the important role of the state has been undermined by neoliberal ideology and mainstream economic perspectives. The neoliberal ideological perspective presents the state as ineffective and market distorting and therefore advocates a reduced role for the state in society. In South Africa, the impact of poor service delivery and state capture has further compromised the reputation of state institutions and public servants. However, while it is important to address corruption and state capture, efforts should be made to highlight the important role played by the state within society. The capacitation of the state and public servants to support innovation will be an important step in preparing the state to develop missions to address key challenges facing the economy, such as unemployment, a deindustrialisation trend, and growing pressure to embrace the green economy and just transition initiatives to mitigate the effects of climate change.

Chapter 17, by Swilling, Callaghan and McCallum, homes in on the microdynamics of intra-state relations that can help in the rebuilding of SOEs and other state institutions through a political settlements approach. They advise that, instead of proposing another round of grand structural reforms, this rebuilding be based on strengthening existing 'pockets of efficiency' where there are skilled public managers 'creating, maintaining and disrupting' institutional cultures, structures and routines in ways that root out corruption and align with current, context-driven demands.

The overarching aim of this book, therefore, is to offer a bigger and more insightful picture of the interplay between economic development and structural transformation. Its premise is that the structure and nature of an economy is more than what the economy produces. The book provides a specific entry point for analysing society beyond sectoral studies and value chains, probing both the global and domestic political economies in terms of the MEC/MEFC acting as a system of accumulation. It recognises that the future sustainability of a democracy and an economy depends on people *not* being excluded and unemployed. It contends that economic perspectives on transformation, which artificially separate the social, environmental and economic aspects of a society (and also ignore global influences), cannot provide appropriate solutions to the multiple crises facing South Africa. It advises that the economy and what it produces – even in a capitalist society – must be influenced and even directed by all members of society, possibly through political settlements and agreements, and that the state has a key role to play in managing the economy.

Finally, the book recognises that, today more than ever, the state must play a developmental role to ensure both environmental and economic sustainability, while also fulfilling the vision of just and equitable transformation, which informed the Freedom Charter and formed the basis of the struggle against apartheid.

REFERENCES

Amsden A. 2008. 'The wild ones: Industrial policies in the developing world', in Narcis, S. and Stiglitz, J. (eds.) *The Washington Consensus Reconsidered: Towards a new global governance*. London: Oxford University Press, 95–118.

Andreoni, A., Mondliwa, P., Roberts, S. and Tregenna, F. (eds.) 2021. *Structural Transformation in South Africa: The challenges of inclusive industrial development in a middle-income country*. Oxford: Oxford University Press.

Chang, H., Grabel, I. and Wade, R. H. 2014. *Reclaiming Development: An alternative economic policy manual*. London: Zed Books.

Chenery, H. B. and Syrquin, M. 1975. *Patterns of Development 1950–1970*. Oxford: Oxford University Press.

Crotty, J. and Lee, K. 2009. 'Was IMF-imposed economic regime change in

Korea justified? The political economy of IMF intervention'. *Review of Radical Political Economics*, 41 (2), 149–169.

Epstein, G. 2009. 'Post-war experiences with developmental central banks: The good, the bad and the hopeful'. G-24 Discussion Paper Series No. 54, February 2009, United Nations, Geneva, http://unctad.org/en/Docs/gdsmdpg2420091_en.pdf, accessed 20 June 2020.

Fine, B. and Rustomjee, Z. 1996. *The Political Economy of South Africa: From minerals–energy complex to industrialization*. London: Hurst.

Freedom Charter (1955), in Karis, T. and Carter, G. M. (eds.) *From Protest to Challenge: A documentary history of African politics in South Africa 1882–1964*, Vol. 3, Challenge and Violence 1953–1964. Stanford University, Stanford: Hoover Institution Press.

Glyn, A. 2007. *Capitalism Unleashed: Finance, globalisation and welfare*. Oxford: Oxford University Press.

Helleiner, E. 1994. *States and the Reemergence of Global Finance: From Bretton Woods to the 1990s*. Ithaca, NY: Cornell University Press.

Hujo, K. 2021. 'Social protection and inequality in the global South: Politics, actors and institutions'. *Critical Social Policy*, 41 (3), 343–363.

Kuznets, S. 1973. 'Modern economic growth: Findings and reflections'. *The American Economic Review*, 63 (3), 247–258.

Lee, J. and Gereffi, G. 2015. 'Global value chains, rising power firms and economic and social upgrading'. *Critical Perspectives on International Business*, 11 (3/4), 319–339.

Lewis, W. A. 1954. 'Economic development with unlimited supplies of labour'. *The Manchester School*, 22 (2), 139–191, Doi.org/10.1111/j.1467-9957.1954.tb00021.x

Mkandawire, T. and Soludo, C. (eds.) 1998. 'Our continent, our future: African perspectives on structural adjustment'. International Development Research Centre, Council for the Development of Social Science Research in Africa, Africa World Press.

Nolan, P. 2003. 'Industrial policy in the early 21st century: The challenge of the global business revolution', in Chang, H-J. (ed.) *Rethinking Development Economics*. London: Anthem Press, 299–322.

Palma, G. 2003. 'The "three routes" to financial crises: Chile, Mexico, and Argentina [1]; Brazil [2]; and Korea, Malaysia and Thailand [3]', in Chang, H-J. (ed.) *Rethinking Development Economics*. London: Anthem Press, 347–376.

United Nations Conference on Trade and Development (UNCTAD). 2020. *Trade and Development Report 2020 – From global pandemic to prosperity for all: Avoiding another lost decade*. United Nations. New York; Geneva.

Van Niekerk, R. 2013. 'Social policy, social citizenship and the historical idea of a social democratic welfare state in South Africa'. *Transformation: Critical Perspectives on Southern Africa*, 81 (2), 115–143.

Von Holdt, K. 2019. 'The political economy of corruption: Elite-formation, factions and violence'. SWOP Working Paper 10, University of the Witwatersrand, https://www.swop.org.za/post/2019/02/18/working-paper-10-the-political-economy-of-corruption-open-access, accessed 20 June 2020.

NOTES

1 Corporations in developing countries, particularly South Korea and China, have managed to make some headway in leading global value chains.

Part One

Evolving Structure of the South African Economy

TWO

Locating industrial policy in developmental transformation: Lessons from the past, prospects for the future

Ben Fine and Seeraj Mohamed

INTRODUCTION

This chapter discusses economic and industrial transformation within the context of capitalism's current stage, defined as neoliberalism, which is fundamentally underpinned by, but not reducible to, financialisation. The chapter explains that countries' structural economic transformation, including industrial development, should be analysed in the light of the shift to the financialised phase of capitalism and its neoliberal practices, interests and ideologies, which are themselves embedded in global economic and financial relations.

Apart from its ideology of reducing the role of the state, neoliberalism entails transformation of the role of the state in the provision of welfare and social security, industrial development, the (de)regulation of trade, labour and finance, and the reorientation of both domestic macroeconomic policies and global financial architectures.[1] Thus, neoliberalism involves shifting the boundaries of governance and the application of power within societies, particularly in favour of the elite as well as domestic and foreign big business interests. Furthermore, the formulation of development and industrial policies has been subject to reinterpretation and dilution, as concepts relating to development and the developmental state have been omitted or degraded when incorporated into mainstream economics and policy discourses.

In the development context, neoliberalism's first phase (from the late 1970s) was promoted by the Washington Consensus (WC), which stunted the (industrial) transformation of developing countries by encouraging policies that favoured the (especially financial) interests and power structures of foreign businesses and corresponding domestic interests and activities (Fine, 2021). In ideological and policy discourses, the concept of development became degraded by the view that things should simply be left to the market, while industrial policy tended to disappear from the official policy agenda (although pursued in practice in a piecemeal but largely incoherent fashion, as dictated by evolving powers and vested interests). The extent to which countries have been transformed through neoliberalism in general and financialisation in particular has been far from uniform, even if prompted by common (global) forces.[2] Both the incidence and impact of financialisation have been highly variegated.

When seeking alternatives to the WC, a natural starting point is the lessons provided by late-industrialising countries, such as the Asian Tigers, which achieved relatively high levels of industrial transformation in the 20th century. Achieving such transformation entailed a departure from orthodoxy, especially its analytical reduction – and even implosion – of concepts such as development and industrial policy, which derive from the WC. It is crucial to take a critical look at the limitations of current mainstream economic approaches within the context of the redefined and degraded notions of development and the role of the state, which is deployed defensively in response to the idea that developmental states played a key role in the economic transformation of the late industrialisers.

Prior to the WC, pioneered by the World Bank from the early 1980s, there was a two-pronged conventional wisdom: that development depends on industrialisation and industrialisation depends on significant state intervention. While the WC tended to accept the central role of industrialisation (unavoidable from historical experience), contingent upon it being driven by market forces, it came down heavily against the role of the state in achieving it. With deindustrialisation having occurred in the developed world for several decades, and even in the wake of the post-Washington Consensus (PWC), there has been a growing presumption that not only is industrial policy unnecessary and even counterproductive, but also that industrialisation itself is superfluous, as the tertiary sectors offer an alternative pathway towards developmental success.

The conventional wisdom regarding finance prior to the WC was informed by the call, particularly by Western, developed countries, to rein in and stabilise finance after the Great Depression of the 1930s (Helleiner, 1994). The regulation of finance and international financial relations was reinforced through the implementation of a fixed exchange rate system and the endorsement of capital controls by the United States (US) and other Western governments. The regulation of finance and international financial flows was also seen as important for upholding the macroeconomic policy sovereignty of the interventionist welfare states of the post-Second World War era, the industrial countries, as well as for supporting efforts to maintain stable exchange rates and rebuild a liberal international trading order. The US, influenced by the Cold War and the containment of the influence of the Union of Soviet Socialist Republics (USSR), endorsed state intervention in finance, particularly capital controls. The US also encouraged Western European states and Japan to use controls to prevent capital flight to support post-war recovery efforts and to allocate finance to achieve policy imperatives.[3]

For countries gaining independence after the Second World War, Amsden (2008: 95) states: 'Nevertheless, unlike in the period after 1980, the United States did the developing world a great favour. It left it relatively alone – a new form of "laissez faire". To create modern factories and skilled employment, the developing world could use unorthodox economic policies rather than laissez-faire.' Industrial policy and the adoption of import-substitution policies in developing countries, particularly the Asian Tigers, were supported by active state involvement in, and regulation of, financial markets and flows. Financial regulation increased state control over savings and direct state involvement in the allocation of finance towards industrialisation plans.

While the WC may have transitioned into its PWC version, the idea of development itself (as indicated) became and has remained degraded. Economic transformation or structural change is seen as merely altering an economy's sectoral composition. Social policy is reduced to the provision of safety nets, either directly in response to perceived temporary adverse circumstances or to remedy deficiencies in the provision of health, education, housing, and so on. Deregulated financial markets, which are inevitably destabilising, either in themselves or through resistance to and/or avoidance of (re)regulation (which prompts the misallocation of finance in economies), are seen as beneficial. They are depicted as more or less efficient/effective and even as malleable vehicles (from a policy perspective) for financing development and sustaining developed economies. The massive levels of support that financial deregulation received following the global financial crisis (GFC) were indicative of the popularity of such a concept. Instead of being seen as drivers of contemporary capitalism, financial institutions have become misrepresented as merely (in)efficient intermediators and allocators of capital. They are largely absent and blameless in erstwhile mainstream, neoliberal accounts of the problems that plague economies, such as macroeconomic instability, deindustrialisation, high unemployment, growing inequality, and heightened and irreversible environmental damage and calamities (see Chapter 3 and Chapter 9 in this volume).

The contribution of this chapter is that it restores what has been so notably excised from the concept of (economic) development. As indicated, across scholarship, ideology and policy (which together create a world vision), the WC so reduced the notion of development both in scope and depth that few avenues have since opened up to compensate for these omissions. The new neoliberal orthodoxy has created its own ragbag of heterodox alternatives, including the

PWC. As captured by Margaret Thatcher's claim that her greatest achievement was New Labour, so the WC's greatest achievement has been to limit alternatives, suppress the confidence with which they may be advanced, and promote compromises in principle and in practice. This is all despite the transparent and self-confessed deficiencies of the orthodoxy in the wake of the GFC, which should not have happened, but did, and which cannot be put right.

Much heterodoxy, including its central thrust, has been compromised through the forward march of neoliberal scholarship. The latter, which is more or less removed from past and contemporary realities, has two anchors. One is mainstream development economics, with analytical framing around optimisation, (in)efficiency, equilibrium and the appropriate mix of institutions and policymaking to correct whatever market imperfections can be identified. This reflects the position of the PWC, with the WC suggesting that interventions would be worse than the imperfections themselves, in view of market-distorting rent seeking. The other anchor is neoliberal ideology, especially with the demise of the Soviet Bloc and its attachment to state ownership and planning and the presumption that markets work well and state intervention does not.

What is striking about these conventional wisdoms is the degree to which they deviate from contemporary and past realities. The historical record shows that developmental success has always involved extensive state intervention and industrial development. As Chang (2002) neatly puts it, any advice to the contrary is not only a denial of developed countries' own pasts but also the pulling away of the ladder for those that wish to follow. Furthermore, the more recent examples of developmental success – the East Asian newly industrialised countries (NICs), with Japan in the lead followed by South Korea, Taiwan, Singapore and others – have all industrialised on the basis of a comprehensive industrial policy. Even with a small dose of realism, it is clear that China has proven this rule to be correct.

What is significant is that, in response to the WC, the developmental strides made by the East Asian NICs inspired a strand of literature on the developmental state, led by Johnson (1982), Amsden (1989) and Wade (1990). These scholars sought to demonstrate the role of industrial policy in bringing about industrialisation and industrial competitiveness. Their work was supplemented by another strand of literature – with the two strands tending to run in parallel – which focused on the human face of development. This second set of scholars argued that regardless of the (at times questionable) developmental successes of WC policies, they invariably hit the poorest the hardest.[4]

The twin critiques of the WC had specific goals: to justify industrial policy on the strength of the evidence from the East Asian NICs and to show how structural adjustments and stabilisation policies were hurting the already poor. As such, while each was compelling and valid in its own right, at the very least the goals should have been combined to convey a more rounded impression of economic and social transformation. Tellingly, neither the WC nor the PWC offered any clear or detailed conceptualisation of development – only the means through which to achieve non-specific outcomes, i.e., leave everything to the market or apply piecemeal corrections to market and institutional imperfections (Fine and Van Waeyenberge, 2006).

Not surprisingly, the limitations of mainstream economics have, to a greater or lesser extent, inspired both radical and constructive (but still critical) alternatives. A leading, and recent, contribution to the new heterodoxies is the invaluable volume edited by Andreoni et al. (2021), which covers both general principles and their application to South Africa in effecting economic transformation. There are many areas in which the Andreoni et al. (2021) approach resonates with our approach as set out in this chapter, but there are also examples of dissonance (also briefly discussed in this chapter). This highlights the distinctiveness of our approach in deviating from the typically incomplete reactions to the continuing influence – if not subtle stranglehold – of the (P)WC. The Andreoni et al. (2021) volume aligns with the political settlements approach in which structures of interests within evolving institutional contexts determine outcomes in the form of (more or less) developmentally advantageous (re)distribution of rents – from whatever policies are adopted. This, however, ignores the extent to which new (structures of) interests are formed: in the global context, there are the emerging financial elites who are gaining strength and stature, while in the South African context, there is the newly formed big black business elite.

In addition, seeing outcomes in terms of access to, and appropriation of, 'rents' either makes every rent sui generis in the light of its own individual circumstances or, as is the case in practice, it unduly homogenises different structures, processes, agencies and relations. Financialisation and the appropriation of interest, in turn, are seen as distinct from, say, rents derived from (mineral) landed property or monopoly profits derived from corporate control over competitiveness. A further weakness or gap is the focus placed on the cutting edge of industrial value added in the context of global value chains (GVCs). Yet this leads to the neglect of the more mundane but still vitally important role of domestic production in satisfying basic consumption needs at the domestic level in relation to clothing, food, housing, and so on (see Chapter 13 in this volume).

To address the issue of developmentalism, our approach rests on the longstanding view of South Africa as a national system of accumulation within a global context. Such a system has been specified as the minerals–energy complex (MEC), now incorporated into a globalised, financialised and neoliberal order. The acknowledged presence of the MEC against a backdrop of financialisation (with Andreoni et al. (2021) mentioning each concept in passing) has given rise to a new term: the minerals–energy–finance complex (MEFC).[5] This is indicative of both new political settlements and new partners in those newly constituted means of settling, with some long established and others dramatically emerging.

In this chapter, however, we are concerned with general principles. First, for contemporary conditions, we revisit the nature and role of industrial policy. Second, we derive lessons from the developmental state paradigm and discuss how to draw on these lessons in contemporary circumstances. Third, we turn to the relationship between economic and social development. Throughout, we are mindful that neoliberalism is underpinned by financialisation, with finance constituting much more than simply one other factor or variable to be taken into account. More generally, we are critical of simple, pervasive dichotomies as ways of containing and steering policy scholarship and discourse – whether they centre on macro and micro (or macro/micro as against an ill-defined and 'grab-all-for-everything-else' meso); the state (and other institutions more generally) versus the market; finance and the real economy; or the economic and political (or social more generally).

Determining the nature of economic and social transformation, and how best to achieve it, requires an understanding of evolving economic, political and ideological interests and how they are represented and fought for within *and* across the above-mentioned dichotomies. With these insights, we conclude by reassessing the role (to be) played by macro policy as a product of a globalised financialised economy as well as the prospects of forging a developmental state, a transformative industrial policy and a progressive social policy.

FROM DEFINITIONS OF INDUSTRIAL POLICY ...

Regarding industrial policy, we begin with two questions. First, how should industrial policy be defined? A definition is necessary to assess, formulate, evaluate and reassess the role of industrial policy in broader policymaking – although this sequence of actions cannot be taken for granted if industrial policy is used primarily to favour certain interests because then it would have minimal ex ante rationale and would deserve ex post scrutiny. Second (a definition of industrial policy is necessary here too), is industrial policy back on the agenda, especially in the wake of the GFC of 2007/2008 and the interventionist responses to the COVID-19 pandemic, each of which gave a justifiable beating to the nostrum of leaving everything – from manufacturing, let alone finance and healthcare – to the market (Wade, 2012)?

Perversely, we answer the second question first, even though an answer to the first is needed for the second. This is because, like Wade (2012), we believe that industrial policy has never been off the agenda, notwithstanding neoliberal and WC ideology. Rather, industrial policy has remained extensive, with Wade himself suggesting that the US (especially in terms of its military expenditure and innovation) has heavily supported industry and can itself be considered a developmental state.[6] Nonetheless, although industrial policy is more openly discussed, it is considerably more limited in scale and scope than it was previously, although new or revitalised issues have come to the fore – especially around technology and the environment.

Indeed, industrial policy has only been put back on the agenda in mainstream circles, in one or other form, to contain it rather than to promote it.[7] Furthermore, if industrial policy were seriously back on the agenda, it would extend to policies that have not in general been restored (such as the active promotion of state ownership and the reversal of privatisation, other than in the case of dramatic private-sector failures) and close attention would be paid to drawing lessons from the role of industrial policy in developmental states' successes. But, as discussed below, the prominence of the role of the developmental state in the new industrial policy has been limited, whether in its classic or more recent, diluted form.

We now return to the question of how industrial policy should be defined. Traditionally – consciously or otherwise – this has followed two paths. One is to define it very narrowly by referring to one or other aspect of policy affecting industrial performance – usually reflecting a particular intervention that is fashionable at the time. Unsurprisingly, given the many policies and factors affecting industrial performance, definitions of industrial policy are wide-ranging and evolving. Such policies and factors might include trade policy, competition, downsizing, regional development, technology, privatisation, small and medium enterprises (SMEs), entrepreneurship, the business climate, the environment, human capital and management skills, industry finance, and more. In some cases, highlighting one or other of these factors would enable the others to be ignored.

Because there are so many different influences on industrial performance, including economic and social infrastructure and workers' wages and living conditions, almost any factor could be construed as falling within the ambit of industrial policy – and the identified factors could potentially be at the expense of other factors. This then gives rise to alternative definitions of industrial policy rather than an accepted definition based on a single, preferred factor.

Our definition of industrial policy is methodologically motivated. The idea is not to have a (more or less) narrow definition of what affects industry, nor a template of factors to be ticked off as having been addressed (or otherwise) in industrial policy (although this is essential). Rather, we regard the nature, and hence definition, of industrial policy as being determined by its context and specificity, whether by sector, country or circumstance. A recent, dramatic example of this are the policies adopted by pharmaceutical companies in the face of the pandemic. In other words, industrial policy should be inductively defined by how it is understood in situ by those implementing it, assessing it or seeking to contest and shift it. This is very different from perceiving industrial policy as, for example, the means through which to correct market imperfections – although it is compatible with such an approach.

To the above considerations can be added other factors relating to industrial policy, such as environmental impact, issues surrounding gender and race, poverty alleviation, employment creation, sources of finance, technological change and skill enhancement. Whether and how these (and indeed still other) factors impinge on industrial performance and help to provide policy goals and levers depends on the context.

... TO THE DEVELOPMENTAL STATE

What we term the developmental state paradigm (DSP) came to prominence within the context of the economic successes of the East Asian NICs, distinct from the WC. It was at its zenith from the mid-1980s to the mid-1990s, but it suffered reputational damage in the wake of the Asian financial crisis of 1997/1998 and the launch, around the same time, of the more state-friendly PWC (which, ironically, studiously ignored the DSP, even though it was prompted in part by the growing dissatisfaction with the WC). We will return in due course to the evolving status of the DSP but will begin by highlighting its core features.[8]

First and foremost, the DSP was (as previously mentioned) inspired by revealing empirically the complete fallacy that is the WC. The East Asian NICs were shown to have enjoyed latecomer, catch-up industrialisation, with strong growth in per capita income and movements up and across value chains through substantial state intervention in general and targeted industrial policy initiatives in particular.

Second, unsurprisingly, the DSP departed theoretically from the WC by emphasising the important role played by the state in correcting market imperfections, especially under the auspices of developmental industrial policy. Its analytical framing has drawn on 'old' or classical development economics in search of economic and social transformation, not putatively efficient, market-led equilibrium.

Third, the literature on the DSP can roughly be divided into two schools. The 'economic' school focuses on identifying those types of industrial policy that lead to success, such as achieving economies of scale and scope, driving coordination upstream and downstream, making industry finance available, expanding both domestic and export markets in sequence, and providing essential infrastructure, amongst others (Chang, 2002).[9] The 'political' school pays less attention to policy as such; instead, it interrogates the circumstances in which a state becomes developmental because it acts to support development rather than being, for example, corrupt and/or inefficient. In other words, the political school defines a developmental state as one that is able and willing to adopt developmental policies.[10]

Fourth, the scope of the DSP has been limited, especially amongst those in the economic school, to the favoured East Asian NICs. This has two aspects to it. On the one hand, as its WC critics observe, successful case studies of state intervention used to bring about industrialisation are self-selecting. Accordingly, Africa has tended to be excluded from the DSP conversation.[11] On the other hand, as emphasised above, the DSP has tended to confine itself to latecomer, catch-up industrialisation. This begs the question: why does the DSP focus exclusively on the intermediate stages of industrialisation and not apply to earlier and later stages of development as well, with the transition from agrarian economies at one extreme and the vanguard of industrialisation at the other extreme (in other words, get in front of, not just level with)? Furthermore, the preoccupation with industry reflects a narrow, albeit core, aspect of development with limited regard for health, education and welfare and for the role of labour (other than as 'human' capital).

Fifth, the DSP is primarily, if implicitly, wedded to what is termed methodological nationalism, which in this case means that the problems of development can be and are confined to intra-national considerations. At most, global factors are treated as just one of many factors when in reality they are driving conditions under which developmentalism may (or may not) be possible.

Sixth, within this methodological nationalism, the DSP adopts the same analytical framing of the WC in order to contest it – the dualism of the state versus the market. The two sides of the dispute differ over the relative emphasis placed on the role to be played by each and how the state and the market should be coordinated, if at all.

Seventh, the DSP overlooks how the state and the market are always heavily intertwined, but the relations and relative balance between the two are conditioned by how more fundamental economic, political and ideological (class or fractional) interests are formed and expressed, both through the state and the market as well as through their interactions with each other. Consequently, especially through the political school and empirical case studies, the DSP has focused primarily on the capitalist class and its relations with the state (or, to narrow it down further, to industry–ministry relations) at the expense of capital–labour relations and the overall role of labour, other than merely as a factor of production.

THE EVOLUTION OF THE DEVELOPMENTAL STATE PARADIGM

In short, on the basis of the experience of the East Asian NICs and beyond, the DSP established a sound, if incomplete, basis on which to construct alternative policies and the conditions under which they might be adopted. However, from the mid-1990s, the DSP went into decline for several reasons.

First, there was the damage inflicted by the Asian crisis of 1997/1998 and, even earlier, by denials by mainstream economists that there had ever been a miracle – they posited that there had merely been an accumulation of physical and human capital.[12] Prominent at the time was the World Bank's (1993) report on the East Asian Miracle (EAM) which came to the remarkably contorted, self-serving conclusion that there had been substantial state intervention in the East Asian NICs.

Yet it only did what the market would have done if the market had been working.

Second, again before the Asian crisis, the literature had begun to cast doubts on whether developmental states could be sustained because of the shifting balances of (class) power induced by their success.[13] For Latin American import-substituting industrialisation, it was argued that this brought about a strengthening of working-class populism and demands for higher wages and improved social provision at the expense of industrial competitiveness. For East Asia, the strengthening of corporate capital (the chaebol in South Korea, for example) enabled it to increasingly defy government control and coordination – from directing who would invest in what (to ensure matched capacity within and across sectors) and who would not (to allow for economies of scale and scope), to constraining speculative financial investments, in particular. Significantly, then, the developmental state had a limited window of opportunity to nurture favourable industry–state relations. Yet, from an analytical vantage point, this signalled how the DSP set aside the evolving economic (and political and ideological) interests underpinning developmentalism (or not) until forced to confront them in the apparent erosion of class relations and corresponding state-led developmentalism.

Third, each of the above two assaults on the DSP ultimately, and ironically, offered some paving stones along the way for the PWC, which was more state-friendly, in scholarly and ideological terms, than its predecessor. It based itself on the need to identify and correct, where beneficial to do so, institutional and market imperfections. Subsequently, over the past two decades, the DSP has been described as a failed buzzword/fuzzword because it has been freely used, if casually and imprecisely.[14] More specifically, the term DSP has been used whenever and wherever any state intervention has been interpreted as successful – most frequently at some microeconomic level rather than at the level of economic transformation in general and successful industrialisation in particular. With some exceptions, the single most successful developmental state (in the original sense of the word) in the neoliberal era, China, has been studiously ignored or simply set aside as an exception rather than used to provide developmental lessons – thus suffering a similar fate to that of the DSP in the transition to the PWC.

FINANCIALISATION AND ECONOMIC STRUCTURE

The changing relationship between finance and productive sectors occurs within a framework that is influenced not only by government ideology but also by conflict and struggles within society, as well as with and within government. Evolving views and struggles over the role of the state in social provisioning, industrial development, and macroeconomic and finance policies, including state influence over the allocation of finance, affect not only the structure but also the size of the productive and financial spheres of the economy. Moreover, they influence the level of commodification and privatisation in services and the reproductive spheres of the economy. As economies become increasingly financialised, larger segments of non-financial spheres – including non-financial firms, households and public entities – are drawn into a context in which their routine operations are influenced by financial motives and linked to financial activities. Therefore, financialisation has an important impact on economic dynamics within countries, which goes unappreciated by mainstream neoclassical economics.

The impact of financialisation is not simple or straightforward; it can lead to accumulation or constrain such accumulation. This support for, or constraint to, accumulation will occur unevenly. As mentioned by Fine (2022: 57), 'Variegated financialisation is not just differentiation due to different variables and contexts being present but because of the complex interaction of underlying forces. Widespread liberalisation and growth of finance were integral to the emergence of the neoliberal era.' As observed, financialisation has also been an important component of the degradation of the DSP, including the reduced role of the state in promoting industrial transformation, economic development and redistributive social policies.

FINANCIAL LIBERALISATION AFTER THE BRETTON WOODS PERIOD

The regulation of domestic financial markets and international financial relations, including cross-border financial activities, was a central function of developmental states. This role was more easily carried out when there was greater coordination between countries in the global financial system under the Bretton Woods arrangements following the Second World War. However, the US and Britain undermined the Bretton Woods arrangements in an effort to boost their own financial sectors after losing ground to competition in global trade. The Bretton Woods arrangements, aimed at rebuilding economies after the war, subscribed to the view – influenced by Keynes – that a stable global economy and the economic recovery of countries required financial regulation, both within countries and in relation to cross-border financial flows.

The architects of the Bretton Woods agreement recognised that, to rebuild the global trading system, it was necessary to have a regulated, coordinated global financial architecture. According to Helleiner (1994), the US made pragmatic political choices in support of embedded liberalism after the war. However, the US would then drive an increasingly imperialist and neoliberal global agenda as the Cold War intensified, and as it intervened in European politics and instigated war in Korea and Vietnam. In part, the US chose these actions to support the global expansion of its corporations and its efforts not to adjust its economy in the face of growing government budget and current account deficits.

Neoliberal policies did not support economic growth in the way that advocates of neoliberal policies suggest – that is, by freeing private entrepreneurs from state constraints so that they can profit from their activities. The main proponents of neoliberal policies, including the US and Britain, experienced increased industrial competition from Germany, Japan and later the East Asian NICs. These countries, particularly Japan and the Asian Tigers – South Korea, Singapore and Malaysia – had policies that in many ways were the opposite of policies advocated by neoliberal economists (Amsden, 1989; Chang, 2002; Wade, 1990). They had activist developmental states that intervened in markets, directed the allocation of finance towards productive investments, and implemented industrial policies to support job creation and exports. Industrialisation and job creation were the main components of their strategies to address poverty. The state provided infrastructure not only to enable businesses to thrive but also to support household reproduction and education systems, thereby contributing to a reduction in poverty and improved labour productivity and skills development. Financial and macroeconomic policies were supportive of these developmental goals and were aligned to these states' fiscal requirements. Rapid economic growth and the developmental state's directing of credit allocations meant that public finances remained in a healthy state.

The US and Britain, faced with increasing competition in their productive sectors, suffered deepening current account and fiscal deficits. Instead of adjusting their economies to support productivity and competitiveness in manufacturing, they looked to their financial sectors for solutions to their balance of payments and government debt problems. The rise of the Organization of the Petroleum Exporting Countries (OPEC), the two oil crises of the 1970s and the war in Vietnam exacerbated these problems. Foreign financial inflows were required to offset negative current account balances, while taxes from growing financial sectors helped to offset tax losses from deindustrialisation (Block, 1977; Panitch and Gindin, 2012). This refocusing on finance in the US and Britain formed an important link between increased financial liberalisation, increasingly integrated international financial markets and the growing dominance of neoliberal policies.

Instead of addressing industrial competitiveness, the US took advantage of having the global reserve currency to print more dollars in order to cover its current account and budget deficits. By 1971, there was such a glut of dollars in global markets that the US was forced to abandon its commitment to exchange dollars for gold, and so unilaterally undermined the fixed-exchange-rate global monetary system agreed on at the Bretton Woods Conference in 1944. Vernengo (2021) argues that the collapse of the Bretton Woods exchange-rate arrangements, which were supported by large US businesses and banks that had become increasingly internationalised, prompted the imposition of a global fiat currency system under the hegemony of the US dollar.

The US and British governments deregulated their own financial sectors and, as they became more dependent on finance and foreign capital inflows, they pushed for the deregulation of capital controls and rules pertaining to foreign ownership of financial institutions in other countries. Financial deregulation in the US and Britain helped to offset their trade deficits and poor real sector economic performance by supporting growth of their financial sectors and attracting more financial flows from other countries. These two countries also showed the world that they would turn a blind eye to the growing Eurodollar market, which helped multinational enterprises (MNEs) and individuals to contravene capital and exchange controls in their home countries. Large corporations that expanded through internationalisation were eager to avoid capital controls and lobbied for deregulation and the growth of offshore capital markets. The response of countries to the breakdown in the Bretton Woods arrangements around capital controls was to rapidly deregulate their financial sectors and to remove capital controls.[15] Those that did not do so might have faced serious balance of payments difficulties because of the risk of large outflows of capital to other countries that already had deregulated financial markets.

CORPORATE RESTRUCTURING, VALUE CHAINS AND FINANCIALISATION[16]

Neoliberal ideology suggested that if government stepped aside, and markets were freed from state distortions and red tape on businesses was removed, then economies could thrive and grow. The actual historical experience was that much of the implementation of policies relating to neoliberal ideology in the advanced capitalist countries was linked to these countries' rapid liberalisation of their financial sectors and the reshaping of trade agreements to suit their interests. The liberalisation of trade markets in developed countries, at a time when the opening up of the Indian and Chinese economies brought almost a billion low-paid workers into the global labour market, put further pressure on developed countries' industrial businesses.

One response from the industrialised, Western countries' businesses to changes in the global economy was large-scale restructuring of their own industrial corporations and GVCs. They moved large parts of their production/assembly operations abroad to developing countries, particularly in Asia where wages and production costs were cheaper, but kept branding, design and technology development at home (Mohamed, 2010). The large corporations in developed countries were also able to use their economic power and geopolitical (including military) power to become lead corporations that dominated GVCs.

The growth of developing-country firms into large MNEs has occurred in two waves. The first wave was during the 1970s and continued into the 1980s (see Kumar and McLeod, 1981; Lall, 1983; Wells, 1983). Many of the first wave of developing-country MNEs emerged from the successful East Asian Tiger countries. The second wave of developing-country MNEs has occurred in a much more integrated and concentrated global economy where inter-firm influence is evident throughout value chains. Goldstein et al. (2006: 369) refer to the growth of MNEs from developing countries, saying, 'The emergence of a "second wave" of developing-country MNEs in a variety of industries is one of the characterising features of globalisation in the most recent years.'

The movement of developed-country MNEs into developing countries to reduce costs and take advantage of expanding markets created opportunities for growing developing-country corporations. In general terms, the second wave of developing-country MNEs has been constrained by the type of globalisation that has taken root since the 1980s and the influence of the financialisation of the developed-country lead firms on GVCs. Therefore, while many developing-country corporations have been able to grow, they have more often than not been limited to being providers of raw materials, low value-added intermediate products and low-cost assembly. While the various value chains assume different characteristics and forms of governance, the general picture is one of an inequitable division of labour, where financialisation allows rentiers to extract profits through lead GVC corporations. These rentiers pressure the lead corporations for high, short-term returns on their investments. The lead corporations then govern the chains to ensure that they capture most of the profits by squeezing those in other parts of the chain. Froud et al. (2014: 47) illustrate the difference between the first and second waves in the auto sector and the impact of financialisation on the second wave:

When the Japanese sold cars in the United States in the 1970s and 1980s, the contest was a productionist one between compact nationally enclosed supply chains in Japan and Detroit with lower wages sustaining Japanese advantage so that firms like Toyota could reinvest profits and grow market share as they built their own brands. The position in the 2000s is complicated by financialisation and long trans-Pacific supply chains where power is often wielded by US firms which act as proxies for the stock market and boost profits by multiple tactics which include control of design, consumer marketing and the use of contract power to take profits at the expense of margins in their Chinese suppliers.

NEOLIBERALISM, FINANCIAL LIBERALISATION AND FINANCIALISATION IN DEVELOPING COUNTRIES

Hujo (2021: 346) describes the impact of neoliberal policies on developing countries during the 1980s:

> State-led development strategies promoting full employment and public social services adopted by developmentalist governments concerned with catching-up (typically represented by Latin America and East Asia), as well as by newly independent states striving to overcome the legacies of colonialism (typically represented by sub-Saharan Africa), were replaced with stabilisation and structural adjustment policies (SAP), what was later called the Washington Consensus.

The damage to developing countries caused by SAPs and the WC will not be covered here as it is well documented (Beckman, 1992; Cornia et al., 1987; Mkandawire and Soludo, 1998). Industrial policy and the adoption of import-substitution policies in developing countries, particularly the Asian Tigers, were supported by active state involvement in, and regulation of, financial markets and cross-border financial flows. The role of the state in finance extended to increased state control over savings, state influence over the allocation of finance by private financial institutions towards national industrialisation plans, development finance institutions, capital and exchange controls, and the management of exchange and interest rates (Eichengreen, 2008; Epstein and Grabel, 2007).

Increased state control over developing-country financial institutions and the allocation of finance was crucial because colonial powers and imperial banks had shaped financial systems to support wealth extraction from the colonies and to service colonial and settler businesses and populations (Mohamed, 2010). Mainstream economists used the term 'financial repression' to dismiss state regulation and involvement in finance as distortionary, saying it starved poor developing countries of the capital required for investment (McKinnon, 1973; Shaw, 1973). The WC called for the liberalisation of financial markets and the PWC, while recognising that unregulated finance and capital flows were dangerous, at least post the GFC, proposed continued liberalisation of finance and (at best) the temporary use of capital controls within a mainstream approach to macroeconomic policy (IMF, 2012).

During the 1980s and 1990s, many developing countries engaged in sweeping financial liberalisation, removal of capital controls and also, notably, the establishment and rapid expansion of stock markets (Singh, 1997). Financial liberalisation initially led to massive surges in capital inflows through foreign bank lending in the 1980s. After the 1980s international debt crisis, developing countries saw a spike in capital inflows largely in the form of short-term portfolio capital flows. According to Palma (2000: 5), 'No matter how hard financially liberalised LDCs [least-developed countries] have tried in the last quarter of a century to deal with the problem of sudden and massive surges in capital inflows, they have ended up in a financial crisis.' Palma (2000) indicates how different developing countries absorbed surges in capital inflows in different ways. The respective roles of financial institutions, non-financial corporations and the state all influenced how surges in capital inflows were used in the host economies. For example, in Brazil, a large proportion of the short-term foreign capital flows were sterilised; in Thailand and the Philippines, they were directed towards financial and real estate speculation and debt-driven consumption; and in South Korea, they were (unwisely) used to finance uncoordinated and excessively long-term, fixed investments by the private sector.

Short-term capital flows in a volatile market environment create systemic financial instability as they have the potential to trigger panic amongst foreigners and residents alike, and thus capital flight out of the countries concerned. Surges in short-term flows are also associated with macroeconomic fragility as they affect key macroeconomic variables, notably the exchange rate and movements in both the current account and the financial account in the balance of payments. In addition, they affect the dynamics and sentiment in domestic financial markets, including private and sovereign debt markets. Furthermore, as many developed-country governments realised after the Second World War, open capital markets reduce countries' macroeconomic policy sovereignty to implement redistributive welfare and infrastructural and industrial development programmes. The liberalisation of capital controls has led to speculative booms and busts in stock markets, which have steered the allocation of capital away from long-term, productive investments. Currency and maturity mismatch risks make short-term capital flows unsuitable for long-term investments in industrial and (re)productive sectors.

The liberalisation of cross-border capital flows is not a form of financialisation as such, but it has been a catalyst for increased financial activities, the 'deepening' of financial markets and financialisation in many countries. This is especially the case where these flows have been absorbed into speculation in financial and real estate markets and increasing household debt. The increased flows have intensified the use of derivatives, including securitisation of debt. Over the past two decades, they have resulted in private finance and credit rating agencies having a greater influence over governments and foreign institutional investors than domestically listed firms. Developed-country institutional investors have been at the vanguard of the shareholder value movement, demanding higher short-term returns on their portfolio flows (Lazonick and O'Sullivan, 2000). Developing-country institutional investors have followed this practice. Institutional investors in both developed and developing countries have expanded as global capital flows have risen and have also increasingly diversified their portfolios out of their host countries (Fichtner, 2020; Pazarbaşıoğlu et al., 2007).

Although both finance and the power of institutional investors have grown during the neoliberal era, the role of the state (and its potentially enhanced role) in the allocation of finance and in financial market formation and regulation should not be dismissed or underappreciated. Finance operates under conditions and regulations decided by the state. The extent to which countries have become neoliberalised, the degree of financialisation, and the role and influence of finance all occur within parameters set by the state. The growing number of financial crises since the start of the neoliberal era shows that neoliberalisation of finance and financial markets requires the active role of the state. Helleiner (1994) reveals that neoliberalism and financial market deregulation did not lead to a smaller role for the state. Rather, he observes how the role of the state grew as it evolved from introducing regulation to avert financial crises, to cleaning up and bailing out finance after crises. The experience after the GFC of 2007/2008 reinforced the fact that inadequately regulated finance requires the state to play a more active role.

States are also able to influence the evolution of the financial system within a country through financial market formation and the structure and regulation of institutions involved in trading, as well as through price formation of financial instruments. Regulation and governance include the role of the state and state ownership, control over institutions, and transactions within these markets. Petry et al. (2021: 15) describe variegation in capital markets as 'the extent to which the quest for private profit is allowed to reign freely in these capital markets'. They also make the important point that profit creation does not have to be the only function of these markets and that the latter can also be organised to facilitate the realisation of broader state objectives.

DEVELOPMENTALISM WITHIN THE NEOLIBERAL ERA

Drawing on the lessons on economic transformation from the discussion of the global/macro context, industrial policy and the DSP, we highlight a number of issues. First, we draw attention to the nature of contemporary global capitalism, not least as the context within which national policymaking is proposed and implemented, with corresponding outcomes. As emphasised in the introduction to this chapter, we have examined the role of globalised production and the neoliberalisation of economic and social reproduction – aspects that render current circumstances considerably different from those prevalent during the golden age of the DSP. Specifically, neoliberalism has been underpinned by financialisation and the associated proliferation and accumulation of financial assets. This has not necessarily led to satisfactory levels of investment in either the public or private sector, quite apart from rendering the (global) economy susceptible to (financial) crises. The strengthened presence of financial interests has been felt across the economy, politics, ideology and cultures.

Indeed, the burgeoning literature on financialisation across the heterodox political economy and social science fields, although negligible within mainstream economics, has emphasised not only that there is too much finance but also that the more finance there is, the more severe the economic and social dysfunctions are. The core reason for this is that financialisation is strongly attached to (the interests of) short-term, speculative finance at the expense of longer-term, productive or other functional goals. Given the extent to which financial markets have expanded, particularly with the spread of asset types, alongside poor economic and social performance relative to the post-war golden age, it is inevitable that simple correlations will be made between growing finance and poorer performance, especially in the wake of the GFC. However, we emphasise that the association of financialisation with lesser real investment in favour of speculative investment is far from universal. Financialisation can also, for example, be associated with the political economy of excess, most obviously in the extensive reliance on fossil fuels as well as in the oversupply and maldistribution of food (with as many suffering from malnutrition through obesity as through undernutrition across the globe).

This points to deeper issues surrounding financialisation. Not only can financialisation have differentiated effects across various areas of activity, but the mechanisms that it uses are themselves highly differentiated – as are the incidence and impact of finance from sector to sector and from country to country. This is the first way in which we can upgrade or update the DSP. Certainly, the success of the East Asian NICs depended on targeted finance and support from the state, in conformity with the industrial policies adopted. But this was not seen as particularly problematic in terms of the potential obstacles presented by financial interests.[17] The situation in contemporary capitalism is very different, what with the deregulation of financial markets and the limited and ineffective reregulation in the wake of the GFC – in contrast to state command over, and direction of, financial resources directed at concerted policymaking. Of significance is the fact that the glaring developmental success of China has been based on unprecedentedly heavy reliance on bank finance for productive investments. Yet such finance has been directed by the state in pursuit of its designated policies.

In short, developmentalism depends on taking command of financial resources to guarantee appropriate levels of directed investment, in conformity with targeted policy. Paradoxically, in what might be termed the third phase of neoliberalism,[18] and despite its ideology to the contrary, closer relations have been forged between the state, finance and private enterprise in an attempt to rekindle profitable growth through such collaborations, with economic and social infrastructure being brought to the fore.[19] This is illustrated in the rise of public–private partnerships.[20]

Such initiatives point to a second reason for upgrading the DSP: to extend its scope beyond industrial policy to other sectors of the economy, even if industrialisation is central to economic and social transformation. But that is not to denigrate the roles played by agriculture, services, and economic and social infrastructure. One reason for incorporating these into the DSP is that there is a clear convergence and overlap with 'industry', especially in the light of the adoption of new technologies. Manufacturing can both subcontract and incorporate services; agriculture is (increasingly) industrialised; and social and economic infrastructure is vital for industrial performance, from efficient energy and transport to a healthy, housed and educated workforce.

As observed, a major limitation of the DSP has been its neglect of social policy. Significantly, this neglect, as Mkandawire (2010: 50) observes, is complemented by the presumption that developmental states no longer offer the potential on which to construct social policy, let alone include social policy as part of the developmental state:

> One quite remarkable feature of the new social policy focused on MDGs [Millennium Development Goals] ... is that the status and the requisite capacity of the state differ radically from the historical 'success stories'. Thus far, these policies are tethered to the demise of the 'developmental state', both as a reality and as an aspiration.

First, there is no need to treat social policy differently from industrial policy, as outlined previously. Quality education, housing and health systems are imperative for industrial performance, and industrial policy neglects them at its peril. Second, even if often primarily within the scope of the public sector, social policy is akin to industrial policy because it is sectoral, using inputs through a chain of provision to provide outputs, even if these might be designated as public goods (and subject to various degrees of commercialisation, including privatisation).

Until the WC, mainstream social policy was dominated by the notion of economic and social transformation leading to the creation of a welfare state, an aspect of modernisation. It had its counterpart in critical literature in terms of whether welfare provision was adopted to be functional for the capitalist economy (in material and legitimising roles) or as a response to the working-class struggle to ameliorate conditions under capitalism (the so-called political economy of the welfare state). Over the period of neoliberalism, these mainstream traditions have been lost and displaced by a now less-than-novel approach to social policy, associated with the 'new welfare economics'. It has taken the neoliberal antipathy to welfare (and its own commitment to privatisation and user charges) as a point of departure, seeing welfare provision as a game in which the state and citizens strategise in relation to one another on the basis of different information and objectives, such as meeting minimum standards of living at minimum cost (what the state desires) but maximising income for minimum work (what the individual desires).

Such an approach to social policy is deficient in two respects. First, in specifying social policy as a response to individual risk and vulnerability, it overlooks the systemic and enduring nature of economic and social reproduction. In other words, it treats social policy as if it were the response to short-term shocks rather than as a component part of development itself. Second, it is based on universal deductive principles (merit goods, optimisation, market imperfections, amongst others) and is therefore insensitive to the contextual differences between countries and their policies in respect of welfare provision. For example, child education means different things in different places at different levels of development; it also poses and is confronted by different types of challenges, depending on the context.

The question then is how to deal with the specificity of particular elements of social policy, given their diverse causes, content and consequences, without losing sight of the bigger picture. According to the United Nations Research Institute for Social Development (UNRISD), the emphasis should be on locating welfare provision within a developmental welfare state framework, which has the advantage of foregrounding systemic change in targeting development, welfare and the role of the state. This approach also remains sufficiently open to a possible need to accommodate different aspects and trajectories of development and welfare provision.

Where does this leave the promotion of social policy and alternative public-sector provision as we contemplate the future? Initially, we can highlight two general lessons. There is a need to insulate public provision against financialisation (the direct or indirect effects of turning provision into a financial asset, however near or distant). Privatisation incorporates finance directly, with provision being increasingly subject to the vagaries of stakeholder value on the stock market. Subcontracting incorporates it indirectly as the firms involved require their own financial imperatives to be observed.

In short, the vulnerability of public-sector provision to erosion and distortion is a consequence of the absence of broad, supportive institutions and policies following three decades of neoliberalism. Alternative public-sector provision and new, broader policymaking capacity, as well as corresponding means and sources of finance, must be built in tandem with the differentiated contexts of specific locations and what is being provided across the water, health, energy, transport and housing sectors, amongst others.[21]

CONCLUSION

Drawing on both our development experience and the development scholarship, we have attempted in this chapter to push for a more critical and rounded approach to economic and social transformation – especially in the light of the skewed terms in which it has been framed. This is despite the diverse reactions that have been directed at extreme manifestations of neoliberalism, which have been prompted by unavoidable hardships – from the GFC to the environment and the pandemic. However, we are equally mindful that this remains a necessary, if academic, exercise. There is a view, which people hold to a greater or lesser extent, that economists rule the policy world, even beyond the economic, and that the demise of Keynesianism and interventionism more generally and the corresponding rise of various forms of monetarism are clearly reflected in neoliberal policymaking.

Our view is different, as we place much less emphasis on the role of economists as such. When Mrs Thatcher first rolled out the British version of monetarism, it had been intellectually inspired by one or two academic economists held in low regard by their peers, with 364 professors signing a letter to *The Times* deploring the policies involved. The point is not that academic endeavour is without influence or is even futile. Rather, it must be placed within the context of those ideas that are likely to be picked up and acted upon, in contemporary circumstances. In this regard, neoliberalism has done its work in ways that have gone far beyond the harnessing and dissemination of ideas.

The alleged rolling back of the state in deference to the market has not transpired. Rather, the state has continued to be highly interventionist, albeit more attuned to the needs of capital in general and those of finance and financialisation in particular. What have in fact been rolled back are the institutions, and the powers that informed them, associated with more progressive policymaking, notably in the wake of the declining strength and influence of trade unions and civic movements. Moreover, what have been rolled out are more centralised, authoritarian and closed forms of governance in which the revolving doors between politics, policymaking, commerce and the media have come to the fore. These have been accompanied by more (or less) maverick and corrupt leadership as progressive forms of checks and balances have been eroded and democracy and democratic participation have been devalued and reduced to a media show.[22]

It follows that developmental transformation in progressive directions will entail building and rebuilding progressive, well-coordinated movements for change, focusing with sufficient detail on the specific issues at hand. Where these opportunities will emerge and how successful they are likely to be remain uncertain. Yet opportunities will arise out of what will increasingly become the inadequacies of globalised, financialised and neoliberalised economic and social reproduction and the increasingly transparent deployment of the state to promote the interests of the few at the expense of the many.

In short, the policy implication of our contribution is to emphasise that the politics is at least as important as the economics. What, then, should be said about the economics? Here a few important conclusions can be drawn. An appropriate policy cannot be derived by taking short cuts and by punting conventional (which these days are typically neoliberal) mantras. Picking policies off the shelf does not guarantee that the right choices will be made or, indeed, whether it is the right shelf in the first place. Whether the decision is to privatise or to nationalise, to liberalise or to subsidise, there is no substitute for policymaking grounded in carefully studied realities. Horses must be picked for the correctly identified courses.

But there is a danger in allowing metaphors to run riot. So, in a more concrete sense,[23] for industrial policy – narrowly conceived as industry and the like – there are interventions to be made at the sectoral and economy-wide levels. As far as sectors are concerned, it is essential to situate them within their forward and backward linkages (suppliers and consumers) and to consider the following factors: investment; financing; technology; environment; basic needs and equity; product composition and quality; markets served; labour issues, including wages and conditions; role of trade unions; skills and training; competitiveness; and so on. Forms of ownership, in turn, will depend on how best to achieve policy-related goals, not by prior ideological predilections. Similar considerations apply to economic and social infrastructure, social reproduction, social policy welfare or whatever term is reserved for housing, education, health, transport, and so on. These must be understood as crucial sectors of the economy and vital to economic and social wellbeing.

This is not to neglect macroeconomic considerations. First and foremost, in contrast to conventional wisdom, macro policy should be the servant of industrial and other policies, not the other way around. Rather than constraining economic and social policy and development by imposing self-fulfilling constraints (austerity) in pursuit of various domestic and foreign balances (for fear of government indebtedness, inflation or currency crises), macroeconomics and macro policy must be reconceived as something different from, and more than, macroeconomic aggregates. How the macroeconomy functions cuts across such aggregates, while being impacted by financialisation, globalisation, neoliberalisation and, inevitably, the power of big business and corresponding economic and political elites (since there is no economics without politics).

Policy must be as much about addressing or relaxing constraints (by adopting further measures as necessary, such as state-directed finance) as it is about observing them. It must also be subject to critical and democratic scrutiny, going through cycles of (re)formulation, implementation and (re)assessment; it should not involve staggering from one policy fad to the next. Such are the lessons from successful developmental states.

Significantly, the above views and remarks are borne out by the cycle of responses, first to the GFC and then to the pandemic. Initially, if only briefly, reflationary measures were adopted in both fiscal and monetary policy, but they were soon followed by austerity measures.[24] Currently, at the time of writing and in the wake of the Ukrainian, energy and other market crises (and in conformity with the diluted Keynesianism that now passes for orthodox policymaking), austerity was being accompanied by interest rate hikes from historically low levels in order to squeeze out inflation and inflationary expectations.

This could be summed up as follows: 'You have to be hit hard to believe there will no longer be inflation so that you can prove yourself correct.'

It is not our intention to reflect on the veracity of such arguments (they are wrong) but rather to illustrate how much they overlook – not least how the financial system allocates funding for different sorts and levels of investment as opposed to effecting marginal increases in the cost of investment (and consumer credit). As experience under neoliberalism has shown us (if we are willing to learn), finance has to be brought under control for the purpose of targeting developmental state policies. Otherwise, the scope and content of policy will be limited by the imperative of meeting the speculative short-termism associated with financialisation, which underpins neoliberalism and its policy-induced postures.

REFERENCES

Amsden, A. 1989. *Asia's Next Giant: South Korea and late industrialization.* New York: Oxford University Press.

Amsden, A. 2008. 'The wild ones: Industrial policies in the developing world', in Narcis, S. and Stiglitz, J. (eds.) *The Washington Consensus Reconsidered: Towards a new global governance.* London: Oxford University Press, 95–118.

Andreoni, A., Mondliwa, P., Roberts, S. and Tregenna, F. (eds.) 2021. *Structural Transformation in South Africa: The challenges of inclusive industrial development in a middle-income country.* Oxford: Oxford University Press.

Ashman, S., Fine B. and Newman. S. 2013. 'Systems of accumulation and the evolving South African MEC', in Fine, B., Saraswati, J. and Tavasci, D. (eds.) *Beyond the Developmental State: Industrial policy into the 21st century.* London: Pluto, 245–267.

Bayliss, K. and Fine, B. 2021. *A Guide to the Systems of Provision Approach: Who gets what, how and why.* Basingstoke: Palgrave MacMillan.

Beckman, B. 1992. 'Empowerment or repression? The World Bank and the politics of adjustment', in Gibbon, P., Bangura, Y. and Ofstad, A. (eds.) *Authoritarianism, Democracy and Adjustment: The politics of economic reform in Africa.* Uppsala: Scandinavian Institute of African Studies, 83–105.

Block, F. 1977. *The Origins of International Economic Disorder: A study of United States international monetary policy from World War II to the present.* Berkeley, CA: UCLA Press.

Block, F. 2008. 'Swimming against the current: The rise of a hidden developmental state in the United States'. *Politics and Society*, 36 (2), 169–206.

Bohrt, M., Graizbord, D. and Heller, P. 2020. 'Toward a spatial measure of twenty-first-century developmental state capacity'. *Sociology of Development*, 6 (2), 250–274.

Boschma, R. 2021. 'Global value chains from an evolutionary economic geography perspective: A research agenda'. Papers in Evolutionary Economic Geography No. 21.34, Utrecht University, https://www.researchgate.net/publication/355929162_Global_Value_Chains_from_an_Evolutionary_Economic_Geography_perspective_a_research_agenda, accessed 5 January 2022.

Chang, H-J. 2002. *Kicking Away the Ladder: Development strategy in historical perspective*. London: Anthem Press.

Cornia, G., Jolly, R. and Stewart, F.; UNICEF. 1987. *Adjustment with a Human Face: Protecting the vulnerable and promoting growth*. London: Oxford University Press.

Cornwall, A. and Eade, D. (eds.) 2010. *Deconstructing Development Discourse: Buzzwords and fuzzwords*. Warwickshire: Practical Action Publishing.

Eichengreen, B. 2008. *Globalizing Capital: A history of the international monetary system*. Princeton: Princeton University Press.

Epstein, G. 2005. 'Central banks as agents of economic development'. Working Paper No. 104, Political Economy Research Institute. Amherst: University of Massachusetts.

Epstein, G. 2009. 'Post-war experiences with developmental central banks: The good, the bad and the hopeful'. G-24 Discussion Paper No. 54. Geneva: United Nations Conference on Trade and Development (UNCTAD).

Epstein, G. and Grabel, I. 2007. 'Financial policy training module'. Brasilia: International Poverty Centre, United Nations Development Programmme (UNDP), http://www.ipc-undp.org/pub/IPCTrainingModule3.pdf, accessed 2 January 2022.

Fichtner, J. 2020. 'The rise of institutional investors', in Mader, P., Mertens, D. and Van der Zwan, N. (eds.) *The Routledge International Handbook of Financialization.* Abingdon: Routledge, 265–275.

Fine, B. 1996. 'Some perspectives on the provision of social and economic infrastructure'. Prepared for, but not presented at, Workshop for South African Policy Makers, June 1996, https://eprints.soas.ac.uk/32961/1/MERGINTR.docx, accessed 2 January 2022.

Fine, B. 2011. 'Locating the developmental state and industrial and social policy after the crisis'. Background Paper No. 3, in *The Least Developed Countries Report 2011: The potential role of South–South cooperation for inclusive and sustainable development.* Geneva: United Nations Conference on Trade and Development (UNCTAD), https://eprints.soas.

ac.uk/13440/3/Fine_unctadnotrack.pdf, accessed 2 January 2020.

Fine, B. 2014. 'The continuing enigmas of social policy'. UNRISD Working Paper 2014–10. Project: Towards Universal Social Security in Emerging Economies, Geneva: United Nations Research Institute for Social Development (UNRISD), http://www.unrisd.org/80256B3C005BCCF9/%28httpAuxPages%29/30B153EE73F52ABFC1257D0200420A61/$file/Fine.pdf, accessed 2 January 2020.

Fine, B. 2016. 'Across developmental state and social compacting: The peculiar case of South Africa'. ISER Working Paper No. 2016/1. Grahamstown: Institute of Social and Economic Research, Rhodes University, https://eprints.soas.ac.uk/34148/1/iserwp.pdf, accessed 2 January 2022.

Fine, B. 2019. 'Post-apartheid South Africa: It's neoliberalism, stupid!', in Reynolds, J., Fine, B. and Van Niekerk, R. (eds.) *Race, Class and the Post-Apartheid Democratic State.* Pietermaritzburg: University of KwaZulu-Natal Press, 75–95.

Fine, B. 2020. 'Financialisation and development', in Desai, V. and Potter, R. B. (eds.) The *Companion to Development Studies,* 4th edition. London: Routledge.

Fine, B. 2021. 'The vagaries and volatilities of mainstream development economics: A personal account', mimeo (for prospective edited collection).

Fine, B. 2022. 'From Marxist political economy to financialisation or is it the other way about?' in Fasenfest, D. (ed.) *Marx Matters.* Leiden: Brill, 43–66.

Fine, B. and Mohamed, S. 2022. 'Locating industrial policy in developmental transformation: Lessons from the past, prospects for the future'. SOAS Department of Economics Working Paper No. 247, London: SOAS University of London, https://www.soas.ac.uk/sites/default/files/2022-10/economics-wp247.pdf, accessed 8 August 2022.

Fine, B. and Pollen, G. 2018. 'The developmental state paradigm in the age of financialisation', in Hyland, M. and Munck, R. (eds.) *Handbook on Development and Social Change*. Cheltenham: Edward Elgar, 211–227.

Fine, B. and Rustomjee, Z. 1996. *The Political Economy of South Africa: From minerals–energy complex to industrialisation.* London: Hurst, and Johannesburg: Wits University Press.

Fine, B. and Van Waeyenberge, E. 2006. 'Correcting Stiglitz: From information to power in the world of development'. *Socialist Register*. London: Merlin Press, 146–168.

Fine, B. and Van Waeyenberge, E. 2013. 'A paradigm shift that never was: Justin Lin's new structural economics'. *Competition and Change*, 17 (4), 355–371.

Freund, B. 2018. *Twentieth Century South Africa: A developmental history.* Cambridge: Cambridge University Press.

Froud, J., Johal, S., Leaver, A. and Williams, K. 2014. 'Financialization across the Pacific: Manufacturing cost ratios, supply chains and power'. *Critical*

Perspectives on Accounting, 25 (1), 46–57.

Gideon, J. and Unterhalter, E. (eds.) 2020. *Critical Reflections on Public Private Partnerships.* London: Routledge.

Goldstein, A., Bonaglia, S. and Mathews, J. 2006. 'Accelerated internationalisation by emerging multinationals: The case of white goods'. *Journal of International Business Studies,* 42 (4), 369–383.

Haggard, S. 2015. 'The developmental state is dead: Long live the developmental state!', in Mahoney, J. and Thelen, R. (eds.) *Advances in Comparative-Historical Analysis (Strategies for Social Inquiry).* Cambridge: Cambridge University Press, 39–66.

Helleiner, E. 1994. *States and the Reemergence of Global Finance: From Bretton Woods to the 1990s.* Ithaca, NY: Cornell University Press.

Hockmuth, K. 2021. 'The developmental sources of South Korean neoliberalism'. *Fudan Journal of the Humanities and Social Sciences,* 15, 41–61, https://rdcu.be/cmLbj, accessed 2 January 2022.

Hujo, K. 2021. 'Social protection and inequality in the global South: Politics, actors and institutions'. *Critical Social Policy,* 41 (3), 343–363.

International Monetary Fund (IMF). 2012. 'The IMF's institutional view on capital flows in practice', https://www.imf.org/external/np/g20/pdf/2018/073018.pdf, accessed 2 January 2022.

Johnson, C. 1982. *MITI and the Japanese Miracle.* Stanford: Stanford University Press.

Jolly, R. 1991. 'Adjustment with a human face: A UNICEF record and perspective on the 1980s'. *World Development,* 19 (12), 1807–1821.

Krugman, P. 1994. 'The myth of Asia's miracle'. *Foreign Affairs,* 73 (6), 62–68.

Kumar, M. and McLeod, K. (eds.) 1981. *Multinationals from Developing Countries.* Lexington, MA: Lexington Books.

Lall, S. 1983. 'The new multinationals: The spread of Third World enterprises'. *Journal of Development Economics,* 19 (1–2), 210–213.

Lazonick, W. and O'Sullivan, M. 2000. 'Shareholder value as a new ideology of corporate governance'. *Economy and Society,* 29 (1), 13–35.

Mabasa, K. 2020. 'The developmental state and black economic empowerment: Lessons from East Asian capitalist models', in Cawe, A. and Mabasa, K. (eds.) *Beyond Tenderpreneurship: Rethinking black business and economic empowerment.* Johannesburg: Mapungubwe Institute for Strategic Reflection (MISTRA), 121–147.

Macroeconomic Research Group (MERG). 1994. *Making Democracy Work: A framework for macroeconomic policy in South Africa.* New York: Oxford University Press, https://eprints.soas.ac.uk/14614/1/MERG.pdf, accessed 2 January 2022.

Mader, P., Mertens, D. and Van der Zwan, N. (eds.) 2020. *International Handbook of Financialization.* London: Routledge.

McKinnon, R. 1973. *Money and Capital in Economic Development.*

Washington DC: The Brooking Institute.

Mkandawire, T. 2001. 'Thinking about developmental states in Africa'. *Cambridge Journal of Economics*, 25 (3), 289–314.

Mkandawire, T. 2010. 'How the new poverty agenda neglected social and employment policies in Africa'. *Journal of Human Development and Capabilities*, 11 (1), 37–55.

Mkandawire, T. 2012. 'Building the African state in the age of globalisation: The role of social compacts and lessons for South Africa'. Mapungubwe Institute for Strategic Reflection, Inaugural Annual Lecture, MISTRA, https://mistra.org.za/mistra-media/building-the-african-state-in-the-age-of-globalisation-the-role-of-social-compacts-and-lessons-for-south-africa/, accessed 2 January 2022.

Mkandawire, T. and Soludo, C. (eds.) 1998. *Our Continent, Our Future: African perspectives on structural adjustment*. Dakar: Council for the Development of Social Science Research in Africa, with International Development Research Centre and Africa World Press.

Mohamed, S. 2010. 'The state of the South African economy', in Southall, R., Pillay, D., Naidoo, P. and Daniel, J. (eds.) *New South African Review 1: Development or Decline*. Johannesburg: Wits University Press, 39–64.

Ortiz, I. and Cummins, M. 2022. *End Austerity: A global report on budget cuts and harmful social reforms in 2022–25*. New York: Initiative for Policy Dialogue, http://www.eurodad.org/end_austerity_a_global_report, accessed 30 September 2022.

Palma, J. G. 2000. 'The three routes to financial crises: The need for capital controls'. Schwartz Center for Economic Policy Analysis (SCEPA) Working Paper No. 2000–17. New York: The New School, http://www.economicpolicyresearch.org/scepa/publications/workingpapers/2000/cepa0318.pdf, accessed 2 January 2022.

Panitch, L. and Gindin, S. 2012. *The Making of Global Capitalism: The political economy of American empire*. London and New York: Verso.

Pazarbaşıoğlu, C., Goswami, M. and Ree, J. 2007. 'The changing face of investors'. *Finance and Development: A Quarterly Magazine of the IMF*, 44 (1), https://www.imf.org/external/pubs/ft/fandd/2007/03/pazar.htm, accessed 2 January 2022.

Petry, J., Koddenbrok, K. and Nölke, A. 2021. 'State capitalism and capital markets: Comparing securities exchanges in emerging markets'. *Environment and Planning: Economy and Space*, 1–22.

Pirie, I. 2018. 'Korea and Taiwan: The crisis of investment-led growth and the end of the developmental state'. *Journal of Contemporary Asia*, 48 (1), 133–158.

Rethel, L. and Thurbon, E. 2020. 'Introduction: Finance, development and the state in East Asia'. *New Political Economy*, 25 (3), 315–319.

Shaw, E. 1973. *Financial Deepening in Economic Development*. New York:

Oxford University Press.
Singh, A. 1997. 'Financial liberalisation, stock markets and economic development'. *Economic Journal*, 107 (442), 771–782.
Thurbon, E. 2020. 'The future of financial activism in Taiwan? The utility of a mindset-centred analysis of developmental states and their evolution'. *New Political Economy*, 25 (3), 320–336.
Vernengo, M. 2021. 'The consolidation of dollar hegemony after the collapse of Bretton Woods: Bringing power back'. *Review of Political Economy*, 33 (4), 529–551.
Wade, R. 1990. *Governing the Market: Economic theory and the role of government in East Asian industrialization*. Princeton, N.J.: Princeton University Press.
Wade, R. 2012. 'Return of industrial policy?' *International Review of Applied Economics,* 26 (2), 223–239.
Wade, R. 2017. 'The developmental state: Dead or alive?', *Development and Change*, 49 (2), 518–546.
Wells, L. 1983. *Third World Multinationals: The role of foreign direct investment from developing countries.* Cambridge, MA: MIT Press.
Williams, M. (ed.) 2014. *The End of the Developmental State?* London: Routledge.
Wong, P. 2020. 'State–market–society alliance: The evolving nature of the 21st-century developmental state'. WIDER Working Paper No. 2020/103, August, https://www.wider.unu.edu/publication/state%E2%80%93market%E2%80%93society-alliance, accessed 2 January 2022.
World Bank. 1993. *The East Asian Miracle: Economic Growth and Public Policy*. New York: Oxford University Press.
Young, A. 1993. 'Lessons from the East Asian NICs: A contrarian view'. NBER Working Paper No. 4482, https://ssrn.com/abstract=227317, accessed 2 January 2022.

NOTES

1 This chapter is a shorter, less wide-ranging version of Fine and Mohamed (2022) which provides fuller references to our own and others' (longstanding) work.
2 There is now extensive literature on financialisation by topic, discipline, definition and approach. See Mader et al. (2020) and Fine (2022) and, in the context of development, Fine (2020). For some coverage on South Africa, see the collection edited by Ashman et al. (2013).
3 The shifting role of central banks is uncovered here (Epstein, 2005, 2009).
4 For a retrospective view, see Jolly (1991).
5 See Fine (2019) for a recent account and Fine and Rustomjee (1996) for

the classical account. Uneven and in embryonic form, the MERG (1994) report adopted the approach suggested here.

6 The idea of the hidden (US) developmental state derives from Block (2008). See also Rethel and Thurbon (2020).

7 As concluded by Fine and Van Waeyenberge (2013), in response to Justin Lin's attempt to promote industrial policy at the World Bank. He failed to gain much support from within, despite his position as Chief Economist (Wade, 2012) – much as Stiglitz's push for change proved futile, leading to his (enforced) departure.

8 Regarding the DSP, see Fine and Pollen (2018); and for South Africa as a putative developmental state, see Fine (2016). For strong claims of the apartheid state being developmental, as opposed to post-apartheid, see Freund (2018).

9 Such is the thrust of Chang's (2002) historical work, which traces the developmentalism of state intervention from Alexander Hamilton forward. It gives rise to a law of economics: wherever there is development, it will be seen to have been the result of a developmental state. South Africa offers a perversion of the law, declaring itself a developmental state in the making as the Mbeki regime desperately sought to support itself ideologically while in its death throes.

10 Thus, for example, Thurbon (2020) places considerable emphasis on a developmental mindset.

11 See Mkandawire (2001, 2012) for South Africa's prospects in this regard.

12 Such a position was initiated by Young (1993) and promulgated by Krugman (1994).

13 See the 'death and end' literature, with the more positive responses emphasising the continuing role of interventionism, even if there is erosion of the developmental state – Williams (2014), Haggard (2015), Wade (2017), Pirie (2018), Wong (2020), Rethel and Thurbon (2020) and Hockmuth (2021).

14 See Cornwall and Eade (2010) for buzzwords and fuzzwords in the development lexicon. Their success and prominence depend, even as critical points of departure, upon their adoption by the World Bank.

15 Helleiner (1994) uses the term 'competitive deregulation' when referring to the frenzy of capital account deregulation that occurred.

16 To examine this in the context of evolutionary economic geography, see Boschma (2021).

17 At least until the South Korean chaebol sought to engage in speculative and international financial markets in conflict with state policy, with some considering this to have underpinned the Asian financial crisis of 1997/1998.

18 The first phase might have the short moniker, shock therapy, and the second might be regarded as third wayism (with financialisation as a common motif). In a South African context, these phases have tended to overlay one another; see Fine (2019).

19 To examine this in the context of the DSP and its latest incarnation as a piecemeal intervention, see Bohrt et al. (2020).
20 See Gideon and Unterhalter (2020).
21 See Bayliss and Fine (2021) whose beginnings can be found in an introductory section of the MERG report on social and economic infrastructure, which was not published but is available as Fine (1996).
22 To examine how this has impacted the South African developmental state (or the lack thereof) within the context of black economic empowerment (BEE), see Mabasa (2020).
23 For an extended discussion on what follows in arriving at policy details, see Fine (2011) and Fine (2014).
24 See especially Ortiz and Cummins (2022) and the earlier reports that they cite.

THREE

Beyond the MEC? Limits and prospects in the development of South African capitalism

SAMANTHA ASHMAN

INTRODUCTION

The South African economy is clearly failing and was doing so long before COVID-19 made its untimely appearance. Without a doubt, there are profitable, 'healthy' sectors (discussed in this chapter), which help to explain the extraordinarily high levels of income and assets concentrated in the top tiers of society. However, unemployment has reached unprecedented levels (and is still climbing), with distinctive racial and spatial dimensions. Across both the economy and society as a whole, there are multiple intersecting crises: of poverty, unemployment and inequality; of basic needs and social reproduction generally; and of deindustrialisation combined with deagrarianisation within the context of an intensifying climate crisis.

Fetishistic discussions about 'the economy' prevail – all too often appearing to overlook the fact that 50 per cent of the population are excluded from employment and therefore lack any income other than social grants. The unrest that gripped certain parts of South Africa in July 2021, on a scale that was unprecedented in the post-apartheid era, highlighted the depth of the socioeconomic fissures in the country. Also worrying is that, despite its chronic, longstanding carbon dependence, South Africa is only just beginning to discuss what may constitute a just transition, particularly in coal-dominated Mpumalanga province. The failure, since the start of the new democratic dispensation, to diversify away from mining-dependent energy at the core of the economy has simply reinforced South Africa's dependence on mining, notwithstanding periodic downturns in commodity prices. Mining remains central to the economy, accounting for just under 50 per cent of exports in the post-apartheid period.

South Africa is not alone in facing these crises. Certainly, as Fraser (2021) argues, global warming is intertwined with a general social crisis, precipitating a combined struggle over energy, labour, politics and care. Some speak of 'catastrophe capitalism', highlighting the combined ecological, epidemiological and economic nature of global crises and how circuits of capital are tied to the aetiology of disease through agribusiness and global value chains or supply chains (Foster and Suwandi, 2020; Wallace et al., 2020). Tooze (2020) accurately depicts COVID-19 as 'the first economic crisis of the Anthropocene ... the era in which humanity's impact on nature has begun to blow back on us in unpredictable and disastrous ways'. The flooding in the Durban/eThekwini area in April 2022, for example, demonstrated the devastating consequences of climate change amidst extreme inequality and corruption.

South Africa cannot be understood outside of the global context. Yet the crisis in the country is particularly acute and is playing out in extreme ways, against the backdrop of all the peculiarities of South Africa's racially based capitalism (Ashman, 2022). This chapter traces the roots of the crisis to the failure to tackle colonial-/apartheid-era legacies during the post-1994 democratic period and, moreover, to the perpetuation of many features of the past. Instead of diversifying away from the minerals–energy core, the post-apartheid government, by adopting a neoliberal globalisation- and financialisation-dominated trajectory, has compounded many of the problems from the apartheid era. This has undermined already-skewed production structures, exacerbated inequality, triggered periods of jobless growth, entrenched low wages and precarity amongst many who are employed, stimulated debt-driven consumption and reinforced reliance on fossil fuels. These are all central features of global capitalism today. Playing out in the South African context, they are having an extremely negative impact (Ashman, 2021a). Compounding all these things is the crisis of public provision, combined with endemic corruption in dealings between the state and non-state agencies.

I argue in this chapter that while it is accurate to say that the minerals–energy complex, or MEC (discussed below), has become fragmented, not all sectors are losers. Many of the most successful sectors since the advent of democracy come under the aegis of the old MEC conglomerates which constructed and greatly benefited from the racial domination and cheap labour system of apartheid and colonialism before it. Some of the 'success' stories are discussed in this chapter. Yet the deep crisis gripping the economy reflects MEC fragmentation. Importantly, no one is driving, or appears capable of driving, a reindustrialisation strategy. Corruption has become widespread, the restructured conglomerates cherry-pick the most profitable sectors, and mainstream macroeconomic policy rules the day. Radical shifts are necessary. Yet remarkably (or even predictably?), fiscal contraction and austerity are still advocated, risking a (possibly permanent) downward structural shift in the economy. Pressure from civil society has preserved the special COVID-19 grant, but its survival remains tenuous.

In the ensuing sections I provide an overview of what I regard as the major trends and their interconnections, many of which are explored in more detail in subsequent chapters in this volume. Space limitations, however, dictate that I cover them quite schematically. First, I examine the MEC thesis, as put forward by Fine and Rustomjee (1996), discussing the concept of a system of accumulation from a global vantage point and how the MEC has evolved into a minerals–energy–finance complex, or MEFC, since finance drives so much. I argue that this remains the best framework for understanding the economy today, while also pointing to some of the major consequences of this trajectory. Second, I look at the biggest companies in the economy and how 'the winners' from the transition have directed their strategies at the globalised, financialised world. In this regard, I provide a general overview of the top 40 companies on the Johannesburg Stock Exchange (JSE) and then focus on three examples – Naspers, Remgro and Shoprite – to illustrate both the changing foci of investment and the continuing importance of old-order capital. Third, I draw some brief conclusions by looking at the fragmentation of the state and corruption within the context of the climate crisis.

FROM MINERALS–ENERGY COMPLEX TO MINERALS–ENERGY–FINANCE COMPLEX

The idea of the South African economy being dominated by an MEC has gained some currency in recent years, albeit often in deracinated and denuded forms. For example, Roger Baxter, the former CEO of the Minerals Council South Africa (formerly the Chamber of Mines) referred to the term in his presentation to the Presidential Climate Commission in September 2021 (Baxter, 2021). However, the MEC analysis was not developed to champion the economic pre-eminence of mining (as would be the inclination of the Minerals Council) – far from it. The idea of the economy being dominated by the MEC was put forward by Fine and Rustomjee (1996) some 27 years ago. It was not *only* a sectoral analysis pointing to the importance of specific economic sectors (minerals, mineral processing, metallic products, energy), the strong linkages between them and the weak linkages with the rest of the economy, and the need to diversify away from these sectors. It was also an analysis aimed at understanding a historically specific mode of capital accumulation and its internal tensions: the historically built, exploitative, class- and race-based development of the economy. This pattern of development produced two powerful forms of concentration: concentration of specific sectors and concentration of ownership. Finance capital was always centralised, given the scale of funding required for the mines. Afrikaner capital would later join English capital, with Sanlam, in particular, channelling Afrikaner savings into investment (O'Meara, 1983). Over time, the project produced both a sectorally skewed economy and one dominated by big conglomerate groupings, with mining, finance and other, manufacturing interests under their wings.

The MEC was identified as South Africa's specific system of accumulation (Ashman et al., 2013a; Fine and Rustomjee, 1996; Freund, 2010), a meso-level theory aimed at understanding the emergence and development of class relations in terms of time and space. Any system of accumulation is necessarily embedded in the global system. As class relations develop, an economic structure emerges from production, linkages, institutions (including the state), strategies (including of the state) and fissures within classes, which change over time.[1] Countries have different experiences of industrialisation, as determined by the pattern of linkages that emerges; thus, industrialisation can be viewed as a 'changing structure of linkages' (Fine and Rustomjee, 1996: 39). Development economist Albert Hirschman emphasised the importance of linkage development, but his conceptualisation was limited by its lack of emphasis on class relations, strategies and dynamics in industrialisation processes (Ashman et al., 2020). A system of accumulation can be seen in broad or narrow terms. In a narrow sense, it can be viewed as a core set of sectors, as demonstrated in input–output tables. This is important from an empirical standpoint. More broadly, these core sectors emerge from class relations and value creation and need to be positioned in relation to the state and finance.

Fine and Rustomjee (1996) identified the following core MEC sectors based on the input–output linkages between them (and relatively weaker input–output linkages with 'non-MEC' sectors): coal, gold, diamond and other mining activities; electricity; non-metallic mineral products; iron and steel basic industries; non-ferrous metal basic industries; and fertilisers, pesticides, synthetic resins, plastics, other chemicals, basic chemicals and petroleum. However, in accounting for development in South Africa, emphasis was placed on linking class and economic structure with the key role played by the state and industrial policy. The MEC analysis therefore empirically identified input–output linkages between economic sub-sectors, which were understood in relation to fractions of capital, industrial sectors and the state, and how class relations and conflicts emerge, develop and are reflected in patterns of accumulation and economic and social reproduction over time.

While the MEC core developed under apartheid and had cemented itself by the 1980s, it rested on previously laid socioeconomic foundations. Colonial conquest globally and across Africa turned great swathes of land over to private control and monocropping. Land alienation and enclosure, with the violent expansion of the frontier and the destruction of commons under the Dutch, British and Afrikaner settlers, had massive consequences for land use and ecology. Following the discovery of minerals, capital and the state became established. Over time and through trial, error and war, a migrant labour system emerged in which Africans migrated from 'reserves' to work for periods of time on the mines. African labour was also 'allocated' to farming capital and later to the new urban centres. Land dispossession underpinned this process, as embodied in the 1913 Land Act, while the entrenchment and expansion of the reserves/ Bantustan system during apartheid (Freund, 1984) resulted in the systematic perpetuation of underdevelopment, which was deepened by apartheid spatial planning. Indeed, I would argue that the labour regime is given insufficient emphasis in the original 1996 formulation of the MEC thesis. The legacy of this forced labour system remains evident throughout the economy and society, as the basis of South Africa's transformation was the pursuit of gold to support the global monetary system (Ashman, 2022).

From 1948 onwards, the state actively promoted and developed key sectors – particularly electricity and steel, which helped to satisfy the mining houses' need for a stable supply of (preferably cheap) electricity. Eskom ensured an electricity supply to the mines, agriculture and industry. The (now privatised) parastatals Iscor (steel) and Sasol (chemicals) made a further contribution to the development of infrastructure and the supply of energy and chemicals. Sasol remains a major producer and consumer of coal. Mining, petrochemicals, metals and related activities typically consumed 40 per cent of the country's electricity, leaving South African industry heavily dependent on coal for its primary energy requirements as well as heavily energy intensive and reliant on low-price electricity, which was provided to large corporate users.

Gradually, the disjuncture between English and Afrikaner capital blurred, particularly in the late 1950s and 1960s. Conglomerate groupings emerged in the 1970s and 1980s, which combined mining, manufacturing and financial interests. There was expansion in the acquisition of financial assets throughout the 1980s and 1990s but by that stage it was less driven by the pursuit of shareholder value (as it is today), which 'crowds out' investment at the level of the firm. Rather, capital was 'trapped' in South Africa by sanctions, yet there was still reluctance to invest fixed capital in the face of political turmoil and uncertainty. This increased the size and depth of capital markets so that stock market capitalisation as a ratio of gross domestic product (GDP) was high, greater than in the United States (US) even, in the 1980s. At that stage, the growth of finance was driven more by political uncertainty. This changed in the 1990s, though, following the deregulation of the 1980s, as recommended by the De Kock Commission, which helped to facilitate this change (Ashman et al., 2013a; Ashman et al., 2013b).

FROM THE CLASSIC TO THE FINANCIALISED MEC – THE POST-APARTHEID TRAJECTORY

Global neoliberalism and the financialisation of accumulation have been the most significant shifts in the global economy since the economic crisis of the 1970s. Driven by the economic slowdown in North America and Western Europe after the post-Second World War boom, the collapse of the Bretton Woods System and the liberalisation of international capital flows, the internationalisation of productive capital and the 'hollowing out' of the state, financialisation – while global in nature – has specificities in different national contexts. Conglomerate groupings have undergone extensive restructuring. Famously, or infamously, a mere six conglomerates – Anglo American Corporation, Sanlam, SA Mutual, Rembrandt, Anglovaal and Liberty Life – controlled 84 per cent of the JSE in the mid-1980s. Today the picture is radically different (as discussed below), but the South African economy remains highly concentrated, and 'old-order' capital,[2] rooted in the classic MEC, remains central. This unbundling has led to the emergence of distinctive financial corporate groupings with growing domestic power, both economic and political, as the financialisation of the economy has intensified and as conglomerates have restructured in pursuit of both global ownership and control and global production networks – but with varied outcomes.

Moreover, this restructuring of the South African economy has been an important element (and consequence) of macroeconomic policy since 1994. Macroeconomic policy has facilitated a great deal of capital flight and corporate restructuring, particularly through the decision to allow major conglomerates to relist overseas (Ashman et al., 2011). Favourable exchange rates have facilitated high levels of capital exports. Short-term inflows, attracted by historically high interest rates, have – though creating instability – been necessary to cover the ensuing balance of payments deficits. Furthermore, wages have fallen as a share of national income and there has been a steep rise in wage inequality, which has helped to fuel rising levels of consumer debt as the financial system has been liberalised. The financialisation of the MEC has had significant and disastrous consequences for investment, as the financial system has channelled money towards short-term speculation and lending to households and away from long-term, productive investment. This has been accompanied by attacks on labour, deemed to be responsible for the low levels of investment, and policies designed to lower the cost of labour.

The growth of the financial sector and the shrinking of manufacturing have been accompanied by the growth of services and rising debt levels, since financialisation, indebtedness and inequality are closely connected. Finance has also become an important driver of inequality globally, as the wealthy have gained from financial assets either directly or indirectly. Formal bank lending to the poor and informal lending activities have increased substantially. Service sectors have grown, both in terms of investment and employment, but this has been partly due to debt-driven consumption and the outsourcing of cleaning and other services (Mohamed, 2017). Inequality of access to mortgage credit and its spatially determined distribution means that those with higher incomes have enjoyed greater increases in wealth through house price inflation and through the acquisition of financial assets (unit trusts, ordinary shares, pension proceeds and insurance products). While the JSE has changed, oligopolies still prevail, enjoying significant market power in major sectors. The continuing lack of basic infrastructure and social provision has given rise to a crisis of social reproduction.

The change that South Africa has undergone can be usefully characterised as a shift from an MEC to an MEFC. Standalone finance (now detached from the conglomerates) acts to reinforce the investment patterns of the past, but it also increases debt through the growth of predatory finance and lending. Financialisation increasingly drives the strategies of big companies, while a large proportion of the population remains essentially excluded and indebted. As capital has shifted away from productive activities, the result has been declining levels of fixed capital investment, particularly in sectors outside the core of the MEC, and increased capital intensity in manufacturing. Minerals–energy finance is responsible for some 50 per cent of GDP but only 25 per cent of employment. Consequently, the South African economy has been unable to absorb the expanding working-age population and, exacerbated by the pandemic, has seen a contraction in absolute employment numbers (see Chapter 2 in this volume).

REAPING WHAT YOU SOW

The crises of poverty, unemployment and inequality are a consequence of this pattern of development. The richest 10 per cent of South Africans now 'earn' 66.5 per cent of the country's total income and own 85.7 per cent of the total wealth (Chancel et al., 2022). This, critically, is driven by the high levels of unemployment (and reliance on social grants for survival) along with poverty-level pay for many of those who are in work. Poverty-level pay since 1994 has been encouraged by the decline in unionised employment, outsourcing and a widespread disregard for legislation aimed at the protection of labour (Marais, 2020). The expanded unemployment rate, which includes 'discouraged' job seekers, currently stands at 46.6 per cent (StatsSA, 2021), and patterns of unemployment and working poverty are highly skewed along racial lines. Between 1994 and 2021, the narrow unemployment rate increased from 23 per cent to 34.9 per cent, while the expanded unemployment rate increased from 30.9 per cent to 46.6 per cent. In addition, the proportion of long-term unemployed – that is, those who have been unemployed for over a year – increased from 57 per cent to 79 per cent.

Between 2008 and 2021, the share of employment in the manufacturing industry fell from 15 per cent to 10 per cent, while the share of employment in the financial sector rose from 12 per cent to 17 per cent (StatsSA, 2021). COVID-19 has, of course, exacerbated the crisis of unemployment, with widespread job shedding a direct result of the lockdowns (which in turn were not accompanied by adequate social support). Only the informal sector has seen a slight increase in its employment share. New technologies, including digital platforms, threaten to cut traditional jobs further but also create new forms of employment, including platform work (see Chapter 14 in this volume).

Importantly, deindustrialisation and deagrarianisation have gone hand in hand. Large-scale commercial agriculture has made small-scale farming uncompetitive. In many rural areas, little farming takes place. Instead, government social grants (pensions or child-support grants) are the primary means of support. The commercial farming sector is highly concentrated, with a small minority of farms producing the bulk of the country's agricultural produce. Perhaps 20 per cent of farms produce 80 per cent of value (Cousins, 2016). Rural areas remain the poorest. While contemporary finance has extended its tentacles into rural areas, recipients of social grants have also been preyed upon by internationalised financial interests (Torkelson, 2020). Land has not diminished in importance as the basis of social reproduction. Cousins et al. (2018) argue that it remains vital (albeit in changing ways) for the maintenance of a homestead for daily and generational reproduction, at a significantly lower cost than in urban areas. Labour migration persists, however, and is increasingly associated with informal and casualised work and gravitation towards informal settlements in or near urban areas. This circular migration pattern pivots on a rural home and applies also to the many young women who leave their children with the grandmothers in the rural areas. Many had faced the collapse of both agrarian and wage livelihoods even before COVID-19 (Schotte and Zizzamia, 2021).

South Africa has, certainly in relative African terms, a unique pattern of generalised rural poverty where small-scale agriculture is marginal and there is little formal employment. The deagrarianisation of rural areas and the widespread dependence on social grants have been accompanied by the spread and increasing importance of supermarkets as sources of food for communities. Supermarkets and social grants are now major features of rural areas.

WHITHER THE CONGLOMERATES?

The above discussion reveals several concerning trends. Yet the picture of the South African economy is not one of unremitting doom for all. As noted in the introduction to this chapter, several sectors have prospered significantly. Indeed, financialisation globally and the ongoing importance of fossil fuels have facilitated high levels of profitability combined with low levels of investment in an economy that continues to be extremely concentrated, where the restructured conglomerates retain their dominance. Having said that, Anglo American no longer dominates as it once did, and mining and finance are now joined by much-expanded retail and telecoms sectors.

Table 3.1 presents the top 40 companies on the JSE in 2022. The share of the economy controlled by these companies and groups is examined further in Chapter 6 in this volume, as is the changing composition of the JSE. For present purposes, I use the top 40 to demonstrate the ongoing, albeit changing, presence of the MEC. Of course, the exact position of these firms varies at different points in time. Furthermore, cross-company ownership and management linkages remain important. My aim here is to highlight the longevity of key sectors and groups, the importance of the new retail and telecoms sectors, the relative weakness of newer black capital, and how some – if not all – of the new sectors have deep roots in the past, against a backdrop of changing investment strategies linked to evolving ownership patterns across the economy.

Table 3.1: Top 40 companies on the JSE, February 2022

Company/ Group	Sector(s)	Major subsidiaries/ brand names	Roots
BHP Group (formerly BHP Billiton), the world's largest mining company by market capitalisation	Mining, metals and petroleum, particularly iron ore, copper and coal	Numerous global subsidiaries	Gencor (Afrikaner capital) bought the mining wing of Billiton; Billiton was absorbed into BHP; Gencor was absorbed into Gold Fields (part of Sanlam)
Prosus	E-commerce, classified advertising, online payments/ fintech, food delivery, travel	In South Africa: Takealot, Mr D Food, Superbalist, Media24, Autotrader, Property24, WeBuyCars	Naspers (Afrikaner capital, media group), Koos Bekker
British American Tobacco (BAT)	Tobacco, cigarettes	Camel, Rothmans, Lucky Strike, Benson & Hedges, Dunhill, Peter Stuyvesant	Richemont/ Rupert
Anheuser Busch Inbev (AB Inbev)	Beer	50 countries, 500 brands, beer and retail outlets	Formed through an international merger, bought out SABMiller in 2016; South African Breweries, previously dominant in South Africa, expanded from 1990 onwards

Company/ Group	**Sector(s)**	**Major subsidiaries/ brand names**	**Roots**
Glencore, the biggest mining company globally, amongst the top 40 biggest companies in the world	Mining, metals, minerals, energy	Numerous, global; merged with Xstrata	Ivan Glasenberg, former CEO of Marc Rich & Co.
Compagnie Financière Richemont SA	Luxury goods		Ruperts/ Rembrandt Group
Anglo American	Mining		Anglo American (English capital)
Naspers	Media, e-commerce	M-Net, Supersport, Multichoice	Naspers (Afrikaner capital, media group), Koos Bekker
Amplats (Anglo American Platinum)	Mining – platinum group metals, chrome, nickel		Anglo American
FirstRand	Finance – banking, financial services	First National Bank, Rand Merchant Bank, WesBank, Ashburton, Aldermore, The FirstRand Corporate Centre	Rembrandt/ Volkskas (Afrikaner capital)
MTN Group	Telecoms	Largest mobile group in Africa and in the top 10 globally; Supersonic Internet	Founded in 1994 with support from the South African government; 35% market share in Nigeria

Company/ Group	Sector(s)	Major subsidiaries/ brand names	Roots
Vodacom Group	Telecoms	Operates in South Africa, the Democratic Republic of Congo (DRC), Lesotho, Mozambique and Tanzania	Formed in 1993 by Telkom, Vodafone and VenFin; now Royal Bafokeng and other black economic empowerment (BEE) partners have a 6.5% share
Standard Bank	Finance	Biggest lender in Africa and South Africa by assets; Liberty Life; Industrial and Commercial Bank of China owns 20%	Key source of finance for goldfield development (English capital)
Capitec, owned by the PSG Group	Finance	PSG banking the 'unbanked'	Led by former head of Distillers/ Rembrandt representatives
South32	Mining, metals	Bauxite, aluminium, coal, manganese, nickel, silver, lead, zinc	Unbundled from BHP Billiton
Impala Platinum	Mining – platinum group metals	Impala, Marula, Momosa, Zimplats	Unbundled from Gencor in 2003
Kumba Iron Ore	Mining	Sishen	Owned by Anglo American
Sasol	Chemicals		Formerly state owned
Mondi	Paper and packaging, timber	33 countries globally	Formerly owned by Anglo American

Company/ Group	Sector(s)	Major subsidiaries/ brand names	Roots
Sibanye Stillwater	Mining, gold, platinum group metals	Southern Africa, US	Unbundled from Gold Fields
Gold Fields	Mining, gold	International	Merger of Gold Fields and Gencor; original founder was Cecil Rhodes
Absa Group	Finance, banking	Barclays Africa	(Afrikaner capital)
Sanlam Limited	Finance	Largest insurance company in Africa	(Afrikaner capital)
AngloGold Ashanti	Mining, gold		Anglo American
Shoprite, the 100th biggest retailer globally	Food retailers and wholesalers, furniture, clothing, liquor, medication	Shoprite, Checkers, Checkers Hyper, OK Stores, Meat Market, 7-Eleven, Computicket, Medirite	Christo Wiese (Afrikaner capital); expanded to 15 countries in Africa
Bid Corporation	Food retailers and wholesalers	30 countries globally	Owned by Bidvest Group
Nedbank Group	Finance – banking, insurance, asset management, property		Old Mutual
Discovery	Financial services, insurance, private healthcare	Discovery and Vitality; operates in 20 countries	Rand Merchant Investments controls 25%

Company/ Group	Sector(s)	Major subsidiaries/ brand names	Roots
Aspen Pharmacare	Pharmaceuticals	Largest drug company in Africa; operates globally; expanded via mergers/ acquisitions	Established in South Africa in 1850 by an Irish chemist
Sasol	Energy, chemicals, mining (coal)		Formerly state owned
Northam Platinum	Mining	Platinum group metals	Unbundled from Gold Fields
Pepkor	Retail, clothes, furniture, appliances, electronics, building materials, fintech	Pep, PepAfrica, Ackermans, Dunns, Shoe City, Tekkie Town, Incredible Connection, The Building Company	Christo Wiese/ Steinhoff (Afrikaner capital)
Remgro	Diversified industries – banking, insurance, healthcare, infrastructure	FirstRand, Rand Merchant Investments, Mediclinic, Distell, RCL Foods	Ruperts/ Rembrandt Group
RMI (Rand Merchant Investments)	Insurance, financial services, health	Discovery, Outsurance	Remgro, Rand Merchant Bank; Royal Bafokeng has a 15% stake
Clicks Group	Retail, distribution	Chemist chain across South Africa and southern Africa	Jack Goldin (started Pick n Pay); 800 shops in South Africa

Company/ Group	Sector(s)	Major subsidiaries/ brand names	Roots
Bidvest Group	Diversified industries	Logistics, automotive, financial services, freight, office and print supplies	Brian Joffe
Exxaro	Mining, coal	Previously called Kumba Resources, merged with Eyesizwe	Unbundled from Anglo
Reinet Investments	Equity Investments		Rupert family (including their BAT stake)
Nepi Rockcastle	Real estate, commercial property	Shopping centres	Largely focused on Central and Eastern Europe
Old Mutual	Financial services		Nedbank, BarlowRand mines; demutualised in 1999

Source: Who Owns Whom (2020)

It is particularly noteworthy how well Afrikaner capital has done in the globalised and financialised world. From small beginnings, some powerful global interests are now firmly rooted in Afrikaner capital and its development through the Afrikaner economic movement, apartheid and beyond.[3] The most dramatic trajectory has been that of Naspers, but the former Rembrandt Group – now Richemont and Remgro – has also fared well and remains at the core of the South African economy, even if largely divested of its manufacturing operations. Retail and food sectors have been major growth areas, with Shoprite coming to the fore.

Below I discuss the three entities of Naspers, Remgro and Shoprite to illustrate both the changing patterns of investment *and* the continuing importance of old-order capital.

NASPERS/PROSUS

Naspers and its international arm, Prosus, are two of the biggest groups on the JSE and are examples of extraordinarily successful internationalised and financialised South African capital – in this case, Afrikaner capital. Naspers is now Africa's biggest media group, controlling pay television in 48 countries on the continent. Koos Bekker, former CEO and current chair, is a dollar billionaire and one of South Africa's and Africa's richest individuals. According to Forbes, in February 2022, he was the fourth-richest person in South Africa, the tenth-richest person in Africa and the 1 332nd-richest dollar billionaire in the world.

Formed in 1915 as De Nationale Pers, Beperkt (The National Press Limited), the company established *Die Burger* and grew to become the main Afrikaans media group, with many subsidiaries, publishing houses, newspapers, magazines and books falling under its control. It was also a key donor to and propagandist for the National Party. From this base in print media, Naspers expanded into pay-per-view television, one of the first two networks of this kind outside the US. Pay TV was competition to the South African Broadcasting Corporation (SABC), but Naspers was nevertheless awarded a licence to offer this service, provided it did not provide news. This network became M-Net, in which Naspers had a majority stake. It later established Supersport and MultiChoice, eventually becoming the largest satellite media group in Africa. M-Net also launched MTN, but later sold its share in the latter. Naspers listed in 1994, and by the 2000s it was concentrating on e-commerce.

In 2001, Naspers bought a 50 per cent stake in Tencent – one of China's largest internet companies, the owner of the messaging platform WeChat and the largest video gaming company in the world, with interests in music, e-commerce, internet services, smartphones, mobile games, online games and payment systems. Although Naspers sold 20 per cent of its stake in 2018 – 'unlocking' US$10 billion in liquidity – it still owns 30 per cent of Tencent. In its recent profile on Bekker, Forbes describes Naspers's buying into Tencent as 'perhaps the greatest venture investment ever' (Forbes, 2022). In 2019, Naspers acquired a dual listing (Amsterdam being one), for the purpose of maximising shareholder value by focusing on growing (global) online industries, particularly online classifieds, food delivery, fintech and payment systems. Naspers's international assets trade under the name Prosus and include Tencent, OLX, Swiggy (Indian online food delivery), Avito (Russia's biggest online classified site) and Mail.ru, which has recently been renamed VK (Russia's biggest internet company, with interests in gaming, social media and e-commerce).

Tencent is currently the largest media group outside the US, while Prosus is the largest consumer internet company in Europe. Prosus operates in 120 countries and is a major shareholder in Delivery Hero, a large online food delivery company based in Germany. In South Africa, Naspers continues to own Media24, Autotrader, Property24, WeBuyCars and Takealot, which is South Africa's largest online retailer. It also owns Superbalist (online fashion retail) and Mr D Food (online food delivery, previously called Mr Delivery), which has the largest share of the online food delivery market in South Africa, ahead of Uber Eats.

FROM REMBRANDT TO RICHEMONT AND REMGRO

If any one group embodies state-of-the-art accumulation in South Africa today, it is Remgro. Remgro is the single most important South African business group, with its CEO, Johan Rupert, vying with Nicky Oppenheimer of Anglo American for the status of richest man in South Africa. Both feature in Forbes' list of the world's dollar billionaires, along with Koos Becker of Naspers and Patrice Motsepe of African Rainbow Minerals (Mille, 2022). On the JSE, the Rupert family's interests are spread across Remgro, Richemont, FirstRand, Reinet Investments and RMI. Remgro, of course, began as Rembrandt under Anton Rupert, Johan's father, and was the epitome of Afrikaner capital. The company's trajectory was impressive, with Rupert leading its expansion from tobacco and alcohol in the Western Cape into mining, finance, steel and engineering, and petroleum.

Over the years, Rembrandt has undergone extensive restructuring and has pursued a deindustrialisation strategy (Ashman, 2019), including winding up its engineering operation, Dorbyl, the single biggest engineering company in South Africa's history (Zalk, 2017), and splitting its interests between Richemont and Remgro. Remgro remains a diversified group, but has focused on finance and financial services, private healthcare, telecoms and regional expansion, while its manufacturing interests are dominated by food, wine and spirits. Compagnie Financière Richemont focuses on luxury goods in Europe, including watches, jewellery, leather goods, pens and tobacco, as well as online distribution. It owns Cartier, Montblanc, Alfred Dunhill, Chloe, Jaegar, Watchfinder, Net-a-Porter, Ralph Lauren (watches and jewellery), and assorted investment property companies. It was formed by combining the Rembrandt Group's luxury suite of assets with its interests in Rothmans tobacco. Apparently, Rupert was clear about the motives underpinning this restructuring, reportedly telling Cyril Ramaphosa, then of the Congress of South African Trade Unions (COSATU), in 1990, 'I have to protect the assets of my stakeholders, the shareholders, against your stakeholders – so that if they want to steal them, they won't be able to do so' (Dommisse, 2021: 85). VenFin houses Remgro's technology and telecommunications interests. The group has also supplied leading personnel to other important post-apartheid firms, such as Capitec.

SHOPRITE

The growth of supermarkets, or the 'supermarketisation' of retail, over the last 30 or so years, is an important global trend (Lang, 2020) and has been accompanied by the financialisation of food (Ghosh, 2010) and land as both productive and speculative assets. Food systems globally are in a critical state, requiring transformation from the perspectives of health, wellbeing and the environment (IPES-Food & ETC Group, 2021). Inequality, of course, perpetuates food poverty, and diet-related ill health has become normalised. In South Africa, malnutrition, hunger and stunting are pervasive, with obesity and diabetes also on the rise.[4]

South Africa has the most developed grocery retail sector in Africa. In South Africa, supermarket chains account for 60 per cent of all retail sales (Das Nair, 2020). The internationalisation of supermarkets through foreign direct investment (FDI) beyond the original home base has been an important trend. For example, Shoprite was the first South African grocery chain to move out of South Africa, paving the way for internationalisation/regionalisation by South African supermarket groups in southern Africa and by Kenyan supermarket groups in East Africa. Shoprite has expanded mainly through the acquisition of existing stores, although there has been some greenfield investment. Shoprite is the largest retailer in southern Africa and, according to Deloitte (2022), is currently the 100th largest retailer in the world.

The spread of South African supermarkets across the southern African region has been a consequence of post-apartheid liberalisation as well as liberalisation more generally across southern Africa in the 1990s and 2000s. Under apartheid, white urban areas were largely served by supermarkets, whereas smaller retailers and spaza shops dominated the townships. The two major figures in South African retail circles remain Whitey Basson and Christo Wiese. Basson built Shoprite, acquiring OK Bazaars from South African Breweries (SAB) in 1997 and Checkers from Sanlam in 1990. He retired as Shoprite CEO in 2016 and remains a billionaire. His friend and collaborator, Wiese, focused on clothing, building the PEP clothing store chain, and at one time was the chair of both Pepkor and Shoprite. PEP focused on rural and poor areas and customers, selling cheap, basic clothing items. The two groups separated in 1986. PEP is now the largest single-brand retailer in Africa, with 2 500 stores, although Wiese lost his status as South Africa's richest man in the wake of the Steinhoff scandal.

Post 1994, supermarkets (except Woolworths) expanded into townships, peri-urban areas and rural areas, targeting low-income consumers and diversifying their formats (hypermarkets, supermarkets, small stores, garage forecourts and food outlets) (Das Nair, 2020). Intraregional FDI may not have been as extensive as some predicted it would be, but it has still had major consequences. These trends are not only important for the shifting relations between commercial and non-commercial farmers (and the struggle for survival by those who are marginalised) but are also linked to changing patterns of consumption and employment (Kenny, 2018).

An important dimension of concentrated markets and the abuse of buyer power is the locking in of retail space in shopping malls, with big supermarkets acting as anchor tenants with 'exclusivity' clauses in their leases. These agreements benefit supermarkets, mall owners and landlords/property developers, while also homogenising development and further squeezing out informal traders. Financialisation is evident in Shoprite, although firm-level analysis reveals different forms and degrees of financialisation (King, 2021; Mohamed, 2020).

FRAGMENTATION, CORRUPTION AND THE CLIMATE CRISIS: MUTUAL RUINATION OF THE CONTENDING CLASSES?

And so, apartheid's state-led MEC has morphed into a neoliberal and financialised one, following the patterns of global accumulation – with a strong role played by the state in facilitating these processes. As we know, neoliberalism and finance have radically altered the role of the state, with devastating consequences for South Africa. This shift, and its connection to the climate crisis, is nowhere better encapsulated than in the trajectories of the three state-owned enterprises (SOEs) that were at the heart of the apartheid state's 'development' project. The three SOEs that were central to the construction of a racist and exclusionary, but in some ways successful, industrialisation project have fragmented. Eskom's crisis is deep and multi-layered. Underinvestment and a lack of planning, combined with rising debt and corruption, have, almost ironically, triggered a crisis of supply to businesses as well as households. Medupi and Kusile power stations have further embedded coal-generated power and run up more debt. Steel production, though a complex story, has essentially been dismantled through exposure to international markets, which privatisation facilitated. Sasol, now a private-enterprise 'success story', is a climate nightmare – its Secunda plant being the world's biggest single-point emitter of greenhouse gases (Ashman, 2021b).

The MEC has accordingly fragmented. The state is no longer driving an industrialisation strategy. Yet the dominant sectors in the economy remain relatively unchanged and, in many areas, are controlled by the same corporate groupings that grew up under, and benefited from, the systems and structures erected by colonialism and apartheid. They now benefit from the state's assistance towards their globalisation and financialisation efforts. The growth of finance and services, of media and telecoms, and of e-commerce has coincided with deindustrialisation and deagrarianisation and rising levels of household debt. Black capital has made only limited inroads (see Chapter 7 in this volume). All the while, social services have been commodified, producing a crisis of basic needs. Labour is in a deep crisis, and the crisis of reproduction is borne by African women.

This collective crisis is a consequence of the changing nature of South African capital's integration into the global economy and the strategies the country has pursued within this global economy. Indeed, this chapter argues that deindustrialisation is best understood as a strategy, as the restructured conglomerates have directed their attention at global growth industries, the gains from which have come at the expense of employment and structural change. As a result, the economy maintains its dependence on minerals for export revenues, with macroeconomic policy facilitating the shifts discussed in this chapter.

The crisis, then, is deep. Moreover, it is compounded by a climate crisis that goes well beyond greenhouse gas emissions and air pollution; it also encompasses drought, land degradation and food insecurity. Events in Durban in April 2022 demonstrated all too vividly the complex interconnections between climate change, inequality and corruption. While the energy mix is certainly changing, coal remains central to South Africa's export earnings, as do other minerals. Many are now clamouring to add offshore oil and gas to the mix – to steer the transition away from coal towards more fossil fuels!

One way 'forward', unfortunately, is to continue in the same way, plundering the natural environment, relying on cheap labour, and spreading predatory finance amongst a large, racialised, surplus population (Bernards and Soederberg, 2022). Of course, the kind of rapid decarbonisation that South Africa needs can only be brought about through rapid, far-reaching and economy-wide change. For a transition to be just, it must include the creation of public-sector climate jobs and the extension and deepening of economic democracy and planning.

While South Africa has so far squandered many opportunities

for socioeconomic transformation during the period of neoliberal democracy, the climate crisis presents – somewhat fortuitously – the opportunity to reconsider and re-engage with socioeconomic transformation. In other words, the country has a second chance to reflect on the scale of the crisis and the measures needed to tackle it effectively and urgently. However, at a time when we need public-sector investment more than ever, it appears that there is a race as to who will dismantle the state most decisively – will it be the corrupt elite (in the public and private sectors) and/or the champions of neoliberalism? The former has scant regard for the consequences of their self-enrichment, while the latter now use the crimes of the former to justify more privatisation and the further shrinking of public assets. Undoubtedly, the road ahead will continue to be rough.

REFERENCES

Ashman, S. 2019. 'Class interests and formation in the de-industrialization of South Africa'. Presented to Africa: Connections and disruptions, 8th European Conference on African Studies. University of Edinburgh, 11–14 June.

Ashman, S. 2021a. 'South Africa: An economy of extremes', in Veltmeyer, H. and Bowles, P. (eds.) *The Essential Guide to Critical Development Studies*. Abingdon: Routledge, 171–178.

Ashman, S. 30 August 2021b. 'South Africa's climate crisis is embedded in coal and exports'. *New Frame* website: https://www.newframe.com/sas-climate-crisis-is-embedded-in-coal-and-exports/, accessed 30 March 2022.

Ashman, S. 2022. 'Racial capitalism and South Africa's changing race–class articulations'. *New Agenda: South African Journal of Social and Economic Policy*, 84, 29–35.

Ashman, S., Fine, B. and Newman, S. 2011. 'Amnesty international? The nature, scale and impact of capital flight from South Africa'. *Journal of Southern African Studies*, 37 (1), 7–25.

Ashman, S., Fine, B. and Newman, S. 2013a. 'Systems of accumulation and the evolving South African minerals–energy complex', in Fine, B., Saraswati, J. and Tavasci, D. (eds.) *Beyond the Developmental State: Industrial policy into the 21st century*. London: Pluto, 245–267.

Ashman, S., Mohamed, S. and Newman, S. 2013b. 'Financialization of the South African economy: Impact on the economic growth path and employment'. Discussion Paper for United Nations Department of Economic and Social Affairs: UNDESA.

Ashman, S., Newman, S. and Tregenna, F. 2020. 'Radical industrial policy', in Chang, H-J., Cramer, C., Kozul-Wright, R. and Oqubay, A. (eds.) *The Oxford Handbook of Industrial Policy.* Oxford: Oxford University Press, 178–206.

Baxter, R. 23 September 2021. 'Keynote Address on behalf of the Minerals Council of South Africa', Presidential Climate Commission just transition framework: Dialogue on the coal value chain. https://pccommissionflow.imgix.net/uploads/images/1eb85a_33b4c64e84e74318a12bbcb7f7bd469f.pdf, accessed 30 March 2022.

Bernards, N. and Soederberg, S. 2022. 'Relative surplus populations and the crises of contemporary capitalism: Reviving, revisiting, recasting'. *Geoforum,* 126, 412–419.

Castel-Branco, C. 2022. 'The historical logic of the mode of capital accumulation in Mozambique'. *Review of African Political Economy,* 49 (171), 11–45.

Castel-Branco, C. and Greco. E. 2022. 'Mozambique – neither miracle nor mirage'. *Review of African Political Economy,* 49 (171), 1–10.

Chancel, L., Picketty, T., Saez, E. and Zucman, G. 2022. *World Inequality Report 2022* website: https://wir2022.wid.world, accessed 30 May 2022.

Cousins, B. 2016. 'Land reform in South Africa is failing, can it be saved?' *Transformation,* 92, 135–157.

Cousins, B., Dubb, A., Hornby, D. and Mtero, F. 2018. 'Social reproduction of "classes of labour" in the rural areas of South Africa: Contradictions and contestations'. *The Journal of Peasant Studies*, 45 (5–6), 1060–1085.

Das Nair, R. 2020. 'The "supermarket revolution" in the South', in Crush, J., Frayne, B. and Haysom, G. (eds.) *Handbook on Urban Food Security in the Global South.* Cheltenham UK and Northampton USA: Edward Elgar, 113–144.

Deloitte. 2022. 'Global powers of retailing 2022: Resilience despite challenges', Deloitte website: https://www2.deloitte.com/content/dam/Deloitte/at/Documents/consumer-business/at-global-powers-retailing-2022.pdf, accessed 30 May 2022.

Dommisse, E. 2021. *Fortunes: The rise and rise of Afrikaner tycoons.* Johannesburg: Jonathan Ball Publishers.

Du Toit, P. 2019. *The Stellenbosch Mafia: Inside the 'billionaires' club.* Johannesburg, Cape Town, and London: Jonathan Ball Publishers.

Fine, B. and Rustomjee, Z. 1996. *The Political Economy of South Africa: From minerals–energy complex to industrialization.* London: Hurst.

Forbes. 2022. 'Forbes profile: Koos Bekker', Forbes website: https://www.forbes.com/profile/koos-bekker/?sh=26a23ee7416d, accessed 1 June 2022.

Foster, J. B. and Suwandi, I. 1 June 2020. 'COVID-19 and catastrophe capitalism: Commodity chains and ecological–epidemiological–economic crises'. *Monthly Review,* https://monthlyreview.org/2020/06/01/covid-

19-and-catastrophe-capitalism/, accessed 18 May 2022.
Fraser, N. 2021. 'Climates of capital'. *New Left Review*, 127.
Freund, B. 1984. 'Forced resettlement and the political economy of South Africa'. *Review of African Political Economy*, 11 (29), 49–63.
Freund, B. 2010. 'The significance of the minerals–energy complex in the light of South African historiography'. *Transformation: Critical perspectives on Southern Africa*, 71, 3–25.
Ghosh, J. 2010. 'The unnatural coupling: Food and global finance'. *Journal of Agrarian Change*, 10 (1), 72–86.
IPES-Food and ETC Group. 2021. 'A long food movement: Transforming food systems by 2045', IPES-Food website: https://www.ipes-food.org/_img/upload/files/LongFoodMovementEN.pdf, accessed 2 May 2022.
Kenny, B. 2018. *Retail Worker Politics, Race and Consumption in South Africa: Shelved in the service economy*. Switzerland: Palgrave-Macmillan.
King, N. A. 2021. 'Non-financial firms in South Africa: A comparative analysis of the variegated forms of financialization for minerals, beverages, and retail'. PhD thesis, School of Economics, University of Johannesburg.
Lang, T. 2020. *Feeding Britain: Our food problems and how to fix them*. London: Pelican.
Marais, H. 2020. 'The crisis of waged work and the option of a universal basic income grant for South Africa'. *Globalizations*, 17 (2), 352–379.
Mille, R. 2022. 'World's billionaires list: The richest in 2022'. Forbes, https://www.forbes.com/billionaires/, accessed 5 June 2022.
Mohamed, S. 2017. 'Financialization of the South African economy'. *Development,* 59, 137–142.
Mohamed, S. 2020. 'Anglo-American Corporation and corporate restructuring in post-apartheid South Africa'. *International Review of Applied Economics,* 34 (4), 439–455.
O'Meara, D. 1983. *Volkskapitalisme: Class, capital and ideology in the development of Afrikaner nationalism, 1934–1948.* Cambridge: Cambridge University Press.
Rolf, S. 2021. *China's Uneven and Combined Development.* Switzerland: Palgrave Macmillan.
Saad-Filho, A. and Morais, L. 2018. *Brazil: Neoliberalism versus democracy*. Chicago: Pluto Press.
Schotte, S. and Zizzamia, R. 2021. 'The livelihood impacts of COVID-19 in urban South Africa'. SA-TIED Working Paper No. 168, https://sa-tied.wider.unu.edu/sites/default/files/SA-TIED-WP168.pdf, accessed 20 May 2022.
Statistics South Africa (StatsSA). 2021. 'Quarterly Labour Force Survey, Quarter 3 2021', https://www.statssa.gov.za/?p=14957, accessed 15 February 2022.
Tooze, A. 7 May 2020. 'We are living through the first economic crisis of

the Anthropocene'. *The Guardian*, https://www.theguardian.com/books/2020/may/07/we-are-living-through-the-first-economic-crisis-of-the-anthropocene, accessed 20 April 2022.

Torkelson, E. 2020. 'Collateral damages: Cash transfer and debt transfer in South Africa'. *World Development*, 126, 104711.

Wallace, R., Liebman, A., Chaves, L. F. and Wallace, R. 1 May 2020. 'COVID-19 and circuits of capital'. *Monthly Review*, https://monthlyreview.org/2020/05/01/covid-19-and-circuits-of-capital/, accessed 20 April 2022.

Who Owns Whom. 2020. Who Owns Whom? African Business Information, 40th edition. Johannesburg.

Zalk, N. 2017. 'The things we lost in the fire: The political economy of post-apartheid restructuring of the South African steel and engineering sectors'. PhD thesis, Department of Economics, School of Oriental and African Studies, University of London.

NOTES

1 For analyses of capitalist development grounded in Marxist political economy, which deploy the idea of (changing) systems of accumulation in comparable ways to this chapter, see Saad-Filho and Morais (2018) on Brazil, Rolf (2021) on China, and Castel-Branco (2022) and Castel-Branco and Greco (2022) on Mozambique.

2 I owe the term to Zavareh Rustomjee.

3 For hagiographic treatment, see Dommisse (2021) and for the 'Stellenbosch mafia' approach, see Du Toit (2019).

4 For an excellent overview of the British food system in particular, see Lang (2020). While Lang focuses on the UK, the sub-headings in his chapters reveal the key global issues: the money flows send the wrong signals; food damages the environment on which it depends; farm size and labour lock one into intensification; there is a production–consumption mismatch; diet-related ill health has been normalised; food choice and culture are intertwined: the battle for the mind; systemic food waste; social inequalities as a driver of food poverty; food power, competition and control; food labour, education and skills; science, technology and engineering in the age of big data; fraying food governance.

FOUR

Why is the South African economy stuck in chronic crises?

ASGHAR ADELZADEH

'The difficulty lies, not in the new ideas, but in escaping from the old ones.' (Keynes, 1936: Preface)

INTRODUCTION

In South Africa, the African National Congress (ANC) changed its views, from concurring with the heterodox economic views and policies up to the early 1990s to fully embracing mainstream economics and policies within two years of the 1994 election. Such a change was not inconsequential. It has shaped the post-apartheid government's role in the economy, its economic policy choices, and the country's growth and development outcomes for nearly 30 years. The aim of this chapter is two-fold: first, to present both mainstream and heterodox economic views on the outlook and policies of the ANC since the 1940s and the ANC government since 1994; and second, to show the links between government-adopted economic views and policy choices and economic outcomes in the ensuing years, before offering an alternative economic outlook for the future of the country.

The main distinction between the mainstream and heterodox schools of thought in economics fundamentally relates to perceptions of how capitalism works. The debate on the role of the state and economic policy is informed by this distinction. The set of theories making up mainstream economics have their intellectual roots in the neoclassical theory of the 19th century and the neoclassical–Keynesian synthesis of the mid-20th century, most notably formulated by Hicks, Modigliani and Samuelson. During the 1970s, mainstream economics evolved into the real business cycle theory, new classical macroeconomics and early new Keynesian economics. During the 1980s and 1990s, a new synthesis emerged within mainstream economics, which was referred to as the new neoclassical synthesis or new Keynesian economics.[1]

Despite the apparent diversity of views within mainstream economics, the differences become less significant when one considers why they were put under the mainstream economics umbrella. Notwithstanding the different explanations provided for short-term economic disequilibrium, mainstream economics starts with a barter economy and perfect competition, with firms' and individuals' main motivation for participating in the economy being to maximise their profits and utility. In line with this view, a competitive capitalist economy is an inherently self-regulating system that moves towards general equilibrium, while simultaneously eliminating excess demand and supply in factor and product markets.[2] For some mainstream economists, government aggregate demand policies may have a positive effect in the short term, but not in the long term. Finally, the free market is regarded as the ideal vehicle for achieving efficiency and maximum social welfare.

Regarding the role of the state and economic policy, mainstream economics advocates small governments because government dissaving threatens to crowd out any incipient rise in private investment, and thus suppresses economic growth. The economic framework's focus on imperfections, rigidities and frictions as causes of market failures 'leads naturally to a focus on policies that will remove these imperfections and frictions, policies that will make the economy more closely resemble the textbook model of perfect competition' (Marglin, 2021: 2). Therefore, deregulation is promoted because labour, capital and other regulations are regarded as hindrances to the otherwise full employment tendency of the market. More generally, the structural adjustment policies of the International Monetary Fund (IMF) or the well-known Washington Consensus policies best capture the policy corollary of mainstream economics.

By comparison, variants of heterodox economics, such as Keynesian, post-Keynesian, Marxian and institutional economics, originated in the theories of Marx, Keynes, Kalecki, Sraffa and Minsky, amongst others. Unlike mainstream economics, whose starting point is an idealised version of a market economy, heterodox economics is rooted in the real world, which includes historical time, money, financial markets, institutions and uncertainty. There are six distinguishing tenets of heterodox economics.[3] First, capitalism is an inherently dynamic system which is not consistent with the static general equilibrium concept. Second, a market economy is not self-regulating, with an endogenous mechanism that guarantees full employment in the factor and product markets. Involuntary unemployment is a normal and even necessary feature of the system.[4] Third, market failures are not the result of externally induced market imperfections but are normal outcomes of the workings of the market. Fourth, an increase in savings does not induce an equivalent increase in investment. Fifth, aggregate demand is a key short- and long-term determinant of the level of economic activity and the level of employment. Finally, a money economy is fundamentally different from a barter economy.

Given this depiction of capitalism, the heterodox economic view of the role of the state and economic policy differs significantly from the mainstream economic view. Heterodox economists relate growth to income and income distribution and argue for active government participation in the economy to stimulate economic growth, promote high employment and provide a safety net for those marginalised by the workings of the market. Heterodox economists believe that policy activism in the form of state action can result in improvements in market allocations. However, views differ on the role of the state in managing capitalism (Poirot and Pavel, 2008).

In South Africa, the two broad schools of economic thought have influenced the ANC's views both on the economy and economic policy since the 1940s. Understanding this history helps to contextualise and better explain the evolution of South Africa's economic policy and outcomes over the period of 26 years covered in this chapter, from 1994 to 2019.

THE ANC'S ECONOMIC JOURNEY

The ANC's early economic views were formed within the context of a liberation movement, the discussion on the nature of a democratic state, the emergence of Keynesian economics and the concept of the welfare state, and the discussion on the post-Second World War international order. Those ANC leaders who had been exposed to the right-based discourse in the United States (US) and the social rights discussion in the United Kingdom (UK) were inspired by the Atlantic Charter of 1941 and the Beverage Report of 1942. The former articulated the principles that should inform a post-war world and included important provisions such as 'the right of all peoples to choose the form of government under which they will live; and they wish to see sovereign rights and self-government restored to those who have been forcibly deprived of them' and 'the fullest collaboration between all nations in the economic field with the object of securing, for all, improved labour standards, economic advancement and social security' (Atlantic Charter, 1941: Clauses 3 and 5).[5] The latter was instrumental in establishing the welfare state in the UK. The ANC leaders adapted the content of these important documents to the conditions in South Africa. The Africans' Claims in South Africa of 1943 presented the Atlantic Charter (1941) from the African point of view and, under the section on the Bill of Rights, full citizen rights and demands. For example, with respect to the Charter's position on economic collaboration and improved labour standards, the document stated (ANC, 1943):

> We shall understand, 'improved labour standards', 'economic advancement' and 'social security' as referred to in this article

> to mean the following: (a) the removal of the Colour Bar; (b) training in skilled occupations; (c) remuneration according to skill; (d) a living wage and all other workers' benefits; (e) proper and adequate housing for all races and colours.

The section on the Africans' Claims on the Bill of Rights included, over and above civil and political rights, socioeconomic rights such as equal pay for equal work and free medical and health services for all (ANC, 1943).

There was clear continuity between the views embodied in the ANC's Bill of Rights of 1943, as contained in the Africans' Claims in South Africa, and the 1955 Freedom Charter that the ANC conference ratified in 1955. Therefore, in the Freedom Charter, the ANC declared that the 'democratic changes' it envisioned for the country included a state that would ensure that the country's mineral wealth, banks and monopoly industry were shared by the country's population. Furthermore, peasants would receive help; men and women of all races would be equally paid; there would be a 40-hour work week with a national minimum wage; there would be free education and medical care; and the state would care for the aged, orphans, the disabled and the sick.

What the Freedom Charter, and before that the Africans' Claims in South Africa, did not proclaim was a post-apartheid state that would rely on mainstream free-market mechanisms to deliver the stated democratic changes. They advocated socioeconomic rights and state interventions in securing such rights. Both of these were (Timmins, 1995, cited in Van Niekerk, 2013):

> ... compatible with the development of a Keynesian welfare state based on the social rights of citizenship, a state which was interventionist and used the powers of government to ensure that economic arrangements ensured full employment and gave effect to post-war social policies for a national health service, free comprehensive education and a non-stigmatising system of social security.[6]

When the ANC was banned (1960–1990), the fight to defeat the apartheid state and realise universal suffrage overshadowed the discussions on post-apartheid socioeconomic policies. However, the latter gained prominence again with the unbanning of the organisation in 1990 (Van Niekerk, 2013). Therefore, almost 40 years after the Freedom Charter had been ratified, the *Ready to Govern: ANC policy guideline for a democratic South Africa* (RTG) (ANC, 1992) allocated a significant portion of its content to elaborating on the organisation's plan 'to create a strong, dynamic and balanced economy'. It envisioned the establishment of a 'mixed economy' where the democratic state would consider increasing or reducing the public sector. It sanctioned state involvement in economic activity to strengthen the ability of the economy to respond to the massive inequalities in the country. Moreover, it envisioned an active, post-apartheid 'democratic state' with policy measures directed at creating employment, restructuring industry, eliminating poverty, meeting the population's basic needs, realising sustainable growth and curbing monopolies.

The RTG document did not consider the removal of imperfections, frictions and market rigidities as a way of achieving full employment, meeting the population's basic needs or restructuring South Africa's trade and industry. Nor did it view government expenditure as crowding out the private sector or consider that South Africa's future economic growth depended on foreign direct investment.[7] In the RTG document, therefore, the ANC's intent, strategy and specific economic policy ideas continued to reflect a largely heterodox view of the South African economy.

After the ANC national conference in June 1992, which saw the adoption of the RTG policy document, it gradually emerged that the ANC leadership was gravitating towards mainstream economic views and policies. Initially, the ANC supported and led the work on the Reconstruction and Development Programme (RDP) and Macroeconomic Research Group (MERG) initiatives, both of which were guided by predominantly heterodox views on the country's future growth and development path after the 1994 election. Concurrently, however, the ANC leadership was engaging on economic policy issues with advocates of mainstream views and policies, such as the National

Party, representatives of organised domestic capital and international finance agencies.

By the end of 1993, the ANC leadership had clearly decided to distance itself from the MERG analysis and policy recommendations and became a signatory to the IMF-led, mainstream, medium-term economic policy package, referred to as the Statement of Policies, which accompanied an US$800 million loan agreement (IMF, 1993).[8] Moreover, after the ANC adopted the RDP as an integral part of its election manifesto in 1994, the government started to distance itself (following the election) from the RDP-based, heterodox, analytical approach and policy framework. For example, in the RDP White Paper, the six principles of the RDP were subtly infused with mainstream economic views, with distinctive changes made to the RDP policy framework.[9]

Overall, the ANC government moulded the RDP into a mainstream economic policy document in which the analytical and policy framework edged closer to the normative economic model of the apartheid state in its later years. Consequently, in the RDP White Paper, redistribution was dropped as the main RDP objective and the government's role in the economy was reduced to that of managing transformation. Fiscal policy was totally emasculated *a priori* because of the fear that fiscal discipline would be sacrificed, while monetary policy became independent, with no specific measures introduced to make it accountable to the democratic government.

In the two years between the release of the RDP White Paper in 1994 and the release of the Growth, Employment and Redistribution (GEAR) strategy document in 1996, the ANC government took further steps towards accepting the tenets of the mainstream economic framework and its associated policies. Despite references still being made to RDP objectives, the framework underlying the government's fiscal, monetary and international economic policies showed a steady shift away from the original thrust of the RDP.[10]

The government released the GEAR strategy document in June 1996. GEAR was presented to Parliament as a non-negotiable macroeconomic policy framework covering the period 1996–2000. Its main pillars were fiscal contraction characterised by major cuts in the government deficit-to-GDP (gross domestic product) ratio; accelerated trade liberalisation; tight monetary policy; some level of privatisation; and deregulation of financial markets. The government claimed that the economic benefits of implementing GEAR included a higher economic growth rate; higher numbers of formal manufacturing jobs; and increased net inflows of foreign investment, exports, and real private and public investments (National Treasury, 1996).[11]

The significance of GEAR was not that it put forward a totally new set of economic policies. Rather, it was that the ANC government openly declared, in a non-negotiable manner, its belief in and preference for mainstream economics and the associated Washington Consensus package of policies going forward. In his address to the South African Communist Party's (SACP) 10th National Congress in 1998, President Mandela stated (Nelson Mandela Foundation, 2022):

> I want to tell you that GEAR is the fundamental policy of the African National Congress. We are not going to change it because of your pressure. We will not do that. You must choose what role you want to play. ... [w]e are convinced that this is the strategy that eventually will put our economy on a sound basis, which will make it internationally competitive. We have no hesitation about that.

After adopting GEAR as its main macroeconomic policy framework, the government took further steps to institutionalise its key policies. In this regard, two measures that were adopted are worth mentioning, namely the multi-year Medium-Term Expenditure Framework (MTEF) for budgeting purposes and inflation targeting as the lynchpin of monetary policy. The first measure enabled the government to integrate GEAR's fiscal policy position into an economic policy planning process, which extended beyond GEAR's original five-year plan. The second measure made the management of inflation the primary goal of monetary policy. By the end of the 1990s, the ANC government had fully adopted mainstream macroeconomic views and policies to underpin South Africa's post-apartheid economic system.

However, low levels of investment and economic growth as well as rising unemployment and income inequality made it increasingly apparent that the adopted policy framework was failing. At the end of GEAR's official five-year timeline, President Mbeki acknowledged that government economic policy had not propelled the economy onto a suitably growth-geared and inclusive path. In 2001, he stated, 'The reality remains that our rate of growth is still too low as are the aggregate savings and investment rates. Similarly, the levels of poverty, unemployment, and underdevelopment in some parts of our country are too high' (Mbeki, 2001). The Minister of Finance, however, decided to gloss over GEAR's unsatisfactory outcomes by stating that the GEAR strategy was designed to achieve stability and fiscal consolidation, which, he claimed, had been achieved (National Treasury, 2001).

Both the President and the Minister of Finance resolved to retain the government's macroeconomic policy, while giving detailed attention to microeconomic issues to move the economy onto a path of expansion.[12] This forward-looking recalibration of the GEAR strategy – of using macroeconomic policy to maintain macroeconomic balances and microeconomic reforms to achieve higher economic growth and employment – constituted another milestone in the evolution of the ANC government's economic views. It brought the ANC's economic views into line with the latest mainstream thinking in economics, which saw the economy as 'a dynamic general equilibrium system that deviates from an efficient allocation of resources in the short run because of sticky prices and perhaps a variety of other market imperfections' (Mankiw, 2007).

Subsequently, for more than two decades, a significant portion of the government's policymaking capacity has been channelled into employing the growth diagnostic approach of Hausmann et al. (2005) to: (a) identify the 'binding constraints' in the South Africa economy; and (b) devise national and provincial government interventions aimed at lifting or relaxing the most severe constraints.[13]

The growth diagnostic approach, according to its architects, will unlock the economy's potential for accelerated growth and employment because, in the absence of rigidities, frictions and market failures, the economy will, through the normal operation of the market, produce the necessary growth with full employment.[14] This mainstream general equilibrium view of the economy informed the majority of the government's economic plans (underpinned by the growth diagnostic approach) during the 2000s and 2010s, which promised high growth and employment. For example, after GEAR had failed to boost the economic growth rate to 6.1 per cent and non-agricultural formal employment to 4.3 per cent by 2000, a succession of alternative strategies was adopted. The Accelerated and Shared Growth Initiative for South Africa (AsgiSA) promised to halve the poverty and unemployment rates by 2014, and to accelerate economic growth to an average annual rate of at least 4.5 per cent from 2005 to 2009 and to at least 6 per cent from 2010 to 2014. The New Growth Path (NGP) undertook to create 5 million new jobs by 2020. The National Development Plan (NDP), in turn, promised to achieve an economic growth rate of 5.4 per cent, reduce the unemployment rate to 6 per cent and totally eradicate poverty by 2030.

Table 4.1 highlights the factors that the government's various economic plans identified as impediments to high growth and employment, using the growth diagnostic approach. The list includes mainly microeconomic supply-side factors.

Table 4.1: Constraints to high growth and employment identified in selected government economic plans, 2004–2019

Constraints	AsgiSA	NDP	Nine-Point Plan[15]	2019 Austerity Plan[16]
Relative currency volatility	X			
High cost and inefficiency of national logistics systems; infrastructural weaknesses	X	X	X	X
Shortage of suitably skilled labour; disjointed spatial settlement patterns	X	X	X	X
Barriers to entry (market access) and competition in various economic sectors	X			X

Constraints	AsgiSA	NDP	Nine-Point Plan[15]	2019 Austerity Plan[16]
Regulatory burden and uncertainty (including property rights); deficiencies in state organisations, capacity and strategic leadership impacting delivery	X	X		X
Poor physical planning and network infrastructure (e.g., ports, telecommunications)		X	X	
Limited access to and affordability of public transportation				X
Energy generation and distribution challenges, and high prices		X	X	X
Challenges with licensing and supply of water, and waste-water management		X	X	X
Inadequate supply of highly skilled labour		X		
Weak institutional arrangements for regulating and executing public–private partnerships, and limited capacity in government departments and other spheres		X		
High public-sector wage bill			X	
Inadequate capital availability				X
Regulatory constraints to investment				X
Delays in digital migration and spectrum allocation process				X
Lack of harmonisation of standards and pricing across the Southern African Development Community (SADC)				X

Source: Author's compilation

In 2019, the National Treasury published an economic strategy document that also relied heavily on the growth diagnostic approach for its analysis and policy recommendations (National Treasury, 2019). However, in contrast to earlier plans, the document did not claim that the implementation of its recommendations would lead to high rates of economic growth and employment. In fact, the document's quantification section showed that the adoption of its recommendations was likely to add only an estimated 2.3 percentage points to the baseline growth rate of 1.5 per cent and create 1 million jobs over a 10-year period, which was well short of the nearly 10 million jobs needed (National Treasury, 2019). Two years later, a joint National Treasury, World Bank and IMF estimation of the impact of the National Treasury's recommendations showed that the average annual economic growth rate, including the baseline growth rate, would be 1.5 per cent between 2022 and 2026, with the unemployment rate gradually increasing to 38.3 per cent by 2026 (World Bank, 2021).

Therefore, the government's longstanding conviction that the removal of binding constraints would lead to medium- to long-term accelerated economic growth and employment has, since 2019, given way to the current understanding: that even with all identified constraints removed, the economy would still be stuck in a cycle of low growth and high unemployment. This deviates from the government's long-held positive outlook on the country's economic and economic development prospects, as advanced, for example, in the NDP targets since 2012. The ANC government thus stands at a historically important crossroads and needs to make a decision: either to continue with the mainstream economic views and policies of the post-1996 era, which the party now knows will not deliver the needed levels of economic growth and employment, or to learn from other countries, especially in East Asia, which have followed heterodox economic policies over the past 50 years to influence the workings of market economies and have achieved much better outcomes.

PAST OUTCOMES AND THE FUTURE OUTLOOK

Over the past (nearly three) decades, the government's pursuit of mainstream economic policy solutions to address South Africa's growth and development challenges has left its empirical imprint on the evolution of policy and outcome indicators, some of which are discussed below.

Performance of key macroeconomic policy indicators (1996–2019)

Since GEAR, the government's fiscal policy has centred on two main aims, namely to avoid permanent increases in the country's overall tax burden and to use medium-term deficit targets to eliminate government dissaving (National Treasury, 1996). In practice, these aims have curtailed the government's ability to raise taxes and/or to borrow to help finance the expected post-apartheid socioeconomic transformation.[17] Fiscal policy data covering more than two decades reflect the implementation of this framework.

Between 1996 and 2019, total annual government revenue was on average equivalent to 24 per cent of GDP, while the annual deficit-to-GDP ratio was on average 3 per cent (see Figure 4.1). This means that the total annual government expenditure envelope was on average equivalent to 27 per cent of GDP. Figure 4.1 shows that these fiscal estimates were observed during the period in question, regardless of government economic plans and their underlying development goals. Put differently, from 1996, all government development plans have adhered strictly to the medium-term, expenditure-envelope fiscal framework that was established under GEAR.

Figure 4.2 compares South Africa's fiscal indicators with equivalent data for Organisation for Economic Cooperation and Development (OECD) countries for the period 1995–2020. It shows that the South African government's average annual revenue-to-GDP ratio of 23.9 per cent was 41.6 per cent lower than the average annual revenue-to-GDP ratio for OECD countries (see Figure 4.2A). Consequently, relative to the OECD countries, the South African government spent the lowest share of the country's GDP on delivering public goods and

Figure 4.1: Fiscal policy indicators, 1996–2019

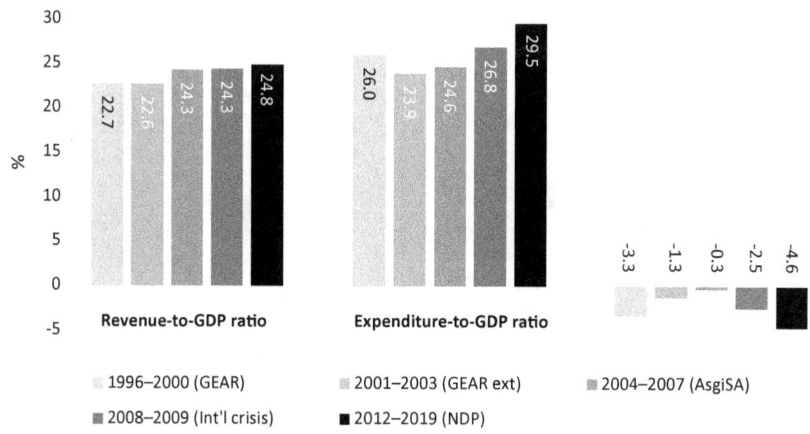

Source: Adelzadeh, 2022, based on South African Reserve Bank Time Series Data on Public Finance, 1996–2019

services and providing social protection (see Figure 4.2B).

Over the 26 years in question, the government's average annual expenditure relative to GDP, namely 27.3 per cent, was about 37 per cent (or 16 percentage points) lower than the average expenditure-to-GDP ratio of OECD countries. This is an astonishing finding, considering that, during the same period, South Africa became the most unequal country in the world. Currently it ranks first amongst 164 countries in the World Bank's latest global poverty database (World Bank, 2022).

Figures 4.2A–D, which provide an international comparison of fiscal policy indicators over a period of 26 years, also show that a government's quest to limit its dissaving is not conditional upon keeping the overall tax burden low.[18] This implies that if the South African government's main concern has been to eliminate government dissaving, it could have pursued this goal without limiting its ability to raise revenue through its tax policy.

The South African government's decision to not only limit its dissaving but also to avoid permanent increases in the overall tax burden has significantly benefited the country's well-off classes and has been supported by international agencies.[19] In reality, however, this has been at the expense of the majority of South Africans who have had

Figures 4.2A–D: South Africa's fiscal indicators relative to those of the OECD countries, 1995–2020

4.2A: Revenue-to-GDP ratio

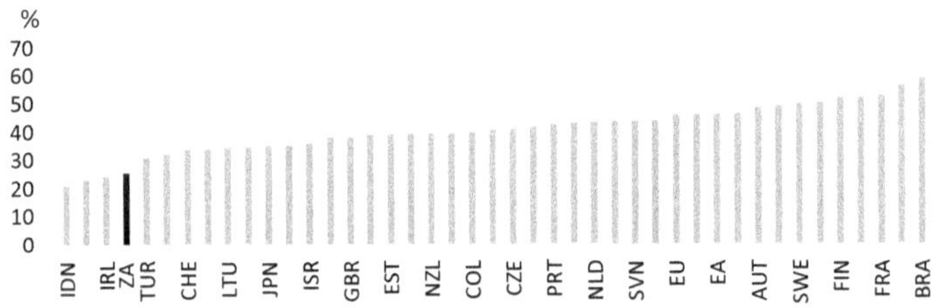

4.2B: Expenditure-to-GDP ratio

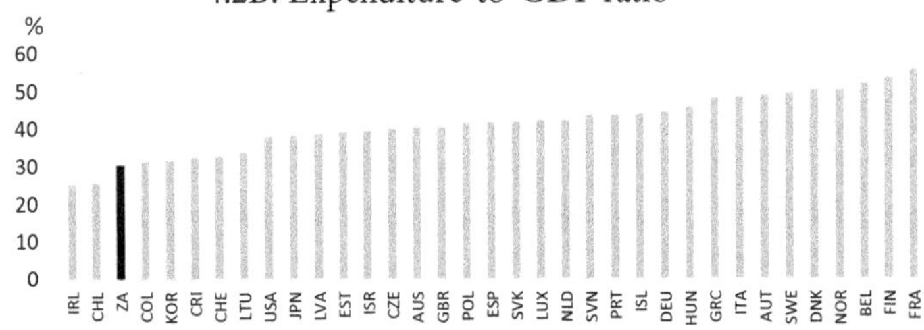

4.2C: Deficit-to-GDP ratio

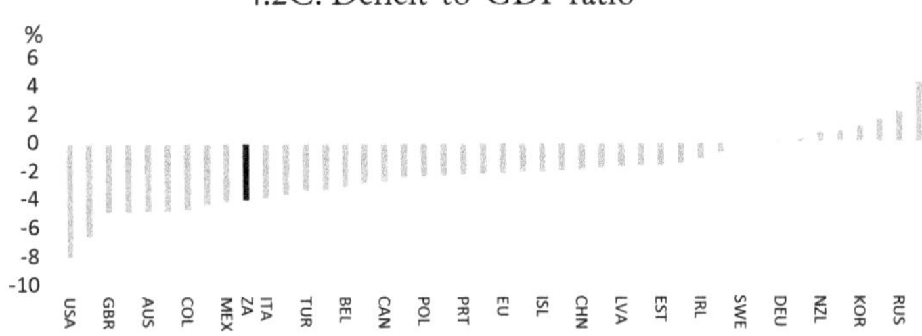

4.2D: Debt-to-GDP ratio

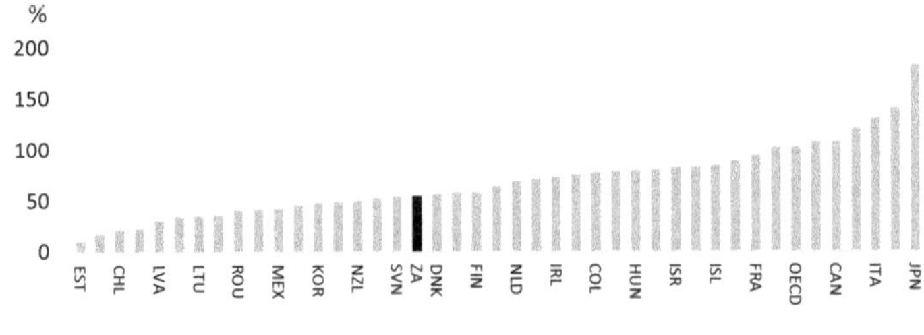

Source: OECD, 2022a. General government spending (indicator)

Notes: The country data used were calculated as average annual figures for 2017–2020 (revenue-to-GDP), 2017–2019 (expenditure-to-GDP), 2017–2020 (deficit-to-GDP) and 1995–2020 (debt-to-GDP).

to endure the direct negative impact of the policy (on the mobilisation of resources) on the scope and pace of post-apartheid socioeconomic transformation.[20] The impact of the policy on the level of available annual resources has been even more severe, given the country's poor economic growth performance.

Figure 4.3: Income tax relative to GDP, 1996–2020

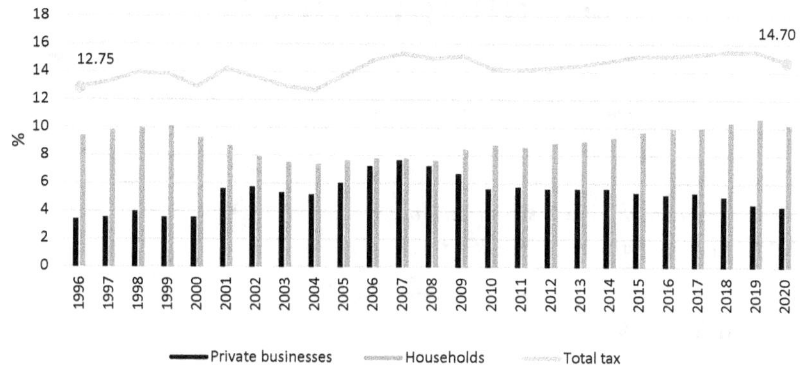

Source: Adelzadeh, 2022, based on South African Reserve Bank Time Series Data on Public Finance, 1996–2020

A common argument for maintaining low tax rates and low government spending is that they boost private investment. This thinking corresponds with the mainstream view that saving determines investment and, therefore, that measures that help to increase savings will automatically stimulate private investment. However, Figures 4.4 and 4.5 show, historically, a positive correlation between the levels of private investment and government spending, and a similar relationship between the growth of real private investment and government consolidated expenditure.

The data on monetary policy indicators confirm that the monetary authorities in South Africa have successfully adhered to the mainstream economic approach of using monetary policy tools mainly to fight inflation. Therefore, as in the case of fiscal policy, monetary policy has been restrictive over the period in question. The direct effects of the Reserve Bank's inflation targeting policy are evident in the data pertaining to interest rates, credit extensions and money supply.

Despite persistently low growth and high unemployment rates,

Figure 4.4: Correlation between private investment and government expenditure, 1996–2019

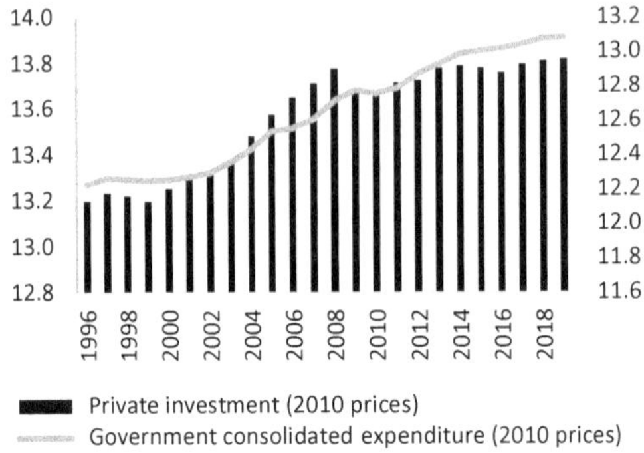

Source: Adelzadeh, 2022, based on South African Reserve Bank Time Series Data on Public Finance, 1996–2019

Figure 4.5: Annual growth of private investment and government expenditure, 1996–2019

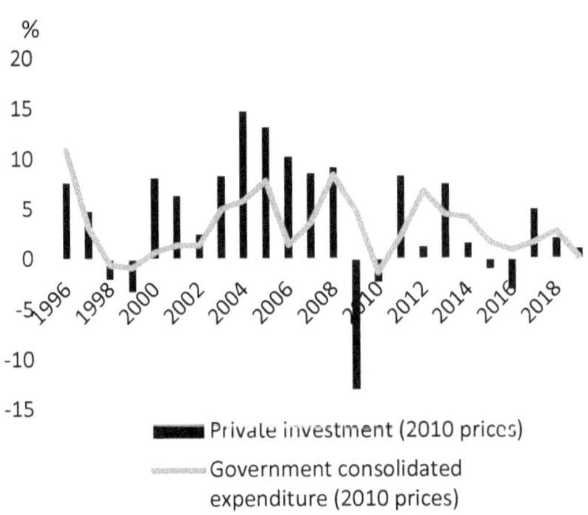

Source: Adelzadeh, 2022, based on South African Reserve Bank Time Series Data on Public Finance, 1996–2019

short-term interest rates, which affect borrowing costs for everyone, were positive in real terms for 21 out of the 24 years between 1996 and 2019 (see Figure 4.7). Similarly, long-term interest rates, which are one of the determinants of business investment, were above the real GDP growth rate for 18 out of the 24 years (see Figure 4.6). Internationally, as Figures 4.8 and 4.9 show, South Africa's short- and long-term interest rates have consistently been almost the highest compared to OECD countries.

Figure 4.6: Trends in real interest rates and economic growth, 1996–2019

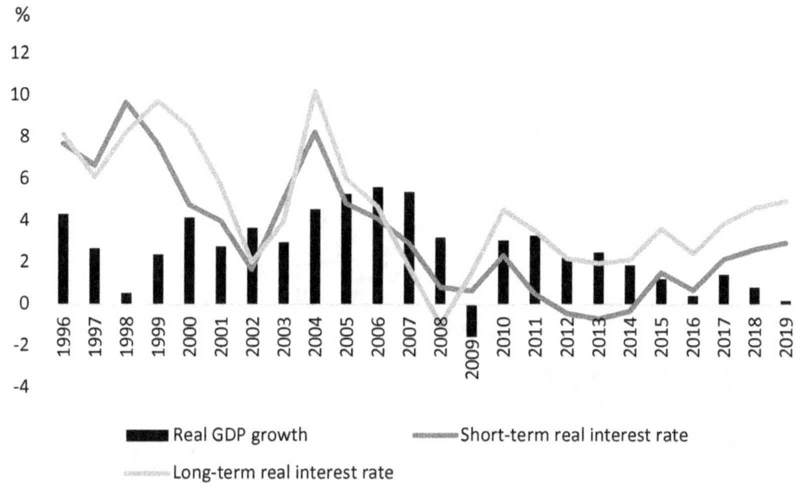

Sources: OECD, 2022b. Short-term interest rates (indicator), long-term interest rates (indicator); South African Reserve Bank Time Series Data on GDP (2010 prices); Adelzadeh, 2022, based on South African Reserve Bank Time Series Data on Public Finance, 1996–2019

Figure 4.7: Short-term interest rates: South Africa relative to OECD countries, 1995–2020

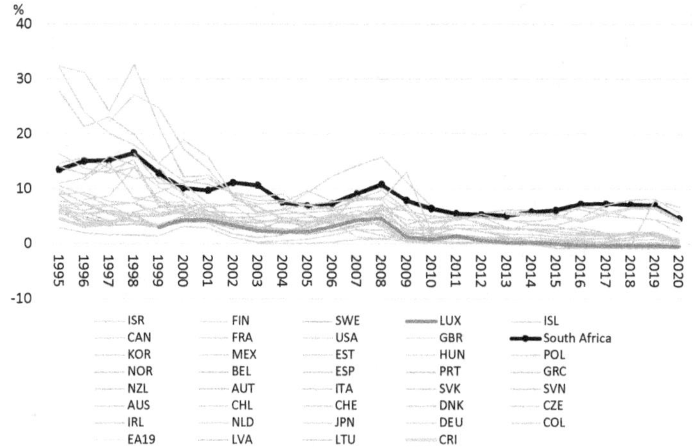

Source: OECD, 2022b. Short-term interest rates (indicator)

Note on Figure 4.7: Short-term interest rates are the rates at which short-term borrowings are effected between financial institutions or the rate at which short-term government paper is issued or traded in the market.

Figure 4.8: Long-term interest rates: South Africa relative to OECD countries, 1995–2020

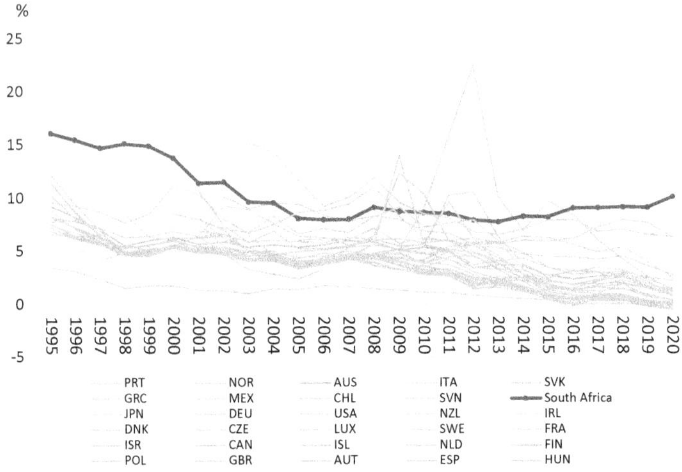

Source: OECD, 2022c. Long-term interest rates (indicator)

Note: Long-term interest rates refer to government bonds maturing in 10 years.

High real interest rates have not only inversely impacted private investment but have also contributed to the rise in the debt-to-GDP ratio. As Figure 4.9 shows, annual changes in the debt-to-GDP ratio positively relate to the annual differences between the long-term real interest rate and the economic growth rate. In other words, the debt-to-GDP ratio increases (decreases) when the real interest rate is greater (less) than the real GDP growth rate.[21]

Access to credit (i.e., borrowing) is another important determinant of private investment (Galindo and Schiantarelli, 2003). Figure 4.10 reflects a close, positive relationship between the private sector's ability to borrow (i.e., access credit) and private real investment in South Africa during the period in question. Despite their potential to support private investment and economic growth, data on the credit extensions highlight another restrictive dimension of monetary policy in South Africa.

Figure 4.9: Monetary policy and debt-to-GDP ratio, 1996–2019

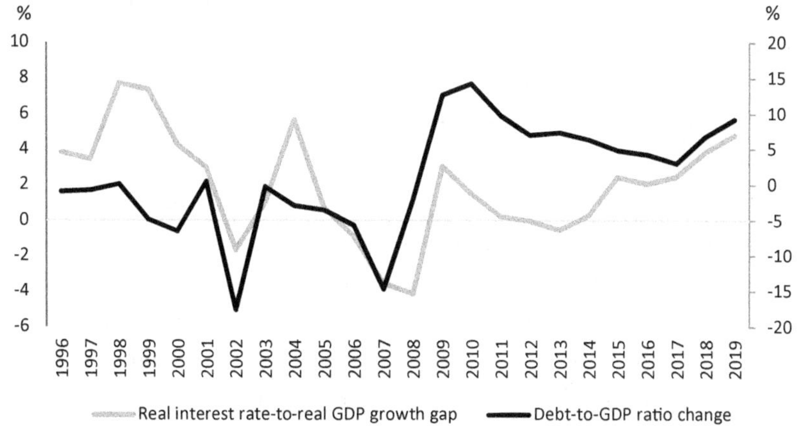

Source: Adelzadeh, 2022, based on South African Reserve Bank Time Series Data on Public Finance, 1996–2019

Notes: Total national government (RB4114J) and nominal GDP (RB6006J) for the calculation of the debt-to-GDP ratio. Calculated the real interest rate using OECD South Africa data on CPI inflation and the long-term interest rate. Used South African Reserve Bank Time Series data for the real GDP growth rate (RB6006Y).

Figure 4.10: Credit extensions to private sector and private investment, 1996–2019

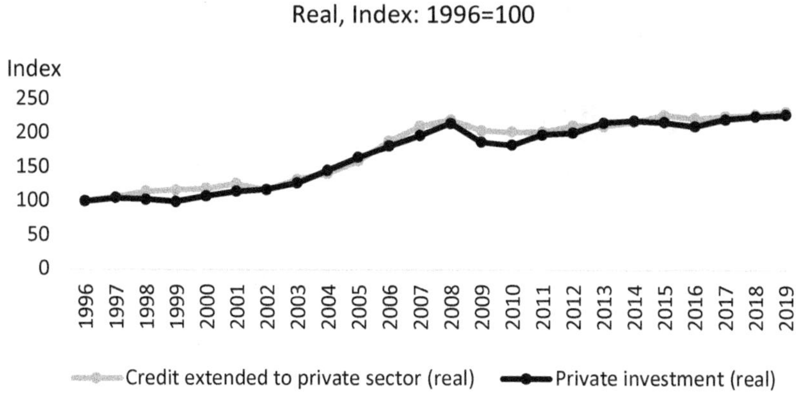

Source: Adelzadeh, 2022, based on South African Reserve Bank Time Series Data on Public Finance, 1996–2019

During the GEAR period (1996–2003), the real value of credit extensions to the private sector grew at an average annual rate of 4.6 per cent. Private-sector investment grew in parallel to credit extensions, at an average annual rate of 4.1 per cent. During the AsgiSA period (2004–2007), the average annual growth rate of credit extensions to the private sector was 12.6 per cent, which was almost three times higher than the average annual growth rate during the GEAR period. Again, parallel to this, private-sector investment during the period 2004–2007 grew at an average annual rate of 12.7 per cent.

After the global financial crisis of 2008–2009, a highly restrictive lending policy was introduced which led to the average annual growth rate of credit to the private sector falling significantly to roughly half a per cent (0.6 per cent) in real terms between 2010 and 2019. This directly impacted private investment growth, which fell spectacularly to an average annual rate of 0.7 per cent. Consequently, the average GDP growth rate recorded was 2.6 times lower than the corresponding rate for the period 1996–2008, i.e., 1.4 per cent against 3.6 per cent.

Figure 4.11: Access to credit, private investment and economic growth

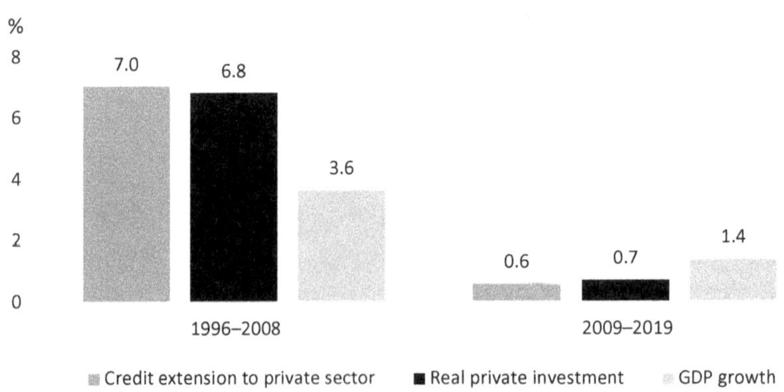

Source: Adelzadeh, 2022, based on South African Reserve Bank Time Series Data on Public Finance, 1996–2019

The increase in broad money in real terms further confirms that monetary policy has been highly restrictive, especially since 2009. Figure 4.12 shows that, in the period 2009–2019, the average annual growth rate of the real money supply dropped below the average annual GDP growth rate. The Reserve Bank's tight money supply policy during this period contributed to the persistence of a sluggish economy after the global recession of 2008–2009.

Figure 4.12: Real money supply and GDP (average annual growth rates), 1996–2019

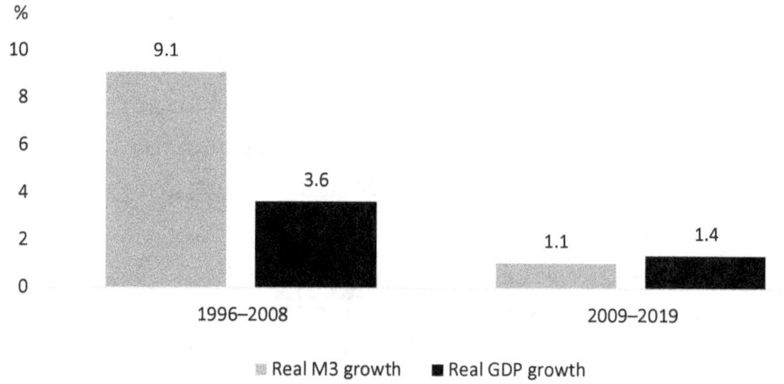

Source: Adelzadeh, 2022, based on South African Reserve Bank Time Series Data on Public Finance, 1996–2019

Overall, during the period in question, the monetary authorities achieved their mandate of keeping inflation rates within the specified band. However, they did this through high interest rates, low growth in credit extensions to the private sector and a highly restrictive approach to growth of the money supply. As demonstrated, these elements of South Africa's macroeconomic policy framework have played significant roles in creating the conditions for persistently low rates of investment and economic growth. Yet they have largely been overlooked amidst the government's singular focus on the microeconomic sources of low economic growth.

KEY MACROECONOMIC OUTCOMES (1996–2019)

The South African economy grew at an average annual rate of 2.8 per cent between 1996 (when GEAR was introduced) and 2019 (the year before the start of the COVID-19 pandemic). During those years, the economy was characterised by at least four periods: the GEAR extended period of 1996–2003, the AsgiSA period of 2004–2007, the global crisis period of 2008–2009 and the NDP period of 2010–2019.

In 1996, a largely complete package of mainstream economic policies was rolled out as 'a broad bridge between the present constrained economic environment and an improved growth and employment performance in the period up to 2000' (National Treasury, 1996: 4). The government claimed that GEAR would, within five years, yield superior outcomes relative to a policy scenario that did not prescribe GEAR policies (i.e., the base scenario). This included promises of high, sustainable economic growth rates, major additions to annual employment figures and improvements in export growth by the year 2000.

In terms of actual outcomes, the government succeeded in institutionalising GEAR's restrictive fiscal and monetary policies, but the policies did not produce the promised outcomes in the areas of economic growth, employment and exports. GEAR policies failed dismally to promote private investment and did not make much of a difference in terms of increasing the pace of non-gold exports (see Figure 4.13).

Figure 4.13: GEAR projections versus actual outcomes, 1996–2000

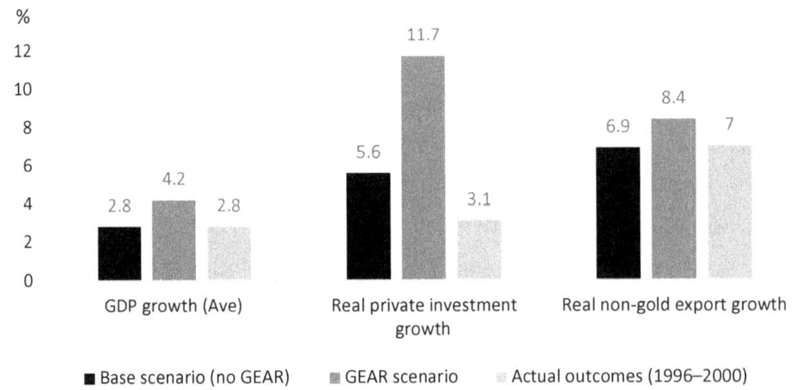

Sources. Adelzadeh, 2022, based on South African Reserve Bank Time Series Data on Public Finance, 1996–2019

Notes: Values for the base and GEAR scenarios are from tables titled 'Base Scenario Projections: 1996–2000' and 'Integrated Scenario Projections: 1996–2000' on pages 4 and 7 of the Growth, Employment and Redistribution strategy (National Treasury, 1996). Actual outcomes are calculated using South African Reserve Bank Time Series Data.

South Africa's economic growth performance did not improve much until the AsgiSA period, when the average annual real GDP growth rate almost doubled, from 2.8 per cent during the GEAR period (1996–2000) to 5.2 per cent in the AsgiSA period (2004–2007). What contributed to this improved outcome was not the removal of the six binding constraints that had been identified in the plan but rather significant increases in public and private expenditures.[22] During the AsgiSA period, the average annual growth rate of total government expenditure increased more than seven-fold in real terms, from 0.8 per cent during GEAR to 5.9 per cent in the period 2004–2007. This included substantial growth in public investment, especially investment by public corporations (see Table 4.2). However, the considerable increase in government expenditure during the AsgiSA period was not limited to an increase in investment expenditure. The average annual growth rate of government final consumption expenditure, in real terms, also increased from 1.4 per cent during GEAR to 4.8 per cent during AsgiSA.

The significant rise in total government expenditure did not crowd out private investment growth, which almost quadrupled, from an average annual growth rate of 3.1 per cent during the GEAR period to 11.7 per cent during the AsgiSA period. This was supported by a significant increase in credit extensions to the private sector, from a real annual growth rate of 5 per cent during the GEAR period to 12.6 per cent during the AsgiSA period. The increase in private-sector investment was also accommodated (facilitated) by a similar increase in the average real annual growth of the money supply (see Table 4.2).

Moreover, contrary to GEAR's fiscal policy reasoning, the expansion of aggregate demand through increased public investment and current spending by government produced relatively lower average inflation rates and deficit-to-GDP and debt-to-GDP ratios. What GEAR promised to achieve in five years, AsgiSA achieved in four years by disregarding at least the fiscal policy elements of the GEAR strategy.

The global economic recession of the late 2000s brought with it a major tightening of the credit market across the world. In South Africa, private-sector access to credit fell sharply, from an average real growth rate of 11.3 per cent during the AsgiSA period to -1.3 per cent

Figure 4.14: Economic growth, 1996–2019

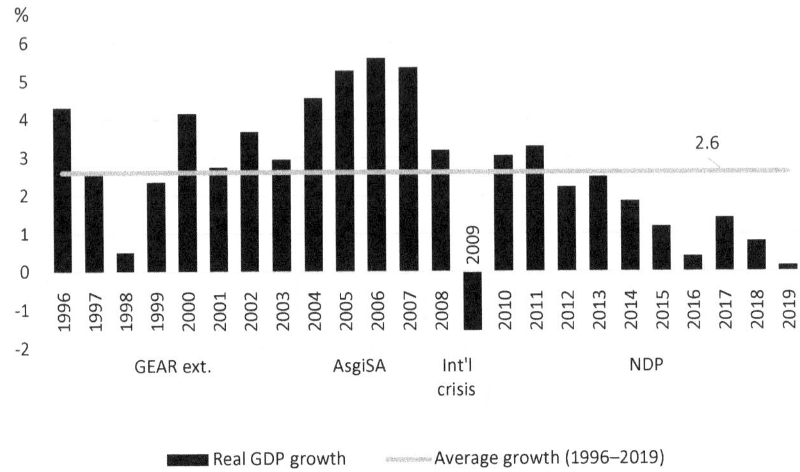

Source: Adelzadeh, 2022, based on South African Reserve Bank Time Series Data on Public Finance, 1996–2019

in the period 2008–2009. The global recession also led to the collapse of South Africa's non-gold real exports, from a high average annual growth rate of 8.8 per cent during AsgiSA to -7.3 per cent in the period 2008–2009. The growth of the real money supply almost came to a halt. During this period, however, real public investment continued to grow, especially investment by public enterprises (see Table 4.2).

In the period following the global recession, which is loosely referred to in this chapter as the NDP period (2010–2019), the fiscal and monetary policy measures were gradually tightened and became more austere. As a result, during the 10-year, post-crisis period, the average economic growth rate dropped to 1.7 per cent, as public investment, especially investment by public corporations, declined in real terms. The government's current spending grew slowly in real terms, while the average real growth rate of private-sector investment dropped to 2.1 per cent, from 8.8 per cent during the AsgiSA period (see Table 4.2).

Overall, to put into perspective South Africa's economic performance after the adoption of GEAR's mainstream policies, Figure 4.15 compares compound annual growth rates (CAGR) of GDP for the G20 countries in the period 1995–2019.[23] Amongst this group of large and medium-sized economies, South Africa's CAGR of GDP was the third lowest, above that of Saudi Arabia and Japan.

Figure 4.15: South Africa within the G20 countries: growth performance (US$/capita, current PPPs, CAGR) 1995–2019

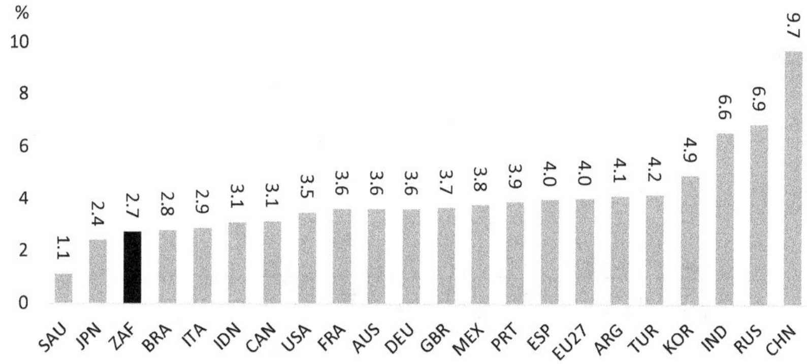

Source: OECD, 2022d. Gross domestic product (GDP) (indicator)

Government's mainstream economic policies have also not produced the desired levels of employment. For more than two decades, South Africa's official unemployment rate has been consistently above 20 per cent. In 1995, the unemployment rate was 16.4 per cent. By 2002, it had reached 30.5 per cent. During the AsgiSA high-growth period, the unemployment rate dropped to 21.5 per cent. However, it increased once again to about 23.1 per cent during the global recession of 2008–2009. From 2010 to 2019, when the average annual GDP growth rate fell to less than 2 per cent (i.e., 1.7 per cent), the unemployment rate continued to rise.

By 2019, before the advent of COVID-19, the official unemployment rate had reached 28.7 per cent. According to the Quarterly Labour Force Survey (QLFS), the official unemployment rate reached 35.3 per cent during the fourth quarter of 2021 (StatsSA, 2022). Figure 4.17 shows that South Africa's unemployment rate has consistently been much higher than that of all the other G20 countries over the period in question.

Table 4.2: South Africa's macroeconomic policy and outcomes, 1996–2019

		Average values (%)					
	Input and output indicators	1996–2000 GEAR official	1996–2003 GEAR extended	2004–2007 AsgiSA	2008–2009 Global financial crisis	2010–2019 NDP	**1996–2019 Overall**
Policy inputs	Total govt expenditure growth rate (real)	0.80	1.87	5.87	6.85	3.19	**3.50**
	Govt final consumption expenditure growth rate (real)	1.42	2.55	4.82	5.22	1.90	**2.88**
	Total public investment growth rate (real)	3.96	4.97	14.77	14.03	-1.07	**4.84**
	General govt investment growth rate (real)	4.57	4.90	11.88	-0.10	0.94	**4.00**
	Public corp. investment growth rate (real)	4.70	6.15	18.86	29.02	-2.64	**6.51**
	Short-term interest rate (SA)	13.96	12.66	7.72	9.36	6.29	**8.91**
	Long-term interest rate	14.80	13.31	8.38	8.90	8.55	**10.14**
	Long-term real interest rate	8.13	6.54	5.68	0.26	3.38	**4.55**
	Total private-sector credit extensions growth rate (real)	5.00	4.60	12.56	1.33	1.34	**4.07**
	Broad money supply (M3) growth rate (real)	5.44	6.70	14.46	0.28	1.78	**5.41**
Macro-economic outcomes	GDP growth rate (real)	2.80	2.92	5.20	0.83	1.68	**2.61**
	Unemployment rate	29.9	30.7	28.4	23.1	26.0	**27.7**
	Private business enterprise investment growth rate (real)	3.1	4.1	11.7	-1.9	2.1	**4.0**
	Non-gold export growth rate (real)	6.97	5.43	8.78	-7.30	2.71	**3.79**
	CPI inflation rate	6.67	6.78	2.70	8.64	5.17	**5.58**
	Deficit-to-GDP ratio	-3.28	-2.52	-0.35	-2.50	-4.62	**-3.03**
	Debt-to-GDP ratio	46.0	42.9	31.5	28.3	47.8	**41.8**
	Wage share relative to GDP	48.6	47.1	48.1	43.6	46.6	**45.9**
	Profit share relative to GDP	41.0	42.5	45.0	45.7	41.5	**42.8**

Source: Adelzadeh, 2022, based on South African Reserve Bank Time Series Data on Public Finance, 1996–2019

Notes: Reserve Bank time series data were used for all data in this table, except the data for interest rates, which came from the OECD, as cited previously. The national income and product account data on compensation of employees and gross operating surplus were used for wages and profits respectively.

Figure 4.16: Unemployment rate, 1996–2019

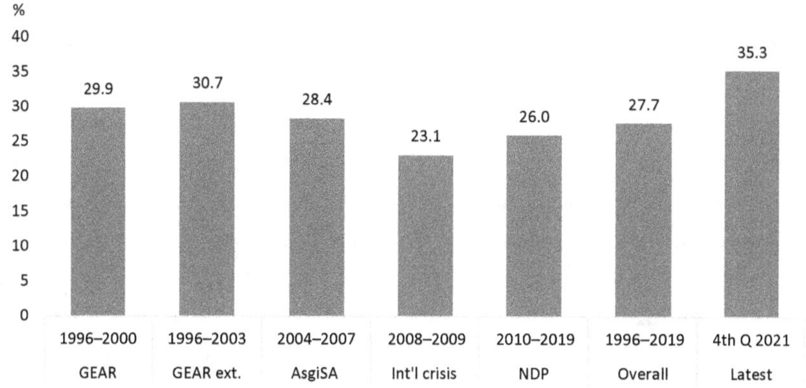

Sources: Macrotrends data, 1996–2007. Used Macrotrends data for 1996 to 2007 and used StatsSA Quarterly Labour Force Surveys for the data after 2007.

Note: The data represent official unemployment rates which are based on the strict definition of unemployment.

Figure 4.17: South Africa within the G20 countries: unemployment rate, 1995–2019

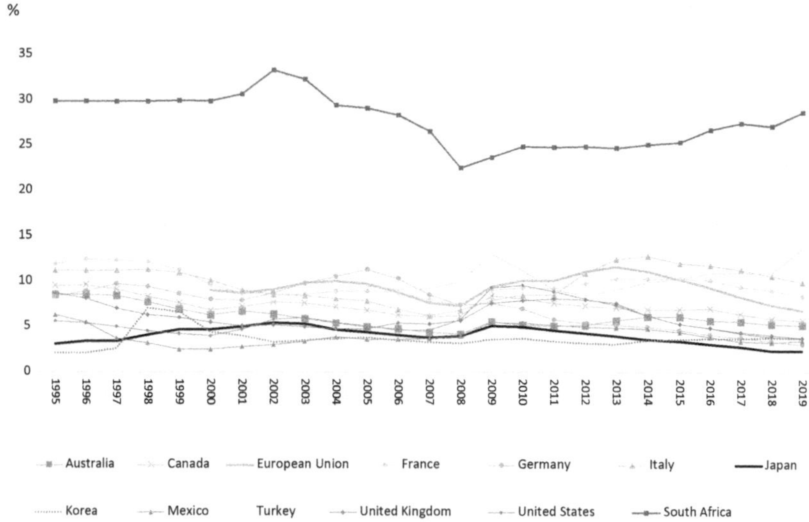

Source: OECD, 2022e. Unemployment rate (indicator)

Note: Data on South Africa unemployment rates are from Macrotrends (1995–2007) and the StatsSA Quarterly Labour Force Surveys (2008–2019).

Despite claims by proponents of mainstream economics that their suite of policy recommendations would expand exports and enhance international competitiveness, Figure 4.18 shows that the earlier, positive gap between the export and import shares of GDP gradually diminished over the period in question. Meanwhile, the South African economic policy mix since 1996 has led to structural transformation, but in the direction of deindustrialisation. Trade liberalisation and financialisation of the economy reduced the share of manufacturing employment in total employment from 15.6 per cent in 1996 to 9.2 per cent in 2020 (see Figure 4.19). In contrast, the shares of financial sector services in total output and employment, respectively, increased. Moreover, the financial sector's output share increased from 15.9 per cent in 1996 to 23.4 per cent in 2020, which is a 7.5 percentage point increase. The share of employment increased from 12.6 per cent in 1996 to 17.6 per cent in 2020, which is a 5 percentage point increase.

Figure 4.18: Trends in the gap between export and import shares of GDP, 1996–2019

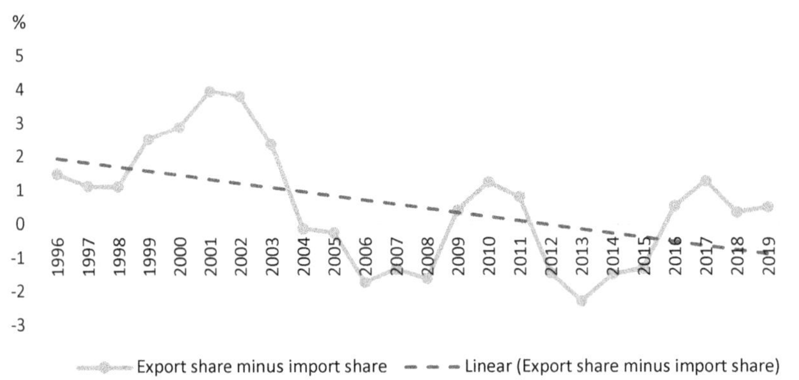

Source: Adelzadeh, 2022, based on South African Reserve Bank Time Series Data on Public Finance, 1996–2019

The United Nations Industrial Development Organization's (UNIDO) Competitive Industrial Performance (CIP) Index (see Figure 4.20) is a composite index of four indicators, namely manufacturing value-added per capita, manufacturing export per capita, industrialisation intensity (i.e., average of the share of manufacturing value-added in GDP and share of medium- and high-technology activities in manufacturing value-added), and export quality (measured as the average of the share of manufactured exports in total exports and the share of medium- and high-technology products in total exports). The CIP for South Africa declined by 17 per cent between 2000 and 2019 (see Figure 4.20). By contrast, the CIP indices for China, Vietnam and South Korea increased by 120 per cent, 262 per cent and 10 per cent, respectively, during that period.

GOVERNMENT'S MACROECONOMIC OUTLOOK (2022–2030)

Since 2019, the South African government has been pursuing a more austere version of its post-1996 fiscal policy. This is especially evident from government revenue and expenditure data. In the Medium-Term Budget Policy Statement (MTBPS) of November 2021, nominal GDP is projected to grow at an average annual rate of 5.9 per cent during the period 2021–2023, which is similar to the average annual growth rate of nominal GDP during the 10 years between 2011 and 2021 (see Table 4.3). Since government revenue grows with nominal GDP growth, the MTBPS projections reveal that total government revenue is expected to grow at an average annual rate of 6.3 per cent during the period 2021–2023, which is also close to the average annual growth rate during the period 2011–2021.

Figure 4.19: Share of manufacturing in total employment, 1996–2020

Source: Quantec EasyData

Figure 4.20: UNIDO Competitive Industrial Performance (CIP) Index, 2000–2019

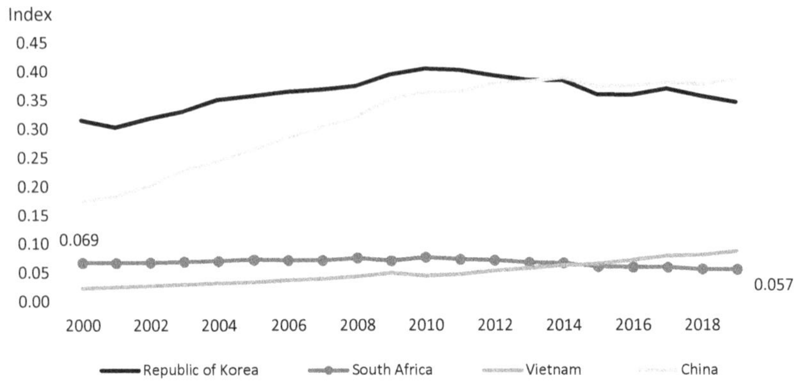

Source: UNIDO, 2020

Despite the two periods' similar GDP and revenue growth rates, the MTBPS data show that government-consolidated expenditure would grow by 1.8 per cent annually during the 2021–2023 period, compared to the much higher 7.8 per cent during the 2011–2021 period. This also means that the increase in government's planned total expenditure would be 2.5 per cent below the expected average inflation rate of 4.3 per cent during the 2021–2023 period (see Table 4.3).

Figure 4.21: Evidence of fiscal austerity, 2011–2020 vs. 2020–2023 (CAGR)

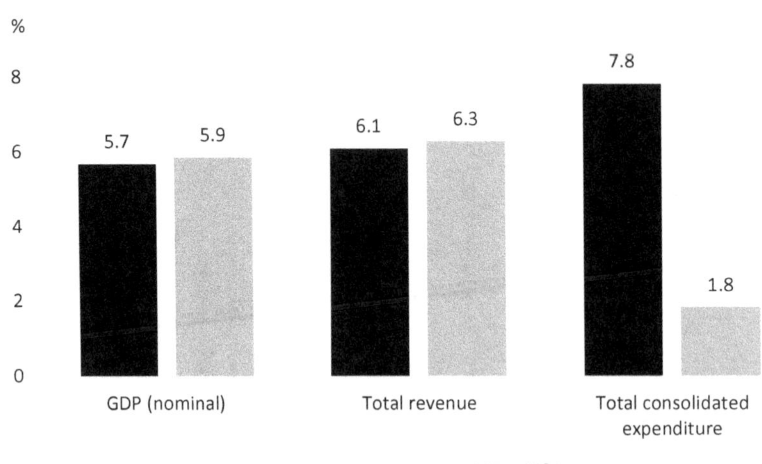

Source: National Treasury, 2021 (MTBPS)

The right-hand panel in Table 4.3 shows that the annual growth rate of the budget allocated to every government function during the 2021–2023 period was lower than the corresponding growth rate during the 2011–2019 period. Overall, during the latest MTBPS period, the annual growth rate of total, consolidated government expenditure is expected to be 6 per cent, or R253 billion, which is lower than the annual growth rate of the budget allocation during the past decade.

Neither the fiscal nor monetary authorities have presented any evidence that the current combination of fiscal austerity, a restrictive monetary policy and a suite of supply-side measures would improve economic and development outcomes. In fact, as stated earlier, the government seems to be pursuing the current economic policy knowing that it will not improve the macroeconomic outlook, as growth is projected to linger at 1.5 per cent during the 2022–2026 period and the unemployment rate is expected to rise to 38.3 per cent by 2026. Furthermore, the National Treasury's projections show that policies that have been advanced to increase savings and investment, reduce government dissaving and improve the debt-to-GDP ratio are unlikely to produce the desired outcomes (see Table 4.4).

In another assessment, Adelzadeh et al. (2021) used an Applied Development Research Solutions (ADRS) economic model of South Africa to design post-COVID-19 recovery scenarios and simulate their impact on key economic indicators for the rest of this decade.[24] One of the scenarios asked what the likely economic outlook would be if the recovery plan implemented economic policies that were even more conservative than those of the post-1996 period. The scenario is set out in the following austere policy roadmap:

- Government spending on goods and services is cut by 10 per cent;
- Government capital spending is cut by 5 per cent;
- Monetary policy is tightened by lowering the current 6 per cent upper bound limit for inflation to 4 per cent; and
- The localisation policy is abandoned and subsidies on products and production are cut by 5 per cent.

Table 4.3: Estimate of fall in budget allocation by function, 2011–2021 and 2021–2023

Consolidated government expenditure: functional	**2011–2021 CAGR (%)**	**2021–2023 CAGR (%)**	**CAGR difference (% points)**	**Allocation difference (R millions)**
General public services	10.4	8.0	-2.4	-19 826
Defence	3.0	1.6	-1.4	-1 330
Public order and safety	5.5	1.0	-4.5	-14 473
Economic affairs	7.2	-0.4	-7.6	-35 746
Environmental protection	6.8	2.7	-4.1	-1 055
Housing and community amenities	6.0	4.3	-1.7	-6 688
Health	7.9	-0.8	-8.6	-43 807
Recreation and culture	8.3	-2.0	-10.3	-3 075
Education	7.2	1.6	-5.7	-46 832
Social protection	9.3	-1.4	-10.7	-76 023
Total consolidated expenditure	**7.8**	**1.8**	**-6.0**	**-253 183**

Source: Author's own compilation based on data in National Treasury, 2021 (MTBPS, Table 8)

The modelling results show that over the coming decade:

- The annual GDP growth rate will on average be 1.8 per cent up to 2030;
- The unemployment rate will be 29 per cent in 2030; and
- The poverty rate will be 37 per cent in 2030.

The future outlook, at least for the rest of this decade, under the current austerity scenario, as quantified by the National Treasury, World Bank and ADRS, presents likely outcomes that are not dissimilar to the economy's performance during the period 2010–2019. It will, however, mean that by 2030 – three and a half decades after the full adoption of mainstream economic views and policies – the country will continue to be trapped in a cycle of low growth and high levels of unemployment and poverty.

Table 4.4: South Africa's future outlook, 2018–2026

	2018	2019	2020	2021	2022	2023	2024	2025	2026
	Estimates				Projections				
National income and prices (annual % changes)									
Real GDP	1.5	0.1	-6.4	5.0	2.2	1.4	1.3	1.3	1.3
Consumer Price Index (CPI) (annual average)	4.6	4.1	3.3	4.4	4.5	4.5	4.5	4.5	4.5
Output gap (% of potential real GDP)	-0.9	-2.0	-9.5	-5.1	-3.2	-2.3	-1.6	-1.0	-0.7
Labour market (annual % change)									
Unemployment rate (% of labour force, annual average)	27.1	28.7	29.2	33.1	34.0	35.8	37.0	37.6	38.3
Savings and investment (% of GDP)									
Gross national savings	13.3	13.3	14.7	16.4	14.1	13.8	13.7	13.7	13.6
Public (including public enterprises)	1.3	1.0	-3.5	-2.0	-0.2	0.4	0.4	0.2	-0.1
Private	12.0	12.3	18.2	18.4	14.3	13.4	13.3	13.5	13.7
Investment	16.5	16.0	12.7	13.5	15.0	15.2	15.4	15.7	16.0
Public (including public enterprises)	4.8	4.3	3.9	3.5	3.6	3.6	3.5	3.5	3.5
Private	11.0	11.1	9.8	9.7	10.1	10.3	10.6	10.9	11.2
Fiscal position (% of GDP) 1/									
Revenue (including grants)	26.4	26.9	25.2	25.1	26.1	26.2	26.3	26.3	26.4
Expenditure and net lending	30.2	31.7	36.0	33.6	33.1	32.5	32.5	32.8	33.2
Overall balance	-3.7	-4.8	-10.8	-8.4	-7.0	-6.4	-6.2	-6.5	-6.8
Primary balance	-0.3	-1.1	-6.6	-4.1	-2.2	-1.2	-0.7	-0.5	-0.2
Gross government debt 2/	51.6	56.3	69.4	68.8	72.3	74.9	77.4	80.2	83.0
Balance of payments (% of GDP unless otherwise indicated)									
Exports of goods and services (volume, annual % change)	2.8	-3.4	-12.0	12.2	1.8	3.1	3.1	2.9	2.9
Imports of goods and services (volume, annual % change)	3.2	0.5	-17.4	15.1	11.3	4.4	4.0	3.6	3.6
Current account balance (US$ billions)	-13.1	-10.6	6.6	11.9	-3.8	-6.3	-7.9	-9.7	-12.8
% of GDP	-3.2	-2.7	2.0	2.9	-0.9	-1.4	-1.7	-2.0	-2.4
Overall balance	0.2	0.5	-1.0	1.1	-0.1	-0.2	-0.2	-0.2	-0.2
Gross reserves (US$ billions)	51.6	55.1	55.5	60.0	59.8	58.7	57.6	56.5	55.4
% of short-term debt (residual maturity)	89.2	98.4	76.7	88.2	86.2	84.3	77.3	75.4	75.5
Total external debt	42.6	47.6	56.4	45.1	44.2	43.5	43.5	44.7	44.6

Sources: This table was originally published by the World Bank (2021: 55). World Bank (2021) states as sources of this table: South African National Treasury, World Bank and Fund staff estimates and projections.

Notes: 1/ Consolidated government unless otherwise indicated

2/ National government

ALTERNATIVE FUTURE OUTLOOK

What if the government were willing to reconsider its mainstream economic views and policies? This section considers the likely outlook for South Africa of adopting a combination of heterodox economic views, represented by an ADRS economic model of South Africa and an alternative, six-pillar policy scenario.

A heterodox economic model of South Africa

The Dynamically Integrated Macro–Micro Simulation Model (DIMMSIM) is a linked, macro–micro model of South Africa. The model's macroeconomic component is a bottom-up, multi-sector econometric model using South African time series data. Additionally, the macro model has two-way links to a full microsimulation model of taxes, transfers, poverty and inequality.

Adelzadeh (2019a) provides a technical presentation of the model. What is relevant to the current discussion is the DIMMSIM's analytical approach, which is in the tradition of the pluralism of heterodox economics. This, amongst other things, means that the model is not based on the neoclassical theory of perfect competition and general equilibrium and does not use calibration methods to develop the model's parameters. Its basis is the specification and estimation of eight industry-level variables (namely output, employment, investment, wage rate, exports, imports, investment prices and sector prices) and detailed categories of household final consumption expenditure, consumer prices, credit extension, money supply, exchange rates and other behavioural equations used in the model.

The specification of the more than 400 estimated equations in the model is informed by the broad theoretical and empirical literature on various subjects, such as the labour market, investment, production, trade, prices and the financial market. As a result, the specification of the model's behavioural variables, in general terms, includes demand-side, supply-side, price and expectation variables, reflecting heterodox theoretical economic views and empirical studies. The adapted broad specification approach is specially used, since the aim of the DIMMSIM is not to impose on the model a particular theoretical proposition but rather to capture the actual law of motion in the South African economy, using a combination of econometric test criteria and economic theory.

For the specific functional form of its estimated equations, the model uses the cointegration technique, in which relationships amongst a set of economic variables are specified in terms of error correction models (ECMs) that allow dynamic convergence towards a long-term outcome. The independent variables in the estimated equations act as the 'long-run forcing' variables to explain the dependent variable. Amongst the various techniques available, the DIMMSIM uses the autoregressive distributed lag (ARDL) estimation procedure, developed by Pesaran (1997) and Pesaran et al. (1999).

Overall, the DIMMSIM is built to capture the dynamics in an evolving economy which is best understood using the broad, heterodox economic theory, verified and validated through a solid statistical analysis. The DIMMSIM therefore differs from a mainstream computable general equilibrium (CGE) model which is built as an idealised representation of a market economy with full employment and perfect competition, which bears little resemblance to the actual South African economy.

An alternative future policy scenario

As an alternative to the mainstream policy framework, the six-pillar policy scenario, developed by Adelzadeh et al. (2021), prioritises economic growth, socioeconomic development and high employment. The six-pillar policy roadmap involves the coordination of macroeconomic, social, microeconomic, trade and industrial policy reforms, private-sector and international support, and inputs from provincial growth and development plans.

Likely aggregate indicator outcomes of the six-pillar policy scenario

Under the six-pillar policy scenario, some of the key model projections are as follows:

- GDP grows at an average annual rate of 6.2 per cent over the period 2021–2030;

Table 4.5: An alternative to the pro-poor policy scenario for South Africa

Pillar	Policy area	Policy scenario
1	**Macroeconomic policy reforms:** This pillar is designed to directly and indirectly enhance economic growth and support other policy pillars, such as the social policy reform pillar (Pillar 2) and the trade and industry policy reform pillar (Pillar 4) to achieve industrial transformation and inclusive economic growth.	• 'What if' the government and public corporations systematically increased their investment in economic infrastructure (e.g., roads, bridges, dams, electricity and water supply), social infrastructure (e.g., schools, hospitals, parks and administrative services) and economic services (e.g., business enterprises) by 10 per cent annually between 2022 and 2030. • 'What if' the Reserve Bank's current solitary mandate under inflation targeting was upgraded to a dual mandate of targeting 6 per cent real gross national product (GNP) and price stability with an upper limit of 9 per cent for the inflation rate. • 'What if' government spending on goods and services (i.e., government final consumption expenditure) increased by 10.5 per cent annually to provide the necessary funding to expand the delivery of individual and collective social services. • 'What if' the monetary authorities adopted the necessary measures to raise the annual growth rate of credit extensions to the private sector to 15 per cent.
2	**Social policy reforms:** This pillar is part of a necessary policy response to both the devastating social impact of the COVID-19 pandemic and the persistently high rates of unemployment, poverty and inequality. The microsimulation component of the DIMMSIM was used to provide not only reliable estimates of the possible number of beneficiaries and programme costs, but also the welfare impact of the proposed measures.	• 'What if' the government began to make Public Works the employer of last resort for the *unskilled unemployed*, with a daily pay rate of R160. The Expanded Public Works Programme would grow to cover about 75 per cent of the unskilled unemployed, with coverage growing by an additional 3 per cent annually after 2022. • 'What if' the government immediately introduced an unemployment grant for the *skilled unemployed* to help them remain or become active in the labour market. The eligible unemployed workers would be entitled to R1000 per month. • 'What if' the government immediately introduced a caregiver grant of R500 per month for the family member who takes care of the child who, in turn, receives either a child support grant or a care dependency grant. • 'What if' the amount of all grants increased by 6 per cent annually.

Pillar	Policy area	Policy scenario
3	**Macroeconomic policy reforms:** Measures under this pillar are designed to increase the competitiveness of the South African economy.	• 'What if' the government's sector-support policies helped exports from the agricultural sector to grow by an additional 1 per cent in 2022 and by an additional 0.5 per cent every year thereafter. Thus, by 2030, exports from the agricultural sector would be expected to be about 6 per cent higher than they would be in the absence of the measures. • 'What if' the government's microeconomic measures succeeded in lowering the cost of the transport, storage and communication sector during the rest of the 2020s by between 5 and 10 per cent annually. • 'What if' the government's microeconomic measures directly boosted labour productivity (an annual positive shock of 1 per cent) in the following sectors: transport, storage and communication; agriculture; food; basic chemicals; iron and steel; trade; and catering and accommodation. • 'What if' microeconomic policy reforms succeeded in improving competitiveness in the following sectors so that their mark-ups gradually declined by 2 percentage points initially and by an additional 1 percentage point in each subsequent year: trade; catering and accommodation; transport, storage and communication; financial intermediation; insurance; real estate; and business services.
4	**Trade and industry policy reforms:** This pillar captures the commitment to three ultimate goals of trade and industrial policy, namely, to raise total investment in the manufacturing sector, to expand exports, and to increase local content and procurement of locally manufactured products.	• 'What if' the industrial policy measures, such as industrial financing incentives, succeeded in directly and indirectly increasing total annual investment in the manufacturing sector by R10 billion (in 2010 prices) over the next nine years (2022–2030). • 'What if' trade and industrial policy measures, such as the special economic zone (SEZ) and African integration programmes, succeeded in increasing total exports by an additional 1.5 per cent after 2021. • 'What if' the government's Proudly South Africa and localisation policies succeeded in gradually reducing import dependency ratios of some sectors by 20 per cent over the next nine years (2022–2030). • 'What if' trade and industrial policy used a range of measures, including the public sector and public–private sector investment practices, to gradually increase the employment intensity of economic growth in South Africa.

Pillar	Policy area	Policy scenario
5	**Private sector and international support:** This pillar considers specific contributions from the private sector and the Public Investment Corporation (PIC).	• 'What if' the Public–Private Growth Initiative (PPGI) increased investment in the South African economy by R500 billion over the next nine years (2022–2030). • 'What if' the Public Investment Corporation (PIC) increased its investment in the South African manufacturing sector by R100 billion between 2022 and 2026 (five years). • 'What if' the level of foreign direct investment in South Africa gradually increased from 0.05 per cent to 0.13 per cent of GDP between 2022 and 2030. • 'What if', in the wake of the recovery from COVID-19, the nominal value of total world imports grew annually by 8 per cent.
6	**Provincial growth and development plans:** As national government policy choices influence provinces' growth and development prospects, provincial economic plans have the potential to affect the country's overall economic performance. This pillar should ideally include input from all provinces. However, the current scenario includes only the likely impact of Gauteng's medium-term Growing Gauteng Together (GPG, 2019) interventions.	• 'What if' the Growing Gauteng Together (GPG, 2019) industrial measures succeeded in increasing the province's total real output by 0.5 per cent in 2022 and by an additional 0.5 per cent each year thereafter. • 'What if' provincial measures to promote African regional trade succeeded in increasing Gauteng's exports to Africa by an extra 0.5 per cent annually. • 'What if' extensive provincial-sector strategies and support measures successfully led to an annual 0.5 per cent increase in investment in Gauteng's agricultural, food, electricity, water, construction, transportation, storage and communication sectors.

Source: Author's compilation based on Adelzadeh et al., 2021

- The unemployment rate drops to 12 per cent, with 8.7 million additional jobs created by 2030;
- The poverty rate is cut by almost 50 per cent to 23 per cent; and
- Income inequality is reduced by 16 percentage points.

At the same time, the six-pillar policy option:

- produces balanced growth, reflected in the simultaneous expansion of both aggregate demand and aggregate supply over the next 10 years (see Figure 4.22);
- generates the funds needed to pay for the scenario's expected increase in government expenditure, because government revenue will grow concurrently with the projected GDP growth rate (see Figure 4.24);

- produces declining annual debt-to-GDP ratios due to the scenario's favourable economic growth rates, real interest rates and primary balance rates (see Figure 4.25); and
- initially increases the cost of social grants relative to GDP, but the ratio will gradually decrease over the rest of the decade because of the scenario's high economic growth outlook. By 2030, the cost of social grants relative to GDP will be 3.1 per cent (see Figure 4.23).

The six-pillar policy framework benefits the poor and the working class because:

- the national poverty rate declines by almost 50 per cent over the rest of this decade as 10 million people are lifted out of poverty and the poverty level falls by 40 per cent by 2030;
- the unemployment rate falls by almost 70 per cent, from 35 per cent in 2022 to 12 per cent in 2030;
- the economy adds 8.7 million jobs to total employment by 2030;
- national income inequality, measured by the Gini coefficient, declines by 16 percentage points, from 71 per cent to 55 per cent; and
- significant improvements in the delivery of social services (e.g., education, health, land reform, housing) and economic infrastructure across the country (e.g., roads, bridges, transportation) improve the living conditions of poor and working-class families.

Figure 4.22: Balanced growth, 2019–2030

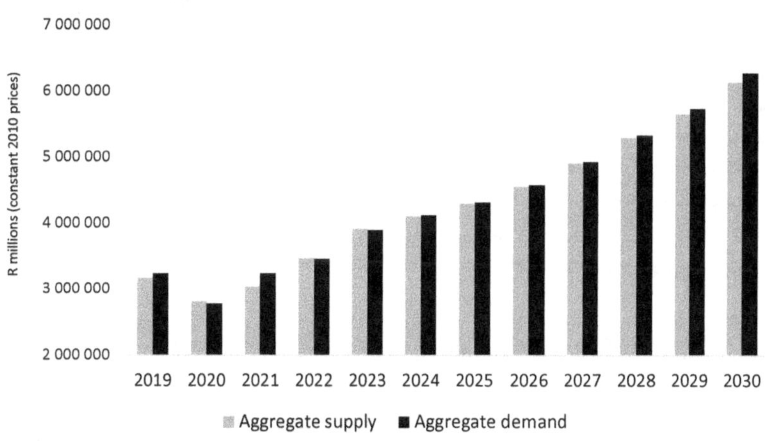

Source: Adelzadeh, 2019b

Note: Aggregate supply is calculated as the sum of model projections of sectoral gross value added at basic prices and the net of taxes on products. Aggregate demand is estimated as the sum of model projections of household and government final consumption expenditures, investment, and exports of goods and services minus imports of goods and services.

Figure 4.23: Cost of social grants to GDP, 2019–2030

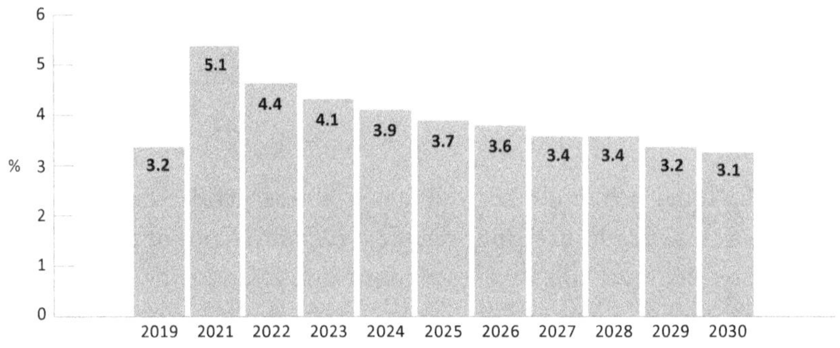

Source: Adelzadeh, 2019b

Figure 4.24: Sustainable fiscal outlook, 2019–2030

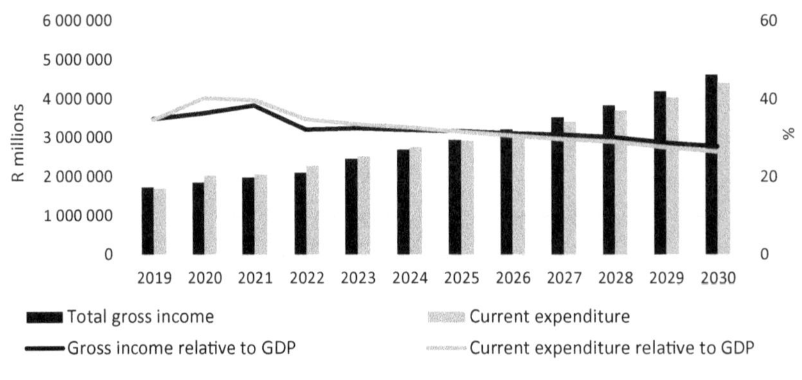

Source: Adelzadeh, 2019b

The six-pillar policy scenario's impact on the business class and the non-poor:

For the rich and the business class:

- real GDP almost doubles over the next decade, which implies a significant expansion of the domestic market;

Figure 4.25: Sustainable debt-to-GDP ratio, 2019–2030

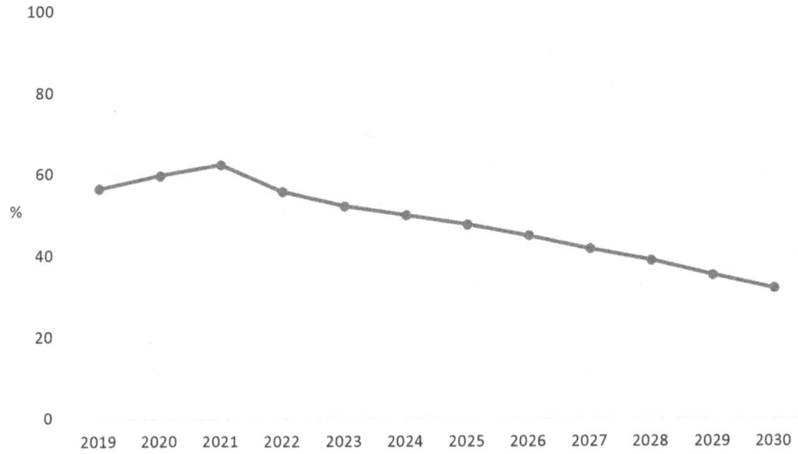

Source: Adelzadeh, 2019b

- the average profit rate remains above 16 per cent;
- improvements in the economy and the overall wellbeing of the population boost the average labour productivity growth rate;
- the government debt-to-GDP ratio gradually decreases, because of the high average annual growth rate, to less than 50 per cent;
- the average investment-to-GDP ratio increases to about 27 per cent; and
- improved social cohesion allows for stable capital accumulation.

Therefore, a heterodox representation of the South African economy, together with a policy framework that includes both macro- and microeconomic policies, is likely to produce high rates of economic growth, employment and socioeconomic development.

CONCLUSION

Heterodox economic views and policies helped the ANC to formulate and advance its popular vision for a post-apartheid South Africa from the early 1940s to the early 1990s, before the organisation embraced mainstream, free-market economics and policies soon after the 1994 election. Today, that shift in the ANC's economic orientation and policies has resulted in South Africa becoming the most unequal country in the world, with the highest unemployment rate and stubbornly low economic growth.

The current state of socioeconomic development and policy formulation in South Africa indicates that, while there is a need for improvement in the government's implementation capacity, there is also an urgent need to respond to the country's ongoing economic stagnation, accompanied by high rates of poverty and inequality. This chapter demonstrated that maintaining the status quo in terms of economic views and policies would – even by the government's own account – simply perpetuate the country's chronic crises of low growth, and high unemployment, poverty and inequality. The chapter revealed that the adoption of heterodox economic views, supported by the alternative, six-pillar policy framework, has the potential to stimulate inclusive growth, with growing prosperity accruing largely to poor and working-class families, rather than to the business class. This alternative approach challenges the economic orthodoxy that continues to underpin the South African government's economic policies and initiatives.

REFERENCES

Adelzadeh, A. 2019a. 'Economic policy scenarios for growth and development of South Africa: 2019–2030'. *Applied Development Research Solutions (ADRS) research report produced for the South African Department of Trade and Industry* website: https://www.adrs-global.com/resources/static/downloads/18973169_ADRS_Report_on_Growth_and_Development_Strategy_for_South_Africa_2019_to_2030.pdf, accessed 25 August 2022.

Adelzadeh, A. 2019b. 'ADRS' dynamically integrated macro-micro simulation model of South Africa (DIMMSIM)'. *Applied Development Research Solutions (ADRS),* https://adrs-global.com/resources/static/downloads/A_Technical_Introduction_to_DIMMSIM.pdf, accessed 25 August 2022.

Adelzadeh, A. 2022. South African Reserve Bank (SARB) Time Series Data on Public Finance, 1996–2019. Figures and trends extracted or calculated based on the data provided by the SARB.

Adelzadeh, A. and Padayachee, V. 1994. 'The RDP white paper: Reconstruction of a development vision'. *Transformation*, 25, https://www.researchgate.net/publication/239567623_'The_RDP_white_paper_reconstruction_

of_a_development_vision', accessed 14 April 2022.

Adelzadeh, A., Malumisa, S. and Benecke, J. 2021. 'COVID-19 and South Africa's future economic outlook'. *Applied Development Research Solutions (ADRS)*, https://www.adrs-global.com/resources/static/downloads/adrs_report_on_covid_19_and_SA_future_economic_outlook.pdf, accessed 5 July 2022.

African National Congress (ANC). 1943. 'Africans' Claims in South Africa'. *South African History Online (SAHO)* website: https://www.sahistory.org.za/archive/africans-claims-south-africa-14-december-1943-alfred-xuma and https://www.marxists.org/subject/africa/anc/1943/claims.htm, accessed 14 April 2022.

African National Congress (ANC). 1992. 'Ready to govern: ANC policy guideline for a democratic South Africa' website: https://www.anc1912.org.za/policy-documents-1992-ready-to-govern-anc-policy-guidelines-for-a-democratic-south-africa/, accessed 14 April 2022.

Atlantic Charter. 14 August 1941. 'Joint declaration by the President of the United States and the Prime Minister of the United Kingdom', https://iowaculture.gov/sites/default/files/history-education-pss-wwii-atlantic-transcription.pdf, accessed 14 April 2022.

Beverage, W. 1942. *Social Insurance and Allied Services*. London: His Majesty's Stationery Office. http://pombo.free.fr/beveridge42.pdf, accessed 14 April 2022.

Galindo, A. J. and Schiantarelli, F. 2003. *Credit Constraints and Investment in Latin America*. Washington: Inter-American Development Bank.

Gauteng Provincial Government (GPG). 2019. 'GGT 2030: Growing Gauteng Together', https://cmbinary.gauteng.gov.za/Media?path=OOP/Documents/Information%20booklets/Growing%20Gauteng%20Together%202030.pdf&Item=1618&Type=Documents&Location=/OOP, accessed 15 August 2022.

Goodfriend, M. and King, R. G. 2020. 'The new neoclassical synthesis and the role of monetary policy'. *NBER Macroeconomics Annual*, 35.

Hausmann, R. 2008. 'Final recommendations of the international panel on ASGISA'. CID Working Paper Series 2008/161. Harvard University, Cambridge, MA.

Hausmann, R., Rodrick, D. and Velasco, A. 2005. *Growth Diagnostics*. The John F. Kennedy School of Government, Harvard University, Massachusetts.

Hirsch, A. 2006. 'Accelerated and Shared Growth Initiative – South Africa. A strategic perspective'. A presentation from the Presidency, November.

International Monetary Fund (IMF). 1993. 'Staff report for the 1993 article IV consultation and request for a purchase under the compensatory and contingency financing facility'. Prepared by the African Department and the Policy Development and Review Department.

International Monetary Fund (IMF). 2014. 'Fiscal and debt sustainability'. Fiscal Analysis and Forecasting Workshop. Bangkok, Thailand, https://www.imf.org/external/region/tlm/rr/pdf/aug7.pdf, accessed 15 August 2022.

Keynes, J. M. 1936. *The General Theory of Employment, Interest and Money*. London: Macmillan.

Luthuli, A. 1955. 'The implications of the Freedom Charter', in Pillay, G. L. (ed.) *Voices of Liberation, Volume One, Albert Luthuli*. Pretoria: Human Sciences Research Council.

Luthuli, A. 1961. 'What I would do if I were Prime Minister'. *South African History Online (SAHO)* website: https://www.sahistory.org.za/archive/if-i-were-prime-minister-article-albert-luthuli-2-december-1961, accessed 19 April 2022.

Macrotrends, 1996–2021. 'South Africa unemployment rate', https://www.macrotrends.net/countries/ZAF/south-africa/youth-unemployment-rate, accessed 21 April 2022.

Mankiw, G. 2007. 'New Keynesian economics'. *Econlib Collection: Government policy*, https://www.econlib.org/library/Enc/NewKeynesianEconomics.html, accessed 1 September 2022.

Marglin, S. 2021. *Rising Keynes*. Cambridge: Harvard University Press.

Mbeki, T. 9 February 2001. 'State of the Nation Address'. *South African History Online (SAHO)* website: https://www.sahistory.org.za/archive/2001-president-mbeki-state-nation-address-9-february-2001, accessed 22 April 2022.

National Treasury. 1996. 'Growth, employment and redistribution: A macroeconomic strategy' website: http://www.treasury.gov.za/publications/other/gear/chapters.pdf, accessed 5 March 2022.

National Treasury. 21 February 2001. 'Budget Speech' website: http://www.treasury.gov.za/documents/national%20budget/2001/speech/speech.pdf, accessed 5 February 2022.

National Treasury. 2019. 'Economic transformation, inclusive growth, and competitiveness: Towards an economic strategy for South Africa' website: https://static.pmg.org.za/190828Economic_Strategy_for_SA.pdf, accessed 5 February 2022.

National Treasury. 11 November 2021. 'MTBPS Medium-Term Budget Policy Statement 2021' website: http://www.treasury.gov.za/documents/mtbps/2021/mtbps/FullMTBPS.pdf, accessed 4 February 2022.

Nelson Mandela Foundation. 2022. '17.6 Alliance contestation around GEAR' website: https://tpy.nelsonmandela.org/pages/part-vi-anc-and-the-transition/17-anc-and-the-transition/17-6-alliance-contestation-around-gear, accessed 22 April 2022.

Organisation for Economic Cooperation and Development (OECD). 2022a. 'General government spending', https://www.oecd-ilibrary.org/governance/general-government-spending/indicator/english_a31cbf4d-en, accessed 22 January 2022.

Organisation for Economic Cooperation and Development (OECD). 2022b.

'Short-term interest rates', https://www.oecd-ilibrary.org/finance-and-investment/short-term-interest-rates/indicator/english_2cc37d77-en, accessed 21 January 2022.

Organisation for Economic Cooperation and Development (OECD). 2022c. Long-term interest rates', https://www.oecd-ilibrary.org/finance-and-investment/long-term-interest-rates/indicator/english_662d712c-en, accessed 12 March 2022.

Organisation for Economic Cooperation and Development (OECD). 2022d. 'Gross domestic product', https://www.oecd-ilibrary.org/finance-and-investment/long-term-interest-rates/indicator/english_662d712c-en, accessed 14 March 2022.

Organisation for Economic Cooperation and Development (OECD). 2022e. 'Unemployment rate indicator', https://data.oecd.org/unemp/unemployment-rate.htm, accessed 1 May 2022.

Padayachee, V. and Van Niekerk, R. 2019. *Shadow of Liberation*. Johannesburg: Wits University Press.

Pesaran, M. H. 1997. 'The role of economic theory in modelling the long run'. *Economic Journal*, 107, 178–191.

Pesaran, M. H., Shin, Y. and Smith, R. J. 1999. 'Bounds testing approaches to the analysis of long run relationships'. ESE discussion paper 46, Edinburgh School of Economics, University of Edinburgh.

Poirot, C. and Pavel, S. R. 2008. 'The state, public policy and heterodox economics: An introduction'. *Forum for Social Economics*, 37 (1), 1–12.

Quantec EasyData. 'Share of manufacturing in total employment, 1996–2020', https://www.quantec.co.za/easydata/industry-subscription/, accessed 2 February 2022.

Republic of South Africa (RSA). n.d. 'Nine-Point Plan', https://www.gov.za/issues/nine-point-plan#:~:text=The%20Nine%2DPoint%20Plan%20has,services)%20in%2044%20municipal%20districts, accessed 12 May 2023.

Sibeko, B. (with contributions by Isaacs, G.). 2019. Institute for Economic Justice, 'The cost of austerity: lessons for South Africa', Working Paper Series No. 2, https://iej.org.za/wp-content/uploads/2020/02/The-cost-austerity-lessons-for-South-Africa-IEJ-30-10-2019.pdf, accessed 12 May 2023.

Skidelsky, R. 2010. *Keynes: The return of the master*. New York: PublicAffairs.

Statistics South Africa (StatsSA). 2008–2019. Quarterly Labour Force Survey (QLFS). Pretoria: Statistics South Africa.

Statistics South Africa (StatsSA). 2022. 'Statistical release P0211: Quarterly Labour Force Survey Quarter 4, 2022'. Pretoria: Statistics South Africa.

Timmins, N. 1995. *The Five Giants: A biography of the welfare state*. London: Harper Collins.

United Nations Industrial Development Organization (UNIDO). 2020.

'UNIDO's competitive industrial performance index 2020: Country profiles published', https://www.unido.org/news/unidos-competitive-industrial-performance-index-2020-country-profiles-published, accessed 14 April 2022.

Van Niekerk, R. 2013. 'Social policy, social citizenship and the historical idea of a social democratic welfare state in South Africa'. *Transformation,* 81/82, 115–143.

World Bank. 2021. 'South Africa COVID-19 response development policy operation', https://projects.worldbank.org/en/projects-operations/project-detail/P174246, accessed 14 April 2022.

World Bank. 2022. 'Inequality in Southern Africa: An assessment of the Southern African customs union', https://documents1.worldbank.org/curated/en/099125303072236903/pdf/P1649270c02a1f06b0a3ae02e57eadd7a82.pdf, accessed 14 April 2022.

ENDNOTES

1 Goodfriend and King (2020) provide a review of the emergence of the new neoclassical synthesis.

2 Leon Walras was the first economist to write about a 'general equilibrium' of the whole economy, referring to the simultaneous clearing of all markets where the sum of excess demand and excess supply across the various markets is zero (Skidelsky, 2010).

3 There is no generally agreed list of tenets of heterodox economics.

4 The Keynesian branch of heterodox economics asserts that with active, demand-management state policies, full employment is possible in a market economy. However, the Marxian branch of heterodox economics views involuntary unemployment (i.e., a reserve army of labour) as a necessary feature of capitalism. State policies can at best help to achieve a low unemployment rate.

5 According to Van Niekerk (2013), discussions took place in the ruling white government of Smuts and the opposition ANC led by Dr AB Xuma on the implications of the Atlantic Charter.

6 In 1955, Albert Luthuli, who was ANC President from 1952 to 1967, stated that the Freedom Charter 'definitely and unequivocally visualises the establishment of a socialist state', even though he personally preferred a 'middle of the road state between the extreme ultra capitalistic state … and the ultra socialistic state' (Luthuli, 1955, cited in Van Niekerk, 2013). Luthuli (1961) visualised a 'democratic social welfare state' as the post-apartheid government.

7 See Section 4 of ANC (1992).

8 On 3 December 1993, at the launch of the Making Democracy Work, the ANC 'effectively disavowed' the MERG policy framework (Padayachee and Van Niekerk, 2019: 99). About a week later, the Transitional Executive

Council, which included the ANC, agreed to the IMF's US$800 million loan agreement which included the IMF's usual economic policy prescriptions.

9 For example, the first RDP principle has been extended to include a commitment to fiscal discipline. See Adelzadeh and Padayachee (1994).

10 For example, the government signed a new General Agreement on Tariffs and Trade and joined the World Trade Organization (WTO) in 1995. This paved the way for the liberalisation of South Africa's international trade, which included a wave of major tariff reductions.

11 See the table showing the expected results of implementing GEAR's 'integrated' scenario (National Treasury, 1996: 7).

12 In his 2001 State of the Nation Address, President Mbeki stated, 'While continuing to focus on the maintenance of the correct macroeconomic balances, we have therefore decided to pay detailed attention to the critical microeconomic issues.' In a section titled 'From macroeconomic stabilisation to microeconomic reform', the 2001 Budget stated, 'Moving our economy onto an expansion path means moving beyond the macroeconomic stabilisation we have achieved.'

13 For an example of this undertaking, see Hirsch (2006).

14 Hausmann (2008: 4) argues that South Africa needs a strategy based on the relative expansion of the trade sector. He proceeds to ask, 'Why is this not happening automatically through the normal operations of the market? In the next section, we shall analyse the binding constraints that may be keeping the economy from realising this potential.'

15 Former President Jacob Zuma announced the Nine-Point Plan to boost economic growth and create much-needed jobs in his 2015 State of the Nation Address (see RSA, n.d.).

16 For an overview of austerity budgeting, including the 2019 details, see Sibeko (2019).

17 In essence, the government implemented IMF fiscal policy recommendations which asked the new South African government to continue the process of reducing the budget deficit. However, given the importance of maintaining a competitive tax structure, the emphasis was on expenditure containment rather than on raising taxes (IMF, 1993: 3).

18 Like in South Africa, the average annual deficit-to-GDP ratio was close to -3 per cent in countries such as Japan, Slovenia, Czech Republic, Italy and Ireland. However, in all these cases, government revenue as a percentage of GDP was significantly higher than in South Africa, thus enabling them to also have higher expenditure-to-GDP ratios relative to South Africa. In the period 1995–2020, the OECD countries' average revenue-to-GDP and expenditure-to-GDP ratios were 30.7 per cent and 38.3 per cent, respectively.

19 The IMF's (1993) Statement of Polices South Africa loan agreement states that the IMF's proposed fiscal framework for South Africa 'will seek to continue the process involved in the reduction of the budget deficit ... but, in light of

the importance of maintaining a competitive tax structure, will emphasize expenditure containment rather than raising taxes' (IMF, 1993: 53).

20 Despite huge income and wealth inequality, which is the highest in the world, taxes on income and wealth relative to GDP have changed only slightly since 1996. Income and wealth tax revenue relative to GDP increased from 12.75 per cent in 1996 to 14.7 per cent in 2020.

21 The change in the debt-to-GDP ratio can be formally written as: dt-dt-1=r-g1+gdt-1-pbt where: d denotes the debt-to-GDP ratio, r is the real interest rate (nominal interest rate minus GDP deflator), g represents the real GDP growth rate, and pb is the prime balance relative to GDP. Based on this equation, one can associate the change in the debt-to-GDP ratio with: interest rate (r1+gdt-1), growth (-g1+gdt-1) and fiscal policy (-pbt). For the derivation of the above debt accumulation equation, see IMF (2014).

22 AsgiSA's six binding constraints were: relative volatility of the currency; cost and inefficiency of the national logistics system; a shortage of suitably skilled labour and disjointed spatial settlement patterns; barriers to entry and competition in various economic sectors; a difficult regulatory environment and an excessive burden on small, medium and micro enterprises (SMMEs); and deficiencies in the state's organisation, capacity and strategic leadership, impacting delivery (Hirsch, 2006).

23 Real GDP per capita grew at a CAGR of 0.95 per cent between 1996 and 2019.

24 Adelzadeh (2019b) provides an overview of the ADRS model, including some of its distinguishing features.

FIVE

Vulnerability in the spotlight: Reflections on macroeconomic management in a polycrisis

EDDIE RAKABE

INTRODUCTION

The post-1994 macroeconomic economic reform process found the South African economy in a vulnerable position, with a pressing social crisis. Macroeconomic stability became the epicentre of South Africa's inceptive economic policies and development plans to support sustainable economic growth, which would in turn bankroll the social transformation programme centred on redistribution and job creation. The adopted pathway to long-term growth and stability was established in 1996 with the implementation of macro policies aimed at moderating inflation and the fiscal deficit, stabilising the exchange rate, and liberalising trade and capital flows under the stewardship of the Growth, Employment and Redistribution (GEAR) strategy (Khamfula, 2004). Compared with the more loosely framed Reconstruction and Development Programme (RDP), GEAR represented a comprehensive macroeconomic strategy, with explicit targets and policy instruments consistent with the overarching macroeconomic stability objective.

Macroeconomic stabilisation was necessitated by the prevailing imbalances, i.e., high inflation and debt levels, a balance of payments deficit and net divestment of foreign funds, and a weak currency at the time, originating primarily in apartheid-induced economic vulnerabilities. These included a deteriorating economy, economic isolation, sanctions on trade and investment, exclusion from global capital markets, autarky and, importantly, socially engineered poverty and inequality levels (see Gelb, 2006; Wright, 1984). The apartheid-driven humanitarian crises, reflected in poor socioeconomic conditions and a lack of access to basic services, necessitated a socioeconomic policy framework that prioritised people's immediate needs. This would entail the RDP underpinned by an economic strategy that incorporated a broad rubric of instruments designed to rebuild the economy and create jobs.

Financial and monetary discipline were viewed as crucial for financing the RDP, while industrial restructuring and the opening up of the economy were intended to remedy some of the lurking structural weaknesses. However, the apartheid debt overhang presented a macroeconomic dilemma for the social reconstruction agenda and the government of the day: how to finance the RDP while maintaining fiscal discipline at the same time. This predicament was acknowledged in the White Paper on Reconstruction and Development (RSA, 1994: 21): 'The immediate challenge facing the Government has been the need to finance and staff the RDP without exacerbating the unacceptably high government debt.'

When it became clear that the social transformation (social demands) programme, the financing thereof and the macro stabilisation objectives were incompatible (at least during the transition), GEAR was touted as a *sine qua non* for building a firm foundation for sustainable growth and development, premised on macro balance. Admittedly, GEAR incorporated a range of other interventions, but its fundamental thrust was macroeconomic stabilisation to address macro vulnerabilities – which to this day continue to draw criticism from detractors as a neoliberal, anti-poor policy. Mckinley (2007: 13) argues that GEAR committed government to: slash government spending (as a means of reducing the budget deficit, to the detriment of the needy); reduce inflation to a single-digit figure (through high interest rates that discourage borrowing and erode the disposable incomes of the middle class and the poor); provide tax cuts and incentives to established industry; phase out exchange controls (which promotes capital flight); create a more 'flexible' labour market; encourage 'wage restraint'; and expedite the privatisation of state entities. These debates are beyond the scope of this chapter.

A resolute commitment to the implementation of GEAR, despite sustained criticism from labour and civil society, led to improvements in key macroeconomic balances by the end of 2000, thus setting in motion a strong and unprecedented positive growth trajectory (with the help of a global commodity boom) which ended in 2008 in the midst of the global financial crisis (GFC). During this period (subsequently called the 'Supercycle'), economic growth averaged 5 per cent per annum, investment as a share of gross domestic product (GDP) increased from 15 to 21 per cent, per capita GDP increased 20-fold and over 1.5 million new jobs were created. In his 2008 Budget speech, the Minister of Finance, Trevor Manuel, attributed the successes to the macroeconomic policies adopted in 1996: 'The prudent fiscal stance, international reserves of $33.6 billion, the inflation targeting, and a floating exchange rate cushioned South Africa against shocks and reduced pressure on interest rates' (RSA, 2008). By this logic, South Africa, as a small open economy, was demonstrating improved resilience against global economic crosscurrents because a solid macro foundation had been laid.

South Africa continued to enjoy favourable macroeconomic conditions during and in the aftermath of the GFC (in the period 2009–2012), made possible by countercyclical monetary and fiscal policy (Hausmann et al., 2022). This period coincided with political change, a more populist ideological orientation (at least in theory) and the introduction of three new strategic plans emphasising various aspects of macro- and microeconomic reforms in response to the prevailing economic circumstances and constraints. These plans have shared a common developmental agenda for growth and a reduction in unemployment, poverty and inequality, but they have lacked explicit attention to macroeconomic vulnerabilities. Stability is taken for granted as an automatic imperative using monetary and fiscal policy instruments (overseen by credible institutions). From their early conception, vulnerabilities have mutated from being strictly macroeconomic in nature to being socioeconomic challenges which, according to Strauss et al. (2019), call for a 'transformative macroeconomic policy framework'.

However, the recent global economic shocks induced by COVID-19 and the Ukraine war have revealed deep-seated faultlines in the macroeconomic framework and adjustment mechanisms that are necessary to support and sustain rapid (V-shaped) economic recovery. Fiscal and monetary policies adopted a countercyclical growth support stance after the GFC, pulling back to a tighter space between about 2012 and 2016. As inflation stabilised from 2017 onwards, the South African Reserve Bank (SARB) loosened monetary policy while fiscal policy continued with its hollow consolidation efforts, resulting in upward pressure on debt, inflation and interest rates (Hausmann et al., 2022). South Africa is once again confronted by a policy predicament over whether to prioritise stabilisation or economic recovery, while social deficits are mounting.

Against this background, this chapter interrogates elements of South Africa's macroeconomic vulnerability (in particular, the nature, trends and channels through which vulnerabilities manifest), the appropriateness of the interventions introduced and the impact of recent negative developments (COVID-19 and geopolitical tensions) on these vulnerabilities. To avoid multiple interpretations of vulnerability, the method of inquiry adopted for this chapter traces vulnerability strictly from a macroeconomic perspective, which focuses on the exposure of the economy to external shocks due to various inherent conditions (Briguglio et al., 2008; Seth and Ragab, 2012). Further novelty is added by making a distinction between inherent macro vulnerabilities which are independent of policy choices (i.e., size of the country) and induced vulnerabilities (i.e., poor policy choices).

The chapter is divided into four sections. The first section provides a theoretical framework upon which the analysis is built. The second section is an exposition of macroeconomic trends and macroeconomic management in South Africa between 1994 and 2022. The third section provides an overview of the policy crises or predicaments precipitated by a confluence of economic headwinds. The last section brings into sharp focus the debates on threshold effects of public debt on economic growth amidst the country's lacklustre economic growth performance. The chapter calls for a comprehensive macroeconomic framework to deal with the sources of macro vulnerability in a holistic sense.

DYNAMISM OF MACROECONOMIC VULNERABILITY AND WHY IT MATTERS

Macroeconomic vulnerability matters because it can unravel the growth and development agenda of economies that are adversely incorporated in the global economy or overwhelmed by internal conflict and mismanagement (Guillaumont, 2011). Vulnerability is understood to be exposure to multivariate economic shocks (large-scale, unpredictable disturbances to economic activity) which can be exogenous, natural or domestic (Briguglio et al., 2008).

Conceptually, economic vulnerability can be analysed from a microeconomic or macroeconomic vantage point. The microeconomic lens focuses on the impact of shocks on individual-level, household-level and firm-level welfare, whereas the macroeconomic lens focuses on the wider implications of shocks on economic growth. Macroeconomic vulnerability manifests as imbalances between domestic demand and output, fiscal revenue and expenditure, the balance of payments, and savings and investment. Such imbalances can trigger domestic fiscal and financial crises and threaten long-term economic growth. Central to the microeconomic analysis is the realisation that shocks may push the incomes of certain households below the poverty threshold at a time when the capacity of government to respond is constrained. This not only elongates but also intensifies the impact of the shock (Seth and Ragab, 2012).

Emerging markets such as South Africa and low-income countries in sub-Saharan Africa are especially vulnerable to acute exogenous economic shocks, which occur more frequently and with greater intensity compared with other countries. Small countries (in terms of geography and population size, as well as remoteness) have similarly been flagged as 'inherently' vulnerable to shocks. This has sparked intellectual interest in the concept of macroeconomic vulnerabilities in the context of small island developing states (SIDs), which has developed into an analytical framework applicable to all countries (Seth and Ragab, 2012). Briguglio (2003) coined the term 'Singapore Paradox' to explain that certain countries are able to achieve high and sustainable economic growth rates, despite being highly exposed to exogenous shocks. This is attributable to such countries having the capabilities to build economic resilience – which implies the policy-induced ability of an economy to withstand, recover quickly and benefit from an adverse shock. Resilience requires a credible macroeconomic framework, sound monetary and fiscal policy instruments, strong institutions and timely responses. From this exposition, vulnerability can be said to be the result of exposure to an exogenous shock, the intensity and frequency of the shock, and the relative capacity to respond to the shock. Similarly, inherent/structural vulnerability suggests that a country has limited control over the natural or induced vulnerability arising from policy actions (or the absence thereof).

Inherent and induced features of vulnerability

This section discusses inherent/structural factors that make countries susceptible to shocks. The analysis includes the macroeconomic channels through which vulnerability to shocks manifests. Studies to date on macroeconomic vulnerability have only interrogated vulnerability in relation to a financial crisis. This is limiting because a financial crisis is a cause but also a consequence of vulnerability. Efforts to develop an Economic Vulnerability Index (EVI) as a criterion for allocating aid to SIDs prompted a wave of studies that identified country size, remoteness and insularity, and proneness to natural disasters as structural characteristics that make SIDs vulnerable to exogenous economic shocks. The later adaptation of the EVI saw a great deal of importance being attached to other structural conditions, such as economic openness, export concentration and dependence on strategic imports (Briguglio, 2003; Crowards, 2004).

Liberalisation or economic openness

Economic openness has been advocated as a fundamental condition for economic growth in recent, post-independence history, especially in African economies. The degree to which a country opens its economy can make the economy vulnerable to global crosscurrents. Openness depends on the size of the domestic market, which affects the exports-to-GDP ratio, and the availability of reserves and production capabilities for diverse goods and services, which affects the imports-to-GDP ratio. Shocks are generally transmitted from the global economy to the national economy through international trade and capital flows. Changes in international prices affect the export revenues of countries that are outward-oriented, thereby leading to a significant decline in growth. The ensuing chain of events then impacts the balance of payments, the value of the local currency, inflation and fiscal balances, depending on the longevity and severity of the shock (Ferrarini, 2007).

Export concentration or instability

Export concentration is an inherent feature of many countries' production bases and the result of restrictions or constraints faced by small economies in their attempts to diversify their export baskets or their export destinations (Briguglio et al., 2008). Volatility in commodity prices and terms of trade are amongst the key factors contributing to economic vulnerability as they can produce shocks in the real economy. Not only does export concentration render macro management and long-term planning difficult but it also tends to force liquidity-constrained economies to choose between two undesirable policy options: low economic activity, unemployment and poverty, on the one hand, and increased indebtedness, in cases of sharp negative price shocks, on the other. Export concentration is especially damaging for very open economies that rely on exports to fuel growth and earn foreign currency to finance imports (Crowards, 2004).

Reliance on strategic imports

Another important, inherent feature of vulnerability is dependence on strategic imports, although this relates not so much to substitutable consumer products but rather to essential products, such as machinery and energy. Exposure to economic shocks is transmitted through various channels in the balance of payments, direct and indirect capital flows, changes in terms of trade and, in some instances, social unrest, as recently witnessed in Sri Lanka (Kollias and Tzeremes, 2022).

The other common external sources of vulnerability are peripherality or distance to major markets, an overreliance on foreign capital flows and exposure to natural disasters. Whereas many of the factors contributing to vulnerability have external origins, in some cases inadequate domestic policy responses (voluntary and involuntary) have intensified inherent vulnerabilities or ignited localised crises. Inadequate domestic policies or induced vulnerabilities can result from excessive borrowing, fiscal profligacy during boom cycles, the absence of countercyclical fiscal policies, unbridled monetary expansion and sub-optimal industrial diversification (Ferrarini, 2007).

Social consequences of macro vulnerability

Seth and Ragab (2012) argue that focusing on a limited number of structural and induced conditions that cause macroeconomic vulnerability, to the exclusion of inequality and poverty, is a flawed approach. Rather than viewing inequality and poverty as consequences of macroeconomic vulnerability, they view them as key determinants of such vulnerability. They theorise that inequality contributes to financial instability through low household income and effective aggregate demand. It also constitutes a source of induced vulnerability by creating a political environment that encourages untimely pro-cyclical policies. Although not directly linked to a shock, poverty reinforces the long-term impact of shocks on productivity and income in the wake of spending cuts on health and education to cope with such shocks.

For Seth and Ragab (2012), the fact that inequality and poverty can aggravate the severity of shocks on economic growth makes them two structural determinants of macroeconomic vulnerability. Keynesian theory views poverty as a consequence of macroeconomic instability and therefore emphasises stability and the provision of public goods through fiscal policy as the key responsibilities of government (Davis and Sanchez-Martinez, 2014). Similarly, unemployment does not make a country any more or any less vulnerable, except that a shock will likely worsen existing labour-market challenges.

Policy responses to macroeconomic vulnerability depend on the nature and source of the vulnerability. As indicated earlier, certain vulnerabilities – either inherent or induced – require resilience, defined previously as the capacity of an economy to withstand, recover quickly and benefit from an adverse shock. The four fundamental factors for building resilience are a sound macroeconomic policy framework, microeconomic market efficiency, good governance and social development (Seth and Ragab, 2012). Even with resilience, responses to the consequences of macroeconomic vulnerability are generally conveyed through fiscal and monetary policy instruments. Both approaches emphasise stability as an overarching, remedial imperative.

Monetary policy ensures price stability to eliminate the possibility that economic shocks affecting inflation are magnified through corresponding price increases. Fiscal policy relies on 'automatic fiscal stabilisers' or 'discretionary fiscal policy' by stimulating aggregate demand and private-sector activity during a downturn and by slackening economic activity during periods of unsustainably strong growth (ECB, 2005). Discretionary fiscal policy tends to be associated with a strong deficit bias. The effectiveness of both monetary and fiscal policy in responding to vulnerability rests on the credibility of and coordination between the relevant authorities.

With reference to the preceding theoretical formulation and in tracing and analysing the evolution of South Africa's macroeconomic vulnerability, this chapter follows the analytical framework depicted in Figure 5.1. The variables of interest are key macroeconomic indicators and their underlying drivers. The direct sources of macroeconomic vulnerability are treated as endogenous to the growth trajectory so that the attention is directed at transmission channels through which shocks manifest. Transmission channels are framed as imbalances that affect stability and the performance of the economy.

Figure 5.1: Macroeconomic vulnerability analytical framework

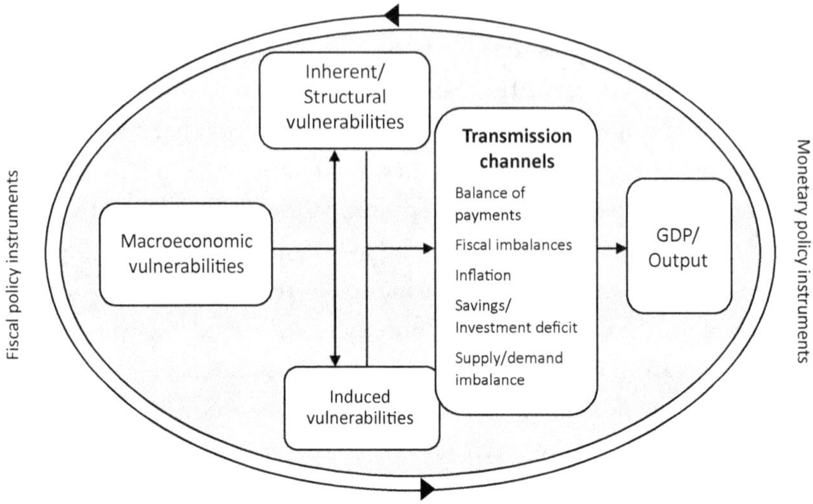

Source: Author's compilation

TRENDS IN ECONOMIC GROWTH AND MACROECONOMIC MANAGEMENT (1994–2019)

The growth spurt foundation

South Africa's economic growth foundations have been built on shaky ground. The end of apartheid and the subsequent democratisation process revealed enduring, previously hidden macroeconomic vulnerabilities that are counterfactual to contemporary views about the sources of economic shocks, as outlined in the preceding section. Instead of promoting economic openness, the white-controlled economy was susceptible to isolation and economic sanctions because it strongly depended on foreign capital for 'first-growth industries', referred to as the minerals–energy complex (MEC) in Chapters 2, 3, 6, 9, 13 and 14 in this volume.

Although the effect of sanctions during apartheid is the subject of ongoing debate, the economy was vulnerable in other ways, which are consistent with the theory outlined earlier. By 1962, when the UN General Assembly proposed a motion of export and import bans against South Africa, exports were highly concentrated in three countries, namely the United Kingdom (UK), the United States

(US) and Japan, with a combined share of up to 50 per cent, while 62 per cent of imports were concentrated in four countries (the UK, the US, West Germany and Japan) (Davis, 1993). The motion failed due to the heavy commercial interest (foreign direct investment) of South Africa's dominant export and import partners. In the wake of the transition to the democratic order, the South African economy was collapsing under its own weight, dragged down by a combination of industry inefficiencies, a hefty bill for maintaining the state security apparatus, external economic shocks and political conflict (Moll, 1991). These factors, albeit not entirely macroeconomic in nature, explain much of the growth spurt that occurred in the late 1990s and early 2000s, supported by interventions aimed at reducing pre-existing macroeconomic vulnerabilities and eliminating macroeconomic imbalances.

Table 5.1 provides a snapshot of the macroeconomic imbalances that prevailed prior to and during the transition. It also contextualises the macroprudential policy stance adopted by the new government in 1994.

Table 5.1: Average macroeconomic imbalances before and during the democratic transition[1]

Macro indicators	Average 1990–1994	Average 1995–2000
Economic growth	0.09%	3%
Inflation	10.75%	6.5%
Interest rate	17.7%	18.6%
Net fiscal deficit (% of GDP)	3.6%	3.2%
Debt-to-GDP ratio	34.4%	41.85%
Current account balance (R millions)	4 527.6	-7 473
Real effective exchange rate (REER)*	1.8	-2.83
Unemployment rate	20%	21.73%

Source: Author's compilation based on data from the World Bank, 2022; SARB, 2022

* This is a price index that describes the strength of the currency relative to a basket of several foreign currencies. An increase in the REER implies an appreciation of the currency against the basket and a decrease implies the opposite.

Moll (1993) argues that, at the dawn of democracy, the South African economy was weak in many ways, but the macroeconomic situation was relatively stable, signalling strong near-term growth prospects boosted by peaceful negotiations surrounding the regime change. Table 5.1 shows that some of the macroeconomic indicators were moving in the right direction prior to 1994, except for high inflation and interest rates, which may have kept the growth rate below 1 per cent. Notwithstanding the low average growth rate trend, the current account balance was positive, deficit levels had fallen to 1 per cent and the accumulated debt stock had grown to 34 per cent of GDP when the new administration took over. The transition period (1995–2000) was characterised by a mixture of deteriorating debt levels and current account balances, rising official unemployment rates and stubbornly high interest rates, juxtaposed against declining inflation and promising green shoots in terms of growth.

The 'passable' macroeconomic picture portrayed in Table 5.1 suggests that the South African economy was sufficiently insulated or resilient to withstand the apartheid era's structural and policy-induced vulnerabilities. Moll (1993) points to labour suppression, underutilisation of labour productivity, an inwardly oriented industrial strategy, industrial decentralisation and self-aggrandising, autarky-style industrial projects as some of the induced vulnerabilities that stalled economic growth in the late 1980s to early 1990s.

First growth spurt – origins of growth plans

With stability seemingly under control, the new government focused its attention on a people-driven approach to undo the systemic legacy of apartheid. The RDP was introduced as a 'coherent socioeconomic framework to meet people's immediate needs, democratise the state and build the economy'. Growth and redistribution were seen as central to development rather than as two contradictory imperatives, as observed in numerous empirical studies (Grundler and Phillip, 2018). The key element of the redistribution programme was not so much tax increases but rather the provision of access to basic services, healthcare, education, transport and training, which required extensive resource allocation (Ndhabi, 2015). However, the overwhelming social demands and the prevailing economic conditions, as shown in Table 5.1, imposed a congenital fiscal constraint, which forced RDP policy to adopt a mild stabilisation stance. The White Paper on Reconstruction and Development (RSA, 1994) made a broad statement about committing to monetary and fiscal policy discipline as well as progressively reducing the deficit and total debt, albeit without explicit targets.

After the successful transfer of power in 1994 and the subsequent rescinding of economic sanctions, South Africa attracted substantial capital inflows, and the SARB responded by engaging in monetary expansion between 1994 and 1995 to avoid currency appreciation. The ensuing inflationary pressure together with the adoption of what were perceived to be 'socialist' RDP and liberalisation policies caused the markets to become jittery over current account imbalances, rising public debt and further inflation risks towards the end of 1995 (see Table 5.1). This set of jitters ignited a three-month-long rand depreciation episode, with up to 25 per cent of its value being lost by April 1996 (Knedlik, 2006). This currency crisis was the first clear manifestation of post-apartheid macroeconomic vulnerability, arising in part from economic openness and a level of mistrust between the nascent democratic government and established capital.

To calm the markets and regain investor confidence following the currency crisis, the government introduced a revised macroeconomic framework through GEAR which, likewise, sought to pursue the socioeconomic transformation goals outlined in the RDP while placing strong emphasis on macroeconomic stability. It is worth mentioning that GEAR incorporated several microeconomic interventions spanning trade and industrial policies, small business development, social and sectoral policies, and training. To this end, the attainment of GEAR objectives was premised on several monetary and fiscal policy interventions:

- Public spending moderation;
- Rapid deficit reduction to contain debt service costs, reduce inflation and crowd in investments;
- Effective maintenance of exchange-rate stability;

- Sound monetary policy to guard against inflation;
- Gradual relaxation of exchange controls;
- Tariff reduction to cushion input costs;
- Tax incentives to stimulate investment in competitive and labour-intensive industries;
- Expedient restructuring of state assets; and
- Concerted public infrastructure investments to address delivery backlogs and binding constraints.

GEAR earned the title of a 'conservative and neoliberal macroeconomic strategy' by explicitly outlining macro-imbalance reduction or stabilisation targets over a period of five years (Fourie, 2022). To some, not least the labour movement, stabilisation targets were synonymous with neoliberal structural adjustment programmes imposed on African economies by Bretton Woods institutions[2] deemed to have had a detrimental effect on growth, development and poor people (Mckinley, 2007).

Table 5.2 depicts GEAR's macroeconomic stabilisation targets, which were mainly premised on fiscal policy tightening (reducing the fiscal deficit and public spending from 5.1 and 19.9 per cent of GDP in 1996 to 3 and 18.1 per cent respectively in 2000) and monetary policy tightening (through high interest rates). Fiscal prudence was required in part to reduce debt service costs and government dissaving, redirect spending towards productive areas, boost investor confidence and, importantly, improve the credibility of government policy. Monetary policy tightening sought to attract foreign capital and savings needed to finance investments. In the wake of these measures, real public and private investments were expected to increase by 16.7 and 17 per cent respectively in 2000.

These interventions were also expected to improve overall macroeconomic conditions in the country, with the economy growing by 6 per cent, inflation stabilising at 7.6 per cent and over 1.3 million jobs being created by the end of 2000. Table 5.2 depicts the GEAR baseline conditions, targets and outcomes.

Table 5.2: GEAR macroeconomic stabilisation and growth targets

Stabilisation instruments	**Baseline 1996 (%)**	**Target 2000 (%)**	**Outcome 2000 (%)**
Fiscal deficit	5.1	3.0	1.7
Real government spending	19.9	18.1	21.4
Average tariff (% of imports)	10	6.0	-
Real average wage growth (private)	-0.5	0.08	-
Real average wage growth (public)	4.4	0.04	5.0
Real effective exchange rate	-8.5	0.0	-1
Real bank rate	7	3,7	6.4
Real public investment growth	3.4	16.7	-
Real state-owned enterprises (SOEs) investment growth	3	10.0	-24.0
Real private investment growth	9.3	17.0	12.0
Real non-gold exports	9.1	10.2	8.0
Macroeconomic goals			
GDP (growth)	3.5	6.1	4
Inflation	8	7.6	5.7
New jobs	126 000	1.3 million	-
Current account deficit % of GDP	2.2	3.1	-1
Real manufacturing export growth	10.3	12.8	8.1
Gross private savings % GDP	20.5	21.9	17.8
Public sector dissaving	3.1	0.6	-

Source: Adapted from RSA, 1994

As with every other macroeconomic framework, GEAR was not without its flaws and contradictions. For instance, the strategy assumed a public wage moderation rate of 1.3 per cent over five years in an environment of labour hostility against the macroeconomic stabilisation stance. Similarly, the fiscal contraction objectives proved to be incompatible with the public investment growth expectations in the light of the known fiscal constraints and muted growth expectations. Its relative success, measured over the six-year period, was also mixed. The strategy was able to achieve successes in policy areas where government had direct control: the fiscal deficit and inflation were reduced to 1.7 and 5.7 per cent respectively (see Outcome column in Table 5.2).

Although not all GEAR targets were met, the economy was in a better state by 2000 than it had been when GEAR was launched. To some, the success came at a huge cost to the social transformation programme, but proponents viewed the six-year GEAR period as a necessary foundation for long-term, sustainable growth. The next set of trends analyses growth spurts in GEAR (and RDP) foundations.

Growth course vulnerabilities

Figure 5.2 depicts South Africa's economic growth performance against that of sub-Saharan Africa (SSA), middle-income countries and the rest of the world. As can be seen, there are two visible periods of sustained, intense growth (growth spurts) during the GEAR period and the 2000–2007 Supercycle driven by the global recovery from the 1998 Asian financial crisis. While the indicators suggest that GEAR built sufficient resilience to support growth, it is also evident that South Africa's growth cycles have been following the global economy and lagging behind those of middle-income countries and SSA.

Economic growth increased rapidly between 2000 and 2007, peaking at 6 per cent in 2006 and allowing government to ramp up spending (well above GEAR targets, enabled by the fiscal surplus), before nosediving in 2009. While the rest of the world recovered from the GFC, the South African economy slowed before weakening further from 2013/14 onwards under the weight of domestic vulnerabilities. The United Nations Development Programme (UNDP, 2016) attributes South Africa's growth pattern partly to its high dependence on volatile primary commodities (export concentration) and the resulting challenges of short-term macroeconomic management and long-term growth channelled through the current account deficit[3] (see Figure 5.2). The sluggish growth rate has resulted in declining rates of GDP per capita as population growth continues to outpace output growth, thereby exaggerating inequalities and social vulnerabilities.

Figure 5.2: South Africa's economic growth performance versus the rest of the world, 1994–2021

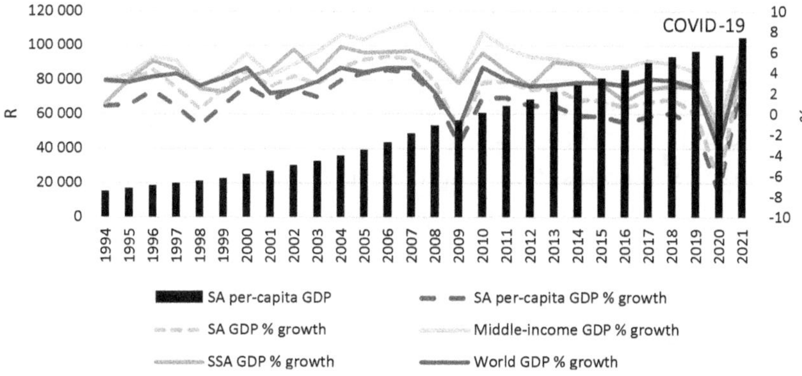

Source: Author's compilation based on data from the World Bank, 2022; SARB, 2022

The country's anaemic growth is further ascribed to several structural impediments, such as deteriorating levels of productivity and private investment, financialisation of the industrial structure, declining business and consumer confidence, electricity supply shortages and soaring tariffs (IMF, 2022; UNDP, 2016). The two key growth drivers, i.e., final household consumption expenditure and private investment, have remained subdued for the rest of the post-Supercycle period (see Figure 5.3). Similarly, savings have not kept pace with investment financing required to sustain long-term growth. Average gross savings as a percentage of GDP remained at 15 per cent over the 22-year period after 1994. High consumption, which in some cases exceeds income, is largely supported by unsecured debt from low-income earners who are themselves vulnerable to shocks and stabilisation responses.

Figure 5.4 shows the growing importance of the tertiary sector to economic growth in South Africa and the structural shift away from the primary (agriculture and mining) and secondary (manufacturing) sectors. These shifts have numerous implications for macroeconomic vulnerability and management. The tertiary sector is crucial for cushioning the economy against external shocks because of its limited exposure to external influence. Yet it can also become an important channel through which the shocks manifest and multiply during financial crises. The secondary sector is essential for industrial diversification and lessening the impact of commodity price shocks. Although its contribution to gross value has declined markedly, the primary sector remains the largest generator of export earnings, which affects fiscal and monetary policy through changes in commodity prices. By this logic, the structure of the economy is crucial not only for output performance, but also for the way in which the economy is affected and responds to macroeconomic shocks.

Figure 5.3: Economic growth drivers,1994–2021

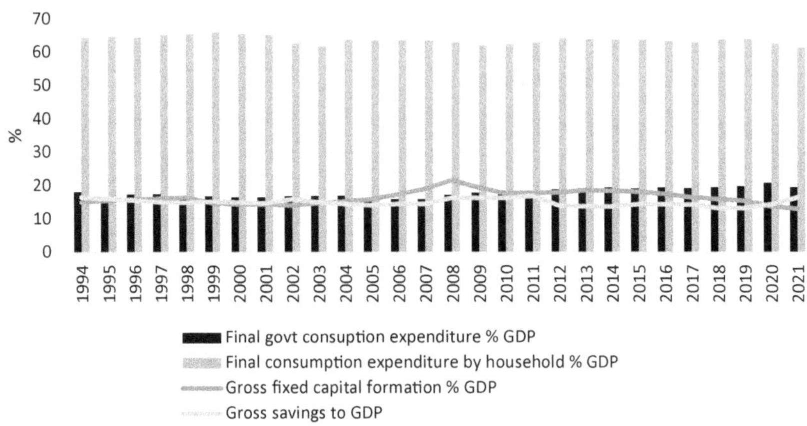

Source: Author's compilation based on data from the SARB, 2022

Figure 5.4: Gross value added by sector, 1994–2021

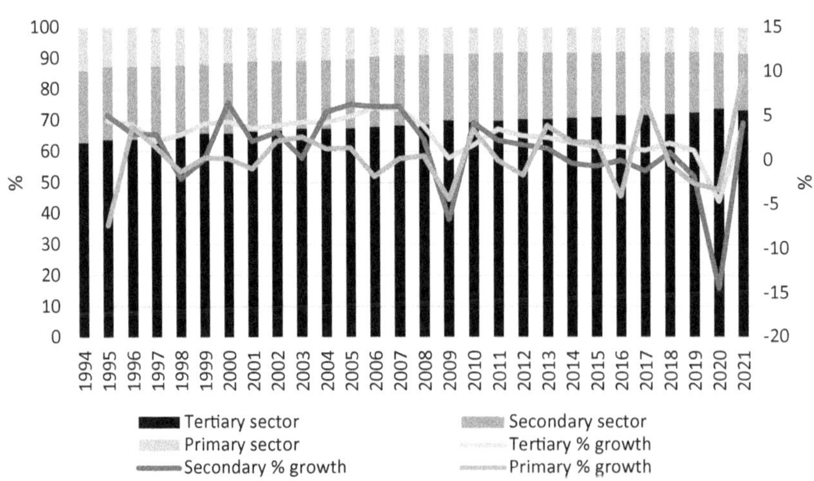

Source: Author's compilation based on data from the SARB, 2022

Table 5.3: Macroeconomic responses over various policy and crises epochs

Year	2006	2007	2008	2009	2010	2011	2012	2013	2014	2015	2016	2017	2018	2019	2020	2021	2022
Overarching strategic plan	**Accelerated and Shared Growth Initiative for South Africa (Asgi-SA); Industrial Policy Action Plan (IPAP)**				**New Growth Path (NGP)**		**National Development Plan (NDP)**										
							IPAP (annual)							**ETIGC (NT)****		**Economic Re-construction and Recovery Plan (ERRP)**	
Crises	Commodity boom		Global financial crisis (GFC)					GFC tail swipe, Marikana strike							COV-ID	Unrest	Ukraine war
Monetary policy stance	**Tightening**				**Easing**				**Tightening**				**Easing**		**COVID easing response**		**Tight-ening**
Stabilisation outcome (average inflation)	6.2%	10.1%	7.2%	4.1%	5.0%	5.7%	5.8%	6.1%	4.5%	6.6%	5.2%	4.5%	4.1%	3.2%	4.6%	4.5%	7.8%*
Fiscal policy stance	**Expansion**		**Countercyclical expansion**					**Mild consolidation**				**Counterfactual**			**Neutrality**		
Stabilisation outcome (average deficit % GDP)	0.2%	0.7%	-0.3%	-4.2%	-4.2%	-3.6%	-4.7%	-4.3%	-4.3%	-3.9%	-3.8%	-4.1%	-3.5%	-5.6%	-9.5%	-5.4%	6.0%*
Key fiscal policy interventions	Strong expenditure growth	Dividend tax reduction from 12% to 10%	Structural budget balance (tax to GDP reaches 29.2)	Countercyclical spending increases (GFC)	Countercyclical spending continues (by borrowing)	Countercyclical spending continues	Counter deficit to narrow by 2014/15	Expenditure moderation	Expenditure ceiling and moderation	Reduced expenditure ceiling and personal income tax increases	Lower expenditure ceiling (new Minister of Finance)	Lower expenditure ceiling and personal income tax increases	VAT increases and free high-er education	Consolidation and reprior-itisation	Wage bill reduction and R500 billion COVID-19 relief	Contraction	Recovery and relief (corporate income tax cut from 28% to 27%)

Source: Author's compilation; framework adopted from Hausmann et al., 2022

* Out of the 3–6% inflation target set by the SARB

** Economic transformation, inclusive growth and competitiveness (Economic Policy Division, National Treasury)

Policy continuity and coherence for sustainable growth

Stuttering or stalled economic growth post the GEAR and Supercycle era begs two fundamental questions: Were GEAR's foundations deep enough to sustain growth and resilience? Did GEAR's policy paradigm find expression in the subsequent overarching strategic plans as well as the intervening fiscal and monetary policy instruments?

Table 5.3 navigates these questions through a chronological depiction of strategic plans and global and domestic crises that shaped the post-GEAR macro framework and how such a framework (responses) may have reinforced or improved macroeconomic vulnerabilities. South Africa has experimented with numerous overarching strategic plans since the end of the Supercycle. Critics have berated such an approach as generally haphazard and inconsistent, but Netshitenzhe (2018) argues that the underlying logic was one of continuity at the level of principle and change at the level of detail. For Hausmann et al. (2022), the common principle relates to economic transformation and the use of state levers to reduce unemployment, poverty and inequality.

Notwithstanding their common theme, each plan focused on a different set of priorities to respond to the prevailing economic circumstances. The Accelerated and Shared Growth Initiative for South Africa (AsgiSA) sought to address six binding constraints to growth and employment, currency volatility being one of them. The New Growth Path (NGP) was a Keynesian, state interventionist approach aimed at stimulating output and employment. The National Development Plan (NDP) was an all-encompassing master plan aimed at improving various aspects of development, from education to healthcare, housing, and so on. Some economic plans emphasised microeconomic reforms and targeted industrial incentives over the course of the period, while the recent Economic Reconstruction and Recovery Plan (ERRP) places a renewed focus on inward industrialisation, electricity/energy market reforms and sectoral development.

As shown in Table 5.3, strategic plans were introduced during various periods of external economic shocks, including the global financial crisis, the COVID-19 pandemic and the Ukraine war. Internal labour ructions in the platinum mining sector and the 2021 civil unrest contributed to the shocks. Yet none of the strategic plans proposes or outlines a macroeconomic framework to address the underlying vulnerabilities, similar to the GEAR approach of setting explicit macroeconomic goals and associated targets. Broader macroeconomic management has become the sole preserve of the SARB and the National Treasury which typically prioritise currency and fiscal stability respectively as their key macroeconomic goals. The absence of an overarching macro policy framework creates an environment in which discordant monetary and fiscal policy decisions can flourish.

Table 5.3 suggests that monetary-tightening cycles tend to offset countercyclical fiscal expansion cycles, or the expansionary fiscal stance creates endogenous inflationary pressures that require monetary tightening during periods of protracted shocks – portrayed in the table as the GFC tail swipe. On balance, the monetary policy stance favouring price stability has been maintained, with inflation remaining within the target range of 3 to 6 per cent for most of the post-GEAR period. Figure 5.5 illustrates further successes in the form of the declining price of credit. The post-GEAR period also saw interest rate reductions and the rapid increase in household credit extension, which precipitated tightening to avoid overheating shortly before the GFC (Hollander and Havemann, 2021). The monetary stance shifted to two monetary-loosening cycles soon after the GFC and the COVID-19 pandemic to boost domestic demand amidst growing calls for growth- and employment-supportive monetary policy.

Figure 5.5: Prime lending rate, 1990–2022

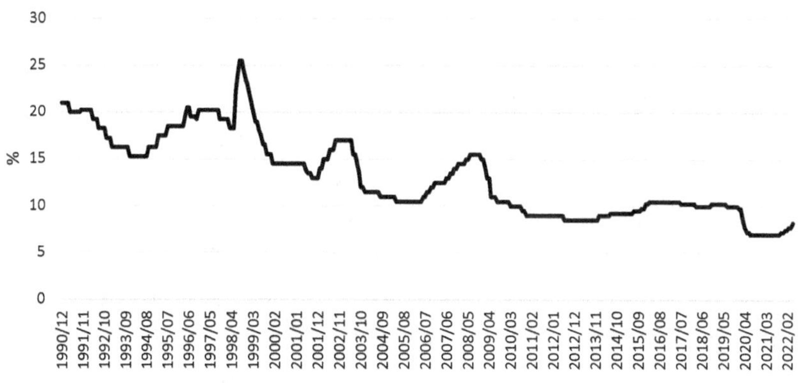

Source: Author's compilation based on data from the SARB, 2022

The fiscal policy trajectory, by contrast, has been broadly nebulous, despite annual budget commitments to keep the deficit within growth-enhancing limits. Unlike in the GEAR era, there are no strong and centralised political commands or strict fiscal rules that impose numerical targets for the budget parameters. As a result, the fiscal policy stance has been characterised by indecisiveness, implementation lags, overly optimistic forecasts (errors), counterfactual gimmicks and neutrality. For instance, fiscal policy adopted a prolonged, discretionary, countercyclical stance following the GFC in the hopes of a near-term recovery[4] while also delaying stringent fiscal adjustments (budget cuts).

Faced with the reality of a slow recovery, the government was forced into expenditure-consolidation mode through the adoption of a system of artificial[5] expenditure ceilings and reprioritisation. Instead of committing to the ceiling (and relying on automatic fiscal stabilisers), fiscal policy opted for a counterfactual approach of increasing taxes during the downturn to minimise the deficit. COVID-19 and the Ukraine war left the South African economy in too weak a state to support a countercyclical response, thus rendering the accompanying fiscal response neutral (unable to stimulate growth).

Figure 5.6 illustrates the deterioration in the fiscal trajectory from when the gap between revenue and expenditure widened for the first time since 2000 due to the GFC. The subsequent annual deficits accumulated into a large public debt stock peaking at 70 per cent of GDP in 2020. The ensuing downside fiscal risks invited unprecedented sovereign credit-rating downgrades, elevated debt service costs (becoming the second-largest spending line item after education) and distorted macroeconomic management due to the persistent large deficit, thus placing pressure on prices, the currency and interest rates.

In the final analysis, there is evidence of continuity of some of the macroeconomic measures contained in GEAR, albeit within a different institutional setting, economic environment and political climate. Monetary stability has been achieved because of the jealously guarded independence of the SARB. Fiscal stability, however, remains elusive because of the complexities in aggregating competing spending demands and managing intra- and inter-party-political power struggles. Other important elements of the macroeconomic framework, in particular savings and investments, are lagging.

Figure 5.6: Fiscal trajectory, 1994–2021

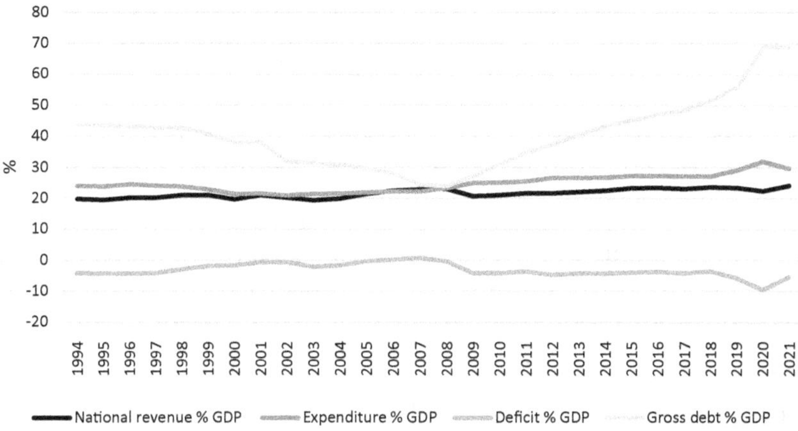

Source: Author's compilation based on data from the SARB, 2022

DEBATES ON MACROECONOMIC MANAGEMENT AND THE ENVIRONMENT

State capture and the macroeconomic environment

South Africa's deteriorating fiscal position coincides with the combined shifting of the power base and ideological orientation within the ruling party; hence, the NGP[6] was premised on increased state intervention in the economy to drive public investment and employment. The period following the change of political leadership and the adoption of both the NGP and NDP became synonymous with a downward spiral into acute kleptocracy, known in South Africa as 'state capture'. State capture enabled unbridled corruption and fiscal profligacy to flourish, while state institutions were left in a state of collapse (Zondo, 2022).

Corrupt activities tend to tilt the scale towards macroeconomic instability by engaging in excessively high levels of public spending (combined with leakages), discouraging investments and redirecting expenditure towards non-productive activities. The direct effect of state capture on macroeconomic stability in South Africa has not been conclusively determined, although rating agencies attribute their downgrades partly to corruption. Similarly, acts of fiscal profligacy cannot be solely ascribed to state capture because debt-financed spending decisions, such as the bailing out of SOEs and the provision of guarantees,[7] were approved via normal budgetary processes. The link between state capture and fiscal deterioration can thus be deduced from the loss of investor confidence, which is channelled into fiscal aggregates through higher bond yields, the current account and higher debt service costs.

Figure 5.7 depicts short- and long-term bond yields as a proxy for investor confidence over time. The state capture era is associated with rising bond yields (junk bonds), signalling a loss of confidence. Interestingly, the average bond yield during the state capture era remained below the yields experienced during the transition and the Supercycle periods.

Figure 5.7: Stock exchange traded bond yields (short, medium and long term), 1994–2021

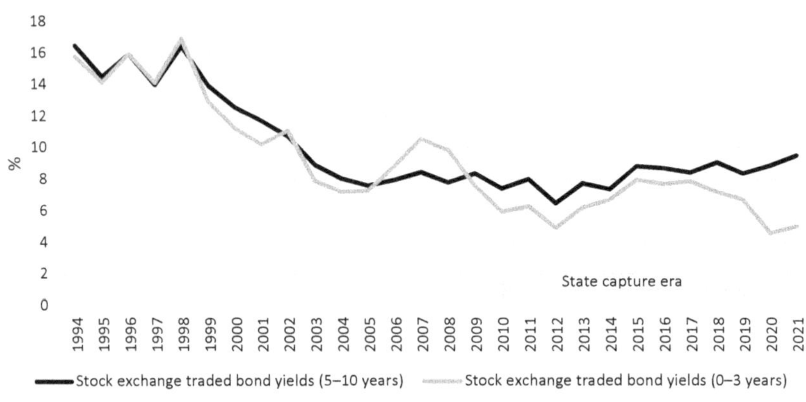

Source: Author's compilation based on data from the SARB, 2022

Debt as a macroeconomic tool for economic reconstruction and recovery

The experience of the post-GFC period buttresses the fact that structural macroeconomic vulnerabilities remain deeply entrenched and continue to hamper growth. Numerous structural reform (macro- and microeconomic) initiatives are yet to yield desirable results because of policy-design weaknesses, implementation inertia, ingrained structural complexities and an outright lack of bold policymaking. The unveiling of the ERRP by the South African government represents another attempt to recommit to the building of a sustainable, resilient and inclusive economy. This latest plan is premised on a combination of interventions spanning infrastructure investment, energy security, localisation and reindustrialisation, public employment and a revised macroeconomic framework – the latter being particularly pertinent to this chapter.

The rationale for the macroeconomic interventions proposed by the plan is two-fold: first, to promote coordination between monetary and fiscal policy (evidence of the gap between the two is shown in Table 5.3); second, to mobilise the necessary funding to implement the plan while maintaining fiscal stability. Achieving the latter would entail using 'debt for productive purposes to generate high growth which will reduce the debt-to-GDP ratio' (RSA, 2021: 24). There is neither a set debt-to-GDP target accompanying the funding requirement nor an estimate of the requisite resources to execute the plan. With debt having been shown to be a key channel through which macroeconomic vulnerabilities manifest and intensify, and a fundamental macroeconomic risk in itself, the question arises as to whether an ERRP debt-financing strategy can be achieved through the dual and simultaneous mobilisation of funding and the pursuit of fiscal sustainability. Efforts to attract private investments in areas traditionally reserved for and controlled by SOEs, such as electricity and freight rail, are slowly crowding in capital, which is likely to ease pressure on the debt requirement. Independent power producers have committed more than R200 billion through the Renewable Energy Independent Power Producer Procurement Programme (REIPPPP).

South Africa's debt-to-GDP ratio peaked at 78 per cent in 2022 from 24 per cent in 2008. Rating agencies and bond holders continued to express their disapproval of the undesirable fiscal trajectory, through credit rating downgrades and shedding of foreign bond holdings. The bond sell-off was particularly acute during COVID-19 (the second half of 2020), resulting in secondary market bond repurchasing by the SARB. The bond market remains actively supported in part by higher comparative yields (i.e., high interest rates) which in turn ensures that the current account balance remains 'relatively' stable. An active bond market does not necessarily imply that debt can be raised beyond market destabilising thresholds. The reason for this relates to the macroeconomic vulnerabilities explained earlier in the chapter. Debt-financed budgetary expansion can be beneficial in the short term to smooth out declining output and macroeconomic fluctuations. In the long term, debt is useful if directed at investments with high rates of return relative to the cost of debt (Kose et al., 2022).

Studies suggest that developed economies with a debt-to-GDP ratio of over 80 per cent and persistent current account deficits experience sudden fiscal deterioration. Countries like Japan have a debt-to-GDP ratio of 226 per cent and still pay low debt service costs. The optimal level of debt depends on a wide range of trade-offs and borrower characteristics, including the political environment (a proxy for fiscal restraint), investor perceptions (a proxy for risk premium) and economic growth (a proxy for ability to repay) (Ljungman, 2008). In the absence of stronger economic growth, South Africa cannot afford a debt-fuelled growth spurt without impairing debt sustainability (the cost of capital is lower than nominal GDP), deepening the threat of financial crises, slowing down investments (at 15 per cent of total government spending, debt service costs crowd out social and investment spending) and constraining countercyclical fiscal measures during downturns.

Polycrisis – a confluence of structural and induced macro vulnerabilities

Macroeconomic developments in the post-Supercycle period, along with internal political machinations, have steered the South African economy into a perfect storm – a policy crisis of epic proportions. Policymakers must navigate, contend with and juggle a polycrisis – a confluence of economic stagnation, embedded fiscal crisis and external crosscurrents, such as COVID-19, electricity supply interruptions and the Ukraine war. By the end of 2019, just before the outbreak of COVID-19, the South African economy was already vulnerable, having grown at an average rate of 1 per cent over five years. Its debt position had become increasingly untenable because of the ongoing and widening revenue gap. Expenditure cuts were the order of the day, with growth limited to social commitments at a rate equal to inflation or below. Such a situation would normally demand countercyclical fiscal responses through increased borrowing, tax cuts and expenditure increases. However, the fiscal space had deteriorated beyond the capacity to effect any counter-cyclical, growth-enhancing interventions.

COVID-19 dealt a severe blow to the macroeconomic situation, with the economy and tax revenues contracting by 6 per cent and 10 per cent respectively in 2020 (National Treasury, 2020) in the wake of disruptions to global economic activity. The pandemic came with fiscal demands for curative and preventative measures on the healthcare front and business and social relief for businesses and households in distress. A comprehensive macroeconomic response comprised nearly two years of consecutive monetary easing by the SARB, a R500 billion (10 per cent of GDP) relief package of reprioritised funding, an International Monetary Fund (IMF) concessional loan and unemployment insurance benefits. Legacy growth and debt challenges also meant that the government could not rely on countercyclical interventions to stimulate rapid (V-shaped) recovery. It was only in 2022 that South Africa's GDP recovered, surpassing pre-COVID-19 levels, but the rest of the world had already recovered in 2021. This prolonged return to growth highlights the peculiar vulnerability of South Africa's economic growth performance to shocks. The economy contracts quickly in times of shocks and recovers slowly during global upturns. For example, South Africa's GDP contracted by 6 per cent in 2020 compared with a 1 per cent contraction in other middle-income countries, 2 per cent in sub-Saharan Africa and 3 per cent across the globe (See Figure 5.2).

A rapid recovery in the pre-COVID-19 economic growth trajectory has been thwarted by self-induced and unending episodes of electricity supply interruptions, with devastating effects on inflation, jobs, productivity and investor confidence. South Africa had to endure 3 767 hours of loadshedding in 2022 alone, with another 2 927 hours before the end of the first half of 2023. Reserve Bank estimates suggests that power cuts are likely to shave 2 percentage points off economic growth in 2023 based on the projected 250 days of loadshedding (SARB, 2023). The energy crisis aggravates pre-existing macro vulnerabilities while creating an uncertain policy and economic environment going forward. Loadshedding-induced economic disruptions not only deter investment but also affect the predictability of tax receipts needed to cushion the poor and other victims, while aggravating uncertainties.

The war in Ukraine has added multifaceted risks to South Africa's macroeconomic performance and created uncertainty about the economy's near-term recovery and/or growth prospects. The economic effects of the war have been felt mainly in high energy and food prices, export and import bottlenecks, and heightened (geopolitical) uncertainty globally. Inflationary pressures arising from these factors require monetary tightening, which will add to the burgeoning fiscal imbalance (UNDP, 2022). Subdued economic growth and narrowing fiscal space make it harder for policymakers to pursue the social transformation goals of unemployment, poverty and inequality reduction. As discussed earlier, this policy predicament is a recurring theme across various phases of national strategic development plans. A persistent state of polycrisis may sow the seeds of discontent and trigger more episodes of civil unrest, such as those witnessed in July 2021.

CONCLUSION

This chapter sought to highlight South Africa's macroeconomic vulnerabilities and the macro management strategies adopted since 1994 to address ongoing, inherent and induced macro imbalances and the broader social transformation agenda. Vulnerabilities, strictly speaking, mean exposure to economic shocks arising from economic openness, import concentration and a lack of export diversification. However, instead of focusing on these underlying drivers of vulnerability, the chapter evaluated the channels through which such vulnerability affects macroeconomic performance. Adopting a historical perspective, the analysis selected a multi-year horizon to identify the origins and assess the continuity of both vulnerability indicators (macroeconomic imbalances) and policy responses.

The findings suggest that the economy's susceptibility to

macroeconomic risks was amongst the top policy concerns when the new democratic government took over in 1994. The RDP, as an inaugural strategic development plan, acknowledged upfront that developmental needs had to be balanced against the fiscal capacity of the economy, at a time when apartheid-inherited social deprivation levels demanded urgent attention. It was not until 1996 that the government committed itself to a systematic, macroprudential stabilisation programme through GEAR, after external economic headwinds had threatened overall macro stability and the reconstruction programme going forward. From this point onwards, macroeconomic stability became a fundamental pre-condition for growth and development, despite strong disapproval from labour and civil society. Stability was viewed by many as a betrayal of the electoral promises because it involved monetary and fiscal policy tightening.

This chapter demonstrated that GEAR's early belt-tightening cycles were followed by unprecedented, strong growth spurts that saw the government achieving a surplus in 2008. Large revenue windfalls from the accompanying commodity boom enabled government to increase social spending. Combined with such constraints as limited infrastructure capacity, skills deficits and low savings rates, this in turn created inflationary pressures and subsequently prompted a tight monetary response. These were the good times: fiscal and monetary policy were well synchronised; the economy was 'seemingly' a well-oiled machine benefiting from the firm foundations laid earlier and therefore resilient 'enough' to withstand macrocosmic vulnerabilities.

Subsequent episodes of economic shocks, including the GFC, COVID-19 and the Ukraine war, revealed that the foundations may not have been firm enough due to protracted periods of pedestrian growth. A suite of policy interventions aimed at changing the course and composition of growth pay little attention to the need for an overall sound macroeconomic framework. Consequently, monetary and fiscal policy have gained prominence as the only two macroeconomic instruments to foster stability. At times, coordination between the two has not been ideal, especially when monetary policy counteracts fiscal policy decisions.

As growth continues to stall, pressure is mounting for fiscal policy to respond adequately to the acute social demands in the country. However, self-induced fiscal constraints prevent fiscal expansion in times of need. This policy crisis may lead to repeat and more intense episodes of social unrest. Addressing this predicament requires a commitment to a credible fiscal rebalancing plan, premised on adherence to automatic rather than discretionary fiscal stabilisation, multi-year deficit reduction through timely expenditure adjustments, and the tackling of non-fiscal drivers of higher debt service costs, appropriate fiscal allocations to improve and encourage investments, and strategic engagement of the private sector in the provision of some public services. Furthermore, strategic development plans must be supported by an all-encompassing macroeconomic framework that addresses the sources of vulnerability holistically and sets clear targets for public and private investment, industrial diversification and savings to drive rapid, strong and sustainable economic growth.

REFERENCES

Briguglio, L. 2003. 'The vulnerability index and small island developing states: A review of conceptual and methodological issues'. Paper prepared for the AIMS Regional Preparatory Meeting on the Ten-Year Review of the Barbados Programme of Action, 1–5 September. Praia, Cape Verde.

Briguglio L., Cordina, G., Farrugia, N. and Vella, S. 2008. 'Economic vulnerability and resilience concepts and measurements'. Research Paper No. 2008/55, United Nations University – UNU WIDER.

Crowards, T. 2004. 'Macroeconomic vulnerability of small developing states: Will it squeeze into a single index?' in Briguglio, L. and Kisanga, E. J. (eds.) *Economic Vulnerability and Resilience of Small States*. Msida: University of Malta, 113–131.

Davis, J. 1993. 'Squeezing apartheid'. *Bulletin of Atomic Scientist*, 49, 9.

Davis, E. P. and Sanchez-Martinez, M. 2014. 'A review of economic theories of poverty: A discussion paper'. Discussion Paper No. 435, National Institute of Economic and Social Research, https://www.niesr.ac.uk/wp-content/uploads/2021/10/dp435_0.pdf, accessed 2 November 2022.

European Central Bank (ECB). 2005. 'The role of fiscal and monetary policy in the stabilisation of economic cycle'. Speech by Otmar Issing, Member of the Executive Board of the ECB International Conference, 'Stability and Economic Growth: The Role of the Central Bank', Mexico City, 14 November 2005.

Ferrarini, B. 2007. 'External debt and macroeconomic vulnerability: A proposal for state-contingent debt contracts to achieve low-income country debt sustainability'. PhD thesis, SOAS University of London, https://doi.org/10.25501/SOAS.00028808, accessed 2 November 2022.

Fourie, D. 2022. 'The neoliberal influence on South Africa's early democracy and its shortfalls in addressing economic inequality, philosophy and social criticism'. *Philosophy & Social Criticism*, https://doi.org/10.1177/01914537221079674, accessed 2 February 2023.

Gelb, S. 2006. 'Macroeconomics in post-apartheid South Africa: Real growth versus financial stability', in French-Davis, R. (ed.) *Seeking Growth Under Financial Volatility*. London: Palgrave Macmillan, 184–218.

Grundler, K. and Phillip, S. 2018. 'Growth effect of inequality and redistribution: What are the transmission channels?' *Journal of Macroeconomics*, 55 (C), 293–313.

Guillaumont, P. 2011. 'Macro vulnerability in low-income countries and aid responses'. CERDI, CNRS and Université d'Auvergne, https://halshs.archives-ouvertes.fr/halshs-00570499/document, accessed 30 August 2022.

Hausmann, R., Sturzenegger, F., Goldstein, P., Muci, F. and Barrios, D. 2022. 'Macroeconomic risks after a decade of microeconomic turbulence – South Africa 2007'. Working Paper 2022/3, United Nations University – UNU WIDER.

Hollander, H. and Havemann, R. 2021. 'South Africa's 2003–2013 credit boom and bust: Lessons for macroprudential policy'. *Economic History of Developing Regions*, 2 (36), 339–365.

International Monetary Fund (IMF). 2022. IMF Country Report No. 22/37. Washington DC: International Monetary Fund.

Khamfula, Y. 2004. 'Macroeconomic policies, shocks and economic growth in South Africa'. School of Economics and Business: University of the Witwatersrand.

Knedlik, T. 2006. 'Signalling currency crises in South Africa'. IWH Discussion Papers No. 19/2006, https://ideas.repec.org/p/zbw/iwhdps/iwh-19-06.html, accessed 20 November 2022.

Kollias, C. and Tzeremes, P. 2022. 'The nexus between social unrest and economic growth in middle east and central Asia countries'. *Review of Economics and Pollical Science*, 7 (2), 74–86.

Kose, M. A., Ohnsorge, F. and Sugawara, N. 2022. 'Benefits and costs of debt: The dose makes the poison'. Policy Research Working Paper 9166. World Bank Group.

Ljungman, G. 2008. 'Expenditure ceilings – A survey'. IMF Working Paper 08/282. International Monetary Fund.

Mckinley. 2007. 'The making of the myth: South Africa's neo liberal journey'. *Discourse,* (35) 2, 10–18.

Moll, T. 1991. 'Did the apartheid economy "fail"?' *Journal of Southern African Studies,* 17 (2), 271–291.

Moll, T. 1993. 'South Africa after apartheid: Prospects for economic recovery'. Collected Seminar Papers. *Institute of Commonwealth Studies*, 45, 161–174.
National Treasury (NT). 2020. 'Budget Review', National Treasury: Pretoria.
Ndhabi, S. 2015. 'The politics of South Africa's macroeconomic policy: A critical study of growth, employment and redistribution strategy (GEAR)'. Dissertation for Master of Arts in Political Science, University of Limpopo.
Netshitenzhe, J. 2018. 'Public policy after apartheid: The fortunes of the Reconstruction and Development Programme'. Keynote lecture, Public Affairs Research Institute (PARI), 28 August 2018.
Republic of South Africa (RSA). 1994. 'White Paper on Reconstruction and Development'. Republic of South Africa: Pretoria.
Republic of South Africa (RSA). 2008. 'Budget Speech'. National Treasury: Pretoria.
Republic of South Africa (RSA). 2021. 'Economic Reconstruction and Recovery Plan'. Republic of South Africa: Pretoria.
Seth, A. and Ragab, A. 2012. 'Macroeconomic vulnerability in developing countries: Approaches and issues'. Working Paper No. 94. International Policy Centre for Inclusive Growth (IPC-IG): Brasilia.
Simpson, Z., Havenga, J. H., Swarts, S. and Witthöft, I. E. 2022. 'Macrologistics supply chains in South Africa'. *Gain Group*, https://www.gaingroup.co.za/index.php/articles/supply-chains-in-south-africa, accessed 7 February 2022.
South African Reserve Bank (SARB). 2022. Economic and Financial Statistics for South Africa, Electronic dataset, https://www.resbank.co.za/en/home/what-we-do/statistics/releases/economic-and-financial-data-for-south-africa, accessed 2 February 2023.
South African Reserve Bank (SARB). 2023. Statement of the Monetary Policy Committee, May 2023. South African Reserve Bank: Pretoria
Strauss, I., Sibeko, B. and Issacs, G. 2019. 'Towards a transformative macroeconomic policy framework for employment in Africa'. Institute of Economic Justice: University of the Witwatersrand.
United Nations Development Programme (UNDP). 2016. 'Primary commodity booms and busts: Emerging lessons from Sub-Saharan Africa', https://www.undp.org/ghana/publications/primary-commodity-booms-and-busts-emerging-lessons-sub-saharan-africa, accessed 1 September 2022.
United Nations Development Programme (UNDP). 2022. 'The impact of the Ukraine war on the South African economy'. Policy Brief, Issue 2/2022, https://www.undp.org/sites/g/files/zskgke326/files/migration/za/Policy-Brief---UNDP-SA---The-Impact-of-the-Ukraine-War-on-the-South-African-Economy.pdf, accessed 1 September 2022.
World Bank. 2022. World Bank Open Data, electronic dataset, https://data.worldbank.org/, accessed 2 February 2023.
Wright, S. 1984. 'Struggling against apartheid: The use of economic sanctions

on South Africa'. *The Review of Black Political Economy*, 13, 37–47.

Zondo, R. M. M. 2022. 'Report of the Commission of Inquiry into Allegations of State Capture', https://www.statecapture.org.za/, accessed 1 September 2022.

NOTES

1 Pre-1994 economic indicators are applied as representative of the whole of South Africa as the Transkei, Bophuthatswana, Venda and Ciskei Bantustan states did not have independent systems of national accounts.

2 These relate to international finance institutions such as the International Monetary Fund (IMF) and World Bank.

3 The nominal exchange rate tends to move in line with the price of gold.

4 This was amplified by overly optimistic economic growth forecasts.

5 Artificial in the sense that the ceiling is set in terms of the ex-post budget outcome rather than the ex-ante budget amounts.

6 Introduced soon after the 2009 elections.

7 Contingent liabilities amounted to R560 billion in 2022.

SIX

The evolution of South Africa's economic structure: Key trends amongst the top 100 firms on the JSE

THANDO VILAKAZI AND TEBOHO BOSIU

INTRODUCTION

Looking through an accumulation lens when analysing South Africa's evolving economic structure is very powerful because it enables an appraisal of the direct and indirect linkages within production systems and the political economy dynamics that shape the interconnections between actors in and across industrial sectors. Importantly, as discussed in Chapter 2 and Chapter 3 in this volume, such an approach requires us to engage with linkages and agency in industrial sectors within the context of the prevailing interactions of 'state, finance, class relations and value creation', as articulated in society (Ashman et al., 2013: 4).

In their discussion of South Africa's system of capitalist accumulation in terms of what they term the minerals–energy complex (MEC), Fine and Rustomjee (1996) demonstrate the powerful links between the core industrial activities in mining (with related energy and manufacturing activities primarily providing inputs to or receiving inputs from mining activity) and the respective roles of finance, political actors and the state in reinforcing this pattern of accumulation. As elaborated in various chapters of this volume, given the growing financialisation of the economy, this dynamic has now been characterised as the minerals-energy-finance complex (MEFC). Fine and Rustomjee (1996) characterise the system as one in which there was limited diversification or investment in economic activities not strongly linked to the MEC core. Over time, a core of family-owned groups and conglomerates, the six 'axes of capital', was formed, namely Anglo American (Oppenheimer family), Sanlam, SA Mutual, Rembrandt (Rupert family), Anglo Transvaal (Anglovaal) and Liberty Life, which collectively controlled about 84 per cent of the Johannesburg Stock Exchange (JSE) in 1985 (Ashman et al., 2013). These groups ultimately came to represent Afrikaner and English capital (notwithstanding the contests between them) and controlled, both directly and indirectly, the extraction of value across almost all the important production and finance sectors by the 1980s (Ashman et al., 2013; Fine and Rustomjee, 1996; Freund, 2017). As a result, the diversification of the economy into other productive sectors, particularly in manufacturing, never truly took off.

A few decades on from the analysis by Fine and Rustomjee (1996), the South African economy remains highly concentrated and dominated by large firms in key sectors (Bosiu et al., 2017a; CCSA, 2019; World Bank, 2021). This has occurred despite the unbundling and restructuring of many of the conglomerate and family-owned groups throughout the 1980s and 1990s (Buthelezi et al., 2019; Chabane et al., 2006; Fine and Rustomjee, 1996), as we discuss below. Furthermore, the country's economy is still heavily reliant on minerals and resource-based industries, such that the extraction of and trade in commodities continues to play a significant role in the overall economic structure, including during the commodity price boom in 2021 (Bosiu et al., 2017a; World Bank, 2021). The contribution of high value-adding sectors, such as manufacturing (particularly manufacturing outside the

MEC-linked activities) to gross domestic product (GDP), has in turn declined since the late 1980s (Bell et al., 2018; Bosiu et al., 2017a). For example, South Africa's manufacturing value-added as a percentage of GDP in 2015 (13.4 per cent) lagged behind that of other middle-income countries (which stood at 20.8 per cent) (Bell et al., 2018). Economic diversification outside the core sectors has not taken place, and firms in domestic supply chains have not developed the requisite capabilities in manufacturing to drive the structural transformation of the economy (Andreoni et al., 2021a; Bell et al., 2018).

Despite high levels of corporate profitability by international standards, the economy is trapped in a cycle of low fixed investment and growth, suggesting a lack of reinvestment of profits in the real economy (Bell et al., 2018; Bosiu et al., 2017a; Zalk, 2021). In addition, recent studies show that the market power of large firms within value chains such as food processing, metals and machinery, and chemicals and plastics, remains entrenched (CCSA, 2019; Goga and Mondliwa, 2021; Mondliwa and Roberts, 2019; Vilakazi et al., 2020).

In this chapter, we provide an analysis of patterns of continuity and change in South Africa's economic structure by focusing on the role and positions of the largest firms in the economy over time. Our interest is in those firms listed in the top tiers of the JSE, as representative of the lead firms in South Africa.[1] We focus specifically on these firms for several reasons. First, for the most part these are the largest firms in the economy overall and in any given sector, such that their strategies, investments and orientation provide insights on patterns of accumulation in the economy as a whole. Second, their scale and size in most cases mean that their investment decisions and ownership of fixed and current assets have significant impacts on the economy overall as well as specific sectors. Third, the largest listed firms are in many ways still representative of those large firms and conglomerates that comprised the core 'axes of capital' identified by Fine and Rustomjee (1996), albeit in very different forms. As such, we are able to arrive at some insights on how their positions of control and influence have evolved over time by mapping present outcomes to the earlier assessments.

This chapter draws primarily on publicly available data on the top 100 firms listed on the JSE (ranked by market capitalisation), with the data broadly organised in terms of a periodisation in decadal intervals from 1990 to 2020, allowing an assessment of the evolving structure of the South African economy. This entails examining the changing composition of the largest corporations with a focus on key parameters – sectoral composition and primary business activities, ownership and control, investment patterns and assets, and market capitalisation. As a starting point, the chapter analyses how the composition of the top 100 firms listed on the JSE has evolved in terms of concentration, composition by firm and sector, and ownership. It then considers how firm performance and strategies have evolved over the period of the analysis, viewed within the context of the wider economy. The chapter concludes with some reflections on the key trends and the broader implications for understanding the evolving system of accumulation in the economy.

CHANGES AND CONTINUITY IN ECONOMIC STRUCTURE AND INVESTMENT

Nearly three decades since South Africa's democratic transition in 1994, the economy remains trapped in a low-growth, low-investment cycle. Whereas the early 2000s were characterised by macroeconomic stability and rising global commodity prices (reflected in strong mining returns and foreign exchange earnings), in broad terms investment in new enterprises and diversification has remained constrained (Bosiu et al., 2017a). The global financial crisis in the late 2000s brought with it significant challenges for emerging market economies, although South Africa benefited from an increase in gross fixed capital formation (GFCF) linked to a period of major, state-led investments in infrastructure in the late 2000s, as evidenced in total GFCF far exceeding private-sector investment in this period (Figure 6.1). At issue, however, is the fact that the positive effects of commodity price increases and infrastructure investments did not necessarily translate into a sustained shift towards diversification in terms of firms, capabilities and business activities, nor greater economic inclusion as a key social and economic imperative (Andreoni et al., 2021a). This outcome was perhaps unsurprising, given the fundamental structural constraints in the economy with respect to the concentration of wealth and investment in MEC-linked sectors (propped up by the commodity price boom in the 2000s) and growing outflows of capital through internationalised South African firms, without the requisite investments in new, dynamic capabilities domestically.

Figure 6.1: Top 100 firms on the JSE by capital expenditure (capex) and GFCF (constant 2015 prices), 1990–2020

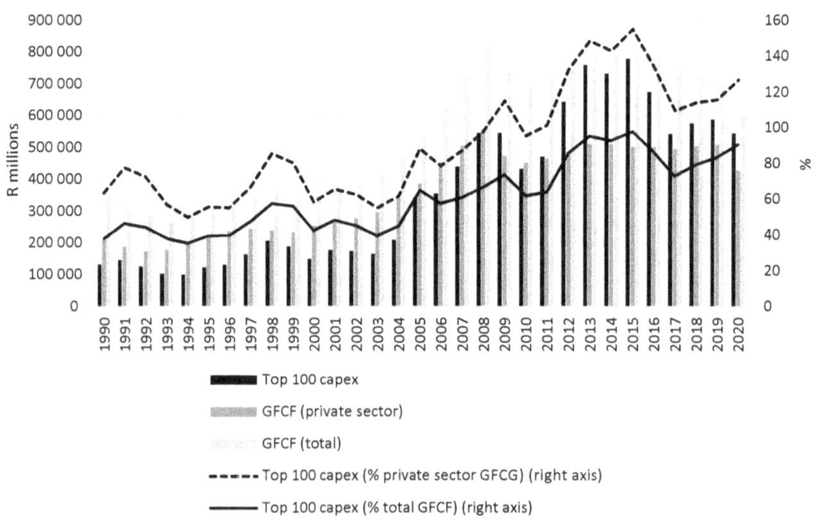

Sources: SARB, 2022; Quantec EasyData, 2022; IRESS, 2022

*Note: Top 100 capital expenditure represents expenditure per year as reported in company annual reports (in constant 2015 prices adjusted). This includes company investments outside South Africa, which leads to capex in some years exceeding private-sector GFCF. GFCF includes the acquisition of produced assets, which are those that emanate from production processes, excluding acquisitions of land and natural resources (https://data.oecd.org/gdp/investment-gfcf.htm). The JSE top 100 firms' capex is not adjusted for annual changes in the composition of those 100 firms.

The investment shifts of the largest 100 firms on the JSE in any given year are telling. There is a significant stagnation of private-sector GFCF from the period after the global financial crisis in the late 2000s, although investments by the lead firms (the top 100) continued to increase – which can be explained by large-scale mergers and acquisitions by these firms during the period (Bosiu et al., 2017a), replacement capital expenditure (rather than expansionary investments) in domestic fixed assets, as well as external acquisitions and new investments in Africa and elsewhere, which is consistent with a pattern of internationalisation of South African capital (Bosiu et al., 2017b; Das Nair and Chisoro-Dube, 2015, 2017; Nhundu et al., 2017). Furthermore, investments made by the JSE firms relative to those made by the private sector domestically occurred in a relatively fixed ratio to one another throughout the period until the mid-2000s, which was most likely driven by higher investments made by large firms outside South Africa (Bosiu et al., 2017a) and stagnation in domestic private-sector investment in an economy that had been gripped by low growth and low domestic demand in later years.

The pattern of internationalisation amongst South Africa's large, listed firms has evolved in different ways, including direct expansion of operations outside South Africa, mergers with and acquisitions of foreign firms, listings on international stock exchanges and foreign acquisitions of South African firms. For example, retail groups and telecommunications companies have expanded outside South Africa through greenfield investment in Africa primarily. There has, however, also been significant merger activity as well as international listings over the past few years. For example, at least 130 transactions have been recorded since 2010 – valued at no less than R280 billion (in real terms) – involving the JSE top 100 firms acquiring foreign companies (Who Owns Whom, 2022). Yet, in 2021, the JSE top 100 group consisted of 43 cross-/dual-listed firms (see Table 6.A2 in the Appendix).

The implication of internationalisation for South Africa is that lead firms raise capital from the domestic economy to largely fund international investments rather than local productive investments. Moreover, firms have invested heavily in short-term, non-fixed assets and/or paid out dividends to shareholders (as we elaborate below). While this phenomenon is rooted in the country's liberalised capital markets and the opportunities that arose to access capital from international markets (Chabane et al., 2006), it may also signal increasing returns on investment in financial assets relative to those economic activities that may require significant fixed-capital outlays.

The challenge of stagnant investment, particularly in the most recent decade up to 2020, is a pervasive one, perhaps even more so in those sectors and activities that are also labour-absorptive, innovative and linked to higher value addition through manufacturing. It is striking in this context that the aggregate value of shares traded on the JSE and at the level of individual firms has grown substantially over the period analysed here, from a total market capitalisation in nominal terms of around R383.2 billion in 1990 to R15.6 trillion in 2020 (IRESS, 2022). Although market capitalisation is only a proxy for underlying value, firm size and investment, it does provide a useful starting point for benchmarking the contribution of the largest listed firms against the universe of listed firms in South Africa and within the context of the economy, as analysed below.

Stock markets are understood to be platforms through which individuals and institutions with disposable cash reserves can invest capital in financial markets and firms, thus providing a source of capital for firms (traditionally in the real economy) which then leverage these equity investments by shareholders to invest in their operations and productive activities. Other things being equal, the expectation is that an increase in value in stock markets is underpinned by an increase in value and investment in the real economy. However, both in South Africa and globally, there has been a 'delinking' of investments in the financial markets and the real economy (Andreoni et al., 2021b), evidenced in the value of financial assets (including debt and equity held) far exceeding that of real-economy, productive investment. Moreover, the past three decades have seen a pattern of increasing financialisation of South Africa's largest firms, such as in mining where financial markets have been leveraged to fund speculation (leading also to market volatility) rather than productive investment (Bowman, 2018; Karwowski, 2015). In a narrow sense, and for our purposes, this form of financialisation refers to (1) the increased disbursement of firms' profits to shareholders (through dividends and share repurchases) relative to reinvestment in long-term capital goods, and (2) the increased use of debt relative to retained profits and equity to fund investments (Andreoni et al., 2021b; Davis et al., 1994; Krippner, 2005; Lazonick, 2010).

Figure 6.2: Dividend payouts and debt accumulation over time, 1990–2020

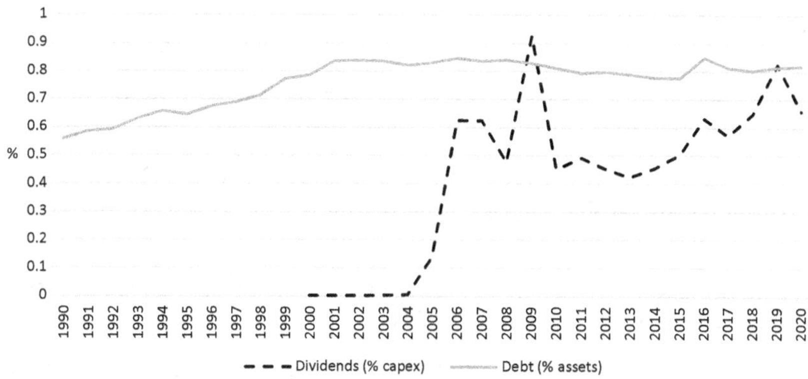

Source: IRESS, 2022

The JSE's top 100 firms' stock of debt has remained high over the past three decades, increasing in value from around 56 per cent of total assets in 1990 to about 83 per cent of total assets in 2020. This implies that a growing share of returns is used to service debt (Figure 6.2). Moreover, dividend payments have increased substantially relative to capital expenditure since the mid-2000s, reaching about 82 per cent of the value of capital expenditure in 2019. This is a further illustration of the diversion of profits away from productive investments. The effect of this, when viewed together with that of internationalisation, partly explains the pattern of stagnant GFCF (domestic investment in productive assets), which is in stark contrast to the rising value in stock markets in South Africa.

'A ROSE BY ANY OTHER NAME...' – OWNERSHIP, CONTROL AND THE TOP 100

To a large degree, the picture with regard to ownership and control in the early 1990s was, as expected, consistent with the underlying productive activity in the real economy, embodied in mining activity as a share of aggregate production in South Africa (and in the absence of other significant productive activity beyond mining). Indeed, in that period and well before it (Fine and Rustomjee, 1996) – and prior to extensive internationalisation by the major conglomerates and increased inward investment in South African markets by foreign investors – South African finance groups (Sanlam, Old Mutual, Liberty Life) were the only other major equity investors in South African stock markets, beyond the major family and conglomerate groups of Anglo American, Remgro (Rembrandt), Sasol and SAB (South African Breweries), which had production operations in South Africa (Mondliwa and Roberts, 2021) (Table 6.1).

Table 6.1: Percentage ownership and control of JSE total market capitalisation by firm/group, 1998–2019

	1998–99	2000–04	2005–09	2010–14	2015–19
Absa	0.00	0.44	0.58	0.00	0.00
Altech	0.00	0.00	0.00	0.04	0.02
Anglo American Corp	19.85	22.42	17.43	9.20	4.02
Anglovaal	0.75	0.00	0.00	0.00	0.00
Bidvest Group	0.95	1.02	0.95	0.88	1.20
Investec	2.95	1.54	0.98	0.74	0.80
Liberty Life/Standard Bank	7.20	5.10	3.88	2.48	0.42
Naspers	0.00	0.00	0.00	0.00	10.52
Old Mutual (SA Mutual)	9.75	9.04	4.20	2.90	1.80
PSG	0.00	0.00	0.00	0.38	1.70
Remgro (Rembrandt)	9.70	9.32	6.53	7.18	7.46
RMB/FirstRand	4.20	4.14	3.63	3.02	2.58
SABMiller	0.00	3.70	5.50	8.34	2.50
Sanlam	11.55	7.20	1.58	1.38	1.40
Sasol	2.40	3.26	4.65	1.48	0.00
Black groups	7.15	5.10	5.85	3.34	0.88
Directors	12.90	7.48	8.00	8.10	10.50
Foreign	3.95	10.80	22.20	30.36	31.40
Institutions	6.70	8.72	12.45	19.96	22.54
State	0.00	0.74	1.95	0.20	0.24
Total	100	100	100	100	100

Source: Who Owns Whom, 2022

Notes: We relied on the categorisations and calculations provided in the Who Owns Whom methodology in the table. Who Owns Whom incorporates the full market capitalisation of a firm after control has been established for a particular owner/group. It defines black- and director-controlled companies by level of empowerment or directors' holding exceeding 26 per cent, with no other dominant shareholder. It also defines institutional investors (asset managers, life insurance companies and stockbrokers) as those investing on behalf of others with the objective of getting the best investment returns. Anglovaal ceased operating in the late 1990s.

The significant shifts in the composition of lead firms at the commanding heights of the economy (in terms of the JSE and, by implication, the economy overall) have occurred throughout the 2000s up to the present day and have been driven by a range of factors. First, even though mining companies remained powerful actors in the productive economy, and were lifted by the boom in the 2000s, the value of their shares declined, partly due to significant divestments of assets, including to black-owned groups as part of compliance under black economic empowerment (BEE) policies, and offshoring of business activities (Chabane et al., 2006). Notably, however, black groups' share of ownership was significant only in the period up to the mid-2000s (Table 6.1), although it was still very small relative to the racial composition of South Africa's population and despite the implementation of the government's BEE programmes from the late-1990s onwards.

Second, there was a stronger presence of firms in diverse service sectors (retail, banking and insurance, medical, telecommunications, media and property, amongst others), many of which were built through capital investments by firms linked to the six lead conglomerates, as we discuss below in the sectoral analysis. Third, and perhaps most significantly, there was rapid growth in stock ownership by foreign investors/traders (averaging 4.7 per cent up to 2002, rising to 30.8 per cent by 2014 and peaking at 42 per cent in 2016) and institutional investors (averaging 4.9 per cent by 2002, rising to 19 per cent between 2009 and 2014, and peaking at 30.8 per cent in 2018) (Mondliwa and Roberts, 2021).

Taking these three factors into account meant, in the simplest terms, that a more diverse set of investors acquired interests in a wider mix of firms, underpinned by shifts in the underlying composition of productive activities – which mainly took the form of consumer goods and services consumption fuelled by household debt. Investing (as shareholders) in domestic finance houses, banks and investment groups, which held very diverse portfolios of interests across a range of economic sectors, became a key feature in and of itself, such that the value of the stocks of banks and investment houses (including Standard Bank, FirstRand, Investec, Sanlam and Absa, amongst others) increased along with their total capitalisation and ranking in the top 100, as discussed below.

Ownership has in fact diversified away from the major groups that formed part of the axes of capital. However, the underlying firms over which these groups exercised control and influence have in many cases remained as lead firms. In other words, in our view, the factors that reinforced and entrenched their dominance in specific sectors have not been eroded, partly because those arrangements have remained in place since 1994, such as long-term rights to key mineral resources or the regulatory favours still enjoyed by lead firms such as Sasol in the post-apartheid period (Mondliwa and Roberts, 2019). This observation is important. When viewed in a narrow sense, the MEC – as initially understood through productive and ownership linkages – has evolved somewhat, having been replaced by a system in which finance (notably private equity rather than that of influential family groups) serves as a key platform for coordinating the flows and distribution of surpluses. This is even as the core mining-related interests, including firms in other sectors built in the apartheid and transition eras on the back of mining rents, remain in place behind a wall of economic barriers that entrench market dominance.

Indeed, economic concentration is extremely high across economic sectors (CCSA, 2019). Key examples of this are Rand Merchant Bank (RMB) and FirstRand, finance companies that emerged from Remgro/Rembrandt (the Rupert family group) and by the 2000s had become two of the largest finance groups in the country, with direct and indirect investments in lead firms in key productive sectors. In this regard, the Rupert family, through various trust and company structures, retained an interest in the firms that were unbundled, such that their direct control of the firms was reduced in favour of more indirect influence. Consider, for example, the Rembrandt Trust which was entitled to 42.57 per cent of voting rights in Remgro, alongside bank nominee investors, by 2015 (Bosiu et al., 2017b).

COMPOSITION OF THE LEAD FIRMS AND SECTORS

It is useful at this point to reflect on the aggregate picture of the significance of these lead firms during the period of analysis. Concentration in terms of the ownership of productive assets is not necessarily problematic in the context of small, open economies where scale economies necessitate concentration in production to decrease unit costs. However, it can be a concern when returns from concentrated markets reflect and sustain a lack of rivalry and economic dynamism (high profits without reinvestment), the abuse of market power (as evidenced in competition law cases) (CCSA, 2019), or the accumulation or retention of assets that reflect entrenched positions that are not necessarily attributable to superior effort, performance, innovation and investment.

Using market capitalisation as a simple proxy for the order of magnitude of concentration rather than underlying value, we observe significant concentration amongst the largest firms. The top 100 listed firms accounted for a very high proportion (83 per cent) of the total JSE market capitalisation in 1990, increasing to 97 per cent in 2020 (Table 6.2). Notably, the composition of firms at the highest deciles by capitalisation has changed significantly, as we discuss below.

Table 6.2: Top 100 firms on the JSE by market capitalisation, 1990–2020

	1990	2000	2010	2020
Top 100 market cap (R billions)	317	1 495	5 779	15 151
Percentage of total JSE market cap	83%	91%	94%	97%

Source: Authors' compilation based on IRESS, 2022

Within the top 100 firms, the proportions of market capitalisation and assets (total and fixed) attributable to the largest firms have increased over time. The 10 largest firms accounted for 38 per cent of the total capitalisation of the top 100 firms in 1990, compared to 70 per cent in 2020, and for over half the fixed assets of all firms considered throughout the period (Table 6.3). The share of fixed assets, however, has remained relatively stable over time (across the bands of the largest 10 and 20 firms), even as their shares of total assets have in most cases risen along with shares of market capitalisation. Other things being equal, this suggests a pattern of accumulation of non-fixed assets (which can include financial portfolios, amongst others), rewarded by the market through a higher valuation of company shares, without corresponding increases in fixed investments (largely machinery, plant, and so on).

This outcome, tantamount to 'sweating the assets', is likely to be seen in concentrated economic sectors where profits may increase as returns on existing assets, without effective competitive disciplines that would otherwise stimulate new investment to maintain market shares and compete for way above-normal economic profits. There are persistently high levels of concentration in those sectors in which many of the largest firms in the economy trade. This is borne out by recent evidence (CCSA, 2019) – even though it is often challenger firms or new entrants that are the most dynamic, innovative and likely to invest in new capabilities for the benefit of consumers and customers (Vilakazi et al., 2020).

The scale of the 20 largest firms is better understood through a disaggregation of firm data into sectors and individual companies. To observers of South Africa's corporate structure, the largest firms have very familiar faces, such is the pervasive influence of mining and banking players (Table 6.4). In the 1990s, the axes of capital in their primary incarnations as mining companies and finance houses accounted for the bulk of the value on the JSE (Chabane et al., 2006; Fine and Rustomjee, 1996). A powerful illustration of this is that, on average between 1995 and 2002, Anglo American Corporation (linked to the pervasively influential Oppenheimer family group) accounted for approximately a quarter of total JSE market capitalisation (Mondliwa and Roberts, 2021). This was down from the more than 40 per cent of JSE market capitalisation that it held around 1994, when accounting for its various interests in an array of firms, including SAB, First National Bank (FNB) Holdings, Mondi and Tongaat Hulett (Chabane et al., 2006). By 2002, Anglo's (direct) interests had decreased due to a series of divestitures and the restructuring of its portfolio (Chabane et al., 2006), as was the case with other leading groups, including Remgro.

Table 6.3: Distribution of top 100 firms on the JSE by market capitalisation and assets, 1990–2020

Bands	Top 100 ranked by:	1990	2000	2010	2020
Top 10	Market cap	38%	50%	55%	70%
	Assets	51%	63%	70%	54%
	Fixed assets	53%	50%	56%	58%
Top 20	Market cap	56%	69%	72%	81%
	Assets	67%	77%	85%	78%
	Fixed assets	68%	67%	72%	72%
Top 50	Market cap	82%	90%	89%	94%
	Assets	88%	91%	95%	93%
	Fixed assets	90%	89%	90%	89%

Source: Authors' compilation based on IRESS, 2022

Anglo American in its various forms remains one of the largest firms in South Africa, along with longstanding lead firms now internationalised (and mostly dual listed – see Table 6.A2 in the Appendix), including Richemont, Sasol, SABMiller (later Anheuser-Busch), Naspers (later acquiring and listing Prosus, a global media, internet and technology firm), BHP Group (mining), British American Tobacco (unbundled and separately listed from Remgro), Old Mutual (formerly SA Mutual) and Standard Bank (previously as Liberty Life as well).

The list of the top 20 firms in 1990 does not include any banks or financial services firms – in fact, each of the 20 firms can be linked primarily to mining or industrial and manufacturing activities. Moreover, the representation of mining firms in this period was significant (Table 6.4). The shifts since this period are remarkable. First, we note that by 2000 and throughout the remainder of the period analysed, there was a substantial increase in large banks and finance houses in the top tiers, including Old Mutual, FirstRand, Standard Bank, Nedbank, Sanlam, Investec and Absa. This is partly a function of unbundling and new listings of existing entities. For example, FirstRand was established in its present form in 1998 but emerged in the 1970s through the Anglo American Corporation, and later under the Momentum vehicle.

Second, the 2000s saw the emergence of a more diversified group of firms alongside financial firms in the upper tiers, including telecommunications firms (MTN and later Vodacom), a range of property groups (with most without substantial operations in South Africa) and retail groups (Shoprite at first, and later Massmart, amongst others), linked in part to the rapid growth in consumer and household spend – and underpinned by rising household debt – in the 2000s.

Third, considering the wider top 50 and 100 firms (see Table 6.A1 in the Appendix), a large proportion of them are still involved in various mining activities, but there has been rapid expansion amongst private healthcare, investment, apparel retail, property, media, medical products, logistics, insurance and consumer goods firms. Nevertheless, it is important to recognise that the diversification of representation of firms on the JSE is not reflective of diversification of primary economic activities in the economy, which would typically be associated with structural transformation (upgrading linked with manufacturing). This is notwithstanding the significant growth of the services sector in terms of contribution to the economy since the 1990s. Indeed, even in this context, significant value has been attributed to mining activity, followed by manufacturing (which is a very broad group ranging from food to pharmaceutical production), as evidenced in the number and market capitalisation of the top 100 firms per broad sector (Table 6.5). In the context of industrialisation and structural transformation, the general expectation would be that the representation of firms involved in 'manufacturing' activities would end up being far greater over time than that of individual mining firms involved in primary extractive activities. Yet this is not the case in reality.

By 2020, the grouping of firms involved in media- and technology-related activities had grown in terms of value. This is reflective of a global shift in which technology and internet-based firms have come to lead in terms of firm value in the wake of the rapid growth of the internet and e-commerce-based activities. Naspers has always held a strong position in the media and other service sectors in South Africa, which can be traced back to the apartheid era. However, Naspers's internationalisation and acquisition of Prosus (a global internet

Table 6.4: Top 50 firms on the JSE (ranked by market capitalisation), 1990–2020

	1990	2000	2010	2020
1	De Beers Consolidated Mines Ltd	Anglo American Plc	BHP Group Plc	Prosus NV
2	Anglo American Plc	Compagnie Fin Riche (CFR)	British American Tobacco Plc	Anheuser-Busch InBev SA
3	Gencor Ltd	De Beers Consolidated Mines Ltd	Anglo American Plc	British American Tobacco Plc
4	Compagnie Fin Riche (CFR)	Anglo American Platinum	SABMiller Plc	Naspers
5	SABMiller Plc	Old Mutual Plc	MTN Group	BHP Group Plc
6	Lonmin Plc	BHP Group Plc	Sasol Ltd	Compagnie Fin Riche (CFR)
7	Anglo American Investment Trust	Dimension Data Holdings Plc	Compagnie Fin Riche (CFR)	Glencore Plc
8	Minorco Société Anonyme	FirstRand	Anglo American Platinum	Anglo American Plc
9	Sasol Ltd	Standard Bank Group	Standard Bank Group	Anglo American Platinum
10	Rembrandt Group	Nedbank Group	Naspers	FirstRand
11	Gold Fields	SABMiller Plc	Impala Platinum Holdings	Vodacom Group
12	Anglo American Platinum	MTN Group	Kumba Iron Ore	Standard Bank Group
13	Barloworld	Rembrandt Group	AngloGold Ashanti	Kumba Iron Ore
14	Gold Fields of SA	Sasol Ltd	Vodacom Group	Sibanye Stillwater
15	Gencor Ltd	Impala Platinum Holdings	FirstRand	Mondi Plc
16	Johnnic Holdings	Sanlam Ltd	Absa Group	Capitec Bank Holdings
17	Anglo American Gold Investment Co.	Remgro	Gold Fields	Impala Platinum Holdings
18	Anglo American Industrial Corporation Ltd	AngloGold Ashanti	Old Mutual Plc	AngloGold Ashanti
19	Tiger Brands	Investec	Nedbank Group	South32 Ltd

	1990	2000	2010	2020
20	Samancor	Lonmin Plc	Sanlam Ltd	Sanlam Ltd
21	Rembrandt Group	Absa Group	Remgro	Gold Fields
22	AngloGold Ashanti	Liberty Group	Shoprite Holdings	Sibanye Gold Ltd
23	Beverage and Consumer Industry Holdings	Rembrandt Group	Bidvest	MTN Group
24	CG Smith Ltd	Intu Properties Plc	Exxaro Resources	Northam Platinum Holdings
25	Kloof Gold Mining Co.	Johnnic Holdings	RMB Holdings	Discovery
26	ArcelorMittal SA Ltd	Elementone	African Rainbow Minerals	Absa Group
27	CG Smith Ltd	Bidvest	Lonmin Plc	Bid Corp
28	Engen	Sappi	Aspen Pharmacare Holdings	Sasol Ltd
29	Free State Consolidated Gold Mines	Imperial Logistics	Steinhoff International Holdings NV	Shoprite Holdings
30	Standard Bank Group	Gold Fields	Tiger Brands	Nedbank Group
31	Charter Consolidated Plc	CG Smith Ltd	Harmony Gold Mining Co.	Clicks Group
32	Sappi	Gencor Ltd	ArcelorMittal SA Ltd	Multichoice Group
33	Liberty Holdings	Tiger Brands	Truworths International	African Rainbow Minerals
34	Impala Platinum Holdings	RMB Holdings	African Phoenix Investments Ltd	Aspen Pharmacare Holdings
35	Western Deep Levels	BOE	Massmart Holdings	Nepi Rockcastle Plc
36	Safmarine & Rennies Holdings	Barloworld	Investec Plc	Old Mutual Ltd
37	Sun International (SA) Ltd	VenFin	Intu Properties Plc	Quilter Plc
38	Genbel South Africa	Genbel Securities	Imperial Logistics	Reinet Investments SCA

	1990	2000	2010	2020
39	Southern Life Association	Investec Holdings	Growthpoint Properties	Bidvest
40	Southvaal Holdings	Liberty Holdings	Assore	Remgro
41	Elandsrand Gold Mining Co.	Tigon	Momentum Metropolitan Holdings	Pepkor Holdings
42	Anglo American Coal Corporation	Technical Investment Corporation Ltd	Uranium One Inc	Exxaro Resources
43	Anglovaal	Pick n Pay Stores	Discovery	Rand Merchant Investment Holdings
44	Nampak	Momentum Metropolitan Holdings	Pick n Pay Stores	Comair Ltd
45	Nedbank Group	Coronation Holdings	Woolworths Holdings	Assore
46	AECI Ltd	Amalgamated Beverage Industries	Reinet Investments SCA	Harmony Gold Mining Co.
47	Edgars Consolidated Stores	Technical Investment Corporation Ltd	Dimension Data Holdings	Mr Price Group
48	Avi Ltd	Nampak	Netcare Ltd	Growthpoint Properties
49	Hartebeesfontein Gold Mining Co.	Alexander Forbes	Foschini Group Ltd	Mediclinic International Plc
50	Absa Group	Fedsure Holdings	Redefine Properties	Woolworths Holdings

Source: Authors' compilation based on IRESS, 2022

and media group) and its listing on the JSE as a standalone entity contributed significantly to the value of media-related stocks, which came to match the value of the 20 mining firms combined.

Nonetheless, these shifts do not dispense with the fact that the activities of mining and financial services firms remain at the core of the economy and that these firms also dominate in terms of total assets (Table 6.6).

Notably, the categorisation and ranking of firms on the JSE by

Table 6.5: Sectoral composition of top 100 firms on the JSE by number of firms and market capitalisation (nominal Rands), 1990–2020

1990			2000			2010			2020		
	Market cap	No.		Market cap	No.		Market cap	No.		Market cap	No.
Mining	175.8bn	40	Mining	494.6bn	15	Mining	2.0tn	20	Manufacturing	4.2tn	15
Manufacturing	79.2bn	26	Financial services	324.6bn	19	Manufacturing	1.6tn	22	Media and internet	3.9tn	3
Financial services	20.9bn	11	Manufacturing	266.0bn	21	Financial services	709.6bn	13	Mining	3.9tn	20
Diversified industrials	14.7bn	4	Diversified industrials	103.5bn	7	Telecoms	386.9bn	3	Financial services	1.3tn	14
Retail	9.6bn	8	IT	80.3bn	5	Retail	295.5bn	13	Retail	401.3bn	10
Hospitality	4.2bn	2	Investment services	60.2bn	6	Media and internet	157.5bn	1	Telecoms	357.4bn	3
Wholesale/Distribution	3.7bn	1	Media and internet	42.9bn	6	Investment services	130.1bn	5	Real estate	250.6bn	11
Logistics	3.2bn	2	Telecoms	40.9bn	1	Real estate	122.6bn	8	Investment services	180.2bn	9
IT	2.3bn	3	Retail	33.6bn	9	Diversified industrials	116.6bn	3	Healthcare	159.9bn	5
Unknown	1.3bn	1	Logistics	16.6bn	3	Healthcare	106.9bn	5	Diversified industrials	104.3bn	2
Construction	898.3m	1	Real estate	15.4bn	1	Construction	39.5bn	3	Airlines	46.9bn	1
Healthcare	886.3m	1	Hospitality	7.9bn	3	Logistics	37.6bn	2	Logistics	35.9bn	3
			Healthcare	3.5bn	2	IT	22.3bn	1	IT	30.6bn	2
			Construction	2.7bn	1	Hospitality	11.7bn	1	Energy	21.4bn	1
			Wholesale/ Distribution	2.3bn	1				Stock Exchange	9.7bn	1

Source: Authors' compilation based on IRESS, 2022

underlying assets reveal the growing significance of large property groups (8 in 2010, up from only 1 in 2000) and the influence of financial and investment services groups (26 in total in 2020). This is especially noteworthy given that the financial services companies also have substantial interests in other firms on the JSE and in non-listed firms as well as through investments, cross ownerships and board memberships (Table 6.6). The large asset bases of banks may not necessarily reflect their own investments resulting from the use of internally retained resources. This is because bank (and insurance company) assets are largely financed through debt (loan book balances financed by deposits; asset portfolios financed by pension fund contributions, and so on) (Bosiu et al., 2017a). The significance of the financial sector from as early as the 1990s, together with the emergence of the investment services sector in the 2000s through to 2020, shows how the sector-based structure of the South African economy has evolved from a purely MEC-based structure to what some describe as a 'financialised MEC' (Ashman and Fine, 2013), thus corroborating analyses by Fine and Rustomjee (1996) and, by extension, Chabane et al. (2006) and Freund (2017). Although the increasingly prominent role played by finance has had a positive impact on employment directly, it has had other, growth-restricting consequences as well. For example, it has led to reductions in the share of investment in long-term physical assets as financial conglomerates have reoriented themselves towards short-term and speculative investments (Ashman et al., 2013, Bosiu et al., 2017a).

It is striking that of the 17 real estate firms in the JSE's top 100 firms (by assets) in 2020, 15 had most of their assets outside South Africa, suggesting that the South African stock market is leveraged simply as a source of capital to be invested elsewhere. Those with an investment presence in South Africa have very large, fixed asset portfolios, just as the major retail groups (food, clothing, apparel, and so on) have extended their property portfolios, numbers of stores and distribution infrastructure over time (Table 6.7). Furthermore, during the 2000s specifically, the number, assets and capitalisation of major construction firms grew on the back of the construction and infrastructure boom at that time. Even within this 'new' context, which only emerged in the 2000s, the mining firms feature strongly, while the number of

Table 6.6: Sectoral breakdown of top 100 firms on the JSE (ranked by total assets), 1990–2020

1990	No. of firms	2000	No. of firms	2010	No. of firms	2020	No. of firms
Manufacturing	31	Financial services	25	Mining	20	Financial services	17
Mining	25	Manufacturing	18	Manufacturing	17	Real estate	17
Financial services	19	Mining	14	Financial services	15	Mining	15
Retail	7	Retail	10	Real estate	10	Manufacturing	11
IT	5	Investment services	8	Retail	8	Retail	9
Diversified industrials	4	Diversified industrials	6	Investment services	7	Investment services	9
Hospitality	2	IT	5	Construction	4	Logistics	5
Construction	2	Hospitality	2	Diversified industrials	4	Diversified industrials	5
Investment services	2	Logistics	2	Healthcare	3	Healthcare	4
Logistics	1	Healthcare	2	Telecoms	3	Telecoms	3
Wholesale/ Distribution	1	Construction	2	Logistics	3	Media and internet	3
Media and internet	1	Telecoms	2	IT	2	IT	1
		Media and internet	2	Hospitality	1	Construction	1
		Real estate	1	Agriculture	1		
		Agriculture	1	Energy	1		
				Media and internet	1		

Source: Authors' compilation based on IRESS, 2022

manufacturing firms amongst the lead firms in terms of control of fixed assets is in fact on the decline (noting, however, that some firms may have delisted from the JSE as part of a recent delisting trend).[2]

Table 6.7: Sectoral breakdown of top 100 firms on the JSE (ranked by fixed assets), 1990–2020

1990	No. of firms	2000	No. of firms	2010	No. of firms	2020	No. of firms
Manufacturing	34	Manufacturing	25	Manufacturing	23	Real estate	29
Mining	22	Real estate	13	Mining	17	Manufacturing	15
Retail	7	Financial services	10	Real estate	17	Retail	10
Logistics	7	Retail	10	Financial services	9	Mining	9
IT	6	Mining	6	Retail	7	Financial services	8
Real estate	6	IT	6	Logistics	5	Investment services	5
Financial services	5	Logistics	6	Healthcare	4	Logistics	5
Diversified industrials	4	Diversified industrials	4	Construction	4	Diversified industrials	5
Hospitality	2	Hospitality	3	Diversified industrials	3	Healthcare	4
Healthcare	2	Media and internet	3	Telecoms	3	Media and internet	3
Construction	1	Investment services	2	Investment services	2	Telecoms	3
Wholesale/ Distribution	1	Healthcare	2	Hospitality	2	Hospitality	3
Energy	1	Construction	2	Media and internet	1	Education	1
Investment services	1	Telecoms	2	IT	1		
Unknown	1	Wholesale/ Distribution	1	Energy	1		
		Education	1	Agriculture	1		
		Agriculture	1				
		Unknown	1				

Source: Authors' compilation based on IRESS, 2022

REFLECTIONS ON THE EVOLVING ECONOMIC STRUCTURE AND SYSTEM OF ACCUMULATION IN SOUTH AFRICA

The lens through which we have chosen to view the top 100 listed firms is a narrow one, given that there is a very wide range of firms making up the rest of the JSE and the private sector. However, it was useful to isolate at least some of the largest firms in the economy, for which good data were available for analysis. We have demonstrated the significance of these firms within the context of the broader economy, not least in terms of their investments and ownership of productive assets. The analysis of this group in terms of firms and sectoral composition, as well as ownership linkages and investment outcomes, has provided insights on South Africa's broad economic structure and how it has (or has not) changed over time. These aspects are considered against the backdrop of other detailed expositions of different facets of the economy, which are covered in this volume. The assessment was necessarily conducted alongside an input–output analysis to demonstrate with greater accuracy the linkages in the economy that give rise to its distinctive structure.

Overall, we find a pattern of both continuity and change in South Africa's broad economic structure, as viewed through the lens of the largest listed firms in the country. Finance and mining remain at the core of the economy (and have even strengthened somewhat), while a diverse range of business and consumer services are peripheral to this core.

From the perspective of fostering structural transformation and reindustrialisation, it is telling that manufacturing firms, although present in significant total numbers and values, exist at the periphery. Moreover, it should be borne in mind that the 'manufacturing' group, as we have categorised it in the data, in fact represents manufacturing activities across a very wide range of industries. When decomposed as a group, we find many of the same lead firms (SABMiller, Sasol, British American Tobacco, and so on) that have been at the centre of productive activities in the economy since the apartheid era. There are few emerging rivals to these lead firms involved in manufacturing activity, which is partly attributable to limited growth and opportunities in the domestic market and a lack of effective policies to support new investments and reduce barriers to entry (Vilakazi et al., 2020).

While there is evidence of continuity in many respects, one of the significant changes since the 1990s is the increasing propensity towards financialisation and internationalisation of the lead firms, as a function of their evolving orientation and strategies. A lack of diversification into other productive activities and new investments is symptomatic of a range of underlying issues that we have discussed in this chapter. These factors include a tendency towards high profit retention and dividend payouts, as well as firms' preference for significant portfolio and short-term assets over expansionary, fixed investments. Furthermore, a low-demand, low-growth environment as well as relative instability in the prevailing political atmosphere have fuelled an apparent reluctance on the part of the largest firms in the economy to engage in large-scale, new investments at the domestic level. Rather, they prefer to sweat their existing assets and market positions, despite the absence of dynamic rivalry in many key sectors.

High profit levels have not been matched by more robust investment. Indeed, the persistence of this pattern is perhaps one of the greatest economic conundrums facing South Africa at present, which will inevitably exacerbate the pronounced inequality and high unemployment levels and constrain the country's growth prospects for the foreseeable future.

REFERENCES

Andreoni, A., Mondliwa, P., Roberts, S. and Tregenna, F. 2021a. 'Framing structural transformation in South Africa and beyond', in Andreoni, A., Mondliwa, P., Roberts, S. and Tregenna, F. (eds.) *Structural Transformation in South Africa: The challenges of inclusive industrial development in a middle-income country*. Oxford: Oxford University Press, 1–27.

Andreoni, A., Robb, N. and Van Huellen, S. 2021b. 'Profitability without investment: How financialization undermines structural transformation in South Africa', in Andreoni, A., Mondliwa, P., Roberts, S. and Tregenna, F. (eds.) *Structural Transformation in South Africa: The challenges of inclusive industrial development in a middle-income country*. Oxford: Oxford University Press, 213–236.

Ashman, S. and Fine, B. 2013. 'Neo-liberalism, varieties of capitalism, and the shifting contours of South Africa's financial system'. *Transformation*, 81/82, 144–178.

Ashman, S., Fine, B. and Newman, S. 2013. 'Systems of accumulation and the evolving MEC', in Fine, B., Saraswati, J. and Tavasci, D. (eds.) *Beyond the Developmental State: Industrial policy into the 21st century.* London: Pluto, 245 – 267.

Bell, J., Goga, S., Mondliwa, P. and Roberts, S. 2018. 'Structural transformation in South Africa: Moving towards a smart, open economy for all'. Industrial Development Think Tank. Johannesburg: CCRED.

Bosiu, T., Nhundu, N., Paelo, A., Thosago, M. and Vilakazi, T. 2017a. 'Growth and strategies of large and leading firms: Top 50 firms on the Johannesburg Stock Exchange'. CCRED Working Paper 17/2017.

Bosiu, T., Nhundu, N., Paelo, A., Thosago, M. T. and Vilakazi, T. 2017b. 'Research project on large firms and system for regular tracking of their strategies and decisions: Remgro Limited company assessment'. CCRED Working Paper 11/2017, https://static1.squarespace.com/static/52246331e4b0a46e5f1b8ce5/t/59847ed4cd39c369f617016a/1501855455559/CCRED+Working+Paper+11_2017+IDRP_Remgro.pdf, accessed 3 March 2022.

Bowman, A. 2018. 'Financialization and the extractive industries: The case of South African platinum mining'. *Competition & Change*, 22 (4), 388–412.

Buthelezi, T., Mtani, T. and Mncube, L. 2019. 'The extent of market concentration in South Africa's product markets'. *Journal of Antitrust Enforcement, 7* (3), 352–364.

Chabane, N., Roberts, S. and Goldstein, A. 2006. 'The changing face and strategies of big business in South Africa: More than a decade of political democracy'. *Industrial and Corporate Change*, 15 (3), 549–577.

Competition Commission South Africa (CCSA). 2019. 'The Data Services Market Inquiry', https://www.compcom.co.za/wp-content/uploads/2019/12/DSMI-Non-Confidential-Report-002.pdf, accessed 14 February 2022.

Das Nair, R. and Chisoro-Dube, S. 2015. 'The expansion of regional supermarket chains: Changing models of retailing and the implications for local supplier capabilities in South Africa, Botswana, Zambia, and Zimbabwe'. WIDER Working Paper 2015/114. Helsinki: UNU-WIDER.

Das Nair, R. and Chisoro-Dube, S. 2017. 'The expansion of regional supermarket chains: Implications on suppliers in Botswana and South Africa'. WIDER Working Paper 2017/26. Helsinki: UNU-WIDER.

Davis, G. F., Diekmann, K. and Tinsley, C. 1994. 'The decline and fall of the conglomerate firm in the 1980s: The deinstitutionalization of an organizational form'. *American Sociological Review,* 59 (4), 547–570.

Fine, B. and Rustomjee, Z. 1996. *The Political Economy of South Africa: From minerals–energy complex to industrialisation.* London: Hurst, and Johannesburg: Wits University Press.

Freund, B. 2017. 'The significance of the minerals–energy complex in the light of South African economic historiography'. *Transformation*, 71 (1), 3–25.

Goga, S. and Mondliwa, P. 2021. 'Structural transformation, economic power, and inequality in South Africa', in Andreoni, A., Mondliwa, P., Roberts, S. and Tregenna, F. (eds.) *Structural Transformation in South Africa: The challenges of inclusive industrial development in a middle-income country*. UK: Oxford University Press, 165–188.

IRESS, 2022. Electronic dataset, https://expert.inetbfa.com/#Logon, accessed 3 November 2022.

Karwowski, E. 2015. 'The finance–mining nexus in South Africa: How mining companies use the South African equity market to speculate'. *Journal of Southern Africa Studies*, 41 (1), 9–28.

Krippner, G. R. 2005. 'The financialization of the American economy'. *Socio-Economic Review*, 3, 173–208.

Lazonick, W. 2010. 'Innovative business models and varieties of capitalism: Financialization of the US'. *Business History Review*, 84, 675–702.

Mondliwa, P. and Roberts, S. 2019. 'From a developmental to a regulatory state? Sasol and the conundrum of continued state support'. *International Review of Applied Economics*, 33 (1), 11–29.

Mondliwa, P. and Roberts, S. 2021. 'Corporate structure, industrial development, and structural change in South Africa', in Oqubay, A., Tregenna, F. and Valodia, I. (eds.) *The Oxford Handbook of the South African Economy*. UK: Oxford University Press, 349.

Nhundu, N., Paelo, A., Thosago, M. O. and Vilakazi, T. 2017. 'Growth and strategies of large and leading firms – food production and processing sector assessment'. CCRED Working Paper 10/2017, https://static1.squarespace.com/static/52246331e4b0a46e5f1b8ce5/t/59847eb7e6f2e181003dbdf9/1501855424616/CCRED+Working+Paper+10_2017_IDRP+Food+Sector-NNAPMTTV.pdf, accessed 16 April 2022.

Quantec EasyData. 2022. 'Gross fixed capital formation: By type of organisation: Private business enterprises'. Electronic dataset, https://www.easydata.co.za/, accessed 28 February 2022.

South African Reserve Bank (SARB). 2022. Quarterly Bulletins: Download information from xlsx data files, https://www.resbank.co.za/en/home/publications/publication-detail-pages/quarterly-bulletins/download-information-from-xlsx-data-files/2022/Downloadinformationfromxlsxdatafiles, accessed 25 February 2022.

Vilakazi, T., Goga, S. and Roberts, S. (eds.) 2020. *Opening the South African Economy? Barriers to entry and competition*. Cape Town: HSRC Press.

Who Owns Whom. 2022. Electronic dataset, https://www.woweb.co.za/?_ga=2.51650857.148956917.1675858920-851327146.1675858920, accessed 1 March 2022.

World Bank. 2021. 'Building back better from COVID-19, with a special focus on jobs'. *South Africa Economic Update: Edition 13*, https://documents1.worldbank.org/curated/en/161431626102808095/pdf/Building-Back-Better-from-COVID-19-with-a-Special-Focus-on-Jobs.pdf, accessed 16 April 2022.

Zalk, N. 2021. 'Structural change in South Africa: A sectoral historical perspective', in Andreoni, A., Mondliwa, P., Roberts, S. and Tregenna, F. (eds.) *Structural Transformation in South Africa: The challenges of inclusive industrial development in a middle-income country*. Oxford: Oxford University Press.

APPENDIX

Table 6.A1: Top 50–100 firms on the JSE (ranked by market capitalisation), 1990–2020

	1990	2000	2010	2020
50	Absa Group	Fedsure Holdings	Redefine Properties	Woolworths Holdings
51	First National Bank (FNB) Holdings	Steinoff International Holdings NV	Liberty Holdings	Tiger Brands
52	Pick n Pay Stores	MIH Holdings	PPC Ltd	Spar Group
53	Sun International	Datatec	Telkom SA Soc	Foschini Group Ltd
54	Palabora Mining Co.	New Africa Investment	Mondi Plc	Santam Ltd
55	Premier Group	Naspers	Mediclinic International	Ninety-One Plc
56	First International Trust	Discovery	Sappi	Investec Plc
57	Avmin	JD Group	Aquarius Platinum	Pick n Pay Stores
58	Technical Investment Corporation Ltd	Nedcor Investment Bank Holdings	Aveng Group Ltd	Life Health Group Holdings
59	Consol	Shoprite Holdings	The Spar Group	Avi Ltd
60	Beatrix Mines	Mutual and Federal Insurance	Mr Price Group	Capital & Counties Prop
61	African Oxygen Ltd	Tongaat-Hulett	Northam Platinum Holdings	Momentum Metropolitan Holdings
62	Orange Free State Investments Ltd	Northam Platinum Holdings	Santam Ltd	Vivo Energy Plc
63	Hunt Leuchars and Hepburn	Cadbury Schweppes	Life Health Group Holdings	Distell Group Holdings
64	Technical Investment Corporation Ltd	Santam Limited	Barloworld	Hammerson Plc

	1990	2000	2010	2020
65	Malbak	African Oxygen Ltd	Distell Group	Sirius Real Estate
66	Zozo Holdings	Harmony Gold Mining Co.	Investec	Italtile
67	Wooltru	Sun International (SA) Ltd	Nampak	Redefine Properties
68	Anglovaal	Clicks Group	Capitec Bank Holdings	Barloworld
69	Amalgamated Beverage Industries	African Phoenix Investments Ltd	Murray & Roberts Holdings	Sappi
70	Northam Platinum Holdings	ArcelorMittal SA Ltd	Reunert	Dis-Chem Pharmacies
71	Pep	Coronation Holdings	Illovo Sugar	Netcare Ltd
72	PPC Ltd	Profurn	Sun International	Liberty Holdings
73	Bankorp Holdings	Avi Ltd	Clicks Group	Resilient REIT Ltd
74	Oryx Gold Holdings	Pick n Pay Holdings	Tongaat-Hulett	Royal Bafokeng Platinum
75	Tongaat-Hulett	Sun International	Hosken Consolidated Investments Ltd	Textainer Group Holdings
76	Assmang	Aveng Group Ltd	Pioneer Foods Group	Transaction Capital
77	Pick n Pay Holdings	Comparex Holdings	Royal Bafokeng Platinum	Truworths International
78	Evraz Highlight Steel & Vanadium	PPC Ltd	Mvelaphanda Resources Ltd	Fortress REIT
79	Evander Gold Mines	Reunert	Pick n Pay Holdings	Bytes Technology Group
80	African Rainbow Minerals	Woolworths Holdings	Avi Ltd	Telkom SA Soc Ltd
81	RD Foods Ltd	African Rainbow Minerals	Adcock Ingram Holdings	DRD Gold
82	Murray & Roberts Holdings	Rebserv Holdings	JD Group	Coronation Fund Managers Ltd
83	Huntoor	Allied Technologies	AECI Ltd	Zambezi Plat Ltd
84	Rand Mines	Duiker Mining	Hyprop Investments	Cartrack Holdings
85	Adcock Ingram	Caxton Publishing and Print	Capital & Counties Properties Plc	Montauk Holdings
86	Wooltru	Tempora Investments	Wilson Bayly Holmes-Ovcon Ltd	Globe Trade Centre SA

	1990	2000	2010	2020
87	Deelkraal Gold Mining Co. Ltd	Safmarine & Rennies Holdings	Grindrod	PSG Group
88	Randfontein Estates	Massmart Holdings	Pangbourne Properties	Ninety-One Ltd
89	Altron Ltd	AECI Ltd	Resilient REIT Ltd	PSG Konsult Ltd
90	Liberty Investors	Assmang	Evraz Highveld Steel & Vanadium	Investec
91	Allied Technologies	Caxton & CTP Publishers and Printers	Great Basin Gold	Equites Property Fund
92	Trans Natal Coal Corp Ltd	Delta EMD	Eastern Platinum	Pan African Resources Plc
93	Foschini Group Ltd	Hosken Consolidated Investments	Lewis Group	Motus Holdings
94	Trencor	Western Areas	Mondi	JSE
95	Cadbury Schweppes	Super Group	PSG Group	AECI Ltd
96	Federale Volksbeleggings	Mediclinic International	Caxton & CTP Publishers and Printers	EPP NV
97	Pep Stores	Aspen Pharmacare Holdings	Optimum Coal Holdings	Massmart Holdings
98	Irvin & Johnson	Del Monte Royal Foods Ltd	African Oxygen Ltd	MAS Real Estate Inc.
99	Technology Systems International	Truworths International	Emira Property Fund	Super Group
100	Ingwe Coal Corporation	Real Africa Holdings	Mutual and Federal Insurance	African Oxygen Ltd

Table 6.A2: List of cross-/dual-listed firms, 2021

Firm	Sector	Secondary listing
Prosus NV	Media and internet	Euronext
Anheuser-Busch InBev SA	Manufacturing	Euronext, Bolsa Mexicana, New York Stock Exchange
British American Tobacco Plc	Manufacturing	London Stock Exchange
Naspers Ltd	Media and internet	London Stock Exchange
Glencore Plc	Mining	London Stock Exchange
BHP Group Plc	Mining	Australian Securities Exchange Limited, London Stock Exchange

Firm	Sector	Secondary listing
Anglo American Plc	Mining	Botswana Stock Exchange, London Stock Exchange, Namibian Stock Exchange, New York Stock Exchange
FirstRand Ltd	Financial services	Namibian Stock Exchange
Standard Bank Group	Financial services	Namibian Stock Exchange
South32 Ltd	Mining	Australian Securities Exchange Limited, London Stock Exchange
Sasol Ltd	Manufacturing	New York Stock Exchange
Mondi Plc	Manufacturing	London Stock Exchange
Impala Platinum Holdings	Mining	London Stock Exchange
Sibanye Stillwater Ltd	Mining	New York Stock Exchange
Sanlam Ltd	Financial Services	Namibian Stock Exchange
Gold Fields Ltd	Mining	New York Stock Exchange
AngloGold Ashanti Ltd	Mining	Australian Securities Exchange Limited, Ghana Stock Exchange, New York Stock Exchange
Shoprite Holdings Ltd	Retail	Lusaka Stock Exchange, Namibian Stock Exchange
Nedbank Group	Financial Services	Namibian Stock Exchange
Old Mutual Ltd	Financial Services	Namibian Stock Exchange, Zimbabwe Stock Exchange, Malawi Stock Exchange, London Stock Exchange
Reinet Investments SCA	Financial Services	Luxembourg Stock Exchange, Euronext
Quilter Plc	Financial Services	London Stock Exchange
Mediclinic International Plc	Healthcare	London Stock Exchange, Namibian Stock Exchange
African Rainbow Minerals Ltd	Mining	London Stock Exchange
Investec Plc	Investment Services	London Stock Exchange
Momentum Metropolitan Holdings	Financial Services	Namibian Stock Exchange
Ninety-One Plc	Investment Services	London Stock Exchange
Harmony Gold Mining Co. Ltd	Mining	London Stock Exchange, New York Stock Exchange
Textainer Group Holdings Ltd	Logistics	New York Stock Exchange
Santam Ltd	Financial services	Namibian Stock Exchange
Capital & Counties Properties Plc	Real estate	London Stock Exchange

Firm	Sector	Secondary listing
Vivo Energy Plc	Energy	London Stock Exchange
Sirius Real Estate Ltd	Real estate	London Stock Exchange
Barloworld Ltd	Manufacturing	London Stock Exchange, Namibian Stock Exchange
Bytes Technology Group	IT	London Stock Exchange
Truworths International Ltd	Retail	Namibian Stock Exchange
Sappi Ltd	Manufacturing	New York Stock Exchange
Investec Ltd	Investment services	Botswana Stock Exchange, Namibian Stock Exchange
PSG Konsult Ltd	Investment services	Stock Exchange of Mauritius Ltd, Namibian Stock Exchange
Globe Trade Centre SA	Real estate	Warsaw Stock Exchange
Steinhoff International Holdings NV	Retail	Frankfurt Stock Exchange
Thungela Resources Ltd	Mining	London Stock Exchange
Vukile Property Fund Ltd	Real estate	Namibian Stock Exchange

Source: Authors' compilation based on IRESS, 2022

NOTES

1 Notwithstanding the presence of a very large, growing and well-resourced, non-listed private sector in some parts, see the announcement in 2022 by the PSG Group, a large, diversified investor, of its intention to delist from the JSE: https://www.news24.com/fin24/companies/investment-holdings/end-of-an-era-psg-to-delist-from-the-jse-20220301

2 See article, for example, on listing and delisting in recent decades: https://businesstech.co.za/news/finance/529244/south-africas-shrinking-jse-investors-explain-whats-going-on/

SEVEN

Confronting the industrial and empowerment implications of the energy transition in South Africa

AYABONGA CAWE

INTRODUCTION

Broad-based black economic empowerment (B-BBEE) in the Broad-Based Black Economic Empowerment Act 53 of 2003 refers to a wide variety of integrated socioeconomic strategies and actions (including skills development, preferential procurement, and facilitation of ownership and management control). All of these are aimed at ensuring that an 'increasing number of black people' own, manage and control 'enterprises and productive assets'. The latter relate to productive assets, not just 'stakes' or distributional access to capital gains or dividends, which is a marked departure from the deal structures that were prevalent prior to the promulgation of the Act. Recently, the more aggressive push for B-BBEE through the creation of black industrialists and exporters and the broadening of their participation in the economy with the help of various policy tools (localisation, designation and preferential procurement as 'rents') has become central to the structural transformation policy objectives of the post-apartheid era.

This chapter considers B-BBEE within the context of the energy transition. It examines the role of the state in using rents and policy instruments, such as preferential procurement and designation for local production, to foster the adoption of new technologies, deepen the sophistication of local industrial value chains, and broaden ownership opportunities and economic participation amongst historically disadvantaged persons, groups and communities. The focus of this chapter is on how these 'rents' have been used in successive waves of the Renewable Energy Independent Power Producer Procurement Programme (REIPPPP), which is aimed at bringing additional megawatts into the electricity system through private investment in wind, solar, biogas and hydro energy generation technologies.

The chapter is an outcome of qualitative interviews conducted with project owners, financiers from both development finance institutions and commercial banks, government officials and a representative from an original equipment manufacturer (OEM) which also supplies engineering, procurement and construction (EPC) services to REIPPPP projects.

The chapter critically engages with the topic, drawing on the literature on global production networks and the role of the state as an incumbent and dominant energy producer. In the context of the just energy transition, this role also encompasses acting as a dominant buyer of renewable energy and a catalyst for the adoption of new energy generation technology. It considers Eskom's annual reports between 1938 and 1992 and finds that OEMs and lead firms in critical global production networks linked to energy generation have played a critical role (before, during and after apartheid), and will continue to do so, in any build process and subsequent after-sales services, as well as broadly across the energy generation landscape and related industrial interests in South Africa. This reality has introduced a global value chain dimension in light of the shift towards renewable technology, but it also highlights the role of global production networks in the old energy paradigm. This has implications not only for the shift towards renewables, but also for the immediate challenges confronting the existing (and ageing) coal-fired generation fleet.

The chapter addresses a number of issues. First, it considers how B-BBEE has unfolded in the energy generation sector in South Africa and discusses the role of 'coal rents' in black economic empowerment (BEE) programmes. It also comments on the fact that weak outcomes in the spread of ownership, management and control of productive assets in industrial sectors have given rise to the Black Industrialists Programme, alongside preferential procurement (and associated designation). The programme is designed to leverage the capacity of the state to unlock the industrial potential of black-owned and -managed businesses operating in industrial sectors through targeted policies and financial and non-financial support measures.

Second, the chapter considers the evolution of the South African energy sector, from the electric telegram lines of the 1800s and the streetlights that were erected in Kimberley after the diamond rush,[1] to the intricate ties formed between energy investments, the mining of coal, and the scale and pace of investments in the mining and associated sectors. In addition, the chapter touches on the historical path of investments in coal-fired electricity in the 20th century at Eskom, at generation plants that are in some cases still part of Eskom's fleet.

Third, in relation to the restructuring of the energy sector, the chapter focuses on post-apartheid energy policy and the unveiling of a policy roadmap for the introduction of new energy generation technologies. It focuses primarily on wind energy technology and the role of procurement-linked rents and BEE frameworks, which act as vehicles for enhanced economic participation, the acquisition of technological capabilities and the introduction of structural change in associated secondary industries.

The chapter concludes with some recommendations aimed at informing future regulatory and policy reflection, while also considering the role of state actions and public instruments in shaping market outcomes in ways that facilitate structural change and the restructuring of historical colonial- and apartheid-era production structures.

COAL RENTS AND BROAD-BASED BLACK ECONOMIC EMPOWERMENT

It is not coincidental that most, if not all, of the current power stations in South Africa were built in the former Eastern Transvaal (now Mpumalanga), close to where the coal that fuelled the power plants was mined. This coal was extracted, on the basis of long-term contracts, from what were called 'cost-plus' mines. Eskom and the colliery co-financed the establishment costs of these mines, paid all the costs of operating the colliery and paid the coal miner a net income based on an agreed return on investment, the latter influenced by a flat rate of return and a return based on the tonnage delivered (Eberhard and Mtepa, 2003).

In a sense, these coal contracts served as a rent to upstream miners, a critical feature of what would later be called the minerals–energy complex (MEC), where coal rents were used to develop the upstream and downstream elements of minerals-linked value chains (Fine and Rustomjee, 1996). Furthermore, more than 100 years of coal-fired production had a far-reaching influence on cost and production structures in South Africa, which favoured energy-intensive aluminium, ferroalloy and steel refineries (Makgetla and Patel, 2021).

However, attention is also given to whether, in the post-apartheid era, corporate restructuring within this rent distribution network has unlocked control, management and participation amongst black players, as required by B-BBEE policy. In the case of electricity generation, opportunities have emerged for black players in respect of build, coal mining and transportation activities. In the discussion below, coal mining rents are regarded as critical catalysts that have, for instance, influenced the scope and scale of black players' participation in coal freight and logistics. Furthermore, the coal procurement landscape has long been a key factor in plant design and performance.

During the past decade, Eskom has introduced a procurement policy requiring coal players to have black ownership of 50 per cent or more. This policy has had two related outcomes. The first is growth in dealmaking amongst incumbent coal players, thus opening the space for black players. This has been evidenced in recent years in the emergence of players like Exxaro (unbundled from Kumba's coal assets and a tie-up with Eyesizwe) and Seriti (spawned from the unbundling of South32 and servicing Lethabo, Tutuka and Kriel Eskom power stations and Salungano, formerly known as WesCoal).

The second outcome of the changed procurement policy was significant shifts in terms of how these coal contracts were structured and the move away from cost-plus towards fixed-cost arrangements. In 2002, just under 23 per cent of the 104.9 million tonnes of coal procured by Eskom were sourced from black suppliers, but by 2021, the top 10 coal suppliers largely comprised what had become relatively large black coal producers. The latter included Exxaro Coal, Seriti Coal and Wescoal (now the Salungano Group). By 2021, many of Eskom's top 10 coal suppliers, while largely black, were subject to fixed rather than long-term, cost-plus pricing, with seven of these contracts subject to fixed-price rather than cost-plus procurement arrangements.

While Eskom now expects lower production from cost-plus mines going forward, many of these mines remain in need of significant investment and recapitalisation. This investment need suggests that while short- to medium-term contracts are more expensive for Eskom than, say, fixed-price contracts, which are more expensive than cost-plus mining ventures, they are more expensive for black enterprises because of the capital investment requirements that they have to shoulder alone, rather than alongside the utility. Cost-plus contracts, while ensuring long-term price predictability and cost advantages, which can in turn be passed on to downstream industrial and household users, have significant upfront capital requirements.

Yet, from the perspective of coal miners, the co-investment by Eskom historically de-risked these plants and provided a secure, long-term customer, effectively creating a rent for these coal miners. However, this element in the rent distribution framework is missing for many of these new black producers, as the share of cost-plus production fed into power stations declined to less than one-third of the value of coal purchased in 2021 (Eskom, 2021). While this may be seen as a disadvantage for the coal miners, the renegotiation in some cases, such as with the Seriti and Duvha power stations, of coal sales agreements between Eskom and many legacy mines now in black hands allows for some production to be exported as and when global coal prices improve.

Potential access to export markets became important because some coal miners faced financial hardship, as their coal sale agreements with Eskom were priced below the cost of mining. However, while this may be beneficial for black-owned coal miners, at the 'right export prices' it may create a supply challenge for the remaining coal-fired stations which may experience rising costs, since the pricing of fixed-cost and shorter-term contracts may introduce significant risks. These risks were particularly evident in the 2021–2022 period when global coal prices were hovering above the US$400/ton mark, in contrast to the 2014–2018 period when prices were below US$100/ton (Slater, 2022).

The implications of this are significant. First, as investment in coal-fired power declines, so too will the scope for long-term, black participation in coal-related rents. As discussed above, Eskom-driven rents may also decline in the current environment, considering the widening gap between the dollar tonnage cost of coal in global spot markets and the cost of fixed-term (and even cost-plus) contract arrangements between coal miners and Eskom.

Second, this decline requires that consideration be given to which areas can be leveraged while the energy sector restructures, with a view to unlocking black participation in new products and technologies, which are critical for such restructuring – both in the existing coal sector, which, as the Integrated Resource Plan (IRP) suggests, should still prevail into the near future, and in enhanced generation from renewable technologies.

Third, this entails not only the transition to new technologies but also the economic opportunities arising from the transitional costs of making such a shift, in the reorientation of the transmission and distribution of electricity. For instance, Eskom announced R178-billion capital expenditure plans to build new transmission capability to complement the diverse spatial profile of sources of new generating capacity from wind and solar. In this regard, what service and other product opportunities exist for black players in Eskom's plans for new transmission capability? The new generation activities relating to wind and solar, along with investment in transformers, present opportunities for localisation of key components and participation of black players.

Furthermore, while coal reserves might seem abundant, the costs of transporting the coal to Eskom's plants have become increasingly prohibitive, with increasing volumes transported by road rather than conveyor belt. The shift away from cost-plus mines has also contributed to a shift away from 'tied-colliery' deals which complemented the cost-plus mines, for the same reasons mentioned above – ostensibly to create new 'coal-related' rents for BEE players.

By 2016, Eskom had 58 transport contracts in place, moving 124 kilotonnes of coal through 30 to 40 haulage routes. This created not only significant costs but also opportunities for corrupt dealings, where RB3 grade coal used at Eskom power plants was replaced by waste coal discard, affecting plant performance (Eskom, 2016). These corrupt activities, triggered by a favourable export price for coal, occurred in tandem with other corrupt schemes, such as the use of the Optimum Coal Mine by the Gupta family for a sophisticated money-laundering operation.

All these opportunities and challenges frame the role that B-BBEE can play in the evolution of the energy sector. Yet to understand this evolution, it is important to first understand the successive waves of change in South Africa's energy sector in the post-First World War era.

THE EVOLUTION OF SOUTH AFRICA'S ENERGY SECTOR

The development of South Africa's energy sector has seen five distinct phases, each with spatial, environmental, social, political and industrial implications. In each phase, which was affected by loadshedding and declining energy availability problems, there was a 'trigger' or 'catalyst' for the expansion of generating capacity, mostly in sectors with growing energy needs (and, in this case, mining) and industrial concerns.

In 1910, the Transvaal colonial government passed the Power Act. This Act defined electricity as a 'public good' rather than a commodity to be exchanged for profit and made provision for the future expropriation of private electricity undertakings after 35 years. Further legislative advances, such as the passing of the Electricity Act of 1922, laid the foundation for the development of an electricity supply sector in South Africa whose role was to provide 'wherever required, a cheap and abundant supply of energy' (Eberhard, 2004: 3).

Eskom or the then 'Commission' regarded 'cheap power as an important factor in promoting industrial development' (Eskom, 1923: 5). The Act facilitated the creation of a new institution, the Electricity Supply Commission (Escom, now Eskom). Eskom undertook the electrification of railways and began the construction of new power stations in Cape Town, Durban, Sabie and Witbank.

The first phase (1922–1945) involved the co-existence of private generation activities alongside municipally run but relatively small-scale generation and distribution, located in the former Pretoria, Witwatersrand and Vereeniging (PWV) area, the Cape, Witbank, Durban and other industrial areas. Technologies included oil- and hydro-powered generation, together with coal-fired steam power stations in Natal, Klip, Cape Town and Witbank. There was limited transmission of electricity beyond the mining and growing industrial sector, the railways and urban residential users. During this phase the catalyst for expansion in generating capacity was the growing energy demand from the mining sector.

The second phase (1945–1983), after the Second World War, was characterised by major expansions in Eskom's coal-fired generation fleet, in response to growing industrial demand (Eskom, 1972). The rollout of build programmes from the 1960s onwards was in response to this growing demand. Spatially, generating assets were located close to the fuel (coal) supply, mainly in the former Eastern Transvaal. This stage also coincided with more streamlining of distribution and transmission activities, with municipalities discouraged from building their own generating capacity and expanding transmission, which effectively created a 'national grid'. During this phase, Eskom moved from six coal-fired power stations in 1945 to 20 coal-fired power stations by 1983. Eskom's capital expenditure on new plants created economic relationships between Eskom, boiler, turbine and generator manufacturers, and coal mines (Eskom, 1983).

This phase coincided with much higher electricity sales to

industrial and bulk distribution customers than to the mining sector. Despite significant investment during this period, in response to growing industrial needs, the ambitious build programme in the 1970s experienced operational challenges. These included boiler tube leaks and slagging issues, and Eskom experienced loadshedding despite building new generating capacity. By 1981, a year in which Eskom faced generation and transmission challenges from Cahora Bassa and voluntary loadshedding by intensive users, Eskom reported that it had eight power stations under construction (Eskom, 1981).

The third phase (1983–2008) seems to have been about reductions in generating capacity and the management of supply, the organisational restructuring of Eskom, and the 'transformation' of its management and supply contracts. By 1983, Eskom had 22 260 MW under construction or on order. Between 1975 and 1991, eight new power stations were completed. Following the recommendations of the De Villiers Commission in 1983, Eskom was reconfigured into a new two-tier governance structure and its capital development fund was scrapped, while excess generating capacity led to the postponement of the construction of some plants and the mothballing of others.

From 1994 onwards, a national electrification programme increased the number of African and black households with access to electricity. By 2003, the number of residential users of Eskom's electricity had risen to 3.3 million households, from just under 400 000 households in 1992. The national electrification programme and rising residential demand, along with a surge in demand from traditional mining and metals industries (linked to the commodity price boom in the 2000s), absorbed much of the earlier excess capacity and led to shortages that required the return to service of mothballed legacy plants. At this stage, the 138 largest industrial customers consumed 40 per cent of the energy generated.

Around 2008, operational challenges led to the first post-apartheid wave of loadshedding. It was caused by a combination of lower-than-expected coal volumes from collieries, lower coal quality, higher load factors and the absence of regular maintenance, amongst other factors (Chettiar et al., 2009). Loadshedding during this period is estimated to have cost the South African economy R50 billion. Coincidentally

– like in the early 1980s – these supply challenges occurred at a time when new coal-fired generating capacity was in the early stages of construction.

The fourth phase (2008–2021) largely coincided with attempts to improve energy availability through improvements to existing plant performance and the adoption and deployment of new-generation technologies and capacity. This phase gave rise to the IRP, which was based on a combination of new-generation technology options. The IRP gave due consideration to the installation of renewables capacity (hydro, gas and nuclear) alongside the existing capability in coal. This was partly in response to an emissions constraint of 275 million tonnes of carbon dioxide per annum after 2024.

The design and construction of the Medupi and Kusile power stations continued during this phase, with the opening of five bid windows for renewables, which stimulated a considerable amount of interest from financiers, project developers and the broader investor community. However, the procurement process for new generating capacity also had to consider socioeconomic imperatives (BEE, local content and community participation) and how these imperatives could be advanced, together with the provision of security of investment to local industry, to build capabilities. The two-decades-long power purchase agreements entered into with independent power producers (IPPs) under this programme represent 'rents' insofar as they lock in a price per kWh which, depending on the technology and product life cycle of these technologies, may be subject to significant change over the 20-year period.

What can be gleaned from this contemporary phase is that the century-long energy-generation project, which Hendrik van der Bijl had spearheaded, collapsed under the weight of the industries it had been designed to support, while also being overtaken by rapid social change. Furthermore, as Makgetla (2021: 33) observes, the previously held assumptions about the generation model no longer applied:

> [There was no longer] continued robust growth in demand from big customers in the mining value chain (alongside) the absence of technologies that are able to compete with large-scale

> coal generation and [the absence of the] ability to externalise the pollution caused by coal use and the supply of low-cost coal. All four assumptions began to fail in the 2010s, ultimately generating the vicious cycles that plagued the electricity system.

The age-old challenge identified by Van der Bijl – how to link the energy paradigm with lower industry costs and enhanced competitiveness – is still very prevalent in South Africa today. The existential crisis that threatens Eskom and the entire energy generation sector not only emphasises the urgent need for new electricity capacity. It also creates opportunities for, but also constraints to, the broadening of economic participation and pricing energy appropriately to attract investment and spur industrial and structural change in South Africa's value-added sectors.

OPPORTUNITIES FOR, AND CONSTRAINTS TO, INDUSTRIAL UPGRADING AND BROADENING OF PARTICIPATION

In South Africa's energy mix, the state acts as a procurer of first resort, in exchange for a technological shift in how energy is generated. This introduces not only new technologies, but also the possibility of acquiring new capabilities in the design, installation, maintenance and repair of new technologies in the generation and transmission of electricity.

The ease with which these new capabilities are acquired is determined by how political-economy relationships play out between technology manufacturers, OEMs and the state (as the guaranteed buyer and transmitter of the energy procured), and local industrial interests. These relationships determine who does what and how value is distributed between the different actors. By implication, this impacts South Africa's development path, with the terms, usage and economic relationships linked to the energy supply also determining the social relations between different economic actors. The next section considers whether the policy objectives of B-BBEE (and structural change through local content designation) have been met through a focus on procurement of wind energy under the auspices of the REIPPPP.

THE RENEWABLE ENERGY PROCUREMENT POLICY ENVIRONMENT AND IMPLICATIONS FOR BROAD-BASED PARTICIPATION AND INDUSTRIAL DEVELOPMENT

Three key policy frameworks shape the establishment of the renewable energy sector and its envisaged impact on industrial development and broad-based participation: the 2003 White Paper on Renewable Energy, the IRP and the REIPPPP. One can add to these the Preferential Procurement Policy Framework Act (PPPFA) of 2000 whose regulations incorporate requirements for subcontracting and, for the purposes of the ensuing discussion, designation for local content.

The IRP is a 20-year electricity infrastructure development plan, based on 'least-cost electricity supply' and balanced user demand, between 2010 and 2030. It brought forward the installation of renewable generating capacity 'to accelerate a local industry' (DoE, 2011: 6). Notwithstanding this, the 2010 IRP also suggested bringing forward, earlier than previously envisaged, 'planned new coal builds', while recognising that additional coal capacity would be undermined by a future carbon tax regime. Moreover, in its modelling of different scenarios, the plan recognised the localisation potential of energy technologies and 'the potential to localise the technology industry' through the communication of a 'regular build profile' (DoE, 2011: 27), which is discussed below.

The REIPPPP is a competitive bid procurement process that serves as a key mechanism to realise the goals of the IRP. The procurement is undertaken in different 'bid windows'. There have been five windows to date (excluding emergency rounds). The evaluation framework, while mainly considering price and tariff structures in delivering the generated energy, places considerable emphasis on non-price criteria, such as employment and socioeconomic development, as outlined in the 2003 White Paper on Renewable Energy. The price considerations constitute 70 per cent of the bid score, while the remaining 30 per cent is made up of B-BBEE elements (ownership, management control, and enterprise and supplier development), community participation and local content.

The 2003 White Paper on Renewable Energy suggests that the choice of renewable technologies to generate electricity should not only consider 'technologies that are currently available in South Africa' but also that 'the local content of equipment needs to be maximised to minimise the costs associated with implementation and operation, as well as the promotion of employment opportunities' (DoE, 2003: xi).

The energy procured under the IRP and related REIPPPP is bought from IPPs which are limited-liability, investor-owned enterprises generating electricity for bulk sale to Eskom or any other industrial or public customers, subject to certain conditions. By the time the 2019 draft IRP was released, over 6 422 MW of renewable energy had been procured. Once the bidder meets all the requirements in Part A to Part C of the request for proposals and their bid is successful, they enter into a power purchase agreement and an implementation agreement with Eskom and the Department of Mineral Resources and Energy (DMRE), respectively.

Broadening black participation

BEE is a key policy instrument used to broaden participation and ownership. Ownership refers to equity ownership in the project company selling energy into the grid, while 'participation' for the purposes of our discussion considers 'local content', setting thresholds for expenditure on local goods and services. In addition to these thresholds, the ownership element specifies targets for shareholding in the project company by citizens, black people and local communities. The 'participation' element also factors in the participation of black contractors in the construction and operational phases of the project, as a critical demographic category.

The threshold for black ownership is 30 per cent, with a target of 40 per cent, while the threshold for black contractors is 25 per cent during construction and operations, with a target of 40 per cent as well. Shareholding by local communities is apparently optional, as the threshold stands at zero per cent, with a target of 2.5 per cent.

Local content

Local content requirements are a key measure to enable technological transfer and industrial upgrading. Local content refers to the proportion of project expenditure spent in South Africa on goods produced locally. This excludes finance charges, land and other fees related to the project (Baker and Sovacool, 2017; DoE, 2011). Evaluation criteria for bids show a preference for South African products and project-level expenditure during the construction and operational phases by imposing local content thresholds during bids on designated products. These thresholds have increased from a 25 per cent local content requirement in wind projects in Bid Window 1 to a 40 per cent local content requirement in Bid Window 5.

The thresholds also involve 'sub-thresholds' at the product and component levels. For instance, in the case of wind technology, steel products and components for the construction of renewables projects, such as fasteners, reinforcing bars and coils, are designated for 100 per cent local content in view of existing local capabilities in downstream steel production. Meanwhile, batteries and connectors used in two-way radio terminal equipment are designated at a local content threshold of between 25 and 30 per cent. In the case of wind towers, the addition of locally manufactured concrete or steel towers to meet the higher local content thresholds in later bid windows may influence some key investment decisions. From Bid Window 4 onwards, local production of towers is mandatory. Towers generally account for 12 to 14 per cent of project costs (Baker and Sovacool, 2017).

If bidders cannot meet the threshold, they are obliged to apply to the Department of Trade, Industry and Competition (DTIC) for an exemption at least one month before the bid submission date. From Bid Windows 1 to 4, according to the DTIC, there was a minimum target in the aggregate, which rose from 25 per cent to 40 per cent by Bid Window 4. By Bid Window 5, specific products and components were designated for local content, and an agreement between the DTIC and the DMRE gave rise to an exemption process, where exemptions given to one player (for a specific product) would in principle be granted to all players.

HOW HAVE THESE POLICY FRAMEWORKS DRIVEN THE MARKET RESPONSE IN THE WIND ENERGY SECTOR?

The wind energy sector consists of a broad range of market participants, OEMs, developers, owners and operators of the projects. However, the vertically integrated nature of the global wind technology supply chain means that the OEMs in many cases also serve as providers of EPC services. EPC is the largest cost item in the budget, at 60 to 75 per cent of the total project cost (Baker and Sovacool, 2017; Eberhard and Naude, 2017). Therefore, cost management of the EPC function is critical for a competitive bid tariff.

WHAT DRIVES THE BID TARIFF DETERMINATION?

The tariff price is largely determined by component-related factors. According to a wind energy project owner, much of what the feed-in tariffs to the grid operator (Eskom) cover are the costs of the actual wind turbine and its components, the rotor blade, the nacelle, the generator inside the nacelle and gearbox, and the tower (and cables running into the tower), as well as the EPC costs. Furthermore, the technology requirements of each project influence the possibilities open to local subcontractors and qualifying small and medium enterprises (SMEs) which can undertake balance-of-plant activities, and auxiliary and related tasks across the lifecycle of the project (Baker and Sovacool, 2017).

Some foreign firms complied with local content rules in earlier bid windows by setting up subsidiaries in South Africa to act as project developers, OEM providers and EPC contractors, or by forming joint ventures and other strategic alliances with domestic players (Bazilian et al., 2020). Expenditures in the construction phase were the major source of local content compliance, as local capabilities in balance-of-plant activities could be drawn in.

Some REIPPPP project-level examples reinforce this point, namely the Nojoli Wind Farm and the Wesley–Ciskei Wind Farm, which are discussed below.

Distribution of value at a project level

The Nojoli Wind Farm is an instructive case of how the different economic activities and market participants interact at a project level. While owned by Enel Green Power SA and Pele Energy, the farm employs turbines manufactured by Vestas, a Danish manufacturer and installer of wind turbines. Vestas is not only critical for the diffusion of technologies and capabilities, but it also frames the distribution of value in the capital structure of these projects. This role is often required by financiers, whose funding is contingent on an EPC service provider that has completed a certain number of analogous projects. The two critical implications of Vestas's involvement are as follows:

- First, Vestas is also the manufacturer of the 10 Vestas V126–3.45 turbines found on the wind farm. This suggests that value is captured both in the construction and the operational phases. In the latter case, the wind turbine generator (WTG) supply contract effectively includes both manufactured final products and after-sales service and operations.
- Second, the EPC element of Vestas's contract allows for strong influence to be exercised over procurement decisions relating to sub-contractors, in fulfilment of enterprise and supplier development obligations underpinning the bid process. This means that Vestas can have significant operational influence over the selection of providers of balance of plant and any other local suppliers that perform civils, electrical work and other service functions. Conversely, it can also exclude, in the face of requirements for 'standards' and 'specifications', any prospective suppliers that may not currently meet these requirements.

This suggests that a key driver of the price (which accounts for 70 per cent[2] of the evaluation criteria) is the commercial decision-making matrix that confronts the tier 1 OEMs that provide the technology and the EPC services.

Put differently, the bargaining or balance of power between project owners and OEMs/EPC service providers determines the price path of many renewables projects. In turn, as one project owner suggested,

OEMs' bargaining considerations would be informed by the scale and volume of the orders in question and the demand conditions broadly, with smaller projects affording project initiators and owners relatively weaker bargaining power relative to that of these OEMs. The implications of this for broadening black participation and encouraging industrial and structural change are that procurement schedules need to have a sufficiently long-term horizon and adequate scale to incentivise both stronger bargaining by local and black project owners and upstream investment in complementary industrial component manufacturing and supply.

The issue of scale is important as it is a key factor determining the degree to which local content can be maximised. The White Paper on Renewable Energy identified this challenge, suggesting that '[to] make local manufacture viable, economies of scale, that is significant demand will be required ... [this] will be partly a function of Government support' (DoE, 2003: 40). A quick scan of the products and components that were granted such exemptions indicates that even the parts that can be localised will be subject to supply pressures if the design of the procurement process makes no provision for the time lags between investment in supply and the realisation of such supply. In the wind sector, recent exemptions included those for steel plates heavier than 10 tonnes, flanges with a diameter of more than 3 metres and imported, fully built nacelles (DTIC, 2021). Conversely, exemptions were denied for power cables and transformers.

While larger-scale projects and predictable, longer-term procurement schedules may afford project owners at the operational level of wind projects more favourable access to the energy generation domain, these may be a necessary but insufficient condition for upstream black industrialists across the components described earlier. Complementary support packages for black industrialists to facilitate their entry into these global production networks must include tax (depreciation allowances on capital investment), industrial and other incentives, in addition to those in the renewables and green economy space. Incentives under the black industrialists scheme have comprised extended financial and non-financial support to black firms in activities 'incidental' to value creation in the renewables sector. For instance, between 2016 and 2021, the four firms supported under this scheme, instead of being in component supply areas covered by designation, were in waste management, bio-charcoal, insulation and metering (DTIC, 2022).

The bulk of incentives to upstream industrial sectors have focused on industrial infrastructure (special economic zones (SEZs) and industrial parks), automotive, agro-processing, steel and metal fabrication, with just over 1 per cent of departmental incentive approvals going to industrial firms in renewables and the green economy. Mechanisms to help black industrialists meet the demand of the REIPPPP will require supply-side incentives and industrial financing support to reduce the scale and number of exemptions from local content requirements. Such support must incentivise the local assembly of components and later manufacturing, through intellectual property licensing frameworks or local joint ventures with black industrialists and OEMs and/or research institutes. Furthermore, consideration ought to be given to the rationalisation of trade policy, through the alignment of the tariff regime on components and that on final manufactured panels in the solar photovoltaic (PV) market, for instance (as suggested in the draft South African Renewable Energy Masterplan), and the use of import tariff frameworks (including rebates and drawbacks where necessary) on related components where early investments are being made to 'incubate' the local market.

LESSONS INFORMING POLICY AND REGULATORY REFLECTION AND ACTION

As discussed in the preceding sections of this chapter, the South African energy market has made the transition from a system based on coal rents and cheap energy supplies to industry, to one where private generation, financed (and refinanced) by private and development financiers, provides for the adoption of new technologies through predictable and secure two-decade agreements. In return for this 20-year rent, project initiators compete on tariffs and the ability to derive socioeconomic benefits for the domestic economy and communities in the vicinity of solar and wind operations.

The next section considers some of the lessons emanating from this shift, and possible policy and regulatory steps that could be taken to influence the distributional and industrial outcomes of the REIPPPP – particularly as energy from the programme will constitute a growing proportion of the country's energy mix going forward.

- **Improve the scale and frequency of bid windows to incentivise investment in industrial capabilities**

The White Paper on Renewable Energy stresses that economies of scale are essential if the local manufacture of renewable energy components is to be viable. Thus, the public demand for renewables must be of a sufficient magnitude to incentivise investment. Many of the participants interviewed noted that the scale of renewable projects (with a cap of 140 MW on onshore wind) did not allow for an improved bargaining dynamic with OEMs and EPC service providers. In addition, the stop–start cycles, due to Eskom's refusal in earlier years to sign power purchase agreements (PPAs), has resulted in the closure of upstream component manufacturing facilities, with many others experiencing distress.

Where South African policymakers are interested in developing renewable energy-linked industrial capabilities, then the projects need to be larger and the time horizon between different bid windows needs to be shorter, thereby smoothing out demand surges and providing opportunities for supplier firms to invest in machinery, know-how and additional capacity. In addition, future procurement windows and the timing associated with different stages of project cycles (financial close, construction, operations) need to be communicated to the ultimate buyer, which is the taxpayer, via the PPAs and implementation agreements with the DMRE.

- **Gradually increase the scope of local content beyond balance of plant, through targeted improvements in local industrial supply of key components, stringent monitoring and exemption processes**

Local content requirements in the REIPPPP have largely applied to products and components already produced locally, which have relatively limited industrial complexity. Subsequent bid windows need to expand the scope of local content beyond balance of plant, to components that can – with investment, partnerships and the requisite licensing – be assembled or manufactured in South Africa. This can be complemented by industrial financing and trade policy support measures which can 'incubate' many of these early-stage investments, improving capacity utilisation, accessing new markets and ultimately incentivising further firm-level fixed investment. Bid processes could also, using notional points, reward project owners that have improved their local content performance in successive bid windows as well as those that have appointed OEMs, which in turn have invested in local, upstream component assembly and/or manufacturing. Furthermore, the exemption process needs to include supply reviews of key components designated for local content and stringent monitoring of compliance with stated local-content commitments, especially during the construction and build phase.

- **Encourage black ownership in key project activities (civils, electrical work, earthwork and transmission) to facilitate transformation and economic empowerment**

A few REIPPPP consortia include black-owned firms in the engineering, steel, electrical work, civils and related sectors acting as 'project owners', while others have investment holding firms acting as 'black investors'. The difference between these two sets of project investors is that the first set of investors can participate directly in construction-related EPC activities and acquire skills, knowledge, certifications and standards, which allow them to compete as investors/EPC service providers in self-generation projects beyond the REIPPPP, both in South Africa and abroad. Some investment holding firms have effective but not operational interests in many of the projects. Policymakers may wish to consider making provision, in the bid evaluation criteria, for 'bonus points' for the participation of black firms and SMEs owned by designated groups, which are already engaged in incidental or related activities. This would be aimed at building the requisite capabilities and ensuring value capture at the construction, operational and allocative (dividend, distribution or capital gain) levels.

- **Improve consultation and participation in socioeconomic development spend**

Many studies have lamented the weak consultative processes, before and even after project commencement, which give rise to community empowerment vehicles and the decline in target thresholds for community participation (Tait et al., 2013). Freely provided, prior and informed consent by community representative structures need to be proven in bid processes, with communities enjoying the right to review the commitments made in their name and register their happiness or concerns. Notwithstanding this, the free carry provision in many of the projects in Bid Window 5 needs to be institutionalised.

Moreover, where vendor financing or mezzanine financing is used, the option of a 'trickle dividend' – where a portion of the dividend pays down debt and the rest is allocated to the community trust – needs to be institutionalised. This would ensure that many of these trusts are cashflow positive from day one and that distributions due to them flow throughout the project, not only when debt has been paid down. Furthermore, community trust dividends need to be allocated to a collection of developmental (bursaries, infrastructure upgrades, and so on) and cash-generative opportunities to ensure the sustainability of the trusts and their ability to benefit from other opportunities and finance-linked organisational activities.

CONCLUSION

Failing generation units and an ongoing battle to keep the lights on are the unfortunate and sadly unavoidable legacy of South Africa's 20th-century energy generation model, which was designed to exploit vast deposits of inexpensive, low-grade coal to supply cheap energy mainly to the high-demand mining sector. Contrary to what many might believe, this energy paradigm is set to remain with us. Yet within it and alongside it is an emerging political economy of renewable and alternative energy supply systems, fuelled by public procurement in line with the IRP, with numerous actors and competing economic interests.

This chapter examined both the industrial and technological landscape of this political economy, as well as the distribution of value and socioeconomic risks across comparable energy-generating 'build' cycles. Regarding onshore wind technology, consideration was given to how shifting procurement-related rents facilitate the participation of BEE and community actors in the renewable energy procurement process, and how the configuration of economic relationships suggested by the REIPPPP encourages the building of capabilities that can drive structural change in related secondary industries. Achieving this outcome will require the sustainable and equitable distribution of value from the procurement of renewable energy. To this end, policy must leverage existing capabilities and production networks in steel, engineering, electrical work and civils as well as other infrastructure-related sectors to advance local content and ensure meaningful economic empowerment.

The chapter has not examined the Hydrogen Society Roadmap launched by the government, particularly the Department of Science and Innovation (DSI, 2022), because it is still at a nascent stage. Building on the Hydrogen South Africa (HySA) strategy developed more than a decade ago, the Roadmap straddles the mining and processing of platinum group metals, the manufacturing of fuel cells and their components, as well as the production of green hydrogen and power fuels for export and domestic use. Already, across this value chain are significant black players such as African Rainbow Minerals (in mining) as well as Bambili Energy and Mitochondria Energy Company which are involved in the production and deployment of fuel cells, the generation of electricity and possible future mobile applications. The evolution of the hydrogen economy in South Africa was led by government working with universities and the private sector in a Triple Helix approach. How this subsector will evolve going forward is a matter of conjecture; but the lessons with the other green technologies outlined in this chapter should stand the country in good stead.

REFERENCES

Baker, L. and Sovacool, B. K. 2017. 'The political economy of technological capabilities and global production networks in South Africa's wind and solar photovoltaic (PV)'. *Industries Political Geography,* 60, 1–12.

Bazilian, M., Cuming, V. and Kenyon, T. 2020. 'Local content rules for renewables projects don't always work'. *Energy Strategy Reviews*, 32.

Chettiar, M., Lakmeeharan, K. and Koch, G. 2009. 'Review of the January 2008 electricity crisis'. *Energize*, https://www.ee.co.za/wp-content/uploads/legacy/Energize_Oct09/01_GT_Review.pdf, accessed 2 August 2022.

Department of Energy (DoE). 2003. 'White Paper on Renewable Energy'. Pretoria: Department of Energy.

Department of Energy (DoE). 2011. 'Integrated Resource Plan (IRP)'. Pretoria: Department of Energy.

Department of Science and Innovation (DSI). 2022. 'Hydrogen Society Roadmap of South Africa for 2021'. DSI: Pretoria, https://www.dst.gov.za/images/South_African_Hydrogen_Society_RoadmapV1.pdf, accessed 20 June 2023.

Department of Trade, Industry and Competition (DTIC). 2021. 'List of companies applying for exemptions for the REIPPPP and Bid Window Five'. Pretoria: Department of Trade, Industry and Competition. (Unpublished and confidential.)

Department of Trade, Industry and Competition (DTIC). 2022. 'List of recipients of Black Industrialists Scheme, 2016/17–2021/22'. Pretoria: Department of Trade, Industry and Competition. (Unpublished and confidential.)

Eberhard, A. 2004. 'The political economy of power sector reform in South Africa'. Working Paper WP-06. Programme on Energy and Sustainable Development, Stanford University.

Eberhard, A. and Mtepa, M. 2003. 'Rationale for the restructuring and regulation of a low-priced utility: A case study of Eskom in South Africa'. *International Journal of Regulation and Governance*, 3 (2), 77–102.

Eberhard, A. and Naude, R. 2017. 'The South African renewable energy IPP Procurement Programme', https://www.gsb.uct.ac.za/files/EberhardNaude_REIPPPPReview_2017_1_1.pdf, accessed 29 August 2022.

Eskom. Annual reports, 1923–2021.

Fine, B. and Rustomjee, Z. 1996. *The Political Economy of South Africa: From minerals–energy complex to industrialisation*. New York: Routledge.

Makgetla, N. 2021. 'Industrial policy and the electricity value chain'. Pretoria: Trade and Industrial Policy Strategies.

Makgetla, N. and Patel, M. 2021. 'The coal value chain in South Africa'. Pretoria: Trade and Industrial Policy Strategies.

Slater, D. 13 May 2022. 'South African coal consumers face tough decisions as miners prioritise exports over domestic offtakers – Jones'. *Engineering News*, https://www.engineeringnews.co.za/print-version/south-african-coal-consumers-face-tough-decisions-as-miners-prioritise-exports-over-domestic-offtakers-jones-2022-05-13, accessed 20 June 2022.

Tait, L., Wlokas, H. L. and Garside, B. 2013. 'Making communities count: Maximising local benefit potential in South Africa's Renewable Energy Independent Power Producer Procurement Programme (REIPPPP)'. London: International Institute for Environment and Development.

NOTES

1 Streetlights came to Kimberley in 1882, before similar lighting was available in London.

2 It also seems that the respective weightings of price and socioeconomic contribution shifted from 70/30 in the earlier bid windows to 90/10 in Bid Window 5.

Part Two

Structural Change and Sector Balances

EIGHT

Post-1994 sectoral evolution and structural transformation in the automotive and agro-processing manufacturing sub-sectors and the grocery retail sector

REENA DAS NAIR AND JASON BELL

INTRODUCTION

Since the dawn of the democratic republic in 1994, South Africa has struggled to address the structural ills of longstanding and stubborn unemployment, persistent inequality, pervasive economic stagnation and the exclusion of the majority of the population from meaningful economic participation. Furthermore, the South African economy is characterised by massive divergence and duality across several sectors, such as agriculture, manufacturing and retail. These sectors are crucial for the country's broader goals of structural transformation.

Structural transformation recognises the importance of industrialisation in facilitating sustained economic growth through an evolution from low-productivity sectors towards higher-productivity sectors, which encompasses the upgrading of economic activity towards greater complexity and higher value-added production. Structurally transforming the South African economy has been identified as essential for economic and social equality and development in the post-apartheid era (Bell et al., 2018). However, it requires significant changes to the current economic structure (Zalk, 2021). Since 1994, however, South Africa has managed to transform only specific sectors and industries, and this record has been uneven and discontinuous (Andreoni et al., 2021). South Africa has instead experienced limited structural transformation evidenced by, amongst other things, a continued path dependency on lower-productivity and energy-intensive, resource-based activities (Fine and Rustomjee, 1996), increased financialisation (Ashman, 2015) and a proliferation of services (Bhorat et al., 2015), all of which have contributed to worsening levels of value addition in the manufacturing sector (Bell et al., 2018).

The poor performance across the manufacturing sector has been exacerbated by premature and ongoing deindustrialisation (Tregenna, 2016), poor export diversification and a hollowing out of capabilities (Bell et al., 2018). Several markets that were already concentrated have seen increasing levels of concentration, with a few firms wielding significant market power in several value chains and presenting high barriers to entry (Buthelezi et al., 2019; Makhaya and Nhundu, 2015; Roberts, 2010; Roberts, 2016).[1] The country lacks meaningful participation and inclusion and weak institutional support in many sectors (Goga et al., 2019; Vilakazi and Bosiu, 2021). Combined, these factors have conspired to keep South Africa in the middle-income trap (Andreoni and Tregenna, 2020, 2021).[2]

Drawing mainly on our previous research and that by the Centre for Competition, Regulation and Economic Development over several years, this chapter assesses these themes and related trends since liberalisation in two sectors: manufacturing and retail. We employ a value chain framework to understand dynamics that affect participation, upgrading and structural transformation, focusing on power and governance in the manufacturing sub-sectors of automotives and agro-processing. We augment value chain principles with insights from industrial organisation treatments of market power and buyer power and look through a political economy lens to provide richer insights on the distribution of power amongst the players in value chains (for value chains, see Bamber et al., 2016; Das Nair and Chisoro, 2017; Gereffi and Lee, 2016; Gereffi et al., 2005; Ponte et al., 2019a; for political economy, see Andreoni and Chang, 2019, 2020; Behuria et al., 2017; Gray, 2016; Ponte, 2020; for issues concerning power in value chains, see Bell and Monaco, 2021; Das Nair, 2021; Goga et al., 2020; Ponte, 2021). Our analysis is pitched primarily at a microeconomic level, and while we acknowledge that macroeconomic factors are important to understand the lack of structural transformation in manufacturing in South Africa, an assessment thereof is beyond the scope of this chapter. In using the value chain framework, we also note that our analysis focuses primarily on supply-side issues. This, though, is not to discount the importance of demand-side factors that have impeded industrialisation and structural economic transformation.

We argue that a key failure in manufacturing is weak technological progress and upgrading (Bell et al., 2019; Monaco et al., 2019). Upgrading, more broadly, refers to the dynamic movement in the value chain, which is evidenced in producers shifting between different stages of the chain, while governance focuses on the strategies used by countries, regions and other economic stakeholders to maintain or improve their positions in the global economy (Fernandez-Stark et al., 2012). Principles of upgrading can be extended to improving positions in local and regional value chains (RVCs).

Technological upgrading is a critical factor in inducing economic growth in developing economies (Hausmann and Hidalgo, 2009; Hidalgo et al., 2007). The process of technological upgrading is complex and multidimensional and is fraught with difficulties that firms and policymakers need to overcome to ensure its success (Andreoni and Anzolin, 2019; Radosevic and Yoruk, 2016). Moreover, upgrading is not a homogeneous process across all sectors and industries. For some industries, upgrading is directly and intimately related to technological sophistication and progress, whereas in others, process and product upgrading are less directly linked to technology.

The central thread in this chapter is the power dynamics between firms and between firms and the state, which impact participation and upgrading in the context of structural transformation. Within manufacturing, for instance, South Africa's automotive sector provides a rich case study of the problems stemming from power imbalances in the value chain. The South African automotive value chain faces challenges arising from large multinational corporations' (MNCs) concentration of value addition, which has implications for the required level of technological capabilities and smaller firms' ability to upgrade. This chapter's discussion of power, structural change and technological capabilities leverages the ongoing debates around the role of power imbalances along the automotive value chain (vertical) and within the plastic automotive components value chain (horizontal) in the context of technological upgrading, with a view to evaluating the sector's evolution post 1994.

In addition, within manufacturing, the agro-processing sub-sector is evaluated in conjunction with the downstream grocery retail sector, given the close linkages with supermarket chains as essential routes to market for processed food and beverage products. High concentration levels characterise both agro-processing and grocery retail, and the chapter explores how power dynamics at the retail level reinforce concentration at the processing level. This has implications for the participation and upgrading of small and medium enterprises (SMEs). Understanding these and other forms of power which shape the development of automotive and agro-processing-to-retail value chains is critical in understanding structural transformation in these sectors, or the lack thereof.

Our selected approach to understanding these concepts through a value chain framework, by its very nature, can only be adopted in respect of a limited number of value chains. Although general, high-level trends in the post-apartheid period are presented in this chapter, we see certain outcomes as best illustrated through in-depth reflections on specific value chains. While some generalisations can be extended to other value chains within manufacturing and retail, the value thereof is limited and can lead to erroneous impressions, given the specific contexts and value chain nuances.

In automotives, we find that power imbalances in favour of MNCs create barriers to entry that have hindered locally owned South African automotive component firms from effectively competing against more technologically advanced firms (often foreign-owned or subsidiaries of MNCs). As a result, South Africa's automotive sector lags behind that of other middle-income countries in terms of competitiveness and technological advancement. In the South African food system, we show that high concentration has persisted at different levels of food value chains, particularly at the agro-processing and grocery retail (supermarket) levels. The power of large, lead firms at these levels has resulted in a clear dualism in which SMEs struggle to participate and upgrade to produce higher value-added products in formal value chains.

The rest of this chapter provides the following: an expanded discussion on the frameworks used to evaluate outcomes in the selected sectors and sub-sectors; a presentation of the broad trends in manufacturing post liberalisation; a discussion on how power in value chains and technological change affect outcomes, as illustrated through the case studies on automotive and plastic automotive component industries; an assessment of the development trajectory in agro-processing-to-grocery retail value chains, focusing on types of power that shape outcomes; and a final conclusion.

POWER, GOVERNANCE AND UPGRADING IN VALUE CHAINS – THE IMPLICATIONS FOR STRUCTURAL TRANSFORMATION

Value chains (VCs) are a prominent feature of the global manufacturing system and are characterised by complex systems of production facilitated by growing technological infrastructure. Global value chains (GVCs) refer to the international fragmentation of production and division of labour, which has created cross-border networks of investment, trade and production linking countries, firms and workers around the globe (Fernandez-Stark and Gereffi, 2019; Ponte et al., 2019b).

In the past, GVCs were seen to be one way for countries to

industrialise, where participation allowed firms to enter and upgrade within the GVCs. This was evidenced, for example, in the development of manufacturing capabilities in Southeast Asian countries like South Korea and China (in the case of phone manufacturers such as Huawei and Xiaomi) and Thailand (in particular, the automotive sector) (see Monaco et al., 2019). However, developing countries' participation in GVCs has stubbornly remained in upstream production, with African firms supplying mainly low-value primary and intermediate products (Andreoni, 2019). This has been for different reasons, including the impact of power, control and governance of the value chain by lead firms in the Global North, which makes it difficult for developing-country firms to upgrade into higher value-added activities.

In contrast, firms from developed economies, typically large MNCs, operate further down the value chain in higher value-added activities. The result is the concentration of value addition. Through this, a concentration of market power and bargaining power affords lead firms the ability to influence the direction of entire industries and markets. Over the past 10 years, the promise of GVCs acting as a pathway to development for developing countries has dimmed, given, amongst other reasons, the increasing frequency of trade conflicts and uncertainty in global markets (Boys and Andreoni, 2020). Developing countries have not necessarily benefited from participating in GVCs, as was initially expected. Furthermore, new production technologies, such as digital production technologies (smart manufacturing) and the Internet of Things (IoT) (under the banner of Industry 4.0), have enabled less fragmentation and more local production and the 'backshoring' of production activities to home countries (Dachs and Pahl, 2019). As a result of these developments, RVCs have been gaining more attention recently as a way of opening up new markets and opportunities (Das Nair, 2021).

Key concepts of governance and upgrading in the value chain framework, irrespective of geography, are nonetheless critical for understanding outcomes in South Africa. Governance and power are closely linked. Governance refers to how certain actors with power over others control and coordinate a value chain (Fernandez-Stark and Gereffi, 2019; Gereffi et al., 2005). This directly affects upgrading because it dictates which firms can engage in the process of upgrading. Firms with market power or buyer power govern value chains by impacting what they sell, and at what price and quality, or by setting standards and requirements for their suppliers, which shape participation and investment decisions along the value chain. This includes investments in the development of technological capabilities required to produce higher value-added products. While this governance can stimulate upgrading along the value chain, it can also hinder it, especially for SMEs that cannot afford to meet the standards and requirements.

Upgrading involves transitioning into higher value-added activities and can take the form of product (moving into more sophisticated product lines), process (transforming inputs into outputs more efficiently by reorganising the production system or introducing superior technology), functional (acquiring new functions to increase the overall skill content of the activities) or chain or inter-sectoral upgrading (moving into new but often related industries) (Fernandez-Stark and Gereffi, 2019). Technological change and upgrading are defined as accumulating new technological capabilities and capacity (Bell and Pavitt, 1992). These higher value-added activities are fundamental for economic development and job creation in an economy (Cattaneo et al., 2013). Given that structural transformation is the transition from low- to higher-productivity sectors, upgrading (which includes technological change) is an essential component of this process. Without upgrading, path dependency on low-value products will persist. Different forms of power directly impact the ability to participate and upgrade, and therefore an understanding of power cannot be separated from an understanding of structural transformation, or a lack thereof.

The aspect of power in traditional value chain literature has tended to focus on direct and dyadic relationships between players at different nodes and how these players shape the development of the value chain through their requirements, procurement and sales practices (Dallas et al., 2019). We argue that this typical power assessment can be enriched by applying the industrial organisational principles of market power, buyer power and barriers to entry. Market power is exerted in critical markets in various ways: by abusing dominant positions through excessive pricing of key inputs for production in value chains; by limiting access to critical inputs covered by intellectual property (IP) rights, including patents; by engaging in price discrimination and exclusionary practices, which affect the ability of rivals to compete effectively, or by collective abuse in the form of collusion, which serves to keep new entrants out. These examples allow a deeper understanding of the impacts on participation and upgrading. Similarly, abuse of buyer power by dominant firms or those that are 'gate keepers' to key markets, such as large supermarket chains, serve to limit participation (Das Nair, 2021; Das Nair and Chisoro, 2017; Paelo and Vilakazi, 2016; Roberts, 2010; Vilakazi and Bosiu, 2021). We also apply this in our analysis of the selected sectors later in this chapter but acknowledge that power is not limited solely to market or buyer power of firms.

Dallas et al. (2019) present a typology or framework that helps us to better understand the multiple dimensions of power that shape value chains. These types of power operate directly or diffusely through dyadic, firm-to-firm interactions or collective forces. For instance, institutional power operates through government and multi-stakeholder groups and manifests in industrial policies, standards and best practices. Collectives such as industry organisations can exert collective power to benefit their members, including lobbying to shape value chain outcomes.

Overall, a complex political economy characterises most VC-linked industries and sectors. This political economy is formed through the relationships between powerful players operating across the entire spectrum of a value chain (Andreoni, 2019; Behuria, 2020; Ponte, 2020; Ponte et al., 2019a; Teye and Nikoi, 2021). In most industries, this can be envisioned as a power triad featuring the state, large firms (or MNCs) and smaller firms operating at different levels of the value chain (Bell and Monaco, 2021). Each of these three key players possesses differing degrees of power. The nature of each player's power contributes to their relative power position within the industry. Possessing power also affords those individuals the ability to engage actively in upgrading.

STRUCTURAL TRANSFORMATION, POWER AND TECHNOLOGICAL CHANGE IN SOUTH AFRICAN MANUFACTURING

General trends in manufacturing

Despite the assumed benefits of participation in GVCs for developing economies like South Africa, the historical record of South Africa's involvement in manufacturing-related VCs has been confined to upstream, primary production with limited avenues for value addition (Andreoni, 2019). It is also well documented that South Africa is facing significant challenges in transforming its economy along multiple lines, from diversifying exports and embracing technological change to addressing problems of concentration and inclusion (Bell et al., 2018). These have taken place in the context of an evolving political settlement and a conflicting macroeconomic policy landscape that has emphasised stability and structural reforms, which have in fact hindered the performance of South Africa's manufacturing sector (Bell et al., 2018).

With the exception of Brazil, South Africa's manufacturing lagged in several categories relative to other developing economies between 1994 and 2020 (see Table 8.1). Specifically, South Africa has seen noticeable shifts in its manufacturing performance in different periods, in line with recognised changes and swings in domestic and international markets. For instance, manufacturing value-added saw significant gains between 2003 and 2008, in line with the increased global demand for commodities. However, relative to most comparator countries and country groupings, South Africa lagged in terms of value-added growth in the period immediately after the financial crisis of 2008, worsening between 2016 and 2020 in response to the crash of global commodities markets. South Africa's manufacturing value-added (as a share of gross domestic product (GDP)) and manufactured exports (as a share of merchandise exports) saw consistent declines throughout the 1994–2020 period. These declines were commensurate with a hollowing out of manufacturing capabilities, evidenced in stagnant gross fixed capital formation and, at times, extremely high levels of import penetration in several key industrial sectors, such as automotives.[3]

Table 8.1: South Africa's manufacturing performance compared to that of other developing economies, 1994–2020

		Brazil	Malaysia	South Africa	Thailand	Turkey	Middle income	Upper middle income
Manufacturing value-added growth	1994–2002	0.8%	6.5%	3.1%	4.0%	3.6%		
	2003–2008	4.5%	6.0%	5.0%	5.4%	7.9%		
	2009–2015	-0.3%	5.1%	1.8%	2.7%	8.7%		
	2016–2020	-0.2%	3.0%	-3.1%	-0.1%	2.7%		
Manufacturing value-added (% of GDP) average	1994–2002	14.2%	28.7%	19.7%	27.1%	20.3%		
	2003–2008	14.4%	27.7%	16.8%	30.0%	16.8%	20.7%*	21.6%*
	2009–2015	11.4%	23.1%	13.0%	28.6%	16.0%	20.3%	21.8%
	2016–2020	10.4%	21.8%	12.3%	26.3%	18.1%	20.3%	22.0%
Manufactured exports (% of merchandise exports) average	1994–2002	53.8%	77.6%	52.1%	73.2%	77.8%	70.1%	73.8%
	2003–2008	49.4%	70.9%	53.9%	75.1%	81.6%	69.9%	73.9%
	2009–2015	34.0%	64.1%	45.1%	72.7%	75.5%	68.4%	72.7%
	2016–2020	31.7%	69.3%	43.3%	73.7%	77.4%	70.7%	74.3%

Source: Authors' calculations based on World Bank, 2022

Notes: Missing values are due to missing data. * = 2004–2008.

Table 8.2: Manufacturing relative to other sectors in the South African economy

Sector	Real output			Real value added			Total employment			Real gross fixed capital formation		
	Growth (1994–2020)	Share of total		Growth (1994–2020)	Share of total		Growth (1994–2020)	Share of total		Growth (1994–2020)	Share of total	
		1994	2020		1994	2020		1994	2020		1994	2020
Agriculture, forestry and fishing	3.7%	3.7%	4.3%	2.3%	3.0%	3.1%	-1.1%	12.9%	7.2%	0.2%	5.5%	3.4%
Mining and quarrying	-0.2%	13.0%	6.2%	-1.2%	11.8%	5.0%	-1.0%	5.7%	3.3%	1.2%	7.7%	6.2%
Manufacturing	2.2%	27.0%	23.7%	1.2%	15.9%	12.7%	-0.8%	15.1%	9.2%	0.7%	12.1%	8.5%
Electricity, water and gas	1.2%	4.0%	2.7%	0.4%	3.9%	2.5%	0.9%	0.5%	0.4%	4.3%	6.4%	11.4%
Construction	2.6%	4.0%	4.0%	2.6%	2.6%	2.9%	1.4%	5.0%	5.3%	4.4%	0.5%	0.8%
Tertiary sector	3.5%	48.2%	58.6%	2.7%	62.8%	73.7%	2.0%	60.8%	74.5%	2.2%	67.8%	69.7%
Total economy	2.7%	100%	100%	2.1%	100%	100%	1.2%	100%	100%	2.1%	100%	100%

Source: Authors' compilation based on Quantec, 2021, 2022

Note: Real values are deflated using constant 2015 prices.

The South African manufacturing sector's performance within the broader economy since 1994 has also declined across several key indicators, such as output, value addition, employment and gross fixed capital formation (Table 8.2). The decline in the importance of manufacturing (often termed deindustrialisation) in South Africa's economic structure has occurred over the same period in which the tertiary sector (led by retail) has acquired an increasing share.[4] Moreover, the growth experienced across all the key indictors emphasises the disparity between the tertiary and manufacturing sectors. This tertiary-sector growth outpaced the growth recorded by the total economy in all cases between 1994 and 2020.

This deindustrialisation that has characterised the South African economy's development path since 1994 has occurred simultaneously with increasing concentration across various product markets (Buthelezi et al., 2019). Additional studies conducted by the Competition Commission South Africa (CCSA) have highlighted persistently high levels of concentration and unilateral dominance (defined by the Competition Act as a firm having a market share in excess of 45 per cent) in a large number of markets. Based on Herfindahl-Hirschman indices, highly concentrated markets include those in communication technologies, energy, financial services, food and agro-processing, infrastructure and construction, intermediate industrial products, mining, pharmaceuticals and transport.[5] Also, as we highlight in the next section, markets in the formal retail services sector are highly concentrated (CCSA, 2019).

Some industries that display high degrees of concentration (such as automotives) also have poor rates of technological adoption amongst locally owned South African firms, thus creating stark technological divides and power imbalances within and across the automotive GVC (see Monaco et al., 2019 for a discussion on South Africa's automotive technological capabilities and the discussion in this chapter on the plastic automotive sub-sector). The persistence and intensification of these technological divides have led to a splintering of production, exacerbating inequalities in many countries (Aguiar de Medeiros and Trebat, 2017). These inequalities have in turn created the conditions for additional, deeper technological divides in South African manufacturing sub-sectors by limiting the ability of locally owned firms to develop advanced technological capabilities.

Pervasive barriers to entry, such as a lack of adequate financial and human capital and weak infrastructural and operational capabilities, further constrain the ability of South African firms to engage in successful technological upgrading. Over time, these have served to consolidate and strengthen existing power positions amongst established players in value chains, thus limiting opportunities for meaningful integration by developing economies with weaker industrial and technological ecosystems. Moreover, this creates a vicious cycle of ever-weakening technological capabilities amongst South African firms, while foreign-owned firms are better equipped to improve their technological infrastructures.

Evidence from the automotive and plastic components industries

Using the framework discussed earlier in this chapter, we provide cross-country perspectives and evidence from the automotive and plastic automotive component industries, highlighting the complexities of structural transformation in the context of power imbalances, how this impacts technological upgrading and how this has, in turn, affected the success of South Africa's attempts to structurally transform these critical sectors. We delve into the specific power dynamics in these sectors and how vertical and horizontal power imbalances in the value chain have impacted their development.

Structural transformation and vertical power imbalances in the South African automotive sector

The globalised and producer-driven structure of the automotive VC gives rise to complex and dynamic interdependencies involving multiple actors spanning, amongst others, but most notably, technological, organisational and institutional dimensions (Figure 8.1; see also Andreoni, 2019; Wad, 2009). Yet crucially, in the context of structural change and power, the automotive supply chain features very high concentration levels. These extreme concentration levels have culminated in a few large MNCs accounting for a substantial share of production and assembly (Lejarraga et al., 2016). The oligopolistic nature of many manufacturing-related sectors, including the automotive sector, implies a considerable amount of power in the hands of a few large lead firms. This has negative implications for the development of value chains, where technological sophistication and productive capabilities are far less developed.

Figure 8.1: A stylised representation of the automotive value chain

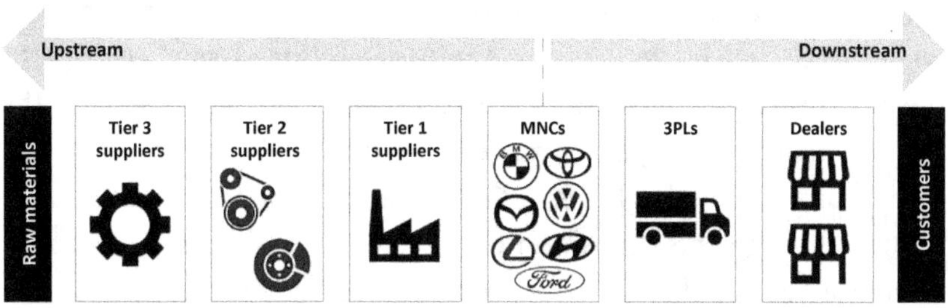

Source: Monaco et al., 2019: 6

MNCs with market power in the automotive value chain play a significant role in shaping the direction of development of local supply chains through their ability to influence industry-wide investment (Monaco et al., 2019). The power of MNCs to direct investment, location and technological direction can alter the landscape of an entire industry, leading to situations where smaller and less experienced firms, generally with limited access to capital, expertise and new technology, are unable to integrate and participate at their respective levels of the value chain (see Johansson and Olhager, 2017). This curtails significant market changes, which can also come from smaller players through dramatic and wholesale changes to the entire industry.

We can think of Tesla's explosion into the electric vehicle market, which catalysed the mainstream green consumer electric vehicle movement. Tesla's cornering of the electric vehicle market led to other large MNCs following suit. Tesla's success and massive growth were also partly due to the large subsidies it received, along with substantial changes in regulations governing the transport sector (Mazzucato, 2011). These factors highlight the integral role of the state and effective regulations in shaping the development of value chains, especially in creating an enabling environment for greater participation.

Another downside of a concentration of power amongst a few large MNCs is that this power can be, and in many cases is, exercised in a variety of ways to achieve different objectives and industry outcomes that favour these powerful and influential firms and nurture a system of value extraction. In such a system, power can also be exercised systematically and strategically, leading to entry barriers limiting the participation of smaller firms (Monaco et al., 2019). For example, barriers to entry can be created through exclusive arrangements where large and powerful firms limit the ability of smaller firms to operate and compete in the industry effectively. This can take the form of exclusive supplier arrangements that lock out locally owned firms from the supply chains of these large MNCs. Other barriers are created through the imposition of patents, technological and quality standards, copyright provisions and trademarks. These then dictate what and how products are produced, where they can be sold and who is allowed to sell them.

The development of the automotive sector is considered to be a crucial component of South Africa's structural transformation efforts. In this section, we explore the challenges faced by South Africa's automotive value chain to upgrade across multiple levels in the context of increasing global concentration and barriers to entry.

Despite the adoption of targeted and full-scale industrial policy interventions since 1994,[6] domestic firms in South Africa's automotive value chain have struggled to upgrade and meaningfully integrate into the global automotive value chain. This lack of integration has been worsened by a lack of investment and high import penetration rates.[7] To add to this poor performance, South Africa's automotive sector remains concentrated in its value addition, with MNCs controlling 40 per cent, tier-1 component suppliers controlling 40 per cent, and lower-order component producers contributing only around 20 per cent of value addition (Figure 8.2). These failures have come despite past attempts by the state to develop South Africa's automotive sector through industrial policies, such as the Motor Industry Development Programme (MIDP) and the Automotive Production and Development Programme (APDP). Despite being praised in some quarters, these programmes ultimately failed to achieve their respective targets due to the developmental state and liberalisation agendas pursued by the government, amongst other factors (Black et al., 2018).

Figure 8.2: Value addition breakdown of the global and South African automotive value chains

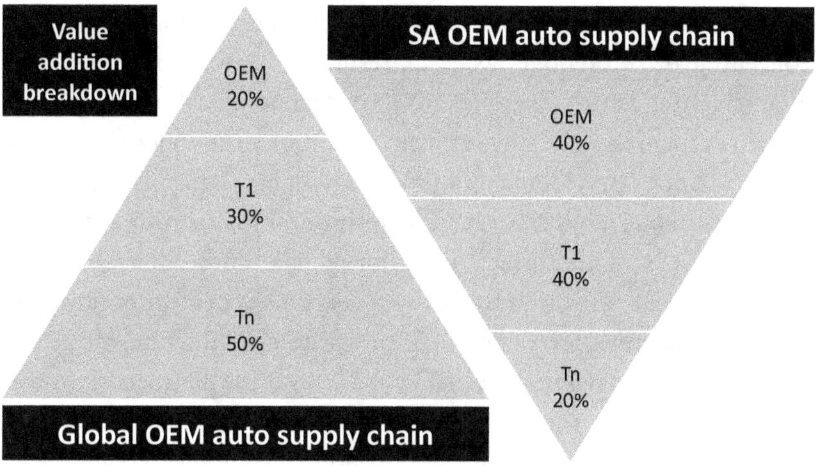

Source: Barnes, 2014

This concentration means that the South African automotive supply chain tends to assume an inverted pyramid shape, in contrast to the global automotive supply chain which boasts much deeper and more inclusive automotive markets. International automotive supply chains operate with a greater share of value addition derived from lower-tier component suppliers (50 per cent) which are typically smaller in size than firms operating downstream in the value chain. The latter firms often operate on a significantly larger scale than these lower-tier component suppliers. The inverted nature of the South African automotive supply chain offers insights into the power and technological chasms that exist between the MNCs and lower-order component suppliers (Bell and Monaco, 2021).

The state's ability to formulate and effectively implement good policies is crucial for the successful development of a domestic value chain. Effective policies will be able to direct investments through subsidies and regulation to foster an enabling technological environment that creates new higher value-added opportunities for local firms.

The strength of the state's policy-setting ability (notwithstanding the relative power positions of the other players) will be reflected both in its institutional power and bargaining power. The stronger the state's bargaining position vis-à-vis the MNCs, the more easily the state's policy agenda will be advanced over time. However, where the state's bargaining position is weak, this power imbalance within an already-concentrated automotive VC can result in skewed outcomes and regressive trends (for example, a lack of technological upgrading and limited deepening of the supply chain over time) in the wider automotive sector and poor development of linkages with cross-cutting sectors.[8]

For example, a weak bargaining position on the part of a state can mean that its structural transformation agenda can become an avenue for further rent extraction by key players. This is evident in powerful firms or collectives leveraging their power to alter the transformation agenda in their favour. In other words, how the balance of power manifests amongst the players over time can determine the overall direction of development, the rate and depth of technological adoption, and barriers to entry.

In the early stages of the government's automotive policy under the apartheid regime, high levels of protectionism prompted large MNCs (Ford and General Motors) to set up operations in South Africa in the 1920s (Barnes and Kaplinsky, 2000). Careful and concerted governance efforts on the part of the apartheid state meant that the automotive sector enjoyed decent growth until sanctions eventually limited expansion and development at several levels of the domestic value chain. This commitment to develop a globally competitive automotive sector was reaffirmed in the early post-apartheid era as the new, democratic South African state sought to attract large-scale investments by adopting a liberalisation policy agenda under a pseudo-developmental state policy narrative, similar to that in Japan, South Korea and Taiwan (Masondo, 2018).

Furthermore, the outcomes that characterised South Africa's lack of automotive sector development in the post-apartheid era served to further weaken the state's power in relation to the ever-growing and increasingly influential power bases of the global automotive MNCs. This weakened position of the state was further exemplified in paradoxical policy interventions (which attempted to pursue both neoliberal and developmental state agendas) that paved the way for the strong position enjoyed by the MNCs, limiting the ability of the state to effectively negotiate with these firms as they enjoyed their newfound power (Hamann et al., 2008). The result was that the MNCs were able to easily leverage their more substantial bargaining power to influence the structure and conditions of policies in their favour, to the point where the South African automotive value chain and, specifically, locally owned component suppliers were subject to the decisions, directions and influence of international investors.

For example, South Africa's early negotiations with automotive producers failed to deliver on the state's local development objectives, such as its targets for local content. Moreover, the state's various institutional departments, such as the Department of Trade, Industry and Competition (DTIC), tasked with assisting in the creation and nurturing of locally owned companies, were unable to influence large MNCs' investment decisions effectively. By contrast, in the 45 years between 1960 and 2005, Thailand's automotive sector grew from 30 firms to 300 suppliers with regional and, in some cases, global exporting capacity (Wad, 2009). The evidence from Thailand's automotive sector's developmental patterns and trends emphasises the positive developmental role that the state was able to play to ensure that the influx of Japanese foreign direct investment (FDI) was conditional on the investment being used to assist in the facilitation of productive and technological capacity building of local firms.

The technological situation in the South African automotive sector stands in stark contrast to the well-coordinated and technologically advanced Thai automotive value chain. This technological divide along the different levels of this value chain has crucial implications for South Africa's attempts to achieve its Automotive Master Plan 2021 objectives, especially in a global manufacturing environment that is seeking more efficient, environmentally conscious and better-quality components. However, this 'vertical' imbalance of power amongst MNCs and component producers is only half the story. An additional manifestation of power is the imbalances between producers operating at the same levels of value chains. We assess these horizontal power imbalances amongst plastic automotive component producers in South Africa's automotive value chain below.

Structural transformation and horizontal power imbalances amongst South African plastic automotive component producers

From a horizontal perspective, these power differences emerge between firms producing similar products that compete to be integrated into the supply chains of MNCs. Unlike the vertical manifestation of power discussed above, where the dependence on automotive MNCs has hindered the growth and technological upgrading of upstream component suppliers in the domestic market, the differing rates of technological adoption amongst plastic automotive component producers in South Africa have given rise to 'horizontal' power imbalances and also created technological divides in the different types, ages and places of origin of the machinery and equipment employed in their production systems. This relationship between power and technological divide is also bi-directional and extends beyond production systems (Schradie, 2020).

South Africa's plastic automotive component sector is considered a valuable facilitator of technological accumulation and upgrading within the South African automotive value chain. However, the nature of this level of the automotive value chain (tier 3 in Figure 8.1) is such that there is a large discrepancy between the size of firms and the quality and quantity of the technologies and machinery utilised in their respective production processes (Bell et al., 2019). These discrepancies have failed to create an enabling technological environment, unlike in Thailand where plastic automotive component producers have managed to acquire more sophisticated technological infrastructures through the careful governance of Japanese capital by the Thai government. The latter move created the conditions for component producers to develop technologically through joint ventures with technologically advanced original equipment manufacturers (OEMs) (Monaco et al., 2019).

The favourable conditions in Thailand were further advanced by the Thai government's super-cluster policies, which were combinations of special economic zones (SEZs) designed to position Thailand as a major player through R&D, high-technology industries and capital-intensive manufacturing. These super-cluster and other policies were successful because of the relatively greater institutional coordination and cooperation between the Thai government's agencies responsible for industrial development (Monaco et al., 2019). This institutional coordination and cooperation were also instrumental in the fostering of a vibrant regional trade network that served as a strong demand base for Thailand's automotive exports.

Conversely, South Africa's case is one of fragmentation and a lack of institutional coordination, which has given rise to the specific automotive sector currently operating in the country. An empirical analysis of survey data collected on South African manufacturing firms across three broad sector groupings produced evidence that large firms were more inclined to engage in export activities, while also possessing significantly greater technical capabilities (Avenyo et al., 2022).[9] Yet successful technological change and upgrading in firms in developing economies (typically SMEs) are often hindered by various constraints, such as a lack of financial and human capital, which affect the rate and degree of technological adoption.[10] Additionally, when forced to compete against internationally linked component producers, these (often smaller) South African plastic component and producers lack the requisite technological capabilities to meet the quality standards and scale of international markets. This creates a vicious cycle of inadequate technological infrastructures and low levels of investment, which further weakens the power positions of South African plastic automotive component producers on both the horizontal and the vertical axes of the automotive value chain.

The differing abilities of smaller firms to integrate into the value chains controlled by MNCs can create a situation where many South African firms, particularly those that lack the requisite technologies compared to others that are intimately tied to the production networks of MNCs as subsidiaries, are increasingly being locked out of the supply chains of these large, technologically advanced MNCs. By being locked out of a supply chain, they are prevented from upgrading their existing technological capabilities. By contrast, firms integrated into an MNC's supply chain can benefit from learning and technology spillovers. The use of joint ventures with Japanese MNCs saw the Thai automotive sector flourish over time, with the creation and nurturing of a vast number of component producers at multiple levels of the value chain continuing apace, to the extent that the Thai automotive value chain resembled the global value chain (Monaco et al., 2019).

To meet these changing standards, plastic component producers are forced to import more advanced machinery and equipment due to a lack of capabilities locally. On the balance of evidence, however, data on imports of plastic-producing machinery show that the South African plastic product and component industry has not increased its import demand since 1994 (Figure 8.3). These lacklustre technological imports have, despite the apparent need for competitiveness, created a situation where the physical and technological infrastructure of smaller firms operating in the South African plastics industry are ageing, causing them to lose competitiveness against more modern machinery and equipment found in larger firms and in international firms that already possess upgraded technologies. These larger firms are often subsidiaries of MNCs operating at this specific tier of the automotive value chain.

Figure 8.3: Imports of plastic-producing machinery into South Africa, 1994–2018

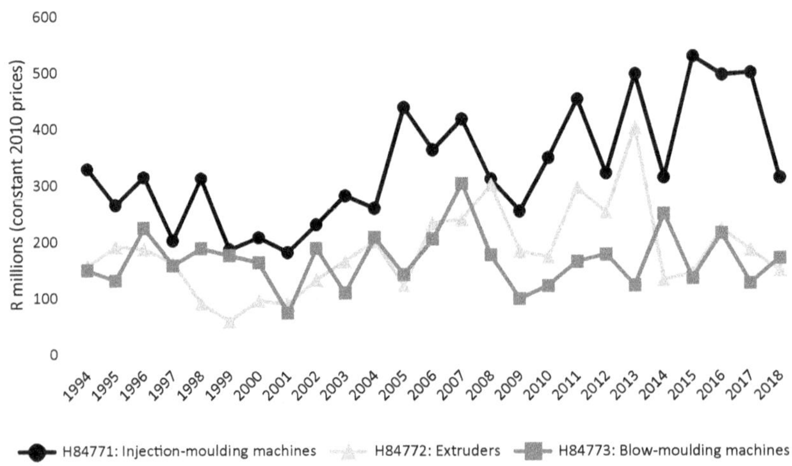

Source: Bell et al., 2019: 15

This lack of technological sophistication is exacerbated by the origin of the firms' machinery within their technological infrastructures. A crucial point worth noting here is the generally high cost of machinery for producing plastic inputs. Between 1994 and 2018, the technological sophistication of South African plastic-producing firms appeared to be on the decline because the mix of the machinery employed in their production had shifted from European origin to Asian origin (Bell et al., 2019). The more expensive European machines are perceived to be of much higher quality, which would enable South African component producers to meet the strict demands of international markets and MNCs. However, many South African firms are opting to employ a mix of both European and relatively cheaper and lower-quality Asian machinery to respond to different demands and pressures from their buyers.

Because South Africa's plastic-producing firms are often smaller in size with very limited production scope and scale, they usually lack adequate financial resources to purchase only European machinery. Typically, though, firms with links to MNCs can afford to invest in European machinery. For example, a producer of plastic automotive components in South Africa is an MNC subsidiary, giving it the financial resources and operational capabilities to more quickly and easily employ the most advanced European technologies in its production line. It is also able to internalise its R&D activities.

By contrast, another South African firm with no ties to a well-funded company is forced, primarily by its resource constraints and a lack of market demand, to utilise an extensive mix of machinery of different origins and ages. While this technology mix gives the firm some ability to supply larger MNCs, its products generally fail to meet the standards demanded by international automotive assemblers.[11] Instead, these firms are usually limited to producing and supplying lower-quality products for low-value markets, such as general houseware and other plastic products that have not yet been forced to adopt the strict standards that are becoming more pervasive as consumer preferences shift to more climate-conscious products (Bell et al., 2022). These firms also opt to forgo investing in newer and European-made machinery that more easily adheres to the strict quality standards required for production and trade. Instead, they hold on to older machinery, which is often over 30 years old. This lack of incremental technological upgrading means that locally owned South

African firms can only make marginal gains in their positions within the value chain.

However, through the formation of associations such as the National Association of Automotive Component and Allied Manufacturers (NAACAM), South African component producers have achieved significant gains in their collective power position within the industry. The institutionalisation of these component producers has proceeded to serve their interests through active participation in recent large-scale industrial policy initiatives, such as South Africa's Automotive Master Plan process (NAACAM, 2019).

Locally owned South African plastic component producers, with their comparatively weaker and outdated technological infrastructure, therefore find it challenging to improve their positions in their respective markets, particularly in high-value and technologically advanced markets, such as automotives. By contrast, larger and more powerful MNCs have achieved this. The wide disparity between the plastic automotive component producers operating in South Africa is evidence of this continued imbalance of power and technological capacity, which, along with the government's failure to stimulate structural transformation in manufacturing, will only worsen in response to changing regulations in major export markets such as the European Union (Bell et al., 2022).

The relatively powerful positions of large MNCs have weakened the South African government's ability to enact meaningful structural transformation across high-value value chains, such as automotives and plastics. So far, a lack of meaningful inclusion and competition has led to a dearth of technologically competitive, locally owned South African firms that can compete in their respective markets. Moreover, these constraints have hindered the ability of these firms to integrate into the supply chains of large MNCs and, by extension, to gain a competitive footing in GVCs. If left unaddressed, this will limit the prospects for economic and social progress in the South African automotive industry.

POWER DYNAMICS SHAPING OUTCOMES IN FOOD VALUE CHAINS: AGRO-PROCESSING-TO-GROCERY RETAIL VALUE CHAINS

General trends in agro-processing and grocery retail

Agro-processing is a sub-sector within manufacturing, with essential value-added products including food, beverages and tobacco. Overall, the weak trends seen in manufacturing are reflected in the muted growth in real output, value added and investments in agro-processing and a decline in total employment between 1994 and 2020 (Table 8.3). The share of agro-processing in the total economy for these variables has also declined over the period.

There has, however, been growth in exports of food and beverages, particularly to the Southern African Development Community (SADC) region, as seen in Figure 8.4. This has important implications for the growth and development of RVCs, as we discuss below. South Africa is a net exporter of many processed food products. This net export status has grown since 1994 in several categories, with increasing exports to SADC. A notable exception is imports of meat and edible meat offal, which increased significantly between 1994 and 2020. This is mainly due to increases in poultry imports (primarily from South America) to cater for the growing demand for chicken meat.

Driven by the spread of South African supermarket chains into the SADC region, the value of exports of processed food products has increased significantly, particularly exports of beverages, spirits and vinegar; miscellaneous edible preparations; sugar and confectionery; and dairy produce. This increase highlights the growing importance of regional markets for South African processed food and beverage products and highlights the capabilities that South African agro-processors have developed to penetrate regional markets (Figure 8.4).

The trade in processed foods is largely a one-way arrangement out of South Africa, with limited reciprocal imports from the region. While this partly reflects limited production capabilities in agro-processing in other countries, a vicious cycle is nevertheless perpetuated in which South African agro-processors continue to dominate (mainly South African) supermarket shelves in the region. Agro-processors outside

Table 8.3: Agro-processing economic trends, 1994–2020

	Real output			Real value added			Total employment			Real gross fixed capital formation		
	Growth (1994–2020)	Share of total		Growth (1994–2020)	Share of total		Growth (1994–2020)	Share of total		Growth (1994–2020)	Share of total	
		1994	2020		1994	2020		1994	2020		1994	2020
Agro-processing	2.0%	6.0%	5.1%	1.3%	3.5%	2.8%	-0.1%	2.8%	2.0%	0.8%	3.3%	2.4%
Total economy	2.7%	100%	100%	2.1%	100%	100%	1.2%	100%	100%	2.1%	100%	100%

Source: Authors' compilation based on Quantec data, 2021

Note: Real values are deflated using constant 2015 prices.

Figure 8.4: Value of South African exports of processed food and beverage products to SADC (excluding SACU), 1990–2021

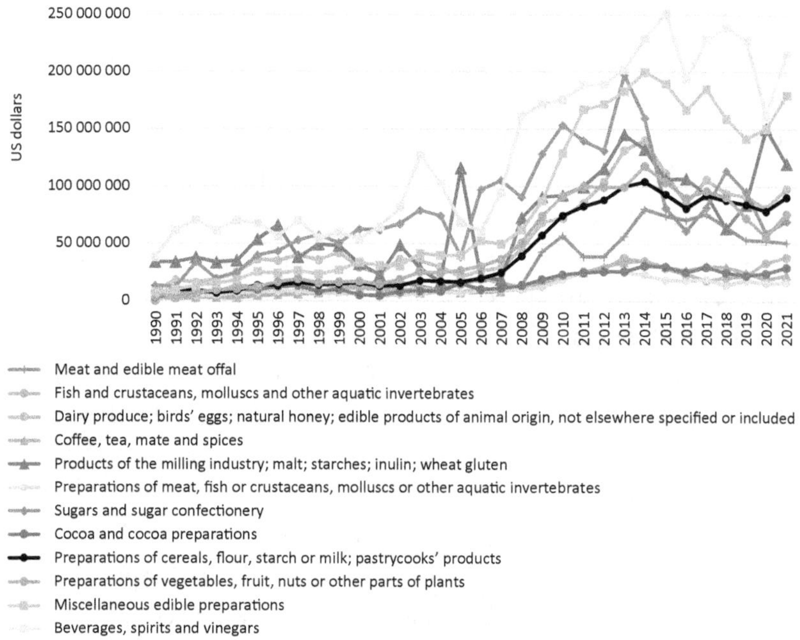

Source: Quantec data, 2022

South Africa cannot access supermarket shelves for reasons that we explain below, limiting their growth and ability to develop production capabilities.

With one-way trade patterns persisting, this asymmetry has created tensions and antagonism towards South African FDI and exports in the region. Despite the different countries belonging to the same regional economic community (REC), this has also led to the imposition of protectionist measures, such as import bans and duties. There has been limited progress in the development of RVCs in agro-processing, which hampers greater regional integration and undermines the objectives of the African Continental Free Trade Area (AfCFTA) agreement (Das Nair, 2021). In concentrated food value chains, the power of lead firms, typically South African or international MNCs operating in or exporting to the region, is a major determinant of these patterns. We return to this below.

Evidence from agro-processing-to-grocery retail value chains

Like other manufacturing sub-sectors, many key food markets in South Africa are concentrated (Buthelezi et al., 2019; CCSA, 2021; Chisoro-Dube et al., 2018; Das Nair and Chisoro, 2017). This concentration, coupled with vertical integration along value chains, bestows significant market power on key players who control inputs, processing and storage infrastructure or access to final markets. Understanding the development trajectory of agro-processing in South Africa and the SADC region involves understanding the forms of governance, control and power exerted at different levels in value chains by lead firms and specific stakeholders.

Ownership of the production of critical inputs in agricultural production, such as fertilisers, seeds, agro-chemicals and the IP rights to breeding stock for animal protein production, is in the hands of a very small number of players both globally and in South Africa, and there is a trend towards even greater consolidation globally (Clapp, 2021; IPES-Food, 2017). In South Africa, critical agricultural input markets are often controlled by monopolies or oligopolies. These players can extract greater margins from the value chain than would be the case if there was more competition and lower barriers to entry. They can use their market power to reduce rivalry or exploit customers at subsequent levels in the value chain, which can ultimately negatively impact consumers. This abuse of market power is evident in the competition cases that have been investigated and, in some instances, prosecuted by the CCSA in fertiliser, grain storage, dairy, poultry and other markets. Competition cases in these markets have included abuse of dominance through excessive pricing and exclusionary practices as well as collusive conduct (for summaries of these cases, see CCSA, 2009, 2019).

There have also been significant mergers in critical input markets, such as seeds. A contentious case involved an essential South African seed producer (Pannar) being bought out by the MNC DuPont Pioneer. The conditional approval of this merger by the Competition Appeal Court has been widely criticised as negatively impacting food security and sovereignty in South Africa, primarily through the reduced incentives for the dominant merged entity to invest in R&D for the development of cultivars (Bosiu et al., 2017).

The agricultural or primary production level has, in several value chains, seen consolidation since the liberalisation of the sector in the 1990s. An apparent duality at this level, which flows throughout food value chains, has emerged. In the first leg of these dual value chains, the majority of primary production is by large, predominantly white commercial farmers who are well resourced and possess strong production capabilities. These large commercial farmers generally benefited from extensive state support on pricing and market access when markets were tightly controlled and regulated under the Marketing Act during apartheid. The Act was abolished in 1997, and the various control boards were shut down as the last steps in the deregulation process of food markets (Chisoro-Dube et al., 2018; Greenberg, 2017; Vink and Kirsten, 2002; Louw et al., 2007). The sector was abruptly forced to operate in a free market system with no price and other controls. With limited support during this transition, many smaller players exited the sector. Large primary producers became larger, aided by technological developments in the sector.

In the second leg of these dual value chains, there are highly fragmented and dispersed small and medium farmers. These smaller farmers are vulnerable to margin squeezes due to high input prices (fertilisers, seeds, and so on), the buyer power of large agro-processors at the secondary processing level and the buyer power of supermarket chains at the retail level (discussed below). Small and medium farmers face numerous barriers to entry and experience difficulties in accessing final markets. However, there are some notable exceptions. For instance, in the citrus industry, smaller citrus growers have been able to penetrate high-value export markets with the support of well-functioning industry associations that have state-of-the-art R&D and innovation capabilities. South Africa is the second-largest exporter of high-value citrus products globally and has largely been able to meet the stringent phytosanitary and other high standards needed to access European markets (Chisoro-Dube and Roberts, 2021). Dubbed the 'industrialisation of freshness' by Cramer and Sender (2019), South Africa's success in the citrus value chains is an exceptional case of structural transformation and upgrading in GVCs.

The agro-processing or secondary (or midstream) level of several

Table 8.4: High levels of concentration in food and beverage markets, 2017

	Relative contribution of 5 largest enterprises (%)	**Relative contribution of 10 largest enterprises (%)**	**Relative contribution of 20 largest enterprises (%)**
FOOD AND BEVERAGES (income) (2017)	**29.4**	**38.7**	**50.1**
Production, processing and preserving of meat and meat products	25.9	39.5	53.7
Processing and preserving of fruit and vegetables	51.0	64.6	77.2
Manufacture of vegetable and animal oil and fats	58.0	77.2	96.9
Manufacture of dairy products	59.5	71.6	84.7
Manufacture of grain mill products, starches and starch products	65.8	75.9	87.8
Manufacture of prepared animal feeds	45.4	61.7	77.0
Manufacture of bakery products	66.6	72.3	80.3
Manufacture of sugar, cocoa, chocolate and sugar confectionery	81.5	92.3	96.8
Manufacture of macaroni, noodles, couscous and similar farinaceous and other food products n.e.c.*	44.8	59.5	70.1
Manufacture of alcoholic and non-alcoholic beverages	77.7	84.9	89.9

Source: StatsSA, 2017

Note: n.e.c. refers to 'not elsewhere classified'.

food value chains is also highly concentrated (Buthelezi et al., 2019; CCSA, 2021). Table 8.4 shows that five enterprises account for almost 30 per cent of the total income in food and beverages, while 20 enterprises account for half the total income. The concentration levels are even higher in specific processed food markets, as can be seen in the table.

The duality in primary agriculture cascades into the secondary processing level, with large farmers typically supplying large processors, who supply value-added processed food and beverages to large supermarket chains. By contrast, SME farmers supply SME processors and generally supply processed products to formal and informal, independent wholesalers, cash and carry outlets, and retailers. SME processors supply these 'alternative' routes to market mainly because they cannot meet the requirements of the large supermarket chains.

The agro-processing level is dominated by large MNCs, both South African and globally owned. These players have the power both to extract margins from suppliers, particularly suppliers with limited bargaining power, and to charge higher prices in output markets. At this level of food value chains, several cases of anticompetitive conduct have been investigated by the CCSA in the bread, milling, milk, edible oils, tea and fish markets, amongst others. The CCSA has also intervened in numerous agro-processing product markets through merger decisions, which have involved conditions requiring parties to commit to certain outcomes, such as local procurement and supplier development (CCSA, 2009, 2019).

Different forms of power affect participation and upgrading in different agro-processing markets. For example, in the poultry value chain, there is a high degree of vertical integration, with four large firms (three South African and one Zimbabwean) either owning or controlling key inputs of animal feed and the licences for breeding stock in the region. With these licences (representing the IP of only a few firms globally), these firms control breeding stock and sales of parent stock and day-old chicks in the southern African region. By controlling these inputs, they essentially control who can enter and the terms of their participation. New players must source these and other inputs, such as animal feed, from the incumbents who are also their rivals. They are therefore exposed to possible exclusionary strategies by these rivals (Das Nair, 2021; Ncube, 2018; Ncube et al., 2016). Such forms of 'hierarchical' governance or control have led to competition investigations of exclusive supply agreements forcing a new entrant to source breeding stock from a competitor (Bosiu et al., 2017).

In the face of increasing concentration levels and competition concerns, such as abuse of dominance and cartel cases, there have been interventions in food markets. In addition to interventions by the competition authorities and new competition legislation in agro-processing and retail (discussed below), industrial policy tools have targeted the processing sub-sector. These tools have included the DTIC's R1-billion Agro-Processing Support Scheme (APSS) which forms part of the Industrial Policy Action Plan (IPAP) 2018/19–2020/21. Core aims of the scheme were increasing the capacity of processors, supporting the modernisation of machinery and equipment, and improving competitiveness. Other support programmes have included the Black Industrialists Programme and various tax incentive and funding programmes run by the Industrial Development Corporation (IDC) and other development finance institutions.

While realising some of their stated objectives, the above-mentioned programmes have been only marginally successful in transforming agro-processing. Significant challenges have centred on the qualifying conditions and the inability of agro-processors to meet local content requirements, given a lack of capabilities amongst local suppliers. Another challenge includes the complex application process for which beneficiaries often have to incur additional costs to secure the assistance of consultants. The lack of coordination between different government departments responsible for the various levels of food value chains has also resulted in wastage and inefficient allocation and use of public resources.

The most recent, ongoing joint policy initiative between the Department of Agriculture, Land Reform and Rural Development (DALRRD) and the DTIC is the Agriculture and Agro-processing Master Plan.[12] This plan takes a value chain approach and is intended to address some of the most pressing challenges in food value chains through a coalition between the private sector, government, labour and civil society. The core aims of the Master Plan are to achieve greater participation, particularly by SMEs, greater transformation and inclusion, food security, expansion of markets, job creation, improved access to finance for the purposes of growth and competitiveness, and greater competition, amongst others.

Grocery retailers as 'gate keepers' to final consumers

The development of agro-processing markets is intrinsically linked to the dynamics in the grocery retail sector as an important route to market for food and beverage processors. In South Africa, the duality in food systems is most stark at the retail level. This reinforces the duality at other levels in food value chains. The Master Plan recognises the importance of grocery retail in developing food value chains. It aims to address bottlenecks in retail and other routes to market, reinforced by the Competition Commission's role in addressing anticompetitive practices by large players in food value chains.

Large, sophisticated supermarket chains dominate the formal grocery retail space in South Africa. The five main supermarket chains, Shoprite, Pick n Pay, SPAR, Woolworths and Massmart, account for 64 per cent of sales in grocery retail nationally (CCSA, 2019). Food Lover's Market, which entered the retail space after the incumbents, expanded from initially focusing on providing a niche fresh produce offering to becoming a fully fledged grocery retail supermarket chain. Only Massmart and SPAR have international ownership. Massmart became part of Walmart following a takeover in 2012, and the SPAR brand is part of SPAR International, based in the Netherlands (Das Nair, 2019).

Since the 1990s, these chains have spread from urban areas into peri-urban, township and rural areas. They have also spread into the African continent, with Shoprite having store networks in 14 African countries and Pick n Pay in nine. These chains exist in multiple formats, tailored to different customer requirements and income groups in specific areas. Through centralised procurement practices at highly sophisticated distribution centres, these chains have superior distribution networks and logistics which surpass even the South African government's ability to reach outlying areas. Such sophistication is evident from the extensive role played by Shoprite and other supermarket chains in distributing social and other government grants through their store networks (which benefits them as it crowds in spending in their stores by grant recipients).

The main supermarkets play an important role in compelling suppliers to upgrade, thereby affecting the full value chain. They act as lead firms that drive investments in supplier value chains, not just through the requirement to meet basic legal standards, but also to meet their individual, often higher, private standards. For instance, most supermarkets have additional food safety certifications, like the Hazard Analysis Critical Control Point (HACCP), International Organization for Standardization (ISO) or Food Safety System Certification 22000 (FSSC 22000). While these and other requirements are beneficial for consumers, they also challenge suppliers. They are expensive and difficult to meet and maintain, including the need for regular audits, which are costly, particularly for small suppliers. Supermarkets with centralised procurement practices also require suppliers to be able to sell the necessary quantity and quality of products across all the stores in their networks, which is impossible for SMEs given their capacity constraints.

In addition to supermarket requirements, the highly skewed power distribution between large chains and SME suppliers means that negotiations of trading terms are often heavily in favour of the main chains. Several studies have highlighted the costs that supermarket chains impose on suppliers. These costs range from support/listing fees to rebates, advertising allowances, promotion fees, merchandising fees, returns charges, spoilage fees, new store opening fees and delayed payment fees. Such fees extract 10–15 per cent (Bosiu et al., 2017; Das Nair, 2019, 2021) or, according to other estimates, 3–20 per cent, from the earnings of suppliers, thereby squeezing their margins. It is unclear if some of these fees are justified by the underlying costs borne by the supermarkets in dealing with suppliers or whether they include rent extraction by supermarkets and the supply costs and risks that they unfairly pass on to suppliers.

The implication is that SME suppliers typically cannot afford to supply the leading supermarket chains and are forced to sell through alternative retail channels, which creates a pronounced dualism at the retail level. Only large agro-processors with countervailing power can successfully supply supermarket chains, which perpetuates high concentration at the processing level. As supermarket chains spread into the continent, such requirements and practices spill over borders. The consequence is that suppliers of other countries are often unable to supply the South African supermarket chains, which negatively affects their ability to build production capabilities and limits the development of regional food value chains (Das Nair, 2021).

In South Africa, alternative retail models have shown surprising resilience, even though the main supermarket chains have increasingly encroached on their traditional strongholds in peri-urban, township and rural areas. These retailers account for 30–40 per cent of total grocery retail sales and comprise formal and informal independent wholesalers and retailers targeting mainly the low-income consumer segment. They include models in which largely foreign-owned, independent retailers and wholesalers fall under buyer groups or voluntary trading organisations in peri-urban and township areas. Buyer groups support multiple stores by collectively sourcing and supporting branding, advertising and marketing activities (Das Nair, 2019). Buyer groups and wholesalers, such as cash and carry outlets, also supply informal spaza shops. Spaza shops are an essential feature of the retail grocery space in South Africa, especially in townships, rural and informal settlements, offering low prices, convenience in terms of location and operating hours, flexibility and credit extension. These alternative routes to market are critical for small agro-processors who cannot supply supermarket chains, yet the policy space has not supported these players in the period following liberalisation. They face significant barriers to entry and expansion, including those of a regulatory nature. It is envisaged that the latest Master Plan will provide the impetus to address some of these barriers.

These and other concerns emanating from the concentration of the retail grocery sector prompted the CCSA to conduct a Grocery Retail Market Inquiry in 2015. In 2019, the inquiry released its final report, highlighting the significant market power that the supermarket chains have and how they can shape participation, not only at the retail level but also amongst suppliers, given their buyer power (CCSA, 2019).

The Competition Act was amended in 2020 to explicitly include a buyer power provision to ensure that SME suppliers in the agricultural and agro-processing sectors are not exploited and their margins are not unfairly squeezed by large buyers, such as supermarket chains and large agro-processors. Recommendations were also made for supermarket chains, as lead firms in food value chains and considering their critical role as gatekeepers on routes to market, to expand their supplier development programmes to incorporate more SME suppliers. These recommendations have been incorporated into the Master Plan to secure voluntary commitments by supermarket chains to grow their supplier development programmes, over and above current commitments as part of the AgriBEE (agricultural black economic empowerment) requirements, with complementary support from the government.

Building local supplier capabilities through supplier development programmes is essential for ensuring the development of domestic value chains and RVCs, as identified and mandated in the conditions set by the competition authorities in Walmart's takeover of Massmart in 2012. Given concerns, following the merger, that Walmart would use its vast global procurement power to source products from other countries, particularly China, and bypass South African suppliers, the competition authorities imposed conditions on the approval of the merger, which included a R240-million fund set aside to support and build local suppliers (Mandiriza et al., 2016). As part of the Master Plan, such interventions recognise the buyer power of large lead firms in driving the development trajectory of agro-processing value chains and aim to leverage this buyer power to support greater and more diverse domestic and regional participation.

The implication of buyer power and market power, both of which are closely linked to the governance of food value chains, is that participation is limited to a few, mainly large firms that are able to countervail these forms of power. Smaller players are mostly excluded in view of the challenges associated with upgrading and the barriers they face in producing higher value-added products. Therefore, while there are clear implications for inclusion, there are also important implications for structural transformation, which remains within the scope of only a few large firms. Growth, upgrading and structural transformation of SMEs are curtailed. The result is a non-diverse food system, with an overreliance on a few, powerful firms for food production and distribution. This has consequences for food security and nutritional outcomes.

CONCLUSION

Using a value chain framework and focusing on understanding the power dynamics that shape participation and upgrading, this chapter traced the evolution of the manufacturing sub-sectors of automotives and agro-processing as well as the grocery retail sector since liberalisation.

It showed that understanding the declining trends in the selected manufacturing sub-sectors and the evolution of the grocery retail landscape requires an understanding of the power imbalances in value chains and the implications thereof for participation, upgrading and structural transformation. Tapping into insights from the automotive and plastic component industries, the chapter highlighted the power imbalances that have manifested along with the vertical and horizontal levels of the value chain, thus creating challenges for broader participation and upgrading and entrenching technological divides.

The power imbalances favouring large, lead firms have created barriers to entry that have prevented locally owned, South African automotive component firms from effectively competing against more technologically advanced firms. These barriers to entry have largely remained in place due to the weak institutional power of the South African government, which prevents the latter from effectively leveraging policy to steer the development and technological upgrading of the local automotive industry. As such, South Africa's automotive industry lags well behind that of other middle-income countries, notably Thailand, in terms of competitiveness and technological advancement, where the Thai government has successfully governed the actions of MNCs operating in the local automotive value chain to stimulate local value addition.

Power dynamics have also shaped the evolution of South Africa's food system. The chapter showcased persistently high concentration levels at different levels in food value chains, particularly at the agro-processing and retail levels. High barriers to entry have exacerbated these levels of concentration, with some at least being the result of the conduct of lead firms with market power. We acknowledge that several other demand- and supply-side factors have negatively affected upgrading within food value chains, which are not explored in this chapter. Rather, we focused on showing how power imbalances have resulted in dualism in food value chains and how concentration at one level reinforces concentration at others. Interventions by the competition authorities have aimed to address these power imbalances, while recent policies are attempting to leverage the power of large, lead firms to facilitate the upgrading of SMEs in their supply chains. However, policymakers have not given enough attention to the regional dynamics surrounding large, South African MNCs operating in the SADC region.

Power imbalances between countries in the region have created political and policy tensions, set against the backdrop of deindustrialisation in neighbouring countries caused by South African products on supermarket shelves displacing locally produced products in these countries. Regional economic development, as envisioned by the AfCFTA, requires such power imbalances to be understood and addressed through policies that can be viewed through a more regional lens. This is even more critical in the food space, given the challenges posed by climate change and the need for drought-stricken and water-scarce countries like South Africa to ensure access to food in the future. If the power imbalances in food value chains at a regional level are not addressed, the objectives of the AfCFTA will be undermined.

The challenges and issues presented in this chapter speak to several longstanding and systemic problems that are hindering efforts to structurally transform the South African economy. Since the dawn of the democratic era, the persistence of these problems has weakened key South African economic sectors, such as manufacturing, agro-processing and retail, widely considered to be crucial enablers of South Africa's long-term economic development. However, as discussed, the overarching problem of power imbalances resulting in significant barriers to entry and exclusion in these sectors will, if left unaddressed, merely exacerbate the lack of evolution within these sectors and the broader South African economy. Tackling these problems should be considered a priority as South African industries attempt to gain ground on their competitors from more developed and, in many cases, technologically advanced economies. However, this will require coordination and buy-in from all key stakeholders operating in the South African economy.

REFERENCES

Aguiar de Medeiros, C. and Trebat, N. 2017. 'Inequality and income distribution in global value chains'. *Journal of Economic Issues*, 51 (2), 401–408.

Andreoni, A. 2019. 'A generalized linkage approach to local production systems development in the era of global value chains, with special reference to Africa', in Noman, A. and Stiglitz, J. (eds.) *Quality of Growth in Africa.* Columbia University Press.

Andreoni, A. and Anzolin, G. 2019. 'A revolution in the making? Challenges and opportunities of digital production technologies for developing countries'. Background Paper for the UNIDO Industrial Development Report 2020: Industrializing in the Digital Age. Vienna: UNIDO.

Andreoni, A. and Chang, H. 2019. 'The political economy of industrial policy: Structural interdependencies, policy alignment and conflict management'. In Andreoni, A., Chang, H. and Scazzieri, R. (eds.) *Frontiers of Industrial Policy: Structures, institutions, and policies.* Amsterdam: Elsevier.

Andreoni, A. and Chang, H. 2020. 'Industrial policy in the 21st century'. *Development and Change,* 0 (0), 1–28.

Andreoni, A. and Tregenna, F. 2020. 'Escaping the middle-income technology trap: A comparative analysis of industrial policies in China, Brazil and South Africa'. *Structural Change and Economic Dynamics,* 54, 324–340.

Andreoni, A. and Tregenna, F. 2021. 'The middle-income trap and premature deindustrialization in South Africa', in Andreoni, A., Mondliwa, P., Roberts, S. and Tregenna, F. (eds.) *Structural Transformation in South Africa: The challenges of inclusive industrial development in a middle-income country.* Oxford: Oxford University Press, 234–260.

Andreoni, A., Mondliwa, P., Roberts, S. and Tregenna, F. 2021. 'Framing structural transformation in South Africa and beyond', in Andreoni, A., Mondliwa, P., Roberts, S. and Tregenna, F. (eds.) *Structural Transformation in South Africa: The challenges of inclusive industrial development in a middle-income country.* Oxford: Oxford University Press, 1–27.

Ashman, S. 2015. 'Financialisation and the South African economy'.

Amandla! Issue 40.

Avenyo, E., Bell, J. and Nyamwena, J. 2022. *Digitalisation and Manufacturing: Insights from South African firms.* Webinar: Digitalisation, innovation and structural transformation, 13 June 2022.

Bamber, P., Fernandez-Stark, K. and Gereffi, G. 2016. 'Peru in the mining equipment global value chain: Opportunities for upgrading'. Technical Report, https://dukespace.lib.duke.edu/dspace/handle/10161/12449, accessed 30 April 2022.

Barnes, J. 2014. 'Localisation opportunities within OEM supply chains: What have we learnt from the AAS?' Presentation at the National Localisation Indaba. International Convention Centre, Durban, 5 June 2014.

Barnes, J. and Kaplinsky, R. 2000. 'Globalization and the death of the local firm? The automobile components sector in South Africa'. *Regional Studies,* 34 (9), 797–812.

Behuria, P. 2020. 'The domestic political economy of upgrading in global value chains: How politics shape pathways for upgrading in Rwanda's coffee sector'. *Review of International Political Economy*, 27 (2), 348–376.

Behuria, P., Buur, L. and Gray, H. 2017. 'Studying political settlements in Africa'. *African Affairs,* 116 (464), 508–525.

Bell, J. F. and Monaco, L. 2021. 'Power and supply chain development in the South African and Thai automotive industries: What lessons can be learnt?' *Journal of International Development*, 33 (3), 457–471.

Bell, J. F., Goga, S., Mondliwa, P. and Roberts, S. 2018. Structural Transformation in South Africa: Moving towards a smart, open economy for all'. CCRED Working Paper Series, https://static1.squarespace.com/static/52246331e4b0a46e5f1b8ce5/t/5ad9e4baf950b767531fe8a9/1524229357942/IDTT+Structural+Transformation+in+South+Africa+Moving+towards+a+smart%2C+open+economy+for+all.pdf, accessed 25 April 2022.

Bell, J. F., Goga, S. and Robb, N. 2022. 'Climate change policies and trade: Implications for industrial policy in South Africa'. CCRED Working Paper Series, https://static1.squarespace.com/static/52246331e4b0a46e5f1b8ce5/t/62f92860408b4b366da8a572/1660495974819/IDTT+5+WP5_Climate+change+policies+and+trade_202208.pdf, accessed 26 April 2022.

Bell, J. F., Mondliwa, P. and Nyamwena, J. 2019. 'Technological change and productive capabilities in the plastics industry'. CCRED Working Paper Series, https://static1.squarespace.com/static/52246331e4b0a46e5f1b8ce5/t/61922e588190350ecc1cca31/1636970076429/WP4+Technological+change+and+production+capabilities+in+the+plastics+industry_FINAL.pdf, accessed 25 April 2022.

Bell, M. and Pavitt, K. 1992. 'Accumulating technological capability in developing countries'. *The World Bank Economic Review,* 6 (1), 257–281.

Bhorat, H., Rooney, C. and Steenkamp, F. 2015. 'Understanding and characterizing the services sector in South Africa', in Newfarmer, R., Page, J. and Tarp, F. (eds.) *Industries Without Smokestacks.* Oxford: Oxford University Press.

Black, A., Barnes, J. and Monaco, L. 2018. 'Structural transformation in the auto sector: Industrial policy, state–business bargaining and supply chain development'. CCRED Working Paper Series, https://static1.squarespace.com/static/52246331e4b0a46e5f1b8ce5/t/5acc481203ce649b2a8d4c10/1523337237824/Structural+Transformation+in+the+Auto+Sector+Invite.pdf, accessed 25 April 2022.

Bosiu, T., Das Nair, R, and Paelo, A. 2017. 'The global food value chain and competition law and policy in BRICS countries: Insights from selected value chains in South Africa'. CCRED Working Paper 21/2017, https://static1.squarespace.com/static/52246331e4b0a46e5f1b8ce5/t/59f7468e53450a54db6b39b2/1509377866778/CCRED+Working+Paper+21_2017_BRICS+Global+Value+Chain+BosiuDasNairPaelo.pdf, accessed 16 April 2022.

Boys, J. and Andreoni, A. 2020. 'Value chain directionality, upgrading, and industrial policy in the Tanzanian textile and apparel sectors'. WIDER Working Paper 2020/93, https://www.wider.unu.edu/publication/value-chain-directionality-upgrading-and-industrial-policy-tanzanian-textile-and-apparel, accessed 28 May 2022.

Buthelezi, T., Mtani, T. and Mncube, L. 2019. 'The extent of market concentration in South Africa's product markets'. *Journal of Antitrust Enforcement*, 7 (3), 352–364.

Cattaneo, O., Gereffi, G., Miroudot, S. and Taglioni, D. 2013. 'Joining, upgrading and being competitive in global value chains: A strategic framework'. World Bank Policy Research Working Paper 6406, https://openknowledge.worldbank.org/handle/10986/14444, accessed 10 April 2022.

Chisoro-Dube, S. and Roberts, S. 2021. 'Innovation and inclusion in South Africa's citrus industry'. Innovation and Inclusive Industrialisation in Agro-Processing project (IIAP), Working Paper 1, https://iiap.info/wp-content/uploads/2021/11/IIAP_South-Africa-Citrus-Working-Paper_October-2021.pdf, accessed 30 May 2022.

Chisoro-Dube, S., Das Nair, R., Nkhonjera, M. and Tempia, N. 2018. 'Structural transformation in agriculture and agro-processing value chains'. CCRED Working Paper 2018/8, https://static1.squarespace.com/static/52246331e4b0a46e5f1b8ce5/t/5be16ed44fa51a60aeb93631/1541500650026/CCRED+Working+Paper+8_2018+IDTT+AGRIC+DubeDasNairNkhonjeraTempia.pdf, accessed 5 December 2021.

Clapp, J. 2021. 'The problem with growing corporate concentration and power in the global food system'. *Nature Food,* 2, 404–408.
Competition Commission South Africa (CCSA). 2009. 'Unleashing Rivalry: Ten years of enforcement by the South African competition authorities 1999–2009', https://www.compcom.co.za/wp-content/uploads/2017/11/10year.pdf, accessed 25 May 2022.
Competition Commission South Africa (CCSA). 2019. 'Unleashing more rivalry', https://www.compcom.co.za/wp-content/uploads/2020/01/Competition-Commission-20-year_V9.pdf, accessed 25 May 2022.
Competition Commission South Africa (CCSA). 2021. 'Essential food pricing monitoring', https://www.compcom.co.za/wp-content/uploads/2021/09/EFPM-Report_Aug-2021.pdf, accessed 25 May 2022.
Cramer, C. and Sender, J. 2019. 7. 'Oranges are not only fruit: The industrialization of freshness and the quality of growth', in Norman, A., Stiglitz, J. E. and Kanbur, R. (eds.) *The Quality of Growth in Africa.* Columbia University Press, 209–233.
Dachs, B. and Pahl, S. 2019. 'Are global value chains in decline?' Global Investments and Local Development: The London School of Economics and Political Science, https://blogs.lse.ac.uk/gild/2019/07/26/are-global-value-chains-in-decline/, accessed 21 January 2022.
Dallas, M., Ponte, S. and Sturgeon, T. 2019. 'Power in global value chains'. *Review of International Political Economy,* 26 (4), 666–694.
Das Nair, R. 2019. 'The spread and internationalisation of South African retail chains and the implications of market power'. *International Review of Applied Economics,* 33 (1), 30–50.
Das Nair, R. 2021. 'Southern African regional value chains and integration', in Oqubay, A., Tregenna, F. and Valodia, I. (eds.) *The Oxford Handbook of the South African Economy.* London: Oxford, 396–418.
Das Nair, R. and Chisoro, S. 2017. 'Growth and strategies of large, lead firms–Supermarkets'. CCRED Working Paper 8/2017, https://static1.squarespace.com/static/52246331e4b0a46e5f1b8ce5/t/5a8d250e652deac0dfeaf83a/1519199519799/CCRED%2BWorking%2BPaper%2B8_2017_IDRP%2BSupermarkets+%281%29.pdf, accessed 5 May 2022.
Fernandez-Stark, K. and Gereffi, G. 2019. 'Global value chain analysis: A primer', in Ponte, S., Gereffi, G. and Raj-Reichert, G. (eds.) *Handbook on Global Value Chains.* s.l.: Edward Elgar Publishing.
Fernandez-Stark, K., Bamber, P. and Gereffi, G. 2012. 'Upgrading in global value chains: Addressing the skills challenge in developing countries'. Duke Center on Globalization, Governance & Competitiveness at the Social Science Research Institute. Duke University.
Fine, B. and Rustomjee, Z. 1996. *The Political Economy of South Africa: From minerals–energy complex to industrialisation.* Boulder, CO: Westview Press.
Gereffi, G. and Lee, J. 2016. 'Economic and social upgrading in global value

chains and industrial clusters: Why governance matters'. *Journal of Business Ethics*, 133, 25–38.

Gereffi, G., Humphrey, J. and Sturgeon, T. 2005. 'The governance of global value chains'. *Review of International Political Economy*, 12 (1), 78–104.

Goga, S., Bosiu, T. and Bell, J. 2019. 'Linking IDC finance to structural transformation and inclusivity in post-apartheid South Africa'. *Development Southern Africa*, 36 (6), 821–838.

Goga, S., Mondliwa, P. and Roberts, S. 2020. 'Economic power and regulation: The political economy of metals, machinery and equipment industries in South Africa', in Francis, D., Valodia, I. and Webster, E. (eds.) *Inequality Studies from the Global South*. s.l.: Routledge, 75–98.

Gray, H. 2016. 'Access orders and the "New" new institutional economics of development'. *Development and Change*, 47 (1), 51–75.

Greenberg, S. 2017. 'Corporate power in the agro-food system and the consumer food environment in South Africa'. *Journal of Peasant Studies*, 44 (2), 467–496.

Hamann, R., Khagram, S. and Rohan, S. 2008. 'South Africa's charter approach to post-apartheid economic transformation: Collaborative governance or hardball bargaining?' *Journal of South African Studies*, 34 (1), 21–37.

Hausmann, R. and Hidalgo, C. 2009. 'The building blocks of economic complexity'. *PNAS*, 106 (26), 10570–10575.

Hidalgo, C., Klinger, B., Barabási, A. L. and Hausmann, R. 2007. 'The product space conditions the development of nations'. *Science*, 317, 482–487.

IPES-Food. 2017. 'Too big to feed: Exploring the impacts of mega-mergers, concentration, concentration of power in the agri-food sector'. Brussels: International Panel of Experts on Sustainable Food Systems.

Johansson, M. and Olhager, J. 2017. 'Manufacturing relocation through offshoring and backshoring: The case of Sweden'. *Journal of Manufacturing Technology Management*, 29 (4), 637–657.

Lejarraga, I., Kouzul-Wright, A., Primi, A., Toselli, M. and Wermelinger, M. 2016. 'Upgrading pathways in the automotive value chain'. Background document for the 7th Plenary Meeting of the OECD Initiative for Policy Dialogue on GVCs, Production Transformation and Upgrading. Paris: OECD.

Louw A., Vermeulen, H., Kirsten, J. and Madevu, H. 2007. 'Securing small farmer participation in supermarket supply chains in South Africa'. *Development Southern Africa*, 24 (4), 539–551.

Luiz, J. 2016. 'South Africa's growth trap – Explaining poor policy choices'. *The Journal of the Helen Suzman Foundation*, 78.

Makhaya, T. and Nhundu, N. 2015. 'Competition, barriers to entry and inclusive growth – CAPITEC case study'. CCRED Working Paper 12/2015 https://static1.squarespace.com/static/52246331e4b0a46e5f1b8ce5/t/56b4aaaec2ea510a3adf4fe9/1454680756804/

CCRED+Working+Paper+12_2015+Barriers+to+entry+_Capitec+case+study.pdf, accessed 10 April 2022.

Mandiriza, T., Sithebe, T., and Viljoen, M. 2016. 'An ex-post review of the Wal-mart / Massmart merger'. Competition Commission Working Paper Series No. CC2016/03, http://www.compcom.co.za/wp-content/uploads/2017/11/CC201603-Mandiriza-T-Sithebe-T-and-Viljoen-M-2016-An-expost-evaluation-of-the-Walmart-Massmart-merger.pdf, accessed 2 May 2022.

Masondo, D. 2018. 'South African business nanny state: The case of the automotive industrial policy post-apartheid, 1995–2010'. *Review of African Political Economy,* 45 (156), 203–222.

Mazzucato, M. 2011. 'The entrepreneurial state'. *Soundings,* 49 (49), 131–142.

Monaco, L., Bell, J. and Nyamwena, J. 2019. 'Understanding technological competitiveness and supply chain deepening in plastic auto components in Thailand: Possible lessons for South Africa'. CCRED Working Paper Series 1/2019, https://static1.squarespace.com/static/52246331e4b0a46e5f1b8ce5/t/5ccff70c51e58c0001f67154/1557133077398/IDTT+2+Plastics+1+Working+Paper+1.pdf, accessed 20 May 2022.

National Association of Automobile Component and Allied Manufacturers (NAACAM). 2019. 'NAACAM media statement: SA automotive masterplan 2035', https://naacam.org.za/naacam-media-statement-sa-automotive-masterplan-2035/, accessed 23 November 2021.

Ncube, P. 2018. 'The southern African poultry value chain: Corporate strategies, investments and agro-industrial policies'. *Development Southern Africa*, 35 (3) 369–87.

Ncube, P., Roberts, S. and Zengeni, T. 2016. 'Development of the animal feed to poultry value chain across Botswana, South Africa, and Zimbabwe'. Working Paper No. 2016/ 2. Helsinki: UNU-WIDER.

Paelo, A. and Vilakazi, T. 2016. 'Barriers to entry for low-cost carriers in the South African airline industry: Competitive dynamics and the entry, expansion and exit of 1Time airline'. CCRED Working Paper 8/2016, https://static1.squarespace.com/static/52246331e4b0a46e5f1b8ce5/t/58cb9ab920099ef564bbf460/1489738442129/BTE_Airlines_FINAL_September+2016.pdf, accessed 5 February 2022.

Ponte, S. 2020. 'Green capital accumulation: Business and sustainability management in a world of global value chains'. *New Political Economy,* 25 (1), 72–84.

Ponte, S. 2021. 'Sustainability and green capital accumulation: Lessons from the South African wine value chain', in Andreoni, A., Mondliwa, P., Roberts, S. and Tregenna, F. (eds.) *Structural Transformation in South Africa: The challenges of inclusive industrial development in a middle-income country.* Oxford: Oxford University Press, 143–164.

Ponte, S., Gereffi, G. and Raj-Reichert, G. 2019a. 'Introduction to the handbook on global value chains', in Ponte, S., Gereffi, G. and Raj-Reichert, G. (eds.) *Handbook on Global Value Chains.* s.l.: Edward Elgar Publishing, 1–28.

Ponte, S., Sturgeon, T. and Dallas, M. 2019b. 'Governance and power in global value chains', in Ponte, S., Gereffi, G. and Raj-Reichert, G. (eds.) *Handbook on Global Value Chains.* s.l.: Edward Elgar Publishing, 120–137.

Quantec. 2021 and 2022. https://www.quantec.co.za, accessed 5 August 2022.

Radosevic, S. and Yoruk, E. 2016. 'Why do we need a theory and metrics of technology upgrading?' *Asian Journal of Technology Innovation,* 24 (sup1), 8–32.

Roberts, S. 2010. 'Competition policy, competitive rivalry, and a developmental state in South Africa', in Edigheji, A. (ed.) *Constructing a Democratic Developmental State in South Africa: Potentials and challenges.* s.l.: HSRC Press, 222–237.

Roberts, S. 2016. 'An agenda for opening up the South African economy: Lessons from studies of barriers to entry'. CCRED Policy Brief, https://static1.squarespace.com/static/52246331e4b0a46e5f1b8ce5/t/589057b65016e1497f652286/1485854652883/Agenda%2Bfor%2BAction_Overarching.pdf, accessed 2 May 2022.

Schradie, J. 2020. 'The great equalizer reproduces inequality: How the digital divide is a class power divide'. *Political Power and Social Theory,* 37, 81–1001.

Statistics South Africa (StatsSA). 2017. 'Manufacturing industry: Financial, 2017', http://www.statssa.gov.za/publications/Report-30-02-03/Report-30-02-032017.pdf, accessed 2 February 2022.

Teye, J. K. and Nikoi, E. 2021. 'The political economy of the cocoa value chain in Ghana'. APRA Working Paper 53. Brighton: Future Agricultures Consortium.

Tregenna, F. 2016. 'Deindustrialisation, structural change and sustainable economic growth'. Inclusive and Sustainable Industrial Development Working Paper Series 02, 1–64.

Vilakazi, T. and Bosiu, T. 2021. 'Black economic empowerment, barriers to entry, and economic transformation in South Africa', in Andreoni, A., Mondliwa, P., Roberts, S. and Tregenna, T. (eds.) *Structural Transformation in South Africa: The challenges of inclusive industrial development in a middle-income country.* Oxford: Oxford University Press, 189–212.

Vink, N. and Kirsten, J. 2002. 'Pricing behaviour in the South African food and agricultural sector: A report to the National Treasury', http://www.sarpn.org/documents/d0000327/P280_Pricing.pdf, accessed 20 November 2021.

Wad, P. 2009. 'The automobile industry of Southeast Asia: Malaysia and Thailand'. *Journal of the Asia Pacific Economy,* 14 (2), 172–193.

World Bank 2022. 'World Development Indicators', https://datatopics.

worldbank.org/world-development-indicators/, accessed 14 April 2022.
Zalk, N. 2021. 'Structural change in South Africa: A historical sector perspective', in Andreoni, A., Mondliwa, P., Roberts, S. and Tregenna, F. (eds.) *Structural Transformation in South Africa: The challenges of inclusive industrial development in a middle-income country.* Oxford: Oxford University Press, 28–52.

NOTES

1 The South African economy under the apartheid system was similarly characterised by excessive concentration of ownership and control, inadequate restraints on anti-competitive trade practices, and unjust restrictions on full and free participation in the economy (Buthelezi et al., 2018).
2 The middle-income trap refers to a situation in which a country experienced high economic growth rates in the past but has since become stuck in a middle-income zone which has seen its growth rates decline. These countries struggle to transition to high-income status (Luiz, 2016). Andreoni and Tregenna (2020) explore this concept further, linking the middle-income trap to a lack of technological capabilities as well as structural and institutional configurations that are not conducive to increasing domestic value addition.
3 These insights were drawn from Quantec's Manufacturing Trends Tables downloaded in April 2022. Between 1994 and 2020, import penetration (proxied through the import–domestic demand ratio) averaged 61 per cent.
4 The tertiary sector comprises wholesale and retail trade, catering and accommodation; transport, storage and communication; finance, insurance, real estate and business services; general government; community, social and personal services.
5 Cited in Government Gazette No. 41294, 1 December 2017.
6 South Africa's automotive sector has received significant state support through programmes such as the Motor Industry Development Programme (MIDP, 1995–2012), the Automotive Production and Development Programme (APDP) (2013–2020, revised in 2021) and the Agriculture and Agro-processing Master Plan (2021).
7 Using Quantec Trend Tables, South Africa's automotive sector's value addition has shown limited upward progress since 2010. Investment, proxied through gross fixed capital formation, has fallen since 2010 to levels just above those in 1994. Employment, too, has seen drastic swings, with its 2020 figure (105 413) lower than in 1994 (119 922). Import penetration has, for lengthy periods between 1994 and 2020, been above 60 per cent, with an average of 57.4 per cent during the 26-year time span.
8 'Deepening' in this context is used as a catch-all term for supply chain

developments on several levels. These include technological change and sophistication and the development and nurturing of component suppliers and producers contributing to the manufacture of ever-increasing numbers of value-added products.

9 The Digital Skills Survey was designed in cooperation with the South African Research Chair in Industrial Development (SARChI-ID) and supported by the DTIC. The survey covered firms that are associated with the Chemical Industry Education and Training Authority (CHIETA), the Manufacturing, Engineering and Related Services Sector Education and Training Authority (merSETA), and the Fibre Processing and Manufacturing Sector Education and Training Authority (FP&M SETA).

10 Based on a presentation given at the symposium held at the University of Johannesburg on 'Structural Transformation and Inclusive Industrial Development: The Relevance of South Africa's Challenges and Experience', 3 November 2021.

11 Based on an interview and factory tour with this South African firm in 2018.

12 The finalisation of the Agriculture and Agro-processing Master Plan was under way at the time of writing.

NINE

From the minerals–energy complex to a just transition?

Lucy Baker and Jesse Burton

INTRODUCTION

South Africa's political economy has been characterised by its minerals–energy complex (MEC) (Fine and Rustomjee, 1996), a concept that offers both a description and an analytical framework for understanding the country's unique and evolving system of accumulation. This capital-, energy- and carbon-intensive system was founded on cheap and abundant sources of coal for the generation of cheap electricity, which, combined with cheap labour along racial divisions, provided input into export-oriented mining and mineral processing and beneficiation. The historical heart of the MEC has been further characterised by evolving relationships and linkages between highly concentrated ownership structures of various institutions of the state and state-owned enterprises,[1] corporate capital and a powerful financial system (Ashman and Fine, 2013).

While South Africa's gross domestic product (GDP) is the 39th highest in the world (World Bank, 2020), the MEC has created one of the world's most socioeconomically unequal societies, with an accompanying legacy of political and racial marginalisation and environmental injustice. This inequality has continued since the post-apartheid, democratic transition of 1994 (Hallowes, 2014). For instance, as of December 2021, unemployment, which has been exacerbated by the COVID-19 pandemic, stood at 35 per cent of the labour force or 46.6 per cent if one uses the expanded definition to include those who are available for employment but have given up seeking work (StatsSA, 2021).

Owing to the carbon intensity of the MEC, South Africa is the world's 14th largest emitter of greenhouse gases (GHGs) and the largest emitter in Africa, contributing 1.8 per cent of global emissions (WRI, 2021). The country's primary energy consumption is ranked 17th globally and its electricity grid is the world's most carbon intensive (Theunissen, 2021). In addition to its emissions, the country faces significant environmental challenges associated with mining, including coal mining and its ultimate use as the main source of electricity generation. These challenges have had seriously negative impacts on land integrity, water quality, local economic sectors, livelihoods, human and animal health, and the quality of life of communities in the vicinity of these developments.

In recent years, notable shifts have taken place within the MEC's core institutions, processes and structures. These shifts include: the declining contribution of heavy industry to the economy, alongside the rise of finance; the unravelling of central relationships between and within institutions of the state, the private sector and trade unions; the declining economic significance of the coal value chain; the country's overt commitment to net zero emissions, climate change mitigation and the just transition; the electricity crisis and potential breakup of the previously omnipotent, state-owned, monopoly electricity utility, Eskom; and the introduction of renewable electricity generation by private-sector actors. With specific reference to the electricity sector and the coal value chain, we analyse some of these key changes for a potential low-carbon economy and consider what they may mean for the future of the MEC.

The rest of this chapter addresses a number of issues. First, it establishes the MEC's core processes and institutions. It then discusses some of the significant shifts that have taken place within the MEC, particularly since the end of apartheid, as well as more recent developments in national climate change mitigation policy and the extent to which these may contribute to a 'decarbonised MEC'. In addition, it examines the evolving national discourse on the 'just energy transition' and some of its potential contradictions. Thereafter, it focuses on changes within the electricity sector, including the anticipated unbundling of the state-owned monopoly utility, Eskom, and the introduction of electricity generation by the private sector, both at the utility and decentralised levels. Finally, it reflects on these developments and how they may or may not be realised in future decades as well as who some of the winners and losers of the transition, just or otherwise, may be.

THE MINERALS–ENERGY COMPLEX

To understand the MEC is to understand the socioeconomic, political and environmental legacy of apartheid and the accompanying nature of state and capital relations in contemporary South Africa (Padayachee, 2010). The MEC has been referred to as an 'architecture' (Freund, 2010) that encompasses critical links and networks of power between the financial sector, the government, the private sector and state-owned enterprises, as well as a system of 'overlapping policy networks ... coordinated by what can be termed an "industrial policy elite" ... with close connections to the political elite' (Marquard, 2006: 71). These interlinkages have been characterised by a particular historical dynamic of 'conflict and coordination' which continues today (Baker et al., 2015: 7).

The significant set of actors and institutions within South Africa's MEC includes the Energy Intensive Users Group (EIUG), which has 25 members largely from the mining, minerals beneficiation and materials manufacturing sectors, including iron and steel, non-ferrous metals, ferroalloys and chemicals. The EIUG claims to account collectively for over 40 per cent of national electricity consumption and 20 per cent of gross domestic product (GDP) (EIUG, 2021).

Several EIUG members were also amongst the country's largest coal mining companies, including Sasol, Exxaro, Anglo American, Glencore and South32 (spun out of BHP Billiton in 2015), although this has shifted in the last decade, as explained below. Other key industrial representative bodies whose membership overlaps to some extent with that of the EIUG include the Minerals Council South Africa (MCSA), which 'acts as a principal advocate for mining in South Africa' (MCSA, 2022), and Business Unity South Africa (BUSA), which, with its approximately 35 company members, represents the country's 'cross-cutting organised business interests' (BUSA, 2018).

Two of the largest and most powerful institutions at the heart of the MEC are also the country's highest GHG emitters. First, the coal-dependent, state-owned, monopoly electricity utility, Eskom, is the primary generator and sole transmitter of electricity via the country's high-voltage transmission grid and is responsible for 60 per cent of distribution (discussed in more detail below). Over 80 per cent of Eskom's total nominal generating capacity of 46.5 GW comes from coal-fired power stations. The utility is responsible for approximately 45 per cent of the country's emissions (Eskom 2021c: 6). Second, the coal-to-liquid (CTL) and petrochemicals multinational and former parastatal, Sasol, is one of the country's largest coal producers. Sasol accounts for approximately 12 per cent of the country's emissions (DFFE, 2021a) and its CTL plant at Secunda is the single biggest point source of GHGs in the world. There has been a strong historical political alliance between the MEC's incumbent companies, Eskom and the government department responsible for mining and minerals policy, currently the Department of Mineral Resources and Energy (DMRE).[2] Until very recently, the MEC's energy- and carbon-intensive incumbents were highly resistant to policy measures pertaining to climate change mitigation and renewable energy, which they saw as a threat to their core economic interests (Baker et al., 2015).

As the main source of electricity generation, a contributor to industrial processes, a major employer[3] and a source of export revenues, coal is a core MEC resource, of which South Africa produced an estimated 258.9 million metric tonnes in 2019 (MCSA, n.d.). Coal currently accounts for over 80 per cent of the country's electricity generation via Eskom (Eskom, 2021a), and 20 per cent of national liquid fuel production through Sasol (Makgetla and Patel, 2021). Eskom is the single largest buyer of South Africa's thermal coal, accounting for about 45 per cent of local demand (Erasmus, 2022). Coal also contributes close to 80 per cent of the country's total GHG emissions, of which 45 per cent come from electricity generation and 12 per cent from CTL fuel production alone (see Figure 9.1).

Figure 9.1: South Africa's GHG emissions by sector, 2000–2017 (excl. forestry and other land use (FOLU))

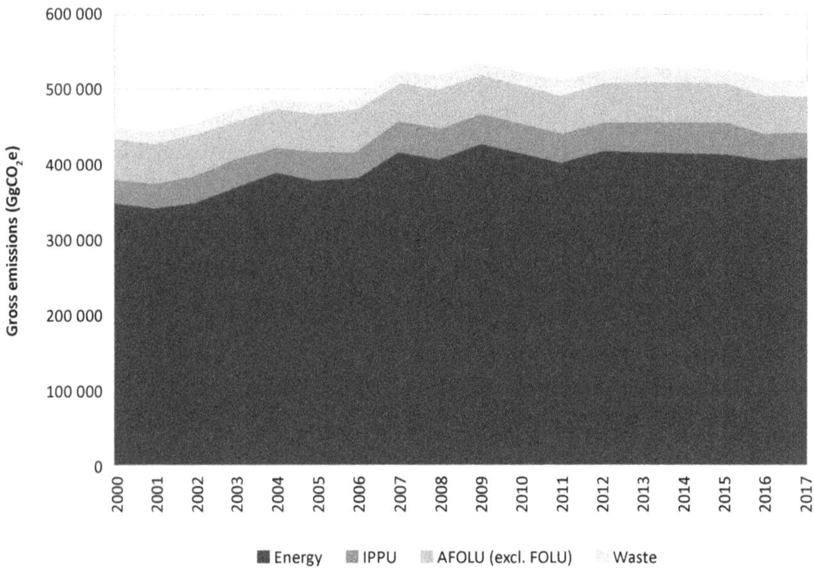

Source: Based on data from DFFE, 2021a: 111

Note: IPPU = industrial processes and product use; AFOLU = agriculture, forestry and other land use.

The country's reliance on coal was actively driven and strongly supported by the state, and the coal value chain has benefited, either directly or indirectly, from significant public subsidies over the past 50 years (Bridle et al., 2022; Burton et al., 2018). These subsidies continue today, with pricing and regulation actively promoting coal use, of which Sasol and Eskom have been key beneficiaries. In the case of Sasol, regulated, import parity fuel pricing allows the company to over-recover its costs of production from CTL. In the case of Eskom, state bailouts have continued to prop up the utility's coal-fired electricity generation. Beyond Sasol and Eskom, other beneficiaries of these subsidies include large, energy-intensive users that have benefited from under-priced electricity over many decades,[4] and coal mining companies that have received direct and indirect support from Eskom and their shareholders. Meanwhile, the health and environmental costs and externalities of coal mining and coal-fired electricity generation in South Africa are often overlooked (Bridle et al., 2022). In 2018, these costs were estimated to range from R11 billion to R30 billion (COBENEFITS, 2019).

Approximately 28 per cent of national coal production is exported, mainly through the Richards Bay Coal Terminal, making South Africa the fourth largest coal-exporting country in the world (DMRE, n.d.). In 2020, the country's coal exports accounted for 5.2 per cent of the global coal trade and 3.7 per cent of global coal production (BP, 2021). In 2019, coal sales were the largest contributor to national mineral sales (at R90.9 billion or 44.6 per cent) and the second largest contributor to export sales (at R57 billion or 17.6 per cent), after platinum group metals (StatsSA, 2021). While coal exports fell from 7 per cent of South Africa's total foreign earnings in 2011 to 4.6 per cent in 2020, coal still ranks ninth in South Africa's top 10 export commodities (Makgetla and Patel, 2021).

TOWARDS A DECARBONISED MINERALS–ENERGY COMPLEX?

Despite the enduring legacy of the historical core of the MEC, some of the key features of South Africa's carbon- and energy-intensive economic growth path and associated political, social and institutional relationships are subject to change and challenges. Many of the MEC's supporting structures and institutions have experienced significant economic, political and technological shifts in the wake of a combination of national and global developments.

As discussed in this section, shifts have taken place in relation to the MEC's core economic sectors; the coal value chain; ownership structures in the coal mining industry; an enhanced national commitment to climate change mitigation; the introduction of a carbon tax; and international trade agreements that may undermine demand for South Africa's high-carbon exports. Moreover, most of South Africa's formerly powerful state-owned companies are now severely constrained economically, including Eskom. The MEC's historical dynamic of 'conflict and coordination' therefore continues, but with new and evolving networks and alliances.

The first major change within the MEC is the decline in the economic contribution of the mining and manufacturing sectors to GDP (Karwowski et al., 2018) and, in parallel, the growing significance of finance in relation to GDP. This includes the financialisation and internationalisation of the MEC's conglomerates, leading to what has been described as a 'financialised MEC' (Ashman and Fine, 2013: 146). The finance, insurance, real estate and business services (FIREBS) sector is now the single largest economic sector in terms of contribution to GDP, accounting for 25 per cent (SARB, 2022). By comparison, the collective contribution of the mining and quarrying, and manufacturing sectors currently stands at approximately 21 per cent of GDP (SARB, 2022).[5] The mining and quarrying sector, in which South Africa's beneficiated exports play a key role, is particularly vulnerable to volatility in international commodity markets (Karwowski et al., 2018) and, at the time of writing, had a high value, following a spike in prices in the aftermath of the COVID-19 pandemic. Along with these economic changes, South Africa has for several years experienced a budget deficit, where rising debt levels have led to higher interest rates and higher debt costs, and increased debt. The costs of servicing this budget deficit are now crowding out social spending (Sachs, 2021).

The second change is that the era of abundant and cheap coal as a core MEC input for both electricity and industrial processes is over, which in turn has affected the competitiveness of the country's energy-intensive industries and exports. Despite the continued importance of coal to the South African economy, its production, consumption and economic contribution have stagnated due to several interrelated changes (BP, 2021; Makgetla and Patel, 2021). The higher cost of coal is one of the reasons, amongst many others, that electricity prices are no longer cheap by historical national standards. Electricity prices have risen more than six-fold over the past decade and are now the second-largest cost component after salaries for deep-level and electricity-intensive mines (Ganie, 2021).[6] New-build coal generation and Eskom's average tariffs[7] are now more expensive than new electricity generation from the country's utility-scale renewable energy projects (CSIR, 2020; Merven et al., 2021). Although some would argue that South Africa's electricity prices are still competitive by international standards, the increasing unreliability due to loadshedding can have a far more detrimental impact on production.

The last decade has seen an increase in coal exports to India, in particular, which buys about half of South Africa's coal exports, as well as Pakistan, Vietnam and, increasingly, China. This has resulted in growing competition between Eskom and exporters for the country's lower-quality coal, which historically had been used only by Eskom (Erasmus, 2022). European demand for South Africa's coal has also decreased over the last decade, although in recent months it has increased slightly in the wake of Russia's invasion of Ukraine, an increase in natural gas prices, a European Union (EU) ban on imports of Russian coal and the reactivation of various European coal plants (Banya and Reid, 2022).

A third change has been the diversification of South Africa's thermal coal mining sector by the country's new black economic and political elite, who emerged after the introduction of black economic empowerment (BEE) legislation (upon the demise of apartheid) and, more recently, the country's Mining Charter and minerals legislation. Until a decade ago, the thermal coal mining sector was dominated by a small number of large multinational conglomerates (as mentioned above), including Sasol, Exxaro, Anglo American, Glencore and BHP Billiton (Baker et al., 2015). As the conglomerates started to divest, financialise and sell their operations to the country's emerging black elite, the share of foreign ownership in the coal sector declined rapidly through the 2010s. By 2020, six companies, only half of them foreign owned, accounted for three-quarters of production (see Figure 9.2). However, the smaller and newer black-owned companies in the coal sector have not had strong enough balance sheets to support investment and their operations have suffered as a result. This, in turn, has contributed to the rising costs of coal (Erasmus, 2022; Makgetla and Patel, 2021).

These shifts have also contributed to a decreasing share of Eskom's coal supply being purchased from mines co-located next to power stations under long-term contracts, and therefore to rising coal costs and electricity prices. Eskom now purchases 44 per cent of its coal from smaller, often black-owned coal mines which are located further away from its power plants. In such cases, the coal is generally transported by truck, which increases transport costs – often by as much as 25 to 30 per cent (Burton et al., 2022; Eskom, 2021b).

Figure 9.2: Share of Eskom coal purchases versus national production by supplier (FY 2020)

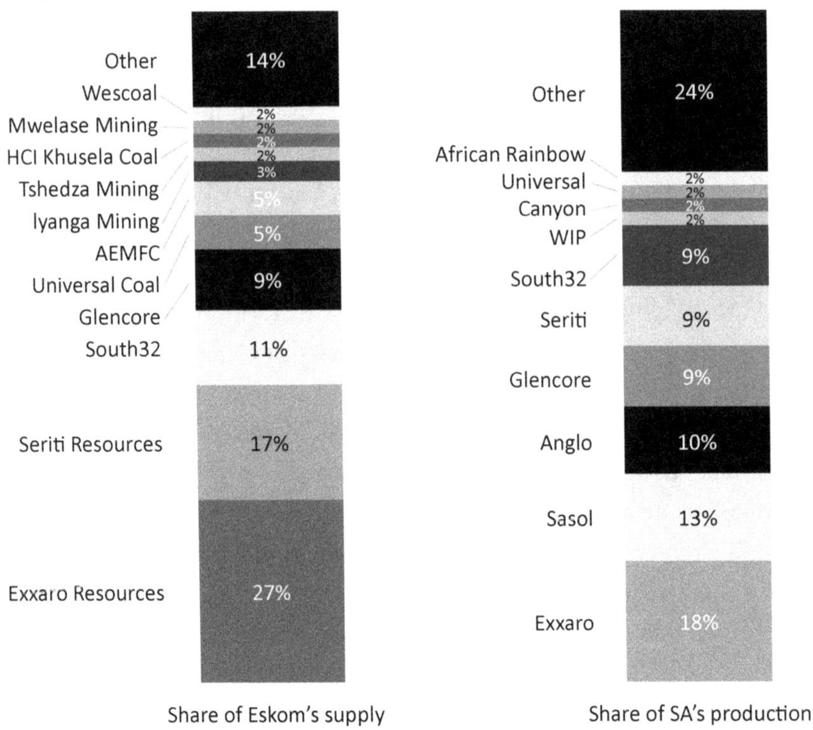

Source: Eskom, 2021b

A fourth significant change in the MEC's historical structures is the growing national visibility and recognition of the country's commitment to net zero emissions and climate change mitigation policy. Until about a decade ago, the key mitigation challenge was to develop policies capable of addressing the cost gap between a high-emissions, 'business-as-usual' future based on abundant sources of cheap coal and a more expensive, low-emissions future (Baker et al., 2015). However, the global and national political economy of climate change mitigation has changed profoundly in recent years. South Africa's national commitment to climate change mitigation was cemented most recently through the submission of a much more ambitious Nationally Determined Contribution (NDC) under the UN Framework Convention on Climate Change (UNFCCC) at Glasgow's 26th Conference of the Parties (COP 26) in November 2021. The new NDC target range of 350–420 metric tonnes of carbon dioxide-equivalent (CO_2e) by 2030 requires absolute emissions reduction from current levels of around 470 metric tonnes of CO_2e, which is far more ambitious than the previous range of 398–614 metric tonnes of CO_2e (RSA, 2021).

Most, though not all, emissions reductions during the current decade will take place in the power sector (Marquard et al., 2021; PCC, 2021). In this regard, the pathway can be growth neutral or even growth enhancing, depending on the policy choices that the government makes. Overall, additional renewable energy capacity is needed to meet the lower, 1.5 degrees Celsius-compatible end of the NDC range, but the planned retirement and reduced use of Eskom's coal fleet will contribute materially to the achievement of this goal.

As climate change has become more of a priority at the national and global levels over the last two years, so GHG emissions have become an increasingly important consideration for asset managers. Financial-sector trends are now showing investors moving away from carbon-intensive lending and starting to price in environmental, social and governance risk criteria when allocating capital (Creamer, 2022; Erasmus, 2022). For this reason, in addition to Eskom's lack of creditworthiness, securing finance for new South African coal operations has become more challenging. It is now much harder for a thermal coal mine to secure a commercial or development bank loan. Given this context, many of South Africa's carbon-intensive and energy-intensive institutions and their representative bodies have recently started to acknowledge the significance of climate change mitigation and to take practical and/or discursive steps towards implementing low-carbon alternatives, particularly in the energy sector. For instance, some large emitters have recently signed up to net zero commitments by 2050, including Eskom, Sasol, Anglo American and Exxaro (Creamer, 2021a).

Another national development highlighting the prominence given to climate change in national priorities is the approval by the cabinet in September 2020 for the establishment of the Presidential Climate Commission (PCC), which has a mandate to coordinate South Africa's just transition to a low-carbon, resilient economy by 2050. Chaired by President Ramaphosa, the PCC has a diverse membership of 22 commissioners, which brings together the full spectrum of government ministers from (amongst others) the Department of Forestry, Fisheries and the Environment (DFFE), the Department of Mineral Resources and Energy (DMRE), the National Treasury, the Department of Trade, Industry and Competition (DTIC), the Department of Transport (DoT), the Department of Public Enterprises (DPE), the Department of Agriculture, Land Reform and Rural Development (DALRRD), the Department of Water and Sanitation (DWS), the Department of Higher Education and Training (DHET) and the Department of Science and Innovation (DSI), as well as representatives of civil society, trade unions and business.

The PCC has changed the nature of South Africa's climate politics quite substantially, including constructing a new framework for climate policy and the just transition and playing a key role in enhancing the ambition of the updated NDC (PCC, 2021). The PCC has also strengthened the position of the DFFE, a department that has never been politically influential – least of all vis-à-vis key MEC institutions and more powerful government departments such as the DMRE (Tyler and Hochstetler, 2021).

Finally, after almost a decade of delays, a carbon tax was introduced by the National Treasury in 2019. Although its first phase contains some significant 'get-out' clauses for the country's highest emitters, the carbon tax requirements are likely to be strengthened in its second phase, which (according to the February 2022 Budget Review) will now begin in 2026 instead of 2023, as previously stated (National Treasury, 2022). An additional but related challenge facing the MEC is the anticipated introduction of a carbon border adjustment mechanism (CBAM) by the EU, which would effectively mean an import levy on South Africa's carbon-intensive products. The proposed levy would be notional from 2023 and fully effective from 2026. The CBAM would ultimately replace an element of the EU Emissions Trading Scheme (ETS) and form part of an EU-wide strategy to reduce the trading bloc's emissions by 55 per cent by 2030 and to incentivise both EU and international companies to reduce their emissions (Theunissen, 2021). The proposed mechanism may undermine demand for South Africa's high-carbon exports, in particular aluminium, iron and steel, given that close to 40 per cent of the country's aluminium exports and about 15 to 20 per cent of its crude steel exports go to the EU (Business Day TV, 2021).

THE JUST TRANSITION

As the climate change agenda has gained traction, the just transition – or, more recently, the 'just energy transition' – is increasingly at the heart of South Africa's national public discourse. The term is used by labour (COSATU, 2022), various government ministries (NPC, 2012), civil society (Overy, 2018), academia (Cock, 2019), industry (MCSA, 2020) and finance (Smith, 2021), despite some scepticism about the latter's adoption of it (Patel, 2021).

Given that the term has been embraced by multiple constituencies and institutions, there are now diverse, competing and sometimes nebulous interpretations regarding what the just (energy) transition means; how, where and through which policies it should be operationalised and measured; under what time frame; how much it will cost (PCC, 2021); what it means for labour and employment, and vulnerable communities living in the vicinity of coal mines; how the winners and losers of any just transition should be compensated and supported; which constituency carries the greatest responsibility; and how the state, local government, private sector and civil society should participate in its implementation. There is thus no overarching, coherent national consensus to date.

However, multiple initiatives have been devised to advance the just transition at the national and sub-national levels and incorporate it into plans and policies. At the governmental level, these include Chapter 5 of the National Development Plan (NDP) (NPC, 2012), the draft Climate Change Bill and the recently updated NDC (DFFE, 2021b). The PCC also recently held a series of just transition dialogues covering diverse topics, such as coal, water and finance, and culminating in the release of a draft national just transition framework. In addition, the PCC has published a discussion document on a just energy transition implementation framework whose overarching, stated objective is 'to provide a structure to monitor the socio-economic impacts of the transition and to support the decarbonisation of the mining and energy sectors in a socially acceptable manner while contributing to the economic development of the country' (DMRE, 2021: 5). Mpumalanga, the province that is socioeconomically most dependent on coal mining and coal power, has developed a phase 1 just transition strategy and is considered a test case in this area. However, a process has not yet been designed to institutionalise the just transition at district and local government levels.

The National Business Initiative (NBI) recently undertook a Just Transition Pathways exercise to map out a technically and financially feasible set of pathways for South African business to follow to achieve carbon neutrality by 2050 (NBI, 2021, cited in PCC, 2021: 15), with a focus on how to ensure the competitiveness of firms and sectors, including mining, power and synfuels-based chemicals, in a changing global context. This was followed by a political declaration, another key outcome of the UNFCCC's COP 26 in Glasgow in November 2021, alongside the more ambitious NDC (discussed above) that developed countries would support South Africa's just transition. The Just Energy Transition Partnership (JETP) is a US$8.5 billion (R157 billion) financial support package for South Africa, approved by the United Kingdom (UK), France, the United States (US), Germany and the EU and comprising grants, concessional finance and other climate finance instruments, which is to be mobilised over the next three to five years. The JETP's stated aims are to support the implementation of South Africa's NDC, of which the decarbonisation of the power sector is a major component, as well as to drive economic diversification, small business development and social aspects of transition. However, thus far, the deal is still under negotiation and there is limited transparency as to how it may progress.

It is noteworthy that the above-mentioned processes and actors tend to emphasise aspects of just transition related to their specific interests or the challenges that existing coal use or imminent decarbonisation place on them. However, there is some agreement between stakeholders that economic diversification at a national or regional level is one of the central pillars of a just transition, together with worker transition and labour market support, procedural justice and social dialogue, and social development/service delivery. For the minerals and energy sectors, the emphasis is on the 'critical minerals' needed for a low-carbon economy (DMRE, 2021) and the potential benefits of greater localisation of renewable energy (through the South African Renewable Energy Masterplan). For Eskom and Sasol, the focus is on clean energy and new technology, and, in Eskom's case, on sustainable job creation to secure its place in a low-carbon energy future (Eskom, 2021a). The Congress of South African Trade Unions' (COSATU) Blueprint (COSATU, 2022) explicitly demands a job-creating industrial policy alongside upskilling, reskilling and other progressive demands. It also emphasises the need for publicly owned renewables and support for local manufacturing, together with regional economic development strategies and mine closures.

AN ELECTRICITY SECTOR IN FLUX: FROM ESKOM AND BEYOND

As mentioned, South Africa's greatest opportunity for decarbonising in both the short and medium terms lies in the transformation of its electricity system, which accounts for 45 per cent of the country's GHG emissions and has some of the lowest-cost and most technically feasible mitigation options (PCC, 2021). However, until very recently, the state-owned utility, Eskom, has largely been disconnected from, and even resistant to, the national climate change mitigation agenda and the introduction of renewable energy technologies to generate electricity, both at the utility scale and the decentralised and distributed scale.

As a central MEC actor, Eskom is the primary generator and sole transmitter of electricity via the country's high-voltage transmission grid and is responsible for approximately 60 per cent of distribution. Most of Eskom's sales are to mining and industrial customers and to a lesser extent to residential, international and commercial customers. South Africa's municipalities are responsible for the remaining 40 per cent of distribution, supplying the bulk of the country's residential customer base as well as some businesses and local government entities. Municipalities purchase their electricity in bulk from Eskom and then on-sell to customers, using their markup to cross-subsidise other social services. Until very recently, Eskom also enjoyed significant influence over decision making in the electricity sector, despite being at the centre of various national scandals pertaining to state capture and corruption; longstanding crises of management, finance and supply; and increasingly unsustainable debt levels (Bhorat et al., 2017).

Having long been the recipient of government bailouts and other forms of public finance, including national guarantees, equity injections, and national and international sources of development finance (Baker et al., 2015; National Treasury, 2022),[8] Eskom is no longer stable. With a current debt burden of approximately R400 billion and an outstanding municipal debt of R42.5-billion, the utility is now considered to be a serious national economic liability (National Treasury, 2022). The cost of servicing Eskom's debt, which has been exacerbated by cost and time overruns at the Medupi and Kusile coal-fired power plants, has become unsustainable (Creamer, 2021b). Moreover, the utility's coal-generation fleet is being adversely affected by deteriorating performance, with its energy availability factor having fallen to about 65 per cent in December 2021 (Eskom, 2021a). Loadshedding has been a regular occurrence since 2008, with 2021 being a particularly bad year (see Figure 9.3; Makgetla and Patel, 2021). According to Walsh et al. (2020), loadshedding is estimated to have cost the South African economy nearly R35 billion in the 12 years between 2007 and 2019, with severe ramifications for agriculture and manufacturing (see Figure 9.3).

Owing to South Africa's economic isolation under apartheid, Eskom resisted the global trend towards power sector reform in the 1980s and 1990s and underwent only partial liberalisation, thereby retaining its monopoly control (Baker et al., 2020). Under apartheid, Eskom was

Figure 9.3: Loadshedding, 2015–2021

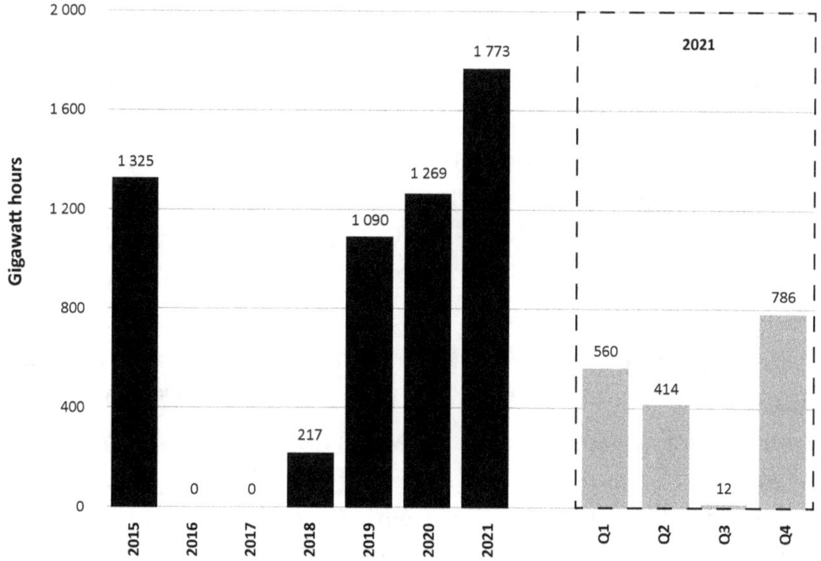

Source: National Treasury, 2022: 21

responsible for all electricity planning and decisions relating to the construction of new generating capacity. Formal and legal structures for energy policy and planning were only introduced at the end of the 1990s, including the 1998 White Paper on the Energy Policy of the Republic of South Africa, the National Regulator Act of 2004, the Electricity Regulation Act of 2006 and the National Energy Act of 2008, which delineated certain planning powers for the Minister of Energy and allowed for the procurement of privately generated power. Since then, a number of significant developments have taken place.

First, the country's first planning document for the electricity sector, the Integrated Resource Plan (IRP), was introduced in 2011 after several years of contested negotiations. Under section 34 of the Electricity Regulation Act of 2006, new generating capacity can only be installed and procured if it has been identified in the IRP. The latest update of the plan, which was eventually released in October 2019 after significant delays, projects a diversification away from coal towards renewable energy, gas and potentially new nuclear energy. The IRP 2019 further projects no new coal plants being built after 2030. Several older, coal-fired power stations that are nearing the end of their life are due to be decommissioned between now and 2030, with some units in the fleet having already been retired. However, despite the potentially progressive gains of the 2019 update, coal will remain dominant in the energy mix until 2030 at least. Moreover, the emissions reductions it projects are not substantial enough to realise the ambitious target of the recently submitted NDC (Tyler and Mgoduso, 2022: 11).

Second, the Renewable Energy Independent Power Producer Procurement Programme (REIPPPP) for utility-scale renewable energy projects was initiated in 2011, also after a lengthy and contested negotiation process. Despite the programme having stalled between 2015 and 2018, by March 2021 6.4 GW of electricity had been procured from renewable energy sources, of which just over 4 GW have already been connected to the national electricity grid. The highly competitive nature of the REIPPPP, coupled with the falling costs of wind and solar technology across the globe, has contributed to a more than 50 per cent decline in the average tariff at which independent power producers (IPPs) have sold electricity to Eskom over the last five years. By 2019, the levelised cost of electricity generated from projects under the REIPPPP had fallen to below Eskom's average cost of supply from its new, coal-fired power plants (Creamer, 2021a; CSIR, 2020). While these developments have been celebrated, concerns have also been expressed over the growing financialisation of the programme and the extent to which the programme will in fact boost local socioeconomic development and ownership (Baker, 2021; Nkoana, 2018).

Third, advances have been made towards the implementation of decentralised and distributed electricity systems from solar photovoltaic (PV), which until recently faced significant regulatory obstacles. Many energy-intensive users have now started to implement their own self-generation projects from renewable energy technologies, both in the interests of energy security and emissions reduction. The implementation of these systems has been further enabled by legislation introduced in 2021 to raise the licence exemption cap on distributed and self-generation plants of up to 100 MW in size. Such projects can now be built without a licence and can 'wheel' or transport electricity through the existing grid infrastructure, either for self-consumption or sale to third-party consumers. This move constitutes a potentially positive step towards reduced reliance of commercial and industrial, agricultural and, to a lesser extent, residential consumers on coal-generated electricity from Eskom or municipalities; it also improves security of supply. However, the supply of decentralised electricity by producer–consumers ('prosumers') to a distribution grid controlled by municipalities has not always been welcomed because it poses a direct threat to municipal revenue generation and the technical management of the distribution grid. Municipalities generate, on average, 26 per cent of their revenue from electricity sales, which they use to cross-subsidise the provision of basic services, including health, education, housing and electricity, to low-income households (Baker and Phillips, 2018).

Finally, despite several decades of failed attempts by some within government to unbundle the utility and Eskom's resistance to significant technological innovations in decentralised and renewable electricity systems, recent years have seen genuine steps being taken towards the creation of three different companies. Eskom's unbundling now seems inevitable. As of June 2023, the recently established National Transmission Company of South Africa had been separated from Eskom and is anticipated to become operational later in the year (Creamer, 2023). However, how Eskom's debt will be allocated across the newly created companies and how this may be passed on to electricity consumers and/or the taxpayer is still unclear and remains a strongly contested issue.

CONCLUSION

As discussed in this chapter, the significant changes taking place across South Africa's political economy suggest that the country may be moving towards a 'decarbonised MEC', given that many of the incumbent institutions and relationships have started to unravel. However, serious questions remain regarding the extent to which any low-carbon transition will be just and inclusive, how this concept may come to be operationalised by numerous actors, given its diverse and often contradictory acknowledgements at the level of discourse, and the extent to which these new developments and ongoing shifts will be able to address the longstanding and severe political and racial marginalisation and environmental injustice.

First, several of the MEC's structures, which have been based on the country's historical dependence on cheap coal, labour and electricity to drive an economy underpinned by mining and mineral beneficiation, are now fragmenting. Coal and coal-fired electricity are no longer cheap relative to historical prices, and many of the elite institutions and the strong interlinkages between them no longer have the same level of political and economic influence over this system of accumulation that they had in the past. Pressure from national climate change mitigation targets and new institutions, such as the PCC, and the emergence of an economically viable renewable energy sector are pointing to a fundamental change in the relationships between natural resources, technologies, and the country's political, economic and social institutions in both the public and private sectors.

Second, two key developments at the UNFCCC's COP 26 in November 2021 have formalised South Africa's climate change commitments at the international level. The first is the adoption of a more ambitious NDC for 2030, while the second is a proposed financing deal under the Just Energy Transition Partnership, which offers international support for power sector decarbonisation, economic diversification and just transition. However, the extent to which this financing deal will ultimately lead to the transformation of Eskom, and the electricity sector more generally, as well as the realisation of the country's emissions reduction commitments, is currently unclear. Not only is the pledge far smaller than what the country needs if it is to meet its NDC (RSA, 2021), but the design of the package and financing terms will be important, given the financial circumstances in which key actors find themselves.

Third, while some of the country's most carbon- and energy-intensive institutions have started to make discursive commitments to net zero, as well as to the just transition, there is some scepticism surrounding the extent to which such commitments may be translated into social and/or environmental action in the years ahead. However, it could well be external pressures that force their hand. For instance, while a more punitive phase 2 of South Africa's carbon tax regime was recently postponed from 2023 until 2026, the introduction of a CBAM may instead encourage carbon-intensive, export-oriented emissions reductions. As one energy economist (anonymised) cautioned: 'If we don't start shifting, the world will shift us, at our expense' (in a webinar held on 31 January 2022).

Fourth, transition to a low-carbon economy requires minerals such as platinum group metals (PGMs), copper and manganese, and rare earth minerals, amongst others, some of which South Africa has in abundance (IEA, 2021). In addition, the Hydrogen Society Roadmap has identified opportunities for South Africa to produce, utilise and export green hydrogen, with PGMs playing a central role. This is meant to build on the Hydrogen SA (HySA) fuel cell strategy developed about a decade ago (DSI, 2022). In this context, along with renewable energy generation (wind and solar PV), this may lead to new value chains across industries, from mineral extraction to processing, manufacturing and services. Thus may emerge a new MEC, this time undergirded by the transition to a low-carbon future.

While the decarbonisation of the energy sector, particularly the coal value chain and the electricity sector, are an essential, core element of the country's climate change mitigation policy, on its own it is insufficient to bring about a just transition. As Mohamed and Montmasson-Clair (2022: 69) note, the 'longstanding promotion of an extractive and polluting industrial development model is at the root of the very problems' that any just transition must address. From an industrial perspective, there may be significant opportunities in new, low-carbon sectors such as renewable energy as well as a need to manage the risks of an unplanned transition, such as in the coal sector but also in petrochemicals and automotive manufacturing. Structural transformation will be a necessary component of a just transition, but it will not be enough to transform existing firms so that they embrace cleaner production if social dialogue, decent work and service delivery are not pursued with equal vigour.

Finally, it is impossible to achieve justice and sustainability simply through a 'techno fix'. As research initiatives, dialogues and other developments on the just transition multiply and spread, the challenge is, first, how to reach a national consensus on the definition and interpretation of this term, specifically for the South African context, and, second, how to operationalise it across multiple sectors and spheres of community and governance. Such challenges are technical, financial, political, social and cultural. Therefore, instead of being a linear process based on optimal techno scenarios, it is likely to be a messy process of conflict and coordination, in which power and political economy play key roles.

REFERENCES

Ashman, S. and Fine, B. 2013. 'Neo-liberalism, varieties of capitalism, and the shifting contours of South Africa's financial system'. *Transformation,* 81 (82), 144–178.

Baker, L. 2021. 'Procurement, finance and the energy transition: Between global processes and territorial realities'. *Environment and Planning E: Nature and Space*, 0 (0), 1–27.

Baker, L. and Phillips, J. 2018. 'Tensions in the transition: The politics of electricity distribution in South Africa'. *Environment and Planning C: Politics and Space*, 37 (1), 177–196.

Baker, L., Burton, J. and Trollip, H. 2020. 'The energy politics of South Africa', in Hancock, K. J. and Emmons, J. (eds.) *The Oxford Handbook of Energy Politics*. New York: Oxford University Press, 711–730.

Baker, L., Burton, J., Godinho, C. and Trollip, H. 2015. 'The political economy of decarbonisation: Exploring the dynamics of South Africa's electricity sector'. Cape Town: Energy Research Centre, University of Cape Town.

Banya, N. and Reid, H. 3 May 2022. 'South African coal miners turn to trucks as rail service deteriorates'. *Reuters,* https://www.reuters.com/world/africa/south-african-coal-miners-turn-trucks-rail-service-deteriorates-2022-05-03/, accessed 27 May 2022.

Bhorat, H., Buthelezi, M., Chipkin, I., Duma, S., Mondi, L. et al. 2017. 'Betrayal of the promise: How South Africa is being stolen'. Public Affairs Research Institute (PARI), https://pari.org.za/wp-content/uploads/2017/05/Betrayal-of-the-Promise-25052017.pdf, accessed 11 May 2022.

BP. 2021. 'Coal: statistical review of world energy 2021', website: https://www.bp.com/content/dam/bp/business-sites/en/global/corporate/pdfs/energy-economics/statistical-review/bp-stats-review-2021-coal.pdf, accessed 11 May 2022.

Bridle, R., Muzondo, C., Schmidt, M., Laan, T., Viswamohanan, A. and Geddes, A. 2022. 'South Africa's energy fiscal policies: An inventory of subsidies, taxes, and policies impacting the energy transition'. Manitoba: International Institute for Sustainable Development, https://www.iisd.org/system/files/2022-01/south-africa-energy-subsidies.pdf, accessed 14

April 2022.

Burton, J., Baker, L., Marquard, A. and Lehmann-Grube, P. 2022. 'From MEC to net-zero: The role of the energy sector in the just transition', in Xaba, N. and Fakir, S. (eds.) *A Just Transition to a Low Carbon Future in South Africa*. Johannesburg: Mapungubwe Institute for Strategic Reflection, 117–151.

Burton, J., Lott, T. and Rennkamp, B. 2018. 'Sustaining carbon lock-in: Fossil fuel subsidies in South Africa', in Van Asselt, H. and Skovgaard, J. (eds.) *Politics of Fossil Fuel Subsidies and Their Reform*. Cambridge: Cambridge University Press, 229–245.

Business Day TV. 9 December 2021. 'Is carbon border tax a revolution or protectionism? Michael Avery talks to Andrew Gilder, director of climate legal at EY Cova, and Duane Newman, partner', https://www.businesslive.co.za/bd/companies/2021-12-09-watch-is-carbon-border-tax-a-revolution-or-protectionism/, accessed 13 April 2022.

Business Unity South Africa (BUSA). 12 March 2018. 'Carbon tax presentation to the select committee on finance', website: https://busa.org.za/wp-content/uploads/2019/03/BUSA-Carbon-Tax-Presentation-12-March-2019.pdf, accessed 14 April 2022.

COBENEFITS. 2019. 'Improving health and reducing costs through renewable energy in South Africa: Assessing the co-benefits of decarbonising the power sector', https://www.cobenefits.info/wp-content/uploads/2019/10/COBENEFITS-Study-South-Africa-Health.pdf, accessed 8 May 2022.

Cock, J. 2019. 'Resistance to coal inequalities and the possibilities of a just transition in South Africa'. *Development Southern Africa*, 36 (6), 860–873.

Congress of South African Trade Unions (COSATU). 2022. 'Just transition: Blueprint for workers', http://mediadon.co.za/wp-content/uploads/2022/04/COSATU-Just-Transition-Blueprint-Full-version.pdf, accessed 29 May 2022.

Council for Scientific and Industrial Research (CSIR). 2020. 'Statistics of utility-scale solar PV, wind and CSP in South Africa in 2019'. CSRI Energy Centre, https://researchspace.csir.co.za/dspace/bitstream/handle/10204/11464/Calitz_2020_edited.pdf?sequence=4&isAllowed=y, accessed 13 April 2022.

Creamer, T. 7 October 2021a. 'PCC's Olver sees updating IRP to exclude new coal as key policy priority'. *Engineering News*, https://www.engineeringnews.co.za/article/pccs-olver-sees-updating-irp-to-exclude-new-coal-as-key-policy-priority-2021-10-07, accessed 12 February 2022.

Creamer, T. 15 December 2021b. 'Eskom releases interim result'. *Engineering News*, https://www.engineeringnews.co.za/article/eskom-releases-interim-results-2021-12-15, accessed 13 April 2022.

Creamer, T. 16 March 2022. 'Standard Bank halts new coal power funding but backs gas as transition fuel'. *Engineering News*, https://www.

engineeringnews.co.za/article/standard-bank-halts-new-coal-power-funding-but-backs-gas-as-transition-fuel-2022-03-16/rep_id:4136, accessed 14 April 2022.

Creamer, T. 2023. 'South Africa's new grid company could be operational by mid-year if licence and lender conditions are met', *Engineering News*, https://www.engineeringnews.co.za/article/south-africas-new-grid-company-could-be-operational-by-mid-year-if-licence-and-lender-conditions-are-met-2023-04-11, accessed 7 June 2023.

Department of Forestry, Fisheries and the Environment (DFFE). 2021a. 'National GHG inventory report South Africa 2017', https://www.dffe.gov.za/sites/default/files/docs/nir-2017-report.pdf, accessed 16 April 2022.

Department of Forestry, Fisheries and the Environment (DFFE). 2021b. 'South Africa's first NDC under the Paris Agreement, updated in 2021', https://www.dffe.gov.za/sites/default/files/reports/draftnationalydeterminedcontributions_2021updated.pdf, accessed 14 April 2022.

Department of Mineral Resources and Energy (DMRE). 2021. 'Towards a just energy transition framework in the minerals and energy sectors', https://cdn.ymaws.com/southafricanenergyassociation.site-ym.com/resource/collection/604B4B63-5AC4-42BC-9C4E-E7599014C1A5/DMRE_Towards_a_JET__Framework_Discussion_Document_Nov_2021.pdf, accessed 12 April 2022.

Department of Mineral Resources and Energy (DMRE). n.d. 'Coal resources overview', website: http://www.energy.gov.za/files/coal_overview.html, accessed 12 April 2022.

Department of Science and Innovation (DSI). 2022. Hydrogen Society Roadmap of South Africa for 2021. DSI: Pretoria, https://www.dst.gov.za/images/South_African_Hydrogen_Society_RoadmapV1.pdf, accessed 12 April 2022.

Energy Intensive Users Group SA (EIUG). 2021. https://eiug.org.za/, accessed 11 March 2022.

Erasmus, D. 9 February 2022. 'SA coal will remain on fire in 2022 even as prices drop'. *Business Day*, https://www.businesslive.co.za/bd/companies/mining/2022-02-09-sa-coal-to-remain-on-fire-in-2022-even-as-prices-drop/, accessed 14 April 2022.

Eskom. 31 March 2021a. 'Integrated report: Towards a new energy future', https://www.eskom.co.za/wp-content/uploads/2021/08/2021IntegratedReport.pdf, accessed 11 April.

Eskom. 2021b. 'Multi-year price determination (MYPD) 5 revenue application for FY2023–FY2025 submission to NERSA', https://www.eskom.co.za/wp-content/uploads/2021/12/Eskom-Holdings-Summary-Submission_MYPD5.pdf and https://www.eskom.co.za/wp-content/uploads/2021/12/Generation-Licensee-Submission_MYPD5.pdf, accessed 17 April 2022.

Eskom. 2021c. 'Emissions', https://www.eskom.co.za/dataportal/emissions/, accessed 13 August 2022.

Fine, B. and Rustomjee, Z. 1996. *The Political Economy of South Africa: From minerals–energy complex to industrialisation*. London: C. Hurst & Co. Publishers.

Freund, B. 2010. 'The significance of the minerals–energy complex in the light of South African economic historiography'. *Transformation: Critical Perspectives on Southern Africa*, 71, 3–25.

Ganie, Z. 24 November 2021. 'Mining industry can help to supplement Eskom energy supply'. *ESI-Africa* website: https://www.esi-africa.com/industry-sectors/generation/mining-industry-can-help-to-supplement-eskom-energy-supply/, accessed 18 February 2022.

Hallowes, D. 2014. 'Slow Poison: Air pollution, public health and failing governance'. *Groundwork,* https://static.pmg.org.za/141028slow_poison_2014_groundwork.pdf, accessed 18 February 2022.

International Energy Agency (IEA). 2021. 'The role of critical minerals in clean energy transitions', https://www.iea.org/reports/the-role-of-critical-minerals-in-clean-energy-transitions accessed 20 February 2022.

Karwowski, E., Fine, B. and Ashman, S. 2018. 'Introduction to the special section: Financialization in South Africa'. *Competition and Change*, 22 (4), 383–387.

Makgetla, N. and Patel, M. 2021. 'The coal value chain in South Africa'. *TIPS* website: https://www.tips.org.za/research-archive/trade-and-industry/item/4161-the-coal-value-chain-in-south-africa, accessed 18 February 2022.

Marquard, A. 2006. 'The origins and development of South African energy policy'. PhD thesis, Faculty of Engineering and the Built Environment, University of Cape Town.

Marquard, A., Hartley, F., Merven, B., Burton, J., Hughes, A. et al. 2021. 'Technical analysis to support the update of South Africa's first NDC's mitigation target ranges'. Energy Systems Research Group, University of Cape Town report, https://zivahub.uct.ac.za/articles/report/Technical_Analysis_to_support_the_update_of_South_Africa_s_First_NDC_s_mitigation_target_ranges_UCT_2021_/16691950, accessed 2 August 2021.

Merven, B., Burton, J. and Lehmann-Grube, P. 2021. 'Assessment of new coal generation capacity targets in South Africa's 2019 integrated resource plan for electricity'. Energy Systems Research Group, University of Cape Town.

Minerals Council South Africa (MCSA). 2020. 'Advancing the just transition', website: https://www.mineralscouncil.org.za/special-features/1175-advancing-the-just-transition,%20accessed%2012%20April%202022, accessed 12 April 2022.

Minerals Council South Africa (MCSA). 2022. 'Purpose and vision', website:

https://www.mineralscouncil.org.za/about/purpose-and-vision, accessed 12 April 2022.

Minerals Council South Africa (MCSA). n.d. 'Coal', website: https://www.mineralscouncil.org.za/sa-mining/coal, accessed 12 April 2022.

Mohamed, N. and Montmasson-Clair, G. 2022. 'Applying a normative framework to assess the just transition to a net zero carbon society in South Africa', in Xaba, N. and Fakir, S. (eds.) *A Just Transition to a Low Carbon Future in South Africa.* Johannesburg: Mapungubwe Institute for Strategic Reflection, 58–85.

National Planning Commission (NPC). 2012. 'National Development Plan (NDP): Chapter 5', http://www.sustainable.org.za/uploads/files/file132.pdf, accessed 12 April 2022.

National Treasury. 2022. 'Budget review', website: http://www.treasury.gov.za/documents/nationalper cent20budget/2022/default.aspx, accessed 25 February 2022.

Nkoana, E. M. 2018. 'Community acceptance challenges of renewable energy transition: A tale of two solar parks in Limpopo, South Africa'. *Journal of Energy in Southern Africa*, 29 (1), 34–40.

Overy, N. 2018. 'The role of ownership in a just energy transition'. *Project 90 by 2030*, https://90by2030.org.za/wp-content/uploads/2018/04/Just-Energy-Transition-The-Role-of-Ownership-in-a-Just-Energy-Transition.compressed.pdf, accessed 25 February 2022.

Padayachee, V. 2010. 'Re-introducing the minerals–energy complex'. *Transformation: Critical Perspectives on Southern Africa*, 71, 1–2.

Patel, M. 2021. 'Towards a just transition: A review of local and international policy debates'. Pretoria: Presidential Climate Commission.

Presidential Climate Commission (PCC). 2021. 'Recommendations on South Africa's draft updated nationally determined contribution (NDC)', website: https://www.climatecommission.org.za/, accessed 24 February 2022.

Republic of South Africa (RSA). 2021. 'South Africa first nationally determined contribution under the Paris agreement', website: https://www4.unfccc.int/sites/ndcstaging/PublishedDocuments/Southper cent20Africaper cent20First/Southper cent20Africaper cent20updatedper cent20firstper cent20NDCper cent20Septemberper cent202021.pdf, accessed 25 February 2022.

Sachs, M. 22 November 2021. 'South Africa faces a slowly worsening chronic fiscal crisis'. *The Conversation*, https://theconversation.com/south-africa-faces-a-slowly-worsening-chronic-fiscal-crisis-172247, accessed 13 April 2022.

Smith, M. 17 February 2021. 'Banks' fossil fuel exposure criticized as South Africa plans just transition'. *S&P Global Market Intelligence,* https://www.spglobal.com/marketintelligence/en/news-insights/latest-news-headlines/banks-fossil-fuel-exposure-criticized-as-south-africa-plans-just-transition-62560008, accessed 24 February 2022.

South African Reserve Bank (SARB). 2022. 'Economic and financial statistics for South Africa', website: https://www.resbank.co.za/en/home/what-we-do/statistics/releases/economic-and-financial-data-for-south-africa, accessed 12 April 2022.

Statistics South Africa (StatsSA). 2021. 'Mining industry 2019 report No. 20-01-02', http://www.statssa.gov.za/publications/Report-20-01-02/Report-20-01-022019.pdf, accessed 18 February 2022.

Theunissen, G. 21 June 2021. 'Dependence on Eskom puts SA exports at risk from EU carbon tax'. *BusinessDay,* https://www.businesslive.co.za/bd/national/2021-06-21-dependence-on-eskom-puts-sa-exports-at-risk-from-eu-carbon-tax/, accessed 18 February 2022.

Tyler, E. and Hochstetler, K. 2021. 'Institutionalising decarbonisation in South Africa: Navigating climate mitigation and socio-economic transformation'. *Environmental Politics*, 30, 184–205.

Tyler, E. and Mgoduso, L. 1 March 2022. 'South Africa's central climate mitigation policy instruments and their impact on the power sector'. Briefing note. Meridian Economics.

Walsh, K., Theron, R., Seedat, A. and Reeders, C. 2020. 'Estimating the economic cost of load shedding in South Africa'. *Nova Economics*, https://www.nersa.org.za/wp-content/uploads/2021/09/Appendix-C_Estimating-the-Economic-Cost-of-Load-Shedding-in-South-Africa-Report.pdf, accessed 12 September 2021.

World Bank. 2020. 'Gross domestic product 2020', https://databank.worldbank.org/data/download/GDP.pdf, accessed 30 May 2022.

World Resources Institute (WRI). 2021. 'Changes in the world's top 10 emitters', website: https://www.wri.org/insights/interactive-chart-shows-changes-worlds-top-10-emitters, accessed 21 May 2022.

NOTES

1 Corporations that are wholly or majority owned by the government, including the electricity utility, Eskom.

2 The DMRE was formed in 2019 through the merger of the Department of Energy and the Department of Mineral Resources.

3 According to the Minerals Council South Africa, the coal sector employed 92 230 people in 2019, representing about 19 per cent of total mining sector employment (Minerals Council, n.d.).

4 Older 'special pricing agreements' are now referred to as negotiated pricing agreements (NPAs) (Eskom, 2021b) and highlight the challenge of higher prices for an energy-intensive industry. Eskom states that NPAs are 'specifically structured to provide opportunities to sustain existing businesses that are at risk of failure and permit others that have closed

production capacity in recent years, owing to their inability to compete in their markets, to restart these assets' (Eskom 2021b: 39).

5 Based on figures for the fourth quarter of 2021.

6 Eskom's coal costs have risen significantly above the producer price index (PPI) (Eskom, 2021b), driven by industry-wide cost increases, unit-cost inflation from tied mines and shifts to shorter-term contracts with higher transport costs. Coal costs were ~R42/tonne in 1999, rising in 2020 to R380/tonne for fixed price, R578/ton for cost-plus and R641/ton for short-/medium-term contracts (Burton et al., 2022).

7 In 2022, Eskom's average tariff was R1.33/kWh and Eskom had applied for a further 46 per cent increase to R2.03/kWh by 2025 (Eskom, 2021b). By way of comparison, Eskom's average tariff in 2003 was 16c/kWh, rising to 106c/kWh in 2021 (Eskom tariff book available at https://www.eskom.co.za/distribution/tariffs-and-charges/tariff-history/)

8 Eskom has received approximately R200 billion in state bailouts in recent years, required to address debt sustainability and solvency. For instance, according to Bridle et al. (2022), in FY 2020–2021, Eskom received a state bailout of R56 billion: tax-free emission allowances for energy production under the carbon tax regime were estimated to result in R47 billion of foregone revenue; electricity subsidies stood at R16 billion, and oil and gas subsidies stood at R35 billion (Bridle et al., 2022).

TEN

The role of spatial development, logistics and transport in the South African economy: Reflections on immediate and longer-term priorities

IRVINDRA NAIDOO, MONDE GQOLI, VUKANI NKASA AND NKULULEKO GOBHOZI

INTRODUCTION

The distribution of economic activity and development in South Africa has been characterised by 'spatial lumpiness', resulting in concentrated economic activity and the perpetuation of spatial economic inequality (Krugell and Naudé, 2005). Consequently, economic development has been centred on three primary hubs – provinces – namely Gauteng, the Western Cape and KwaZulu-Natal. In 2017, these three hubs contributed approximately 65 per cent to total economic activity in the country, with Gauteng accounting for the largest share at 34 per cent

(Mahofa, 2017; StatsSA, 2019). The growth of Gauteng as the primary economic hub in South Africa was driven by the location of valuable mineral deposits (e.g., gold) on its reef and the capital-intensive extraction technology used to operate the mines, which required the development of supporting infrastructure, such as rail and electricity networks (Krugell and Naudé, 2005).

Similarly, the growth of KwaZulu-Natal and the Western Cape into commercial centres was partly influenced by mining, as the exploration of various inland deposits (e.g., diamonds in the Northern Cape and gold in Gauteng) helped these hubs evolve from colonial trading points into modern port and maritime trade-driven commercial hubs to support the export of commodities (Krugell and Naudé, 2005). See Figure 10.1 for a map showing economic hubs in relation to the country's transport network.

Figure 10.1: Production points in relation to main urban and export centres in South Africa (gross value added)

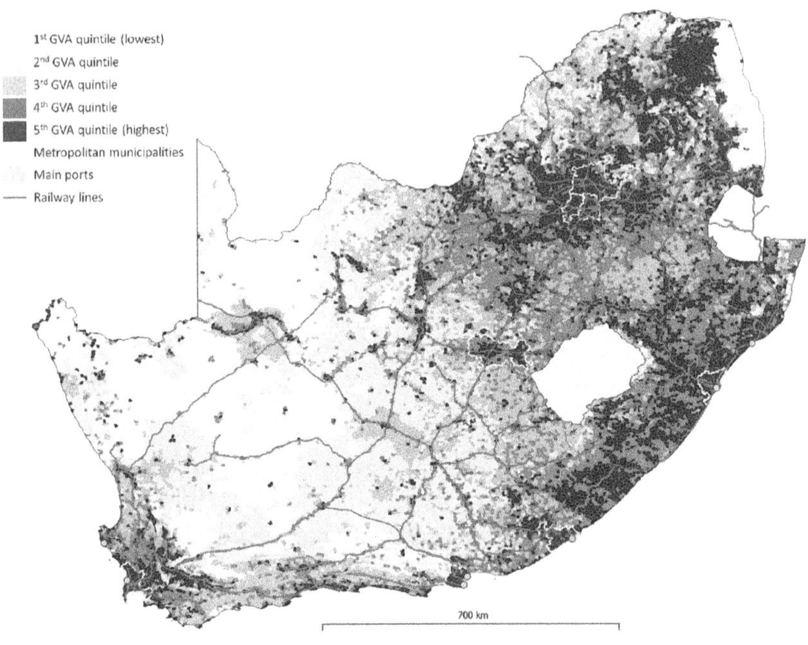

Source: Data sourced from Greenbook, 2022 and QGIS software used to plot the GIS heatmap

Developments within the commercial hubs do not, however, address the challenge of vast distances between the country's closest port(s) of entry and exit to inland commercial activity. For example, the distance (by rail) between Johannesburg and the port of Durban is approximately 690 km and between Johannesburg and the port of Cape Town is approximately 1 400 km. By way of comparison, other emerging economy peers, such as Brazil and India, have established commercial hubs that are located closer to points of entry and exit. In the case of India, a well-established commercial hub such as Ahmedabad in Gujarat state is located approximately 200 km from the port of Kandla (Invest India, 2020). Similarly, in Brazil, the distance between the commercial hub of São Paulo and the ports of Santos and São Sebastia (a bulk port) is approximately 90 km and 200 km respectively (Invest SP, 2022).

This highlights the inherent challenges of the spatial configuration of the South African economy (De Villiers, 2017; Morton et al., 2006). According to Ittmann and King (2010: 2), the result of this spatial configuration of the economy is 'long supply chains for local products to get to the global marketplace' and the need for 'world-class' and cost-effective supply chains to ensure effective distribution. The development of world-class supply chains is also a key enabler of the competitiveness of the local economy and firms in the global arena. For example, potential customers have adopted a more integrated outlook that no longer assesses the competitiveness of products or commodities solely; rather, they use an integrated approach that assesses overall supply chain competitiveness (De Villiers, 2017).

This chapter examines the crucial role played by efficient logistics in achieving competitive supply chains in South Africa and reflects on the immediate and longer-term activities required to improve South Africa's logistics competitiveness, paying particular attention to challenges in key industrial supply chains. The chapter conducts an analysis at two levels: the first is a macro-level analysis of freight system challenges; the second is a meso-level analysis of the challenges confronting a limited number of industrial supply chains. The meso-level analysis is important because freight system optimisation is fundamentally about supply chain optimisation as a whole rather than optimisation of individual transport modes. The following sub-sector supply chains are analysed in this chapter: agricultural, bulk mining, beneficiation and consumption.

OVERVIEW OF SOUTH AFRICA'S TRANSPORT AND LOGISTICS SYSTEMS

According to Logistics Performance Index (LPI) rankings published by the World Bank, South Africa has a relatively well-developed logistics system. This is reflected in its overall mean ranking of 29 out of 160 countries. South Africa is also setting a leading example by having an integrated logistics system on the African continent, outcompeting its economic competitors, Nigeria and Egypt, which are ranked 103rd and 60th respectively (Fitchsolutions, 2022; World Bank, 2018). South Africa's logistics system is underpinned by an extensive infrastructure, including vast road, pipeline and rail networks connecting key economic hubs to neighbouring countries and ports of entry, which forms part of aviation and maritime networks (Fitchsolutions, 2022). The country's surface transportation system moves approximately 865 million tonnes annually through a combination of rail, road and supporting infrastructure, including terminals and distribution centres (Simpson et al., 2021).

Furthermore, the overall performance of South Africa's logistics system is better than that of other emerging markets, such as the other members of the BRICS (Brazil, Russia, India, China, South Africa) alliance, with India, Russia and Brazil having mean LPI rankings of 42, 85 and 56 respectively in 2018 (World Bank, 2018). In addition to South Africa's infrastructure and international shipments being the strongest components of its logistics ranking, the country's overall consistent performance has resulted in it being ranked among the top performers amongst upper middle income countries on the LPI (World Bank, 2018).

A key contributor to South Africa's relatively strong rating for transport infrastructure is its extensive and well-developed road network which achieved an overall score of 5.1 on a 7-point scale, placing it second on the continent, behind Namibia (WEF, 2016). This road network consists of approximately 747 000 km of roads of which approximately 156 100 km are paved (making the country's road network the 10th largest in the world by length). This road network links the main urban and production centres to consumption markets, thereby facilitating trade (DoT, 2021).

South Africa's road network is complemented by a 30 400 km rail network consisting of an approximately 21 000 km route network (International Union of Railways, 2014). This route network is further divided into an approximately 12 800 km 'core network'. The core network connects economic nodes and is responsible for most of the freight transported by rail. There is a further 'branch-line' network that 'service(s) communities and activities not directly on the main corridors' and spans the remaining approximately 9 000 km of network (Transnet, 2017: 35).

Land-based freight movements largely follow a set pattern along predetermined corridors which link the main urban population and consumption centres in the country. As Figure 10.2 indicates, the main corridors include the Gauteng-to-Durban corridor which is the most heavily traversed in the country and the Gauteng-to-Cape Town and Gauteng-to-Eastern Cape corridors (Gain Group, 2020).

This surface transportation network is complemented by a network of eight commercial ports which provide maritime connectivity to key trading partners. This network of ports consists of five general service ports, namely Durban, East London, Ngqura, Gqeberha (previously Port Elizabeth) and Cape Town, which also provide maritime connectivity to centres of production in the country that are linked by road and rail networks (Transnet, 2017). The general service ports support the handling of various types of freight, such as breakbulk, automotive and liquid bulk; however, containers are the main freight type handled (Transnet National Ports Authority, 2020). The port of Durban is the largest port in southern Africa, with a container capacity of 3.6 million twenty-foot equivalent units (TEUs). It is also the most important in the network as it is best placed to service the commercial hub of Gauteng and other southern African markets (e.g., Zimbabwe and Botswana) (PricewaterhouseCoopers, 2018).

This network of general service ports is complemented by two

Figure 10.2: Gauteng-to-Durban, Gauteng-to-Gqeberha and Gauteng-to-Cape Town corridors

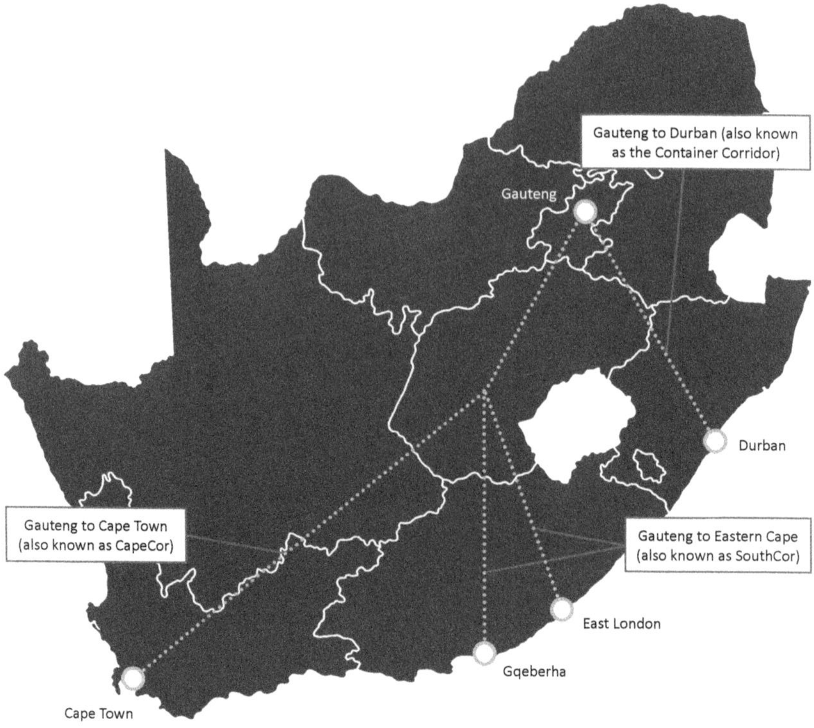

Source: Authors' formulation, 2022

dedicated dry bulk ports located on the western and eastern coasts of the country, namely Saldanha Bay and Richards Bay (Transnet, 2017). These ports form part of the key mineral freight corridors that are driven by rail logistics and enable the efficient export of bulk freight, such as iron ore (Saldanha Bay) and coal (Richards Bay) (PricewaterhouseCoopers, 2018). The dry bulk ports provide approximately 180 million tonnes of export capacity (60 million tonnes for Saldanha and 120 million tonnes for Richards Bay) for the mineral supply chains across their various terminals (Transnet, 2017).[1]

Notwithstanding the foregoing analysis, the South African logistics system has encountered challenges that have hindered its development and potential efficiency gains over the last two decades. These include underinvestment in, and underutilisation of, the rail network,

Table 10.1: South Africa's performance on the Logistics Performance Index, 2010–2018

		2018	2016	2014	2012	2010
Overall LPI	Ranking	33 ↓	20 ↑	34 ↓	23 ↑	28
	Score	3.38 ↓	3.78 ↑	3.43 ↓	3.67 ↑	3.46
Infrastructure	Ranking	34 ↓	18 ↑	42 ↓	26 ↑	31
	Score	3.17 ↓	3.60 ↑	3.11 ↓	3.35 ↑	3.22
Customs	Ranking	36 ↓	21 ↑	38 ↓	19 ↑	29
	Score	3.19 ↓	3.78 ↑	3.20 ↓	3.79 ↑	3.42
International shipments	Ranking	22 ↑	23 ↑	25 ↓	20 ↑	31
	Score	3.51 ↓	3.62 ↑	3.45 ↓	3.50 ↑	3.26
Logistics quality & competence	Ranking	39 ↓	22 ↑	24 ↓	24 ↑	25
	Score	3.19 ↓	3.75 ↑	3.62 ↑	3.56 ↓	3.59
Tracking and tracing	Ranking	35 ↓	17 ↑	41 ↓	16 ↑	24
	Score	3.41 ↓	3.92 ↑	3.30 ↓	3.83 ↑	3.73
Timeliness	Ranking	34 ↓	24 ↑	33 ↓	20 ↑	57
	Score	3.74 ↓	4.02 ↑	3.88 ↓	4.03 ↑	3.57

↓ Declined ↑ Improved

Source: World Bank, 2018

reduced port efficiency, overreliance on road haulage as the primary means of transporting freight, high transport intensity and costs, and limited integration into the planning processes for the various modes of transport (Fitchsolutions, 2022; Havenga, 2015; Stellenbosch University, 2015).

PERFORMANCE OF THE LOGISTICS SYSTEM

While South Africa's logistics system is rated as one of the top performers in the upper middle-income group of economies and is the leader on the African continent, its overall performance has nevertheless deteriorated over time. For example, South Africa's global ranking on the LPI declined from 20th in 2016 to 33rd in 2018 (World Bank, 2018) (See Table 10.1). This was due to a general decline across the attributes used to assess logistics competitiveness. The greatest decline was evident in the attributes of logistics quality and competence and infrastructure quality (World Bank, 2018).

The deterioration of South Africa's logistics system has also been reflected in the reduced operating efficiency of the country's container ports, as documented in the 2020 Port Performance Index (PPI). The latter put Cape Town in 347th position, Gqeberha in 348th position, Durban in 349th position and Ngqura in 351st position respectively on a list of 351 ports that were considered to be in a state of decline. This decline has also been exacerbated by COVID-19-related restrictions and lockdowns (World Bank, 2021).

THE SPATIAL CONFIGURATION OF THE SOUTH AFRICAN ECONOMY AND ITS IMPACT ON LOGISTICS

Owing to the geospatial layout of the country, South Africa is a transport-intensive economy, requiring goods to travel great distances for the purpose of trade (Stellenbosch University, 2015).[2] This geospatial layout is the result of the country's historical economic development, which was largely shaped by concentrating productive capacity near the mineral complexes inland and far from the coastal areas (Havenga, 2010). As a result, the country has had to put effort into operating a more efficient logistics system than would typically be required and managing logistics costs to ensure competitiveness within the global arena (Havenga, 2010).

According to a macro-logistics and costs assessment conducted in 2016, South African logistics costs accounted for approximately 12 per cent of gross domestic product (GDP), having risen by approximately 0.8 per cent between 2011 and 2016 (Havenga et al., 2016). By contrast, markets with more mature logistics networks, such as North America and the European Union (EU), averaged around 8.2 per cent and 9.2 per cent of GDP respectively (Havenga, 2015).[3] These costs were largely driven by the transport element, which accounted for approximately 59 per cent of overall logistics costs. This rate was almost 20 per cent higher than the global average of 40 per cent (De Villiers, 2017).

In addition to geospatial layout challenges, South Africa's logistics costs are further exacerbated by the sub-optimal modal mix for surface transportation, which is heavily biased towards road transport. Some 74 per cent of all freight is transported by road, which has a higher cost burden due to its reliance on imported oil-based fuel (Havenga, 2015). These fuel costs account for up to one-third of total supply costs. The country's logistics costs have also adversely impacted logistics efficiency. For example, the country has achieved limited integration across supply chains. This is attributable in part to its ageing transport infrastructure (e.g., intermodal terminals) which has not developed in line with global standards[4] (National Treasury, 2019).

The transition to a dependency on road transport has in part been driven by the deterioration in the country's rail industry and the deregulation of the road transport industry which began in 1989 and expanded over time (PMG, 2012). Over and above its operational challenges, the rail industry's effectiveness has been adversely affected by a shortage of locomotives to support operations and legal restrictions which have prevented the acquisition of additional tractive units (Derby, 2022). Consequently, the capacity and performance of the country's rail system have declined over time.

SPATIAL LOCATION OF SUPPLY AND DEMAND IN FREIGHT LOGISTICS

Regarding the spatial location of freight logistics supply and demand, the period from 1994 to 2021 has not been characterised by significant variations at the national or district level. The patterns of freight demand in the economy, first identified in 1998 by the Department of Transport (DoT) in the seminal Moving South Africa (MSA) report (DoT, 1998), have not significantly rearranged themselves and continue to consolidate along a small number of dense corridors. These patterns of freight demand have been perpetuated by a combination of factors, including the absence of a coherent rail policy that drives industry reform, underinvestment in rail infrastructure over time and declining operational performance on the part of Transnet. Consolidating long-distance freight along a small number of freight corridors and transitioning towards hub-and-spoke logistics supply and distribution models are key global trends that South Africa must capitalise on.

The adoption of this philosophy may lead to the creation of a logistics industry that would be in a position to negotiate solutions to the longstanding challenges that are confronting the freight system, while also adapting to the new challenges of the future. At the micro level, i.e., the level of the individual supply chain, significant changes have taken place in how logistics services are provided and the infrastructure that is required. For example, the European division of the global fast-moving consumer goods (FMCG) company, Proctor & Gamble (P&G), has adapted its logistics systems so that it can use rail to service its Euro cluster distribution centre, thus eliminating 4.2 million truck km (Islam and Zunder, 2018). This reduction has aided supply efficiency by reducing costs through the adoption of intermodal solutions and has improved the company's carbon footprint by reducing greenhouse gas (GHG) emissions through the use of rail rather than road.

SECTORAL SHIFTS FROM RAIL TO ROAD

In this section, we review the micro-level supply chains of key commodity groups, such as bulk mining and agricultural products, highlighting how the patterns of trade have evolved and consolidated around key corridors, and the changes that have occurred over the last three decades.

In the case of bulk mining products, there has been an increase in the volume demanded by commodity-consuming markets, resulting in higher volumes of freight being transported by road, particularly non-traditional commodities, such as chrome and manganese (Havenga et al., 2022). Rail, however, remains the primary means of transporting mining bulk, and was responsible for transporting approximately 154 million tonnes in 2019[5] (Fitchsolutions, 2022; Transnet, 2020). The dominance of rail has arisen through historical investments made by the state rail operator, Transnet. The support given to mining bulk has continued, as demonstrated by Transnet's recent investments in the expansion of the manganese rail capacity between Hotazel (Northern Cape) and the port of Gqeberha (Eastern Cape) (Buthelezi, 2012; Transnet 2020). This investment has seen flows of manganese on this route increase to 16 million tonnes. The investment has also enabled efficiency improvements in train operations, enabling Transnet Freight Rail to increase the number of wagons from 342 to 375, resulting in a train that is 4 km long (Buthelezi, 2012; Transnet, 2020) with a payload of 22 500 tonnes. This translates into approximately 562 fewer trucks on the road and a reduction of road haulage-related externalities, e.g., GHG emissions.

Investments have also been made to increase capacity across other parts of the bulk network, as seen in the coal line running between the Waterberg (Limpopo) and Richards Bay (KwaZulu-Natal). In this case, additional network infrastructure upgrades (e.g., network loops and double sections) were completed in 2016, contributing to an increase in capacity between Lephalale (Limpopo) and Richards Bay Coal Terminal (KwaZulu-Natal) from 400 000 tonnes to 2 million tonnes and to an overall increase in export coal volumes of 13.1 per cent between 2017 and 2018[6] (Likhethe, 2014; Transnet, 2018). This investment in capacity has also enabled improved operational efficiency, with the number of wagons increasing from 50 to 100, without any disruptions to oncoming traffic due to loops and improved service frequency (from two to five trains per week) (Likhethe, 2014).

Notwithstanding these improvements, the investment in rail network capacity has proved to be insufficient as it has not been able to keep up with the increasing demand for bulk transport services for mining products, particularly in the face of favourable commodity prices, prompting increased production by mining companies. The constrained and shrinking rail capacity across the network in South Africa has been a key driver in the rail-to-road modal shift for mining and agricultural bulk commodities.

When it comes to agriculture, Transnet Freight Rail used to move 5 metric tonnes of agricultural products per year, but this declined to 3 metric tonnes between 2021 and 2022. Critical factors have driven the agricultural sector's shift and consolidation of freight volumes from rail to road. Certain types of agricultural products are not well suited to rail transportation as they lack density and are geographically dispersed, which renders rail transport costly. In addition, relatively low volumes are transported and the centres of agricultural production are dispersed (Havenga et al., 2022). In the past, the spatial dispersion of agricultural production was mitigated by farmers sending their products to central points, where they would be aggregated and loaded onto trains.

The industry has, however, moved to individual producer loading, which not only exacerbates the spatial dispersion problem, but produces low volumes – and low profitability for Transnet Freight Rail. The challenge of low volumes and the erosion of the sustainability of rail for agricultural products was further compounded by the general lack of central funding provided by government for rail infrastructure. Consequently, the rail industry was forced to prioritise higher-margin services and freight (e.g., mining bulk and chemicals) which led to more marginal services receiving dwindling resources over time. This reduction of and/or disinvestment from the rail branch-line network had a severe impact on the agricultural sector, as the branch-line network linked the rural areas to the main line. This led to increased utilisation of modern trucks and trailers which are lighter and have higher axle-load ratings (e.g., multi-axle super links capable of carrying 50 tons in multi-trailer combinations), which also influenced the consolidation of the modal shift to road (Braun, 2017).

This modal shift means that the logistics industry and broader economy have become increasingly exposed to exogenous shocks (e.g., oil price increases). This has resulted in a general rise in the costs of logistics for the product supply chains (e.g., delivery costs), which negatively impacts the mining and agricultural sectors' global competitiveness (Havenga, 2015; Simpson et al., 2021).

SPATIAL CONFIGURATION CHALLENGES AND THEIR IMPACT ON LOGISTICS

The Moving South Africa (MSA) diagnostic (DoT, 1998) identified two specific areas of concern in the freight system:

- Lack of support for export competitiveness; and
- Low levels of system sustainability.

The first issue described a lack of alignment between value-added, ocean-bound exports and cross-border Southern African Development Community (SADC) traffic, which have faced many barriers since the 1980s – and which still exist today. To improve trade competitiveness, solutions to the enduring problems of long delays at border posts, high transport costs and low levels of maritime connectivity in the region have to be found.

The freight system sustainability challenge centred on the high externality cost (such as road accidents, emissions and congestion) of domestic freight and the deteriorating quality of the overall system (despite some investment in heavy haulage channels), which were partially driven by historical underinvestment in rail infrastructure (Morton et al., 2006). The financial sustainability of the road and rail networks was a key concern, and remains so today, as is the deteriorating quality of the freight system. Concerns about the deterioration of the rail network have been further compounded in the COVID-19 pandemic and subsequent periods, which have seen the electrified rail network come under threat from cable thieves (Derby, 2022).

The MSA strategy set out three strategic objectives:

- Build density in the transport system by directing freight flows through selected corridors – achieved by supporting and reinforcing current trends to build the backbone of the system, while at the same time reducing complexity and investment requirements (rationalisation of the network);
- Build economies of scale within the different modes by sharpening their respective roles, maximising scale economies within each mode and offering differentiated services where economically sustainable; and
- Improve firm-level competitiveness by removing obstacles, improving integration, ensuring sufficient reinvestment to maintain quality infrastructure and operations, restoring price and value signals between customers and providers, and building an industry platform that drives differentiation and innovation.

These recommendations to improve freight-system performance developed by the MSA strategy remain valid today and focus on developing implementable programmes and solutions to realise the strategic actions under the MSA. However, Transnet needs to adopt a more regional outlook in terms of the freight system and ensure that it extends beyond South Africa's borders. Going forward, there needs to be better regional economic integration and intraregional trade as critical foundation pillars of the post-COVID-19 economic recovery plan. In this regard, particular attention must be given to improving the efficiency and effectiveness of cross-border infrastructure networks, reducing goods' standing time at borders, and increasing regional maritime and air connectivity.

The adoption of regionally focused development strategies, such as the SADC Indicative Strategic Development Plan (ISDP), and the continentally focused African Continental Free Trade Area (AfCTFA) trade agreement mark the start of a journey towards more harmonised markets, which will reduce both physical and administrative trade barriers in the region and across the continent (SADC, 2021; World Bank, 2022). According to the World Bank (2022), the AfCTFA agreement (and its possible future iterations) could lead to the doubling of intra-African trade, induced primarily by the manufacturing sector which would require the support of effective and efficient supply chains to reach end customers[7] (World Bank, 2022).

The National Development Plan (NDP) (NPC, 2012) envisages a freight transport sector that, by 2030, facilitates domestic and cross-border movement across supply chains to enable industrialisation, diversification, and trade and development. To this end, the sector will have to be efficient, reliable, resilient, financially sustainable and consistent with a low-carbon future.

In addition to the strategic challenges and responses identified by the MSA, the following system-level challenges must be resolved to ensure the long-term competitiveness of the freight system.

Table 10.2: South Africa's freight-system challenges and long-term requirements

Freight-system challenges	Requirements for long-term competitiveness
• The road–rail market share is unbalanced and leads (in the case of road transport) to high costs, high carbon intensity and vulnerability to international oil price volatility.	• A large-scale modal shift from road to rail to address the problems of high costs, congestion and carbon emissions. • A low-carbon, energy-efficient freight system that will reduce vulnerability to oil price volatility.
• Global and regional maritime connectivity is poor, limited to well-established lines linking SADC to main shipping hubs, such as Singapore.	• The creation of international hub ports. • Increased maritime connectivity between regional ports.
• The regional freight system is weakly integrated and delivers a poor performance.	• A high-performing core transport network in the region which will enable growth in intraregional trade.
• The demand for transport infrastructure across all modes is due to rise significantly in view of the forecasted increase in the demand for freight.	• A robust infrastructure-funding model capable of ensuring capacity ahead of demand.
• There is a shortage of skills across most areas in the freight system.	• Targeted skills development strategies.
• The supplier industries for all transport modes are underdeveloped.	• Coordinated investment across international networks. • A supplier development plan linked to a long-term infrastructure investment plan.
• There is little understanding of customers' needs and what drives competitiveness at a supply chain level.	• Service offerings tailored to supply chain needs rather than individual modal requirements. • Flexible positions in respect of investment development options, including the role of the public and private sectors within the different supply chains.

Source: Authors' formulation; DoT, 2016; NHFS, 2019

South Africa's freight transport system challenges are relatively well known and have proven to be difficult to resolve. Indeed, several of the challenges identified in the 1980s through the 1987 National Transport Policy Study (DoT, 2016) and in the 1990s through the MSA strategy are still impacting the sector today (DoT, 2016). The persistence of these challenges has hindered the evolution of the freight system and has prompted the formulation of certain critical objectives (such as the road-to-rail transition for freight), as highlighted in key transport strategies and policies, e.g., the Green Transport Strategy for South Africa: 2018–2050 (DoT, 2018).

The rail freight transport system has served traditional industries, such as mining, fairly well and developed dedicated 'bulk logistics systems' (e.g., an iron-ore line) that connect mines to export and manufacturing nodes relatively efficiently (Stellenbosch University, 2015: 13). However, it has not made sufficient progress in improving its service to non-traditional industries and agriculture, the sectors meant to drive future growth, dynamism and employment creation. The inadequate development of the freight transport system (particularly the rail and intermodal components) can partly be explained by a sub-optimal funding model, very limited private-sector participation and weak regulation. Moreover, policy integration between modes of transport has been limited, although multimodal transport is essential – particularly in industries that are meant to drive South Africa forward.

Going forward, the logistics industry will need to transform further to orientate around supply chains. Customers, including rural and emerging commercial farmers, miners and manufacturers, should be able to reach domestic and international markets easily and competitively. The reform of the freight system must incorporate the following key characteristics:

- a transition towards a supply chain orientation, with a focus on enhanced efficiency to improve national competitiveness;
- holistic and integrated transport regulations and supporting models to provide all-encompassing governance over multiple modes and functions;
- a redefined national rail-operating model characterised by well-

classified network infrastructure (multi-tier network) which supports participation by the private sector through third-party access; and
- enhanced collaboration between surface transport stakeholders with the aim of improving integration between surface transport modes and greater flexibility in one's approach.

THE IMPACT OF FREIGHT SYSTEM CHALLENGES ON SUPPLY CHAINS

South Africa's macro-level freight logistics network is made up of a number of industry-level supply chains which enable the movement of goods between value chain participants, including sources of production (e.g., farms), intermediate and final manufacturing (e.g., milling), and consumption centres (e.g., retail stores) (Havenga and Simpson, 2022). Accordingly, the challenges faced across the broader freight system also have adverse impacts on these industry supply chains, reducing the efficiency and competitiveness of the industries due to higher transport costs for goods (De Villiers, 2017; Ittmann and King, 2010). In line with this, it is necessary to apply an industry 'lens' to assess the impact of the challenges on the micro-level supply chains. This can be done by reviewing the impact on the four primary supply chains, namely agricultural, mining, beneficiation and consumption (Havenga et al., 2022).

Agricultural supply chains

South Africa's relatively well-developed agricultural sector (e.g., grain farming) regularly produces surplus harvests which can be exported once local demand has been met. This was the case during the 2017 and 2021 grain seasons when record maize crops of 16.2 million tonnes and 16.8 million tonnes respectively were produced (Van der Vyer, 2022). The ability of the sector to export has, however, become increasingly constrained over time due to the reduced service capacity of the rail system which faces a multitude of challenges, such as ongoing and an escalation in cable theft and underinvestment in the rail network, particularly the rural branch network (Braun, 2017; Derby, 2022). Agricultural freight is today primarily transported by road (Senwes, 2022), one of the reasons being the shortcomings within the rail network. Another reason is innovation on the part of agricultural companies which have expanded their operations downstream to develop bulk agriculture transport solutions – of which a leading example is Grainovation (a joint venture between Senwes and Imperial Logistics).

This transition to road freight has, though, had an adverse impact – cost-wise – on the agricultural supply chain, with the transport element being the highest cost component, ranging between 63 and 67 per cent, depending on the corridor traversed (Havenga et al., 2022; Van der Vyer, 2022). Figure 10.3 indicates the potential agricultural volumes that are transported primarily by road, alongside key rail corridors, as well as the well-developed silo network that supports the country's logistics system. These volumes include a selection of grains, such as maize, wheat and sorghum, on the Cape Town-to-Gauteng (CapeCor) and Durban-to-Gauteng (NatCor) rail corridors. Maize that is grown and stored predominantly in the inland maize triangle (the dotted-line triangle in Figure 10.3) is located within an area covered by an extensive grain silo network, which is integral to the logistics system used to transport the products to coastal processors. Likewise, wheat and sorghum farmers near the coast leverage the same logistics system to transport products to processing and consumption centres inland.

Figure 10.3: Map of potential grain movements along CapeCor and NatCor corridors

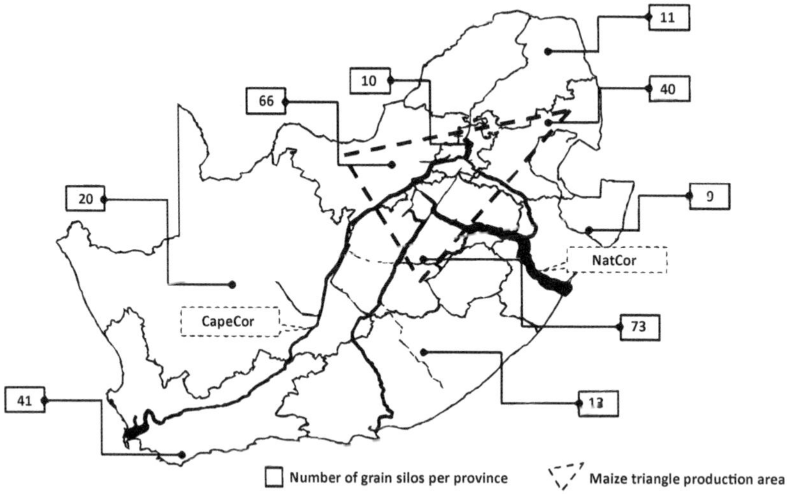

Source: Adapted from Havenga et al., 2022

Mining bulk supply chain

South Africa's mining industry remains an important player in the overall economy, employing approximately 460 000 people and contributing R78.1 billion to GDP (in the form of taxes) in 2021 (MCSA, 2022). Further analysis shows that the base minerals segment, which produces minerals such as coal and iron ore (amongst others), employs about 162 540 people and contributes approximately R7.8 billion in mining royalties (MCSA, 2022). Most of the minerals produced in the base minerals segment are exported in their raw state as mining bulk and are thus adversely impacted by the limited rail and port capacity (Bulbulia, 2022).[8]

The limited access to rail capacity has resulted in higher transportation costs within the supply chain as higher freight volumes (which can be as high as 50 per cent of production) are allocated to road hauliers to compensate for the rail capacity and reliability challenges (Seccombe, 2021). This sub-optimal road haulage-based solution means that the transport cost component of some of these bulk commodities is as high as 75 per cent of the total logistics cost (Havenga et al., 2022). Furthermore, these bulk mining supply chains and, in particular, non-traditional bulk commodities such as chrome – which are often transported on 'rural routes' by road hauliers – are also challenged by various externalities, which have an adverse impact on mining activity by adding to the stress on the rural road network (Havenga et al., 2022).

These supply chains opt for road freight despite the latter's high cost and despite their having a natural 'high rail conformance' because of their products' characteristics. In this regard, they would derive optimal benefit from conveyor belt-like supply chains with dedicated supporting infrastructure (e.g., sidings), which would reduce the logistics costs associated with getting the products to market (Havenga and Simpson, 2022). The supply chains' relatively high rail conformance is driven by several key factors, including the uniformity of a mining product, which is a non-fragile, standard ore body, its terminal density, which results from large volumes being handled at sidings, and its point-to-point density, as the goods repeatedly traverse the same route (Havenga and Simpson, 2022).

Domestic mining bulk, which flows between local mines and domestic beneficiation centres (e.g., iron ore between Sishen and Newcastle), has a moderate share of the rail market, with up to 50 per cent of freight being transported by road (Bulbulia, 2022; Havenga and Simpson, 2022; Seccombe, 2021). By contrast, large-volume exports, which flow from local mines to dedicated export terminals at maritime ports (e.g., manganese between Hotazel and Gqeberha), have a relatively high share of the rail market, although their share has declined somewhat due to capacity constraints and reduced reliability of rail services (Bulbulia, 2022; Havenga and Simpson, 2022; Seccombe, 2021).

Beneficiation supply chains

South Africa has relatively well-developed beneficiation supply chains that predominantly support large-scale manufacturing of industrial inputs (e.g., steel coils), which are used to manufacture products consumed by households in the tertiary sector (Simpson et al., 2021). These supply chains transport heavy breakbulk items over relatively long distances and typically follow conventional corridors for export (e.g., Gauteng to Durban). Although some heavy breakbulk items are transported by rail, most of the beneficiation supply chains are reliant on road hauliers who carried approximately R32.6 billion worth of freight in 2016 (Mazareanu, 2020). Over time, as the performance of the country's rail system has worsened, road hauliers have managed to extend their service coverage beyond high-value goods and perishables to traditional bulk freight, such as coal and iron ore (Morton et al., 2006).

The transition to road haulage presents a challenge to the industry as the nature of beneficiated products (e.g., manganese alloys) does not allow for meaningful product differentiation; therefore, local producers cannot secure a competitive advantage from their products, relying instead on 'costs advantage' within their supply chains to be globally competitive (Van Zyl et al., 2019). However, the dominance of the road-freight industry is reflected in the relatively high logistics costs associated with moving heavy breakbulk across the corridors. It is also reflected in the share of the transport component, which ranges from 56 per cent for the Gauteng-to-Durban and Gauteng-to-Eastern

Cape corridors to 58 per cent for the Gauteng-to-Cape Town corridor, making it difficult for the industry to compete on the global stage (Havenga, 2015; Van Zyl et al., 2019).

Consumption supply chains

South Africa's ports handled approximately 4.6 million TEUs in 2019 (prior to COVID-19). This confirms the existence of a relatively large market for palletised goods and light breakbulk and presents an opportunity for improved use of rail-based intermodal solutions, particularly for the line-haulage component of these supply chains (Havenga and Simpson, 2022; Islam and Zunder, 2018; World Bank, 2021). Most of the freight for consumption supply chains, however, is transported to its final destination either by road in TEUs or in palletised form. The innovative decision to palletise goods increased the efficiency of road-freight services as road hauliers can load 24 per cent more pallets in the same area compared with a 6 m and 12 m TEU combination (De Villiers, 2017). In addition to transporting additional volumes, the palletisation of consumption freight creates the additional benefits of time saving through direct delivery from warehouses adjacent to the port and cost savings through the processing of shipping containers at the port of origin rather than at inland container depots.

In a recent study (2018) conducted on low-density, high-value (LDHV) goods in Europe, it was noted that specialised terminals were key enablers of 'carrying LDHV goods by intermodal rail in a cost-efficient manner' (Islam and Zunder, 2018: 4). Efficient scale could be achieved through the use of block or unit trains to transport containerised (intermodal) palletised goods and light breakbulk to specialised consolidation terminals in the Gauteng hinterland (De Villiers, 2017). The shift from road- to rail-driven supply chain solutions would present an opportunity to optimise the transport component of the palletised and light breakbulk supply chain costs, which currently account for between 46 per cent and 56 per cent for palletised freight and 57 per cent and 65 per cent for light breakbulk, depending on the corridor (Havenga and Simpson, 2022; Havenga et al., 2022).

Although at face value this freight may seem to have 'low rail conformance', it can be unitised (packaged together) onto pallets and transported by rail in specialised pallet containers to high-consumption urban centres (e.g., Cape Town, Johannesburg and Durban). Achieving this modal transition would also be reliant on the provision of supporting intermodal infrastructure (e.g., specialised container-handling facilities); it cannot be achieved through the provision of a standalone, long-haul rail solution.

CONCLUSION AND THE WAY FORWARD

Improvement in the performance of the various commodity supply chains is paramount for the continued and/or enhanced competitiveness of various freight segments, ranging from agriculture through to manufacturing, such as the globally competitive automotive sector (Derby, 2022). Attracting adequate freight volumes and densifying corridors using optimal modes of transport are key to overcoming the challenges created by the spatial configuration of the economy and achieving improved logistics performance through the 'balancing' of the freight volumes transported by the surface modes (Braun, 2017).

As part of balancing the modal share, the industry needs to optimise transport solutions to meet the unique requirements of the freight segments being catered for (Derby, 2022). Of particular importance is the shifting of potential rail-friendly bulk cargo (uniform, relatively dense and handled in terminals) to rail from road freight. The enhancement of rail capacity and services within the country is a critical factor in attracting freight and reducing the costs associated with the transport component of supply chains (Havenga et al., 2022). The ensuing modal shifts would improve global competitiveness through the lower delivered costs for commodities, enhanced environmental sustainability of supply chains in the country and fewer adverse externalities for the economy overall (e.g., road degradation).

The enhancement of rail capacity and services will require a collaborative effort from the various stakeholders involved in the logistics industry, including policymakers, logistics service providers and Transnet. This collaborative effort should focus on allocating industry resources in ways that will best deliver value-adding solutions and forge meaningful partnerships that will improve cost efficiency and responsiveness to the requirements of different freight segments. To this end, it is important to explore alternative rail-operating models (e.g., third-party operators) (Derby, 2022). Furthermore, international experience, particularly in the North American market, suggests that South Africa should opt for a multi-tiered rail freight model that is able to accommodate integrated rail systems for the dedicated heavy-haulage channels, an open-access model for the core general freight network and private operators on the branch-line networks as a means to improve efficiency.

This is in line with the National Treasury's assertion that South Africa's economy requires an efficient logistics system to facilitate both intra- and inter-country trade and to drive economic development (National Treasury, 2019). To achieve greater efficiency, the country's supply chain systems will need to undertake several reforms, which can be categorised into three overarching approaches:

- using optimal transportation modes within the logistics elements of supply chains;
- densifying supply chains by luring freight back to rail from road and presenting collaboration opportunities to logistics service providers and infrastructure owners; and
- improving the global competitiveness of domestic industries (e.g., steel industry) and the goods they produce through the development of cost-efficient supply chains which ensure effective and dependable goods delivery.

Use of optimal transportation modes

South Africa's bulk supply chains (particularly non-traditional mining and agricultural supply chains) have, over time, become reliant on the road freight industry, owing to rail's capacity and reliability challenges. However, this modal solution is sub-optimal. Yet an opportunity exists to improve efficiency through a modal shift (Braun, 2017; De Villiers, 2017). The characteristics of some mining and agricultural products, including product uniformity and relatively high density, have led to their having a 'high rail conformance' and being suitable for efficient rail transport (Havenga and Simpson, 2022). This, coupled with the reality that these supply chains often have access to existing rail-aligned logistics infrastructure (e.g., silos and mine sidings), presents a great opportunity to utilise rail as the primary mode of transporting these goods to improve efficiencies (IOL, 2010; Van der Vyer, 2022). In the case of agricultural freight, where density and geolocation of farms could be a challenge, the existing silo network needs to be better utilised as consolidation points where large volumes of uniform agricultural products are stored in rail-friendly infrastructure, which is integrated into the existing rail network[9] (Braun, 2017; Havenga et al., 2022).

The transition would help to reduce the direct transport and handling costs associated with bulk supply chains and enable producers to be more competitive in the market. The transition to an optimal transport mode for mining and agricultural products would also have a positive impact on the cost of externalities linked to the supply chains – notably, reductions in emissions and less wear and tear of the rural road network.

Densification of supply chains

South Africa's geospatial make-up means that freight is transported over vast distances to reach its site of beneficiation and/or consumption, resulting in higher-than-average logistics intensity in the country (Stellenbosch University, 2015). A possible way to overcome this problem is to improve route densities through the use of 'rail-driven' intermodal solutions to support some agricultural supply chains, particularly consumption supply chains. The implementation of this solution would necessitate the provision and integration of various intermodal and rail elements, including focused intermodal infrastructure, such as automated transhipment, temperature-controlled consolidation and distribution services (e.g., warehouses). These in turn are complemented by key operational support services (e.g., drayage and customs services) and service planning to provide the industry with an integrated, 'total supply chain' solution (Islam and Zunder, 2018).

Furthermore, the facilitation of the transition to rail would require integration between the predictable intermodal rail solution (e.g., line haul) and the other surface transport modes, with road transport being required for the first- and last-mile stages, which it is well placed to provide. The integration of stakeholders into a total supply chain solution, with optimised consolidation facilities and services, would benefit all parties through efficiency gains and streamlined rail services (De Villiers, 2017).

Figure 10.4 demonstrates the potential integration of rail-based intermodal solutions (image on the right) to act as long-haul components of palletised goods supply chains.

Figure 10.4: Model shift opportunity provided by palletised freight

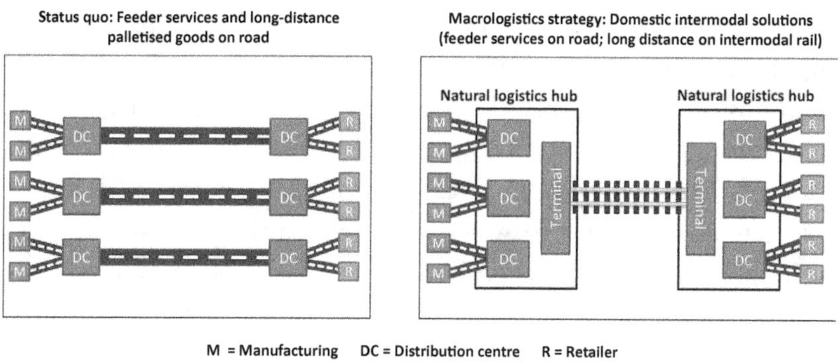

Source: Simpson et al., 2021: 194, cited in Havenga et al., 2022

Cost-efficient supply chains

As national supply chains have become more reliant on costlier road hauliers, their competitiveness has declined, and this is compounded by their inability to differentiate their offerings through other elements, such as product quality (De Villiers, 2017; Ittmann and King, 2010). These supply chains, particularly beneficiation supply chains (e.g., intermediate and final manufacturing) which are 'cost sensitive' and compete globally, could potentially benefit from initiatives designed to improve logistics costs and efficiency. Such initiatives would potentially lead to the optimisation of operations and enhance the cost efficiency of supply chains through the infusion of rail, which would allow densification and reduce overall transport costs, particularly in the case of heavy breakbulk (Havenga et al., 2022).

The envisaged efficiency gains would depend on making better use of rail-focused infrastructure. This could be achieved through the leveraging of dedicated sidings and bulk material-handling equipment (which are prevalent across several beneficiation sites) to improve handling efficiency, which could account for between 10 per cent and 13 per cent of logistics costs (National Treasury, 2019; Havenga et al., 2022). The modal switch from road to rail would also potentially eliminate the need for the last-mile activity currently required in road transport, since the beneficiated product would be delivered to a dedicated siding at the 'point of final intermediate input' (Havenga et al., 2022: 10).

Improvements in the operating efficiency of South Africa's national supply chains will require the implementation of multiple, focused, supply chain-specific interventions which will provide bespoke solutions for the challenges (e.g., cost and/or reliability) faced by the four primary supply chains, as opposed to generic solutions being adopted. The interventions developed will also require collaboration between modes and between state and private-sector logistics operators, in line with their competitive capabilities, to overcome the inherently high and spatially driven transport intensity of the country.

REFERENCES

Braun, M. 2017. 'The role of transport in logistics of agriculture', https://www.namc.co.za/wp-content/uploads/2017/10/The-Role-of-Transport-in-Logistics-of-Agriculture.pdf, accessed 27 January 2022.

Bulbulia, T. 9 May 2022. 'South Africa's mine production value exceeds R1 trillion for the first time in 2021'. *Mining Weekly*, https://www.miningweekly.com/article/south-africas-mine-production-value-exceeded-r1tr-for-the-first-time-in-2021-2022-05-09, accessed 13 August 2022.

Buthelezi, N. 26 October 2012. 'TFR to increase Hotazel–Port Elizabeth manganese throughput to 16Mt/y'. *Mining Weekly*, https://www.miningweekly.com/print-version/distributed-power-for-transnets-hotazel-port-elizabeth-rail-link-tested-2012-10-26, accessed 1 June 2022.

Department of Transport (DoT). 1998. *Moving South Africa Strategy: The Action Agenda: A 20-year strategic framework for transport in South Africa*. Pretoria: Government Printer.

Department of Transport (DoT). 2016. 'National transport master plan 2050 – synopsis update', https://www.transport.gov.za/

documents/11623/39906/00_TableContents2017.pdf/1f534d84-dba9-4bff-b252-b5acb3a97deb, accessed 16 August 2022.

Department of Transport (DoT). 2018. 'Green transport strategy for South Africa: 2018–2050', https://www.transport.gov.za/documents/11623/89294/Green_Transport_Strategy_2018_2050_onlineversion.pdf, accessed 4 May 2022.

Department of Transport (DoT). 2021. 'Overview: South Africa's road network', https://www.transport.gov.za/roads, accessed 5 May 2022.

Derby, P. 21 March 2022. 'Portia Derby: How we are getting Transnet back on track'. *BusinessLive*, https://www.businesslive.co.za/bd/opinion/2022-03-21-portia-derby-how-we-are-getting-transnet-back-on-track/, accessed 18 April 2022.

De Villiers, G. July 2017. 'Improving competitiveness of companies in South Africa through logistics and supply chain management'. 36th Annual Southern African Transport Conference 2017, https://repository.up.ac.za/handle/2263/62699, accessed 12 May 2022.

Fitchsolutions. 7 January 2022. 'South Africa freight transport & shipping'. *Fitch Connect,* https://app.fitchconnect.com/entity/GRP_80442220/industry-risk/freight-transport-&-shipping/reports, accessed 25 January 2022.

Gain Group. 30 March 2020. 'Sector study: Logistics – South Africa'. Netherlands Enterprise Agency, https://www.rvo.nl/sites/default/files/2020/08/sector-study-logistics-in-south-africa.pdf, accessed 17 February 2022.

Greenbook. 2022. 'Green Book: Adapting settlements for the future', https://greenbook.co.za/, accessed 2 May 2022.

Havenga, J. 2010. 'Logistics costs in South Africa – The case for macroeconomic measurement'. *South African Journal of Economics,* 78 (4), 460–471.

Havenga, J. 2015. 'Macro-logistics and externality cost trends in South Africa – Underscoring the sustainability imperative'. *International Journal of Logistics*, 18 (2), 118–139.

Havenga, J. and Simpson, Z. 2022. 'The future of heavy haul'. South African Heavy Hauls Association (SAHHA) Conference, 3 August 2022.

Havenga, J. H., De Bod, A., Simpson, Z. P., Swarts, S. and Witthöft, I. E. 2022. 'Macrologistics supply chains in South Africa'. Gain Group website: https://www.gaingroup.co.za/index.php/articles/supply-chains-in-south-africa, accessed 7 February 2022.

Havenga, J., Simpson, Z., King, D., De Bod, A. and Braun, M. 2016. 'Logistics Barometer South Africa 2016'. Stellenbosch University, https://www.sun.ac.za/english/faculty/economy/logistics/Documents/Logistics%20Barometer/Logistics%20Barometer%202016%20Report.pdf, accessed 17 February 2022.

Independent Online (IOL). 8 October 2010. 'Poor rail systems impact on silo owners'. *IOL,* https://www.iol.co.za/business-report/economy/poor-rail-systems-impact-on-silo-owners-809661, accessed 30 May 2022.

International Union of Railways. 2014. 'Railway statistics synopsis', https://uic.org/IMG/pdf/synopsis_2014.pdf, accessed 29 January 2022.

Invest India. May 2020. 'Great places for manufacturing in India', https://www.investindia.gov.in/great-places-for-manufacturing-in-india, accessed 30 May 2022.

Invest SP. 2022. 'Why São Paulo', https://www.en.investe.sp.gov.br/why-sao-paulo/infrastructure/ports/, accessed 30 May 2022.

Islam, D. Z. and Zunder, T. H. 2018. 'Experience of rail intermodal freight transport for low-density high value (LDHV) goods in Europe'. *European Transport Research Review*, 10 (24), 1–14, https://etrr.springeropen.com/articles/10.1186/s12544-018-0295-7, accessed 04 May 2022.

Ittmann, H. and King, D. 2010. 'The state of logistics – an overview of logistics in South Africa'. Council for Scientific and Industrial Research, https://researchspace.csir.co.za/dspace/bitstream/handle/10204/4254/Ittmann_2010.pdf?sequence=1&isAllowed=y, accessed 29 April 2022.

Krugell, W. and Naudé, W. 2005. 'The geographical economy of South Africa'. *Journal of Development Perspectives*, 1 (1), 85–128, https://journals.co.za/doi/pdf/10.10520/AJA20062184_55, accessed 3 May 2022.

Likhethe, M. 16 July 2014. 'Transnet marks significant step in increasing capacity on the coal line', https://www.transnet.net/Media/Press%20Release%20Office/Transnet%20marks%20significant%20step%20in%20increasing%20capacity%20on%20the%20coal%20line.docx, accessed 9 June 2022.

Mahofa, G. 2017. 'The spatial dimension of economic activity in South Africa: The role of regional crime and business environment'. PhD thesis, University of Cape Town, https://open.uct.ac.za/bitstream/handle/11427/27835/thesis_com_2018_mahofa_godfrey.pdf?sequence=1, accessed 4 May 2022.

Mazareanu, E. 2020. 'Income from road freight transport services in South Africa in 2016, by commodity'. *Statista,* https://www.statista.com/statistics/1072163/income-road-freight-transport-storage-industry-south-africa/, accessed 16 February 2022.

Minerals Council South Africa (MCSA). 2022. 'Facts and figures 2021 – changing mines, changing lives', https://www.mineralscouncil.org.za/downloads/send/16-featured/1875-facts-and-figures-2021, accessed 15 August 2022.

Morton, B., Visser, A. and Horak, E. 2006. 'A life cycle cost analysis of the Gauteng to Durban freight corridor: Introduction to study'. Conference paper for 25th Southern African Transport Conference, https://www.researchgate.net/figure/Gauteng-to-Durban-freight-corridors-for-road-and-rail-freight-transport-The-Gauteng-to_fig3_228367859, accessed 3 May 2022.

National Planning Commission (NPC). 2012. 'National Development Plan 2030: Our future – make it work', https://www.gov.za/documents/national-development-plan-2030-our-future-make-it-work, accessed 23 May 2022.

National Treasury (NT). 2019. 'Economic transformation, inclusive growth, and competitiveness: Towards an economic strategy for South Africa', http://www.treasury.gov.za/comm_media/press/2019/Towards%20an%20Economic%20Strategy%20for%20SA.pdf, accessed 17 February 2022.

New Horizon Freight Solution (NHFS). 2019. 'Challenges in the South African freight industry', https://www.nhfs.co.za/5-challenges-in-the-south-african-freight-industry/, accessed 13 August 2022.

Parliamentary Monitoring Group (PMG). 2012. 'Reduction of transportation by road and a shift toward rail: An update by the Department of Transport', https://pmg.org.za/committee-meeting/13907/, accessed 24 May 2022.

PricewaterhouseCoopers. 2018. 'Strengthening Africa's gateways to trade', https://www.pwc.co.za/en/publications/african-ports.html, accessed 3 May 2022.

Seccombe, A. 2021. 'Tharisa is the latest company to flag Transnet constraints', https://www.businesslive.co.za/bd/companies/mining/2021-04-13-tharisa-is-the-latest-company-to-flag-transnet-constraints/, accessed 3 August 2022.

Senwes. 2022. 'Company profile', http://www.senwes.co.za/en-za/about-senwes/company-profile, accessed 1 May 2022.

Simpson, Z., De Bod, A., Havenga, J., Van Dyk, E. and Meyer, I. 2021. 'Intermodal solutions for the South African fast-moving consumer goods sector'. *World Review of Intermodal Transportation Research*, 10 (3), 179–201.

Southern African Development Community (SADC). 2021. 'SADC Regional Indicative Strategic Development Plan (RISDP) 2020–2030', https://www.sadc.int/sites/default/files/2021-08/RISDP_2020-2030.pdf, accessed 13 August 2022.

Statistics South Africa (StatsSA). 2019. 'Four facts about provincial economies', https://www.statssa.gov.za/?p=12056, accessed 3 May 2022.

Stellenbosch University. 2015. 'Logistics Barometer South Africa 2015', https://www.sun.ac.za/english/faculty/economy/logistics/Documents/Logistics%20Barometer/Logistics%20Barometer%202015%20Report.pdf, accessed 25 January 2022.

Transnet. 2017. 'Long term planning framework', https://www.transnet.net/businesswithus/ltpf%202018/forms/allitems.aspx, accessed 25 April 2022.

Transnet. 2018. 'Integrated Report 2018', https://www.transnet.net/InvestorRelations/Pages/Annual-Results-2018.aspx, accessed 25 April 2022.

Transnet. 2020. 'Annual Report Freight Rail 2019', https://www.transnet.net/InvestorRelations/AR2019/Freight%20Rail.pdf, accessed 18 April 2022.

Transnet National Ports Authority. 2020. 'National ports plan - update', https://www.transnetnationalportsauthority.net/Documents/NPP%20 2019%20Update%20(1).pdf, accessed 1 May 2022.

Van der Vyer, A. 2022. 'Will cable theft and rail inefficiencies derail maize exports?'. SA Grain website: https://sagrainmag.co.za/, accessed 22 May 2022.

Van Zyl, H., Bam, W. and Steenkamp, J. 2019. 'Identifying barriers to growth in mineral value chains'. Mintek, https://www.mintek.co.za/Pyromet/Files/2020VanZyl.pdf, accessed 4 May 2022.

World Bank. 2018. 'Connecting to compete 2018 – The logistics performance index and its indicators', https://openknowledge.worldbank.org/bitstream/handle/10986/29971/LPI2018.pdf, accessed 29 January 2022.

World Bank. 2021. 'The container port performance index 2020: A comparable assessment of container port performance', https://www.maritimes.gr/images/PORTS/Container-Port-Performance_Index-WB-2021.pdf?_t=1620669079, accessed 3 May 2022.

World Bank. 2022. 'Free trade deal boosts Africa's economic development', https://www.worldbank.org/en/topic/trade/publication/free-trade-deal-boosts-africa-economic-development#:~:text=Key%20Findings,159%20percent%20under%20the%20AfCFTA, accessed 13 August 2022

World Economic Forum (WEF). 2016. 'The global economy – Business and economic data for 200 countries', https://www.theglobaleconomy.com/rankings/roads_quality/, accessed 9 February 2022.

NOTES

1 The port of Richards Bay's capacity is dominated by the Transnet-owned Richards Bay Coal Terminal (RBCT), a terminal for privately owned mining companies and commodity traders, with a 91 million-tonne capacity. The terminal has a 30 million-tonne capacity through its dry bulk (21 million tonnes) and breakbulk (9 million tonnes) terminals.

2 South Africa's economic activity is predominantly located in its inland provinces and centred on the urban areas of Gauteng province, which accounts for 34 per cent of GDP.

3 Freight logistics costs relative to GDP, according to Havenga (2015), ranged between 11 per cent and 14 per cent over the decade and remained consistently higher than those in other markets owing to South Africa's reliance on road freight and the impact of fuel costs on this mode.

4 Over time, freight terminals have developed into gateways offering a range of value-added services to cargo owners and transporters (e.g., financing,

light manufacturing/finishing and customs, amongst others). By offering value-added services, these terminals make it easier for their customers to do business and integrate into value chains and to attract a larger share of freight volumes.

5 In 2019, Transnet Freight Rail transported approximately 154 million tonnes of mining bulk, which included the following key commodities: iron ore (58.4 million tonnes), coal (72 million tons), manganese (14 million tonnes), chrome (7.1 million tonnes) and granite (0.5 million tonnes).

6 According to Transnet's 2018 results presentation, coal export volumes increased by approximately 9 million tonnes between 2014 and 2018 to reach 77 million tonnes.

7 According to the World Bank, the AfCFTA agreement could result in incomes increasing by about 7 per cent (US$450 billion) by 2035, while intra-Africa exports could increase by 109 per cent over the same time horizon. Other potential benefits, according to the World Bank, include better wages, higher employment and improved gender equality.

8 The term 'mining bulk' is a composite term used to describe base minerals, such as ores extracted during the mining process; however, it excludes precious metals and precious stones.

9 Based on a study conducted by Havenga et al. (2022) and an article by the director of the South African Cereals and Oilseeds Trade Association, approximately 90 per cent of grain silos are located near rail networks, having been designed to function optimally with a rail mode.

ELEVEN

Lifting the colony while improving the metropolis: Addressing duality in economic development

JOEL NETSHITENZHE

INTRODUCTION

This chapter deals with interventions that could help eliminate the parallel streams of lived economic experiences within the South African economy, referred to in this context as 'the colony' and 'the metropolis'. It starts off by briefly characterising these streams of development to illustrate some of the core features of the entrenched duality. It then posits proposals to facilitate convergence of developmental outcomes by catalysing mass absorption into industrial activity, opportunities in agriculture and support for micro enterprises.

As elaborated on in other chapters in this volume, the structure of the South African economy cannot be separated from its colonial origins. It evolved with two attributes, elements of which continue to define it in the post-apartheid period.

First, during the 20th century, monopolies with ubiquitous

production and/or supply chains across the length and breadth of the country came to dominate the economic landscape. When combined with the suppression of entrepreneurship within the black community, a distorted structure emerged, with much of the 'product space' constituted by 'branded products that are mass produced by large, vertically integrated corporations' (Fourie, 2018b).

Second, the economy was based on a hierarchical system of inclusion and exclusion, with Africans[1] on the lowest rung of the social ladder. Africans were considered to be 'sojourners' in 'white' South Africa and were largely meant to reside in labour reserves.[2] Indian and Coloured communities were also confined to specific geographical areas and a limited range of economic activities. Some of the legal regimes enforcing these constraints were relaxed slightly as the needs of the economy grew, but the apartheid-era system was inherited mostly intact with the attainment of democracy in 1994. Since then, sections of the black community have gradually been integrated into the upper levels of the advanced economy. Yet a large part of the population remains alienated. The dual tracks of South Africa's economic journey have barely shown signs of convergence some three decades into democracy.

Former President Thabo Mbeki (2003) characterised this as 'two parallel economies'. The duality suggested in this chapter draws partly on this observation, but it refers more specifically to dynamic developments in the political economy since 1994. In this sense, it differs from a static characterisation suggesting that the rich and the poor are 'not just set apart by quantitative differences in wealth' but inhabit 'two separate and qualitatively distinct economies' (Callebert, 2014: 119). Indeed, individuals occupying this dual space and their socioeconomic activities are linked in a multiplicity of ways, and their lives – within and across social strata, communities and families – do intersect. As such, the interventions proposed go beyond the binary approach of seeking to elevate the 'second economy' to become part of the 'first economy', as is assumed to be the aim of the South African government (Masondo, 2007: 66–80) or delinking 'poor communities from the depredations of the capitalist labour market' (SACP, 2014: 28).

The interventions proposed in this chapter are aimed at contributing to the narrowing of the economic developmental chasm between the two economic streams. They straddle areas of policy, institutions, resource allocation and implementation mechanisms and they would need to be scaled up in a manner that ensures a catalytic and mass impact.

ATTRIBUTES OF DUAL ECONOMIC DEVELOPMENT AT THE INTERSECTION OF EMPLOYMENT, EDUCATION AND SKILLS

There are many attributes that characterise the dual development tracks. In this section, attention is given to labour-market dynamics.

Employment trends

As reflected in Table 11.1, the unemployment rate is highest amongst Africans. The hierarchy of exclusion is reflected both in the labour absorption ratio and the rate of labour force participation. While the unemployment rate declined significantly in the 2000s during the years of high growth, it has effectively been stagnant during the last decade. The COVID-19 pandemic has worsened the situation amongst all groups, with the devastation felt most keenly amongst Coloureds and Africans.

The marginalisation also manifests in terms of gender, with rates for those not in employment, education or training (NEETs) in the 15–34 age group standing at 39.9 per cent and 42.5 per cent amongst men in Quarter 3 of 2020 and 2021 respectively and 46.1 per cent and 49.6 per cent amongst women in Quarter 3 of 2020 and 2021 respectively (StatsSA, 2021a).

Education and skills

Prospects of employment and wage levels improve 'dramatically with earning a Matric Certificate or more' (Van der Berg et al., 2011: 8), and educational attainment has been improving since 1994. This, however, is not equitably reflected across the population groups, with Africans and Coloureds still having a high proportion of individuals with less than a Matric as a proportion of the expanded labour force (StatsSA, 2017), while also largely experiencing poor-quality education.

Table 11.1: Employment rates (narrow definition) by population group

Population 15–64 yrs rates (%)	Q3 2002 %	Q3 2007 %	Q3 2014 %	Q3 2019 %	Q3 2021 %
South Africa					
Unemployment rate	26.6	21.0	25.4	29.1	34.9
Employed/ population ratio (absorption)			42.6	42.4	35.9
Labour force participation rate			57.1	59.9	55.2
African					
Unemployment rate	31.0	23.9	28.6	32.8	38.6
Employed/ population ratio (absorption)			39.2	39.4	33.1
Labour force participation rate			54.9	58.6	54.0
Coloured					
Unemployment rate	24.9	23.4	24.1	23.5	30.3
Employed/ population ratio (absorption)			49.8	49.3	39.3
Labour force participation rate			65.5	64.5	56.4
Indian/Asian					
Unemployment rate	17.8	9.5	11.5	13.3	22.0
Employed/ population ratio (absorption)			52.5	52.8	43.2
Labour force participation rate			59.3	60.9	55.4
White					
Unemployment rate	6.0	4.1	7.3	7.4	9.2
Employed/ population ratio (absorption)			63.6	63.1	60.8
Labour force participation rate			68.5	68.2	67.0

Source: StatsSA, 2002, 2007, 2014, 2019b, 2021a

The number of enrolled students at tertiary education institutions has almost doubled since 1994. From less than half of the total, African students constituted about 71 per cent in 2018 (SAIRR, 2018). However, the proportion of South Africa's population with tertiary qualifications is low, at 6 per cent for university degrees, compared with other middle-income countries, such as Brazil (15.7 per cent) and Mexico (15.3 per cent) (Nkosi, 2021).

Sectoral skills intensity

How has the post-1994 skills intensity in different economic sectors evolved? As shown in Figure 11.1, between 1995 and 2015, 'every major sector' demonstrated growing skills intensity and, except for agriculture, 'the share of semi-skilled work decreased' (World Bank, 2018: 81). Moreover, it is only retail, utilities, and community, social and personal services (CSP) that have created employment at a rate higher than their rate of growth.

Figure 11.1: Growth of employment shares (%) by sector and skills level, 1995–2015 (left); Composition of employment (%) by sector and skills level, 2015 (right)

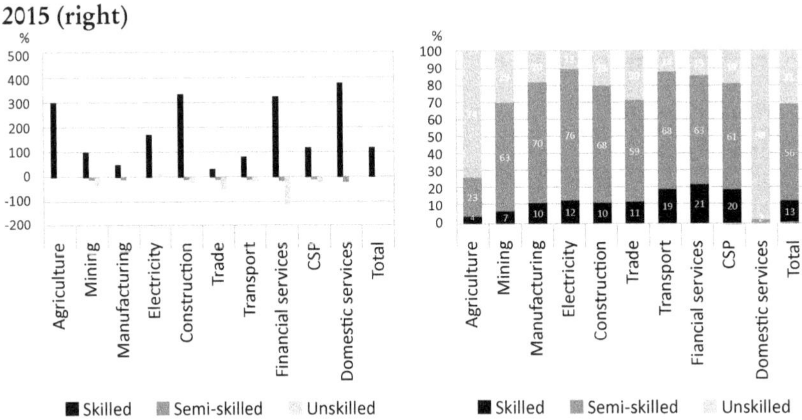

Source: World Bank, 2018: 80

As reflected in Figure 11.2, there are increasing returns as education and skills levels rise, with continuing marginalisation of (especially) the 'missing middle' (World Bank, 2018) and wide variations in incomes. However, because the economy of the metropolis is performing below par, skilled job opportunities are increasingly lagging behind the number of graduates coming out of educational institutions every year.

Figure 11.2: Skills composition of the unemployed and income returns on skills

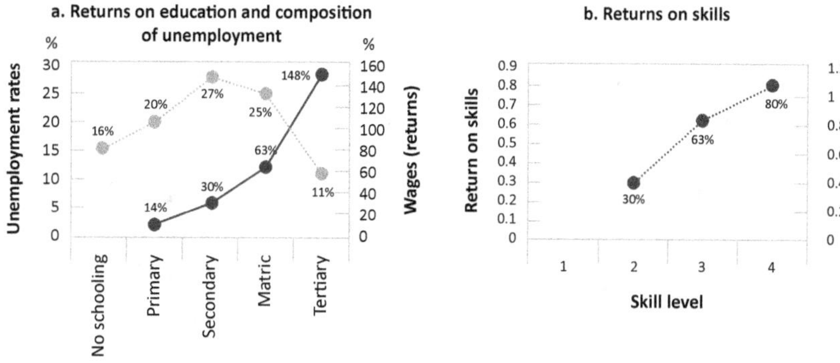

Source: National Income Dynamics Study (NIDS), base = no education for wage regressions. Coefficients from Mincer regression with log wages dependent variables, education, skills, sectors, skills and other repressors included.

Source: NIDS, base = skill level 1 for wage regressions. Coefficients from Mincer regression with log wages dependent variables, education, sectors, skills and other repressors included.

Source: World Bank, 2018: 86

The youth dimension

Figure 11.3 shows that the unemployment rate amongst youth is higher, irrespective of their level of education. Their share of the employed decreased between 1999 and 2019, with the absolute number also decreasing between 2009 and 2019 (Yu and Adams, 2021). The rate of unemployment amongst those aged 25–34 years is more than twice that of those aged 45–54 years (StatsSA, 2019b).

While young people face onerous requirements with regard to professional experience during hiring processes, the National Planning Commission (NPC, 2011: 16) also cites the issue of entry-level wages as an important factor: 'the average starting salary is 60 per cent of the average' in South Africa. By contrast, it is 37 per cent in Organisation for Economic Cooperation and Development (OECD) countries.

ATTRIBUTES OF DUALITY IN EMPLOYMENT EQUITY AND INEQUALITY

Various data point to a gradual improvement in the position of black people at virtually all levels of the labour market in the metropolis. This is accompanied by hysteresis or stubborn persistence, a situation

Figure 11.3: Unemployment rate by education level and age group, 2019

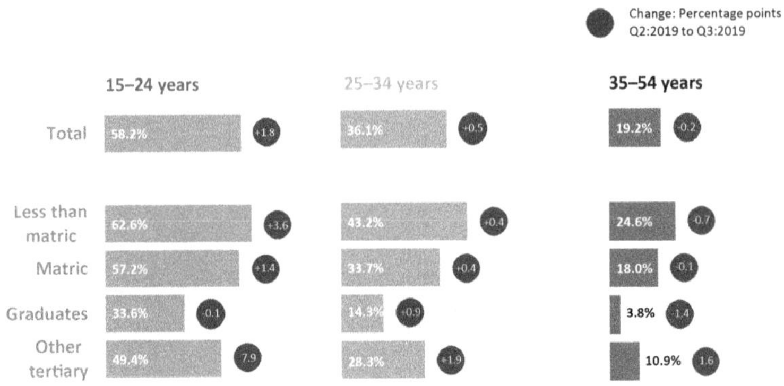

Source: StatsSA, 2019b

in which 'the underlying "equilibrium unemployment rate" may itself be high and possibly increasing' (Yu and Adams, 2021: 1). This is the nub of the contradictory development of the post-apartheid political economy, where a duality also manifests in relation to inequality.

Employment equity and income inequality

Since 1994, more and more black people have been breaking the apartheid 'glass ceiling' and moving into skilled and other senior occupations, though at a slower pace at the top management level. Progress is particularly pronounced in the public sector. Since 2010, blacks have been the majority in both professional and skilled technical occupational categories.

In terms of 'class sizes', the National Income Dynamics Study (NIDS) shows a decrease in chronic poverty from the first report in 2009 until the advent of COVID-19 and a marginal increase in the middle strata and elite (Gumede, 2021). While the average income per person has improved, the functional distribution shows that South Africa has the highest income inequality in the world (World Bank, 2022). Race continues to play a central role, but inequality within the black community has increased, as the 'coefficient of variation for wages of black South Africans has risen substantially … (from 3.83 to 6.37, a 66 per cent rise)…' (World Bank, 2018: 86).

Table 11.2: Trends in employment equity at various occupational levels

Occupational level	2006		2010		2013		2020	
	Black (%)	White (%)	Black (%)	White (%)	Black (%)	White (%)	Black (%)	White (%)
Top management	22.2	74.9	24.1	73.1	33.3	62.7	32.1	64.7
Senior management	26.9	70.6	33.7	64.1	40.1	57.0	44.3	52.5
Professionally qualified	36.5	62.2	50.2	47.7	57.4	40.2	65.5	32.1
Skilled technical	58.4	40.4	70.2	28.5	76.4	22	80.7	17.6

Source: DoL, 2007–2021

Note: The above figures do not include foreign nationals.

Asset inequality

'Wealth inequality is much larger than income inequality' (World Bank, 2018: 52). While there was an improvement in assets amongst Africans between 2009 and 2015, their 'asset scores ... remained the lowest as compare[d] to other population groups, whereas whites had the highest scores' (StatsSA, 2019a: 51).

Black ownership of the Johannesburg Stock Exchange (JSE) market capitalisation is estimated by the National Treasury (2017), using figures from Alternative Prosperity, at 10 per cent in terms of direct ownership and 23 per cent when institutional funds are taken into account. However, much of this is encumbered through debt, and the institutional managers of the pension funds are largely white. Over 150 000 South African workers are share owners through employee share-ownership plans (Esops), and their estimated market value is over R100 billion (Crozier, 2022). Most Esops, however, have not been successful (Hassen, 2020).

As with the income dimension, non-income inequality amongst blacks has increased, with 'within-group' inequality already accounting for some 81.9 per cent of total non-income inequality by 2004 (Bhorat et al., 2006).

DISTILLING THE DEFINING TRENDS AND IDENTIFYING INTERVENTIONS TO UNDERCUT DUALITY

The data cited above starkly illustrate the coexistence of a metropolis and a colony within the integument of one nation state. While there is some integration of segments of African, Coloured and Indian people who are able to take advantage of opportunities at the upper levels of the economy, the broad patterns of exclusion continue to replicate themselves.

The returns to education are clearly evident. However, the economy of the metropolis has difficulty absorbing the middle cohort of semi-skilled workers (with secondary and Matric qualifications). At one extreme, the South African economy mimics attributes of advanced economies. At the other extreme, it exudes high levels of underdevelopment. At the core of this duality is the tendency of the advanced economy to reproduce and regenerate with little regard for those who do not 'belong'. Other chapters in this volume deal with these dynamics in greater depth.

The COVID-19 pandemic has had the effect of slowing down and even reversing some of the progress made in the first 25 years of democracy. As a consequence, the parallel tracks of dual economic development are even diverging. However, the country's regression started well before the pandemic. The irony is that it is precisely in the period after the adoption of the National Development Plan (NDP) in 2012, which outlined 2030 targets for inclusive growth and development, that there was an unfortunate confluence of state degradation, systemic venality and negative per capita gross domestic product (GDP) growth. In Chapter 4 in this volume, Adelzadeh argues that fiscal austerity and tight monetary policy further undermined prospects for economic growth. At the current pace, even if the slow recovery projected by the OECD (2021) does prove somewhat pessimistic, convergence between the dual economic tracks will take scores of years to attain, if at all.

How to deal with the excluded masses, trapped in the colony, is the fundamental question confronting the South African political economy. This is not so much about eliminating duality in the economy altogether; nor is it about 'dragging down' the metropolis in order to lift the colony. Rather, it is a complementary task to facilitate inclusivity: combining the lifting of the colony in terms of developmental outcomes while continuing to improve the metropolis.

The rest of this chapter deals with three interventions, selected for their potential to have a significant and catalytic effect, namely:

- mass absorption of semi-skilled and unskilled workers into industrial activity, with a focus on low-end manufacturing through special economic zones (SEZs);
- land and agrarian reform to position agriculture as a terrain of intense economic activity, productive use of assets and employment; and
- focused support for micro enterprises, especially in the informal sector, tapping energies already extant.

MASS ABSORPTION INTO INDUSTRIAL ACTIVITY – A CASE FOR AN IMPROVED SPECIAL ECONOMIC ZONE PROGRAMME

Two trends are playing out in global manufacturing: first, the persistence of offshoring in the context of integrated value chains; and, second, growing automation and the Fourth Industrial Revolution (4IR), which are linked to some reshoring activity amongst developed economies. Added to this, and associated with the COVID-19 pandemic, are efforts (though still nascent) to shorten supply chains. Neither of these trends is currently dominant and there are many other factors that come into play, including geopolitics.

The analysis in this section proceeds from the perspective that low-end manufacturing, interconnected global value chains and export-led growth have not diminished much in terms of their impact on economic growth and employment, and they will continue to play a significant role.

Hai (2016) refers to a form of historical manufacturing relay race since the Second World War involving Japan immediately after the war, the East Asian Tigers in the 1960s and China in the 1980s. While 9.7 million manufacturing jobs relocated from Japan and later 2.3 million from South Korea as these countries sequentially moved up the manufacturing sophistication ladder from the 1980s into the 1990s, Hai (2016) estimates that 85 million of such jobs are now relocating from China. The manufactures from labour-intensive industries are still in high demand; and – besides countries such as Vietnam and Bangladesh – African countries, including Mauritius, Ethiopia and Rwanda, are taking advantage of this. Can South Africa, in the context of its 'second economy', also benefit?

The African National Congress (ANC) recently pointed to opportunities in low-end manufacturing to absorb low- and semi-skilled workers in a massively expanded SEZ and industrial parks programme (ANC Economic Transformation Committee, 2020). The precise number of jobs that can be created depends on the scale and effectiveness of execution. While the ANC refers to scale, the National Treasury deals with the quality of the programme, questioning whether incentives such as lower tax rates are 'crowding in' the targeted investments and calling for 'a more nuanced understanding of the circumstances under which SEZs are most effective … and whether they are appropriate tools for clustering industrial activity and addressing unequal spatial development'. This would allow for processes 'to improve the design, functioning, and ultimately the impact of SEZs as a key industrial policy tool' (National Treasury, 2019: 49).

In a comprehensive study on South African SEZs, the Centre for Development and Enterprise (CDE) defines such a zone as 'a geographically defined area in which government provides specific services or benefits to firms so that they are able to grow more rapidly' (Altbeker et al., 2021: 2). The government, through the Department of Trade and Industry (DTI),[3] defines such a zone as 'a geographically designated area of a country set aside for specifically targeted economic activities, which are then supported through special arrangements … and support systems to promote industrial development' (DTI, 2012: 8).

SEZs are aimed at, amongst other things, addressing market failures in the rest of the economy, creating low-cost manufacturing opportunities for export, aggregating supply chains and attracting high-level skills. Because such zones demand the commitment of state resources, there naturally needs to be a cost–benefit analysis to make sure that activities attracted would otherwise not have been as commercially viable. The zones should therefore provide clear 'additionality' (Altbeker et al., 2021: 9). Currently, 11 SEZs are operational in South Africa; but, with some R25 billion having been spent on such programmes, 90 per cent of investments and jobs are generated in only three of them – Coega, East London and Dube Trade Port (Altbeker et al., 2021: 7).

South African policymakers have baulked at far-reaching measures to ensure that the zones are indeed special. There has been hesitation, for instance, around a special rate of corporate tax, along with the belief that clustering and subsidised infrastructure are largely sufficient. Consideration also needs to be given to whether activities in such zones should be confined to exports with a provision for duty-free inputs. Furthermore, weaknesses identified by the DTI (2012) still plague the overall approach, such as ad hoc funding arrangements, poor investment promotion targeting, weak coordination with stakeholders, inadequate governance arrangements and, to some extent, faulty design.

A critical deficit, however, is South Africa's approach to integrating the country into global value chains (Olasehinde-Williams and Oshodi, 2021) – that is, adding value across one or more borders before consumption. From comparative studies of 30 developing and industrialised countries, South Africa and Cambodia were the only ones that, between 1995 and 2009, did not improve their integration into global value chains. According to Olasehinde-Williams and Oshodi (2021: 2), 'South Africa has not fully exploited the advantage of global value chains to improve her export performance, although it has the potential of leveraging on its comparative advantages in mining, light manufacturing, agro-business, tourism and textile'. Rather than clamouring only for the production of finished products, the country can use SEZs to also produce 'less sophisticated goods or processes within the global value chain' (Olasehinde-Williams and Oshodi, 2021: 2). As elaborated in Chapter 12 of this volume, the African Continental Free Trade Area (AfCFTA) presents major opportunities for regional integration and division of labour.

In its SEZ programme, South Africa has sought to meet another critical element of successful SEZs, which is location. There have been conscious attempts to escape the path dependency informed by the geography of mineral endowments and to locate the SEZs in port cities and inland trade routes and development corridors. However, a mechanical, spatial levelling up as the objective of the SEZ programme – with scattered locations that have little potential for value addition – should be avoided.

While SEZs and industrial parks can help to reduce spatial inequality, the starting point should be comparative advantage and value addition in the specific locations. The experience of China does demonstrate, though, that SEZs can be used to start new cities and upgrade an underdeveloped area (Ng, 2011). In this context, consideration needs to be given to allocating SEZ status to some of the 'smart cities' that the South African government has proposed (Ramaphosa, 2019). Furthermore, rust belts, which already have some infrastructure, could be revived through SEZs and industrial parks – if indeed they have economic potential.

While this section deals narrowly with manufacturing, it should be recognised that business process outsourcing (or global business services) also has potential to absorb unskilled and semi-skilled workers, especially young people (Mubajwa and Surianarain, 2022).

In as unequal a society as South Africa, and given the rights enjoyed by workers in the metropolis, including a living wage, it is natural that concerns should arise on two fronts, namely whether SEZs would undermine existing worker rights across the economy and would also lead to a dual labour market. Certain principles need to be underlined in this regard.

First, given the extant parallel development paths described above, with profound levels of marginalisation of unskilled and low-skilled workers, using SEZs is a time-bound intervention for the inclusion of the excluded. The aim, over time, should be to climb up the manufacturing sophistication ladder with corresponding improvements in working and living conditions. Second, no one in the country should earn below the minimum wage, and emphasis in the zones should be on youth at the entry level. This can be combined with the employment tax incentive, where employers and the government share the cost of employment by subsidising wages.

Third, if wages are set too low, the reservation wage[4] phenomenon is bound to kick in, thus limiting the number of takers and resulting in unstable labour relations. Fourth, Onaran and Stockhammer (2005: 65) argue that reducing the wage share in most settings does not necessarily stimulate 'accumulation, growth, and employment'. Fifth, the aim and the praxis should preclude the possibility of undermining the status of those already occupying decent jobs. The current labour relations regime, which is constitutionally and otherwise legally enshrined, should be maintained and even improved.

In addition, and critically, as the NDP correctly observes, other interventions should be used to ensure a decent standard of living for all. This includes reducing 'the cost of living in relation to food, transport, education, health and other basic services' (NPC, 2012: 114) as well as social infrastructure and other elements of the social wage. This is not merely a social imperative; it would also help to create a virtuous circle on the demand side both in terms of infrastructure supplies and consumer demand.

OPPORTUNITIES IN AGRICULTURE

This section assesses the role that agriculture can play in relation to marginalised segments of society. Extensive reference is made to proposals in the NDP (NPC, 2012), which posit the creation of 1 million jobs between 2012 and 2030. These proposals were based on the premise that increasing agricultural activity within the 'current structure of farming by merely expanding large-scale commercial farming' would limit the sector's job-creation potential (NPC, 2012: 225). Other issues pertaining to agriculture are dealt with in Chapter 8 in this volume.

In its 2019 General Household Survey, StatsSA reports that 15.3 per cent or 2.6 million of South African households are involved in agriculture. Of these, 'more than three-quarters ... were involved in an attempt to secure an additional source of food' (StatsSA, 2020: 54). Some 65 per cent of these households operate on less than half a hectare of land (NPC, 2012).

Three dimensions of reality have influenced the current structure of agriculture in South Africa. The first pertains to objective circumstances in respect of soil, with South Africa falling into the so-called 'third major soil region', with only 13 per cent of land being arable and 3 per cent having high potential. Large parts of the country are characterised by 'shallow sandy soils' not conducive to agriculture (NPC, 2011: 10). The second dimension is a consequence of historical policy, with subsistence and small-scale agriculture, particularly amongst black people, largely destroyed under colonialism. The third dimension is the evolving structure of the broader economy: the contribution of agriculture has been declining and was estimated 'at just under three per cent of national GDP' in Q2 of 2021 (USB IFR, 2022: 9). Between 2001 and 2016, the sector grew by 1.9 per cent, with employment contracting by 2 per cent (World Bank, 2018).

It is remarkable that those involved in subsistence agriculture evince better levels of food security, underlining the importance of such activity, not only for employment but also for general wellbeing (World Bank, 2018). The approach in the NDP proceeds from the perspective that agriculture can become a more vibrant contributor to employment and self-employment, beyond cyclical and weather-based dynamics. In this regard, it projects the potential to create jobs amongst various categories of farmers, from the smallest to large, labour-intensive and labour-extensive sub-sectors (Table 11.3).

Each of the target groups identified in Table 11.3 requires specific interventions to ensure that its capabilities and employment potential are enhanced. This can be attained through, amongst other things (NPC, 2012: 219):

- identifying regions and sectors with high potential for faster growth and job creation;
- expanding irrigated agriculture from 1.5 million to 2 million hectares through efficient use of water resources and new projects;
- ensuring access to product value chains by also linking small-scale farmers in communal areas to domestic and international markets;
- providing openings for underused land in communal areas for commercial production;
- promoting opportunities for upstream and downstream industrial

Table 11.3: The employment potential of South African agriculture

Target group	Primary jobs created	Secondary jobs created	Assumption
Subsistence farmers with <0.5 hectares	83 000	41 500	The livelihoods of one in 10 of the farmers in this category are improved.
Small-scale farmers with between 0.5 and 5 hectares of land	165 000	82 500	The livelihoods of half the farmers in this category are improved.
Small-scale farmers with >5 hectares of land	75 000	37 500	These farmers employ themselves and two others.
Better use of redistributed land	70 000	35 000	Redistribution beneficiaries employ themselves and two others; one in 10 restitution beneficiaries becomes self-sufficient.
Labour-intensive winners	200 000	100 000	Critically, this requires investment in irrigation, support to smallholder farmers and their ability to grow their businesses.
Labour-extensive field crops	10 000	5 000	This reflects a 'high-road' or optimistic scenario and assumes that the current decline in employment in commercial farming is halted.
Labour-extensive livestock	40 000	25 000	This reflects a 'high-road' or optimistic scenario and assumes that the current decline in employment in commercial farming is halted.
Total	**643 000**	**326 500**	**969 500**

Source: NPC, 2012: 197–198

Note: The employment multiplier between agriculture and its upstream and downstream industries has been taken at a conservative estimate of 0.5 for small-scale farmers.

activities; and

- utilising extensive opportunities in the 'food-away-from-home' platforms, including hospitals, schools, correctional facilities and restaurants, to give a leg up to small-scale farmers.

Systematic interventions such as these require effective support for those with potential – most importantly, to ensure the presence and effectiveness of agricultural extension officers across the length and breadth of the country. It is open to debate as to whether the intentions of the Department of Agriculture, Land Reform and Rural Development (DALRRD) announced in 2021 'to reduce the ratio of extension officers to farmers from 1:850 to 1:250' are adequate (RSA, 2021: 2). While it is commendable that close to R1 billion has been allocated from 2021 to 2024 for the recruitment of about 10 000 extension officers (Erasmus, 2021), the deficit over the years has been so massive that this should rather be considered the beginning of the process.

These interventions should also be informed by an appreciation of the labour intensity and growth potential of various agricultural activities, as illustrated in Figure 11.4. All the categories, located in the spectrum from large-scale commercial activity to small-scale, labour-intensive sub-sectors, deserve appropriate and proportionate support to boost job creation and improve livelihoods. Growing domestic demand and export opportunities in the various markets need to be fully explored through economic diplomacy, efficient transport infrastructure, producer dexterity and other factors.

Large-scale, labour-intensive opportunities exist in areas identified in quadrant 2 of Figure 11.4, including citrus, subtropical fruit and vegetables. For instance, according to the DALRRD, between 2008/09 and 2018/19, avocado production almost doubled and its gross value more than tripled (DALRRD, 2020b). Over and above the labour-intensive sectors, large industries that are less labour-intensive have value chain linkages with immense potential.

The Agriculture and Agro-processing Master Plan, a draft of which was presented in 2020 – some eight years after the adoption of the NDP – seems to have the potential to bring the NDP ideas to life (DALRRD,

Figure 11.4: Agricultural growth and employment potential

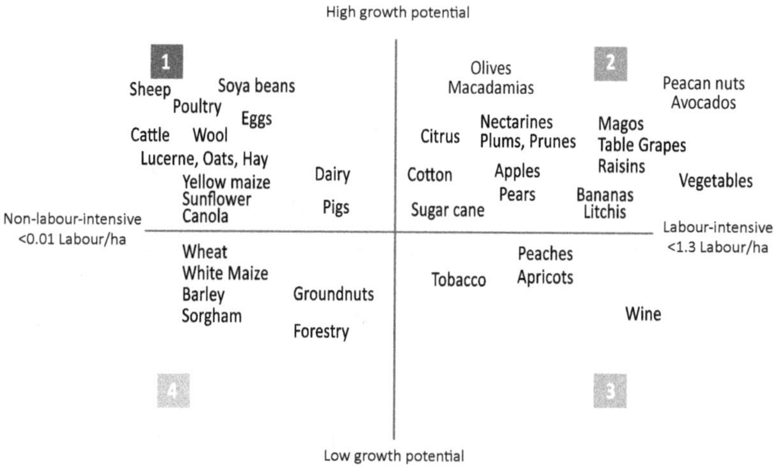

Source: NPC, 2012: 201

2020a). The plan acknowledges the 'dualistic agricultural economy'; it adopts a detailed, district-based, commodity value chain approach; it promotes the implementation of infrastructure investments in priority districts and in relation to priority commodities; and it underlines the importance of comprehensive producer development, which includes millions of farming/rural households. The implementation of the Master Plan will need to be monitored against the timeframes identified.

The University of Stellenbosch Business School Institute for Futures Research (USB IFR, 2022) argues that macro planning for agriculture also needs to consider the possible long-term evolution of the sector at the upper end of the development spectrum. It projects even further adoption of technology and new types of jobs that will attract skilled youth, entailing soft skills such as communication and customer services; systems thinking skills, which include project management and design thinking; 'natural sciences (soil, biology, plant, animal)'; technology integration, which includes engineering and analysis; and data management in relation to storage, analysis, collection and security (USB IFR, 2022: 60).

The issue of ownership is fundamental to land reform.

Redistribution and restitution – with or without compensation – are broadly acknowledged as part of the reform process. The NDP proposes a more systematic and comprehensive approach through envisaged district land committees which would be 'responsible for identifying 20 per cent of the commercial agricultural land in the district and giving commercial farmers the option of assisting its transfer to black farmers' (NPC, 2012: 227). This entails a kind of compact with contributions and sacrifices by all partners (commercial farmers, government and the beneficiaries), and it resonates with the government's recently initiated District Development Model.[5] In the communal areas, there will be a need for tenure security combined with a form of fungibility (the ability to exchange or use as security) which, at the same time, does not result in land alienation in respect of the poor. In addition, the exercising of power by traditional leaders needs to be decisively addressed.

Using agriculture to 'lift the colony' also implies taking conscious steps to address three additional issues. First, the magnitude of the minimum wage needs to ensure an improved standard of living for workers. Farmworkers' minimum wage in 2021 finally reached parity with the national determination (Nxesi, 2022). Yet the improvements should be consistent over time, while objectively balancing this against the imperative of job preservation. Second, land redistribution and tenure security should place ownership opportunities for workers high on the agenda, through such mechanisms as employee share-ownership schemes and appropriately regulated systems of labour tenancy and sharecropping. Third, as argued by South African Reserve Bank (SARB) Deputy Governor, Kuben Naidoo (Erasmus, 2022), there also has to be financial support, with generous terms, for emergent farmers in the former Bantustans, as was the case for white farmers in the six decades from the 1920s. Combined with transport infrastructure, water and storage, this would allow the emergence of thousands of farmers, increased output and expanded job creation. The Land Bank would play a critical role in providing such financial support, but it needs to be subsidised or attract long-term, low-interest-rate deposits.

SUPPORTING MICRO ENTERPRISES WITH A FOCUS ON THE INFORMAL ECONOMY

A significant section of those trapped in the 'colonial' economic mode run or work for micro enterprises, especially in the informal economy. As indicated earlier, the evolution of the structure of the South African economy resulted in a comparatively low proportion of small enterprises. These historical circumstances have proved difficult to reverse, despite many post-1994 efforts on the part of government (Altman, 2007).

According to the Global Entrepreneurship Index, South Africa is behind other developing countries in terms of small business start-ups (The Global Entrepreneurship and Development Institute, 2018: 45). Maduku and Kaseeram (2021: 664) cite the 2013 Global Entrepreneurship Monitor (GEM) as noting that 'the small business failure rate is very alarming in South Africa'. With regard to start-ups, 'South Africa ranks 41st out of 43 countries in the prevalence rate for established businesses'. Also critical to note in their study is the gender dimension: for instance, out of 390 small, medium and micro enterprises (SMMEs) surveyed, 48.46 per cent were owned by women (Maduku and Kaseeram, 2021). Total early-stage entrepreneurial activity amongst the youth (18–34 years) is also lower than the regional (African) average (Yiannakaris, 2021), although there are encouraging initiatives in the area of information and communication technologies (ICTs).

Subjective factors responsible for this include perceptions about whether there are good opportunities and doubts about one's own capabilities and 'fear of failure' (Herrington and Kew, 2018: 7). Many enter the terrain not merely out of necessity but because they identify an opportunity. Moreover, 52.5 per cent of early-stage entrepreneurs are in the wholesale/retail sector (Herrington and Kew, 2018).

What about the informal economy in particular? The definition of the informal economy has evolved over the years, from a rights-based approach in terms of working conditions to a characterisation of 'production units' (Bernabe, 2002: 33) with fewer than five paid employees, on average. A refined International Labour Organization (ILO) definition identifies the informal economy as comprising very small, unregistered economic units of the self-employed, employers and employees, and co-operatives in non-agricultural activities (ILO, 2015).

There are differing conceptual approaches to the informal sector: the 'dualistic school' (which sees the sector as separate from the rest of the economy and believes it will ultimately disappear), the 'legalistic school' (which emphasises the costs associated with formalisation), and the 'structuralist school' (which views the sector as part of a 'continuum within the market' which is linked to the formal sector) (Altman, 2007: 5). The 'structuralist school' seems the most apt, as 'the underclass shares resources and households and families combine both formal and informal sources of income in their livelihoods' (Callebert, 2014: 125).

The sectors in which informal enterprises operate include housebuilding and maintenance, street food and non-food vending, car repairs, hair care, cigarette sales, refuse collection, clothes, and wholesale and retail trade. Some 73 per cent of informal sector jobs are at the 'survivalist' end of the spectrum while the rest are in 'growth-oriented' businesses (Fourie, 2018a).

As shown in Table 11.4, the informal sector makes a significant contribution to economic activity and accounts for around 20 per cent of total employment. Its share of total employment had been rising before the advent of COVID-19. The experience during the pandemic – which saw a reduction of some 300 000 jobs in the informal sector – as well as earlier during the global financial crisis some 15 years ago, tends to dispel the belief that the informal sector serves as a refuge during economic crises (Fourie, 2018a).

Table 11.4: Informal sector proportion of total employment

Date	Percentage (%)	Numbers
2009	17.65	2.1m
2019	21.13	3.0m
2021	18.9	2.7m

Source: StatsSA, 2009, 2019b, 2021a

Two-thirds of the self-employed in South Africa are found in the informal sector, while women in the sector are more likely to be self-employed (80 per cent) than men (55 per cent) (Essop and Yu, 2008). Characterising the informal sector as incorporating both unskilled operators and professionals 'who are starting out on their own', Louise Silver of the South African Informal Traders' Alliance (Saita) argues that they deserve to be in partnership with large companies, beyond procurement. According to Silver, 'They are hard-working self-starters who, with the appropriate training, skills development and business environment, can play a larger, more valuable role in the economy' (Moodley, 2022).

Given all these characteristics, it would have been expected of government to pay particular attention to this sector. But the entrepreneurial policy ecosystem does not allow the sector to flourish. Fourie (2018a) observes that while the Accelerated and Shared Growth Initiative for South Africa (AsgiSA) of the mid-2000s did identify this sector as an area for focused intervention, subsequent plans such as the 2010 New Growth Path (NGP) made hardly any reference to it. The informal sector is also given poor treatment in the economic chapter of the NDP except in the scenarios where it is expected to create some 20 per cent of new jobs by 2030.

The formulation of the 2014 National Informal Business Upliftment Strategy (NIBUS) (DTI, 2014) was the first time since AsgiSA that the government had systematically identified the constraints facing the informal sector and the required interventions. However, there has not been much progress across the spheres of government in dealing with the regulatory burdens, including onerous municipal by-laws, and programmes are in some instances clouded by anti-immigrant sentiments.

A multiplicity of agencies has been set up over the years to address challenges facing SMMEs, such as the Small Enterprise Development Agency (SEDA) for non-financial support and the Small Enterprise Finance Agency (SEFA) for financial support. This culminated in the formation of a dedicated Ministry and Department of Small Business Development (DSBD) in 2014. However, there is a low level of awareness of the state's offerings amongst targeted groups. Some 73.8 per cent of SMMEs are not aware of the DSBD and the number is even worse amongst informal operators (Botha et al., 2020). There is also limited awareness of SEDA and the National Youth Development Agency (NYDA), the latter designed to focus on young people.

Of equal concern is that only a small proportion of those who are aware of the above-mentioned agencies actually use them – only 16.6 per cent in the case of SEDA and 15 per cent in the case of the NYDA (Herrington and Kew, 2018). It is debatable whether government's intended incorporation of SEFA and another agency, the Co-operative Banks Development Agency (GCIS, 2022), into SEDA will improve matters.

Critical interventions to improve the SMME ecosystem, particularly in relation to the informal sector, are briefly outlined below (not necessarily in order of importance).

- *Refine strategies and enhance focus on informal business:* As argued by Fourie (2018a), '[I]f an employment-creation policy does not explicitly tackle the problems and disenabling environment faced by those outside the realms of the formal economy, it is unlikely to make the required impact on unemployment, poverty and inequality'. The approach should not conflate all small businesses under one category; rather it should seek out and assist those already involved or seriously interested in the informal sector (who demonstrate remarkable initiative and resilience). Given the low levels of awareness and take-up of state support, there is quite clearly a need for intensive, mass communication. How the support institutions operate and the challenges of maladministration and inefficiency need to be attended to.
- *Ensure a common approach to the informal sector across all spheres of government and institutionalise a comprehensive, nationwide regulatory impact assessment of all statutes:* The starting point in this regard should be to abandon the pretentious 'first economy' mindset in the approach to the informal economy, in terms of 'trade licensing procedures and charging of municipal rates' (TIPS, 2016: 25). In the context of the COVID-19 pandemic, there was a waiver of permit requirements until December 2022, recognising that permits and registration should not be used as blunt instruments.

- *Undertake a multifaceted and transdisciplinary education and skills development campaign*: The first level involves general education as this has proven to improve the performance of informal-sector operators. The second relates to artisanship, which creates many opportunities for small-scale entrepreneurship. The third focuses on economic know-how and appreciation of business fundamentals – which include planning and forecasting (Maduku and Kaseeram, 2021), creative advertising, as well as such financial practices as 'institutional differentiation between the household and the emerging business enterprise' (Fourie, 2018b).
- *Improve the systems and institutions that offer financial assistance:* According to Maduku and Kaseeram (2021), most small businesses rely on entrepreneurs' own savings (43.08 per cent) and assistance from family members (39.23 per cent). As indicated earlier, state institutions do not fare well in this regard, but the support plan of the DSBD and the COVID-19 lockdown support measures[6] could go a long way towards correcting this weakness. Meanwhile, the requirements for 'registration', 'licensing', 'recording' and 'mainstreaming' complicate matters – though the conceptual differentiation does introduce an interesting hierarchy (discussed below). The establishment of a specialised bank to support micro enterprises and informal businesses (along the lines of the Grameen Bank)[7] needs to be seriously considered.
- *Improve the infrastructure for and assets of informal businesses:* The majority of those in the informal sector cannot afford assets and so they hire some of their tools of trade and use street spaces, homes or backyards for their operations (Maduku and Kaseeram, 2021). The problem of poor infrastructure (operational spaces, electricity and ablution facilities) is widespread. These challenges need to be tackled with both the informal businesses and their patrons in mind – without detracting from health protocols and other responsibilities of local government. The approach should be more facilitative than punitive.
- *Address the challenges of crime and community safety in a systematic manner:* Many of the areas in which informal businesses operate, including townships, informal settlements and city centres,

experience high rates of crime (SAPS, 2021). Added to these are all manner of protection rackets as well as police harassment (Hunter, 2018). This has a negative impact on the businesses and their patrons alike, though there are differing views on the degree to which these factors hinder the initiation and survival of the enterprises. Altman (2007) and Grabrucker and Grimm (2017) place different amounts of emphasis on the impact of crime on informal operators. Yet there is general agreement that crime needs to be addressed both as a community and a business imperative.

Overall, government needs to abandon the 'dualistic' and 'legalistic' mindsets that seem to inform the orientation of policy relating to the informal sector. Furthermore, the policies and programmes should be directed at the sector as a whole as well as at specific industries (Fourie, 2018a).

The notions of 'recording', 'licensing', 'mainstreaming', 'registration' and 'formalisation' need to be fully elucidated. Contained within this hierarchy is a fundamental conceptual issue that requires serious reflection. The 'structuralist' approach – that the informal sector is part of a continuum in the market, from 'pure' informality all the way to formality – is best suited for effective facilitation. A requirement for some form of record of the operators is understandable, if only to ensure that they can be provided with the necessary support and observe health and other necessary obligations. Depending on the industry in which they operate and the size of the enterprise, licensing may be a requirement, especially as the operator moves up the social ladder. However, while the growth and success of informal enterprises should be an objective of policy, it would be folly to expect all the informal enterprises to become part of the mainstream, to be registered with the relevant agencies (in this case, the Companies and Intellectual Property Commission (CIPC) and the South African Revenue Service (SARS)) and to disappear as they become formalised. Given the vagaries of the marketplace, there will be both upward and downward mobility.

The matter of the nationality of informal operators is not dealt with in this chapter, partly because it is of little relevance to the conceptual issues and also because the applicable statutes pertaining to (legal and illegal) migrants are found in a different category of regulation, and this requires its own special treatment.

CONCLUSION

The evolution of the structure of the South African economy after the attainment of democracy has entailed both the integration of large sections of the black community into the advanced economy and the reproduction of mass exclusion. Without deliberate interventions that are both bold in scale and sharp in focus, this trend will continue. An approach that takes into account the actual profile of South Africa's unemployed – to ensure mass absorption into industrial activity, expand opportunities in agriculture and systematically support informal enterprises – can progressively improve economic inclusion.

The economy of the metropolis is going to continue chugging along (hopefully, with improvements as proposed in other chapters in this volume), and it would be disingenuous to put the brakes on the development of the productive forces that it commands. The aim should be to attain a decent quality of life for all, both as participants in economic activity and as beneficiaries of the social wage and an affordable cost of living. This requires a developmental state that gives leadership to economic development, working in a social compact with all social partners.[8]

To exercise such leadership, the state will need to systematically effect the necessary changes in policy, institutions, resource allocation and implementation mechanisms that each of the interventions proposed in this chapter requires. These interventions will need to be scaled up in a manner that ensures a catalytic and mass impact. The convergence of developmental outcomes between the metropolis and the colony and thus the gradual elimination of systemic duality in South Africa's political economy should be the strategic objective.

REFERENCES

African National Congress (ANC) Economic Transformation Committee. 2020. 'Reconstruction, growth and transformation: Building a new, inclusive economy', https://cisp.cachefly.net/assets/articles/attachments/82688_etc_document_final_8_july_2020.pdf, accessed 15 February 2022.

Altbeker, A., Visser, R. and Bulterman, L. 2021. 'What if South Africa had a special economic zone that was actually special?' Centre for Development and Enterprise, https://www.africaportal.org/documents/21258/What-if-South-Africa-had-a-special-economic-zone-that-was-actually-special-1.pdf, accessed 14 February.

Altman, M. 2007. 'What are the policy implications of the informal sector becoming the informal economy?' Concept paper prepared for IZA/WB Conference on Employment and Development. Bonn, Germany: HSRC.

Bernabe, S. 2002. 'Informal employment in countries in transition: A conceptual framework'. LSE STICERD Research Paper No. CASE056, https://papers.ssrn.com/sol3/papers.cfm?abstract_id=1158947, accessed 5 April 2022.

Bhorat, H., Naidoo, P. and Van der Westhuizen, C. 2006. 'Shifts in non-income welfare in South Africa: 1993–2004'. *Development Policy Research Unit* website: http://www.tips.org.za/files/forum/2006/papers/Shifts_in_Non-Income_Welfare-vanderWesthuizen.pdf, accessed 15 February 2022.

Botha, A., Smulders, S., Combrick, H. and Meiring, J. 2020. 'Challenges, barriers and policy development for South African SMMEs – does size matter?' *Development Southern Africa*, 38 (2), 153–174.

Callebert, R. 2014. 'Transcending dual economies: Reflections on popular economies in South Africa'. *Africa Journal*, 84, 119–134.

Crozier, C. 26 January 2022. 'Employee share schemes and public BEE shares create wealth'. *BusinessDay*, https://www.businesslive.co.za/bd/opinion/2022-01-26-carol-crozier-employee-share-schemes-and-public-bee-shares-create-wealth/, accessed 28 January 2022.

Department of Agriculture, Land Reform and Rural Development (DALRRD). 14 May 2020a. 'Agriculture and agro-processing master plan: Presentation to NEDLAC', https://static.pmg.org.za/220607Agriculture_and_Agro-processing_Master_Plan_Signed.pdf, accessed 20 December 2021.

Department of Agriculture, Land Reform and Rural Development (DALRRD). 2020b. 'A profile of the South African avocado market value chain', http://www.dalrrd.gov.za/phocadownloadpap/Agricultural_Marketing_Commodity_Profiles/Avocado%20market%20value%20chain%20profile%202012.pdf, accessed 16 February 2022.

Department of Labour (DoL). 2007–2021. 'Commission for employment equity annual reports', https://www.google.com/search?q=commission+for+employment+equity+report, accessed 28 January 2022.

Department of Trade and Industry (DTI). 2012. 'Policy on the development of Special Economic Zones (SEZ) in South Africa (2012)', http://www.thedtic.gov.za/wp-content/uploads/Policy_SEZ.pdf, accessed 28 February 2022.

Department of Trade and Industry (DTI). 2014. 'Draft National Informal Business Upliftment Strategy (NIBUS)', https://www.gov.za/minister-rob-davies-unveil-national-upliftment-strategy-informal-traders, accessed 28 February 2022.

Erasmus, D. 24 February 2021. 'Agri department wants to recruit 10 000 extension officers'. *Farmers Weekly*, https://www.farmersweekly.co.za/agri-news/south-africa/agri-department-wants-to-recruit-10-000-extension-officers/, accessed 4 March 2022.

Erasmus, D. 19 April 2022. 'Land Bank needs overhaul to help black farmers, says Kuben Naidoo'. *BusinessDay*, https://www.businesslive.co.za/bd/national/2022-04-19-land-bank-needs-overhaul-to-help-black-farmers-says-kuben-naidoo/, accessed 19 April 2022.

Essop, H. and Yu, D. 2008. 'The South African informal sector (1997–2006)'. Stellenbosch Economic Working Papers 03/08, https://resep.sun.ac.za/wp-content/uploads/2017/10/wp-03-2008.pdf, accessed 4 March 2022.

Fourie, F. 2018a. 'Democracy, governance, service delivery and society', in Fourie, F. (ed.) *The South African Informal Sector: Creating jobs, reducing poverty.* Pretoria: HSRC Press.

Fourie, F. 6 August 2018b. 'Creating jobs, reducing poverty III: Barriers to entry and growth in the informal sector – and business cycle vulnerabilities. Edited extracts from REDI3X3 book on informal sector'. *Econ3x3*, https://www.econ3x3.org/article/creating-jobs-reducing-poverty-iii-barriers-entry-and-growth-informal-sector-%E2%80%93-and-business, accessed 18 December 2021.

Government Communication and Information System (GCIS). 2022. 'Statement on the Cabinet meeting of 6 April 2022', https://www.gov.za/speeches/statement-cabinet-meeting-6-april-2022-6-apr-2022-0000, accessed 11 April 2022.

Grabrucker, K. and Grimm, M. 2017. 'Does crime deter South Africans from self-employment?' *Journal of Comparative Economics*, 46 (2), 413–435.

Gumede, V. 2021. 'Revisiting poverty, human development and inequality in democratic South Africa'. *Indian Journal of Human Development*, 15 (2), 183–199. DOI: 10.1177/09737030211032961

Hai, H. 2016. *'Would Africa become the next Manufacturing Floor for the world?* Presentation at China–Africa Think Tanks Forum.

Hassen, E-K. 2020. 'Return-to-workers: Trade union investment companies and ESOPS', in Cawe, A. and Mabasa, K. (eds.) *Beyond Tenderpreneurship: Rethinking black business and economic and economic empowerment.* Johannesburg: Mapungubwe Institute for Strategic Reflection (MISTRA), 278–309.

Herrington, M. and Kew, P. 2018. 'Is there a change in attitude towards the small and medium business sector in South Africa, 2017/18?' *Global Entrepreneurship Monitor,* https://www.gemconsortium.org/file/

open?fileId=50411, accessed 18 March 2022.
Hunter, R. 2018. 'Cities support programme of national treasury'. Township Economies Series No. 1, https://csp.treasury.gov.za/csp/DocumentsProjects/Township%20Economies%20Series%201%20Paper.pdf, accessed 20 February 2021.
International Labour Organization (ILO). 2015. 'Transition from the informal to the formal economy recommendation 2015 (No. 204)', https://www.ilo.org/dyn/normlex/en/f?p=NORMLEXPUB:12100:0::NO::P12100_ILO_CODE:R204, accessed 3 April 2022.
Maduku, H. and Kaseeram, I. 2021. 'Success indicators among black owned informal small micro and medium enterprises (SMMEs) in South Africa'. *Development Southern Africa*, 38 (4), 664–665.
Masondo, D. 2007. 'Capitalism and racist forms of political domination'. *Africanus*, 37 (2), 66–80.
Mbeki, T. 11 November 2003. 'Address by President Thabo Mbeki to the National Council of Provinces'. *Polity*, https://www.polity.org.za/article/mbeki-address-to-ncop-11112003-2003-11-11, accessed 25 January 2022.
Moodley, N. 29 March 2022. 'Can corporate SA and micro businesses collaborate to tackle unemployment crisis?'. *Daily Maverick*, https://www.dailymaverick.co.za/article/2022-03-29-can-corporate-sa-and-micro-businesses-collaborate-to-tackle-unemployment-crisis/?, accessed 30 March 2022.
Mubajwa, F. and Surianarain, S. 30 March 2022. 'How to unlock youth job opportunities in SA's rapidly shifting economy'. *Daily Maverick*, https://www.dailymaverick.co.za/opinionista/2022-03-30-how-to-unlock-youth-job-opportunities-in-sas-rapidly-shifting-economy/, accessed 31 March 2022.
National Planning Commission (NPC). 2011. 'Diagnostic overview report: Chapter 5 economy', https://www.gov.za/sites/default/files/gcis_document/201409/npcdiagnosticoverview1.pdf, accessed 5 April 2022.
National Planning Commission (NPC). 2012. 'National development plan: Vision for 2030', https://www.gov.za/sites/default/files/gcis_document/201409/devplan2.pdf, accessed 5 April 2022.
National Treasury. 2017. 'Ownership of JSE-listed companies – Research report for National Treasury', http://www.treasury.gov.za/comm_media/press/2017/2017100301%20ownership%20monitor%20-%20sept%202017.pdf, accessed 5 April 2022.
National Treasury. 2019. 'Economic transformation, inclusive growth, and competitiveness: Towards an Economic Strategy for South Africa'. *Economic Policy, National Treasury*, http://www.treasury.gov.za/comm_media/press/2019/towards%20an%20economic%20strategy%20for%20sa.pdf, accessed 5 April 2022.
Ng, M. 2011. 'Strategic planning of China's first special economic zone:

Shenzhen city master plan (2010–2020)'. *Planning Theory & Practice*, 12 (4), 638–642.

Nkosi, B. 11 June 2021. 'Only 6% of South Africans have university degrees, report says'. *Independent Newspapers*, https://www.iol.co.za/the-star/news/only-6-of-south-africans-have-university-degrees-report-says-8717cdd0-e701-474b-96f1-2377038b32df, accessed 16 February 2022.

Nxesi, T. 2022. 'Minister Thulas Nxesi announces 2022 national minimum wage increases', https://www.gov.za/speeches/minister-thulas-nxesi-announces-2022-national-minimum-wage-increases-8-feb-2022-0000, accessed 07 March 2022.

Olasehinde-Williams, G and Oshodi, A. 2021. 'Global value chains and export growth in South Africa: Evidence from dynamic ARDL simulations'. *Transnational Corporations Review*. DOI:10.1080/19186444.2021.195983.

Onaran, O. and Stockhammer, E. 2005. 'Two different export-oriented growth strategies: Accumulation and distribution in Turkey and South Korea'. *Emerging Market Finance and Trade*, 41 (1), 65–89.

Organisation for Economic Cooperation and Development (OECD). 2021. 'Economic outlook', https://www.oecd.org/economic-outlook/may-2021/, accessed 20 December 2021.

Ramaphosa, C. 2019. 'State of the Nation Address 2019', https://www.gov.za/speeches/2SONA2019, accessed 1 March 2022.

Ramaphosa, C. 2022. 'State of the Nation Address 2022', https://www.gov.za/speeches/president-cyril-ramaphosa-2022-state-nation-address-10-feb-2022-0000, accessed 10 March 2022.

Republic of South Africa (RSA). 2021. 'South Africa Yearbook 2021/22'. Government Communication and Information System (GCIS): Pretoria.

South African Communist Party (SACP). 2014. 'Going to the root, towards a radical second phase of the National Democratic Revolution (NDR): SACP discussion document on its context, content, and our strategic tasks'. *African Communist*, 187 (4), 28.

South African Institute of Race Relations (SAIRR). 2018. 'Life in South Africa: Reasons for hope'. Johannesburg: SAIRR.

South African Police Service (SAPS). 2021. 'Police recorded crime statistics – Republic of South Africa first quarter of 2021/2022 financial year (April to June 2021)', https://www.saps.gov.za/services/downloads/april_june_2021_22_quarter1_presentation.pdf, accessed 10 March 2022.

Statistics South Africa (StatsSA). 2002. 'Quarterly Labour Force Survey: Quarter 3, 2002', https://www.statssa.gov.za/publications/P0210/P0210September2002.pdf, accessed 7 May 2023.

Statistics South Africa (StatsSA). 2007. 'Quarterly Labour Force Survey: Quarter 3, 2007', http://www.statssa.gov.za/publications/P0210/P02102007.pdf, accessed 24 February 2022.

Statistics South Africa (StatsSA). 2009. 'Quarterly Labour Force Survey:

Quarter 4, 2009', http://www.statssa.gov.za/publications/P0211/P02114thQuarter2009.pdf, accessed 24 February 2022.

Statistics South Africa (StatsSA). 2014. 'Quarterly Labour Force Survey: Quarter 3, 2014', https://www.statssa.gov.za/?p=3453, accessed 24 February 2022.

Statistics South Africa (StatsSA). 2017. 'Whither a demographic dividend in South Africa: An overton window of political possibilities', http://www.statssa.gov.za/publications/OP001/OP0012017.pdf, accessed 2 March 2022.

Statistics South Africa (StatsSA). 2019a. 'Inequality trends in South Africa: A multidimensional diagnostic of inequality', https://www.statssa.gov.za/?p=12744&gclid=CjwKCAjwy_aUBhACEiwA2IHHQA-dsIHwTgCY7D-28sZihsGui7SP8X5RgRI6TXpdDuM1cY188fyWIhoC-agQAvD_BwE, accessed 18 December 2022.

Statistics South Africa (StatsSA). 2019b. 'Quarterly Labour Force Survey: Quarter 3, 2019', https://www.statssa.gov.za/?p=12695, accessed 18 December 2021.

Statistics South Africa (StatsSA). 2020. 'General Household Survey 2019', https://www.statssa.gov.za/?p=14930&gclid=CjwKCAjwy_aUBhACEiwA2IHHQEdkM3_9U-djF7mh-JOf4O3YaAlTjziiM6sPbIjjh3m453bGbLrVxRoCKP0QAvD_BwE, accessed 12 February 2022.

Statistics South Africa (StatsSA). 2021a. 'Quarterly Labour Force Survey: Quarter 3, 2021', https://www.statssa.gov.za/?p=14957&gclid=CjwKCAjwkYGVBhArEiwA4sZLuE56OE6w79xeEeo6SzSxpzQikyu4-d99fwECj3SpxpY8D1UkIza3hRoC0NYQAvD_BwE, accessed 24 February 2022.

Statistics South Africa (StatsSA). 2021b. 'Vulnerability of youth in South African labour market', http://www.statssa.gov.za/?p=13379, accessed 12 February 2022.

Statistics South Africa (StatsSA). 2022. 'Quarterly Labour Force Survey: Quarter 3, 2002', https://www.statssa.gov.za/publications/P0210/P0210September2002.pdf, accessed 24 February 2022.

The Global Entrepreneurship and Development Institute. 2018. 'The Global Entrepreneurship Index', https://www.researchgate.net/profile/Laszlo-Szerb/publication/322757639_The_Global_Entrepreneurship_Index_2018/links/5c040b02a6fdcc1b8d503a9e/The-Global-Entrepreneurship-Index-2018.pdf, accessed 12 February 2022.

Trade and Industrial Policy Strategies (TIPS). 2016. 'Towards a single definition of small business: TIPS Report for Business Unity South Africa (BUSA)', https://busa.org.za/wp-content/uploads/2018/03/Public-2-Towards-a-Single-Definition-of-Small-Business-12-2016.pdf, accessed 25 April 2022.

University of Stellenbosch Business School Institute for Futures Research (USB IFR). 2022. 'Futures of Agricultural employment in South Africa 2035', https://www.usb.ac.za/usb_news/futures-of-agricultural-employment-in-south-africa-2035/, accessed 9 April 2022.

Van der Berg, S., Burger, C., Burger, R., De Vos, M., Du Rand, G., Gustafsson, M., Moses, E., Shepherd, D., Spaull, N., Taylor, H., Van Boekhuizen, H. and Fintel, D. 2011. 'Low quality education as a poverty trap'. Stellenbosch Economic Working Papers 25/11, https://www.ekon.sun.ac.za/wpapers/2011/wp252011/wp-25-2011.pdf, accessed 9 April 2022.

World Bank. 2018. 'Overcoming poverty and inequality in South Africa: An assessment of drivers, constraints and opportunities', https://documents1.worldbank.org/curated/en/530481521735906534/pdf/Overcoming-Poverty-and-Inequality-in-South-Africa-An-Assessment-of-Drivers-Constraints-and-Opportunities.pdf, accessed 28 April 2022.

World Bank. 2022. 'Inequality in Southern Africa: An Assessment of the Southern African Customs Union', https://www.worldbank.org/en/events/2022/03/09/inequality-in-southern-africa-an-assessment-of-the-southern-african-customs-union, accessed 28 April 2022.

Yiannakaris, E. 2021. 'Youth entrepreneurship: A realistic strategy for alleviating youth unemployment?' in De Lannoy, A., Langa, M. and Brooks, H. (eds.) *Youth in South Africa: Agency (in)visibility and national development.* Johannesburg: Mapungubwe Institute for Strategic Reflection (MISTRA), 157–186.

Yu, D. and Adams, C. 15 September 2021. 'Labour market trends in South Africa between 2009–2019: A lost decade?' *The Conversation*, https://theconversation.com/south-africas-labour-market-trends-from-2009-to-2019-a-lost-decade-167645, accessed 5 April 2022.

NOTES

1 In this chapter, 'African' refers to those designated as 'black Africans' in most official documents and statistical presentations, while 'Indian' is also referred to as 'Indian/Asian' and 'Coloured' is used to denote those classified as such in the pre-democracy racial classification system. Combined, Africans, Indians and Coloureds are referred to as 'black'.

2 The 1923 Native (Urban Areas) Act designated urban blacks as 'temporary sojourners' and were accepted only to the extent that they ministered 'to the wants of the white population'.

3 Currently known as the Department of Trade, Industry and Competition (DTIC).

4 A reservation wage is income below which even unemployed workers are not prepared to take up an available job.

5 The government's District Development Model entails the use of districts as spatial units within which plans by all spheres of government find integrated expression.

6 Directions to assist SMMEs during the COVID-19 lockdown, 7 April 2020; the Department of Small Business Development on uplifting informal fruit

and vegetable traders, 20 November 2020; State of the Nation Address, 10 February 2022.

7 A community development bank and microfinance institution established in Bangladesh, now emulated in over 60 countries.

8 This refers to government, business, labour and other sectors of civil society, some of which are not represented in the National Economic Development and Labour Council (Nedlac).

TWELVE

South Africa: Regional integration and structural transformation

ALAN HIRSCH

INTRODUCTION

South Africa's engagement with the rest of the African continent is critical for the structural transformation of the country and the region. As this chapter argues, there is a virtuous cycle deriving from African economic integration, one that promises still greater welfare outcomes as integration deepens. A leading African trade diplomat argues: 'The AfCFTA [African Continental Free Trade Area] is ... not simply a free trade agreement; it is a vehicle for Africa's economic transformation' (Mene, 2021: 7).

Research shows that South Africa's economic engagement in the region has been one of the factors contributing to higher levels of growth in Africa in recent decades. Arora and Vamvakidis (2005) found a strong, direct relationship between South Africa's engagement with other African countries and their rates of growth, largely attributable to South Africa's investment in the region. Arizala et al. (2019) similarly found significant spillovers between the growth rates of nearby African countries, which were traceable to regional economic relationships. They found that 'long-run growth spillovers in sub-Saharan Africa are of similar magnitude to those in other emerging and developing economies' (2019: 5).

It is also evident that African integration strengthens South Africa's prospects of driving domestic industrialisation and structural transformation: other African countries tend to import a considerably larger proportion of manufactured goods from South Africa than South Africa's other trading partners. As Arndt and Roberts (2018: 298) note, 'Africa, driven principally by SADC [Southern African Development Community], has become the largest destination for diversified manufactured exports from South Africa, surpassing the European Union in 2010.' As manufacturing is a key ingredient of structural transformation (Rodrik, 2014), South Africa's economic exchanges with Africa are critical for its prospects of sustained, transformative growth. Were it not for African markets, there would be far fewer export opportunities for South African manufacturers. Africa also imports high-level services from South Africa, which helps to maintain or strengthen key service providers in the country (Turok and Visagie, 2020). Moreover, deeper African integration potentially offers opportunities to build scale and efficiency in South Africa and enhance the country's productivity and growth prospects.

Thus, there is prima facie evidence of the virtuous growth-supporting cycle for South Africa and its integration partners in Africa. And yet resistance in South Africa to importing goods and services and to the immigration of citizens from other African countries could hamper progress towards further regional integration and the mutual benefits it brings to South Africa and its integration partners. South Africa's consultative negotiations model, which entails extensive consultations with organised labour and organised business in the National Economic Development and Labour Council (Nedlac) (Bilal and Laporte, 2004; Ismail, 2012), the strength of domestic anti-import lobbies (Makgetla, 2021) and the national anxiety about immigration, especially from the rest of Africa (Aidi, 2021; Nshimbi and Fioramonti, 2014), have the potential to compromise South Africa's commitment to deepening regional integration and hold back structural transformation in South

Africa and the region.

This chapter first sketches the history of South Africa's economic integration efforts in Africa and some of the factors discouraging wholehearted support for integration. It proceeds to describe economic interactions between South Africa and its African neighbours, focusing on trade, investment, value chains and labour migration. The chapter then assesses the case for deeper integration when its known economic benefits are considered, the impact of key global trends such as digitisation, COVID-19, climate change, and the potential effects of new, growing global rivalries where developing countries are enticed or forced to choose sides in a less open global economy.

SOUTH AFRICA AND REGIONAL INTEGRATION IN AFRICA

Southern African Customs Union

The Southern African Customs Union (SACU) was officially created in 1910 for the convenience of Britain to manage its colonies and protectorates in the region. Its origin can be traced to earlier colonial arrangements. SACU was reconstituted in 1969 in a semi-post-colonial milieu, but on terms imposed by the powerful apartheid state. It has had various member states at different times and currently comprises Namibia, Botswana, Lesotho, Eswatini and South Africa. It is a full customs union and considered to be the oldest active customs union in the world (WTO, 2003).

SACU was renegotiated after South Africa's democratisation, with new consensus-based decision-making procedures and a new revenue-dispensing formula which gives a greater share of revenue, proportionate to their trade, to the smaller and poorer states (McCarthy, 2003). Nevertheless, it is sometimes criticised for favouring South Africa's economic policy interests (Gibb, 2006; Saurombe, 2010). While convenient for trade in the neighbourhood, SACU adds complexity to South Africa's trade negotiation processes and to the trade policies of its partners, as none of SACU's members may enter into external trade agreements without the support of the other members of the union (Ismail, 2012).

Southern African Development Community

The Southern African Development Community (SADC) first appeared in 1992 when colonialism and settler rule was coming to an end in southern Africa. After the liberation of the former Portuguese colonies in the 1970s, countries bordering still-settler-ruled Namibia, Zimbabwe and South Africa organised themselves into the so-called Frontline States. After the liberation of Zimbabwe, a Southern African Development Coordination Conference (SADCC) community of states emerged which was primarily focused on development, while the more informal Frontline States structure continued to focus on the issues of liberation and security (Tjønneland, 2013).

In one of its first legal acts, the newly democratic South Africa acceded to the SADC treaty in August 1994. While trade and investment relationships external to Africa had been more significant for South Africa, SADC represented the first multilateral external commitment for the new government. South Africa, along with its SADC partners, signed onto an unrealistically ambitious Regional Indicative Strategic Development Plan (RISDP) in August 2003, which included the achievement of a series of milestones: a regional free trade area in 2008, a regional customs union in 2010, a common market in 2015, a monetary union in 2016 and a regional currency in 2018. None of these targets has been fully realised and only the regional free trade agreement was implemented in law, although it remains incomplete in practice (Hartzenberg and Kalenga, 2015). SADC's portfolio also covers security issues, but these have been addressed unevenly.

Tripartite Free Trade Agreement

In 2018, South Africa ratified the Tripartite Free Trade Agreement, which it had signed the previous year. The treaty is designed to bring 26 African countries belonging to three existing regional economic communities – SADC, COMESA (Common Market for Eastern and Southern Africa) and the EAC (East African Community) – into a single trade bloc with common rules. The tripartite agreement was first proposed at a joint summit meeting of the three participating groupings in 2008 and, after extensive negotiations and several high-level meetings, was launched in Egypt in 2015. South Africa was the 22nd country out of 26 to ratify the agreement (Ensor, 2018; Erasmus, 2018).

African Continental Free Trade Area

Even while the mega, 26-country, Tripartite FTA was being finalised, a grouping for more than twice as many countries was being planned – the African Continental Free Trade Area (AfCFTA). After negotiations kicked off in 2016, the AfCFTA was formally launched in March 2018 at an extra-ordinary African Union (AU) Summit in Kigali, Rwanda. Some 44 of the 55 AU members signed the text. The first ratifications were announced soon afterwards (Erasmus, 2018).

Erasmus (2018) detected a shift in South Africa's negotiating stance during this period: previously, South Africa had preferred not to enter into such agreements until negotiations were completed; now South Africa was prepared to sign onto and ratify an agreement whose details had not yet been finalised. While the treaty has now been ratified and 'came into force' on 30 May 2019, and while 38 countries had, as of September 2021, ratified the treaty and deposited their instruments of ratification (Tralac, 2021), the rules of the treaty are still being hammered out. Only when a detailed set of rules is finalised will the treaty be implemented.

SOUTH AFRICA'S DEPTH OF COMMITMENT TO REGIONAL INTEGRATION

Trade policy

The South African government's Department of Trade, Industry and Competition (DTIC) issued a trade policy statement in 2021 which reflected both South Africa's commitment to African economic integration and its preoccupation with inward-looking 'localisation'. The government wants to reduce imports by at least 20 per cent, according to DTIC Minister, Ebrahim Patel (Phakathi, 2021).

The starting point in the policy is '(f)ocused programs … to address competitiveness challenges, with the emphasis on localisation and beneficiation'. Nevertheless, '(t)he launching of the AfCFTA represents a significant milestone in Africa's continental integration project'. The

AfCFTA 'will provide greater incentives for new investment to take advantage of a more open and integrated continental market' (DTIC, 2021: 2). South Africa, one of the most industrialised economies on the continent, is of the view that the AfCFTA will attract more investment to the country for activities aimed at the broader African market.

South Africa has pressed hard in the AfCFTA negotiations for tight rules of origin which would favour more industrialised countries in Africa (DTIC, 2021: 4): 'Rules of origin that give preferences to "Made in Africa" products will boost manufacturing and industrial development in Africa. In this context, South Africa will set out the case for rules of origin that increases the level of African value-add.' While the DTIC goes on to say that it has begun consultations with other countries regarding cross-border value chains (building vertical supply chains that cross African political borders), it admits that while 'discussions focusing on [certain] sectors ... are already under way with SACU member states ... we will expand the discussion with others over time' (2021: 5).

South Africa supports African integration as it is 'at the heart of SA's trade policy agenda' (DTIC, 2021: 9), but it approaches the process of integration with great caution. Although the Centre for Competition, Regulation and Economic Development (CCRED), an influential policy centre, has been advocating more ambitious regional value chain strategies for many years, current strategies to build value chains, according to the DTIC's (2021) trade policy statement, are apparently limited to the other four SACU members, which are small economies.

Although South Africa has made commitments in respect of a range of multilateral economic relationships, including the four African trade groupings discussed above, historically it has also enjoyed various bilateral agreements. For example, it has entered into bilateral trade agreements with several of its neighbours, including Zimbabwe, Malawi and Mozambique, all members of SADC. While the Zimbabwe agreement was dissolved by agreement in 2018, there is no clear evidence of the ending of the other two agreements; yet these bilateral agreements are also not reflected in the South African tariff schedule (Hartzenberg, 2021).

A final complexity is that some commentators see South Africa's tendency to pursue relationships with non-African countries or regions on its own, or within SACU at best, as undermining a common African approach to relationships beyond the African continent. The Economic Partnership Agreement (EPA) with the European Union (EU) is one example, according to Saurombe (2010).

Migration

As noted by Nshimbi and Fioramonti (2014), South Africa has, since the apartheid era, preferred using bilateral arrangements in respect of migration in the region. Amadi (2019) believes that the abandonment of the 1995 SADC Draft Protocol on the Free Movement of People and its replacement in 2005 with a SADC Protocol on the Facilitation of the Movement of People was symptomatic of South Africa's and some of its neighbours' preference for bilateralism in migration arrangements. Unlike the earlier SADC Draft Free Movement Protocol, the Facilitation Protocol makes visa-free travel, residence and establishment rights subject to domestic legislation, and encourages member states to develop bilateral agreements for the free movement of persons. It promotes the prevalence of sovereignty and indicates a preference for security management through bilateral agreements and national laws (Amadi, 2019).

Saurombe (2010) notes that, although for a century South Africa depended on migrant labour from neighbouring countries and currently benefits from the influx of skilled professionals from other parts of Africa, laws like the Employment Equity Act discriminate against non-citizens, including people from other parts of Africa.

It may be that the 2021 DTIC trade policy statement marks a break with bilateralism within Africa regarding trade, but there is no indication and little likelihood that the policy towards migration within the region will change soon. The preference for bilateral agreements on migration reflects South Africa's concerns, shared by some of its neighbours and certain other middle-income African countries, about the quality of identification and passport systems, the exchange of criminal and security information, and the presence or absence of repatriation agreements, amongst other factors (Hirsch, 2021).

South Africa's system of trade negotiations and trade remedies

South Africa follows a deeply consultative trade policy process (Bilal and Laporte, 2004; Ismail, 2012). Many stakeholders are consulted, including all key government departments and Parliament. A key part of the process is consultations at Nedlac. The key players at Nedlac are the more powerful business groupings and the stronger trade unions and their federations. For applications for protection outside of trade treaty negotiations, firms or industries may approach South Africa's International Trade Administration Commission (ITAC) which manages both the broader trade negotiations on behalf of South Africa and SACU and, from time to time, the administration of trade remedies, such as anti-dumping measures.

While the consultative nature of the South African trade negotiations system has been justifiably praised on occasion (e.g., Bilal and Laporte, 2004; Ismail, 2012), it is also open to a certain amount of lobbying, which can work against the interests of vulnerable stakeholders in South Africa and SACU. Makgetla (2021) argues that the exposure of the South African system to lobbying has led to excessively high prices for the poor. She shows how tariffs for basic foodstuffs have increased since 2013 and now exceed average tariffs. This has resulted in floor prices for a range of wage goods, especially chicken and wheat, which are detrimental to the poor. She found 'that the main mechanism was the decision-making process on tariffs, which magnified the influence of well-resourced commercial farm and food-processing lobbies' (Makgetla, 2021: 1). The irony is that most of these products could be produced competitively in the region if South Africa was open to establishing regional value chains. For example, a southern African poultry chain, drawing on soya from high-output producers in Zambia, could lower the cost of chicken in South Africa considerably (Ncube et al., 2017).

To move towards the effective development of regional value chains, South Africa will have to find a way to neutralise or win over key protectionist elements amongst the social partners, i.e., business and labour.

PATTERNS OF ENGAGEMENT

Trade

Since South Africa's democratisation and acceptance amongst African states, its trade with other parts of Africa has become increasingly important for the local manufacturing sector. In a country and region largely dependent on the production of primary products, structural transformation initially entails the expansion of manufacturing output, which in turn paves the way for rising productivity in both direct and indirect ways. Especially in an open global economy, when the domestic market is limited and domestic tariff protection is low, exports of manufactures are critical for structural transformation.

In the past, the largest importers of manufactures from South Africa were the countries of the EU. South Africa's exports of manufactures to other African countries grew steadily after South Africa joined SADC and grew stronger still after the launch of the SADC Free Trade Area in 2008. Figure 12.1 shows that in 2010 South Africa's exports of manufactures to the rest of Africa surpassed its exports of manufactures to the EU, with the gap widening steadily for several years. Recently, exports to Europe rose, while exports of motor vehicles grew from 16 per cent of total exports to Europe in 2012 to 51 per cent in 2019, before declining to 40 per cent in 2020 in the wake of COVID-19 (Tshabalala, 2021). A large proportion of South Africa's exports to the rest of Africa, as shown in Figure 12.1, go to other members of SADC. (South Africa's leading exports to SADC are shown in Figure 12.2.)

In contrast, South Africa's imports from the rest of Africa, including SADC, are very low. In 2019, South Africa's gross exports to sub-Saharan Africa were valued at US$23.5 billion, while gross imports from the same region were valued at US$10.2 billion. This imbalance is not atypical of historical patterns and is quite severe (World Bank, 2021).

Much of the trade derives from the link between South African suppliers and the mining industry in the region. The dip in exports after 2012 came after the fall in mineral prices and a slowdown in the expansion of the South African mining sector, while the revival coincided with the resurgence of commodity prices after 2016 (Nkonjera

Figure 12.1: South Africa's exports of manufactures by regional destination, 1995–2020

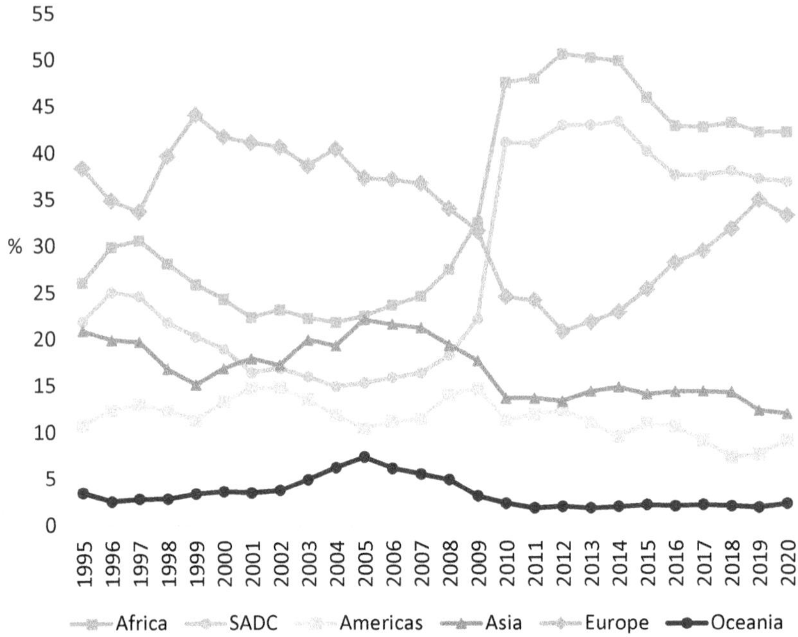

Source: Author's compilation from Quantec EasyData, 2021

Figure 12.2: South Africa's leading exports to SADC countries (excluding basic metals, coke and petroleum and basic chemicals), 1995–2020

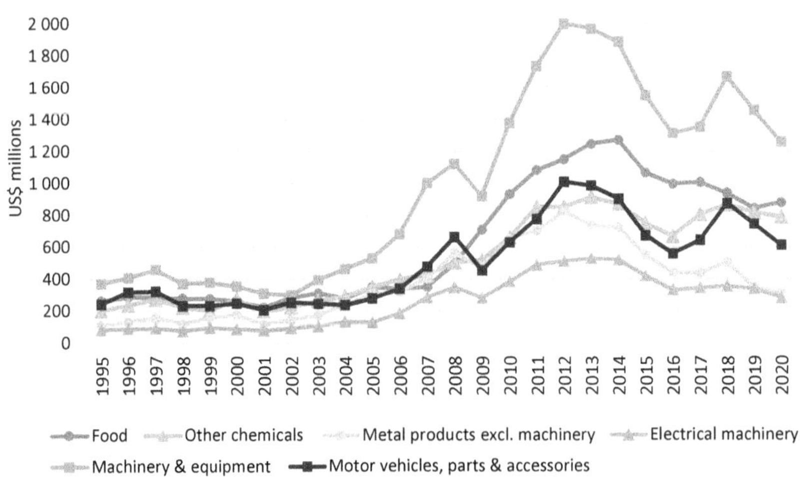

Source: Author's compilation from Quantec EasyData, 2021

and Roberts, 2021). Regional economic growth is similarly sensitive to commodity price cycles, which is one reason why South Africa's food exports to the region also declined. They had risen because of the spread of South Africa-based supermarket chains as well as rising incomes and urbanisation in the region (Arndt and Roberts, 2018).

A key conclusion emerging from this imbalance is that, despite the RISDP and the SADC FTA, South Africa's imports from the region are not contributing significantly to the diversification of poorer economies. Throughout the region, but even more so outside of Eswatini, South Africa, Mauritius and Madagascar, manufacturing accounts for a small percentage of gross domestic product (GDP) compared with developing countries in East Asia. Another reason for low industrialisation in southern Africa, argue Nkonjera and Roberts (2021), is that high volumes of mineral exports inflate the value of currencies in the countries concerned, instead of currencies reflecting the countries' low industrialisation levels.

A rich and varied literature argues that a range of factors – including the diminishing role of manufactures in consumer baskets globally, the rise of automation in manufacturing and the powerful position of East Asia as the manufacturing workshop of the world – make it unlikely that manufacturing in Africa will ever play the same role in structural transformation as it did elsewhere in the world (Rodrik, 2014).

Although the potential contribution of industry as a percentage of GDP or employment is uncertain, African countries can certainly industrialise beyond current levels. Some researchers have been asking how other countries in the region might use the proximity of the South African economy to build their own value-added industries. Arndt and Roberts (2018) have conducted a useful survey of such research. They have argued that for a range of sectors, including mining, minerals and metallurgy, poultry and other food sectors, and plastics, there are ample opportunities for increased exports of value-added products and the addition of value amongst South Africa's neighbours through the deeper integration of value chains in the region. This requires policies to support investment across borders and policies that encourage firms to build cross-border value chains. It will also entail the implementation of deliberate strategies to neutralise or win over key elements in business and labour that have adopted a defensive stance towards regional integration.

Investment

Arora and Vamvakidis (2005) found that there was a significant positive relationship between growth in South Africa and growth in the rest of Africa. They found that South Africa was the only country that produced this effect. While South Africa's exports to the region had a positive impact on the country's growth and its imports from the region had a small positive impact on the exporting countries, trade was not found to be the main connector between South Africa's growth and growth within the region. Instead, Arora and Vamvakidis (2005: 3) posit:

> Spillover effects related to investment and technology transfers could play a role, even if trade flows are relatively small. Furthermore, financial linkages between South Africa and the rest of Africa, such as foreign direct and portfolio investment, may contribute to the estimated growth spillovers, although this effect has been stronger in recent years than earlier.

More recently, Arizala et al. (2019: 5) estimated that 'positive idiosyncratic shocks to regional trading partners' growth significantly increased growth in the average sub-Saharan African country by 0.2–0.5 per cent'. This suggests more generalised returns from regional integration in Africa and points to 'the need to support further continent-wide integration and the associated growth spillovers'.

In this light, patterns of South African investment in the region are pertinent both to Africa's growth and to South Africa's structural transformation. When exchange controls were gradually liberalised by the South African government after the democratic transition in 1994, a more generous provision was made for the export of capital to other parts of Africa, compared with allowances for capital exports to other parts of the world (Hirsch, 2005). Like South Africa signing onto SADC very soon after democratisation in 1994, this showed the Mandela government's commitment to African economic development. Firms led the way: from 1991 to 1995, South African firms increased their total investment in sub-Saharan Africa five-fold, thereby boosting their share of investments in this region to 25 per cent of their total foreign investments. From 1994 to 1998, Africa received 42 per cent of South African companies' outward investments, while the EU received 18 per cent (Carmody, 2002).

The scope of South Africa's Industrial Development Corporation (IDC) was broadened to include other countries in Africa. Indeed, the current mission of the IDC is to 'contribute to the generation of balanced, sustainable economic growth in Africa, and to the economic empowerment of the South African population' (IDC, 2021).

In recent years, some South African firms have pulled back from some of their investments in certain parts of Africa, but the rest of the continent remains an important investment destination for South African firms. Initially, much of the investment was directed at what other African economies shared with South Africa – an abundance of precious and commodity metals and minerals (Carmody, 2002). Later, South African firms identified opportunities in fast-growing African markets, especially as the rate of growth of many African countries was considerably higher than that of South Africa and were also helped by the fact that businesses and consumers had somewhat similar needs and tastes (Turok and Visagie, 2020).

As can be seen from Table 12.1, in recent decades most South African investments in other parts of Africa have been in financial and other business services, telecoms and information and communication technology (ICT), media, food and beverages, and tourism – all industries intent on leveraging the opportunities in Africa's growing economies – although the biggest investment projects have been in metals, minerals, chemicals and construction.

Turok and Visagie (2020) observe that many of South Africa's investments in service sectors in other parts of Africa have value chain effects. Investments by South African supermarket chains have created opportunities for their South African suppliers to supply regional markets as well. Similarly, investments in financial services and ICT often result in contracts for South African suppliers. This means that South African firms can benefit from increasing their scale of production, with

Table 12.1: Direct investment from South Africa in Africa, January 2003–August 2019

Industry cluster	No. of investment projects	Percentage of FDI projects (%)	Size of capital investment (US$ millions)	Percentage of capital (%)	No. of jobs	Percentage of jobs (%)
Financial services	139	28.3%	1 503	3.9%	4 014	6.8%
Telecoms and ICT	82	16.7%	6 377	16.7%	6 482	10.9%
Minerals. chemicals. and metals	54	11.0%	4 839	12.7%	14 453	24.4%
Construction	38	7.7%	7 695	20.2%	16 072	27.1%
Media and marketing industries	37	7.5%	426	1.1%	1 213	2.0%
Other business services	33	6.7%	566	1.5%	931	1.6%
Food and beverages	31	6.3%	1 381	3.6%	7 512	12.7%
Energy	31	6.3%	13 496	35.4%	4 240	7.2%
Tourism	22	4.5%	1 119	2.9%	2 385	4.0%
Other manufacturing	15	3.0%	321	0.8%	1 105	1.9%
Transport and storage	10	2.0%	404	1.1%	875	1.5%
Grand total	**492**	**100%**	**38 128**	**100%**	**59 282**	**100%**

Source: Turok and Visagie, 2020: 12

Note: Actual capital and jobs estimates are forecasted for most projects in the fDi Markets database and are therefore only indicative.

the potential for scale-induced productivity gains, although their exports to other parts of Africa are generally not that large yet.

Das Nair et al. (2018) found that while South African supermarkets operating in other parts of Africa empower their South African suppliers to participate in these markets, they have not used their considerable technology and skills to upgrade suppliers and potential in other African countries. The authors note that regulatory obstacles are part of the problem. Alongside multilateral trade agreements there are 'local content policies, import duties and import quotas that serve to protect national industries' (Das Nair et al., 2018: 347).

The DTIC has lofty integration ambitions (DTIC, 2021: 9–10):

> African economic integration, structural transformation and industrialisation lie at the heart of SA's trade policy agenda. African prosperity, growth and development, industrialisation, market integration and cross-border infrastructure development should create a dynamic for greater prosperity, from which all African economies should benefit. Our engagements beyond the continent should support these objectives, both for Africa and SA, and should be geared to steadily correcting the manufacturing deficit in our international trade profile.

At present, it seems that many of the progressive sentiments contained in the 2021 DTIC trade policy statement are mere ambitions, as they are yet to be accompanied by actions that would lead to the realisation of the objectives.

CONTEMPORARY FACTORS AFFECTING SOUTH AFRICA'S TRADE INTEGRATION STRATEGY

The microchip and digital coding revolutionised computing six decades ago, yet the digital revolution continues apace with enormous implications for the world of work (see, for example, Frey, 2019; Susskind, 2020). So far, relatively little research has been conducted on the experience of developing countries regarding their engagement with emerging digital technologies or on the impact of global trends in digitalisation on emerging economies.

There are both developmental opportunities and pitfalls associated with contemporary digitalisation (which includes automation, robotisation and artificial intelligence). Opportunities include new and more refined technologies, mobile money, suitably scaled management systems and grids, productivity enhancement in agriculture and other key productive sectors in developing countries, regional integration opportunities through systems harmonisation and integration, enhancement of service sectors such as health and education, and improved prospects of employment through various forms of offshoring and outsourcing of services. One widely discussed negative factor is the prospect of more and more developed countries insourcing production and services. This is despite labour being more expensive because of the automation and/or robotisation of productive and service work and the loss of the labour cost advantages of developing countries (Gelb et al., 2020).

Historically, poor countries, where wages are low, have stepped onto the lowest rungs of the industrialisation ladder and engaged in labour-intensive manufacturing of products, such as processed foods, textiles, clothing and footwear. This happened successively in Europe, North America, East and South Asia and, as labour costs and productivity rose, these countries were able to move up the industrialisation ladder. The potential decline in the labour input in production due to the adoption of digitally enabled technologies could wrest this opportunity away from poor countries seeking to progress through industrialisation. African countries had been hoping for more outsourced industrial activities from China. However, there is evidence that China, in response to rising wages, is tending to automate rather than outsource (Xu et al., 2017). There is thus a greater likelihood today than in the past that decisions regarding the location of economic activities will be influenced by proximity to large markets and skilled labour.

As Rodrik puts it (2018: 14):

> (N)ew technologies present a double whammy to low-income countries. First, they are generally biased towards skills and other capabilities. This bias reduces the comparative advantage of developing countries in traditionally labour-intensive manufacturing (and other) activities and decreases their gains from trade. Second, GVCs [global value chains] make it harder for low-income countries to use their labour cost advantage to offset their technological disadvantage, by reducing their ability to substitute unskilled labour for other production inputs.

During the COVID-19 pandemic, the vulnerability of value chains and just-in-time production to massive disruption became evident. Shortages, bottlenecks and rising prices have been some of the consequences. The impact of COVID-19 on GVCs would seem to favour inshoring, at least in the medium term (Makokera and Makokera, 2020).

Climate change also needs to be considered as a parameter for trade policy. There are likely to be constraints to trade, such as carbon border taxes, which may be protectionist in impact, persuading more firms to locate in green energy locations close to large markets. There are also opportunities for the development of green energy sources and climate change adaptation solutions. As the needs and environments are similar in many African countries, there are opportunities for trade in climate change solutions across African borders.

Another factor is the possible emergence of a new cold war, with China and the United States (US) being the two poles of the conflict. '(T)he launch of AUKUS [Australia, United Kingdom and United States alliance] has confirmed that the standoff with China is indisputably the number one foreign policy priority for US President Joe Biden and his administration' (Kortunov, 2021). In such circumstances, there is a risk that African states may be pushed towards choosing sides and in effect becoming client states, where choices about trade and investment are constrained. The impact of the Russian invasion of Ukraine is serving to heighten uncertainty about global economic relationships. The effects of global polarisation, though, could be offset by stronger internal trade and investment links within Africa.

All these factors – the impact of deeper digitalisation on the location of economic activities, the impact of COVID-19 on logistical chains, the impact of climate change on production and trade, and the threat of global polarisation affecting the freedom of developing countries to choose trade and investment partners – point to the need for a deeper and more comprehensive form of economic integration on the African continent. As the DTIC (2021: 6) states in its trade policy, 'For greater economic resilience, now and in the future, SA's trade and industrial policy must focus on building more diversified production centres both in SA and across Africa'.

Although virtually all African countries are committed to the AfCFTA, many are hesitant about opening their borders to other countries on the continent for fear that infant industries will be swamped or that agricultural imports will undermine food security. Another frequent concern is that trade imbalances with larger and more developed countries will grow. Richer countries like Nigeria and South Africa have powerful protectionist lobbies. For these reasons, trade liberalisation measures under the AfCFTA do allow a reasonable amount of flexibility and can be implemented gradually. In addition, successful integration would have to be what some scholars call 'developmental regionalism'. This requires transfers of various kinds to the poorer and less-developed countries in Africa to enable them to participate in regional integration initiatives on more equal terms.

CONCLUSION

Regional integration in the past contributed to structural transformation in South Africa by providing export markets for South African manufactures and skill-intensive services. The DTIC has indicated its commitment to deepening African integration; yet this position is weakened by protectionism in respect of the importation of some products from other African countries, slow movement towards the building of regional value chains, and an ultra-cautious attitude towards giving Africans greater freedom to move across intra-continental borders.

To accelerate the implementation of its regional integration commitments, South Africa needs to devote considerably more resources to developing the capabilities of the public sector and the private sector to advance the integration agenda, as well as to educate citizens about the advantages of African integration.

REFERENCES

Aidi, H, 2021. 'Inequality and political identity in South Africa'. Policy Brief 56/21. Policy Centre for the New South.

Amadi, V. T. 2019. 'Facilitating interregional trade through the movement of people in the Southern African Development Community (SADC)'. LLD thesis, University of the Western Cape.

Arizala, F., Bellon, M. and MacDonald, M. 2019. 'Regional growth spillovers in Sub-Saharan Africa'. IMF Working Paper WP/19/160.

Arndt, C. and Roberts, S. J. 2018. 'Key issues in regional growth and integration in Southern Africa'. *Development Southern Africa*, 35 (3), 297–314.

Arora, V. and Vamvakidis, A. 2005. 'The implications of South African economic growth for the rest of Africa'. *South African Journal of Economics*, 73 (2), 229–242.

Bilal, S. and Laporte, G. 2004. 'How David prepared to talk to Goliath? South Africa's experience of negotiating trade with the EU'. *European Centre for Development Policy Management,* https://www.researchgate.net/publication/265525764_How_David_Prepared_to_Talk_to_Goliath_South_Africa%27s_experience_of_negotiating_trade_with_the_EU, accessed 2 October 2004.

Carmody, P. 2002. 'Between globalisation and (post) apartheid: The political economy of restructuring in South Africa'. *Journal of Southern African Studies*, 28 (2), 255–775.

Das Nair, R., Chisoro S. and Ziba, F. 2018. 'The implications for suppliers of the spread of supermarkets in Southern Africa'. *Development Southern Africa*, 35 (3), 334–350.

Department of Trade, Industry and Competition (DTIC). 2021. 'A trade policy for industrial development and employment growth', http://www.thedtic.gov.za/wp-content/uploads/SA_Trade_Policy.pdf, accessed 15 October 2021.

Ensor, L. 8 August 2018. 'Deal being inked to allow 26 African countries to better trade terms'. *BusinessLive,* https://www.businesslive.co.za/bd/world/africa/2018-08-08-deal-being-inked-to-allow-26-african-countries-access-to-better-trade-terms/, accessed 11 October 2021.

Erasmus, G. 2018. 'South Africa to ratify tripartite and continental free trade area agreements'. *Tralac* website, https://www.tralac.org/blog/article/13467-south-africa-to-ratify-tripartite-fta-and-continental-free-trade-area-agreements.html, accessed 10 October 2021.

Frey, C. 2019. *The Technology Trap: Capital, labour and power in the age of automation.* Princeton: Princeton University Press.

Gelb, A., Ramachandran, V., Christian, J., Meyer, S., Wadhwa, D. and Navis, K. 2020. 'Can Sub-Saharan Africa be a manufacturing destination? Labor costs, price levels, and the role of industrial policy'. *Journal of Industry, Competition & Trade,* 20, 335–357.

Gibb, R. 2006. 'The new Southern African customs union agreement: Dependence with democracy'. *Journal of Southern African Studies*, 32 (3), 583–603.

Hartzenberg, T. 2021. Email correspondence on South African trade agreements.

Hartzenberg, T. and Kalenga, P. 2015. 'National policies and regional integration in the South African development community'. WIDER

Working Paper 2015/056. UNU-WIDER: Helsinki, https://www.wider.unu.edu/sites/default/files/wp2015-056.pdf, accessed 17 October 2021.

Hirsch, A. 2005. *Seasons of Hope: Economic reform under Mandela and Mbeki*. Scottsville: University of KwaZulu-Natal Press.

Hirsch, A. 2021. 'The African Union's free movement of persons protocol: Why has it faltered and how can its objectives be achieved?' *South African Journal of International Affairs*, 28 (4), 1–21.

Industrial Development Corporation (IDC). 2021. https://www.idc.co.za/, accessed 23 October 2021.

Ismail, F. 2012. 'Reflections on a new democratic South Africa's role in the multilateral trading system'. *Global Policy*, 3 (3), 270–280.

Kortunov, A. 29 September 2021. 'Should Russia be worried by the new AUKUS alliance?' *Carnegie Moscow Centre*, https://carnegiemoscow.org/commentary/85451, accessed 23 October 2021.

Makgetla, N. S. 2021. 'Tariffs on basic foods: Evolution and impacts'. South African Reserve Bank Working Paper Series WP/21/19, https://www.econbiz.de/Record/tariffs-on-basic-foods-evolution-and-impacts-seidman-makgetla-neva/10012621363, accessed 22 September 2021.

Makokera, C. G. and Makokera, M. B. 2020. 'South Africa's trade policy post COVID-19'. *South African Journal of International Affairs*, 27 (4), 561–571.

McCarthy, C. 2003. 'The Southern African customs union in transition'. *African Affairs*, 102 (409), 605–630.

Mene, W. 2021. 'African Continental Free Trade Area (AfCFTA) and the WTO: Shaping the future of the multilateral trading system'. WTO Lecture in Honour of Ambassador Chiedu Osakwe, https://www.wto.org/english/news_e/news21_e/acc_28sep21_e.htm, accessed 10 October 2021.

Ncube, P., Roberts, S. and Zengeni, T. 2017. 'The Southern African poultry value chain: Regional development versus national imperatives'. CCRED Working Paper No. 2017/7, WIDER Working Paper 2017/97, https://ssrn.com/abstract=2958098 or http://dx.doi.org/10.2139/ssrn.2958098, accessed 9 October 2021.

Nkonjera, M. and Roberts, S. 2021. 'Regional integration and industrial development in Southern Africa: Where does South Africa stand?', in Bradlow, D. and Sideropolous, E. (eds.) *Values, Interests and Power: South African foreign policy in uncertain times*. Pretoria: Pretoria University Law Press, 140–159.

Nshimbi, C. and Fioramonti, L. 2014. 'The will to integrate: South Africa's responses to regional migration from the SADC region'. *African Development Review*, 26 (S1), 52–63.

Phakathi, B. 16 September 2021. 'Patel says localisation drive will not derail Africa's free trade deal'. *BusinessLive*, https://www.businesslive.co.za/bd/national/2021-09-16-patel-says-localisation-drive-will-not-derail-africasfree-trade-deal/ accessed October 11 2021.

Quantec EasyData. 2021. 'South Africa's exports of manufactures by regional destination'. Electronic dataset, https://www.quantec.co.za/post/3476/south-africa-regional-trade-industry-data-analysis/, accessed 21 October 2021.

Rodrik, D. 2014. 'The past, present, and future of economic growth'. *Challenge,* 57 (3), 5–39.

Rodrik, D. 2018. 'New technologies, global value chains, and the developing economies'. *Pathways for Prosperity Commission,* Background Paper Series No. 1. Oxford.

Saurombe, A. 2010. 'The role of South Africa in SADC regional integration: The making or breaking of the organization'. *Journal of International Commercial Law and Technology,* 5 (3), 124–131.

Susskind, D. 2020. *A World Without Work: Technology, automation and how we should respond.* London: Penguin.

Tjønneland, E. N. 2013. 'Making sense of the Southern African Development Community (SADC)'. *African Security Review*, 22 (3), 190–196.

Tralac. 2021. 'Status of AfCFTA ratification', website: https://www.tralac.org/resources/infographic/13795-status-of-afcfta-ratification.html, accessed 12 October, 2021.

Tshabalala, N. 2021. Correspondence with the author.

Turok, I. and Visagie, J. 2020. 'Building malls or metros? South Africa's exports of tradable urban services to the rest of Africa'. SA-TIED WIDER UNU, https://sa-tied.wider.unu.edu/sites/default/files/pdf/SA-TIED-WP-129.pdf, accessed 26 September 2021.

World Bank. 2021. 'Trade data', https://wits.worldbank.org/CountryProfile/en/Country/ZAF/Year/2019/TradeFlow/, accessed 5 October 2021.

World Trade Organization (WTO). 2003. 'Trade policy review – Southern African customs union 2003', https://www.wto.org/English/tratop_e/tpr_e/tp213_e.htm, accessed 12 October 2021.

Xu, J., Gelb, S., Li, J. and Zhao, Z. 2017. 'Adjusting to rising costs in Chinese light manufacturing: What opportunities for developing countries?' ODI and Center for New Structural Economics, https://set.odi.org/wp-content/uploads/2017/12/SET_Survey-report_Chinese-manufacturing_Final.pdf, accessed 12 October 2021.

Part Three

Governance, Labour and Livelihoods

THIRTEEN

Structural transformation in South Africa: Who bears the cost? The invisible work of social reproduction

Basani Baloyi, Miriam Di Paola and Andrew Mukandila

INTRODUCTION

Structural transformation has typically been seen as a measure of developmental success. Structural transformation is commonly defined as the shift from low-productivity sectors (i.e., agriculture and mining) to high-productivity sectors (i.e., manufacturing), and within sectors from the production of low-value-added activities (i.e., clothing and textiles) to that of high-value-added activities (i.e., capital goods). This definition gives rise to two critical challenges, which this chapter grapples with.

First, the concept of structural transformation is an inadequate measure of development as there is more to development than a shift in the sectoral composition of an economy. Industrialisation may take place, but at a social cost. Therefore, crucially, the link between economic development (which the definition addresses) and social reproduction is missing. This follows on from what Fraser (2016) calls a 'critical separatism' between economic, ecological and social dynamics. On the contrary, while the boundaries have blurred even further in the wake of the marketisation and commodification of care work, the activities taking place in the economic sphere are deeply intertwined with the environment and work in the reproductive sphere. In fact, the exploitation of both the environment and people who bear the brunt of social reproduction, and the racialised and gendered division of labour that characterises production and reproduction, are essential conditions for capitalist accumulation.

Second, the pattern of development in post-apartheid South Africa has continued to be based on the minerals–energy–finance complex (MEFC), while lacking industrial diversification. Instead, the country has experienced massive deindustrialisation which has precipitated a social crisis. The period has been characterised by neoliberal structural reforms underpinned by financialisation, which have contributed to premature deindustrialisation, worsening working conditions and unemployment, and a deepening social crisis which the reproductive sphere has had to absorb.

This chapter explores two ways in which the pattern of uneven development fostered by the MEFC and the crisis of capitalist accumulation have been forced upon the reproductive spheres. Contextually, the interrelationship between economic development and social reproduction is highlighted.

First, we can argue that private accumulation necessarily shirks its reproductive role of ensuring adequate occupational health and safety at the site of production. In South Africa, capital externalises its reproductive role to an under-resourced public sector as well as to communities and households. We use the mining sector, which has been at the heart of the minerals–energy complex (MEC) since the advent of racialised capitalism under apartheid and throughout the democratic period, to demonstrate this point. Second, we can argue that the exploitation of workers involved in reproductive activities (both paid and unpaid workers) is fundamental to the continuation of capitalist development, while austerity measures and financialisation in the healthcare sector have resulted in work restructuring and casualisation. Again, workers' (including health workers') livelihoods are put under strain by the very processes of accumulation that they sustain.

Therefore, the private sector's shirking of its reproductive role and the exploitation of paid and unpaid workers involved in providing care are key drivers behind the perpetuation of capitalist development. Yet the social reproduction of the workforce is jeopardised by economic accumulation through financialisation, privatisation and unaffordable services, widespread casualisation and unsafe working conditions (Fakier and Cock, 2009; Federici, 2014).

The rest of this chapter consists of the following: an outline of our theoretical approach, which highlights the interdependencies between economic and social reproduction in a capitalist society; a discussion of how, instead of structural transformation leading to industrial deepening, patterns of 'economic development' brought about by the MEFC, against a backdrop of apartheid-driven, racialised capitalism and neoliberal accumulation, have been uneven and prone to crisis; and an analysis of the social costs borne by workers due to the private sector abandoning its reproductive role and exploiting workers involved in care.

THEORETICAL APPROACH TO THE INTERRELATIONSHIP BETWEEN ECONOMIC AND SOCIAL REPRODUCTION

There is more to development, as defined by structural transformation, than just a shift in the sectoral composition of an economy. Industrialisation may take place, but partly at a social cost because of the neglect and invisibilisation (Adams, 2022; Federici, 2014) of social reproduction, which is inconsistent with the push for productivity. Social reproduction refers to the activities that nurture future workers (such as childcare and education), regenerate the current workforce (such as cleaning, cooking and sex), and maintain those who cannot work (such as elder care and healthcare). In broad terms, it consists of caring directly for oneself and others, maintaining physical spaces, and organising resources and species reproduction. These tasks have traditionally been performed by women for low or no wages both in and outside the household (Bhattacharya, 2017).

The unequal burden of care work also has a racial and class component because in South Africa and globally, social reproduction work is predominantly performed by black women, migrant women and women belonging to subaltern groups (Mezzadri, 2022). At the same time, jobs that have a strong social reproduction component, as discussed later in this chapter, are systemically undervalued and poorly remunerated. We argue in this section that structural transformation as a measure of development ignores and undervalues both reproductive work in general and, more specifically, the degree to which the productive and social reproduction spheres are deeply entangled.

Marx (1976 [1867]: 711) notes that 'every social process of production is at the same time, a process of reproduction. The conditions of production are at the same time the conditions of reproduction' (Marx, 1976). According to Marx, under capitalism, the reproduction of workers is essential for the maintenance of the 'capitalist relation'. Therefore, it is not the reproduction of life itself that is necessary but rather the reproduction of the labour power embodied by workers, which is strictly linked to capitalist production. Moreover, Marx points to an insuperable contradiction between production and reproduction, which is of specific relevance to this chapter. Under capitalism, the worker is the most indispensable means of production; as a result, it is the responsibility of the capitalist to give the worker a certain amount of capital in return for their labour power. This capital 'is converted into means of subsistence which have to be consumed to reproduce the muscles, nerves, bones and brains of existing workers, and to bring new workers into existence' (Marx, 1976 [1867]: 717). The maintenance and reproduction of the working class remain necessary conditions for the reproduction of capital and, in fact, the value of the labour power and the wage given to the worker must include the means needed for the maintenance and reproduction of the worker and the working class.

At the same time, due to the coercive force of capitalist competition and productivity, capital strives to overwork certain segments of the workforce to the point of exhaustion. In fact, according to Marx, unlike other oppressed classes, such as the serfs under serfdom, 'the modern labourer ... instead of rising with the process of industry, sinks deeper and deeper below the conditions of existence of his own class. He becomes a pauper, and pauperism develops more rapidly than population and wealth. And here it becomes evident, that the bourgeoisie is unfit any longer to be the ruling class in society' (Marx and Engels, 1948: 20).

Structural transformation as a concept, which is determined by the transition from low-productivity sectors to high-productivity sectors, is caught up in a similar tension. This transition would require a change in the composition of capital and possibly an increasingly skilled workforce; or it could involve increased capital formation and less-skilled workers, and fewer of them. The capitalist then extracts a larger surplus but, in the process, creates a contradiction where they place the burden on household reproduction which, over time, could create conditions that undermine the capitalist's quest to keep on extracting a surplus. This is an intrinsic destructive tendency of capitalism, which can be curbed by workers' resistance and the enforcement of specific legislation. Nevertheless, there is an inherent contradiction between the dependency of capitalism on the social reproduction of the worker and the tendency of the capitalist system to exploit the worker (and the environment) until the point of destruction (Cammack, 2020).

We argue that given the historical contradiction between the maintenance of 'the capital relation' and its tendency to exploit workers, the latter tendency is currently dominating. In fact, although the worker is the capitalist's most indispensable means of production (Marx, 1976 [1867]), employers take no responsibility for the social reproduction of the worker – such as providing sufficient subsistence, or a living wage, and adequate health and safety – let alone the reproduction of the working class, such as through taxation. Crucially, the employer has a reproductive role that is embodied in the wages it pays and in the occupational health and safety standards set out in law. As pointed out by Alli (2008: VII): 'Occupational safety and health (OSH) is generally defined as the science of the anticipation, recognition, evaluation and control of hazards arising in or from the workplace that could impair the health and wellbeing of workers, taking into account the possible impact on the surrounding communities and the general environment'.

During the neoliberal era, the privatisation of services and the deterioration in labour conditions and protection have unleashed a *crisis of social reproduction* which characterises both paid and unpaid care work. While households need to take on activities that should be publicly provided by the government, such as caring for elders and the disabled, those workers who are employed in 'socially reproductive services' have experienced worsening working conditions and increased workloads. For decades, mainstream economics has failed to acknowledge the work and the value produced in the reproductive sphere; however, in more recent years, care work has been recognised in social policies, economics and international organisations' documents as an important economic sector which is still largely unaccounted for in the main socioeconomic measures, such as gross domestic product (GDP).

Feminist scholars have always sought to take social reproduction work out of the shadows. The demand for wages for housework, which was brought into the political arena by the feminist movement in the 1970s, was intended to expose the enormous subsidy that capitalism received from women's work in the household, as provided by an unpaid labour force whom capitalism exploited for profit (Costa and James, 1975; Cox and Federici, 1975; James, 2012). At the same time, this wave of radical feminism exposed the fallacy that women were somehow more inclined than men to perform what some scholars refer to as a 'labour of love'. Feminist scholars have used the concept of social reproduction to highlight global production processes and accumulation in the Global South (Bhattacharya, 2017; Fakier and Cock, 2009; Mezzadri, 2020; Stevano et al., 2021).

According to Federici (2014), the way in which women's labour of social reproduction is exploited and made invisible in the household and in communities is mimicked by capital in the workplace. It is colonialism, racism and patriarchy that constitute the foundations of capitalism and characterise its first stages of primitive accumulation. In mainstream economics, the world of reproduction has slowly, albeit only partially, gained visibility in relation to employment patterns and gender. For instance, unpaid care work is now discussed in international fora as the main impediment to women's full participation in the labour market. The United Nations (UN) even recognises social reproduction work in its social and development policies (UN, 2015). However, the policy implications emerging from these perspectives may lead to the further commodification of social reproduction, as evidenced in the empowerment of certain, more privileged women at the expense of others.

Thus, the result of this approach may be increased inequality between the Global North and Global South, and amongst women along class and racial lines. Liberal feminism aims to create opportunities for privileged women through the outsourcing of reproductive work to other, less privileged women (Beier, 2018). However, we seek to overcome the false distinction between production and reproduction and to unmask the systems of oppression that underpin the gendered, racialised division of labour that characterises both productive and reproductive activities. Moreover, recognising the value of social reproduction activities, and not simply their cost, is essential for overcoming the burden that black and migrant women have to bear.

Nevertheless, awareness and social recognition are not sufficient to combat the exploitation to which women are subjected. The following steps need to be taken: first, reverse the impact of financialisation and austerity on labour and healthcare services; second, redistribute resources and service provision between the private and the public sectors; and third, tackle the unequal distribution of care work within households. In this way, women may free themselves from this burden; at the same time, greater social justice is encouraged in society.

STRUCTURAL TRANSFORMATION, ECONOMIC CRISIS AND WOMEN'S PARTICIPATION IN THE LABOUR FORCE

Instead of industrialisation being pursued through a process of structural transformation, the pattern of development in apartheid and post-apartheid South Africa has continued along a trajectory of uneven development based on the MEFC. At one level, this served the logic of racialised capitalism as the state was only concerned about the social upliftment of a fragment of society – white people in general and white men in particular. However, at another level, the predominance of capitalism meant that the system of accumulation was prone to crisis. The period has been characterised by neoliberal structural reforms underpinned by financialisation, which have contributed to premature deindustrialisation, worsening conditions of work, rising unemployment and a deepening social crisis which the reproductive sphere has had to absorb.

We argue in this section that the MEFC under apartheid-driven, racialised capitalism and neoliberal accumulation has brought about uneven development, which is prone to economic crisis and has shaped women's role in the labour force. Two periods of protracted crisis of capitalist accumulation in the productive sphere, marked by a fall in the rate of profitability, are depicted in Figure 13.1 and Figure 13.2 respectively. The first period, the stagnation decades, occurred in the mid-1960s until the mid-1980s. Underpinning the fall in the rate of profitability in the stagnation decades was an increase in capital intensity over that period, resulting in the over-accumulation of capital, as depicted in Figure 13.2. This increase was driven by the growth in gross capital formation[1] in the private and public sectors, as depicted in Figure 13.3.

The notable capital projects that were behind apartheid South Africa's capital-deepening project during this period were in the MEFC and were also driven by the country's public corporations (such as Eskom in the electricity sector, Iscor in the iron and steel sector and Sasol in the petrochemicals sector) and state departments (such as South African Railways & Harbours Administration in their construction of the Richards Bay railway line and port and in their purchasing of new aircraft for South African Airways) (see Prinsloo and Smith, 1997). The stagnation decades were followed by the neoliberal recovery which was associated with a rise in the rate of profitability from the mid-1980s until about 2008.

The second period, the great recession decade, occurred from the late 2000s at around the time of the global financial crisis (GFC) in 2008/2009.

Figure 13.1: Rate of profitability (all listed companies in South Africa), 1960–2016

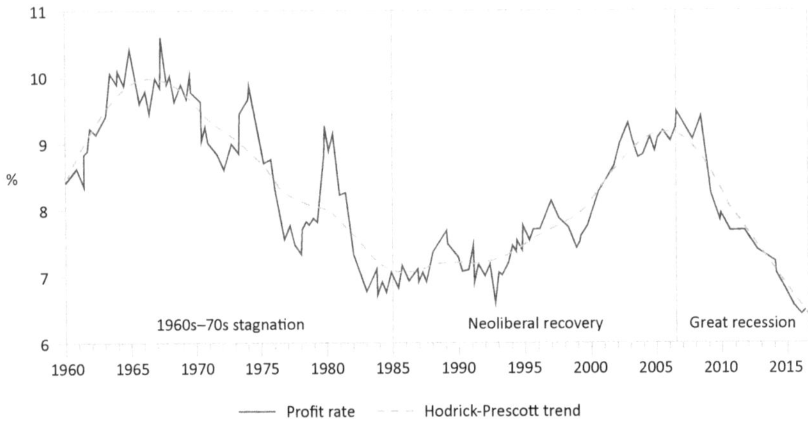

Source: Malikane, 2017: 14–15

Note: The Hodrick-Prescott trend minimises the deviation of the original profitability series from the trend and the curvature of the estimated trend.

From the 1980s, the South African economy set off on a trajectory in which its rate of profitability would be restored through neoliberal reforms. In the early 1980s, during the apartheid era, neoliberal reforms came in the form of the deregulation of the banking system and experiments with privatisation which were formalised through the White Paper on Privatisation and Deregulation released in 1987. In the 1980s, therefore, those with capital in South Africa responded to the crisis of accumulation by reducing their investments in fixed capital stock and investing their financial surpluses in financial assets (see Figure 13.4). This spurred a bull run on the Johannesburg Stock Exchange (JSE) in the first half of the 1980s (see Bond, 2000).

Neoliberal reforms in post-apartheid South Africa shaped the patterns of the economy's uneven development. The macroeconomic framework that was adopted was aimed at achieving 'economic stability', driven by low levels of borrowing, a moderate and stable inflation rate, liberalised international capital and trade accounts, and predictable and moderate levels of taxation, amongst other factors.

Uneven development in post-apartheid South Africa is characterised by three salient features. The first feature is the deep financialisation of

Figure 13.2: Capital intensity and profit share (all listed companies in South Africa), 1960–2016

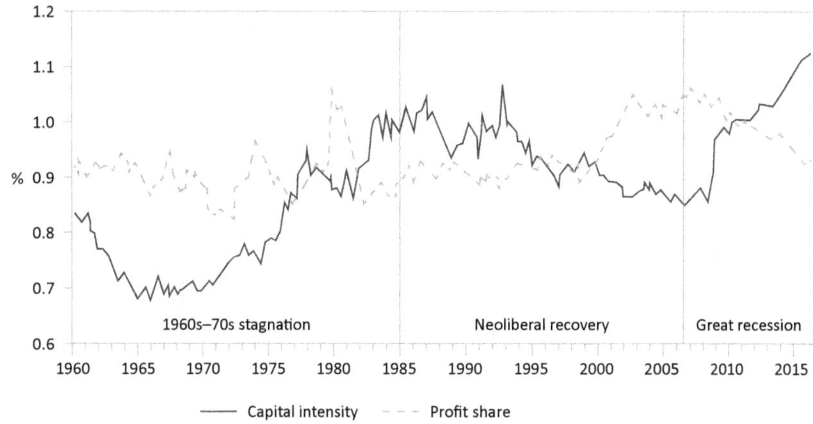

Source: Malikane, 2017:14–15

Figure 13.3: Gross capital formation by private and public corporations at constant 2015 prices, 1960–2016

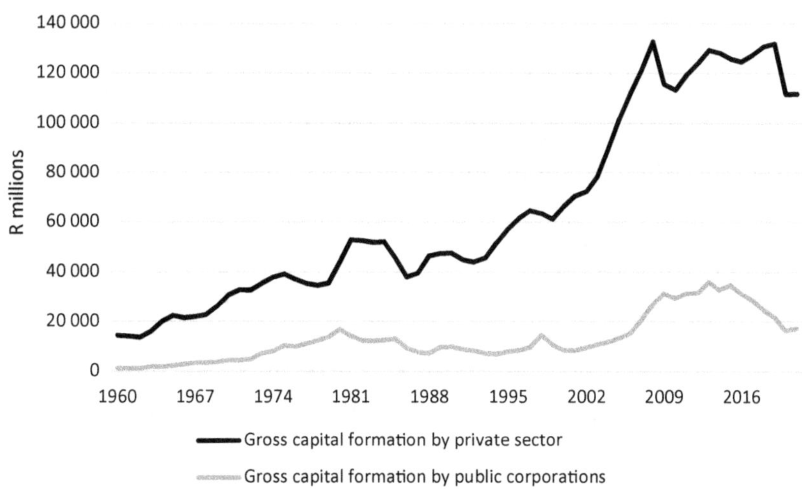

Source: SARB Quarterly Bulletin, extracted from Quantec, 2022 (database)

Figure 13.4: Flow of funds in South Africa at constant 2015 prices, 1970–2020

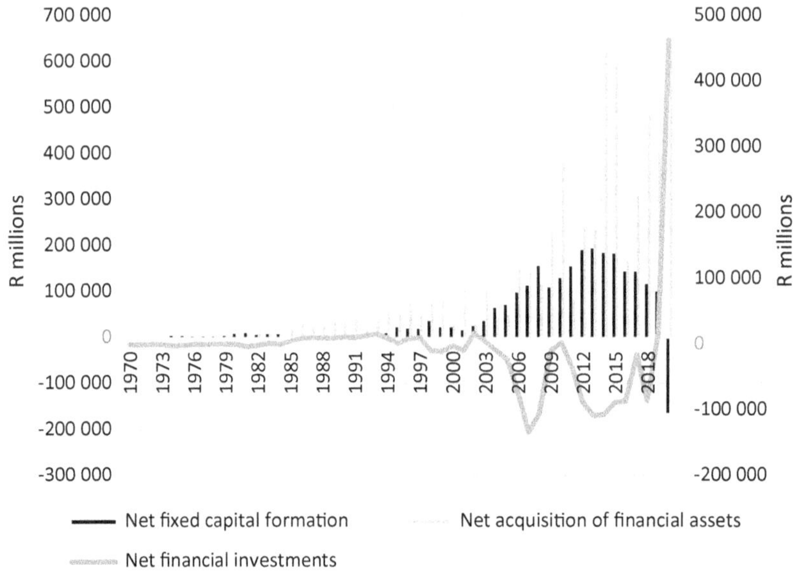

Source: SARB Quarterly Bulletin, extracted from Quantec, 2022 (database)

the economy due to the comparative growth in the financial sector and in financial markets and actors, within an otherwise stagnating economy. The net acquisition of financial assets has seen meteoric growth since the 1980s, with its dominance over net fixed capital formation being plain to see (see Figure 13.4). What is also notable is that the exponential growth of the financial sector since the 1980s has not been accompanied by growth in fixed capital stock (see Figure 13.5). Moreover, the deregulation of the capital account has been associated with short-term portfolio flows rather than foreign direct investment (see Figure 13.6).

Figure 13.5: Change in fixed capital stock at constant 2015 prices and growth in financial sector, 1961–2021

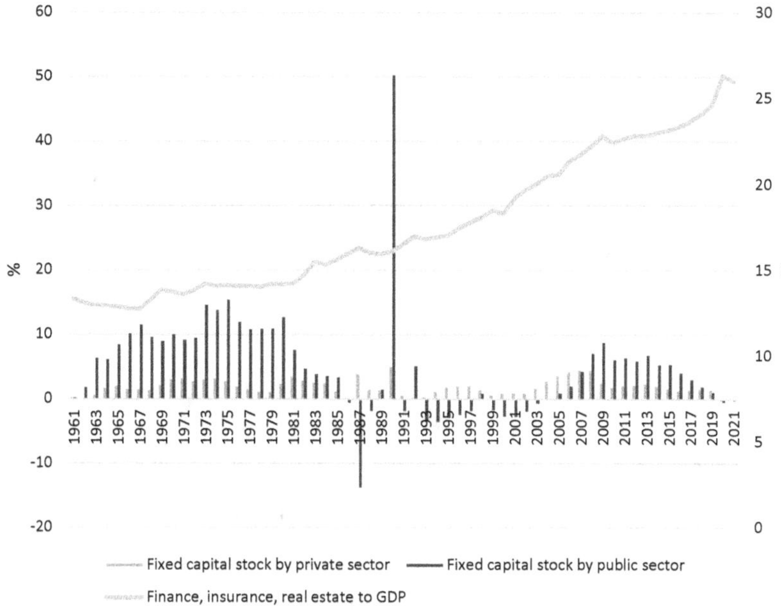

Source: SARB Quarterly Bulletin, extracted from Quantec, 2022 (database)

The second feature is the restructuring of the productive components of the economy in the first decade after the democratic transition, in the wake of the accelerated liberalisation of trade and the capital account as well as the financialisation of the South African economy. As argued by Ashman et al. (2013), the capture of South African conglomerates by institutional investors led to more attention being given to shareholder value, which necessitated the unbundling of non-core assets and a strong focus on the core business. Moreover, accelerated trade liberalisation meant that domestic firms, particularly in the manufacturing sector, faced stiff competition, resulting in a spike in company closures. Company closures fostered by divestments in non-core assets, international competition and the outsourcing of business services together contributed to the premature deindustrialisation of the economy.

Premature deindustrialisation, as observed in a decline in employment in the manufacturing sector relative to, say, the services sector, is particularly noteworthy. Manufacturing sector employment fell from 15 per cent of total employment in 1993 to 9 per cent of total

Figure 13.6: Speculative investments and unemployment in South Africa, 1994–2021

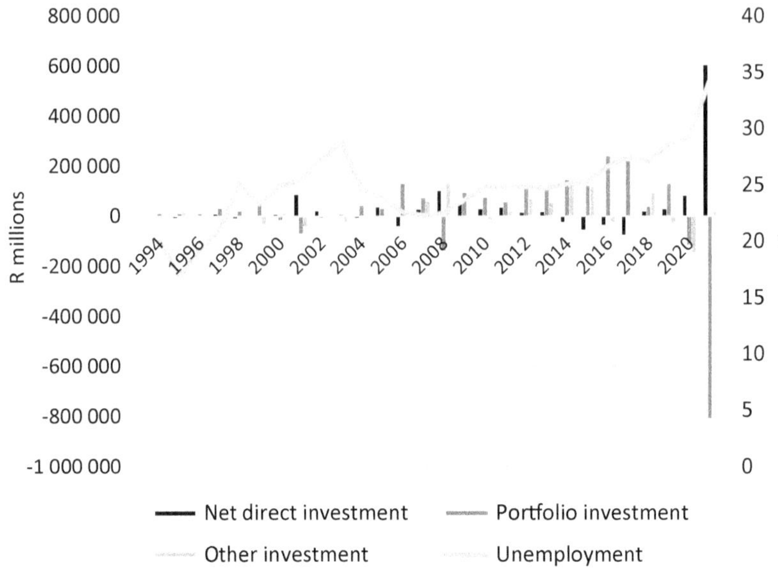

Source: SARB Quarterly Bulletin, extracted from Quantec, 2022 (database)

employment in 2020, while services sector employment (excluding government services) rose from 55 per cent of total employment in 1993 to 68 per cent of total employment in 2020 (Quantec, 2022). Given its capital-intensive nature, the MEFC's ability to create jobs is constrained by the absence of linkages with downstream labour-intensive activities.

The precarity of the services sector *relative* to the manufacturing sector can be seen in Figure 13.7a and Figure 13.7b. Services-sector jobs tend to be relatively insecure compared to manufacturing-sector jobs *on aggregate*. Services-sector jobs (aside from the finance sector) make only a small contribution to formal employment and pay lower wages than manufacturing-sector jobs on aggregate. The gender-based division of labour is also highlighted in Figure 13.7c. Women are underrepresented in the manufacturing sector, particularly within the MEFC.

The third feature is the restructuring of the labour process within the productive spheres of the economy. This has resulted from local producers in domestic markets implementing cost-cutting measures when faced with international competition and the financialisation of the economy, which (as discussed above) has contributed to low levels of investment. According to Englert (2017), South Africa saw a 71 per cent increase in the number of non-core workers between 2004 and 2017, with 40 per cent of the workforce deemed to be in precarious jobs. Again, black workers are most disadvantaged when it comes to outsourcing and casualisation of work.

Moreover, the failure to invest in labour-intensive, productive activities (as discussed earlier) has contributed to structural unemployment in the country. Labour force participation has increased, with unemployment being one of the key factors contributing to greater labour force participation amongst men and women (see Figure 13.8a and Figure 13.8b). In South Africa, this is more apparent amongst black people in general and black women in particular (see Figures 13.9a–d). This is in marked contrast to the international literature on the feminisation of work, which reports that sizeable numbers of women have light manufacturing jobs in developing countries, particularly in Asia.

Figure 13.7a: Sectoral contribution to formal employment, 1993–2017

Source: Newman, 2019

Figure 13.7b: Average remuneration per worker by sector, 1993–2017

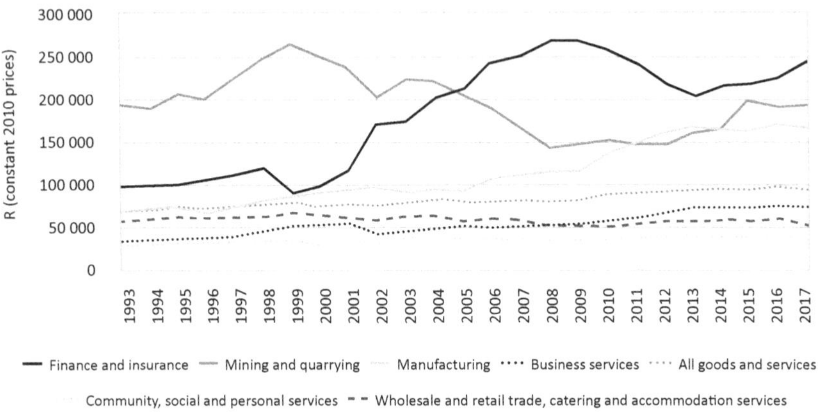

Source: Newman, 2019

Figure 13.7c: Employment and median salary per industry in the manufacturing sector, 2019

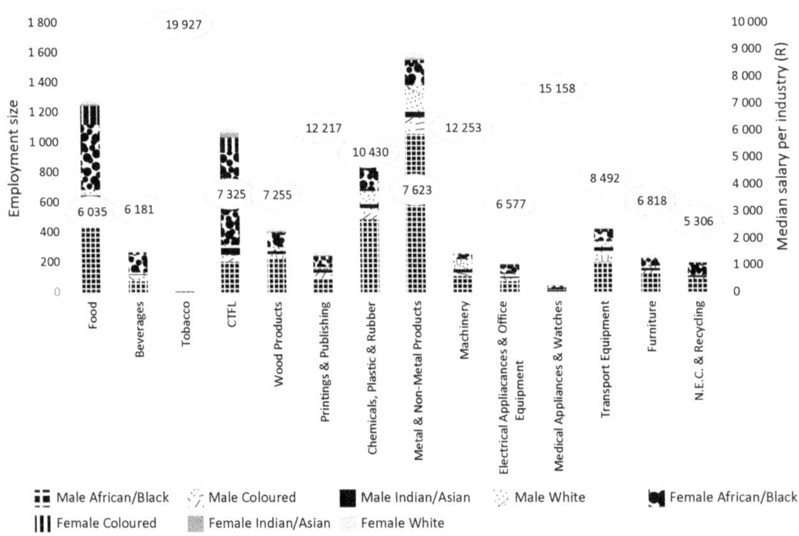

Source: Adapted from Gqubule, 2019, using data from Quantec, 2022 (database)

Figure 13.8a: Female labour force characteristics, 2008–2021

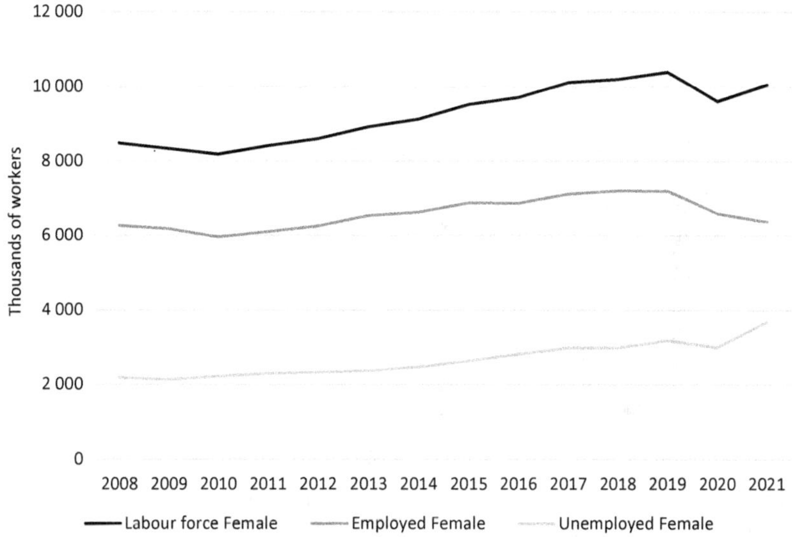

Source: StatsSA Labour Force Survey, 2021, extracted from Quantec, 2022 (database)

Figure 13.8b: Male labour force characteristics, 2008–2021

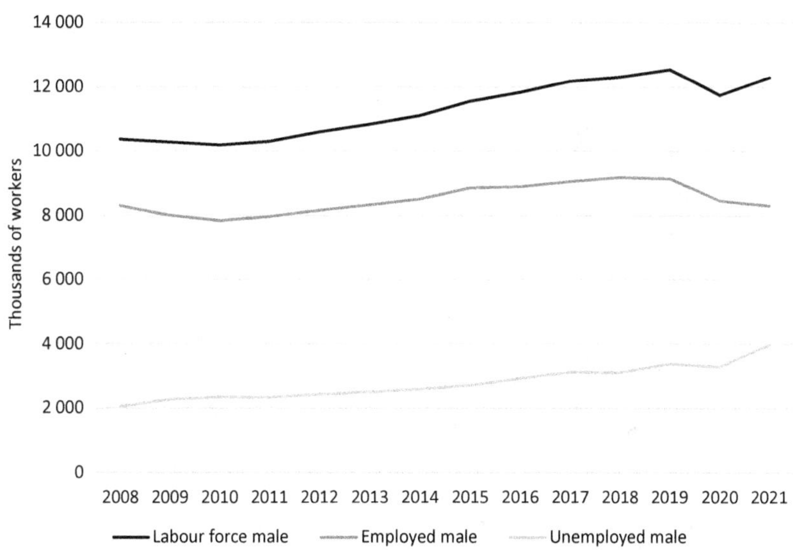

Source: StatsSA Labour Force Survey, 2021, extracted from Quantec, 2022 (database)

Figure 13.9a: Employment status by gender, 2008

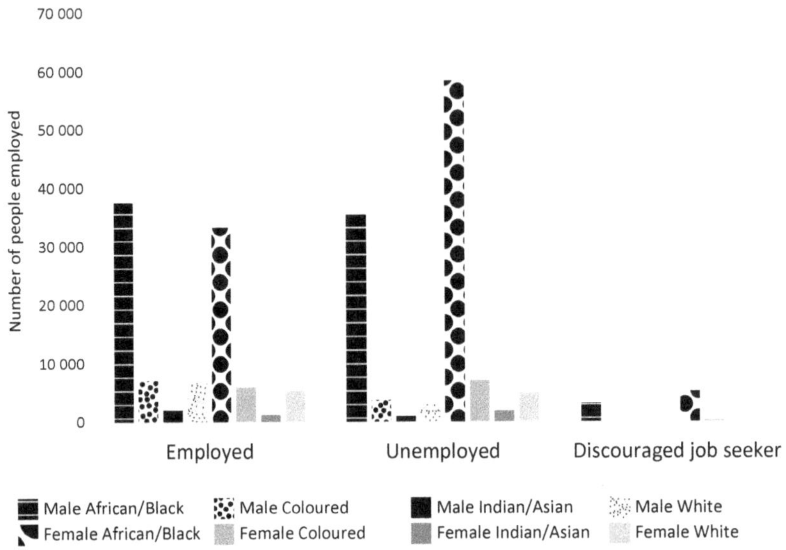

Source: StatsSA, 2019, extracted from Quantec, 2022 (database)

Figure 13.9b: Employment status by gender, 2011

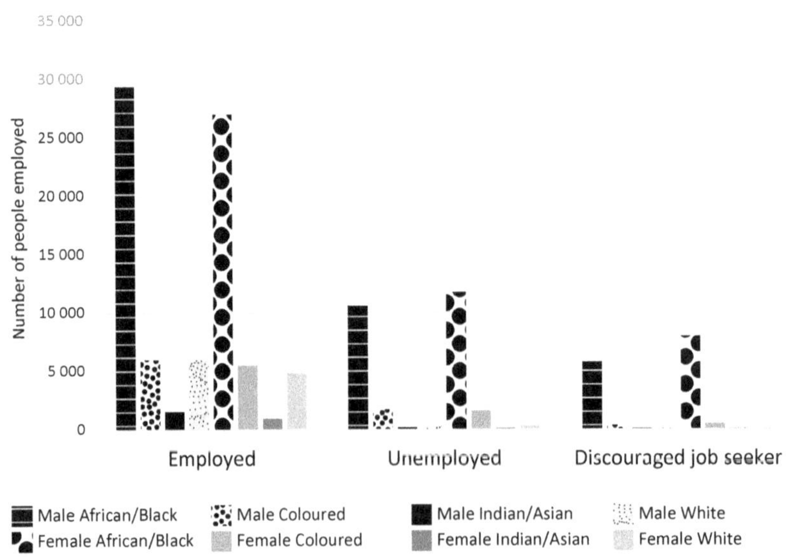

Source: StatsSA, 2019, extracted from Quantec, 2022 (database)

Figure 13.9c: Employment status by gender, 2015

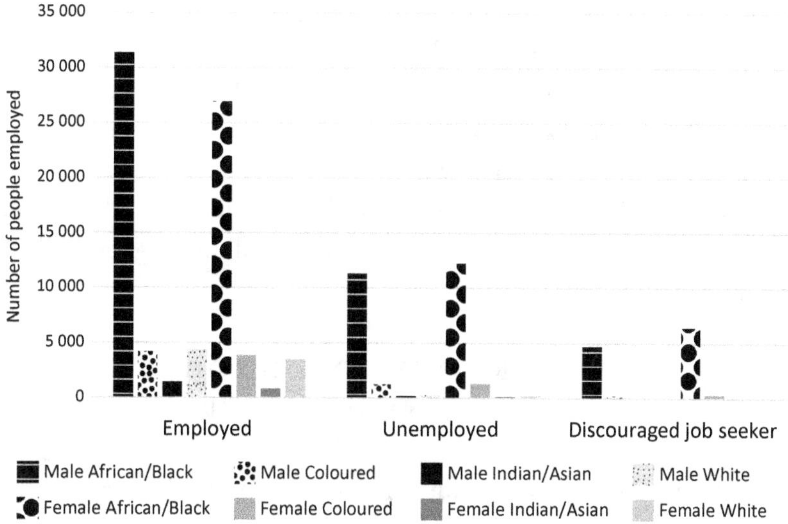

Source: StatsSA, 2019, extracted from Quantec, 2022 (database)

Figure 13.9d: Employment status by gender, 2019

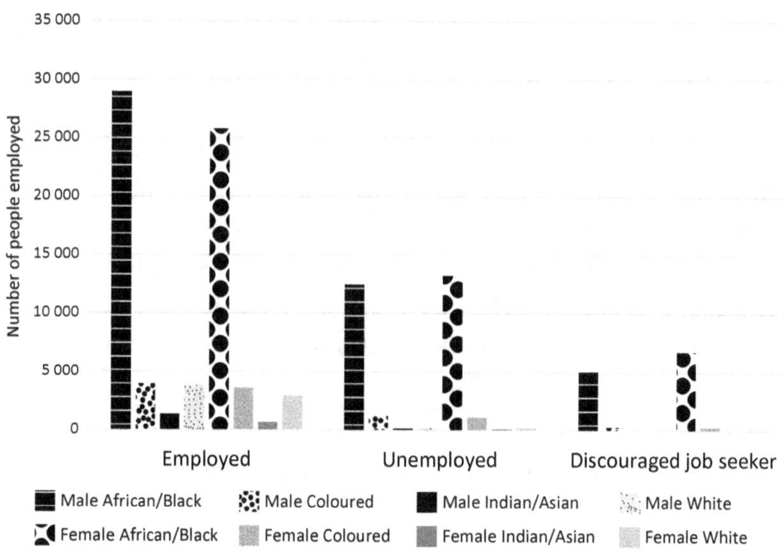

Source: StatsSA, 2019, extracted from Quantec, 2022 (database)

The fifth feature is the austerity macroeconomic agenda, spearheaded by the National Treasury, which has seen cuts in public expenditure over the last decade. Between 2014 and 2018, revenue growth was 2 per cent. However, non-interest expenditure growth was 1.8 per cent, while population growth was 1.6 per cent over the same period (BJC, 2019). The effect of the austerity drive has been to cut essential services, which has further worsened living conditions and increased the burden of care on mostly black women who are left to fill in the gaps left by a shrinking public service system.

THE EMPLOYER'S ROLE IN REPRODUCTIVE LABOUR: AN UNFOLDING CRISIS

One of the biggest disappointments of the post-apartheid labour regime in South Africa is that the progressive gains made by workers to ensure that worker rights are legislated have been undermined by the growth of non-standard work contracts or the informalisation of formal work. As discussed previously, subcontracting and casualisation are strategies employed to cut labour costs and to control the workplace by segmenting the workforce and are an outcome of the financialisation of the South African economy and its accelerated integration into the neoliberal global economy. In this section, we discuss the social costs of financialisation of non-standard work contracts – specifically, the impact of non-standard work contracts on the reproduction of the workforce. We also demonstrate how the pattern of uneven development fostered by the MEFC has been forced upon the reproductive spheres and that the economic and social reproduction spheres are heavily intertwined.

The 1970s were a time of unrest, with watershed industrial strikes during that period shaping the future trajectory of industrial relations in the country. The implementation of adequate occupational health and safety standards was amongst the key demands of the trade union movement, resulting in the establishment of the Erasmus Commission of Inquiry into Occupational Health and Safety in 1974. Unfortunately, none of the recommendations of the Erasmus Commission, which addressed workers' demands, were implemented. Some of the recommendations called on the private sector to prevent occupational diseases through training programmes for workers.

Over the past 20 years, safety in the mining sector has shown a massive improvement. Mining fatalities declined by 400 per cent between 1999 and 2018, while mining-related injuries declined by close to 300 per cent between 1999 and 2020 (see Figure 13.10 and Figure 13.11). Growing agitation by the trade union movement since the 1970s (as discussed above) was one of the factors contributing to this outcome. In terms of the Occupational Health and Safety Act No. 85 of 1993, employers were required to identify, assess and mitigate all workplace risks and to implement systems to contain risks that may not otherwise be easily mitigated. A system of occupational health surveillance, which included occupational health medical practitioners and hygienists, was also required to ensure that workers' health was continuously assessed and monitored in the interests of preventative care. Moreover, workers needed to be adequately trained so that they could perform their tasks safely without risks to their health.

Workers' resistance and state legislation have therefore offset the usual capitalist coercive pressure to maximise profit at the expense of the reproduction of the labour force. As a result, significant progress has been made in protecting mineworkers' lives through improvements to health and safety standards and practices.

Figure 13.10: Mining fatalities, 1999–2020

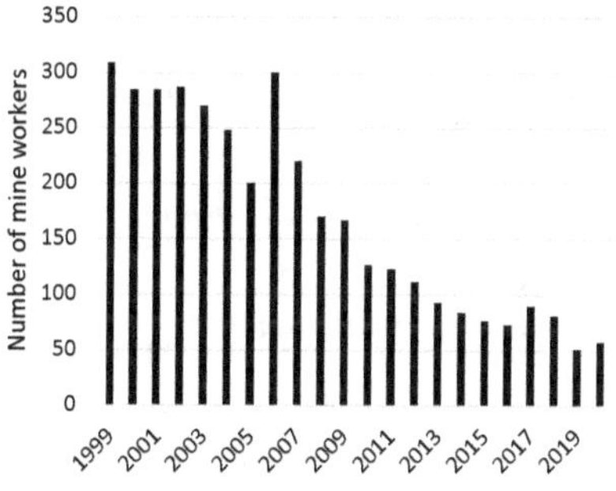

Source: MCSA, 2020: 18

Figure 13.11: Mining injuries, 1999–2020

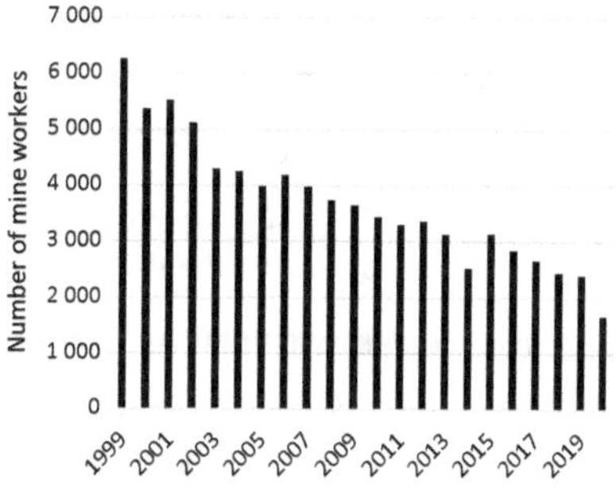

Source: MCSA, 2020: 18

However, these improvements mask the true nature of working conditions faced by mine workers, which have been induced by the financialisation of the mining sector and the integration of the sector into the global economy. The financialisation of the mining sector has taken place in multiple ways, all of which have had a bearing on the mining workforce. The push for increased shareholder value, for example, is linked to the workings of the international capital markets and the aspirations of institutional investors. Some mining companies, such as Anglo American, in opting for dual listings on international stock exchanges, have undergone restructuring, resulting in their focusing on their core business and/or divesting themselves of their industrial interests.

The impact of this form of financialisation, as observed by Ashman et al. (2013), is that the 80 per cent share of market capitalisation on the JSE held by the top five companies (mostly in mining and finance) in 1990 had shrunk to 26 per cent by 2012. Another form of financialisation that has occurred in the mining sector is what Karworski (2015) describes as a liquidity preference, evidenced in rising cash holdings, which are used for financial speculation with respect to mining assets. As observed by Bowman (2018), financialisation has spurred distributional contests between capital and labour over the share of outputs.

Financialisation has contributed to work restructuring. We argue that this has impacted the social reproduction of the workforce at the site of production in two ways. First, the growth in subcontracted work has undermined the effective implementation and monitoring of occupational health and safety standards. Close to half the workforce in the mining sector are employed under non-standard contracts, involving subcontracted work and employment secured via labour brokers (see Figure 13.12). This has been on the rise since the 1990s. A major concern is the two-tiered occupational health and safety regime which governs permanent and outsourced workers respectively. Outsourced workers are not only poorly paid, but they also do not receive the key benefits that permanent workers receive which would help to reproduce their labour power, such as medical aid, sick leave, injury compensation, pension benefit, severance pay, death benefits and free safety equipment (Crush et al., 2001).

Moreover, subcontracted workers are most likely to do the most dangerous jobs, have longer working hours and inferior personal protective gear and to be instantly dismissed in the event of injury or sickness (Stewart et al., 2019). Extended working hours are particularly common amongst subcontracted workers as it is a way of making up for their low pay. Consequently, they are most likely to suffer from fatigue and exhaustion, which in turn makes them injury prone. Importantly, a common problem that affects the mining workforce as a whole is the under-reporting of injuries. Managers would rather make private payments for workers to receive medical attention than work through the mine's medical system, as reporting the injury will affect individual and production team bonuses (Stewart et al., 2019). This informal system mostly affects subcontracted workers as a relatively large proportion of their salary is tied to production bonuses. By presiding over a two-tiered application of the Occupational Health and Safety Act, which discriminates according to contract type, mining bosses are reneging on their reproductive role to ensure the health, safety and wellbeing of their workforce (Stewart et al., 2019).

Furthermore, improvements in the occupational health of workers lag behind improvements in their occupational safety. Workers' exposure to airborne pollution has remained steady in the case of certain types of pollutants (HEG A and B) and has increased in the case of others (HEG C) (see Figure 13.15). Moreover, none of the targets for respiratory crystalline silica has been met during the period in question (see Figure 13.13 and Figure 13.14), meaning that there are more individual workers who are suffering from respiratory disease than the agreed maximum target. This has far-reaching implications for the health of subcontracted workers as many do not have access to medical aid benefits. This does not bode well for them should they fall ill. Again, workers operating under non-standard contracts are worse off, as they are not eligible for continuous health assessments aimed at preventative healthcare.

The financialisation of the economy in general and the mining sector in particular in post-apartheid South Africa has contributed to the growing fragmentation of the workforce, which has had serious repercussions

Figure 13.12: Standard and non-standard employment contracts in the mining sector, 2012, 2015 and 2019

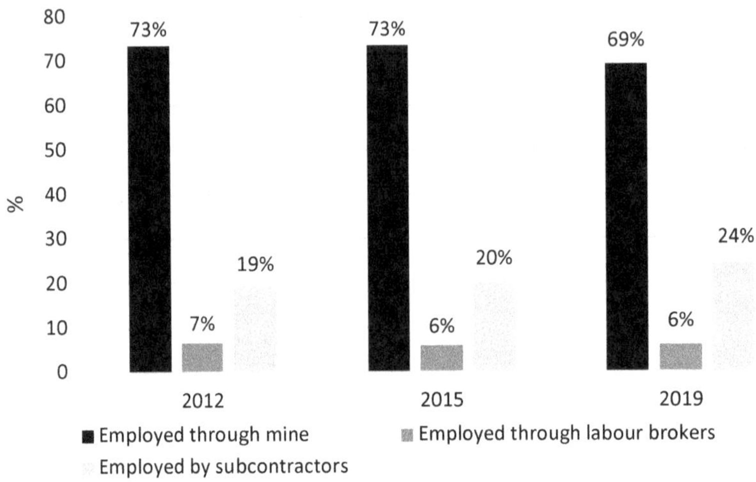

Source: StatsSA, 2012: 5; StatsSA, 2019: 15

Figure 13.13: Progress with respiratory crystalline silica (RCS), 2015–2019

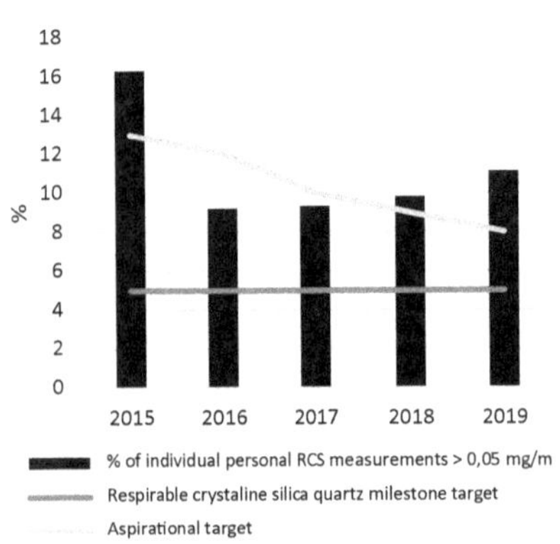

Source: MCSA, 2020: 21

Figure 13.14: Progress with coal dust milestone, 2015–2019

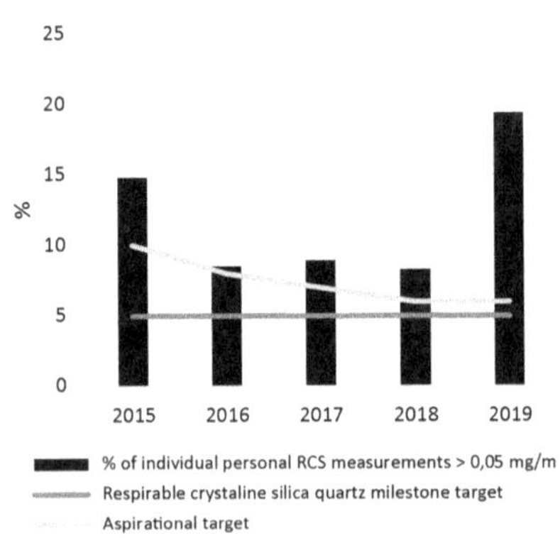

Source: MCSA, 2020: 21

for the reproductive role of the employer, as mentioned above. There is a contradiction here: mine bosses need a healthy workforce for the mine to operate efficiently and generate revenue; yet they are constrained by the compulsion for profits and high dividends through the use of cost-cutting measures, such as workforce segmentation via different contract types and the associated externalisation of mine bosses' reproductive

Figure 13.15: Mineworkers' exposure to airborne pollution, 2009–2019

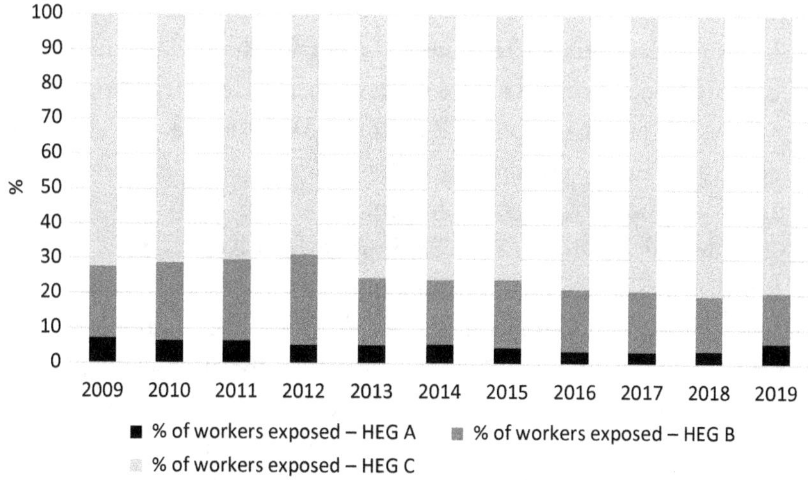

Source: MCSA, 2020: 20

role, which often come at a cost – that is, the cost of workers' lives, wellbeing and livelihoods. Therefore, the social costs of mining (which manifest as a disease burden, injury and death) are externalised, either to the public healthcare system or to households and communities.

WORKING IN REPRODUCTIVE SECTORS: FINANCIALISATION VERSUS OVERBURDENED HOUSEHOLDS

Social reproduction sectors (health, social services and care) have had similar experiences to those of the mining sector in terms of financialisation and cost-cutting strategies, evidenced in both the private and public sectors adopting various forms of austerity measures and work casualisation. We argue that the exploitation of workers involved in care (both paid and unpaid workers) is fundamental for the perpetuation of capitalist accumulation and that austerity and financialisation processes in the health sector have prompted work restructuring and casualisation. Again, workers' lives and livelihoods, including those of health workers, are put under strain by the very processes of accumulation that they help to sustain.

What characterises this reproductive work, specifically under a system of neoliberal capitalism, is the lack of recognition (social invisibility) and the intersecting systems of oppression, including those along gendered, socioeconomic and racial lines. The invisibility of care work performed (for free) by women in families mirrors and reinforces the fact that care work performed in workplaces is similarly undervalued and overrepresented by women globally, particularly women of colour and migrant women.

The democratic government in South Africa has designed a social policy that focuses on cash transfers in the form of social grants (child support, foster-child support, old-age pension and disability grants, amongst others). In April 2020, a temporary social relief of distress (COVID-19) grant was added to the collection. In financial year 2020/2021, 18.44 million social grants were paid, through a private service provider, to 11.45 million beneficiaries. This form of social assistance is considered by government to be the most effective, pro-poor programme currently in place and represents the main source of income for close to a quarter of all South Africans (Parliamentary Budget Office, 2021). However, this approach to social policy entails a shift from the provision of high-quality public services to the financialisation of social policy (Lavinas, 2017; Webb, 2016). As a result, the approach – based on the notion of financial inclusion – ends up reinforcing powerful financial institutions and the commodification of services of public interest and drives up indebtedness amongst the poor.

The South African population is faced with a quadruple burden of disease: communicable diseases, such as HIV/AIDS and tuberculosis (TB) (South Africa has the largest global share of TB cases); maternal and child mortality; non-communicable diseases, such as hypertension and cardiovascular disease, diabetes, cancer, mental illness and chronic lung disease; and injury and trauma. Owing to the unprecedented socioeconomic inequality in the country and the informalisation of work as well as the inadequacy of safe housing and sanitation facilities, the distribution of diseases is higher amongst the working-class black majority.[2] HIV/AIDS disproportionately affects women and is highest amongst black African women. In this regard, African women are the most vulnerable to infection due to factors such as their low socioeconomic status, which may force them into relationships that expose them to a higher risk. Moreover, there are demands on women's time and resources, as they constitute the majority of caregivers (Fakier and Cock, 2009).

The economic system has failed (either through the market or the state) to look after the health of the bulk of the population; as a result, the job of looking after people with poor health has largely fallen to African women, who either nurse patients in underfunded public entities or care for their family or community – often with limited access to electricity and sanitation.

During apartheid, healthcare provision used to be organised along racial and class lines. From the 1980s, due to government policies and global trends, the under-resourcing of public hospitals was accompanied by the growth of private hospitals, leading to what is referred to as the bifurcation of health provision. McIntyre et al. (1995) indicate that the number of private hospital beds in the country doubled between 1988 and 1993. The expansion of the private healthcare sector has continued in post-apartheid South Africa, which has resulted in heightened competition for skilled nursing labour and the emigration of health workers from the public to the private sector and from South Africa to the Global North. The growth of private hospitals has in turn reinforced the historical understaffing of health services available to the black majority.

Government health spending increased substantially between 1995 and 2012 to meet the rising demand for services, especially in the face of the HIV/AIDS epidemic. However, if figures are adjusted for population growth, real per capita (uninsured) public-health expenditure rose from 2012/13 (R157 547 million) until 2018/19 (R174 362 million) and, according to some measures, is now decreasing due to falling numbers of private insurance users (Blecher et al., 2017). From 2011, 'provincial departments of health have increasingly implemented tight restrictions on filling posts. [Consequently], fewer than half the number of professional nurses hired in the period 2006 to 2012 were hired between 2012 and 2016' (Oxfam, 2020b: 24).

What started in the 1980s and has continued in post-apartheid South Africa is a two-tiered health system: a well-resourced and high-cost private health service catering to less than 20 per cent of the population and an extremely under-resourced public service catering to the majority of the population yet relying on less than 50 per cent of public and private investment (Ataguba and McIntyre, 2018). The private system that serves an adequately resourced and generally healthier minority is subsidised by the state through expensive medical tax credits. As pointed out in an Oxfam (2020b: 26) report: 'Instead of giving R35.4 billion medical tax credits to wealthy taxpayers and the private healthcare sector, the government could increase the budget allocated to the public healthcare system by more than 60 per cent.'

Moreover, the Oxfam (2020b) report shows how the highly financialised private healthcare sector prioritises the interests of shareholders when it comes to the quality of its health services. In fact, against the background of the global and then domestic economic crisis: 'From 2016 to 2019, Netcare, Mediclinic and the Lifecare Group made a combined R11.7 billion in net income and paid R19.2 billion to shareholders in dividends and share buybacks. Cash to shareholders exceeded profit, with a shareholder pay-out ratio of 163 per cent' (Oxfam, 2020b: 27). Oxfam also notes that, to cut costs, private companies have accelerated their outsourcing strategies, leading to the deterioration of health workers' employment conditions and the services provided to clients.

The adverse consequences of financialisation and understaffing for the workforce cannot be overstated. Nurses and healthcare community workers (HCWs), who are the frontline workers in the healthcare system, are generally overworked (Cohen and Venter, 2020) and suffer from high levels of chronic stress. Furthermore, the South African black majority is bearing the brunt of systemic under-investment in the public sector and cost-cutting policies, which impact the quality of services. Women, specifically African women, are disproportionately represented amongst healthcare workers (see Figure 13.16) and their jobs are undervalued and poorly remunerated, despite the enormous workloads they carry.

The black majority carries the highest burden of disease relative to the richest white minority. However, the black majority receives the lowest quality and quantity of healthcare services. This is exacerbated by high morbidity rates, which affect the quality of healthcare work. This juxtaposition is a manifestation of the so-called 'inverse care law' (Hart, 1971).

Figure 13.16: Racial distribution of nursing staff by percentage, 1980 and 2001

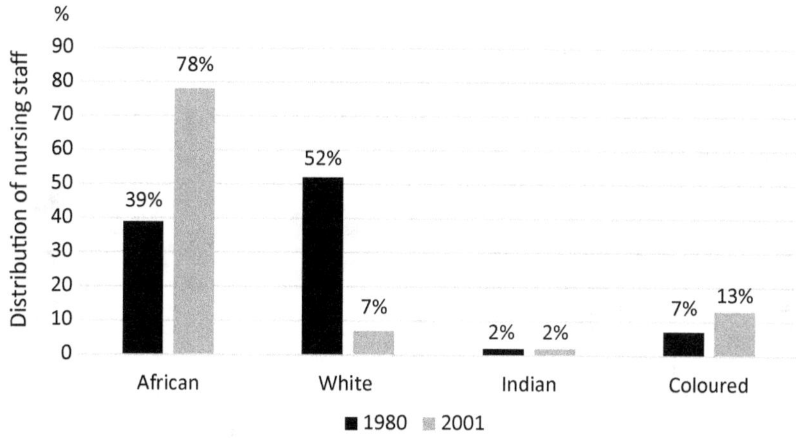

Source: Extracted from Hall and Erasmus, 2003: 539

The restructuring of healthcare services, which began in the 1980s in the context of a widespread lack of social and care services and inadequate preventative health facilities, has caused the amount of unpaid labour in households and communities to rise (Marais, 2007). Globally, socially reproductive activities are mostly performed at home by women, although the unequal distribution of this type of work between genders may vary depending on factors such as the broader socioeconomic environment, prevailing political and cultural values, and (importantly) the availability (or otherwise) of care alternatives outside the home.

The household is the epicentre of unequal, unpaid reproductive work (see Figure 13.17 and Figure 13.18). According to a 2019 time-use survey, women in South Africa spend on average 3 hours 15 minutes per day on unpaid work in the form of care and house maintenance, while men in South Africa spend on average 1 hour and 28 minutes on unpaid work.

Casale and Posel (2020) provide an analysis of women's employment patterns in the South African economy from 1995 to 2020. While pointing to the significant gains made by women since the transition to democracy, the authors also indicate the extent of the gender disparity in the labour market. Casale and Posel (2020) provide some evidence of the centrality of the burden of unpaid labour amongst women participating in the labour market. They conclude that as long

Figure 13.17: Minutes per day spent on unpaid work: Household, care and community, 2019

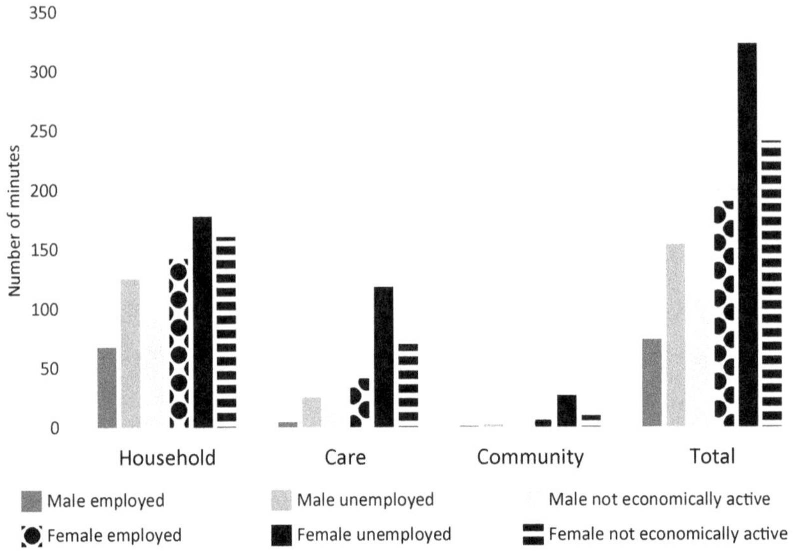

Source: Oxfam South Africa, 2020a: 58

as the provision of care within the household remains the primary responsibility of women, gender disparities will persist.

During apartheid, social reproduction work was rendered invisible by the racial divide that underpinned society and the economy as a whole, under the institutional banner of separate development (Ginsburg, 2021). Black women were employed for low wages in white households where they would perform essential reproductive tasks, such as cleaning the house, doing the laundry, and ironing, cooking and raising their employers' children (at the expense of their own.)

Even today, middle-class households employ domestic workers often for less than the minimum wage and often under informal employment arrangements. Domestic workers in South Africa may work part time, full time or as live-in workers (Oxfam, 2020a) and they may perform part or most of the reproductive work necessary to maintain the household, to raise the children and to look after the elders. Most domestic workers in South Africa are black women, as shown in Figure 13.19.

Historically, social reproduction work performed largely by

Figure 13.18: Minutes per day spent on unpaid service work according to employment status, 2019

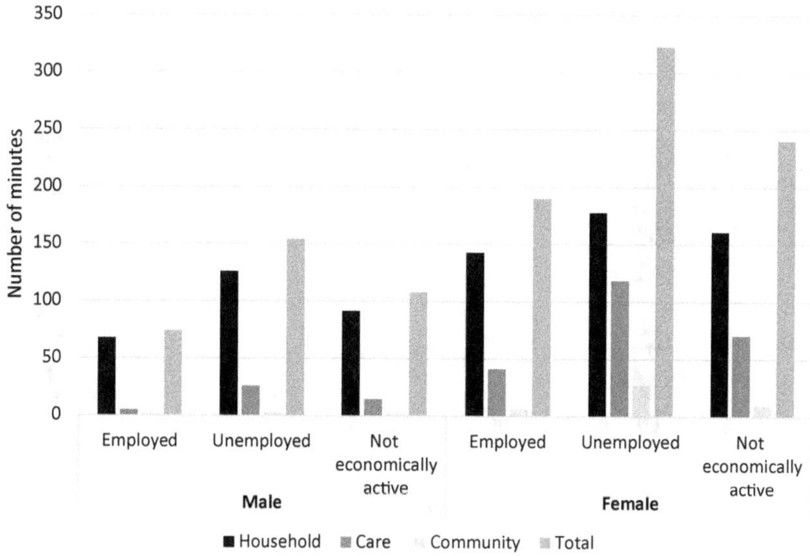

Source: Oxfam South Africa, 2020a: 57

black women in South Africa has been a fundamental characteristic of capitalist accumulation. This is exemplified by the lack of social services available to the black population throughout the periods of colonialism and apartheid and by the material support given to the economy by the black Bantustans in the form of cheap labour and the 'reserve subsidy' (Wolpe, 1972). As a result of the COVID-19 pandemic, the media, policymakers and the general public are finally paying more attention to some of the jobs entailing reproductive activities, describing some of these jobs as 'essential'. Nevertheless, the essential work categorisation is piecemeal and contested. Not only has the 'essential worker' categorisation been applied differently in different countries, but in general it excludes the most precarious or unpaid forms of reproductive work, which has remained invisible to the media and escaped policy attention (Stevano et al., 2020).

Globally, reproductive work is in a state of crisis and, because of the way in which it is organised, it has become a vector for deepening, intersecting inequalities. In South Africa, it is highly feminised and

Figure 13.19: Domestic helpers and cleaners by gender, per population group, 2019

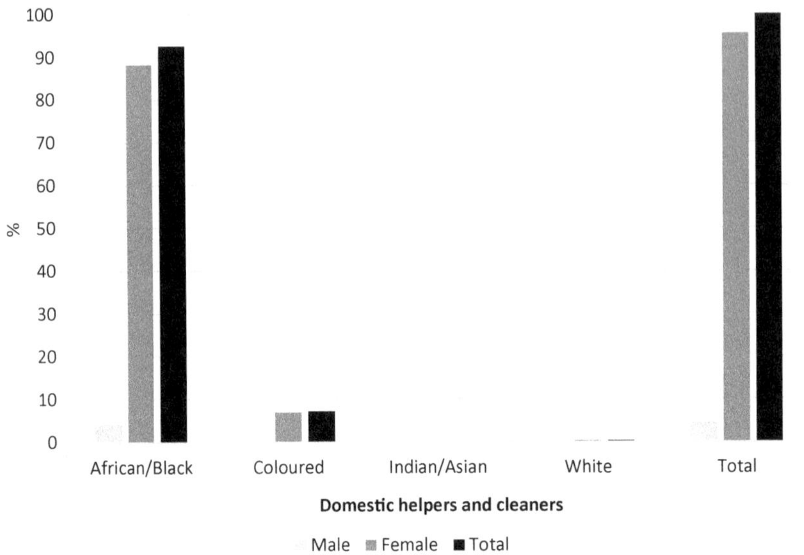

Source: StatsSA, 2019

racialised and is characterised by poor working conditions, which range from unpaid labour to informal labour and a high incidence of overworking in formal employment settings.

CONCLUSION

In this chapter we demonstrated that structural transformation in South Africa has been inadequate as it has failed to include critical dynamics in the economy, particularly those found at the intersection between class, race and gender. Instead of deepening industrialisation, which is itself an insufficient measure of development, structural transformation has continued to be associated with uneven development which has contributed to the crisis of social reproduction. The structure of the economy has continued to rely on the MEFC, giving rise to a crisis of economic production that has had to be absorbed by an undervalued and unrecognised social reproduction sphere.

We presented two arguments. The first argument is that, under apartheid-driven, racialised capitalism and the post-apartheid neoliberal order, private accumulation has shirked its reproductive duty to sustain the life and wellbeing of the workforce through the provision of a living wage and adequate health and safety at the site of production. Indeed, using the mining sector as an example, we demonstrated that capital externalises the costs of reproduction to an under-resourced public sector as well as to communities and households, with black women bearing the brunt of its process. The second argument is that the exploitation of workers involved in reproductive activities (both paid and unpaid workers) is fundamental to the perpetuation of capitalist development. We showed that financialisaton in the health sector, coupled with austerity measures, has resulted in work restructuring and casualisation. Again, the lives of black African women, who constitute the majority of the workforce in the health sector, are put under strain by the economic system that they have to sustain.

To break the cycle of social reproduction crises, it is essential to acknowledge the relevance of social reproduction activities to the functioning of the economy and society more broadly. Moreover, to counter the ongoing onslaught of inequalities, reproductive work must be redistributed between genders in the household and between the household and the state, through the provision of adequate public services and through the private sector, ensuring a living wage for their workers and a healthy and safe work environment.

REFERENCES

Adams, Z. 2022. 'Invisible labour: legal dimensions of invisibilization'. *Journal of Law and Society*, 49, 385–405.

Alli, B.O. 2008. *Fundamental Principles of Occupational Health and Safety*. Geneva: International Labour Organization.

Ashman, S., Mohamed, S. and Newman, S. 2013. 'The financialization of the South African economy and its impact on economic growth and employment'. Discussion Paper. Geneva: UNDESA, file:///C:/Users/27834/Downloads/Susan_retreat_UNDESA.pdf

Ataguba, J. and McIntyre, D. 2018. 'The incidence of health financing in South Africa: Finding from a recent data set'. *Health Economics Policy and Law*, 13 (1), 68–91.

Beier, F. 2018. 'Marxist perspectives on global enclosures and social reproduction'. *Journal for a Global Sustainable Information Society*, 16 (2), 546–561.

Bhattacharya, T. (ed.) 2017. *Social Reproduction Theory: Remapping class, recentering oppression*. London: Pluto Press.

Blecher, M., Daven, J., Kollipara, A., Maharaj, Y., Mansvelder, A. and Gaarekwe, O. 2017. 'Health spending at a time of low economic growth and fiscal constraint', in Padarath, A. and Barron, P. (eds.) *South African Health Review 2017*. Health System Trust, 25–40.

Bond, P. 2000. *Elite Transition from Apartheid to Neoliberalism in South Africa*. London: Pluto Press.

Bowman, A. 2018. 'Financialization and the extractive industries: The case of South African platinum mining', *Competition and Change*, 22 (4), 388–412.

Budget Justice Coalition (BJC). 2019. 'Budgeting in an era of austerity and state capture: A five-year review of budget policies and outcomes'. Submission by Budget Justice Coalition to Select and Standing Committees on Finance, https://iej.org.za/wp-content/uploads/2020/02/IEJ_BJC_presentation_26-02-2019_5_year_review-1.pdf, accessed 1 September 2022.

Cammack, P. 2020. 'Marx on Social Reproduction'. *Historical Materialism*, 28 (2), 76–106.

Casale, D. and Posel, D. 2020. 'Gender and early effects of the Covid-19 crisis in the paid and unpaid economies in South Africa'. National Income Dynamics (NIDS)-Coronavirus Rapid Mobile Survey (CRAM) Wave 1 Working Paper No. 4, https://cramsurvey.org/wp-content/uploads/2020/07/Casale-Gender-the-early-effects-of-the-COVID-19-crisis-in-the-paid-unpaid-economies-in-South-Africa.pdf, accessed 15 July 2022.

Cohen, J. and Venter, W. D. F. 2020. 'The integration of occupational- and household-based chronic stress among South African women employed as public hospital nurses'. *PLoS ONE*, 15 (5), e0231693.

Costa, D. M. and James, S. 1975. *The Power of Women and the Subversion of the Community*. Bristol: Falling Wall Press.

Cox, N. and Federici, S. 1975. *Counter-Planning from the Kitchen: Wages for Housework: A perspective on capital and the left*. Bristol: Falling Wall Press.

Crush, J., Ulicki, T., Tseane, T. and Jansen van Veuren, E. 2001. 'Undermining labour: The rise of sub-contracting in South African gold mines'. *Journal of Southern African Studies*, 27 (1), 5–31.

Englert, T. 2017. 'Precarious workers, their power, and the ways to realise it, the struggle of Heineken labour broker workers'. University of the Witwatersrand Global Labour University Research Report, https://wiredspace.wits.ac.za/items/4d2c8d22-992f-4538-ae68-baf1913ac591

Fakier, K. and Cock, J. 2009. 'A gendered analysis of the crisis of social reproduction in contemporary South Africa'. *International Feminist Journal of Politics*, 11 (3), 353–371.

Federici, S. 2014. 'The reproduction of labour power in the global economy and the unfinished feminist revolution', in Atzeni, M. (ed.) *Workers and Labour in a Globalised Capitalism: Contemporary Themes and Theoretical issues.* United Kingdom: Palgrave Macmillan.

Fraser, N. 2016. 'Contradictions of capital and care'. *New Left Review*, https://newleftreview.org/issues/II100/articles/nancy-fraser-contradictions-of-capital-and-care.pdf, accessed 1 September 2022.

Ginsburg, R. 2021. *At Home with Apartheid: The Hidden Landscapes of Domestic Service in Johannesburg.* Virginia: University of Virginia Press.

Gqubule, B. 2019. 'Women in the economy'. Briefing Paper for Oxfam South Africa. (Unpublished.)

Hall, E. and Erasmus, J. 2003. 'Medical practitioners and nurses', in Human Sciences Research Council *Human Resources Development Review 2003: education, employment and skills in South Africa.* Cape Town: HSRC Press, 522–553, https://www.gtac.gov.za/wp-content/uploads/2022/02/Medical-Practitioners-and-Nurses.pdf, accessed 25 March 2023.

Hart, J. T. 1971. 'The inverse care law'. *The Lancet*, 297 (7696), 405–412.

James, S. 2012. *Sex, Race and Class – The Perspective of Winning: A Selection of Writings, 1952–2011.* Oakland: PM Press.

Karworski, E. 2015. 'The finance–mining nexus in South Africa: How mining companies use the South African equity market to speculate'. *Journal of Southern African Studies*, 41 (1), 9–28.

Lavinas, L. 2017. *The Takeover of Social Policy by Financialization.* New York: Palgrave Macmillan.

Malikane, C. 2017. 'Profitability and crisis in the South African economy'. MPRA Paper No. 76165, https://mpra.ub.uni-muenchen.de/76165/1/MPRA_paper_76165.pdf, accessed 30 May 2022.

Marais, H. 2007. 'The uneven impact of AIDS in a polarized society'. *AIDS*, 21 (3), S21–S29.

Marx, K. 1976 [1867]. *Capital: A Critique of Political Economy. Volume One, translated by Ben Fowkes.* Germany: Vintage.

Marx, K. and Engels, F. 2004 [1948]. *The Communist Manifesto*, English Edition by Andy Blunden, Leesmagazijn.

McIntyre, D., Bloom, G., Doherty, J. and Brijlal, P. 1995. *Health Expenditure and Finance in South Africa.* Durban: Health Systems Trust and World Bank.

Mezzadri, A. April 20, 2020. 'A crisis like no other: Social reproduction and the regeneration of capitalist life during the COVID-19 pandemic'. *Developing Economics.* https://developingeconomics.org/2020/04/20/

a-crisis-like-no-other-social-reproduction-and-the-regeneration-of-capitalist-life-during-the-covid-19-pandemic/, accessed 30 May 2022

Mezzadri, A. 2022. 'Neoliberal capitalism and the commodification of social reproduction, from our home to our classroom'. *Developing Economics* website: https://developingeconomics.org/author/alemezzadri/, accessed 1 September 2022.

Minerals Council South Africa (MCSA). 2020. 'Safety and health industry performance review'. Minerals Council South Africa Integrated Review 2020, https://www.mineralscouncil.org.za/downloads/send/14-current/1572-integrated-annual-review-2020-safety-and-health-industry-performance-review#:~:text=The%202020%20industry%20safety%20performance,fatalities%20year%2Don%2Dyear, accessed 1 September 2022.

Newman, S. 2019. *The Minerals–Energy Complex and Structural Inequality in South Africa.* Johannesburg: Oxfam South Africa. file:///C:/Users/User/Downloads/minerals-council-iar-2020-safety-and-health%20(2).pdf, accessed 17 April 2022.

Oxfam South Africa. 2020a. 'Reclaiming power: Womxn's work and income inequality in South Africa', https://www.oxfam.org.za/wp-content/uploads/2020/11/oxfam-sa-inequality-in-south-africa-report-2020.pdf, accessed 30 May 2022.

Oxfam South Africa. 2020b. 'The right to dignified healthcare work is a right to dignified healthcare for all', www.oxfam.org.za/wp-content/uploads/2020/08/oxfam_care4carers-report_final_20200720.pdf, accessed 30 May 2022.

Parliamentary Budget Office. 2021. https://www.parliament.gov.za/storage/app/media/PBO/National_Development_Plan_Analysis/2021/june/03-06-2021/May_2021_Social_Grant_fact_sheet.pdf, accessed 17 April 2022.

Prinsloo, J. W. and Smith, H. 1997. 'Development in fixed capital stock: 1960–1995'. OECD Capital Stock Conference, Agenda Item IV, https://www.oecd.org/sdd/na/2666708.pdf, accessed 19 April 2022.

Quantec database. 2022. 'Gross capital formation by private and public corporations at constant 2015 prices, 1960–1990'. www.quantec.co.za, accessed 11 September 2022.

Quantec database. 2022. 'Flow of funds in South Africa at constant 2015 prices, 1970–2020'. www.quantec.co.za, accessed 11 September 2022.

Quantec database. 2022. 'Change in fixed capital stock at constant 2015 prices and growth in financial sector, 1961–2021'. www.quantec.co.za, accessed 11 September 2022.

Quantec database. 2022. 'Speculative investments and unemployment in South Africa, 1994–2021', www.quantec.co.za, accessed 11 September 2022.

Quantec database. 2022. 'Employment and median salary per industry in the manufacturing sector, 2019', www.quantec.co.za, accessed 11 September 2022.

Quantec database. 2022. 'Female labour-force characteristics, 2008–2021', www.quantec.co.za, accessed 11 September 2022.

Quantec database. 2022. 'Male labour-force characteristics, 2008–2021', www.quantec.co.za, accessed 11 September 2022.

Quantec database. 2022. 'Employment status by gender, 2008'. www.quantec.co.za, accessed 11 September 2022.

Quantec database. 2022. 'Employment status by gender, 2011', www.quantec.co.za, accessed 11 September 2022.

Quantec database. 2022. 'Employment status by gender, 2015', www.quantec.co.za, accessed 11 September 2022.

Quantec database. 2022. 'Employment status by gender, 2019', www.quantec.co.za, accessed 11 September 2022.

Statistics SA (StatsSA). 2012. 'Mining Industry, 2012'. Report No. 20-01-02 (2012), http://www.statssa.gov.za/publications/Report-20-01-02/Report-20-01-022012.pdf, accessed 16 August 2022.

Statistics SA (StatsSA). 2019. 'Mining Industry, 2019'. Report No. 20-01-02 (2019). http://www.statssa.gov.za/publications/Report-20-01-02/Report-20-01-022019.pdf, accessed 16 August 2022.

Stevano, S., Ali, R. and Jamieson, M. 2020. 'Essential for what? A global social reproduction view on the re-organisation of work during the COVID-19 pandemic'. *Canadian Journal of Development Studies/Revue canadienne d'études du développement*, 42, 1–22.

Stevano, S., Mezzadri, A., Lombardozzi, L. and Bargawi, H. 2021. 'Hidden abodes in plain sight: The social reproduction of households and labour in the COVID-19 pandemic'. *Feminist Economics*, 27 (1–2), 271–287.

Stewart, A., Bezuidenhout, A. and Bischoff, C. 2019. 'Safety and health before and after Marikana: Subcontracting, illegal mining and trade union rivalry in the South African mining industry'. *Review of African Political Economy*, 47 (163), 27–44.

United Nations (UN). 2015. 'Resolution Adopted by the General Assembly on 25 September 2015. A/Res/70/1 Transforming Our World: The 2030 Agenda for Sustainable Development'. New York: United Nations, https://www.un.org/en/development/desa/population/migration/generalassembly/docs/globalcompact/A_RES_70_1_E.pdf, accessed 1 September 2022.

Webb, C. 2016. 'Profiting from poverty in South Africa'. *African Review of Political Economy*, http://roape.net/2016/08/30/profiting-poverty-debt-finance-social-grants, accessed 18 July 2022.

Wolpe, H. 1972. 'Capitalism and cheap labour-power in South Africa: From segregation to apartheid'. *Economy and Society*, 1 (4), 425–456.

NOTES

1 Gross capital formation is the sum of additional capital outlays and fixed assets as well as net inventory level changes.

2 This chapter adopts a Marxian definition of the working class, which includes both unemployed and underemployed workers, which Marx refers to as 'surplus labour' or 'the reserve army of labour' in the Communist Manifesto and in Capital Volume I (Marx, 1976 [1867]).

FOURTEEN

Technological innovation, the changing nature of work and the implications for trade unionism in post-apartheid South Africa

THABANG SEFALAFALA, RUTH CASTEL-BRANCO AND MUSAWENKOSI H. MALABELA

INTRODUCTION

In July 2021, South Africa experienced an unprecedented wave of social unrest, highlighting deep social, economic and political fissures. Since the end of apartheid, income inequality has increased, despite attempts to deracialise the labour market and expand public provisioning (Chancel et al., 2022). Persistently high levels of unemployment and widespread working poverty are amongst the key drivers of inequality. The expanded unemployment rate currently stands at 46.6 per cent (StatsSA, 2021), yet being employed is no guarantee that workers can meet their households' basic needs (Isaacs, 2016). Notably, patterns of unemployment and working poverty are highly skewed along racial lines, pointing to the enduring structure of the apartheid labour market. Despite expectations that the end of apartheid would bring about improvements in working conditions for black workers, these have not materialised (Pons-Vignon and Anseeuw, 2009) amidst a neoliberal order.

Historically, South Africa's economy has been dominated by the minerals–energy complex (MEC), which is characterised by capital-intensive industries associated with the extractive sectors, with few linkages with the rest of the economy (Fine and Rustomjee, 1996). With the end of apartheid and the transition to democracy, the African National Congress (ANC) government adopted a neoliberal macroeconomic framework. This precipitated the internationalisation and financialisation of capital flows, as corporations reoriented their investments towards financial activities (Ashman, 2015). The outcome has been declining levels of fixed capital investment, particularly in sectors outside the core of the MEC, and increased capital intensity in manufacturing (Newman, 2019).

The failure to diversify South Africa's economy and develop labour-intensive light manufacturing has undermined the labour market's capacity to absorb the country's growing working-age population – which has been further exacerbated by the COVID-19 pandemic (StatsSA, 2021). Furthermore, externalisation and outsourcing, together with the flexibilisation of the labour market, have compromised conditions of work and undercut the social basis of trade unions, shifting the balance of power between capital and labour (Webster et al., 2016). Meanwhile, the reorientation of capital inflows towards speculative credit has resulted in rising consumer debt (James, 2014), prompting a reproductive squeeze. The rollback of public provisioning – housing, transportation, health, education – has only amplified this crisis of social reproduction.

It is within this context that a strenuous debate has developed around the impact of digital technologies on the world of work(ers) and inequality in South Africa. Digital technologies are proliferating at an unprecedented pace, even if uneven and contested. The World Bank (2019) contends that this digital revolution has the potential to increase productivity, stimulate growth and catalyse employment outside of the core of the MEC. The role of the state, the World Bank argues, is to ensure that the next generation has the skills to benefit from emerging employment opportunities – a position shared by South Africa's Presidential Commission on the Fourth Industrial Revolution (2020). However, others paint a more disturbing picture of growing inequality, widespread job shedding – estimates for South Africa are between 35 per cent and 67 per cent (Frey and Osborne, 2017) – deskilling and declining wage shares. As digital technologies concentrate capital across sectors and geographies, non-standard and informal employment is likely to spread to new industries (Anner et al., 2019).

Drawing on the labour process theory, this chapter explores how technological innovation is reshaping the world of work(ers) and inequality in South Africa. It focuses on two case studies outside the core of the MEC. The first case is the automotive industry, which has received substantial state support through the Motor Industry Development Programme (MIDP), which in recent years has been superseded by the Automotive Production and Development Programme (APDP) (Mashilo, 2022). The second case is digital labour platforms, which have proliferated in the wake of the COVID-19 pandemic (Webster and Masikane, 2020). While the former is a historically unionised sector, the latter is characterised by hybrid forms of collective organisation outside the trade union movement.

THE CHANGING NATURE OF WORK IN THE POST-APARTHEID PERIOD

Compared to neighbouring countries, South Africa is highly proletarianised – a legacy of colonial land dispossession, repression of autonomous economic activities, and coercive measures aimed at funnelling black women and men into ultra-low-wage, humiliating and permanently insecure labour (Bundy, 1979). Under colonial capitalism, race became the key social differentiator. The black worker was subjected to a racialised wage structure and stripped of their basic rights, including the right to form or belong to a union. In the absence of labour and social protections, labour reserves across southern

Africa carried the full cost of social reproduction. They subsidised black workers' wages, raised a new generation of wage labourers, and absorbed the unemployed during periods of labour surplus (Legassick and Wolpe, 1976). However, the violence of proletarianisation – aimed at creating conditions of absolute deprivation, which left southern Africans with little choice but to sell their labour to colonial capital – ultimately undermined the economic basis of the very reserves on which colonial capital had come to rely, triggering a crisis of social reproduction (Mafeje, 1981).

Despite attempts, at the end of apartheid, to deracialise the labour market and expand public provisioning, inequality has continued to rise. One of the key drivers of inequality has been endemic unemployment. Between 1994 and 2021, the official (strict) unemployment rate increased from 23 per cent to 34.9 per cent, while the expanded unemployment rate increased from 30.9 per cent to 46.6 per cent (StatsSA, 2021) (Figure 14.1). Furthermore, the proportion of the long-term unemployed – that is, those who have been unemployed for over a year – increased from 57 per cent to 79 per cent, pointing to the structural nature of unemployment.

Some argue that high wages and labour market rigidity are at the root of South Africa's unemployment crisis (Bhorat and Cheadle, 2009). Others contend that labour relations are already highly flexibilised due to rampant outsourcing and weak enforcement of labour protections, and that the problem is the result of an increasingly financialised, capital-intensive MEC (Fine and Mohamed, 2022; Newman, 2019). As Newman (2019) illustrates in Figure 14.2, gross fixed capital investment in the post-apartheid era has barely kept up with capital stock, accelerating between 2004 and 2008 due to increased investment in the MEC and financial sectors. With the onset of the recession, sectors outside the MEC core experienced a contraction in investment, deepening unemployment. Today, approximately 50 per cent of South Africa's gross domestic product (GDP) comes from the MEC and financial sector (and adjacent industries) which constitute less than 25 per cent of the total labour share (Figure 14.3).

As Figure 14.3 illustrates, between 2008 and 2021, the share of employment in manufacturing fell from 15 per cent to 10 per cent, exacerbated by the advent of labour-replacing technologies in key industries such as the automotive industry (Naidoo, 2020). Meanwhile, there was a substantial increase in the share of employment in the financial sector, from 12 per cent in 2008 to 17 per cent in 2021 (StatsSA, 2021). This was driven by the expansion of financial services to the previously unbanked and a shift to automated banking systems, which initially required additional labour but subsequently eroded employment gains (SASBO, 2020).

The industries with the highest employment shares during the period were community and social services and trade, which constitute important sources of employment for women. However, as Isaacs (2016) points out, more than a third of those employed in services were below the working poverty line prior to the introduction of a national minimum wage. Working poverty was even higher amongst those employed in trade, hovering around 60.2 per cent. Another important source of employment for women was paid domestic work, which reflected the highest level of working poverty, followed closely by agricultural work (Isaacs, 2016).

Figure 14.1: Unemployment trends, 2008–2021

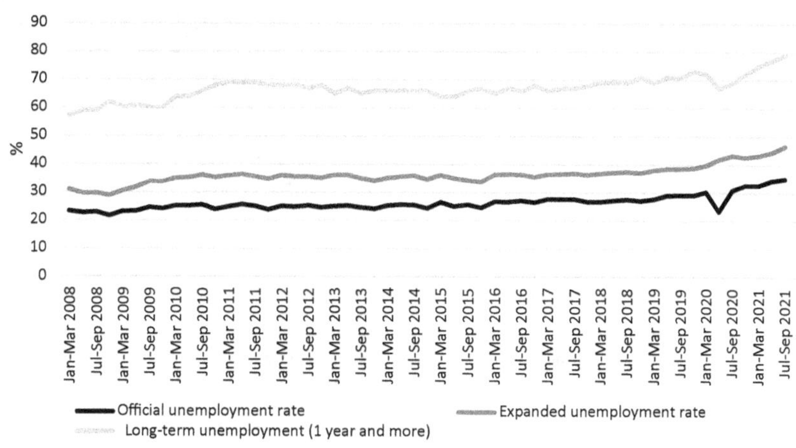

Source: StatsSA, 2021

Figure 14.2: Gross fixed capital investment, 1970–2016

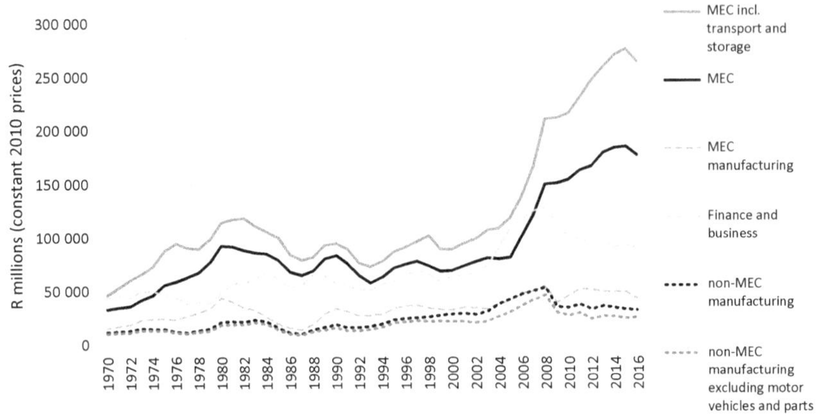

Source: Newman, 2019

Figure 14.3: Trends in employment shares by industry, 2008–2021

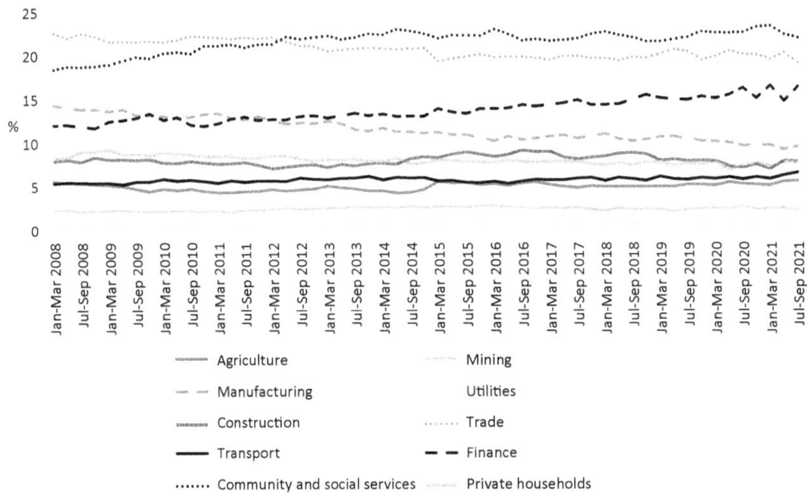

Source: StatsSA, 2021

Of course, widespread unemployment and working poverty are hardly new phenomena. Indeed, as Scully (2016) points out, throughout history and across much of the world, informality has been the norm, and South Africa is no different. According to Statistics South Africa's Quarterly Labour Force Survey, approximately a third of the employed population derive a livelihood primarily from activities outside the formal, non-agricultural sector – a share that has remained more or less constant over the last few decades (StatsSA, 2021). As Figure 14.4 illustrates, the industries with the highest shares of informality include construction, trade and transportation. In reality, the boundaries between formal and informal employment are extremely blurred. Moreover, the scope of informal work is extraordinarily broad and there are more linkages than divisions between the formal and informal economies (Valodia and Devey, 2012).

Despite high levels of unemployment, South Africa's informal economy is small when compared to that of other African countries. Indeed, according to the Quarterly Labour Force Survey, only 4 per cent of those between the ages of 15 and 64 years plough their own fields (StatsSA, 2021). Contributing factors include: the dominance of the formal sector and the concentration of conglomerates, which crowd out informal activities; the absence of state support for small-scale and local production; and limited access to public land and other forms of social provisioning (Francis and Valodia, 2022). The COVID-19 pandemic, in turn, exacerbated South Africa's crisis of social reproduction and unemployment (StatsSA, 2021). For the first time since the Quarterly Labour Force Survey was introduced, South Africa experienced sustained job shedding. Only the informal economy saw a slight increase in its employment share. However, informal workers are largely excluded from labour and social protections.

Rising unemployment and informality have aggravated the crisis facing the trade union movement. Trade union density has been in decline since the late 1990s, driven by neoliberal macroeconomic policy, the introduction of labour-replacing technologies and the increased financialisation of the MEC. Trade unions have struggled to respond, ultimately compromising their own capacity to service members and fostering discontent amongst disgruntled workers. Declining union representation has created the space for new forms of worker representation, some more progressive than others. Sefalafala (2011) notes that there has been a proliferation of legal firms representing workers in unionised workplaces, driven by workers' declining confidence in trade unions. Furthermore, trade unions have struggled

Figure 14.4: Share of informality by industry, 2021

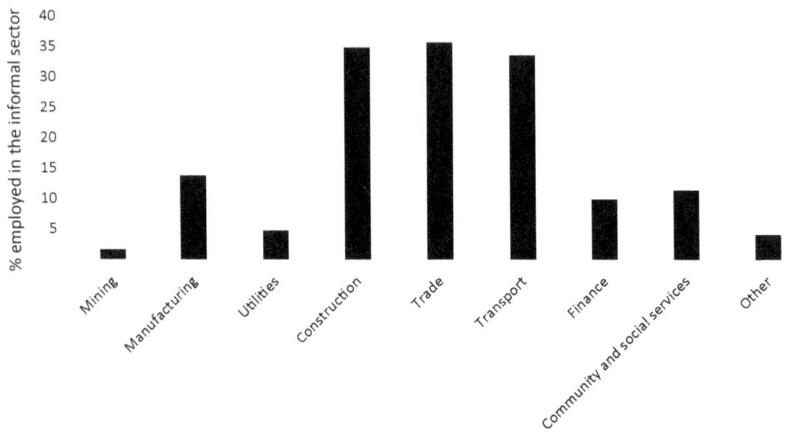

Source: StatsSA, 2021

to organise gig workers, atypical workers and migrant workers – despite having the historical mandate to do so (Lorgat, 2022). Currently, only a third of the South African workforce is unionised (StatsSA, 2021), thus shifting the balance of power from labour to capital.

While technological innovation has the potential to generate new forms of employment (Presidential Commission on the Fourth Industrial Revolution, 2020), the increased uptake of digital technologies threatens to roll back labour and social protections (Anner et al., 2019). It is therefore imperative that trade unions shape the terms of technological innovation. Drawing on the labour process theory, the next section explores the impact of technological innovation on workers in the automotive industry and on digital labour platforms.

TECHNOLOGICAL INNOVATION AND THE CHANGING LABOUR PROCESS

The labour process theory is critical for understanding how production is organised and how it shapes social relations. This is because the conditions of work are inextricably linked both to the circumstances of workers and to the working classes more generally. Any changes in the structure of the working class cannot be understood unless the ongoing transformations in the labour process are analysed. Moreover, the terms of production directly affect the ways in which workers can or cannot effectively organise.

Harry Braverman's *Labour and Monopoly Capital* (1975) proved influential in advancing the labour process theory in South Africa. Braverman was concerned with the relations between labour and management and the role of technology in the processes of capital accumulation and the changing structure of the working class. He understood the labour process, not just as a technical process but also as a social process embedded in the social conditions and relations that emerge at the point where labour and capital converge – that is, the point of production (Braverman, 1975). Three themes have dominated studies on the labour process: skill/deskilling, technology and race/racial Fordism.

Regarding the first theme, debates have centred on the degree to which capitalist developments degraded and eroded the skills of craft workers. The managerial prerogative to separate conception and execution transformed workers into automatons following instructions, as exemplified in the figure of Schmidt, the automaton worker in Taylor's book, *Scientific Management* (Taylor, 2003). Braverman's analysis of the labour process and Taylorism indicates that management is concerned with gathering knowledge for the purpose of controlling the production process and separating the worker from the knowledge underpinning production, confining them to execution. However, as Leger (1992) pointed out in his study on black gold mineworkers in South Africa, mineworkers had tacit skills, developed through accumulated experience and applied knowledge. Despite the changes in the labour process, workers continued to have repositories of knowledge that could be concealed from management and which created opportunities for worker resistance.

Thus, it is important for trade unions to use these repositories to build their bargaining power and ensure that they protect their workers. Trade unions, as key players in South Africa's industrial relations landscape, need to be proactive when it comes to technological changes in the workplace. This is because technology has a direct impact on their power and organisational strength in the respective workplaces where they organise, especially when such changes lead to retrenchments.

Regarding the second theme, debates have centred on the impact of technology on worker power. While management has exercised managerial control, the adoption of machine technology as a weapon was hardly predetermined. Mechanisation could also strengthen the bargaining power of certain groups of semi-skilled workers and facilitate collective action through the concentration of workers under one roof (Webster, 1985). Technological advances in the current epoch tend to disperse workers, allowing them to work remotely. This potentially undermines the earlier forms of solidarity based on worker concentration in one place. Indeed, as unions lose members (see Cloete, 2021), old ways of recruiting and organising workers, used by the erstwhile black trade union movement of the 1970s and 1980s, may not be effective in the face of changes to work patterns induced by digital technologies.

New hybrid forms of worker organising have emerged in parallel to traditional unions, including associations that combine traditional unionism with informal worker organising. Alongside traditional trade unions, workers in the gig economy have developed ways to overcome the switch to the remote and individualised organisation of work by using WhatsApp groups that operate like a trade union, such as the Uganda Bike Drivers Association (Webster and Masikane, 2020).

Lastly, debates have centred on race and racial Fordism. Although race is neglected in Braverman's (1975) analysis of the labour process, it became critical in South Africa where the apartheid state created a system of labour domination through forced proletarianisation, racial despotism (Burawoy, 1985) and the political oppression of black workers (Von Holdt and Webster, 2005). Mass production and the division of labour were structured along racial lines, through the job colour bar and Job Reservation Act, which excluded black workers from skilled and higher-paying positions. Black workers were also excluded from mass consumption, creating a brand of 'racial Fordism' (Gelb, 1987). Although some argue that 'racial Fordism' fell away in the post-apartheid workplace, as an increasing number of black workers moved into skilled and supervisory jobs (Crankshaw, 1997), subsequent investigations into the labour process across sectors exposed the perpetuation of the apartheid legacy (Von Holdt and Webster, 2005).

The remainder of this section analyses contemporary changes in the labour process and working conditions, drawing on two case studies: the automotive industry and digital platform work.

The automotive industry

The automotive industry is one of the industries that has received significant support from the state in the form of various incentives provided by the Departments of Trade and Industry and Economic Development (now merged into the Department of Trade, Industry and Competition) and is a key contributor to the GDP of the manufacturing sector (Mashilo, 2019). Under pressure to increase their productivity and compete within global value chains, manufacturers embarked on a process of economic upgrading. For example, investments in technology, including robotics, by component manufacturing enterprises under contract to original equipment manufacturers (OEMs) increased from 15 per cent in the 1980s to 55 per cent in 2010 (Vulavala and Ulmer, 2014). In South Africa, the automobile body shop is fully automated, while 80 per cent of the paint shop is automated. Technological adoption on the assembly line stands at about 20 per cent, while the use of machines in logistics operations is increasing. These changes in the production process have significantly increased the ratio of 'dead capital' to 'variable capital' and boosted productivity, efficiency, exports and global integration, investments and profitability. However, workers have been displaced and subject to greater control amidst rising labour insecurity in the wake of heightened mechanisation (Chigbu and Nekhwevha, 2020).

Owing to economic upgrading, productivity in the automotive industry has increased. In this regard, the industry's contribution to GDP increased from 0.8 per cent in 2018 to 1.2 per cent in 2019, and is projected to continue to rise. Meanwhile, sales and exports increased, from US$37.57 billion in 2017 to US$38.1 billion in 2018. Exports of automotive components and goods accounted for 14 per cent of total exports or US$13.52 billion in 2018, while close to 30 per cent of the country's total manufacturing output came from the automotive industry. Seven OEMs grew their investments by more than US$545 million in 2018 (NAAMSA, 2019). These industry trends signal increased global integration and profitability in the industry, but they have come at a huge cost to labour (Barnes et al., 2018).

Mashilo (2019) argues that economic upgrading has been detrimental to workers. Between 2000 and 2010, the number of workers required to produce a car steadily dropped, year on year (Hicks and Devaraj, 2015). Investment in technology led to the displacement of over 1 314 workers between 2016 and 2019, while intensifying job insecurity for those remaining due to the ongoing risk of production-line workers losing their jobs to technology. Many human skills have become vulnerable in the face of advancing mechanisation (Ford, 2015). Indeed, 87 per cent of the production jobs shed are casualties of increasing capital intensity, which has in the process improved productivity.

This case study demonstrates how technology has been crucial not only for increasing productivity and efficiency but also for increasing managerial control over workers who face the threat of retrenchment. The concept of social upgrading has been key to understanding the erosion of working and living conditions in the automotive industry (Mashilo, 2019).

Digital platform work

The advent of the COVID-19 pandemic triggered a surge in digital labour platforms, which (now that the COVID risk has subsided) are used by a growing number of industries, as capital has become increasingly concentrated across sectors and geographies (Huws, 2014). Platforms like Uber Eats use a shared business-ownership model, which (mis)characterises workers as own-account entrepreneurs or partners. Consequently, they are excluded from national minimum wage regulations and must work long hours to make ends meet. As own-account workers, they have no access to paid leave, social security benefits or occupational health and safety protections. Because they have to carry the full cost and risk of the business operation – purchasing the motorcycle, paying for petrol, covering the cost of any medical treatment in the event of an accident, and so on – platform workers are frequently in debt (ILO, 2021). In Johannesburg, the vast majority of digital platform workers are immigrants. Many of them lack proper documentation and are therefore particularly vulnerable to police harassment (Webster and Masikane, 2020).

Despite being considered entrepreneurs or partners, digital platform workers are subject to high levels of scrutiny through algorithmic management. To access work, they must log onto the app, which assigns tasks, tracks performance, determines pay and can terminate employment unilaterally. Ultimately, platform workers provide services and produce value for the app on a regular basis, are economically dependent on the app and generally do not own the means of production. Indeed, the app is the point of production (Webster and Masikane, 2020). Yet, by (mis)classifying platform workers as partners, employers avoid the responsibility of ensuring labour and social protections – a common strategy of externalisation.

Digital platform work challenges traditional views of the workplace. Historically, the workplace was a physical location, but in the case of platform work it is also a digital app. However, the key tenets of the labour process theory remain relevant. When it comes to control, workers are not subject to the scrutiny of an identifiable manager on a shop floor. Algorithmic managerialism has become the epicentre of worker control, with anonymous managers creating an uncomfortable backdrop to workers' daily routines. The employment contract that underpinned the traditional employer–employee relationship has also been reconfigured, with platform workers now reframed as business partners rather than workers. Technological innovation has thus been crucial for externalisation and for increasing managerial control, while appealing to workers' desire for autonomy to undermine their resistance.

CONSIDERATIONS FOR TRADE UNIONS AND WORKER ORGANISATIONS

The black trade union movement has been a powerful force for social change since the 1930s. Struggles for better working and living conditions, evidenced in black workers revolting against extreme exploitation and exclusion from meaningful economic participation, have contributed to the trajectory of the South African economy. The South African trade union movement entered the new, democratic dispensation with powerful organisational capacity. In 1994, the

Congress of South African Trade Unions (COSATU) had over 2 million paid-up members, making it the biggest organisation in South Africa. Its strength lay not only in its membership, but also in its commitment to democratic unionism, underpinned by worker education and the principle of worker control. With the transition to democracy and the internationalisation of South African capital, trade unions have been confronted with growing labour insecurity at the global level, while also having to navigate the uneven politics of the Tripartite Alliance at home.

According to Hlatshwayo (2014), trade unions have been on the 'back foot' of technological innovation and have been systematically side-lined from decision making in respect of the organisation of production. They have tended to focus on bread-and-butter issues, such as wage negotiations, conditions of employment and the terms of retrenchment, rather than on proactively influencing the direction of innovation and technological adoption. As Alex Mashilo, a former National Union of Metal Workers of South Africa (NUMSA) shop steward and head of its Organising, Campaigns and Collective Bargaining, notes, unions have struggled to respond appropriately to labour displacement (Mashilo, 2021):

> South African trade unions, more often than not, become active on matters of the changing nature of work when that gives rise to Section 189 notice, which is retrenchment notice. Most of the noise starts coming then, when you read trade union statements, those statements will be opposing retrenchments [...] But when the process begins with the changes in the nature of work and introduction of technology, that process is under management's control. But it is that process that can produce Section 189 or 189a notices (retrenchments). And when a company issues a Section 189 notice that is the tail-end of the process, it is not its beginning.

Responses to technological innovation have been further hindered by the growing fragmentation of the trade union movement, as skilled trade unionists with institutional memory and immeasurable experience leave for greener pastures in business and politics (Buhlungu, 2010).

In the automotive industry, for instance, limited research capacity and inadequate union training programmes have resulted in disarticulated demands during periods of workplace restructuring (Mashilo, 2019).

The inability of trade unions to respond strategically to workplace restructuring has weakened the organisational power of unions on the shop floor, reducing them to mere spectators in the struggle over the terms of technology-induced restructuring. Consequently, unions have found it increasingly difficult to recruit and retain members. According to the Quarterly Labour Force Survey (StatsSA, 2021), only a third of the employed population in South Africa are union members, thus undermining workers' ability to influence the conditions of work.

Indeed, as Table 14.1 illustrates, less than half of those employed have retirement benefits and just over two-thirds have access to paid leave, amongst other legally mandated protections. Women generally have less access to standard employment benefits than men – the only exception being maternity leave. Furthermore, 52 per cent of workers said that wages are set unilaterally by the employer, 7 per cent said that wages are negotiated one-on-one between the worker and the employer, and 6 per cent said that they receive no increment at all (StatsSA, 2021).

Table 14.1: Conditions of work amongst the employed by gender

	Men	Women	All
Union membership	34%	31%	33%
Earn above the working poverty line	49%	42%	46%
Access to retirement funds	50%	44%	47%
Access to paid leave	70%	68%	69%
Access to paid sick leave	75%	74%	74%
Access to maternity/parental leave	53%	58%	55%
Make Unemployment Insurance Fund (UIF) contributions	67%	59%	63%

Source: StatsSA, 2021

As membership numbers dwindle and new forms of worker organisation emerge, the key question is: Will the labour movement become increasingly marginalised or will it manage to revitalise itself? Some people argue that traditional trade unions are obsolete, while others contend that their approach neglects the multiple terrains on which the working class continues to struggle (Kenny, 2020). As the previous section has shown, workers remain critical for the creation of value, albeit in different ways. In the automotive industry, labour is not obsolete and has played an important role in mitigating the erosion of working conditions. However, labour has not yet adjusted and adapted to the challenges posed by digital forms of work and externalisation. The slow pace of trade unions' engagement with and adaptation to digitisation puts them at risk of becoming increasingly marginalised against a fast-changing professional landscape.

The rise of hybrid forms of worker organisation is partly attributed to the declining power of traditional trade unions to organise workers in emerging workplaces. Technology as a socially contested phenomenon has often been used to curtail the power of traditional unions in a variety of ways, including through worker displacement. Where workers have not been displaced, their insecurities have been magnified by the possibility of machines taking over their jobs. Research and innovation are important in helping trade unions to understand the impact of technology and to prepare for technology-driven changes in the organisation of production.

Trade unions will also need to re-invent their organising tools to attract and retain younger workers. Worker education needs to play a crucial role if unions are to conscientise younger workers and capacitate them to participate meaningfully in a union's activities. The full-time shop steward (FTSS), who is an elected worker representative working full time for the union in the workplace and side by side with other workers on the shop floor, requires worker education. In particular, an FTSS needs to be capacitated and upskilled to understand the politics of technology in a broad sense – beyond technology being used as a tool of trade – if they are to be an effective worker leader in the digital age. Furthermore, technology as a political and socially contested force has shifted the power to capital in the interests of profit. This means that if labour is to provide an effective response, collaboration is paramount.

To be clear, technological change is inevitable and is to be welcomed.

However, it becomes problematic when it is used to weaken labour in pursuit of profit. Trade unions, in collaboration with other types of organisations, have the opportunity to shape the use of technology in ways that support the goal of achieving a more equitable distribution of income between labour and capital and across society in general.

From a historical standpoint, it is evident that new managerial control techniques have often suppressed existing worker organisations and worker resistance. However, Webster et al. (2009) suggest that some of the problems confronting trade unions can be tackled through strategic engagements and initiatives. First, it is important to strengthen unions' capacity to research and strategise around technological innovation and workplace restructuring. Second, it is necessary to develop a clear agenda on work and production, in consultation with workers at all levels, thereby giving practical effect to the principle of worker control. Third, shop stewards, union officials and elected office bearers need to undergo training in production-related restructuring options so that they are well equipped to engage in negotiations over the scope and terms of technological change. Workers and shop stewards have 'tacit skills' and applied knowledge repositories which need to be uncovered and leveraged through worker education and research. This will also enable their innate sense of resistance to be awakened. Finally, it is necessary to introduce full-time shop stewards, whose mandate can be expanded, to the intricacies of negotiating with employers over acceptable types of technological change on the shop floor.

Ultimately, unions need to extend their focus beyond bread-and-butter issues, such as wages and working conditions (Hlatshwayo, 2014). NUMSA's approach to organising the automotive industry, for example, has been effective in deflecting the full blow of technological upgrading. Their strategy has involved a value chain approach, where the union organises labour brokers and all the workers in the workplace, regardless of the sectors to which they belong. At a single plant, workers can belong to various sectors, such as security, transport and services. For example, at the BMW plant, NUMSA organises all the workers at the plant, including outsourced cleaners, canteen workers, security personnel and others. This strategy has strengthened trade union power on the shop floor and could be used as a blueprint to organise those workers who, having been overlooked by the unions in the past, have had little option but to seek support from non-governmental organisations (NGOs) to fill 'the representation gap'. As Webster and Masikane (2020) relate:

> What is happening is that you now have what I call trade union substitutionism ... you getting NGOs emerging like the Casual Workers Advice Office (CWAO) who are giving workers some voice but are not membership-based unions. So, you have an NGO like CWAO ... helping workers by giving workers advice, but they are not a trade union, or if they are not an established trade union, they establish committees.

In the automotive industry, NUMSA remains relatively strong with unionisation standing at over 80 per cent, including externalised workers. However, a different picture emerges with digital platform work, where traditional unions risk being marginalised and superseded by non-unionised forms of worker organisation. The strategies that are largely effective for NUMSA in the automotive industry face challenges in areas where work has had to adapt to the digital age.

Some unions have accepted the discourse that platform workers are independent contractors and not workers, which puts them (the unions) at a disadvantage when it comes to organising platform workers. Instead of embracing the inevitable and developing new organising strategies, trade unions have retreated into a defensive position, creating a 'representation gap' in platform work that is being taken up by non-union, hybrid and transnational forms of worker collectives. This was evident in the recent strike in South Africa by platform workers from all the e-hailing services – Uber, Bolt, DiDi and inDrive. These platform workers have organised themselves under the auspices of a group called Unity in Diversity (UID), which represents workers across all the digital platforms. Their spokesperson, Vhatuka Mbelengwa, was quoted as saying, 'The fact that a powerful organisation like COSATU and its affiliates have voiced and said they will support us ... that is an impact we have been struggling to bring about for years' (Banda, 2022).

The trade union movement has an opportunity to align its organising strategies with the needs of platform workers in the 21st century and should be informed by the significant technological changes and innovative paradigm shifts that are occurring in many professional domains.

CONCLUSION

Managerial control and worker resistance are the dynamic, contradictory forces that have shaped the labour process, conditions of work and racial capitalism in South Africa. The end of apartheid came with great expectations of a 'better life for all', in which decent jobs were to play a pivotal role. These expectations turned into disappointment, however, as millions of workers lost their jobs while those lucky enough to hold onto them experienced increasing labour insecurity and working poverty. Declining investment in productive sectors, outsourcing and automation are some of the dominant drivers of structural unemployment.

This chapter explored the role of technological innovation as a contested social force at the interface between managerial control and worker resistance. While technological innovation has the potential to produce the material conditions for unprecedented abundance, liberating humanity from the drudgery of labour and creating a new set of social relations that allow humans to flourish (Bastani, 2019), how it is used and whose interests it serves remain contentious.

Drawing on two case studies – the automotive industry and digital platform work – this chapter used the labour process theory to illustrate how technological innovation has been leveraged by capital to maximise value, enforce managerial control and weaken the social basis of trade unions. However, the chapter also pointed to emerging forms of worker power, challenging Braverman's (1975) theory of deskilling and declining worker power in the wake of technological innovation. Whether the trade union movement can leverage these forms of worker power to influence how and for whom technology is used remains to be seen.

Looking ahead, trade unions need to be far more proactive in defining the terms of technological innovation and social upgrading;

identifying strategic points of organisation and recruiting workers in emerging sectors, including young and casual workers; investing in research, worker education and the upskilling of shop stewards; and collaborating with worker organisations outside the trade union movement.

REFERENCES

Anner, M., Pons-Vignon, N. and Rani, U. 2019. 'For a future of work with dignity: A critique of the World Bank Development Report: The changing nature of work'. *Global Labour Journal*, 10 (1), 2–19.

Ashman, S. 2015. 'Financialisation and the South African economy'. *Amandla!* 40, https://aidc.org.za/financialisation-south-african-economy/, accessed 15 May 2022.

Banda, M. 22 March 2022. 'Uber, Bolt, DiDi and Indrive drivers protest over lack of regulation and app firm exploitation'. *Daily Maverick*, https://www.dailymaverick.co.za/article/2022-03-22-uber-bolt-didi-and-indrive-drivers-protest-over-lack-of-regulation-and-app-firm-exploitation/, accessed 2 February 2022.

Barnes, J., Black, A. and Monaco, L. 2018. 'State–business bargaining, localisation, and supply chain development in the South African auto industry'. The 4th Annual Competition and Economic Development (ACER) Conference. Johannesburg, South Africa, 19–20 July 2018.

Bastani, A. 2019. *Fully Automated Luxury Communism*. London: Verso Books.

Bhorat, H. and Cheadle, H. 2009. 'Labour reform in South Africa: Measuring regulation and a synthesis of policy suggestions'. DPRU Working Paper 09/139, University of Cape Town.

Braverman, H. 1975. *Labour and Monopoly Capital*. New York: Monthly Review Press.

Buhlungu, S. 2010. 'Gaining influence but losing power? COSATU members and the democratic transformation of South Africa'. *Social Movement Studies*, 7 (1), 31–42.

Bundy, C. 1979. *The Rise and Fall of the South African Peasantry*. London: Heinemann.

Burawoy, M. 1985. *Politics of Production: Factory regimes under capitalism and socialism*. London: Verso.

Chancel, L., Piketty, T., Saez, E. and Zucman, G. 2022. 'World Inequality Report 2022: World inequality lab', https://wir2022.wid.world/www-site/uploads/2021/12/WorldInequalityReport2022_Full_Report.pdf, accessed 26 April 2022.

Chigbu, B. I. and Nekhwevha, F. H. 2020. 'The extent of job automation in the automobile sector in South Africa'. *Economic and Industrial Democracy*, 31 (4), 1–22.

Cloete, K. 2 March 2021. 'Labour pains: Trade union membership has declined badly, and bosses are calling the shots'. *Daily Maverick,* https://www.dailymaverick.co.za/opinionista/2021-03-02-labour-pains-trade-union-membership-has-declined-badly-and-bosses-are-calling-the-shots/, accessed 2 September 2021.

Crankshaw, O. 1997. *Race, Class and the Changing Division of Labour Under Apartheid.* London: Routledge.

Fine, B. and Mohamed, S. 2022. 'Locating industrial policy in developmental transformation: Lessons from the past, prospects for the future'. SOAS Department of Economics Working Paper No. 247, https://www.soas.ac.uk/sites/default/files/2022-10/economics-wp247.pdf, accessed 26 April 2022.

Fine, B. and Rustomjee, Z. 1996. *The Political Economy of South Africa: From minerals–energy complex to industrialisation.* New York: Routledge.

Ford, M. 2015. *Rise of the Robots: Technology and the threats of a jobless future.* New York: Basic Books.

Francis, D. and Valodia, I. 2022. 'Chapter 5: The informal economy and informal employment in South Africa'. World Bank, https://thedocs.worldbank.org/en/doc/37511318c092e6fd4ca3c60f0af0bea3-0350012021/related/Informal-economy-Chapter-5.pdf, accessed 2 May 2022.

Frey, C. B. and Osborne, M. A. 2017. 'The future of employment: How susceptible are jobs to computerisation?' *Technological Forecasting and Social Change*, 114 (C), 254–280.

Gelb, S. 1987. 'Making sense of the crisis'. *Transformation*, 5, 33–50.

Hicks, M. J. and Devaraj, S. 2015. 'The myth and the reality of manufacturing in America'. Centre for Business and Economic Research: Ball State University, https://conexus.cberdata.org/files/MfgReality.pdf, accessed 5 May 2022.

Hlatshwayo, M. 2014. 'NUMSA and Solidarity's responses to technological changes at the ArcelorMittal Vanderbijlpark plant: Unions caught on the back foot'. *Global Labour Journal,* 5 (3), 283–305.

Huws, U. 2014. *Labour in the Global Digital Economy: The cybertariat comes of age.* New York: Monthly Review Press.

International Labour Organization (ILO). 2021. 'World employment and social outlook: The role of digital labour platforms in transforming the world of work', https://www.ilo.org/global/research/global-reports/weso/2021/WCMS_771749/lang--en/index.htm, accessed 6 May 2022.

Isaacs, G. 2016. 'A national minimum wage for South Africa'. Summary Report 1. National Minimum Wage Research Initiative. Johannesburg: University of the Witwatersrand.

James, D. 2014. *Money from Nothing: Indebtedness and aspiration in South*

Africa. Stanford: Stanford University Press.
Kenny, B. 2020. 'The South African labour movement: A fragmented and shifting terrain'. *Tempo Social, revista de sociologia da USP*, 32 (1), https://orcid.org/0000-0001-6255-4971, accessed 2 November 2021.
Legassick, M. and Wolpe, H. 1976. 'The Bantustans and capital accumulation in South Africa'. *Review of African Political Economy*, 7, 87–107.
Leger, J. 1992. 'Talking Rocks: An investigation of the pit sense of rockfall accidents amongst underground gold miners'. Unpublished PhD thesis, University of the Witwatersrand.
Lorgat, A. 2022. 'No, we are not fighting against foreign workers, and we'll never fight against foreign workers: Trade unions and migrant rights', in Rugunanan, P. and Xulu-Gama, N. (eds.) *Migration in Southern Africa*. Cham: Springer, 247–260.
Mafeje, A. 1981. 'On the articulation of modes of production: Review article'. *Journal of Southern African Studies,* 8 (1), 123–138.
Mashilo, A. M. 2019. 'Economic and social upgrading in global production networks: The auto components sector in Gauteng'. Unpublished PhD thesis, University of the Witwatersrand.
Mashilo, A. M. 2022. 'Collective bargaining during and after apartheid: Economic and social upgrading in the automobile global value chains in South Africa', in Teipen, C., Dünhaupt, P., Herr, H. and Mehl, F. (eds.) *Economic and Social Upgrading in Global Value Chains: Comparative analyses, macroeconomic effects, the role of institutions and strategies for the global south*. Cham: Springer International Publishing, 227–257.
Naidoo, K. 2020. 'Innovation, digital platform technologies and employment: An overview of key issues and emerging trends in South Africa'. Southern Centre for Inequality Studies (SCIS), Working Paper 9.
National Association of Automobile Manufacturers of South Africa (NAAMSA). 2019. 'Quarterly review of business conditions: New Motor vehicle manufacturing industry automotive sector, 2nd quarter 2019', https://cdn.lightstoneauto.co.za/NAAMSA/2019_2ndQuarter/NAAMSA_QUARTERLY_REVIEW_2NDQUARTER_2019.pdf, accessed 15 June 2022.
Newman, S. 2019. *The Minerals–Energy Complex and Structural Inequality in South Africa*. Johannesburg: Oxfam South Africa.
Pons-Vignon, N. and Anseeuw, W. 2009. 'Great expectations: Working conditions in South Africa since the end of apartheid'. *Journal of Southern African Studies,* 35 (4), 883–899.
Presidential Commission on the Fourth Industrial Revolution. 2020. 'Presidential Commission on the Fourth Industrial Revolution: Summary Report and Recommendations', https://www.gov.za/sites/default/files/gcis_document/202010/43834gen591.pdf, accessed 5 May 2022.
Scully, B. 2016. 'Precarity north and south: A southern critique of Guy

Standing'. *Global Labour Journal*, 7 (2), 160–173.
Sefalafala, T. 2011. 'Mineworkers opt for private legal scheme'. *South African Labour Bulletin,* 35 (4), 24–26.
Statistics South Africa (StatsSA). 2021. 'Quarterly Labour Force Survey : Quarter 3: 2021', http://www.statssa.gov.za/publications/P0211/P02113rdQuarter2021.pdf, accessed 21 February 2020.
Taylor, F. W. 2003. *Scientific Management*. London: Routledge.
Valodia, I. and Devey, R. 2012. 'The informal economy in South Africa: Debates, issues and policies'. *Margin: The Journal of Applied Economic Research*, 6 (2), 133–157.
Von Holdt, K. and Webster, E. 2005. 'Work restructuring and the crisis of social reproduction: A Southern perspective', in Von Holdt, K. and Webster, E. (eds.) *Beyond the Apartheid Workplace: Studies in transition*. Scottsville: University of KwaZulu-Natal Press, 3–40.
Vulavala, H. and Ulmer, J. M. 2014. 'Importance of robotics in automotive manufacturing'. *Insights to a Changing World Journal*, 4, 20–33.
Webster, E. 1985. *Cast in a Racial Mould: Labour process and trade unionism in the foundries*. Johannesburg: Ravan Press.
Webster, E. and Masikane, F. 2020. '"I Just want to survive": The case of food delivery couriers in Johannesburg'. Report of FES & SCIS. Braamfontein: University of the Witwatersrand.
Webster, E., Mashilo, A., Nasondo, T. and Bischoff, C. 2009. 'Changes in the production systems and work methods'. Johannesburg: NUMSA, Friedrich-Ebert-Stiftung, Sociology of Work Unit and Development Institute for Trade Union Support and Education for Labour.
Webster, E., Joynt, K. and Sefalafala, T. 2016. 'Informalization and decent work: Labour's challenge'. *Progress in Development Studies*, 16 (2), 203–218.
World Bank. 2019. 'World Development Report 2019: The changing nature of work', https://www.worldbank.org/en/publication/wdr2019, accessed 21 February 2020.

RESEARCH INTERVIEWS

Mashilo, A. M. 23 December 2021. Interview with Malabela, H. M. Johannesburg.
Mashilo, A. M. 7 January 2022. Interview with Malabela, H. M. Johannesburg.
Webster, E. 8 December 2021. Interview with Malabela, H. M. Johannesburg.
South African Society of Bank Officials (SASBO). 20 April 2020. Interview with Castel-Branco, R. via Zoom.

FIFTEEN

Developmental state, social compacting and economic recovery: South Africa's experiences through the COVID-19 pandemic

Yacoob Abba Omar

INTRODUCTION

The Economic Reconstruction and Recovery Plan (ERRP), unveiled by President Cyril Ramaphosa in October 2020, was the product of a process that had begun under the auspices of the National Economic Development and Labour Council (Nedlac) in the early stages of South Africa's response to the COVID-19 pandemic. A confluence of trends led to that moment, including initiatives aimed at addressing previous economic crises through the coordinated efforts of government, business and labour. These efforts included responding to the global financial crisis of 2007–2008 and addressing the rising levels of unemployment through various job summits. Cited as examples of social compacting, they were influenced by the ruling African National

Congress's (ANC) developmental state orientation, which the ERRP and its subsequent unfolding were meant to consolidate.

This chapter draws on a range of academic debates, institutional reports and records of meetings, and personal interactions between the author and key actors during the drafting of the ERRP[1] as well as conversations since its launch. The methodology used could be located within theories of standpoint ethnography, where standpoint theories refer to the view that knowledge is produced from a position of access and lived experiences (Da Silva and Webster, 2018). The chapter examines the relationship between a developmental state and social compacting, both conceptually and through historical precedents set in South Africa. Of particular value is what Fine (2016) terms the tensions with and between the developmental state paradigm (DSP) and the social compacting paradigm (SCP), which are 'more or less freely applied across a wide range of diverse contexts, without necessary reference to longstanding traditions and experiences and to broader and deeper causal factors and goals' (Fine, 2016: 1).

It is argued that the notion of the developmental state, as advanced by South African policymakers, displays what can be regarded as neopatrimonialism, where resources are used to consolidate power relations. An important issue that the chapter examines is the extent to which a social compacting approach could help to elevate economic growth, increase the rate of employment, and reduce poverty and inequality – all of which have been portrayed ad nauseum as the objectives of the South African state. The ERRP built on and incorporated the findings from the 2018 Presidential Jobs Summit and the 2020 Social Compact on Supporting Eskom – initiatives that many of the decision makers in the drafting of the ERRP were involved in.

This chapter sets out to answer two key questions:

- To what extent has the developmental state orientation of the current regime (notably captured in the 2012 National Development Plan (NDP)) been realised? Chapter 13 of the NDP, titled 'Building a capable and developmental state', explains that 'developmental' refers to the state playing a transformative role when addressing poverty and inequality and that 'this requires well-run and effectively coordinated state institutions with skilled public servants who are committed to the public good and capable of delivering consistently high-quality services, while prioritising the nation's developmental objectives' (NPC, 2012: 409).

It is important to note that much of the conceptualising around the developmental state emanates from the ruling ANC, as has been evident since the release of its 1998 document titled 'The State, Property Relations, and Social Transformation. A Discussion Paper Towards the Alliance Summit' and in its economic transformation policy document prepared for the 2017 policy conference. The ruling party's 2020 policy document states that 'by 2000 the ANC had adopted the concept of the developmental state to frame its approach to governance' (2020: 16).

The ANC combined the notion of a developmental state with Sen's focus on capability, as argued in *Development as Freedom* (Sen, 1999) that the 'freedom of citizens to attain socio-economic well-being is of primary moral importance, and that freedom of citizens to attain this well-being is to be understood in terms of people's capabilities' (ANC, 2020: 172). As an acknowledgement of the turmoil experienced during the administration of President Zuma, when the state was captured by a corrupt elite, the prefix 'ethical' has more recently been added to the term, giving rise to the notion of 'an ethical, capable, developmental state' (ANC, 2022: 135).

- To what extent has the ERRP laid the foundation for a social compact? The ERRP was largely facilitated by Nedlac and was the outcome of months of intense debates involving business, labour, civil society and government, or, in Nedlac parlance, 'social partners'. The ANC's 2022 policy documents point out that 'there has been closer co-operation and compacting amongst social partners – government, business, labour and communities – as mandated by the 54th National Conference. Still, significant scope exists to deepen the process of social compacting around a common programme to achieve agreed economic objectives' (ANC, 2022: 142). This unfinished process of compacting is examined below in relation to the assessment of the ERRP to date.

DEVELOPMENTAL STATE AND SOCIAL COMPACTING: IS THERE A CONNECTION?

Fine (2016: 1) argues that the developmental state paradigm (DSP) was at its height during the East Asian miracle, especially in its opposition to the dogma of the Washington Consensus, although it was in decline prior to the East Asian crisis of 1997/98. He suggests that the concept has 'diluted, shifted and broadened', with Mkandawire (2012: 8) referring to the various forms it has taken as 'competitive', 'social' and 'developmental' pacts. Fine (2016: 1) is concerned that the developmental state has come to refer 'to any positive intervention by the state just as social compacting serves as a rhetorical device to support any cooperative compromise between potentially conflicting interests'.

Mkandawire's (2012: 3) conception of developmental states as 'social constructs brought by states and societies' and Evans' (1995) notion of 'embedded autonomy' shaped the concept of a developmental state in a way that shows that democracy is reconcilable with development. Almost three decades later, in a special edition of *Third World Quarterly* which focuses on the developmental state, Singh and Ovadia (2018: 1034) ask, 'Given that the DS model(s) emerged within specific conditions, what generic policies and state institutions can inform contemporary governing elites to address the challenge of economic and social development especially in the context of states with weak capacity and legacies of inequality, oppression and colonial rule?'

This should not lead one to the conclusion that developmental states are necessarily authoritarian; as shown below, they are in equal measure democratic. Furthermore, in looking at the economic context, a distinction needs to be drawn between the experience of the Southeast Asian countries in the 1980s and that of African states in the 1990s. Perhaps the most important difference is that with the former, the emerging capitalist classes were not yet well developed and required state coordination in various forms – both sector specific and in the economy generally (Leftwich, 1995: 403). This is different from the African context where states are dealing with a range of issues, from nascent to well-developed capitalist classes and business interests.

The experience of the 1980s and 1990s showed that newly

industrialised countries (NICs), labelled developmental states, displayed some common characteristics, such as agency, which Freund (2011: 1) describes as 'the existence of a state formation that transcends or overrules the usual bureaucratic processes. Such agencies are capable of directing capital and defying the logic of market forces which may constrain structural transformation'.

Another feature of the NICs was a pro-business orientation, creating a mutually beneficial alliance between states and big business. Evans (1995) describes situations in which developmental states were able to strike a careful balance between business and other stakeholders, while acting autonomously, using rewards and sanctions to drive their developmental agenda. Woo-Cummings (1999: 4) notes that, in such circumstances, 'a developmental state is not an imperious element lording it over society but a partner with the business sector in an historical compact of industrial transformation'. Another feature was that the NICs were facing huge economic challenges and possibly conflict, creating a structural condition in which national elites had to deal with their 'systemic vulnerability and hence focus on ... development as the principal source of political legitimacy of such states' (Singh and Ovadia, 2018: 1035, 1038).

Singh and Ovadia (2018: 1036) describe Argentina, Brazil, Ethiopia, Rwanda and China as 'newer examples of developmentalist thinking with varying success', with these countries 'centralising rent management, strengthening political ties between government and domestic capitalists and adapting industrial policy and state backed finance to create new competitive advantages'.

Nearly a decade after *Embedded Autonomy* was published in 1995, Evans (2004: 32) called for states to be pragmatic and flexible in responding to new challenges and contexts, thereby avoiding 'institutional mono-cropping and one-size-fits-all approaches to development policy'. In the African context, the notion of developmental patrimonialism has emerged, where it is argued that states behave as a cohesive agent that shapes interest groups. Crook and Booth (2011) comment that 'in some (African) states "patronage politics" seems to produce only predation and economic collapse, while in others the outcomes justify the use of the term "developmental patrimonialism"'.

Amsden (2001) had tried to answer the question posed by Singh and Ovadia more than a decade earlier by factoring in the importance of business interests and the state's regulatory role in managing these interests. Her work on 'reciprocal control mechanisms' describes how developmental states have used state rents and regulatory mechanisms to prevent state capture by narrow or sectarian business interests. Crook and Booth (2011: 104) argue that 'it is possible for a government to pursue successful developmental policies within a political system which operates primarily on the basis of patron–client relations and thus "goes with the grain" of the dominant mode of state–society interaction'.

Mkandawire (2012: 15) points out that 'developmentalist discourse was so pervasive and so much part of conventional wisdom in both African developing and developed countries that it permitted the most extensive violation of human rights to take place as long as "development" was somehow taking place'. Crook and Booth (2011: 99), in examining several African rentier states, observe that 'the most benign combination occurs when there is fully centralised rent control under a unified elite, and long-horizon investment of rents ... such a regime demands and sustains a competent public service which is vertically disciplined … but also given sufficient autonomy to manage and implement development policies – it therefore has "bureaucratic integrity"'. Importantly, though, they warn that 'it is hard to visualise equivalent results being generated under systems of competitive democracy in which incumbents face the actuality or risk of loss of office at frequent intervals, powerfully incentivising them to engage in short-term pillage of public resources' (Crook and Booth, 2011: 101). This is applicable, as seen in the South African context, not only to electoral politics but also to intra-party elections.

According to Singh and Ovadia (2011: 1041–1042), growing authoritarianism notwithstanding, the ability of political elites at the apex of power to generate a consensus or 'political settlement' is the glue that holds together the relationships between contending elites – and between states and social forces. This then provides an enabling environment for national elites, such as organised business, labour and the ruling party, to secure political stability and policy consensus over the trajectory of development planning.

The approach advocated by Mkandawire (2012: 2), who is wary of authoritarianism in many parts of the Third World, is one of 'democratic developmental states' – that is:

> … developmental (in the sense that they facilitate and promote economic growth and structural transformation), democratic (in the sense that they derive their legitimacy through popular participation and [the] electoral process) and socially inclusive (in the sense that they pursue social policies that ensure equitable entitlements of all their citizens to ensure that their capacities and functioning are adequate for a decent inclusion in societal affairs).

Fine (2016: 5) asserts that there are several problems with the DSP, including taking the state–market contradiction as foundational, with class interests 'tend(ing) to be confined to consideration of capitalists alone' and then focusing 'on its (capital's) relationships to the state as more or less exclusively constituted out of the latter's embedded autonomy in administering industrial policy on capital's behalf and in its collective interest'.

Mkandawire (2012) is dismissive of arguments emanating from the developed world on why African states cannot become developmental states. One argument is that Africa was the 'epicentre' of neopatrimonialism which produced states that fatally combined tradition with modernity, with the former built on highly personalised reciprocity as the basis for exchange and the latter based on Weber's legal–rational order. The other argument is that African states 'simply didn't have the human resources' (Mkandawire, 2012: 4) and technical capacity to have developmental states or that globalisation had closed the window to state interventionism, as it left little room for states to effectively intervene in their respective economies (Mkandawire, 2012). The literature on the Asian developmental states tends to focus on state–business relations, while eliding the involvement and position of other classes such as labour or sectors such as civil society. This argument is the basis of the increasing focus on social compacting in more recent conceptualisations of the developmental state.

Mkandawire (2012: 6) provides a succinct, somewhat functional description of social compacts, saying they:

> ... refer to the institutionalisation of consultation and cooperation on economic policy involving representation from the state, capital, labour and other organisations of civil society ... (they are) used to address distributive and growth objectives of society at the micro-level; to improve labour management at the firm level and, as in the current usage of 'social pacts' in Europe, to manage the distributional issues of macroeconomics policies.

A 2020 study conducted by the Mapungubwe Institute for Strategic Reflection (MISTRA, 2020) on compacting gave the examples of Rwanda and Mauritius as instructive for the South African context. Rwanda, for example, built its social compact on the pillars of democratic reforms, truth, justice and reconciliation, and socioeconomic development. The MISTRA report points out that 'it is an important case study that teaches us about successful national development planning, and societal rehabilitation' (MISTRA, 2020: 9). Brautigam and Diolle (2009) identify three pillars that support social compacts in Mauritius: public–private signalling, as indicated by the rapprochement of the new government with the capitalists who dominated the economy; the existence of a peak association that organised the business class across ethnic groups and sectors; and the existence of multiple formal and informal arenas for consultation.

According to a 2013 International Labour Organization (ILO) report, '(i)n Western Europe social pacts have been a preferred route in areas of economic and social policies, and more recently, in order to facilitate the adjustment of national economies to external shocks such as loss of competitiveness or economic/monetary integration' (ILO, 2013: 34). The Republic of Ireland, regarded as the most successful model of 'competitive pacts', saw the country being referred to as the 'Celtic Tiger'. According to Teague and Donaghey (2009), although the Irish experience occurred around the same time as 'social pacts' in much of Europe, it was premised on more developmentalist ideologies and featured trade unions, employer organisations and several civic associations bargaining hard to reach wage agreements. This resulted in the creation of 'a new form of economic and social governance, which is sometimes described as "post-corporatist"' (Teague and Donaghey, 2009: 59).

To sum up, the following emerge as principles that define the relationship between developmental states and social compacting:

- Authoritarian or illiberal regimes are not necessarily preconditions for developmental states or successful social compacting.
- The state needs to be strong enough to act autonomously so that it can extract the required behaviours from business and labour.
- Such state capability ensures that the state can centralise rent management, such that it acts in the broader interests of society.
- A 'political settlement' is fundamental to shaping relationships amongst the elite.
- A long-term perspective is required so that compromises can be agreed to, with the future in mind.

The need for an agency that coordinates and directs the work of the state has been recognised as a critical feature of the developmental state as well as a requirement for social compacting. South Africa has a number of institutions that could potentially play this role, including Nedlac, which falls under the Department of Employment and Labour, and the recently created Operation Vulindlela, a joint initiative of The Presidency and the National Treasury, which aims to accelerate the implementation of structural reforms and support economic recovery. It is overseen by the Deputy Finance Minister and reports directly to the President.

Naidu and Maré (2015), in their assessment of the National Planning Commission (NPC), raise the possibility that the 'the long-term implementation window outlined in the NDP, along with the permanent status granted to the Commission as a special purpose institutional vehicle, might enable it to avoid the diffuse and opportunistic weaknesses of AsgiSA [Accelerated and Shared Growth Initiative for South Africa] and the NGP [New Growth Path]' (2015: 425). The issue of agency is revisited below.

SOUTH AFRICA'S EXPERIENCES OF SOCIAL COMPACTING

Mkandawire (2012: 40) captures the different levels of complexity that South Africa faces in the following extract:

> ... (b)oth the time of liberation and the nature of the struggle have placed on the agenda a whole range of issues that other social compacts may have dealt with separately: the need for nation-building pacts that bridge the racial divide and heal the wounds of past injustice; the 'development pacts' that ensure accumulation and legitimise such accumulation in the eyes of many; 'competitive pacts' that ensure performance in the global market while governing the market; 'social pacts' that produce both 'patient labour' and 'patient capital' and ensure that the burden and returns of economic development are fairly shared and permit redistribution that does not undermine economic development ... Compounding matters is the lack of clarity and timidity by the state about its own long-term projects.

Since South Africa's first democratic election in 1994, four seminal, long-term plans and a plethora of complementary ones have been produced. These can be regarded as one of Mkandawire's (2012) pacts or an example of what Fine (2016) calls neo-corporatism – a broad concept that tends to cover the high levels of interest in and contracting around specific issues. These are the Reconstruction and Development Programme (RDP); the Growth, Employment and Redistribution (GEAR) framework and its complementary Accelerated and Shared Growth Initiative for South Africa (AsgiSA); the New Growth Path (NGP) and the National Development Plan (NDP). An important complementary plan is the Department of Trade, Industry and Competition's (DTIC) Industrial Policy Action Plan (IPAP), which has been produced every three years since 2009.

Fine (2016: 14) sees in the trajectory from the RDP to GEAR and to the NDP the abandonment of the 'progressive policies for the post-apartheid economy ... neo-corporatism was subject to a heavy assault (by) GEAR' because of its 'compromise with the old Afrikaner/white order and international capital'. He has criticised the NDP for 'presuming a unity of purpose and identity that simply does not, and increasingly so, exist' (Fine, 2016: 17–18).

These are important considerations emerging from the most recent attempts at compacting, especially around economic issues. The Presidential Jobs Summit Framework Agreement, the Social Compact on Supporting Eskom and the ERRP are examined in some detail below, after which the chapter concludes with a prognosis on the developmental state and social compacting in South Africa.

It is important to recall the lessons from past social compacting exercises, which were summarised in a report by MISTRA which had been commissioned by the NPC in 2014. These included: 'social compacts should be based on a specific objective or aim, e.g., development, conflict resolution, social policy, labour relations, etc.'; they should 'incentivise creation and maintenance of social partnerships'; they should 'determine non-negotiables', noting that 'some of the case countries had authoritarian governments – do South Africans really want to give up some of their freedoms?'; 'state capacity is imperative'; the 'private sector also needs to come to the party (it's not just about state legitimacy)'; there needs to be 'visionary leadership across society'; and 'there must be a willingness to compromise' (MISTRA, 2020: 15–18).

The case studies at hand (the Presidential Jobs Summit, the Social Compact on Supporting Eskom and the ERRP) are discussed below.

PRESIDENTIAL JOBS SUMMIT

The 2018 Presidential Jobs Summit was seen as a follow-up to a similar one held in 1999, the 2003 Growth and Development Summit, the 2008/9 Framework Agreement in response to the global financial crisis, and a series of social accords on specific themes (skills development, education, the green economy, local procurement and youth employment) which were adopted between 2011 and 2013.

A 2018 Nedlac report observes two key weaknesses in previous attempts to create social compacts:

- Business being asked 'only to tolerate redistributive efforts, rather than contributing to them directly' (Nedlac, 2018:6). This could be attributed to a number of factors, including the capacity of the state to extract greater commitment from business, the distance between a largely white elite and a largely poverty-stricken black population, and the ever-present threat of capital flight.
- An undertaking 'to support industrialisation through programmatic commitments through the development of sector strategies and supplier development' (Nedlac, 2018: 11). This contrasts with the European and Asian approaches that expected government to determine industrial policy. The report further notes that the pacts 'did not include systemic trade-offs around labour markets and remuneration. They also did not incorporate an explicit commitment to managing regulatory burdens or to improving investor certainty' (Nedlac, 2018: 4). This highlights a key weakness in the compacting processes – the focus on micro, supply-side interventions rather than on structural transformation aimed at achieving stability so that an enabling environment can be created to attract investment.

Both weaknesses talk to (what Mkandawire, 2012, calls) the 'timidity of the state' where the post-apartheid state has not felt capable of wielding the carrots and sticks needed for embedded autonomy, as proposed by Evans (2008). Given the experiences of these compacts, a conscious attempt was made not to repeat the mistakes of the past when the 2018 Jobs Summit was convened under the auspices of Nedlac. It was to signal the beginning of the Presidency led by Ramaphosa, who was elected by the National Assembly in February 2018 after the ANC's December 2017 elective conference had ousted his predecessor, Jacob Zuma, as its leader.

In engagements with government and business participants in the ERRP-drafting process, many commentators were critical of the 2018 Jobs Summit Framework Agreement, arguing that in its aftermath government and labour tended to focus on specific projects rather than on macroeconomic interventions. For them, the summit's most significant achievement was the identification of key obstacles to growth and investment, referred to as bottlenecks that needed to be unblocked, which the state was not addressing. The terminology during the ERRP-drafting process morphed from 'bottlenecks' into 'structural reforms' that were needed (personal sources).

The COVID-19 pandemic shifted the political and economic terrain dramatically, with President Ramaphosa, in an address on 21 April 2020, saying that 'the pandemic requires an economic response that is equal to the scale of the disruption it is causing' (Ramaphosa, 2020a). He later added that 'our economic strategy going forward will require a new social compact among all role players – business, labour, community and government – to restructure the economy and achieve inclusive growth' (Ramaphosa, 2020b).

Business for South Africa (B4SA) emerged to lead the business response to COVID-19. Its leading lights were Business Unity South Africa (BUSA), which operates as a federal body for about 35 trade and industry associations, the Black Business Council (BBC), which is an independent membership-based organisation representing professional and business associations and chambers, and Business Leadership South Africa (BLSA), which is a membership organisation consisting of the largest corporations in South Africa. B4SA was able to rapidly mobilise the vast resources of the business sector, assisted by an array of large and small consultancies.

On 10 July 2020, B4SA released a document titled 'Post-COVID-19: A New Inclusive Economic Future for South Africa: Delivering an Accelerated Economic Recovery Strategy (AERS)'. It argued that the key success factors that would shape South Africa's future were a shared vision supported by agreed targets and strong leadership, with a focus on inclusive growth and jobs, increased impetus given to what it termed 'sustainable B-BBEE [broad-based black economic empowerment] and gender equality', regulatory certainty and consistency, and public–private sector collaboration (B4SA, 2020: 4). It identified, from a list of 50 proposals, 12 key projects and initiatives across 10 high-impact sectors (B4SA, 2020: 16).

On 21 July 2020, a document (Nedlac, 2020a: 6) submitted to the Executive Director of Nedlac reported that the:

> ... Jobs Summit partners have agreed to build on the Jobs Summit partnership to support a national plan for a new, more inclusive

> economy and that the existing Jobs Summit Commitments and Institutional Arrangements must be refocused in support of the national economic recovery plan in a manner that retains the social compact that was created through the signing of the 2018 Framework Agreement.

The link that was being drawn between the Jobs Summit and B4SA's proposals indicated a desire amongst those who were involved in the former to curb the latter, especially given the latter's largely business genesis and orientation.

Through Nedlac's various negotiating forums, the social partners agreed to several structural reforms, such as modernising and reforming network industries and the associated state-owned enterprises; reorienting trade policies and pursuing greater regional integration to boost exports, employment and innovation; lowering barriers to entry for businesses start-ups; supporting labour-intensive sectors such as tourism and agriculture; and 'addressing racial, gender, geographical and other inequalities which hamper deeper economic growth, inclusiveness and greater economic development' (Nedlac, 2020b: 15). In the Nedlac document titled 'The social partners' economic recovery action plan', an important point was made: 'Each social partner, not only government, has resources that can enhance job creation, economic growth, transformation, and the capacity of the state. Each social partner understands that trade-offs and sacrifices have to be made in the common good' (Nedlac, 2020b: 3–4). This represented an important shift from the previous pacts where the burden of implementing the agreements had been left largely to the state.

SOCIAL COMPACT ON SUPPORTING ESKOM

The idea of a social compact to support Eskom was first mooted in late 2019 after the Congress of South African Trade Unions (COSATU) said at one of the Presidential Working Committee (PWC) meetings that if a solution was not found to Eskom's mounting debt and inefficiencies, there would be 'a serious crisis which would impact on employment' (personal source). By the time the pandemic struck, the social compact had been largely agreed to, also coinciding with the appointment of a new CEO at Eskom, André de Ruyter. The signing of the agreement, titled the Framework Agreement for a Social Compact on Supporting Eskom for Inclusive Economic Growth, was delayed due to the focus on COVID-19, but it was finally signed in September 2020.

Two key elements underpinned the Framework Agreement: first, the achievement of a turnaround in Eskom's performance, while addressing the corruption that had become endemic in its operations; second, the facilitation by government of measures, such as renewable energy generation and self-generation, to diversify the sources of energy feeding into the national grid to enable energy security. However, the core of the social compact was that organised labour would use their pension contributions in the Government Employees Pension Fund (GEPF) to address Eskom debt, although, to date, this has not occurred because of the controversy surrounding the matter within organised labour.

ECONOMIC RECONSTRUCTION AND RECOVERY PLAN

On 15 October 2020, at a joint sitting of the Houses of Parliament, President Ramaphosa tabled South Africa's Economic Reconstruction and Recovery Plan (ERRP). He shared its lofty goals, saying that 'our challenge is not only to recover to the pre-pandemic levels of economic activity, but to lift ourselves out of an economic decline that has been several years in the making, while seeking to undo structural distortions that were (also) many decades in the making' (Ramaphosa, 2020c: 4). For this to be realised, 'durable social compacts are more important than ever ... We must work together to build this new inclusive economy and to build a South Africa that works'. Ramaphosa (2020c: 18) added:

> The estimated impact of the plan as modelled by National Treasury is about 1.7 per cent GDP growth additional to the 1.3 per cent baseline from a no-policy intervention scenario, bringing the total to about 3 per cent GDP growth on average

over the next ten years. It is also estimated that the plan shall result in an additional 1.6 million jobs over and above the two million jobs in the case of the baseline scenario without further policy interventions. Thus, the plan is projected to add 3.6 million jobs over a period of ten years.

Figure 15.1: Summary of the ERRP

PRIORITY INTERVENTIONS →		KEY ENABLERS →		STRUCTURAL REFORMS →	
1	Aggressive infrastructure investment	1	Resource mobilisation and fighting corruption	1	Modernising and reforming network industries and associated SOEs
2	Employment orientated strategic localisation, reindustrialisation and export promotion	2	Regulatory changes, a supportive policy environment and improving the ease of doing business	2	Re-orienting trade policies and pursuing greater regional integration
3	Energy security	3	Building a capable state	3	Lowering barriers to entry
4	Support for tourism recovery and growth	4	Social compacting	4	Supporting labour-intensive sectors to achieve more inclusive growth
5	Gender equality and economic inclusion of women and youth	5	Skills development	5	Creating greater levels of economic inclusion
6	Green economy interventions	6	Economic diplomacy and further integration into Africa	6	Addressing the weak job-creating capacity of the economy
7	Mass public employment interventions			7	Boosting education and skills development
8	Strengthening food security			8	Promoting greater beneficiation of raw materials
9	Macroeconomic interventions			9	Addressing racial, gender and geographical inequalities

Source: B4SA, 2020: 11

Assessment of the ERRP

Ramaphosa's announcement was greeted with a degree of scepticism by a jaded public who had seen far too many grand plans unveiled and then often never heard of again. The NDP is one such example. Having immersed innumerable sections of South African society in its consultation process, the NDP has barely been mentioned by government departments since its official launch in 2012.

Business leaders were also disappointed that the ambitious plans they had presented at Nedlac ended up being very watered down in the ERRP. Part of the reasoning behind this, according to ministers at the Nedlac forums, was that it was government's responsibility to govern and therefore the state should draw up the final version of the plan. This subtext might have been a reflection of how the developmental state was being interpreted – that the state must lead the country's economic reconstruction and recovery process. But it certainly did not advance the social compacting agenda; rather, it spoke to the distance between the largely white business elite and the largely black government. Labour, not having quite the resources of business, let alone those of the state, was more concerned about the immediate issues affecting its membership – hence its focus on ensuring the adequacy of the Unemployment Insurance Fund (UIF) and special relief grants. It did, however, express its frustration over the slow pace of ERRP implementation.

Thus, less than a year after the ERRP was released publicly, criticisms were being raised about the tardy implementation process, especially on the part of government. In February 2021, Minerals Council South Africa president, Mxolisi Mgojo, said that 'it has been incredibly disappointing that a lack of decisive action has meant that – six months after the proposals were tabled – we still don't have a coherent and inclusive plan ... Government needs to partner with and enable the private sector investment to grow the economy. It can do this by allowing private sector investment into rail, ports, electricity, pipelines, for example' (Mgojo, 2021: 7). Moreover, COSATU's Matthew Parks commented that, although 'we concluded the ERRP fairly quickly between August to October 2020, the one worrying part was the lack of detailed timeframes and financial commitments from government on many of the commitments' (Parks, 2021: 5).

In the latter half of 2021, the Thabo Mbeki Foundation (TMF) engaged in a series of consultations on the ERRP with business, labour, government and civil society and came to the conclusion 'that what President Ramaphosa and the Government had called a Plan was in fact a Vision!' (TMF, 2021: 3). In its report, the TMF acknowledged the work of B4SA, saying 'it seemed to us that indeed serious work had been done by B4SA towards producing (an) implementable plan' (TMF, 2021: 3). The TMF also noted the increasingly prominent role being played by business and that 'for the first time since 1994, business had come together to make a firm commitment to provide the much needed and considerable investment in our economy... The opportunity to do this still exists and requires that government should act to bring the social partners together' (TMF, 2021: 11).

Rudi Dicks (2021), head of the Project Management Office in The Presidency, speaking at a webinar hosted by the Gauteng City–Region Observatory and MISTRA in November 2021, admitted that the implementation of the ERRP had not lived up to expectations. 'Energy supply constraints remain while the need for additional generation capacity especially in renewables was being felt,' he said. While a National Infrastructure Plan 2050 and Country Investment Strategy had been developed, there was 'still insufficient investment (private and public), especially in economic infrastructure and network industries'. He pointed out, though, that progress had been made in drafting various sector master plans, in securing localisation commitments, and in gaining support for the integration of small, medium and micro enterprises (SMMEs) and cooperatives into supply chains.

The TMF (2021: 14) also stated in its report that it had met with 13 ministers and their officials and had concluded that 'it was clear that what was missing from the work of the ministers and their senior officials were time-specific national economic targets which were binding on Government ... In fact, only passing references were made to the ERRP by the ministers and their departments in their Parliamentary Budget Vote submissions between May and July [2021]'.

The TMF (2021) proposed a range of steps to remedy the tardy implementation of the ERRP, including the drafting of an Implementation Plan for Economic Reconstruction and Recovery (IP–ERR), which would set concrete targets and dissolve the mistrust amongst social partners. In the context of the sluggish implementation of the ERRP, the TMF proposed that the lead management of the compact be undertaken by government, instead of Nedlac, as the latter is more of a bargaining council than a negotiation forum. This particular recommendation went against the views of some of the social partners, especially given Nedlac's experience in drafting the compact around Eskom and the supply of electricity as well as its role in coordinating the response to COVID-19 generally.

Lisa Seftel (2021), Executive Director of Nedlac, indicated that an ILO/MISTRA study on the kind of leadership role that Nedlac should play over the next 25 years had made several recommendations. These would entail making amendments to the Nedlac Act, its constitution and its protocol documents with a view to assigning the body a broader mandate than was initially envisaged. The issue of how representation was determined also needed to be examined, 'out of a recognition that Nedlac has become more successful when there is a greater diversity of partners at the table and is regarded as speaking on behalf of "all society" beyond the actual representation of Nedlac' (Seftel, 2021).

BUSA, through its CEO, Cas Coovadia, shared the growing frustration amongst the different social partners with the pace of implementation of the ERRP, calling on the President in January 2022 to address the urgent need for structural economic reforms. Coovadia spoke of the need for 'a clear implementation strategy that demonstrates the importance of the government's commitment to the ERRP', stressing the importance of the President ensuring that 'his government operates in a cohesive manner and that there will not be mixed messages from different departments' (Coovadia, 2022).

The chorus of discordant voices had been heard in the Union Buildings. In his February 2022 State of the Nation Address, President Ramaphosa announced that 'to grow our economy, create jobs and combat hunger we have given ourselves 100 days to finalise a comprehensive social compact' (Ramaphosa, 2022). Carol Paton, writing for *News24*, reported that 'President Cyril Ramaphosa took business and labour by surprise' with this announcement but 'by 11 April 2022, 42 days will have slipped away'. She indicated that 'separate engagement between government and the social partners is starting to pinpoint the issues. However, with the clock running towards deadline, the parties are yet to meet together in one forum' (Paton, 2022). The ERRP remains to date the fulcrum around which attempts at achieving a broad-ranging social compact are focused.

CONCLUSION: A BONFIRE OF PACTS OR A CELEBRATION OF COMPACTS?

South Africa's experience has shown that it is possible for social partners to identify a common cause around which they can cohere. The country's enduring constitutional democracy remains a framework within which such compacting can occur and a developmental state can be consolidated.

However, despite all the effort that went into the formulation of the ERRP and the goodwill that Nedlac's social partners were willing to show towards it, the state of the country at the end of 2021 was not substantially better than the state it had been in at the beginning of the pandemic. According to Statistics South Africa's 2021 Quarter 4 report (StatsSA, 2022), 2.2 million jobs had been shed since January 2020. At the beginning of 2022, 12.5 million South Africans were without a job or an income, and the number of those employed had fallen to 14.2 million, down from 16.4 million in January 2020, with the broadly defined unemployment rate standing at 46.6 per cent.

The question raised by Singh and Ovadia (2018: 1034) as to whether the emergence of a developmental state is possible 'in the context of states with weak capacity and legacies of inequality, oppression and colonial rule' needs to be addressed. Fine's (2016) highlighting of the tension between the DSP and SCP requires South African policymakers to appreciate that there is no silver bullet for South Africa's economic challenges. Perhaps a conceptual error was made in casting all these attempts in the same mould, in contradiction to Mkandawire's (2012) call for a distinction to be made between 'development pacts', 'competitiveness pacts' and 'social pacts'. The different agreements sketched in this chapter must be analysed to determine which category of pact they represent. Doing so will reveal the type of agency required, the format of the negotiations needed to realise such a pact, the social partners to be involved and how implementation is to be achieved. In other words, the tradition of omnibus pacts is not necessarily the answer to the dire socioeconomic circumstances in which South Africa finds itself.

From the experiences of other successful developing countries, it appears that for South Africa to have an effective 'competitiveness pact', the government needs to adopt a pro-business stance, but one that is based on the kind of embedded autonomy prescribed by Evans (2008) – where the state is able to discipline capital using a combination of carrots and sticks. In other words, it is rewarded when it contributes to the goals of the compact and sanctioned when it goes against them. As Heise (2007: 337) suggests, sanctioning could take the form of 'non-cooperation in the next round of interactions ("shadow of the future") or institutional sanctions for defecting parties ("shadow of the law")'.

As other chapters in this volume assert, the South African economy is highly concentrated and the state needs to lead the various compacts with a firm hand. Underlying this process is the need for the kind of elite compacting that has been pursued by countries such as Mauritius or that Singh and Ovadia (2018) call a 'political settlement'. Such elite compacting should involve the leaders of the social partners, with black business, in particular, playing a more responsible role. This facilitates a unified approach to rent management, which is performed in the interests of the country as a whole and not for any particular segment of the well-connected elite.

At the same time, business needs to visibly display a higher level of commitment to the wellbeing of South Africans. South Africa's racially defined inequality perpetuates a political economy with a largely black (and unionised) working class, an army of the unemployed and impoverished sections, all of whom are suspicious of capital which remains largely in the hands of whites. Reducing the number of dual business listings in other domains, thereby making capital more accessible to emerging businesses, and investing the high returns that businesses enjoy in the South African economy would go a long way towards building trust in the private sector.

Another critical element is agency, especially that of the state. Business and labour appear united in their criticism of the poor performance of government as a whole and the individual ministers' inability to work together to implement the various agreements emanating from recent milestones on the compacting spectrum. Perhaps this is what is required for the ERRP – an institutional arrangement that is durable, while Nedlac acts as the forum for social dialogue amongst the various social partners. Yet this type of agency can play only a limited role if state capacity and capabilities remain constrained and the state, because of ongoing infighting, is unable to take a long-term view and fully commit to the plans it rolls out.

Last but not least, a firm foundation needs to be laid so that the various compacts can thrive; a foundation premised on democracy and trust amongst South Africans as a whole and between the various social partners. This will be the basis of a 'social pact', as portrayed in the South African Constitution through the negotiating process, or the nation-building pacts proposed by Mkandawire (2012).

REFERENCES

African National Congress (ANC). 2020. Umrabulo: NGC 2020 discussion documents, Special edition. ANC: Johannesburg.

African National Congress (ANC). 2022. Umrabulo: 2022 Policy conference, Special edition. ANC: Johannesburg.

Amsden, A. 2001. *Rise of the 'Rest': Challenges to the west from late-industrialising economies.* New York: Oxford University Press.

Brautigam, D and Diolle T. 2009. 'Coalitions, capitalists, and credibility: Overcoming the crisis of confidence at independence in Mauritius'. Development Leadership Programme, https://www.dlprog.org/publications/research-papers/coalitions-capitalists-and-credibility-overcoming-the-crisis-of-confidence-at-independence-in-mauritius, accessed 20 February 2022.

Business for South Africa (B4SA). 10 July 2020. 'A new inclusive economic feature for South African presentation', https://www.businessforsa.org/wp-content/uploads/2020/07/B4SA-A-New-Inclusive-Economic-Future-for-South-Africa-Presentation-10-July-Final.pdf, accessed 20 February 2022.

Coovadia, C. 8 February 2022. 'Business Unity SA (BUSA) media release prior to the State of the Nation Address (SONA) 2022: Time for implementation'. BUSA website: https://www.busa.org.za/business-unity-sa-busa-media-release-prior-to-the-state-of-the-nation-address-sona-2022-time-for-implementation/, accessed 3 March 2022.

Crook, R. C. and Booth, D. 2011. 'Conclusion: Rethinking African governance and development'. *IDS Bulletin,* 42 (2), 97–101.

Da Silva, S. M. and Webster, J. P. 2018. 'Positionality and standpoint situated ethnographers acting in on- and offline contexts', in Beach, D., Bagley, C. and Marques da Silva, S. (eds.) *The Wiley Handbook of Ethnography of Education.* New York: John Wiley and Sons, 501–512.

Dicks, R. 11 November 2021. 'Economic reconstruction and recovery plan: Building a new economy'. Presentation at GCRO/MISTRA webinar on 'Rebuilding Economies'.

Evans, P. B. 1995. *Embedded Autonomy: States and industrial transformation.* Princeton, NJ: Princeton University Press.

Evans, P. B. 2004. 'Development as institutional change: The pitfalls of institutional monocropping and the potentials of deliberation'. *Studies in Comparative International Development,* 38 (4), 30–52.

Evans, P. B. 2008. 'In search of the 21st century developmental state'. Centre for Global Political Economy, Working Paper No. 4, University of Sussex, http://www.sussex.ac.uk/cgpe/research/publications/workingpapers, accessed 14 February 2022.

Fine, B. 2016. 'Across developmental state and social compacting: The peculiar case of South Africa'. ISER Working Paper No. 2016/1. Grahamstown: Institute of Social and Economic Research, Rhodes University.

Freund, B. 2011. 'A ghost from the past: The South African developmental state of the 1940s'. *WISER*, https://phambo.wiser.org.za/files/seminars/Freund2011.pdf, accessed 14 December 2021.

Heise, A. 2007. 'Institutions, market constellations and growth: The case of South Africa'. *Annals of Economics and Finance*, 8 (2), 313–340.

International Labour Organization (ILO). 2013. 'National tripartite social dialogue: An ILO guide for improved governance'. International Labour Office, Social Dialogue and Tripartism Unit, Governance and Tripartism Department. Geneva: ILO.

Leftwich, A. 1995. 'Bringing politics back in: Towards a model of a developmental state'. *The Journal of Developmental Studies*, 31 (3), 400–424.

Mapungubwe Institute for Strategic Reflection (MISTRA). 2020. *Social Compacting Report: Case studies*. Johannesburg: Mapungubwe Institute for Strategic Reflection.

Mgojo, M. 2021. 'Minerals-council-address-by-mxolisi-mgojo-state-of-the-mining-nation', https://www.mineralscouncil.org.za/industry-news/publications/presentations/send/7-2015/1369-state-of-the-nation-address-by-mxolisi, accessed 14 February 2022.

Mkandawire, T. 29 March 2012. 'Building the African state in the age of globalisation: The role of social compacts and lessons for South Africa'. MISTRA Inaugural Mapungubwe Annual Lecture: University of the Witwatersrand.

Naidu, V. and Maré, A. 2015. 'Implementing the National Development Plan (NDP)? Lessons from co-ordinating grand economic policies in South Africa'. *Politikon*, 42 (3), 407–427.

National Economic Development and Labour Council (Nedlac). 2018. 'Learning from experience with socio-economic pacts'. Johannesburg: National Economic Development and Labour Council.

National Economic Development and Labour Council (Nedlac). 21 July 2020a. 'Building the new economy: Refocusing the 2018 jobs summit to support the economic recovery plan – Placing employment at the centre'. Johannesburg: National Economic Development and Labour Council.

National Economic Development and Labour Council (Nedlac). 2020b. 'The social partners' economic recovery action plan'. Johannesburg: National Economic Development and Labour Council.

National Planning Commission (NPC). 2012. *National Development Plan 2030. Our future, make it work*, https://www.gov.za/sites/default/files/gcis_document/201409/ndp-2030-our-future-make-it-workr.pdf, accessed 20 September 2022.

Parks, M. 2021. 'A mixed bag of fruit'. *South African Labour Bulletin*, https://www.southafricanlabourbulletin.org.za/a-mixed-bag-of-fruit, accessed 14 February 2022.

Paton, C. 11 April 2022. 'The race is on as Ramaphosa lines up trade-offs for his 100-day social pact'. *News24*, https://www.news24.com/fin24/economy/the-race-is-on-as-ramaphosa-lines-up-trade-offs-for-his-100-day-social-pact-20220411, accessed 15 April 2022.

Ramaphosa, C. 2020a. 'Statement by President Cyril Ramaphosa on further economic and social measures in response to the COVID-19 epidemic', website: https://www.thepresidency.gov.za/speeches/statement-president-cyril-ramaphosa-further-economic-and-social-measures-response-covid-19?msclkid=cb3e5366c5ad11eca74cbd327129b4ac, accessed 14 February 2022.

Ramaphosa, C. 2020b. 'President Cyril Ramaphosa: Engagement with South African national editors forum', website: https://www.gov.za/speeches/president-cyril-ramaphosa-engagement-south-african-national-editors-forum-31-may-2020-0000?msclkid=382076a4c5ae11ec975b6c13febcf1f6, accessed 14 February 2022.

Ramaphosa, C. 2020c. 'Address by President Cyril Ramaphosa to the Joint Sitting of Parliament on South Africa's Economic Reconstruction and Recovery Plan', *SA People News*, https://www.sapeople.com/2020/10/15/full-transcript-address-by-president-cyril-ramaphosa-to-the-joint-sitting-of-parliament-on-south-africas-economic-reconstruction-and-recovery-plan/?msclkid=80768235c5af11ec895143a33deccc23, accessed 14 February 2022.

Ramaphosa, C. 2022. 'State of the Nation Address (SoNA) by President Cyril Ramaphosa, Cape Town City Hall, Thursday, 10 February 2022', website: https://www.gov.za/speeches/president-cyril-ramaphosa-2022-state-nation-address-10-feb-2022-0000, accessed 15 February 2022.

Seftel, L. 12 December 2021. 'Nedlac quick off the mark to mobilise society in the face of Covid'. *Sunday Times*, https://times-e-editions.pressreader.com/article/282037625463797, accessed 11 February 2022.

Sen, A. 1999. *Development as Freedom*, New York: A. Knopf.

Singh, J. N. and Ovadia, J. S. 2018. 'The theory and practice of building developmental states in the global south'. *Third World Quarterly*, 39 (6), 1033–1055.

Statistics South Africa (StatsSA), 2022. 'Quarterly Labour Force Survey: Fourth Quarter 2021', http://www.statssa.gov.za/publications/P0211/P02114thQuarter2021.pdf, accessed 11 April 2022.

Teague, P. and Donaghey, J. 2009. 'Why has Irish social partnership survived?' *British Journal of Industrial Relations*, 47, 55–78.

Thabo Mbeki Foundation (TMF). 2021. *Report of the Thabo Mbeki Foundation on its engagements with the Nedlac social partners and proposals on a way forward*. Johannesburg: Thabo Mbeki Foundation.

Woo-Cummings, M. 1999. *The Development State*. Ithaca, NY: Cornell University Press.

NOTES

1 The author was part of the private-sector delegation to Nedlac while he was working with the Banking Association South Africa in 2020. In drafting this chapter, he had numerous conversations with representatives of business and labour as well as Nedlac staff.

SIXTEEN

Binding constraints to decision making on growth: Perspectives from heads of departments

AMUZWENI NGOMA AND BUSANI NGCAWENI

INTRODUCTION

As South Africa moves towards its third decade of democracy, it faces a host of complex and interrelated challenges that risk the stability of the social order and its stewardship of the growth and development of the economy.

Post-1994, South Africa enjoyed an eight-year stretch of economic growth between 1999 and 2008, averaging 4 per cent per year (Hausmann et al., 2022). However, the end of the commodity boom coupled with the 2008/2009 global financial crisis (GFC), amongst other factors, curtailed growth. By the end of 2019, about four months before the first COVID-19 case was confirmed in South Africa, the country's gross domestic product (GDP) growth rate was almost zero (0.1 per cent) (World Bank, 2022), with growth having averaged 1.7 per cent between 2010 and 2019 (Hausmann et al., 2022).

A combination of high inflation, casualised work, low wages and chronic unemployment amongst young people, as well as the juxtaposition of the indebted poor and working and middle classes, have heightened social discontent throughout the country. Moreover, from an environmental perspective, adverse weather events, besides causing social and financial distress for communities, pose a threat to ageing and poorly maintained economic infrastructure, of which flooded railway lines and rain-damaged power lines are prominent examples.

The state's (in)ability to address these and other risks and challenges facing the economy has been exacerbated by a still-fledgling small business sector, public- and private-sector investment rates that have remained below 30 per cent of GDP – the threshold necessary for growth, as set out in the National Development Plan (NDP) of 2012 – and strained relations between the state and society in the wake of state capture. Together these factors have frustrated the state's ability to take advantage of reindustrialisation, innovation and 'green' economic opportunities and to engage in long-term human capacity building, eliminate poverty, and reduce unemployment and inequality. Former President Thabo Mbeki recently characterised these challenges and pressures facing the country as possibly overwhelming (eNCA, 2022); yet they need to be urgently addressed.

Stiglitz (2021) argues that the health and economic challenges that resulted from the COVID-19 pandemic have highlighted the importance of building better institutions, as well as better governments and markets. This applies to South Africa in particular. Analysts have pointed out that the implementation of various economic reforms, which had been formulated in the pre-COVID-19 era, would likely have improved South Africa's ability to tackle the socioeconomic damage caused by the pandemic. In other words, better implementation of reforms would have increased the economy's resilience and improved its recovery rate from COVID. According to Stiglitz (2021: 1), the effects of the pandemic have reinforced the need to arrive at better 'understandings of the relationship between government, the market, and other institutions within society'. He also emphasises that the current configurations and patterns of relationships between the state and market are insufficient for economic recovery. Therefore, in pursuing the goals of robust, resilient and inclusive economic recovery, nation building and democratic consolidation, the South African government must ensure that the configuration of state–society relations remains consistently aligned with these goals.

This chapter proceeds from the premise that government is central to the creation and support (through the allocation of resources) of effective institutions, the improvement of state–society relations (which are indispensable for economic restructuring), and the achievement of inclusive and environmentally sustainable growth (Mazzucato et al., 2021). The chapter taps into the voices and experiences of senior government officials who have spent years driving economic growth under difficult global and domestic circumstances and conditions, against the backdrop of debates on how the South African economy has evolved and how it should look in the future.

The voices and experiences of the post-1994 heads of departments (HoDs) or directors-generals (DGs) are significant for two reasons. First, as accounting officers or accounting authorities, they are responsible for 'the effective, efficient, economical and transparent use of resources' in terms of the Public Finance Management Act (PFMA, 1999) (Tsheletsane and Fourie, 2014: 45). Second, DGs have made and led many economic choices and interventions relating to research and development, industrial policy, a national innovation strategy, the country's transition to a low-carbon economy and the work of the economic cluster. Third, DGs play a critical role in tracking and exposing the successes and failures of state attempts to bring about structural transformation (Stiglitz, 2021).

As Mazzucato et al. (2021) assert, the state is not just a market fixer, but also a market co-creator and shaper. Thus, in the light of South Africa's 29-year-old (and still unfolding) democracy, both the government and society need to develop a critical understanding of the country's internal mechanics and culture, the effects of policies and initiatives (especially government failures), and possible pathways to overcome shortcomings. If economic growth has a rate and a direction, then it also has a personality which influences its rate and direction. This is evidenced in its ethical blueprint, and social and political values and sentiments (whether coherent or chaotic). In developing countries, government failure may pose a greater risk to economic growth than market failure (Perrot, 2015). If government fails to perform, it will not be able to fix 'market failures', as demanded by neoliberalist thinking, or become an effective developmental state. Knowing what internal factors contribute to government's 'failure' or 'success' is an essential stepping stone on the path towards a developmental state.

DGs derive their mandate and accountability from legislation, with the design of policy, the implementation of plans, the allocation of human, infrastructural and financial resources, and the management of multi-billion-rand budgets falling within their ambit. As a result, senior government leaders share responsibility for the performance of the South African economy. As such, their professional, social and personal experiences in leading economic growth and development initiatives offer useful insights into the nature of the relationship between government and economics – which is atypical of structural transformation debates.

This chapter is divided into four sections. The first section traces selected structural changes that have been made to the macro structure of government over successive administrations. The second section, based on interviews with DGs, highlights the organisational factors, dynamics and cultures that have affected policy choices, resource allocation and implementation and how these are perceived to have affected economic growth. This offers a two-dimensional view of the perceived dynamics in and performance of government (Nabudere, 2006).

The third section determines that the macro organisation of national government and the associated organisational and cultural factors that prevail at the national level have undermined the development of dynamic state capabilities. The conflict at the political and administrative interface appears to be the dominant (and perennial) factor inhibiting the realisation and uptake of key policies and programmes. The conceptualisation of the administrative and political spheres of national government as being separate and distinct from each other serves to perpetuate conflict and the high turnover of DGs, while also weakening the administrative and technical capacities of politicians. DGs perform a critical function, but, in the current circumstances, they are constraining government's ability to positively influence both the rate and direction of South Africa's economic growth. A combination of poor and even contradictory economic policy and regulatory choices and non-strategic, inadequate or delayed industrial and infrastructure investments have conspired to create a low-performing economy.

The fourth and final section provides a suggested framework for approaching the issue of state capacity in South Africa so that it will create the foundation on which goal-driven policies and mega projects can be anchored.

A NOTE ON NOMENCLATURE

To maintain the confidentiality of the DGs interviewed, the chapter applies the national government's cluster system[1] to distinguish DGs and indicate the area in which they operate. Given that the DGs spoken to have worked in and led different clusters, their last place of work is given. National government has five clusters: (1) Economic Sectors, Investment, Employment and Infrastructure Development; (2) Social Protection, Community and Human Development; (3) Governance, State Capacity and Institutional Development; (4) Justice, Crime Prevention and Security; and (5) International Cooperation, Trade and Security. These clusters are listed in Table 16.1, along with the departments they represent.

EVOLUTION OF THE MACRO ORGANISATION OF GOVERNMENT

The analysis in this chapter focuses on selected departments within economic clusters during the period 1999–2020, excluding the Department of Transport, the National Treasury and the Department of Public Enterprises,[2] as their respective structures remained stable over this period. President Mandela's administration was also excluded as it underwent no major changes (Naidoo, 2018), save for the phasing out of the second deputy president position and the dropping of the Minister without Portfolio[3] position which had been responsible

Table 16.1: Clusters and the departments they represent

Economic Sectors, Investment, Employment and Infrastructure Development	Social Protection, Community and Human Development	Governance, State Capacity and Institutional Development	Justice, Crime Prevention and Security	International Cooperation, Trade and Security
DALRRD (Department of Agriculture, Land Reform and Rural Development)	**DALRRD** (Department of Agriculture, Land Reform and Rural Development)	**CoGTA** (Department of Cooperative Governance and Traditional Affairs)	**JCS** (Justice and Correctional Services)	**DCDT** (Department of Communications and Digital Technologies)
DCDT (Department of Communications and Digital Technologies)	**DBE** (Department of Basic Education)	**NT** (National Treasury)	**DMV** (Department of Military Veterans)	**DMV** (Department of Military Veterans)
CoGTA (Department of Cooperative Governance and Traditional Affairs)	**CoGTA** (Department of Cooperative Governance and Traditional Affairs)	**DHA** (Department of Home Affairs)	**NT** (National Treasury)	**NT** (National Treasury)
DEL (Department of Employment and Labour)	**DEL** (Department of Employment and Labour)	**JCS** (Justice and Correctional Services)	**DHA** (Department of Home Affairs)	**DFFE** (Department of Forestry, Fisheries and the Environment)
DFFE (Department of Forestry, Fisheries and the Environment)	**DFFE** (Department of Forestry, Fisheries and the Environment)	**DWYPD** (Department of Women, Youth and Persons with Disabilities)	**DIRCO** (Department of International Relations and Cooperation)	**DIRCO** (Department of International Relations and Cooperation)
DHET (Department of Higher Education and Training)	**DoH** (Department of Health)	**The Presidency**	**Police**	**JCS** (Justice and Correctional Services)
DSI (Department of Science and Innovation)	**DHET** (Department of Higher Education and Training	**DPWI** (Department of Public Works and Infrastructure)	**DPWI** (Department of Public Works and Infrastructure)	**DPME** (Department of Planning, Monitoring and Evaluation)
DHS (Department of Human Settlements)	**DSI** (Department of Science and Innovation)	**DPSA** (Department of Public Service and Administration)	**DSD** (Department of Social Development)	**DWYPD** (Department of Women, Youth and Persons with Disabilities)
DWS (Department of Water and Sanitation)	**DHS** (Department of Human Settlements)	**DPE** (Department of Public Enterprises)	**SSA** (State Security Agency)	**The Presidency**
DIRCO (Department of International Relations and Cooperation)	**DWS** (Department of Water and Sanitation)		**DSDB** (Department of Small Business Development)	**DSAC** (Department of Sport, Arts and Culture)
DMRE (co-chair) (Department of Mineral Resources and Energy)	**JCS** (Justice and Correctional Services)			**SSA** (State Security Agency)
				DTIC (Department of Trade, Industry and Competition)

Economic Sectors, Investment, Employment and Infrastructure Development	Social Protection, Community and Human Development	Governance, State Capacity and Institutional Development	Justice, Crime Prevention and Security	International Cooperation, Trade and Security
NT (National Treasury) **DPWI** (Department of Public Works and Infrastructure) **DPE** (Department of Public Enterprises) **DSBD** (Department of Small Business Development) **DWYPD** (Department of Women, Youth and Persons with Disabilities) **SSA** (State Security Agency) **DT** (co-chair) (Department of Tourism) **DTIC** (Department of Trade, Industry and Competition) **Police** **The Presidency** **DoT** (Department of Transport)	**DSD** (Department of Social Development) **DWYPD** (Department of Women, Youth and Persons with Disabilities) **The Presidency** **DSAC** (Department of Sport, Arts and Culture) **DSBD** (Department of Small Business Development) **DoT** (Department of Transport) **DPWI** (Department of Public Works and Infrastructure)			

Source: Government Information and Communication System (GCIS), 2022

for the Reconstruction and Development Programme (RDP) office (Naidoo, 2018).

The national government machinery in South Africa has undergone extensive changes in the post-1994 period. This has affected state capacity, which relates to the state's ability (or otherwise) to make significant progress in tackling poverty, unemployment and inequality, and to deepen and sustain such efforts. As Figure 16.1 shows, between 1994 and 2019, the number of national departments rose from 27 to 46, the number of ministers rose from 27 to 35 and the number of deputy ministers rose from 14 to 37 (DPSA, 2019).

Figure 16.1: Numbers of ministers, deputy ministers and departments over six administrations, 1994–2022

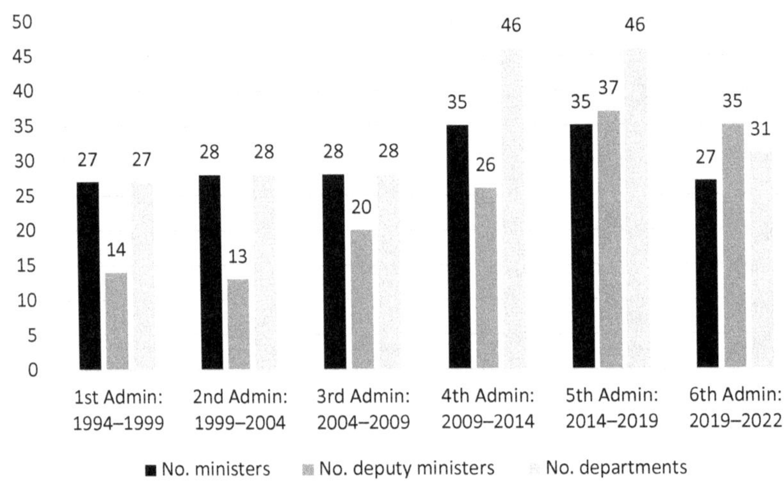

Source: DPSA, 2019; GCIS, 2022

Note: The 6th Administration will end in 2024.

The pattern of change amongst national and provincial entities, respectively, is somewhat different. By the fifth administration, the total number of public entities stood at 277, having peaked at 299 in the previous administration. There has also been a substantial increase in the number of national public entities since 1994, rising from 91 to 205 between 1994 and 2019. Contrary to the national trend, the number of provincial entities has declined steadily since 1994.

Figure 16.2: Numbers of national and provincial entities listed by the Public Finance Management Act (PFMA) over six administrations, 1994–2023

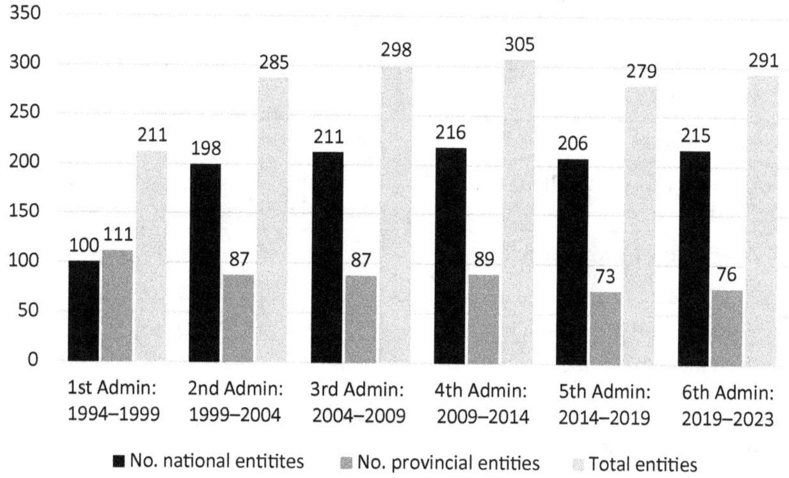

Source: National Treasury, 1999, 2003, 2009, 2014, 2023

Departments within economic clusters have undergone the most change over the period 1994–2022. Tables 16.5 and 16.7 illustrate how some of the critical departments responsible for the promotion of agriculture, land reform, economic development, and trade and industry have changed during this period. In terms of these changes, it is not only the departments' mandates and programmes that have been affected, but also their budget and departmental structures and the scope of the legislation that they administer. The column headings in Table 16.2 reflect the departmental nomenclature at the end of 2022 (new names) and 2018 (old names). The left-hand column reflects the current (sixth administration's) names for the various departments.

Table 16.2: New (as at October 2022) and old (as at November 2018) department names

New names	Old names
Agriculture, Land Reform and Rural Development	Agriculture, Forestry and Fisheries
	Rural Development and Land Reform
Basic Education	Basic Education
Communications and Digital Technologies	Communication, Telecommunications and Postal Services
Cooperative Governance and Traditional Affairs	Cooperative Governance and Traditional Affairs
Military Veterans	Defence and Military Veterans
Employment and Labour	Labour
National Treasury	National Treasury
Forestry, Fisheries and the Environment	Environmental Affairs
Health	Health
Higher Education and Training	Higher Education and Training
Home Affairs	Home Affairs
Human Settlements	Human Settlements
International Relations and Cooperation	International Relations and Cooperation
Mineral Resources and Energy	Energy
	Mineral Resources
Police	Police
Justice and Correctional Services	Justice and Correctional Services
Public Enterprises	Public Enterprises
Public Service and Administration	Public Service and Administration
Public Works and Infrastructure	Public Works
Science and Innovation	Science and Technology
Small Business Development	Small Business Development
Social Development	Social Development
Sport, Arts and Culture	Sport and Recreation
State Security Agency	State Security
The Presidency	The Presidency
The Presidency: Planning, Monitoring and Evaluation	The Presidency: Planning, Monitoring and Evaluation

New names	Old names
The Presidency: Women, Youth and Persons with Disabilities	The Presidency: Women
Tourism	Tourism
Trade, Industry and Competition	Trade and Industry
	Economic Development
Transport	Transport
Water and Sanitation	Water and Sanitation

Source: GCIS, 2018, 2022

Table 16.3: Departmental changes by number and type, 1994–2022 (October)

Type of structural change	Presidencies				
	Mandela	Mbeki	Zuma	Ramaphosa	
	1994–1999	2000–2008	2009–2014	2020–Oct 2022	
Establishing/ founding	3	0	5	Founding	0
Functional splitting	1	1	5	Splitting	1
Functional merging	0	1	1	Mergers	5
Absorption	0	0	1	Absorption	5
Vertical movement	1	2	0	Name change	4
Name change/ functional alteration	4	2	8	Functional transfer	11
Total structural changes	9	6	20	Total structural changes	26

Source: Naidoo, 2018: 12 (for the period 1994–2020); adapted from DPSA, 2020 (for the period 2020 – October 2022)

Table 16.4 illustrates the evolution of key economic policies or plans and their location in government.

Table 16.4: Structural evolution of economic plans and priorities and location in government, 1994–2022

Presidency	Policy/Plan	Lead portfolio	Lead minister(s)	Lead DG	Evolution of priorities
Mandela 1994–1999	RDP (Reconstruction and Development Programme) (1994)	The Presidency	Jay Naidoo	None	5 programmes: meeting basic needs;[4] developing human resources; building the economy;[5] democratising the state and society and implementing the RDP
	GEAR (Growth, Employment and Redistribution) (1996)	NT (National Treasury)	Trevor Manuel	Maria Ramos	Macroeconomic stability and employment creation
Mbeki 2000–2008	GEAR (1996)	NT (National Treasury)	Trevor Manuel	Maria Ramos	Macroeconomic stability and employment creation
	AsgiSA (Accelerated and Shared Growth Initiative for South Africa) (2006)	NT (National Treasury); DTI (Trade and Industry [now DTIC]); DPE (Public Enterprises)	Deputy President Phumzile Mlambo-Ngcuka Trevor Manuel Mandisi Mpahlwa Alexander Erwin	Alan Hirsch[6] (The Presidency) Lesetja Kganyago (NT) Tshediso Matona (DTI [now DTIC]) Portia Molefe (DPE)	6 binding constraints: government incapacity, currency volatility, infrastructure backlogs, skills shortages, sector competitiveness shortcomings, inequality and marginalisation
	IPAP (Industrial Policy Action Plan) I (2007) and II (2010)	Trade and Industry	Mandisi Mpahlwa Rob Davies	Tshediso Matona (DTI [now DTIC]) Lionel October (DTI [now DTIC])	Sectoral development plans: motor industry, etc.

Presidency	Policy/Plan	Lead portfolio	Lead minister(s)	Lead DG	Evolution of priorities
Zuma **2009–2014**	NGP (New Growth Path) (2010)	Economic Development	Ebrahim Patel	Prof Richard Levin	Public investment in infrastructure and public services; green economy and rural development
	NDP (National Development Plan) (2012)	NPC (National Planning Commission)	Trevor Manuel	Cassius Reginald Lubisi	Quality social protection, education and healthcare; 11 million jobs created; new infrastructure; clean energy; low carbon and rural economy development; fight corruption; build capable state; unite society
Ramaphosa **2020–Oct 2022**	ETIGC (Economic transformation, inclusive growth and competitiveness – National Treasury) (2019)	NT (National Treasury)	Tito Mboweni	Dondi Mogajane	Modernisation of network industries; labour-intensive agriculture and services; trade; export competitiveness and ownership/concentration
	ERRP (Economic Reconstruction and Recovery Plan) (2020)	The Presidency	Jackson Mthembu Mondli Gungubele	Cassius Reginald Lubisi Phindile Baleni	Localisation; infrastructure; public employment; green economy; capable state; financing development; skills; energy security; export competitiveness; regulatory easing and macroeconomic stability[7]

Source: Authors' compilation

Portfolio: Agriculture, Land Reform and Rural Development

Between 1999 and 2009, the Department of Agriculture, Land Reform and Rural Development, as it is now called, had one political head and two DGs who were responsible for agriculture and land affairs respectively. Under the 2009 and 2014 administrations, a substantial change took place: the department was split into two, creating the Department of Agriculture, Forestry and Fisheries and the Department of Rural Development and Land Reform. The forestry function was separated from the Department of Water Affairs and Forestry (Levin, 2009). Changes to the executive authority meant that each department obtained a minister and a DG. The 2009 reconfiguration saw three departments undergoing changes: Forestry and Fisheries was split from the Department of Water Affairs and Forestry and the Department of Environmental Affairs and absorbed by the new Department of Agriculture, Forestry and Fisheries (see Table 16.5).

In the sixth administration, which straddles the period 2019 to 2024, further reorganisation of this portfolio and departmental structure took place (see Table 16.5). A new portfolio was created, called Agriculture, Land Reform and Rural Development, with one political head, two deputy ministers and one DG (DPSA, 2019). This change meant that the responsibilities previously carried by two DGs between 1999 and 2014 were now carried by one DG. Along with the added strain on its capacity, the department suffered an incommensurate shrinkage in its budget, despite its expanded functions.

Table 16.5: Configurations of Agriculture, Land Reform and Rural Development

Portfolio/executive authority	New department	Former department/s	Comments on affected departments
Agriculture, Land Reform and Rural Development 2 DMs, 1 DG	Agriculture, Land Reform and Rural Development (DALRRD)	Agriculture, Forestry and Fisheries Rural Development and Land Reform	Agriculture merged with Land Reform and Rural Development Environmental Affairs combined with Forestry and Fisheries

Source: DPSA, 2019; PSC, 2022

Portfolio: Human Settlements, Water and Sanitation

Another important department in the economic cluster which has historically experienced dramatic changes to its mandate, scope and structure is the Department of Water Affairs. From 1999 to 2009, it was called the Department of Water Affairs and Forestry (DWAF), led by one minister and one DG. The DWAF's forestry function was moved to another department, thus creating a new department called the Department of Agriculture, Forestry and Fisheries. In 2009, the DWAF's mandate changed to include environmental affairs, which had been part of the Department of Environmental Affairs and Tourism (DEAT).

Table 16.6: Configurations of Human Settlements, Water and Sanitation

Portfolio/executive authority	New department	Former department/s	Comments on affected departments
Human Settlements 1 DM, 1 DG	Human Settlements	Human Settlements	Transfer of water and sanitation to Department of Human Settlements
Water and Sanitation 1 DM, 1 DG	Water and Sanitation	Water and Sanitation	Split from Human Settlements portfolio

Source: Adapted from DPSA, 2019

Until 2009, there had been a Department of Housing, which then became the Department of Human Settlements (DHS). The DHS also assumed the sanitation function from the former DWAF. In 2014, a new Water and Sanitation portfolio was created, gaining one minister and one DG. Thus, the sanitation function was removed from the DHS (DPSA, 2014). In 2019, the department underwent another structural change, with its consolidation into the Human Settlements, Water and Sanitation portfolio. Its leadership comprised one minister, two deputy ministers and one DG for Human Settlements and one for Water and Sanitation respectively. The rationale for this structure was that having one point of political oversight would help to address the challenge of houses being built without proper connections to water and sanitation infrastructure (DPSA, 2019).

This consolidated arrangement was briefly sustained from 2019 (the start of the sixth administration). However, in August 2021, the portfolio was split again, recreating the Water and Sanitation portfolio.

Portfolio: Trade and Industry

The Trade and Industry portfolio also experienced significant changes in 2009. Since 1999, the department had had one minister, two deputy ministers and one DG. Its scope covered trade, industry and small business development. The department also played a role in the formulation of economic policy, particularly industrial policy. In 2009, the department was split into two, retaining the trade and industry function but allocating the function of economic development to a new portfolio called Economic Development (Levin, 2009). In 2014, a further split was made in the Trade and Industry portfolio, when a new Small Business Development portfolio was created. Therefore, between 2009 and 2014, the original Trade and Industry portfolio was split into three.

The subsequent reconfiguration in 2019 resulted in the economic development function being returned to the Trade and Industry portfolio, with the name change reflected in Table 16.7. Importantly, the transfer of the Presidential Infrastructure Coordinating Commission (PICC) to the Department of Public Works and Infrastructure (DPWI) (its new name since 2019) also included the DPWI receiving the infrastructure development management system (IDMS) function from the National Treasury, with the department thus assuming the coordinating responsibility for all public infrastructure development (DPSA, 2019).

THE PRESIDENCY: THE CENTRE OF GOVERNMENT

The Presidency, which is the centre of government, has also seen changes made to the leadership structures responsible for coordinating the affairs of the state. Gumede (2017: 3) asserts that 'The Presidency must lead decision making, policies, coordination, planning as well as monitoring and evaluation'.

The centralising role of The Presidency was initiated during the second

Table 16.7: Configurations of Trade, Industry and Competition

Portfolio/ executive authority	New department	Former department/s	Comments on affected departments
Trade and Industry 2 DMs, 2 DGs	Trade, Industry and Competition (DTIC)	Trade and Industry Economic Development	Merger Transfer of the PICC from the Economic Development Department (EDD) to the Department of Public Works and Infrastructure (DPWI) Transfer of the economic development function from the Economic Development Department (EDD) to the Department of Trade, Industry and Competition (DTIC)

Source: DPSA, 2019

administration under Thabo Mbeki. Nelson Mandela had occupied the scaled-down 'Office of the President' which consisted of three offices: for the president and his two deputies (Jacobs, 2002). When Mbeki became president in 1999, he merged the offices of the president and the two deputy presidents into a single entity called The Presidency (Jacobs, 2002; Southall, 2007). This created transversal links between ministries, such as international relations, government and administration, social development and education, and trade, industry and investment.

Between 1999 and 2008, there was one minister in The Presidency and one DG who was responsible for administrative functions in The Presidency and the Government Communication and Information System (GCIS), the latter being responsible for government communications. In 2001, the DG of the GCIS was appointed to also serve as head of the Policy Coordination and Advisory Services (PCAS), a position he assumed on a full-time basis in 2006. The Presidency was also responsible for political oversight of its administration and the National Youth Commission (NYC). In anticipation of the impending transition while Mbeki served his last term of office in 2008, the ruling African National Congress (ANC) recommended that its recently elected deputy president be appointed as minister in The Presidency. His role was well defined and was limited to leading government business. In this capacity, he worked with the goverment on the anti-poverty programme. This arrangement changed in September 2008, when Thabo Mbeki stepped down from his position and was replaced by Kgalema Motlanthe. Motlanthe reorganised the cabinet, maintaining the same structure of ministries and departments, but letting go of the position of second minister in The Presidency, which he had occupied.

In 2009, during the fourth administration (2009–2014) led by Jacob Zuma, more changes took place in The Presidency. Two more ministers were added, raising the number to three. Officially, these were the functions that historically had been led by the PCAS, which was disbanded in 2010 (Gumede, 2017). The PCAS was preceded by the Coordination and Implementation Unit (CIU), established in 1997 in the deputy president's office (occupied at the time by Mbeki) to 'equip government with strategic planning and management capacity as required' (Jacobs, 2002: 31). Importantly, the GCIS also had its roots in the deputy president's office. The PCAS was a 'super' branch within The Presidency, reporting to the DG in The Presidency, supporting the president, deputy president and minister. According to Jacobs (2002: 33), from 1998, the PCAS had chief directorates that mirrored cabinet committee clusters:

- the economics cluster (covering the ministries of finance, trade, labour and water);
- the social services cluster (covering the ministries of education, health, housing and welfare);
- international relations (covering the ministries of foreign affairs and defence);
- intergovernmental relations (covering provincial and local government); and
- criminal justice (covering the ministries of safety and security, justice and correctional services).

The PCAS was thus the main engine room where policy proposals and all reforms were thoroughly scrutinised and key reports on economic and social issues were produced, which were translated into five-year strategic frameworks and through which policy coordination took place (Gumede, 2017; Jacobs, 2002; Southall, 2007). It played a key role not only in coordinating the programme of action for economic transformation, but also in leading the thinking on key reforms, working closely with departments like the National Treasury and (as they were then known) Trade and Industry and Minerals and Energy.

The PCAS also carried the responsibility for mainstreaming the programmes for women, youth, children and persons with disabilities across government, which were additional PCAS sub-units (Gumede, 2017). In 2009, three political heads or ministers were appointed to lead this function (Gumede, 2017): the Planning minister; the Performance, Monitoring and Evaluation minister; and the Women, Children and People with Disabilities minister. In addition, the Department of Women, Children and People with Disabilities (DWCPD) assumed the oversight role of the Chapter 9 constitutional body, the Commission for Gender Equality (CGE), which was previously under the Department of Justice and Correctional Services. The new Planning minister was also given the responsibility of supervising Statistics South Africa (StatsSA), which had previously been located in the Finance portfolio (National Treasury).

In 2014, the structure underwent further changes, which saw the Planning ministry dropped and planning combined with the Monitoring and Evaluation portfolio. This also meant that the new Planning, Monitoring and Evaluation minister assumed oversight over StatsSA. The administrative leadership had a hybrid structure comprising two accounting officers, which also changed. Through this change, the secretariat of the National Planning Commission (NPC) was relegated to the status of a branch and subordinated to the DG of the new Department of Planning, Monitoring and Evaluation (DPME). The second significant change that occurred in 2014, which affected the structure of The Presidency, was that the oversight responsibility of the GCIS was relocated from The Presidency to the Communications ministry. This ministry, which itself had undergone changes, having been split into two, was renamed the Ministry of Telecommunications and Postal Services.

These changes disrupted the leadership, implementation and coordination of strategic programmes led by The Presidency as the centre of government. While The Presidency was growing, in reality it was being hollowed out and its functions fragmented, as its strategic functions had been decentralised without the necessary strategic centre of coordination being retained (DPSA, 2019; Naidoo, 2018), a role historically played by the PCAS. In this regard, one of the senior DGs interviewed for this study lamented that 'strong economic leadership must be provided from the centre' of government, meaning The Presidency.

To improve political, implementation and technical capacities, The Presidency acts as a critical centripetal force, particularly in the absence of mission-oriented planning and execution. Building The Presidency up to be the centre of government remains a key objective of the sixth administration. In his budget speech in 2022, President Cyril Ramaphosa stated: 'What we have sought to do over the past four years is to locate The Presidency at the centre of an integrated government. From this centre, we have been leading the drive to reconstruct the nation's economy in a manner that is inclusive, and that leaves no-one behind.'

The sixth administration has maintained the two ministries: Planning, Monitoring and Evaluation; and Women, Youth and Persons with Disabilities. It should be noted that the children's function was removed from the Women, Youth and Persons with Disabilities portfolio and returned to the Social Development portfolio. Significantly, the GCIS function was returned to The Presidency, with a separate DPME minister also responsible for planning. In the cabinet reshuffle of August 2021, State Security was phased out as a ministry and this responsibility was absorbed into the Planning, Monitoring and Evaluation ministry, which is supported by three deputy ministers.

Table 16.8: Configurations of The Presidency

Portfolio/executive authority	New department	Former department/s	Comments on affected departments
President The President is, in line with the Public Service Act, the executive authority of The Presidency.	The Presidency	The Presidency	Transfer of socioeconomic impact assessment functions from the DPME to The Presidency Creation of policy and research services capacity in The Presidency
Minister in The Presidency Deputy Minister in The Presidency	Planning, Monitoring and Evaluation (DPME), including the National Planning Secretariat, Statistics South Africa (StatsSA), Government Communication and Information System (GCIS) • Entity: Media Development and Diversity Agency (MDDA) • Entity: Brand SA	Planning, Monitoring and Evaluation (DPME) Statistics South Africa (StatsSA)	Transfer of socioeconomic impact assessment functions from the DPME to The Presidency. Transfer of GCIS and the following entities from the Minister of Communications to the Minister in The Presidency • Entity: Media Development and Diversity Agency (MDDA) • Entity: Brand SA
Minister in The Presidency: Women, Youth and Persons with Disabilities Deputy Minister	Women, Youth and Persons with Disabilities (DWYPD) • Entity: National Youth Development Agency (NYDA)	Women	Transfer of youth development functions and NYDA from the DPME Transfer of persons with disabilities function from the Department of Social Development to the DWYPD
State Security Deputy Minister	State Security Agency (SSA)	State Security Agency (SSA)	Transfer of State Security Agency (SSA) to The Presidency

Source: DPSA, 2019 (with authors' update on state security)

Figure 16.3 shows the configuration of The Presidency in a way that highlights the many changes that have taken place.

Figure 16.3: Configuration of The Presidency

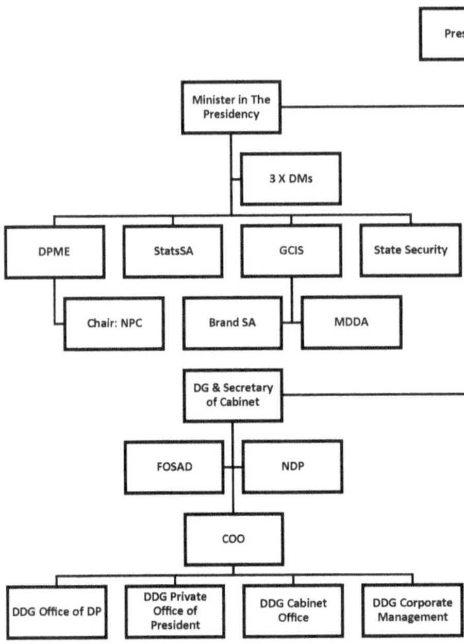

Source: Authors' compilation, adapted from DPSA, 2019; The Presidency Annual Report, 2021–2022

Notes: FOSAD stands for Forum of South African Directors-General; IMCs stands for Inter-Ministerial Committees

HOW THE REORGANISATION HAS IMPACTED THE AGENDAS OF POLITICAL ACTORS

As noted above, the changes in the structure and the programmes of The Presidency as the centre of government have not strengthened its ability to effectively lead economic transformation. As some of the DGs who were interviewed argued, The Presidency has, over the period 1994–2022, been characterised as leading a large number of projects instead of missions, which have had little impact on the real economy. Naidoo (2018: 2) concurs, stating: 'The national machinery has been on an expansive trajectory, although with discernible variation in intensity across different presidential incumbents. Macro-organisational change has unfolded in the absence of a clear strategic blueprint, and in conjunction with a coherent programme of public sector reform.' A DG in the economic sector aptly commented that 'we actually are a personality-driven state', where prioritisation is dependent on the proximity of a particular ministry and department to The Presidency. Thus, the political capital of political heads is used to determine what the state prioritises, resulting in The Presidency becoming merely a conduit for the pursuit of multiple 'pet' projects. The many 'hands on deck' have also created confusion across government, as there are too many entry points into The Presidency, thus weakening its authoritative core.

The formation of the PICC, the management of which was delegated to the Economic Development Department (EDD), created in 2009, stands out for its conceptual and practical flaws. First, the 2009 structural arrangement initiative failed to consolidate government's infrastructure development portfolio. This is because the EDD, as a new department, sat outside the centre of government and was practically incapable of coordinating infrastructure-related departments and state-owned enterprises (SOEs) which, as one DG in the governance cluster put it, 'were already all over the place'.

A further complication was the impression created that, for the competing priorities and projects to get attention from The Presidency, ministers had to use political capital. For example, portfolio functions were dissociated from departments and integrated into The Presidency in an effort to speed up implementation and to elevate or prioritise seemingly intractable implementation challenges. However, in the long run, such an approach prevents departments from developing dynamic capabilities around the challenges, while creating an impractical and overburdened bureaucracy within The Presidency. It also creates competition amongst those seeking The Presidency's attention, which leads to the 'wrong' incentivisation of political heads and encourages missions that do not drive economic transformation.

Thus, reorganisation to bolster the agenda of political actors and to drive policy action, in Naidoo's view (2018), coincides with and/or mutates into the dilution of state capacity. For example, there is a view that infrastructure coordination was shifted to the EDD and received a great deal of attention because of activism on the part of the minister. In this regard, the DGs argued strongly that changes in the structure of government have been inconsistent with the changes in the sectoral structure of the economy, exemplified by the creation of the Department of Telecommunications and Postal Services, when the latter was a sunset industry due to the rise of digital communications.

INSTABILITY IN GOVERNMENT LEADERSHIP

Structural governance issues, policy choices and their links to available capacity were also identified as impediments to building dynamic capabilities over time. The DGs interviewed were of the view that Nelson Mandela's administration was largely defined by the formulation of a new policy landscape and the transformation and creation of one public service. This included the establishment of processes and institutions to drive policy development and coordination (Gumede, 2017). Of this, Naidoo (2015: 24) remarks that the sheer 'scale' of that administration's endeavour 'saw South African policymakers draw inspiration from an accumulated wealth of international experience in public sector reform efforts, especially related to managed development and practice'.

The transition to the next administration, led by Thabo Mbeki, was marked by more intensive policy implementation, which would necessarily transfer the knowledge, skills and competencies accumulated in the previous administration. Importantly, DGs noted that the transition from the formulation of policy and the creation of a single public service became hampered by an emergent 'mismatch between the available capacity to get things done and what we want to do' (DG: Governance cluster). Specifically, a DG in the infrastructure sector noted that by the mid-2000s, a time when South Africa was experiencing higher levels of growth (see Chapters 2 and 5 in this volume), it had become poignantly apparent that the state lacked the necessary capacity to implement its defined policies.

In effect, this had a bearing on the country's ability to fully realise 'good' policies and sustain buoyant levels of economic growth and to transfer these to other areas of development. Indeed, 'increased fiscal space made it possible to broaden access to public services and to social grants, which reduced absolute poverty' (Levy et al., 2021: 1). Yet transferring these gains in a way that built economic resilience proved difficult, given government's capacity shortcomings (see Chapter 5 in this volume).

One factor impacting the capacity of the state and the emergence of dynamic capabilities was government's inability to retain the skills and competencies it had developed. Tsheletsane and Fourie (2014) analysed the turnover rate for accounting officers in 39 national departments between 1999 and 2011, which straddled four of the six democratic administrations that South Africa has had thus far. Their findings revealed a large proportion of DGs (45.8 per cent) in an acting capacity. Van Onselen (2017), in turn, pointed to a 47 per cent increase in the rate of acting DGs between May 2009 and March 2017. As few as 7.3 per cent of DGs served a three- to four-year term, while a sizeable 42 per cent spent less than one year in office. The Departments of Public Works, Correctional Services and Public Service and Administration, and the Public Service Commission had had the highest rates of DG turnover, standing at 11, 9, 8 and 8 DGs respectively in 12 years. Not far behind, the Departments of Agriculture, Forestry and Fisheries, Communications, Health, Rural Development and Transport had all had 7 DGs in 12 years.

There were also significant changes made in respect of cabinet ministers, as shown in Van Onselen's (2017) analysis of the period between May 2009 and July 2017 (over eight years into Jacob Zuma's presidency). By March 2017, the national executive had 74 executive authorities: the president and his deputy, 35 ministers and 37 deputy ministers. The fourth and fifth administrations had 10 cabinets resulting from 10 reshuffles, with the average life of a cabinet being 8.6 months.[8] From May 2009 until March 2017, there were '126 changes to the national executive: 62 changes to ministerial positions, 63 changes to deputy ministerial positions and one change to the deputy presidency' (Van Onselen, 2017: 4).

Besides cabinet ministers and DGs, the public service was generally losing black managerial staff. Pottinger (2008) attributes the high turnover rate of black managerial staff to issues such as reassignment, illness, incompetence and corruption. In addition, there were not enough black 'quality' candidates to go around, with few whites prepared to take up public-sector positions. Within the context of employment equity and its associated requirements, the public service's low retention rates were due to it being outcompeted by the private sector in the search for skilled black managers. As of 1 August 2007, the Personnel and Salaries Management System (PERSAL) reflected 330 978 vacancies at national and provincial level, representing 23.1 per cent of the total funded complement (PSC, 2007).

The high turnover during this period meant instability in the public service leadership (Levy et al., 2021; Tsheletsane and Fourie, 2014), with three likely implications for building the capacity and increasing the performance of the state. First, given the loss of institutional memory, there was a risk of policy drift. This is because efforts to carry through the goals, objectives and priorities from the vigorous transformation undertakings of the previous administration, and their associated pathways and expression, could be diluted. The knowledge, skills and competence accumulated in the first administration – in terms of public service restructuring and policy formulation – could be reduced. Levy et al. (2021: 23) argue that the high turnover of senior bureaucrats and ministers strained 'the political–administrative relations, and enabled appointments suspected of facilitating corruption'.

DGs spoke about the turnover of senior leaders and the loss of capacity during a discussion about the South African National Roads Agency (SANRAL). DGs recognised that SANRAL had a relatively good track record of delivering and maintaining South Africa's road network and running its operations. However, the CEO responsible for the SOE's performance was not retained, though he was available for another term. DGs saw two repercussions from this.

First, as the DG in infrastructure development remarked: 'Then we're going to come back in a year or two and complain about capacity, when capacity is deliberately … being depleted in some of these entities.' Second, DGs recognised that the technical capacity garnered by SANRAL could have been used across the built environment where large infrastructure had to be delivered. The inability to retain these skills served as a future constraint to building dynamic and specialised capabilities across the public sectors, particularly as the emergent capabilities were being weakened, thus thwarting the development of public-sector-wide capabilities in network industries. A DG in the economic sector saw this as the demobilisation of public institutions by government actors. According to the DG in infrastructure development, this ultimately meant that government had 'not mastered the art of ... dynamic capabilities, because dynamic capabilities is about pooling all the available resources to get the job done'.

Third, policy drift could be accompanied by diluted accountability as 'new directors-general cannot give proper account of a department's activities in the previous period when appearing before the Legislature. When asked questions by parliamentary committees, many directors-general simply use their length in office as an excuse. It is also obvious that changes instituted are less likely to be sustained when there is a change in leadership' (Tsheletsane and Fourie, 2014: 48). Policy drift is also associated with policy failure. DGs identified policy contradiction or incoherence as another concrete example that has stifled dynamic capability. For DGs, the PFMA and its attendant regulations have neither curbed corruption nor facilitated conducive environments for innovation and effective policy implementation. Instead, DGs regarded the PFMA as a technical instrument that overburdened the available capacity to implement programmes. Intended to promote prudent resource management, DGs were of the view that the PFMA has instead stifled creativity and innovation and curtailed speedy state responsiveness, agility and implementation. Tsheletsane and Fourie (2014) and Naidoo (2018) note that some public servants have even ignored the PFMA.

Fourth, the structural changes in the macro organisation of government, which took place from 1999 to 2019, as discussed above, have dealt a blow to government's ability to retain departmental competence, implement policies as intended and maintain accountability.

In summary, where accumulated knowledge and learnings have not been well managed within departments and across the state, policy drift and high leadership turnover and conflict have become binding constraints to the development and emergence of dynamic capabilities. Moreover, where such capabilities have been developed, they are diluted and under stress.

AN EMBEDDED CRISIS OF 'SHORT-TERMISM' AND THE ROLE OF DIRECTORS-GENERAL

South Africa's economic policymaking and policy implementation have been plagued by an embedded tendency towards short-termism (short-range decisions that address challenges for a quarter or a year), which have also produced and reproduced outputs without generating sustained outcomes that drive growth. DGs observed that the interactions and sometimes clashes at the political and administrative interface have hampered the effective delivery of economic plans and programmes. According to the DG in investment, DGs in all the clusters have outsourced their leadership of the administration to ministers, with the role of DGs being 'reduced to supporting the ministers'. The DG in governance, in turn, remarked, 'And the politics then tend to dominate planning in government, because if there is a new minister, that new minister in the economic cluster, they would want to see things differently. And the DGs tend to take a back seat.'

Political interference in government planning has disrupted the implementation of long-term economic plans. While DGs tended to have a long-term outlook, ministers were said to be 'more concerned about the term of government'. According to the DG in governance, the political interference resulted in 'many policies, saying the same thing, but with new names'. The DG in institutional development added:

> When looking at our policies ... we rehash the same things. We give them names, but actually substantively, these are the same things that we had said a long time ago. We talked about the nine-point plan. We introduced the 14 confidence-boosting initiatives. And now we're dealing with the 10-point ERRP. If you look at the ERRP, there are 10 points there. And if you look at all of those things that are in the ERRP, number one priority is energy. It was there in the nine-point plan, isn't it? We prioritised energy in the nine-point plan. We talked about it in the 14-point economic boosting initiatives, so to speak. So it could be that we jump from one priority to the next or we jumped from one item to the next without doing much.

One of the DGs in the economic sector called for 'a professionally run, insulated public service that is run by bureaucrats and professionals, rather than, as I said, personality driven'. Fear was another condition identified as preventing the formulation and implementation of plans to drive economic growth, which resulted from a lack of policy legitimisation. A DG in investment observed that in the current economic policy landscape, it appeared that the state was suffering from 'a bit of paralysis' and 'hesitation' in following structural transformation as a growth strategy because of the fear that if structural transformation were publicly announced as the growth strategy, leaders and their associated actors would be 'lynched'. As a result, the DG emphasised, the state was not driving structural transformation well enough, with a focus on growth strategies in sectors such as mining, energy and telecommunications.

STRUCTURE OF GOVERNMENT AS A HINDRANCE TO INFRASTRUCTURE DEVELOPMENT

A DG in the economic sector remarked that the structure of the state hindered its ability to 'energise and dynamise the private sector'. This DG recognised that South Africa had developed multiple 'world-class' products and services, supported by world-class policies and sectors, but had failed to change the structure of the state in tandem and to support and respond to market developments.

Network industries and economic infrastructure were identified as examples of how the structure of government and its operations adversely affected industrial development. The general view was that South Africa had performed well in terms of its road network but had failed in terms of 'energy planning ... the energy infrastructure, the rail infrastructure' (DG in infrastructure development). Thus, the network industries were generally described as perennial challenges that government had failed to 'learn' from and improve on. 'Here (SA) you have a number of infrastructure departments: transport, human settlements, they're sitting all over the place, which perhaps maybe is one of the reasons why we keep changing things (DG in infrastructure development).'

Poor rail and port infrastructure were identified as a hindrance to increasing the volumes of tradable export goods. A DG in the economic sector stated, 'We can't export even our commodities when there's a commodity boom, we can't get enough iron ore, we can't get enough coal even, not to even talk about autos, we can't export our autos at cheaper and faster rates because they have to reach the port by road. The ports are clogged, Durban port is clogged.'

These failures have occurred despite the fact that infrastructure has been a key and consistent policy priority in all of South Africa's successive economic plans. This is because its development, financing and modernisation have been 'fragmented,' with the planning, resourcing and execution of network industry developments dispersed across different departments. These include the DPWI, the DoT, the DPE and the National Treasury. A good example of ongoing fragmentation is that the Infrastructure and Investment Office (IIO) sits in The Presidency. Therefore, while the PICC has moved from the National Treasury to the DPWI (with the latter meant to be the centre of infrastructure development), the IIO remains in The Presidency. The IIO is responsible for driving, coordinating and aligning the public-sector infrastructure ecosystem, improving the efficiency of the delivery programme, and facilitating private-sector cooperation and financing. It also monitors and reports on 'the national infrastructure project pipeline with respect to the gazetted Strategic Integrated Projects (SIPs)' (The Presidency, 2022: 26). Importantly, in 2022, the National Infrastructure Plan 2050, under the stewardship of the DPWI, was approved (see Chapter 17 in this volume).

A DG in governance proposed a more integrated, targeted approach to infrastructure development: 'The only thing I like about Italy is the way the whole infrastructure sector is structured, you have Department of Infrastructure and Transport; everything else falls in there in the Department of Transport and Infrastructure.'

The right kind of clustering or compartmentalising of portfolios was also called for, with a DG in human development reasoning that the separation of portfolios into economic and social clusters had undermined the social sector's 'ability to contribute to … economic sectors'. This was seen most poignantly during COVID-19.

MISSED OPPORTUNITIES

Numerous opportunity costs were identified, each with a significant impact. First, political and administrative leadership failed to examine and address the interface between the political and administrative spheres. For example, the NDP proposed that a head of public administration be created, but this decision was deferred and has not yet been implemented in the sixth administration (NPC, 2020).

A DG in infrastructure development observed that South Africa's energy policy had failed because the country had not adopted an energy mix policy around 2008 when the proposals were first drafted. The proposal, contained in the NGP of 2010, was to adopt gas as a transition fuel away from coal, but the necessary investment to realise this was not made. This was about two years after loadshedding began, where the quick implementation of the energy mix policy and the Independent Power Producer (IPP) procurement programme would have prevented the escalation of loadshedding.

Second, in the current period, South Africa would not be experiencing the level of loadshedding that it is if the energy mix policy had been properly adopted and implemented. Another missed opportunity was that the transition to gas required an intersectoral, multizone strategy in which private investment in gas (as the transition fuel) would be made, thus also spurring the growth of the ocean economy and the further development of Saldanah Bay which was identified as an industrial zone. In addition, biodiesel/biofuel was identified as part of the energy mix, which would reverse the decline suffered by the sugar industry in KwaZulu-Natal in 2010. Biofuel was also seen as an opportunity to 'save SAA [South African Airways] in terms of fuel efficiency,' said one of the DGs.

In further reviewing why the transition to gas was a lost opportunity, this DG explained that it stemmed from the notion that the government had 'a choice'. The idea that there was a choice to be made between 'clean fuels, or clean energy versus the use of coal' was in fact a political 'false choice', characterised as 'policy noise' (Andreoni et al., 2022). South Africa's reliance on coal meant that an energy mix policy was unavoidable, where resources and expertise would need a dual focus –

that is, continued energy from the current sources, while transitioning, using a cascading approach, towards the development of cleaner energy sources. This DG emphasised that South Africa had lost opportunities in the areas of infrastructure implementation and investment because the key (responsible) departments had been bogged down in the idea that 'there is a choice'.

The false choice notion also emerges from the fact that South Africa has been engulfed by myriad ideas and ideologies from different schools of thought which have permeated different sections of government, causing incoherence and, in this case, a lack of implementation. This is well argued by Naidoo (2015: 24), who states that while the espousal and application of variegated interpretations and approaches emanating from the New Public Management (NPM) and post-NPM in the South African public sector has 'combined a wealth of knowledge on comparative public management practice', it has also 'produced a contradictory and inconsistent application of reform approaches in practice'.

Another DG in human development explained that the health sector had multiple technology opportunities which applied to multiple sectors. However, the potential growth of these technologies was seen as hamstrung by the limited imagination of the health sector to add complex products to the economy. Instead, ideas on the role of the health sector in the economy were parochial, with people tending to limit it to the pharmaceutical industry, whereas the country had the opportunity to build sub-sectors, such as pharmaceutical diagnostics and medical devices.

South Africa's economic policy choices are seen as incapable of igniting industrialisation, halting the financialisation of the economy and changing the economic base to a more productive one. The above discussion points less to an incomplete, post-apartheid transition or development of quality public institutions, and more to a regression in accumulated progress and government competency. This is the result not only of state capture, but also of the multiple exogenous and endogenous crises that state institutions have had to simultaneously confront while attempting to drive social transformation.

CONCLUSION: IMPLICATIONS FOR BUILDING A DYNAMIC STATE

Ndletyana and Maimela (2013: 6) assert that now more than ever before, 'the post-apartheid state has the dual mission of transforming and stabilising the South African society while also undertaking this transformation for itself'. In the light of this, this chapter has argued that building dynamic capabilities within the state involves the stabilisation of the South African government across the ideological, political, technical and implementational spheres in the face of numerous, significant failures on the part of government.

Clearly, stabilising the South African state is a 'grand challenge' in itself, with Ndletyana and Maimela (2013: 6) suggesting that this may be likened to 'building the plane while flying it', a metaphor that applies to the post-COVID-19 period. To this end, a mission-oriented approach to stabilising the state is needed, which may need look like (see Figure 16.4):

Figure 16.4: Framework for reimagining the South African state

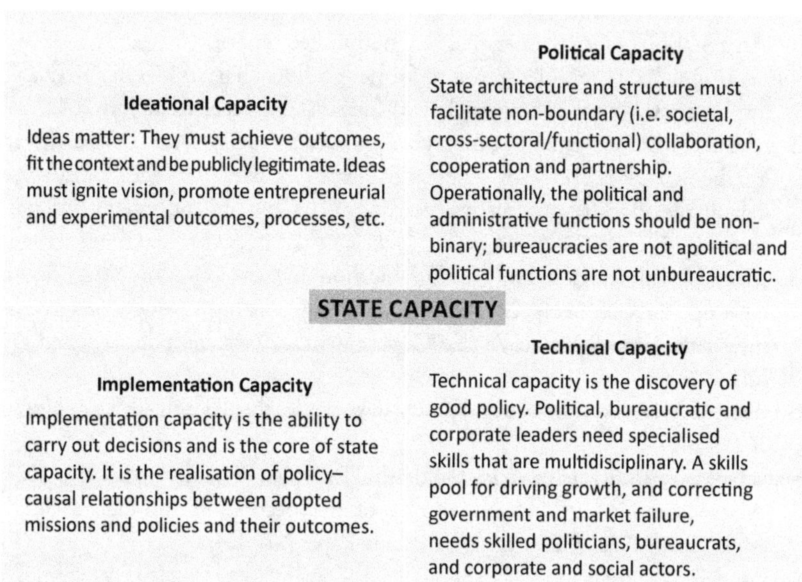

Source: Authors' compilation

The above framework has been conceptually derived from the discussion in this chapter as well as from insights provided in Chang (2004), Cummings and Norgaard (2004), Lindvall and Teorell (2016), NPC (2020) and Stiglitz (2021).

REFERENCES

Andreoni, A., Creamer, K., Mazzucato, M. and Steyn, G. 2022. 'How can South Africa advance a new energy paradigm? A mission-oriented approach to megaprojects'. *Oxford Review of Economic Policy*, 38 (2), 237–259.

Chang, H. J. 2004. *Globalisation, Economic Development and the Role of the State*. New York: Zed Books.

Cummings, S. N. and Norgaard, O. 2004. 'Conceptualising state capacity: Comparing Kazakhstan and Kyrgyzstan'. *Political Studies*, 52, 685–708.

Department of Public Service and Administration (DPSA). 2 June 2014. 'National Macro-Organisation of the State, 2014: National Executive Portfolios and Departments'. Unpublished report.

Department of Public Service and Administration (DPSA). 14 June 2019. 'Terms of Reference National Macro Organisation of Government (NMOG) 2019: Configuration of Portfolios and Departments'. Unpublished report.

Department of Public Service and Administration (DPSA). 2020. 'Annexure A – 6th Administration National Executive and Departments, National Macro Organisation of Government 2019'. Unpublished report.

eNCA, 30 July 2022. 'eNCA speaks to former president Thabo Mbeki'. *YouTube*, https://www.youtube.com/watch?v=dfBjewdO73k, accessed 30 July 2022.

Government Information and Communication System (GCIS). 2018. 'South African Yearbook 2017/2018: Government Systems'. https://www.gcis.gov.za/sites/default/files/docs/resourcecentre/yearbook/11-GovernmentSystems2018.pdf, accessed 30 July 2022.

Government Information and Communication System (GCIS). 2022. 'South African Yearbook 2021/2022: Government Systems'. https://www.gcis.gov.za/sites/default/files/docs/gcis/8.%20Government%20Systems.pdf, accessed 30 July 2022.

Gumede, V. 2017. 'Presidencies and policy in post-apartheid South Africa'. *Politeia*, 36 (1), 1–17.

Hausmann, R., Sturzenegger, F., Goldstein, P., Muci, F. and Barrios, D. 2022. 'Macroeconomic risks after a decade of microeconomic turbulence: South Africa 2007–2020'. CID Faculty Working Paper No. 404.

Jacobs, S. 2002. 'Remaking The Presidency: Coordination versus centralisation'. *Indicator SA*, 9 (1), 30–36.

Levin, R. 12 May 2009. 'Implementing the new macro-structure of national government: Briefing for incoming ministers & deputy ministers'.

Unpublished report.

Levy, B., Hirsch, A., Naidoo, V. and Nxele, M. 2021. 'South Africa: When strong institutions and massive inequalities collide'. Carnegie Endowment for International Peace, https://carnegieendowment.org/2021/03/18/south-africa-when-strong-institutions-and-massive-inequalities-collide-pub-84063, accessed 4 April 2022.

Lindvall, J. and Teorell, J. 2016. 'State capacity as power: A conceptual framework'. Paper presented at the seminar on the State and Capitalism since 1800, Harvard University, https://ces.fas.harvard.edu/uploads/files/Event-Papers/State-Capacity-as-Power-September-2016.pdf, accessed 28 July 2022.

Mazzucato, M., Qobo, M. and Kattel, R. 2021. 'Building state capacities and dynamic capabilities to drive social change: The case of South Africa'. UCL Institute for Innovation and Public Purpose (IIPP) Working Paper Series: IIPP WP 2021/09, https://www.ucl.ac.uk/bartlett/public-purpose/wp2021-09, accessed 6 April 2022.

Nabudere, D. 2006. 'Development theories, knowledge production and emancipatory practice', in Padayachee, V. (ed.) *The Development Decade*. Pretoria: HSRC Press, 33–52.

Naidoo, V. 2015. 'Changing conceptions of public management and public sector reform in South Africa'. *International Public Management Review*. 16 (1), 23–42.

Naidoo, V. 2018. 'Machinery of government change in South Africa's post-democratic public administration'. PARI Working Paper, https://pari.org.za/machinery-government-change-south-africa/, accessed 30 April 2022.

National Planning Commission (NPC). 2020. 'A review of the National Development Plan 2030: Advancing implementation towards a more capable nation', https://www.nationalplanningcommission.org.za/assets/Documents/NDP%20REVIEW.pdf, accessed 23 July 2022.

National Treasury. 1999. 'Public institutions listed in PFMA Schedules 1, 2, 3A, 3B, 3C and 3D as at 30 April 1999', https://www.treasury.gov.za/legislation/pfma/public%20entities/1999-04-30%20Public%20institutions%20Sch%20 1 -3D.pdf, accessed 23 June 2023.

National Treasury. 2003. 'Public institutions listed in PFMA Schedules 1, 2, 3A, 3B, 3C and 3D as at 5 December 2003', https://www.treasury.gov .za/legislation/pfma/public%20entities/2003-12-05%20Public%20institutions%20Sch%20 1-3D.pdf, accessed 23 June 2023.

National Treasury. 2009. 'Public institutions listed in PFMA Schedules 1, 2, 3A, 3B, 3C and 3D as at 20 March 2009', https://www.treasury.gov.za/legislation/pfma/pubIic%20entities/2009-03-20%20PubIic%20institutions%20Sch%20l-3D.pdf, accessed 23 June 2023.

National Treasury. 2014. 'Public institutions listed in PFMA Schedules 1, 2, 3A, 3B, 3C and 3D as at 23 May 2014', https://www.treasury.gov.za/legislation/pfma/public%20entities/2014-05-23%20Public%20institutions%20Sch%20 1 -3D.pdf, accessed 23 June 2023.

National Treasury. 2019. 'Public institutions listed in PFMA Schedules 1, 2, 3A, 3B, 3C and 3D as at 24 May 2019', https://www.treasurv.gov.za/Jegislation/pfma/public%20entities/201 9-05- 24%20Public%20institutions%20Sch%201-3D.pdf, accessed 23 June 2023.

National Treasury. 2023. 'Public institutions listed in PFMA Schedules 1, 2, 3A, 3B, 3C and 3D as at 28 March 2023', https://www.treasury.gov.za/legislation/pfma/public%20entities/2023-03-28%20Public%20institutions%20Sch%201-3D.pdf, accessed 23 June 2023.

Ndletyana, M. and Maimela, D. 2013. *Essays on the evolution of the post-apartheid state: legacies, reforms and prospects.* Johannesburg: Real African Publishers.

Perrot, R. 2015. 'The trojan horses of global environmental and social politics', in Mytelka, L. K., Msimang, V. and Perrot, R. (eds.) *Earth, Wind and Fire: Unpacking the Political, Economic and Security Implications of Discourse on Green Economy*. Johannesburg: MISTRA, 31–52.

Pottinger, B. 2008. *The Mbeki Legacy*. Cape Town: Zebra Press.

Public Service Commission (PSC). 2007. 'Report on the Audit on Vacancy Rates in National and Provincial Departments', https://www.gov.za/sites/default/files/gcis_document/201409/auditvacancyrates0.pdf, accessed 24 June 2024.

Public Service Commission (PSC). 2022. 'Report to the portfolio committee on Public Service and Administration, Performance Monitoring and Evaluation on the National Macro Organisation of Government', https://static.pmg.org.za/PSC_Report_of_the_Public_Service_Commission_to_the_Portfolio_Committee_on_Public_Service_and_Administration_Performance_Monitoring_and_Evaluation_on_the_National_Mac.pdf, accessed 12 January 2023.

Ramaphosa, C. 9 June 2022. 'President Cyril Ramaphosa: The Presidency Budget Vote 2022/23', https://www.gov.za/speeches/address-president-cyril-ramaphosa-9-jun-2022-0000, accessed 30 July 2022.

Republic of South Africa (RSA). 1994. 'Reconstruction and Development Programme (RDP)'. Ministry in the Office of the President, https://www.gov.za/sites/default/files/governmentgazetteid16085.pdf, accessed 18 November 2021.

Southall, R. 2007. 'Introduction', in Buhlungu, S., Daniel, J., Southall, R. and Lutchman, J. (eds.) *State of the Nation: South Africa 2007*. Pretoria: HSRC Press, 1–24.

Stiglitz, J. 2021. 'The proper role of government in the market economy: The case of the post-COVID recovery'. *Journal of Government and Economics,* 1, 1–7.

The Presidency. 2022. 'Annual Report 2021–2022', https://www.thepresidency.gov.za/sites/default/files/The%20Presidency%20Annual%20Report%202021_22.pdf, accessed 9 September 2022.

Tsheletsane, I. and Fourie D. 2014. 'Factors hindering public financial management and accountability in South Africa'. *African Journal of Public Affairs*, 7 (4), 42–56.

Van Onselen, G. 2017. 'Political musical chairs: Turnover in the national executive and administration since 2009: An analysis of the turnover rates for directors-general and ministers in Jacob Zuma's national administration, May 2009 – July

2017'. South African Institute of Race Relations, https://irr.org.za/reports/occasional-reports/files/irr-political-musical-chairs.pdf, accessed 30 April 2022.

World Bank. 2022. 'Global economic prospects: January 2022'. Washington, DC: World Bank, https://openknowledge.worldbank.org/handle/10986/36519, accessed 7 May 2022.

NOTES

1 There are five clusters: (1) Economic Sectors, Investment, Employment and Infrastructure Development; (2) Social Protection, Community and Human Development; (3) Governance, State Capacity and Institutional Development; (4) Justice, Crime Prevention and Security; and (5) International Cooperation, Trade and Security. These are 'groupings of government departments with cross-cutting programmes. Clusters foster an integrated approach to governance which is aimed at improving government planning, decision making and service delivery. The objective is to ensure proper coordination of all government programmes at national and provincial levels. The main functions of the clusters are to ensure the alignment of government-wide priorities, facilitate and monitor the implementation of priority programmes and provide a consultative platform on cross-cutting priorities and matters being taken to the cabinet. The clusters of the Forum of South African Directors-General (FOSAD) mirror the ministerial clusters. The FOSAD clusters provide technical support to the ministerial clusters, https://www.gov.za/faq/guide-government/what-are-government-clusters-and-which-are-they, accessed 9 September 2022.

2 In 2014, Broadband Infraco Limited was transferred from the Department of Public Enterprises to the newly established Department of Telecommunications and Postal Services.

3 Portfolio refers to executive authority, in which there is a ministry. The RDP office's activities were absorbed into the deputy president's office of Thabo Mbeki (Jacobs, 2002).

4 These refer to jobs, land, housing, water, electricity, telecommunications, transport, a clean and healthy environment, nutrition, healthcare and social welfare.

5 This involved focusing on linking reconstruction and development, industry, trade and commerce, and resource-based industries; upgrading infrastructure; labour and worker rights; Southern Africa and regional economic development; strengthening labour; and recognising worker rights (RSA, 1994).

6 DDG: Head of the economic sector in the PCAS.

7 Interestingly, The Presidency (2022: 13) states that the ERRP priority areas are monitored by 'different structures within The Presidency on a day-to-day basis'.

8 Zuma conducted another cabinet reshuffle before the end of his term. This was not included in Van Onselen's calculation.

SEVENTEEN

Political settlements and the rebuilding of South Africa's state-owned enterprises

MARK SWILLING, NINA CALLAGHAN AND WENDY MCCALLUM

INTRODUCTION

In 2012, the National Development Plan (NDP) was approved as the official forward-looking development plan for South Africa through to 2030. Chapter 13 called for the 'building of a capable and developmental state'. Ten years later, in 2022, the Zondo Commission published its reports which documented how state institutions had been looted and hollowed out over the previous decade, with specific reference to several major state-owned enterprises (SOEs). This tragic trajectory from a noble commitment to building a capable and developmental state to address the legacies of the past to the institutional decomposition now referred to as 'state capture' has resulted in a new set of challenges – how to rebuild the SOEs. In 2020, President Ramaphosa set up the Presidential Commission on State-Owned Enterprises (PCSOE) to address a narrowly defined set of governance challenges highlighted in reports by the National Planning Commission (NPC, 2020) which were later amplified by the broadly defined governance challenges described in the Zondo Commission reports.

This chapter brings into focus the more granular micro dynamics of intra-state relations which can enable the rebuilding of SOEs within the wider context of state capability development for post-state capture and post-pandemic economic reconstruction. To achieve this, we draw on the new literature on 'political settlements', which has emerged in recent years to address the persistent challenge of building effective state capabilities to drive economic development, particularly in the African context. The focus on the 'building of a developmental state', which is present both in policy documents (e.g., the NDP) and in academic literature (Edigheji, 2010; Fine, 2010; Gelb, 2006; Lodge, 2009; Makgetla, 2007; Southall, 2006; Swilling, 2008; Swilling et al., 2015; Von Holdt, 2010), is clearly deficient when it comes to framing an approach that results in more beneficial outcomes than have been evident to date.

The 'repurposing of state institutions', which was at the centre of the state capture project (Bhorat et al., 2017; Callaghan et al., 2020), was fully justified in terms of the developmental state narrative, especially when it came to emphasising the need to 'build a black industrial class'. Those who did the 'repurposing' were mandated by a political settlement brokered by the Zuma-centred power elite from 2009 onwards (Bhorat et al., 2017). To rebuild the SOEs, it will be necessary to go beyond the developmental state narrative which has been used too easily to rhetorically justify a wide array of progressive and regressive initiatives. Furthermore, this is necessary because there is no evidence that the PCSOE has even attempted to develop such an approach to help frame its recommendations for rebuilding the SOEs. Nor did the NPC reports that led to the formation of the PCSOE contain such a framework. Instead, the focus of the NPC documents and the PSCOE mandate is on 'fixing the SOEs' rather than reframing their roles within a broader conception of developmental transformation, as envisaged in the NDP (Swilling and Callaghan, 2021).

The core argument that is elaborated on in this chapter is as follows:

to effectively build capable and effective state institutions in general, and SOEs in particular, it is necessary to create politically protected spaces for competent groups of people to initiate, lead and operationalise purposeful, impactful mandates in ways that simultaneously create agile, goal-driven and efficient institutional capabilities. Institutional capabilities are not first built, followed by the right actions. Instead, it will be argued that these capabilities get built through mission-led actions that require the constant expansion of the capacity – in the words of the institutional work literature: to 'create, maintain and disrupt' institutions (Lawrence and Suddaby, 2006).

The next section elaborates on a conceptual framing of the 'political settlements' literature, supplemented with insights from the literature on 'institutional work' (Lawrence and Suddaby, 2006) and 'state capability building' (Andrews et al., 2017) Although the contemporary challenges are the focus of this chapter, what follows is a historical perspective on the evolution of South African SOEs (and development finance institutions (DFIs) which are seen as a subset of SOEs) which demonstrates the significance of political settlement making as a means of building institutional capabilities in the SOE and DFI sector. Three key pre-1994 turning points are identified: 1924 when the Pact Government was formed, 1948 when the National Party (NP) won the white general election, and 1979 when the NP government adopted neoliberal modes of governance. This is followed by a discussion of the post-1994 era, paying particular attention to three key turning points in the governance of SOEs and DFIs: (a) 1996: SOEs during the Mbeki period (1996–2007); (b) 2007: SOEs during the 'state capture' period, in particular after the 2014 election; and (c) 2018: SOEs since the election of Ramaphosa as president and his decisions to massively expand The Presidency as a broker of an array of political settlements in the context of a politically fragmented ruling elite.

POLITICAL SETTLEMENTS

SOEs are important instruments for deploying capital to catalyse economic development. For the purposes of this chapter, SOEs are understood to be state owned institutions that are designed for a specific public purpose. These include those mandated to deliver a particular set of sociotechnical infrastructures (e.g., energy via Eskom, or transport via Transnet/Passenger Rail Agency of South Africa (Prasa)) or DFIs mandated to allocate capital to achieve particular policy goals and/or counter-cyclical investment priorities (e.g., Industrial Development Corporation (IDC), Development Bank of Southern Africa (DBSA)).

It would be a mistake to depict the new 'political settlements' literature as a paradigmatic alternative to the mature and contextually more diverse 'developmental state' literature. This literature shares with the developmental state literature a normative commitment to a developmental role for states, but the focus of these writers is on the contextually specific, granular details of how institutional capabilities are actually built to enable these developmental roles to be realised in practice. That said, however, the developmental state literature pays little attention to SOEs (Nem Singh and Chen, 2018), and next to no attention to the institutional dimensions and configurations of DFIs (Marodon, 2022; Ocampo and Ortega, 2022). The reason for this has much to do with the deficiencies in the developmental state literature identified in the new literature on political settlements, i.e., a lack of attention to the granular details of how developmental capabilities are institutionalised in practice.

The rich and mature literature on the developmental state emerged primarily to make sense of the Asian states which defied neoliberal orthodoxy during the last decades of the 20th century by being highly interventionist, ideologically opportunist, strategically longsighted, politically contested and institutionally sophisticated (Andrews and Nwapi, 2018; Bagchi, 2000; Chibber, 2003; Evans, 1995, 2006; Jordan, 2017; Khan, 2004; Kohli, 2006; Mkandawire, 2001; Noman et al., 2011; Onis, 1991; Ovadia and Wolf, 2018; Zenawi, 2011). Peter Evans originated the well-used notion of 'embedded autonomy' to refer to the way developmentally oriented Asian state institutions were embedded within the strategic requirements of their respective national business elites while enjoying sufficient autonomy to discipline these elites into backing a long-termist developmental vision (Evans, 1995).

Many African academic and political elites (including those in South Africa), concerned about developmental trajectories after the uprisings of the 1990s that displaced the African dictatorships (Branch and Mampilly, 2015), drew on the Asian model to inform African development strategies and policy frameworks (Kelsall, 2013; Mkandawire, 2011; Noman et al., 2011; Whitfield et al., 2015; Zenawi, 2011). They were attracted to the developmental state literature because it tended to describe developmental bureaucracies as relatively autonomous, rational, relatively free of rent seeking, unconstrained by clientelism and institutionally well resourced. Policy-related research in Africa (and in South Africa) thus became a search for the presence or absence of these conditions as a measure of developmental potential; or policy was quite simply about emulating this idealised characterisation of the Asian state. However, as Bowman (2020) argues, this approach risks searching 'for an ideal type of governance that never existed in the first place' (Bowman, 2020: 7).

In the light of developmental experiences and trajectories in Africa since the 1990s, it is now clear that the developmental state literature may have had the advantage of counteracting the neoliberal antipathy towards state intervention, but it tended to create the impression that the construction of a developmentally oriented, state-wide system was somehow a precondition for development itself to happen in practice. Without such a state-wide system, it follows that development would not materialise. Underlying this was the implicit assumption that the developmental state was a kind of ideal 'systemic structure' that needed to be put in place by political elites committed to a developmental agenda. There was no room for 'pockets of efficiency and effectiveness' to instigate incremental changes where conditions made this possible. This idealisation of the Asian experience meant that there was little appreciation for the fact that the state as a 'systemic structure' does not, in reality, exist.

What exists empirically is a vast, ramshackle affair comprising a multiplicity of different kinds of (largely uncoordinated) institutions, with each configured in its own way with more or less capacity to act. As Jessop (2016) argues, 'the state' only exists as a political idea and ideological project. Unsurprisingly, therefore, discussion of the 'developmental state' has tended to ignore the complexities of unevenly distributed and organised institutional capabilities across the state system, focusing instead on an idealised role of the state within the economy and national development strategy (Swilling, 1999). This is why the developmental state literature has paid such little attention to SOEs (Nem Singh and Chen, 2018). They are simply instrumentally significant, not relatively autonomous organisational phenomena in their own right.

The 'political settlements' literature has emerged to address the deficiencies of the developmental state literature by bringing into focus the political deals and agreements that are needed between political elites (including factions of ruling elites), state bureaucrats (depicted as non-homogeneous, often competing interests) and politically connected business elites (organised into different groupings with divergent interests).

We bring into the picture a fourth constituency, namely organised civil society groupings (in particular, labour, but increasingly environmental movements, amongst others). Behuria et al. (2017: 508) describe the political settlements approach as 'a discrete political economy analytical framework that provides a novel way of understanding the drivers and outcomes of contemporary socioeconomic change', going well beyond the idea of a peace agreement or political order. Khan (2018) explains that a political settlement is a power-sharing agreement that directs institutions and policies to produce particular political and economic results, which can be maintained over time. The agreements between political, bureaucratic and business elites within the wider political system (i.e., the political settlements) are about the way that power, risks and benefits are distributed which, in turn, determines the effectiveness (or otherwise) of particular institutions with specific mandates.

Given the renewed popularity of state-led industrial development in Africa, a new literature has emerged which addresses the challenge of state capabilities and political settlements (Nem Singh and Chen, 2018). This literature argues that 'understanding why widely adopted industrial policies succeeded in some instances but not others require extending the analytical frame to encompass the wider distribution of, and struggle for, organisational power and rents amongst social groups within and beyond the state' (Bowman, 2020: 8). What differentiates success from failure is not whether the state is 'autonomous' and 'developmental' in the structural sense, but whether effective intra-state political settlements were forged to allow for the emergence of 'pockets of effectiveness' to flourish (Bowman, 2020: 8; see also Whitfield et al., 2015).

In a recent contribution to the South African debate about building state capabilities, Mazzucato et al. (2021) emphasise the importance of mission-led governance supported by partnership-based delivery systems. Although this influential paper departs from the structuralist focus of the developmental state literature, it also tends to under-emphasise the complexities of diverse, intra-state political interests, conflicts and factions. By contrast, emphasising political settlements means recognising the importance of formal and/or informal deals (or agreements) made by political actors within the state and wider polity (for a good example, see Bowman, 2020). The allocation of rents and the protection of vested interests are built into a political settlement, influencing how capital is allocated and, therefore, which programmes and projects get to be implemented (Khan, 2018; Ovadia and Wolf, 2018).

While each context is different, there are usually unevenly balanced top-down and bottom-up vertical dynamics that shape the way these deals or agreements are negotiated and constituted. Whitfield et al. (2015) describe how political settlements are contested. Where bottom-up pressures are absent, technocratic solutions are imposed, which may later trigger resistance as system feedback loops express their complexity or as groups within the polity organise to contest these solutions. Weak top-down capacity can also result in paralysis, especially in the face of strong bottom-up pressures. There are also horizontal dynamics of (non-) collaboration between different state agencies, departments and political elites that shape political settlements. What matters is how these vertical and horizontal dynamics are managed by leaders from many different sectors, who must find ways to interact to co-create pathways towards shared desired outcomes (Whitfield et al., 2015). No leaders or change agents can act autonomously from their institutional context; nor is there sufficient evidence to suggest that institutional constraints are so overwhelming that leadership for change is impossible (Lawrence and Suddaby, 2006). How agents of change choose to act and lead really matters, as the constraints and boundaries they encounter will not be so inflexible as to determine the outcome beyond the scope and reach of their agency.

The literature on political settlements tends to focus on the interrelationships between three key groups of interests (which are not internally homogeneous): ruling elites, state bureaucrats and business elites. Not taken into account are organised civil society groupings, in particular organised labour and, more recently, environmental movements. Political settlements between sub-sets of these four groups create the space for building capabilities within (and beyond) the state. Following Whitfield et al. (2015), the three primarily economic relationships are as follows:

- 'mutuality of interests' between ruling elites and business elites which can result in agreements to sacrifice short-term rent extraction in return for longer-term gains;
- 'pockets of efficiency' staffed by competent bureaucrats who are backed by ruling elites who accept the need for competence to get things done in relatively autonomous ways, as opposed to political controls aimed at micro-managing the bureaucracy for the sake of servicing bespoke networks; and
- sustained 'learning processes' for continuous productivity improvements enabled by collaborations between state bureaucrats and businesses, in particular via support for innovation and experimentation (Whitfield et al., 2015).

Space constraints allow only the first two economic relationships to be discussed in any detail below. Before that, however, it must be noted that the political settlements literature tends to omit the relationships with civil society, in particular with organised labour. Civil society has historically driven transformation agendas in South Africa and remains a political force capable of shaping partnerships and steering finance, albeit with less political muscle than political and state actors (Suttner, 2014). Nevertheless, it is necessary to include the following key relationships (the dynamics of which are illustrated in Figure 17.1):

- partnerships between businesses and civil society that have developmental impacts beyond pure profit extraction, especially in fora such as the National Economic Development and Labour Council (Nedlac) or in corporate social investment (CSI) programmes;
- accountability of ruling elites to broader civil society constituencies via effective engagements and communicative fora; and
- state bureaucrats who are responsive to, rather than dismissive of, civil society, resulting in the mobilisation of extra-state ideational and implementation capabilities.

Figure 17.1: Key conditions for transforming political settlements

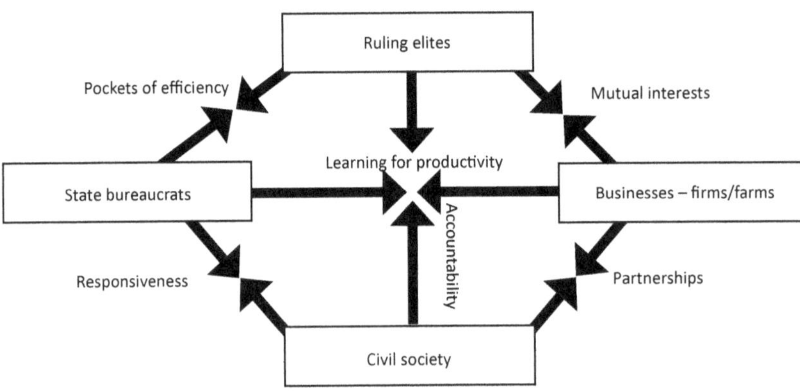

Source: Authors' formulation

The existence or absence of these conditions affects the efficacy and durability of the political settlements reached between key political actors. Factionalism that is allowed to disrupt institution building, for example, reflects the absence of, or weak, political settlements. Weak intra-state political settlements make it difficult to create pockets of efficiency within SOEs and DFIs because these institutions become highly contested and ultimately institutionally fragile. Following Whitfield et al. (2015), two of these six key relational dynamics are discussed here in more detail because they are of particular relevance to the discussion that follows.

- *Mutual interests (ruling elite–business relations):* For investment-led growth to succeed, firms and farms need to conclude that the uncertainty about returns on their investment are low enough to justify the (relatively high) longer-term risk of investing. To reduce uncertainty with a view to unlocking investment flows, ruling elites have an array of state interventions at their disposal to provide, for example, enabling infrastructures, access to low-cost capital, subsidies for labour costs (e.g., via skills training), subsidised R&D, access to land and resources, and negotiated preferential trade agreements.

For this *mutuality of interests* to work, personal relations between businesses and elites can be helpful under certain circumstances. However, if a power imbalance favours one or the other, industrial strategies can fail: if ruling elites become too dominant, they can instigate predatory extraction of rents, which has the effect of disincentivising future investing; or if a powerful business faction gains the upper hand (e.g., exporters or foreign capital-linked local businesses), local value chains can suffer, thus undermining the real economic potential of the country. If ruling elites and business leaders use each other in mutually beneficial ways, the most conducive conditions for long-term investment in industrialisation can follow. If ruling elites gain a reputation for making good on their promises without extracting too much rent, and if businesses agree to just make ordinary profits rather than super profits by accepting their place in the market, then this will be because healthy, mutually beneficial relationships between ruling elites and businesses have been created.

- *Pockets of efficiency (ruling elite–bureaucracy relations):* Departing from the 'developmental state' perspective, instead of making the idealistic assumption that a 'strong state' is required with capabilities spread out across the entire bureaucracy, it is more realistic to anticipate the formation of 'pockets of efficiency' comprising state bureaucrats who can formulate and effectively implement industrial policies in partnership with key investors and business networks (Nem Singh and Chen, 2018; Ovadia and Wolf, 2018; Whitfield et al., 2015). This is tricky work, because it often means tough negotiations to align a range of potentially divergent interests.
- For such a 'pocket' to emerge, the lead faction in the ruling coalition

must ensure that political space is created for a trusted and capable group of state bureaucrats to act, and this group must comprise individuals with the relevant industry knowledge and experience. If such a 'pocket of efficiency' can master the art of building an industry and managing competing factions within the ruling elite and business class, they can be enormously successful. Close, formal and informal personal relations between state bureaucrats and businesses can, under these circumstances, enable effective flows of information and coordination; but when corrupted for personal gain in ways that compromise rather than reinforce certainty, investments can dry up. Ultimately, the aim is to create the certainty needed for long-term investing.

The growth of Mozambique's sugar industry after the civil war is a good example of a political settlement premised on a 'mutuality of interests' between industry players and political elites. The Independent Power Producers (IPP) Office in South Africa is a good example of a 'pocket of efficiency' made possible by a political settlement between key state bureaucracies (DBSA, National Treasury (NT) and Department of Energy (DoE)) and a non-dominant faction in the ruling elite.

EARLY POLITICAL SETTLEMENTS FOR RACIALLY EXCLUSIVE INDUSTRIAL STRUCTURE

SOEs and DFIs have been central to the evolution of the South African economy (Clark, 1994; Freund, 2019; Magubane, 1996). They have been reconfigured during different historical periods in ways that reflected changes in the character of the political regime in response to changing economic conditions, realignments of ruling and business elites, and shifting political settlements.

South Africa's oldest DFI, the Land Bank, was established in 1912 shortly after the formation of the Union in 1910 by a specific political settlement that fused together remnants of the old Boer republics, former colonial land banks, the post-1910 Union Government and the new Union bureaucracy created by 'Milner's Kindergarten' (Dubow, 1997). The bank was intended to support struggling white farmers after the South African War (1899–1902) and the droughts that followed. Sporadic yields and volatile market prices meant commercial banks were wary of extending credit; so state support became the only way to secure long-term finance for this key political constituency.

The oldest SOE was South African Railways & Harbours (SAR&H). Formed in 1910 to coincide with the birth of the Union, SAR&H was the new Union Government's primary SOE for crafting the imaginary, white South African nationhood that became coterminous with a romantic, racially exclusive image of the South African landscape, from the Cape to the Limpopo (Foster, 2003). Inspired by a desire to replicate the modernist sociotechnical infrastructural vision of rail-based mobility that had emerged in 19th-century Europe and North America, a political settlement emerged that linked Cape-based agricultural export businesses, mining houses and influential engineering professionals and a section of the new Union bureaucracy interested in joining together the railway and harbour authorities of the pre-1910 states (Foster, 2003).

Up until the Pact Government in 1924, despite the political significance of the agricultural sector, white minority rule and foreign capital colluded primarily in the extraction of rents from mining and its subsidiary sectors. The state's role during this period was to sustain private capital's desire to externalise profits in exchange for the ability to access finance for industrialisation (Clark, 1994; Magubane, 1996). This political settlement reflected the mutual interests of ruling elites and businesses for long-term benefit in that pre-1924 period. But the mining-centred political settlement that emerged from the gold fields became more unstable as mining profits continued to enrich foreign shareholders with little reinvested to stimulate local industrial development, a factor that began to fracture white politics. This eventually led to the formation of the Nationalist Party-led Pact Government in 1924. This inevitably created new conditions for SOE and DFI formation. The transformation of the Electricity Supply Commission (Escom) from a mere facilitator of electricity for the mines to a key driver of import-substitution industrialisation (ISI) is a case in point.

The decision to establish the Electricity Supply Commission (Escom, now Eskom) was taken during the height of the Rand Revolt in 1922 by the Smuts Government to facilitate the provision of cheap electricity. It came into being in 1923 to provide cheap electricity to the expanding railways (who needed cheap energy for the new electric trains), increasingly deep-level mines and nascent secondary industries. The political settlement between mining magnates (including Ernest Oppenheimer), key industrial planners like Hendrick van der Bijl, railway planners and Escom itself resulted in the complete integration of the electricity industry by 1948 under the auspices of Escom, a public entity. The formation of the Iron and Steel Corporation (Iscor) in 1928 reinforced the ISI programme by providing the booming mining and secondary industries with reliable and affordable energy and steel. After 1924, these two SOEs became the Pact Government's key instruments for driving the ISI programme, especially during the 1940s (Freund, 2013).

As the Second World War loomed and as anti-Smuts, pro-Nazi Afrikaner nationalist sentiment mounted, the pro-British, Smuts-led United Party Government enabled the formation of the Industrial Development Corporation (IDC) in 1939 (Clark, 1994). As a state-owned capital investment agency, the IDC was able to access public funds for reinvestment into South African-owned industrial enterprises, marking the start of a period of expanded inward industrial development (Freund, 2019). The IDC helped fund major industrial clusters, including Anglo American's diversification into industry, Sasol, and the growth of Afrikaner-owned industrial conglomerates after 1948 such as those associated with Sanlam. Without explicit state support for the formation of a white industrial class, it is unlikely that a substantial South African-owned industrial sector would have emerged (Freund, 2019). However, despite his efforts to the contrary, the broad-based white political settlement that Smuts attempted to broker between English and Afrikaner interests, underpinned by ISI policies, failed. Fuelled by the Afrikaner nationalist sense of exclusion from the succession of white political settlements since 1910, by 1948 the National Party had won sufficient support to win the white general election. This marked another turning point in the role of the SOEs and DFIs.

SOEs were a central pillar of the state-building project of Afrikaner nationalism after the formation of the Nationalist Party Government in 1948 (Clark, 1994). Capitalising on the rapid, state-directed industrialisation programme initiated after 1924 and reinforced during the 1940s (Freund, 2013), the post-1948 government focused on supporting the alliance between Afrikaner capital and organised white labour. SOEs proliferated and prospered in the food, fuel, arms, forestry, chemicals, housing, networked infrastructure and even family holiday sector, growing Afrikaner industrialists by reallocating state contracts that gave apartheid its rent-seeking characteristics (Clark, 1994; Khadiagala, 2015). Rapid industrialisation depended on cheap electricity and in 1948 Escom became the primary supplier to the mines, after the Victoria Falls and Transvaal Power Company was bought and nationalised with co-investments from Anglo American (Freund, 2019). Sasol was established in 1951 with financing from the IDC, showing the state's entrepreneurial appetite to invest in the nascent technology of deriving fuel from coal. Global oil markets spiked in 1971 after the fall of the Bretton Woods agreement and surged again in the wake of the 1973 oil crisis, propelling Sasol into a dominant position in the liquid fuel and chemical sector in South Africa (Roberts and Rustomjee, 2009).

The electoral shift in 1948 marked the start of the apartheid era during which a new set of political settlements enabled the establishment of a range of purpose-built state institutions during a period when the 'parastatal sector and state economic ownership certainly became far more pronounced in importance' (Freund, 2019: 83). Some of the existing SOEs, such as Escom, Iscor, SAR&H and the IDC, were repurposed to focus on the Afrikaner nationalist agenda (including employment of white workers), while many new SOEs were constructed, including those that were needed to prop up the Bantustan system. After the cataclysmic Sharpeville shootings in 1960 followed by the banning of the liberation movements, the consolidation of white minority rule led by Afrikaner interests was coupled to the Bantustan political project to counter black nationalist aspirations within an ethnically fragmented paradigm. A vast literature now exists which has documented how South African capitalism was realigned during the post-1948 period around the strategic political primacy of Afrikaner capital and organised white labour (Clark, 1994; Freund, 2019; Magubane, 1996).

By the late 1970s, the post-1948 state-centric economic project had run its course. Reflecting the rise in popularity of neoliberalism in Western countries followed by the electoral victories of Ronald Reagan in the United States (US) and Margaret Thatcher in the United Kingdom (UK), a new political settlement emerged with a focus on 'free markets' and the reversal of state intervention. Responding to economic crisis, local and international political pressures for reforms, and the emergence of influential reformers in the (now well-established, mainly Cape-based) Afrikaner business and academic communities, a set of government commissions triggered policy reforms with respect to labour rights (Wiehahn Commission in 1979) and urban rights (Riekert Commission in 1979). The underlying reassessment of the role of the state reflected in the reports of these two commissions set the stage for a rethink on the SOEs and DFIs.

The DBSA was established in 1983 with a once-off grant to leverage private-sector funding for 'regional economic development', which became a euphemism used by economic reformers like Simon Brand (first CEO of the DBSA) to signal that the Bantustan political project was economically unviable (Cobbett et al., 1986). The turning point came in 1985 when, at the height of a State of Emergency, the De Villiers Commission recommended far-reaching changes to the governance of Eskom (formerly Escom). The 'commercialisation' of Eskom soon followed, with major ripple effects into the present (Johnson, 2021). Together with the 'private-sector' orientation represented in the formation of the DBSA, this new Eskom model became the template for the future role of the state in the economy and marked a decisive break from the post-1948 conception of the role of SOEs and DFIs. Democratisation in 1994 did not result in a fundamental change in this trajectory, as reflected, for example, in the passing of the Eskom Conversion Act in 2001 which incorporated Eskom as a state-owned company.

DERACIALISING NEOLIBERAL GOVERNANCE

The African National Congress (ANC) came to power in 1994 without a clearly articulated vision for the future of SOEs and DFIs within a non-racial, developmentally oriented democracy. After shelving the

1993 Macroeconomic Research Group (MERG) report (Padayachee and Van Niekerk, 2019), the ANC-led government continued with and expanded neoliberal economic policies which were focused more on macroeconomic stabilisation than on investment-led growth by the productive sectors of the economy. The MERG report of 1993 had proposed a development pathway based on the late-industrialising experiences of other countries, such as Malaysia, Taiwan and Brazil, with a strong social-democratic focus that favoured state intervention in regulating and directing the private sector, land reform and growing small business (Nattrass, 1994; Schneider, 2018). Instead, the ANC-led government adopted a neoliberal approach to development which focused on debt reduction, privatisation and trade liberalisation to stimulate growth (Nattrass, 1994; Schneider, 2018). The consequences for SOEs and DFIs were that the neoliberal governance trend initiated in 1979 continued into the democratic era, albeit with a non-racial mandate.

Mcebisi Jonas, the former Deputy Minister of Finance, has argued that the post-1994 social compact was premised on a political settlement between black business who were promised a stake in the economy via black economic empowerment (BEE); organised labour who required the protections afforded by the Labour Relations Act; white business who were assured that nationalisation would not take place; and the unemployed masses who were promised a welfare system (Jonas, 2019). Missing from this political settlement was a bold strategic vision of the developmental role and impact of SOEs and DFIs. During the initial 'RDP years' (1994–1996), they were useful instruments for realising policy goals like infrastructure, energy, housing and social grant programmes, but economic policy did not leverage the SOEs and DFIs to enable investments in industrialisation and the productive economy (Zalk, 2017). Eskom, for example, became the primary instrument for delivering 'electricity for all', but there were limited attempts to restructure the minerals–energy complex inherited from the apartheid era which sustained this energy delivery strategy. Additionally, as Suttner (2014) argues, a statist style of governance resulted in a decline in civil society as a key co-creator of the democratic project.

The Reconstruction and Development Programme (RDP) was

South Africa's first democratic development policy. It set massive welfare initiatives in motion to address apartheid injustices and unequal development. Social grants, free and subsidised housing and health, school feeding schemes, transport networks, electrification and other networked infrastructures were rolled out and the land-reform programme was initiated. Some of these initiatives were financed by DFIs: the Land Bank financed black farmers for the first time, the DBSA expanded from investing in homeland infrastructure to core national infrastructure and the IDC was central in funding BEE initiatives. An entirely new DFI, the National Housing Finance Corporation (NHFC), was formed to make housing finance more accessible to low- to middle-income households, collaborating with the DBSA to build infrastructure in new housing settlements (Khadiagala, 2015). SOEs like Eskom, water boards, Transnet and Prasa were deployed in the RDP's redistributive project, even though some of them were financially constrained and lacked the capacity needed to implement new developmental approaches that required more partnerships and greater coordination between state and private institutions. Many big SOEs continued to be poor revenue generators in the context of massive public investment and inadequate financing. Smaller SOEs were restructured, and privatisation of these non-core assets presented a solution for deficient performance and a way to fund redress.

The absence of a clear strategic vision for SOEs and DFIs persisted during the Growth, Employment and Redistribution (GEAR) strategy years (1996–2005). Relaxed exchange controls, market-related tariffs, integration into the global economy, export-led growth and privatisation were aimed at achieving fiscal consolidation but were unable to realise job creation or restorative justice. By failing to find ways to significantly redistribute wealth after 1994, fiscal consolidation faced resistance as political pressures built up for increased fiscal spending that was, in turn, funded by the raising of debt levels in a low-growth economy. Despite this, the poor effectively became increasingly dependent on an expanding welfare budget, while unemployment levels were not significantly reduced (Mosala et al., 2017).

The adoption of GEAR in 1996 created the context for a gradual shift in the balance of power within the post-1994 political settlement. As this grand pact unravelled in the face of poor economic performance, new political settlements began to emerge around specific political projects. The Mbeki Presidency weakened the ANC as the centre of political gravity, gradually marginalised organised labour and concentrated policy leadership within an increasingly dominant Presidential Office (Gumede, 2005). Around this a political settlement formed which endorsed the economic policies of the Ministry of Finance and cemented a strong alliance between the core of Mbeki's cabinet, white business leaders, the first generation of BEE beneficiaries and a core group of state bureaucrats within government departments and SOEs. Up until 2002, when the 'developmental state' narrative was adopted by the ANC and the government, this coalition strongly favoured the privatisation of some SOEs, inflation targeting and fiscal restraint.

Riding on the back of a debt-financed, consumption-led boom, low government debt levels and tight monetary policies, SOEs and, to some extent DFIs, were not seen as key instruments of development. However, this changed after 2002 when the 'developmental state' narrative justified infrastructure spending to sustain economic growth in the wake of the weakening of debt-funded consumption as an economic driver. It was then realised that SOEs and DFIs would have to play a key role in the national infrastructure programme (Pitcher, 2012).

With a focus on 'binding constraints', the new approach was expressed in the Accelerated and Shared Growth Initiative for South Africa (AsgiSA) implemented in the period 2006–2009. This economic policy recognised the potential of SOEs for a developmental nation-building project, with R78 billion planned for infrastructure expenditure which amounted to 9.7 per cent of gross domestic product (GDP) between 2009 and 2012. Major SOEs like Eskom (electricity), Transnet (transport and ports), the South African National Roads Agency (SANRAL) (roads), the Airports Company South Africa (ACSA) (airports) and the newly formed Infraco (broadband) received substantial capital injections to stimulate infrastructure-led growth, with many projects partially funded by the Public Investment Corporation (PIC), a state-owned asset management entity that also manages the investments of the Government Employees Pension Fund (GEPF).

AsgiSA regarded state intervention in the economy more favourably, but it said little about how to sustain investment levels, rebuild the manufacturing sector and effect economic transformation that would create enough jobs and raise the standard of living for the majority of South Africans (Greenberg, 2006; Smith, 2010). Even when the annual growth rate topped 4 per cent in 2004, a surge in government expenditure, overvalued exchange rates and low interest rates pushed the fiscus into deficit (The Presidency, 2008). Government's big infrastructure investments during this time pushed up demand for imports relative to the value of exports, even though exports climbed to over 30 per cent of GDP in 2006, up from 21 per cent in 1994 (The Presidency, 2008).

AsgiSA was less an integrated development policy framework and more a plan of detailed initiatives supported by growth-enhancing projects, informed in part by the Microeconomic Reform Strategy (MERS) adopted in 2002 (GCIS, 2008). There was a preference for sector-specific investment strategies where labour was concentrated and where opportunities existed for small business development and broad-based black economic empowerment (B-BBEE) (Mosala, 2015). Because it was project based, AsgiSA depended on strong state capacity to implement effective government coordination, monitoring and coherence, all of which were, in the view of The Presidency, inadequate (The Presidency, 2007).

It was during the AsgiSA years that SOEs and DFIs became increasingly significant in the political rhetoric and policy discourse of the ANC and the government. However, they were depicted mainly as implementing institutions rather than core vehicles for capital mobilisation, strategic infrastructure development and community-based development. The 'development package' proposed by the New Growth Path (NGP) published by the newly created Economic Development Department in 2011, headed up by former trade unionist Ebrahim Patel, reiterated the emphasis placed on infrastructure-led economic growth (including 'green economy' investments) and prioritised state-led initiatives across a broad front of economic sectors. The NGP was aimed at rebuilding a progressive political settlement connecting the left wing of the ANC, the Congress of

South African Trade Unions (COSATU), civil society organisations, SOEs, DFIs, small, medium and micro enterprises (SMMEs) and key industrial sectors which were keen to revive production with state support (Tregenna, 2011). COSATU, however, referred to it as 'two steps forward, one step back'.

STATE CAPTURE OF STATE-OWNED ENTERPRISES AND DEVELOPMENT FINANCE INSTITUTIONS

Contrary to what was intended, by bringing SOEs and DFIs into strategic focus, AsgiSA and the NGP set the stage for state capture during the Zuma Presidency (2009–2018) (Callaghan et al., 2020; Chipkin and Swilling, 2018). The Department of Trade and Industry (DTI) published a policy document in 2014 that marked a decisive policy shift by placing SOEs (and to some extent DFIs) at the centre of economic policy. Referring to the procurement spend of SOEs (at around R200 billion per year) as a means of achieving 'radical economic transformation' (RET), the DTI advocated the building of a 'black industrial class' to lead the economic transformation of the South African economy (DTI, 2014). According to this narrative, dismantling the persistent and disproportionate levels of white-owned wealth, otherwise referred to as white monopoly capital (WMC) by Zuma's faction, could only be achieved if a black industrial class could be constructed using the procurement spend of state-owned industries (Callaghan et al., 2020).

The post-Polokwane, Zuma-centred political settlement was supposed to include a range of constituencies that felt politically estranged from the Mbeki Presidency. This included the South African Communist Party (SACP), COSATU, the ANC Youth League, key state bureaucrats and political factions who had fallen out with Mbeki, and increasingly unhappy black business leaders who were impatient with the slow pace of economic transformation. The policy focus on the procurement spend of 'our industries' seemed to satisfy the latter and pacify those whose faith lay in greater state intervention in boosting economic development.

In reality, the post-Polokwane political settlement turned out to be a chimera. Indeed, it was very different from what the left-wing constituencies had hoped for. Instead, the Zuma-centred power elite comprised a set of 'constitutional and shadow state' networks who bypassed these constituencies as well as the ANC itself and executed a 'silent coup' that resulted in the 'repurposing' of a wide range of state institutions, including many key SOEs (Bhorat et al., 2017). Many key personalities who backed the 'Zunami', such as Zwelinzima Vavi and Julius Malema, soon fell out of favour and set up separate political initiatives.

The IDC, a key DFI, found itself entrapped in a shadow state web managed by the Gupta brothers. For example, the IDC granted a loan of R250 million to Oakbay, the family business set up to acquire the Shiva uranium mine. This acquisition was intended to service a fleet of nuclear power stations in the arrested nuclear deal with Russia. A further R90 million of IDC money was lost when Oakbay delisted from the Johannesburg Stock Exchange (JSE) in 2018 after the Guptas' grand plan started to unravel. The IDC had bought shares in Oakbay when the Guptas struggled to pay back their loan (Callaghan et al., 2020).

Shadow World Investigations (2021), an outfit that probes cases of grand corruption, gave evidence at the Zondo Commission in June 2021. In their testimony, they revealed the top 10 sites of state capture, seven being SOEs and one being a DFI (the other three were provincial government offices of the Free State, North West and Mpumalanga provinces). Table 17.1 presents value estimates of what was stolen at these state-owned companies.

Table 17.1: Extent of state capture looting at SOEs

Transnet	R40 billion
Eskom	R7 billion
Denel	R250 million
IDC	R250 million
SABC (South African Broadcasting Corporation)	R62 million
SAA (South African Airways) and SA Express	R26 million
SAFCOL (South African Forestry Company Limited)	R5.7 million

Source: Shadow World Investigations, 2021

More than R47.6 billion was siphoned out of SOEs and one DFI in just the top 10 sites of state capture, not counting the opportunity and social costs. When calculating other sources of rent capture, the cost has been estimated to be as high as R1.5 trillion (Merten, 2019). It is a dark irony, considering Zuma's RET rhetoric, that the loot eventually lined the pockets of mainly white and foreign-owned businesses, including German software company SAP, Swiss-based Liebherr, T-systems, Neotel and Bain & Company, amongst others (Callaghan et al., 2020).

THE EVOLVING ROLE OF DEVELOPMENT FINANCE INSTITUTIONS IN DEVELOPMENT

DFIs have played a pivotal role in shaping the South African economy. DFIs are responsible for the deployment of capital into projects with lower-than-acceptable financial returns on investment, often in exchange for higher social and/or environmental returns on investment and higher-than-acceptable levels of risk in traditional capital markets. The failure of the capital markets to allocate capital to these types of developmentally focused projects necessitates some form of state intervention in the market. DFIs partially fill this gap. In financing development-defining projects, such as the IDC's investments in minerals and energy beneficiation where foreign capital was not accessible owing to apartheid (Le Pere, n.d.), DFIs have been instrumental in financing the government's desired development pathways.

In the post-apartheid period, DFIs continue to contribute to the development agenda of the country, with a specific mandate to redress racialised inequalities of the past. The DBSA, IDC and National Empowerment Fund (NEF), the three largest of the 16 national and local DFIs in South Africa, have had limited success in realising this development mandate, as capital-intensive, resource-oriented energy industries continue to direct the economy, with limited labour-intensive, downstream development (Le Pere, n.d.). This is coupled with the poor economic performance of DFIs, with the exception of the DBSA, which is 'self-financing, has retained a strong balance sheet, and enjoys sound domestic and international credit ratings … and [i]n terms of operational efficiency … performs very well' (Le Pere, n.d.: 12). The relatively strong economic performance of the DBSA has been enabled through effective governance, as 'good governance leads to good financial outcomes, which lead to good development outcomes' (Van Niekerk et al., 2022).

How the DBSA has managed to achieve financial and operational sustainability requires further consideration in terms of the role it plays in the political economy of the country and the degree to which it has achieved its development mandate. The way in which the DBSA could strengthen its approach to achieving its development mandate, in partnership with SOEs, is considered to be a potential model for financing social and economic infrastructure intended to improve the wealth and wellbeing of citizens.

The DBSA's mission is economic development through investment in catalytic infrastructure. It is assumed that the provision of such infrastructure can increase economic output by increasing productive capacity and reducing the cost of production (DBSA, 2021). The DBSA's focus on catalytic infrastructure, cemented over the period 2007–2010 (DBSA, 2021), was likely in response to the ask of AsgiSA. Using funds obtained in the capital markets and from margins made from projects, the DBSA seeks to direct and influence private-sector participation in infrastructure development and to stimulate demand through government expenditure (Fedderke and Garlick, 2008). From 2016 onwards, the DBSA expanded its operations from a narrow financing focus of providing debt and equity finance to the addition of technical advisory services, such as project preparation, project management for implementing infrastructure projects and institutional development support (DBSA, 2021).

An example of the institution's dual commitment to financing high-risk programmes and the provision of institutional support is best illustrated in the DBSA's role in the government's Renewable Energy Independent Power Producer Procurement Programme (REIPPPP). In terms of financing, as of 30 September 2021, the DBSA had invested approximately R20 billion (9.5 per cent of total investments) in 34 renewable energy projects (37 per cent of the total number of projects approved in terms of the REIPPPP), contributing 2.9 GW of the total 6.2 GW of installed capacity that has been constructed. In terms of institutional support, the DBSA played a pivotal role in establishing the Independent Power Producers (IPP) Office in response to the need for a coordinated institutional function, as necessitated by the development of renewable energy generation as a new industry. This office emerged from a strategic partnership between the DoE, National Treasury and the DBSA. The development and nurturing of the REIPPPP is an example of how the DBSA institutionalised the expansion of the traditional role of DFIs to include technical advisory services to support infrastructure development as a lever for inclusive economic development.

Unlike many other SOEs, the DBSA survived the state capture period unscathed. Surrounded by a sea of captured public-sector institutions, the DBSA carefully crafted a fragile political settlement between itself, the National Treasury, key players in the capital markets and international DFIs.

Given the crisis in most municipalities, the DBSA can play a more active and even proactive role in advising, capacitating and generally assisting municipalities in undertaking infrastructure projects, including construction and maintenance. To the extent that it has sought to play this role, the DBSA has had minimal impact. Furthermore, besides its risk averseness, the question as to whether financial interventions (in the form of loans, for instance) are adequately matched by appropriate advisory services is a matter that deserves closer attention.

PUBLIC AND PRIVATE FINANCIAL INSTITUTIONS IN SOUTH AFRICA WELL POSITIONED TO DEPLOY CAPITAL AT SCALE

South Africa has well-developed public financial institutions (PFIs) and highly regulated capital markets. While PFIs include DFIs, there are other key PFIs in South Africa, such as the PIC which manages investments on behalf of public-sector entities, such as the GEPF and the Unemployment Insurance Fund (UIF). The PIC/GEPF is the largest PFI in South Africa and investment decisions are closely aligned with those of private financial institutions (FIs). The DBSA and the IDC, as DFIs, are positioned to de-risk investments by the PIC/GEPF and private FIs. Most of South Africa's critical PFIs are major investors in the existing coal-based energy system and emerging renewables-based energy system.

The GEPF has R2 trillion in assets under management. These are managed by the PIC which invests in different asset classes in domestic and international markets. The PIC/GEPF holds R80 billion of Eskom's R392 billion debt (Sguazzin, 2021) and the DBSA holds R20 billion of its debt (Moody's Investors Service, 2019). Together, this amounts to over a quarter of Eskom's debt. The balance sheet of the PIC/GEPF coupled with the complementary de-risking mandate of DFIs are ideally placed to play key roles in the mobilisation of the large-scale public, private and international funding that will be required to accelerate the energy transition. The REIPPPP to date has largely been funded by domestic PFIs and private FIs. The PIC is the largest institutional investor on the JSE and many private FIs are co-investors in the PIC/GEPF's multi-sectoral projects. Greater investment by the PIC/GEPF in the energy transition, de-risked by domestic DFIs and coupled with governance reforms, may unlock further international finance.

In 2020, the DBSA also established the Infrastructure Fund, South Africa's largest blended finance vehicle, with start-up capital of R100 billion from the fiscus to crowd in R900 billion in private-sector infrastructure co-investments over the next decade. The Fund has a pipeline of projects worth R85 billion across several sectors. It is ready and able to package large-scale, blended finance initiatives aimed at accelerating the energy transition, with a special emphasis on grid extension and transmission. Like the cross-sectoral investments of the PIC, the DBSA's Infrastructure Fund is well placed to manage a new generation of energy infrastructure investments on behalf of the GEPF. The largest share of the IDC's assets, worth R144 billion, is invested in South African coal mines and therefore faces the threat of stranded assets. This provides a clear impetus for its diversification into financing of the clean energy infrastructure that will underpin the transition.

Finally, the recently adopted National Infrastructure Plan (NIP) 2050 emphasises blended finance, with 30 per cent of the R6 trillion earmarked for bulk infrastructure – bulk freight, bulk water, bulk energy and digital infrastructure between 2016 and 2040 – to be publicly funded. The remainder would be sourced through public–private partnerships. The NIP's blended finance targets may prove difficult to attain as public spending on infrastructure has been declining, resulting in a shortfall of R2.1 trillion in 2021 (DPWI, 2022). Herein lies the opportunity for SOEs and PFIs (including DFIs) to strategically coordinate and structure investments to address the current gaps and leverage private funding. This, however, will depend on the emergence of an appropriate political settlement to protect these initiatives, including a major role for the private FIs.

South Africa's SOEs and DFIs are expected to provide and finance infrastructure to 'foster economic and social development' (Le Pere, n.d.). In practice, SOE mandates have been found to be poorly articulated without clear key performance indicators (KPIs) (Makgetla, 2020). Out of a sample of 13 SOEs, governance researcher Neva Makgetla found that responsibility for the entity was split for five of them, while only four had clear mandates (Makgetla, 2020).

Table 17.2: Oversight of priority SOEs and DFIs

Company	Shareholder	Policy department	Other departments affected	Other spheres affected
Eskom	DPE (Department of Public Enterprises)	DoE (Department of Energy)	Economic departments; DEA (Department of Environmental Affairs)	Municipalities
SANRAL	DoT (Department of Transport)	DoT	Economic departments; DEA	Municipalities and provinces
Transnet	DPE (Department of Public Enterprises)	DoT	DTI (Department of Trade and Industry), DMR (Department of Mineral Resources), DAFF (Department of Agriculture, Forestry and Fisheries)	Municipalities and provinces
Prasa	DoT	DoT	DoCG (Department of Cooperative Governance), DTI	Gauteng metros, Cape Town
SAA	NT	DoT	Tourism	Municipalities with airports
Central Energy Fund (CEF)	DoE	DoE	DTI	
Denel	DPE	DTI	Defence, DIRCO (Department of International Relations and Cooperation)	
SABC	DoC (Department of Communications)	DoC	GCIS	

Company	Shareholder	Policy department	Other departments affected	Other spheres affected
SAPO (South African Post Office)	DTPS (Department of Telecommunications and Postal Services)	DTPS	DSD (Department of Social Development)	Provinces and municipalities
PIC	NT	NT	Economic departments	
IDC	EDD (Economic Development Department)	EDD	DTI, DSBD (oversees SEFA/Small Enterprise Finance Agency)	
DBSA	NT	NT	DoCG	Municipalities
Land Bank	NT	DAFF (Department of Agriculture, Forestry and Fisheries)	DRDLR (Department of Rural Development and Land Reform)	Provincial agriculture

Source: Makgetla, 2020: 15

Notes: Several of the names of these departments have recently been changed (see Chapter 16). The Department of Agriculture, Forestry and Fisheries (DAFF) and Department of Rural Development and Land Reform (DRDLR) have been merged to form the Department of Agriculture, Land Reform and Rural Development (DALRRD). The Department of Trade and Industry (DTI) has been merged with the Economic Development Department (EDD) to form the Department of Trade, Industry and Competition (DTIC). The Department of Mineral Resources (DMR) and the Department of Energy (DoE) have been merged to form the Department of Mineral Resources and Energy (DMRE). The Department of Communications (DoC) and the Department of Telecommunications and Postal Services (DTPS) have been merged to form the Department of Communications and Digital Technologies (DCDT).

Eskom is governed by the Department of Public Enterprises (DPE) as its shareholder and takes policy direction from the Department of Mineral Resources and Energy (DMRE). Eskom is also answerable to the Department of Forestry, Fisheries and the Environment (DFFE) (formally the DEA) for environmental compliance as well as to the National Treasury. Eskom's leading role in the just energy transition is therefore dependent on a political settlement between all four government departments. It is unable to decarbonise and ramp up renewables, as required by the DPE, if the DMRE does not align energy policy (i.e., the Integrated Resource Plan) with the lowest-cost energy pathway endorsed in the NIP 2050 document.

For all these dispersed oversight functions, no one department is responsible for energy security, a deeply developmental outcome. Until a political settlement is reached between the key political and economic interests that coalesce around these departments and Eskom, this problem of multiple mandates will persist.

The NPC released a report in 2020 entitled *The Contribution of SOEs to Vision 2030: Case studies of Eskom, Transnet and PRASA* (NPC, 2020) which spelled out four main reasons for what they termed 'chronic underperformance'. This included 'years of uncertain policy expectations, precarious funding strategies, poor institutional accountability and poor governance, and political interference' (NPC, 2020: 9). What the NPC reports did not say, however, was that these conditions were the intentional outcome of concerted action by a particular political settlement, namely the Zuma-centred power elite. This much has now been confirmed by the Zondo Commission reports.

The Presidential SOE Council (PSEC) established in 2020 has been mandated to 'reposition and strengthen the governing framework of state-owned companies as well as address their liquidity challenges including implementing turnaround strategies' (The Presidency, 2021). Changes to the structure of SOEs, and to the overall governance and accountability of SOEs is certainly needed and long overdue. Fundamental reforms will be needed to enhance efficiency, strengthen governance and accounting systems, control corruption, reform procurement, and improve and restore institutional cultures after the impact of state capture. However, for this to happen, it will be necessary for the PSEC to go beyond an operational 'fix-it' approach. What is missing is a shared political vision for the developmental role of all SOEs and DFIs. Establishing a single shareholder governance structure is clearly a step in the right direction. But without articulating a compelling and shared political vision, it will be impossible to build a political settlement between the key political players (DPE and The Presidency, DTIC, DoT, and the SOEs and DFIs themselves) which results in the rebuilding of high-performance institutions capable of attracting the best available talent and galvanising creative, impactful initiatives.

NEW POLITICAL SETTLEMENTS IN THE MAKING

New political initiatives like the Presidential Climate Commission (PCC) are worth noting. Located within The Presidency, its mandate is essentially to build a vision and facilitate intra-state partnerships and partnerships with non-state actors. The PCC is made up of 22 commissioners, 12 of whom are from key government departments while the rest are from labour, academia, business, civil society, traditional leadership and SOEs. This broad social base may enable less politically contested processes and more decisive action. The potential of the PCC's convening power across government is that intra-state relationships can be forged and progress jointly monitored by a multiplicity of departments and stakeholders (Makgetla, 2021).

REFORMED, RENEWED AND REFOCUSED

SOEs are tasked with infrastructure development, maintenance and related service delivery. Most of their investments tend to be capital intensive and long term. Furthermore, innovation is a challenge because of the strictures of the financial regulatory framework prescribed by the Public Finance Management Act (PFMA). DFIs are tasked with facilitating investment into projects that result in a positive developmental impact. To achieve this, DFIs must be able to accept a higher level of risk and lower returns on investment (ROIs) compared to what private financial institutions will accept. This is necessary to leverage private capital into co-investment structures that offer private investors an acceptable level of risk and associated ROIs.

DFIs are tasked with facilitating flows of finance that result in positive social, economic and environmental developmental outcomes. A key challenge is that, in practice, DFIs are in fact risk averse because they need to fund operations from operational profits. South African DFIs are required by the shareholder to self-fund some or all of their operations. In its most recent Integrated Report, the IDC noted that '... financial sustainability remains one of the key pillars and strategic priority imperatives ...' of the institution (IDC, 2021: 16).

Given the current fiscal constraints of the country, including an increasing debt-to-GDP ratio, it is unlikely that DFIs will in the near future receive increased contributions from the government. This forces them to depend on conventional capital markets and, increasingly, foreign funding denominated in US dollars or Euros. The result is the rising cost of capital which contradicts developmental mandates. The R100 billion allocated for the DBSA-managed Infrastructure Fund over the years is a key exception. The National Treasury will avail this funding over a 10-year period to seed coordinated and well-governed infrastructure development which is anticipated to crowd in R900 billion from the private sector (Van Niekerk et al., 2022). This is a bold step because it means a strategic decision was made by the Executive to concentrate this public capital injection to leverage private capital, rather than disperse it across a multiplicity of sectoral initiatives that usually lack the capacity to leverage co-funding.

DFIs do not receive funding from the fiscus. They are therefore totally dependent on their own reserves and capital markets for sourcing capital. DFIs must then use their institutional capacity and intellectual capital to source, prepare and execute projects that generate returns that cover operational costs and the margins required by the capital markets. At the same time, outside the REIPPPP, public–private partnerships (PPPs) play a very minor role – only 2 per cent of the R791 billion infrastructure spend envisaged in the Medium-term Expenditure Framework (MTEF) is allocated to PPPs. What this means is that DFIs are taking on all the risk to achieve developmental outcomes while being forced to generate returns compatible with the requirements of the capital markets. This is why the R100 billion committed for the Infrastructure Fund is so significant – it marks a break from the past because the funds originate from the fiscus, while explicitly incentivising PPPs that can leverage co-investments worth another R900 billion. This would be a significant step forward, representing 17 per cent of the R6 trillion target set by the NIP 2050.

The use of private finance to fund public goods requires astute structuring of deals and good governance. Lessons have been learnt from the first rounds of the REIPPPP. In these first rounds, DFIs loaned capital to communities to fund their share of the project. The way in which these deals were structured meant that communities received dividends only after 10 or more years of operations, but other private national and international investors received dividends almost immediately. This has been corrected in further rounds of the REIPPPP. The flow of finance, interest for debt and dividends for equity must be carefully considered in structuring PPPs. If private finance is to be used to fund the infrastructure funding gap, the use of funding that supports the social security system of South Africa, such as the funds managed by the PIC, is a better alternative to international private finance, where finance flows out of the country. This requires a meeting of minds and mandates, i.e., a political settlement, of institutions responsible for developing catalytic infrastructure, notably SOEs, and institutions responsible for financing catalytic infrastructure, as well as DFIs seeding investments that crowd in private-sector funding, as the Infrastructure Fund is designed to deliver.

As DFIs cluster projects to achieve net zero and Sustainable Development Goal (SDG)-related targets, they will require partnerships with SOEs to then leverage private-sector investments. The digital infrastructure challenge is a case in point: without regulatory alignment, DFI investments and clearly defined roles for public and private institutions, South Africa will remain in the digital stone age. Similarly for energy: DFIs should not be competing with private FIs to fund IPPs. Unlike the decade leading up to 2022, the challenge is no longer the risk profile of renewable energy generation – that business case has been proven. The challenge now is the grid, which requires an investment of R130 billion. Now that the National Transmission Company of South Africa has been established, it can be activated with a viable balance sheet, which would once again attract investments from the DFIs, including the GEPF/PIC. This will crowd in private-sector investments without having to rely on foreign funding.

Amendments to Regulation 28 of the Pension Funds Act is creating the potential for an exciting new political settlement between DFIs, SOEs and South Africa's well-endowed pension funds. If just 10 per cent of South Africa's current pension fund assets were deployed to de-risked infrastructure that can catalyse positive economic and social development, this would equate to investments of approximately R260 billion, equal to 26 per cent of the envisaged R1 trillion to be raised by the Infrastructure Fund. However, none of this will be possible without a political settlement that results in a clearly defined vision and role for the SOEs and DFIs. With The Presidency at the centre, such a political settlement seems to be in the making: the PCSOE is addressing the governance of these institutions, the Presidential Economic Advisory Council (PEAC) has proposed that they should be at the vanguard of mission-led investments, the NPC has proposed a role for itself in implementing the NDP, and Infrastructure South Africa (in The Presidency) is leading the NIP 2050 initiative which is South Africa's first long-term integrated infrastructure plan.

CONCLUSION

This chapter critically reviewed the role that SOEs and DFIs have played during the colonial, apartheid and democratic eras. The essential argument is that state-owned economic institutions such as DFIs and SOEs are essential instruments for promoting and achieving agreed national development goals. During the pre-democratic era, these goals were constrained by a racial paradigm. During the post-1994 era, with key exceptions (e.g., Eskom's 'electricity for all' programme in the 1990s), they have largely failed to realise their full-potential historical mission as primary developmental institutions responsible for infrastructure development and the meeting of basic needs. From experiments in privatisation to achieve fiscal consolidation during the Mandela/Mbeki years to looting during the state capture years, the democratic government has failed to develop a compelling strategic vision of the developmental role of SOEs and DFIs.

Reforms, however, have commenced during the post-Zuma era that could, if handled properly, result in a more appropriate developmental role for SOEs and DFIs. One example is potential new roles for SOEs and DFIs in facilitating a just energy transition for a more equitable, inclusive and decarbonised economy. We have proposed that this can only happen when there are a set of interrelated, purpose-specific political settlements. Reflecting the shared intent of particular political settlements, industrial and infrastructure policies have historically been a vehicle to enact economic transformation and development. Today, the challenge is implementing infrastructure and industrial programmes that catalyse a number of policy priorities, including the just energy transition, the digital transition, sustainable water infrastructure, and bulk freight and transport systems as some of the most important. A new set of political settlements implies a new contract with society, as well as the creation of space for building capacities for learning, experimentation and innovation. Policy, regulation and finance need to be responsive in an uncertain and fast-changing global environment.

REFERENCES

Andrews, M., Pritchett, L. and Woolcock, M. 2017. *Building State Capability: Evidence, analysis, action*. Oxford: Oxford University Press.

Andrews, N. and Nwapi, C. 2018. 'Bringing the state back in again? The emerging developmental state in Africa's energy sector'. *Energy, Research and Social Science*, 41, 48–58.

Bagchi, A. K. 2000. 'The past and the future of the developmental state'. *Journal of World-Systems Research*, 1 (2), 398–442.

Behuria, P., Buur, L. and Gray, H. 2017. 'Studying political settlements in Africa'. *African Affairs,* 116 (464), 508–525.

Bhorat, H., Buthelezi, M., Chipkin, I., Duma, S., Mondi, L., Peter, C., Qobo, M. and Swilling, M. 2017. *Betrayal of the Promise: How South Africa is being stolen*. Stellenbosch and Johannesburg: Centre for Complex Systems in Transition and Public Affairs Research Institute.

Bowman, A. 2020. 'Parastatals and economic transformation in South Africa: The political economy of the Eskom crisis'. *African Affairs*, 119 (476), 395–431.

Branch, A. and Mampilly, Z. 2015. *African Uprising: Popular protest and political change*. London: Zed Books.

Callaghan, N., Foley, R. and Swilling, M. (eds.) 2020. *The Anatomy of State Capture*. Stellenbosch: Centre for Complex Systems in Transition.

Chibber, V. 2003. *Locked in Place: State-building and late industrialization in India*. Princeton N.J.: Princeton University Press.

Chipkin, I. and Swilling, M. (eds.) 2018. *Shadow State: The politics of state capture*. Johannesburg: Wits University Press.

Clark, N. 1994. *Manufacturing Apartheid: State corporations in South Africa.* New Haven and London: Yale University Press.

Cobbett, W., Glaser, D., Hindson, D. and Swilling, M. 1986. 'A critical analysis of reform strategies in the 1980s', in Frankel, P., Pines, N. and Swilling, M. (eds.) *State Resistance and Change in South Africa.* Johannesburg: Ravan Press, 19–51.

Department of Public Works and Infrastructure (DPWI). 2022. 'Section 4 (a) of the Infrastructure Development Act (23/2014): National Infrastructure Plan 2050 ("NIP 2050") for comments', https://www.gov.za/sites/default/files/gcis_document/202203/46033gon1874.pdf, accessed 10 March 2022.

Department of Trade and Industry (DTI). 2014. 'The DTI to create 100 black industrialists in three years'. South African Government website: https://www.gov.za/dti-create-100-black-industrialists-three-years, accessed 20 August 2022.

Development Bank of Southern Africa (DBSA). 2021. 'Integrated annual report', https://www.dbsa.org/sites/default/files/media/documents/2021-09/DBSA%20Integrated%20Annual%20Report%202021.pdf, accessed 29 August 2022.

Dubow, S. 1997. 'Colonial nationalism, the Milner kindergarten and the rise of "South Africanism", 1902–10'. *History Workshop Journal*, 43, 53–85.

Edigheji, O. 2010. *Constructing a Democratic Developmental State in South Africa: Potentials and challenges*. Pretoria: HSRC Press.

Evans, P. 1995. *Embedded Autonomy: States and industrial transformation*. Princeton: Princeton University Press.

Evans, P. 2006. 'What will the 21st century developmental state look like? Implications of contemporary development theory for the state's role', in 'The change role of the government in Hong Kong' conference at the Chinese University of Hong Kong, Hong Kong: Unpublished.

Fedderke, J. and Garlick, R. 2008. 'Infrastructure development and economic growth in South Africa: A review of the accumulated evidence', Policy Paper No. 12. University of Cape Town.

Fine, B. 2010. 'Can South Africa be a developmental state?', in Edigheji, O. (ed.) *Constructing a Democratic Developmental State in South Africa: Potentials and challenges*. Pretoria: HSRC Press, 169–182.

Foster, J. 2003. '"Land of contrasts" or "home we have always known"? The SAR&H (South African Railways & Harbours) and the imaginary geography of while South African nationhood, 1910–1930'. *Journal of Southern African Studies*, 29 (3) 657–680.

Freund, B. 2013. 'A ghost from the past: the South African developmental state of the 1940s'. *Transformation: Critical Perspectives on Southern Africa*, 81 (1), 86–114.

Freund, B. 2019. *Twentieth-Century South Africa: A developmental history*. Cambridge: Cambridge University Press.

Gelb, S. 2006. 'A South African developmental state: What is possible?', in Wolpe, H. Memorial Trust's Tenth Anniversary Colloquium 'Engaging silences and unresolved issues in the political economy of South Africa, 21–23 September 2006'. Cape Town: Unpublished.

Government Communication and Information System (GCIS). 2008. *SA Yearbook 2007/2008 Overview*, https://www.gcis.gov.za/sites/default/files/docs/resourcecentre/yearbook/2008/chapter0_overview.pdf, accessed 24 June 2023.

Greenberg, S. 2006. *The State, Privatisation, and the Public Sector in South Africa*. Harare: Southern African People's Solidarity Network.

Gumede, W. 2005. *Thabo Mbeki and the Battle for the Soul of the ANC*. London: Zed Books.

Industrial Development Corporation (IDC). 2021. Integrated Report 2021, https://www.idc.co.za/wp-content/uploads/2021/09/IDC-Integrated-Report-2021.pdf, accessed 14 August 2022.

Jessop, B. 2016. *The State: Past present future*. Cambridge: Polity Press.

Johnson, E. 2021. 'Between liberalisation and state capture: A deeper look at the case of Eskom', in Callaghan, N., Foley, R. and Swilling, M. (eds.) *The Anatomy of State Capture*. Stellenbosch: Stellenbosch University Media, 97–116.

Jonas, M. 2019. *After Dawn: Hope after state capture*. Johannesburg: Picador Africa.

Jordan, K. 2017. 'Perspectives on the role of the state in economic development: Taking stock of the "developmental state" after 35 years'. IFRPI Discussion Paper 1597, International Food Policy Research Institute website: http://ebrary.ifpri.org/cdm/ref/collection/p15738coll2/id/131049, accessed 14 August 2022.

Kelsall, T. 2013. *Business, Politics, and the State in Africa*. London: Zed Press.

Khadiagala, G. 2015. 'The role of Development Finance Institutions (DFI) in building South Africa's developmental state'. Development Bank of Southern Africa Working Paper No. 29/2011.

Khan, M. 2004. 'State failure in developing countries and institutional reform strategies', in Tungodden, B., Stern, N. and Kolstad, I. (eds.) *Toward Pro-Poor Policies: Aid, institutions and globalization*. New York: Oxford University Press, 65–196.

Khan, M. 2018. 'Political settlements and the analysis of institutions: An introduction'. *African Affairs*, 117 (469), 636–655.

Kohli, A. 2006. *State and Economic Development*. Princeton: Princeton University Press.

Lawrence, T. B. and Suddaby, R. 2006. 'Institutions and institutional work', in Clegg, S. R., Hardy, C., Lawrence, T. B. and Nord, W. R. (eds.) *Handbook of Organisation Studies*. London: Sage Books, 215-254, https://criticalmanagement.uniud.it/fileadmin/user_upload/lawrence-suddaby-2006.pdf, accessed 20 August 2022.

Le Pere, G. L. n.d. 'Repositioning state-owned enterprises (SOEs) and development finance institutions (DFIs)'. Wits School of Governance: University of the Witwatersrand.

Lodge, T. 2009. 'The South African developmental state?' *Journal of Southern African Studies*, 35 (1), 253–261.

Makgetla, N. 2007. 'A developmental state for South Africa'. *New Agenda*, 28 (4), 29–36.

Makgetla, N. 2020. 'The crisis at the state-owned enterprises'. Trade and Industrial Policy Strategies (TIPS) Policy Brief: 1/2020.

Makgetla, N. 2021. 'Governance and the just transition'. Working Paper for the Presidential Climate Commission: Trade and Industrial Policy Strategies (TIPS).

Magubane, B. 1996. *The Making of a Racist State: British imperialism and the union of South Africa, 1875–1910*. UK: Africa World Press.

Marodon, R. 2022. 'Can development banks step up to the challenge of sustainable development?' *Review of Political Economy*, 34 (2), 268–285.

Mazzucato, M., Qobo, M. and Kattel, R. 2021. 'Building state capacities and dynamic capabilities to drive social and economic development: The case of

South Africa'. UCL Institute for Innovation and Public Purpose Working Paper 2021/09.

Merten, M. 1 March 2019. 'State capture wipes out a third of SA's R4.9 trillion GDP – never mind lost trust, confidence, opportunity'. *Daily Maverick,* https://www.dailymaverick.co.za/article/2019-03-01-state-capture-wipes-out-third-of-sas-r4-9-trillion-gdp-never-mind-lost-trust-confidence-opportunity/, accessed 25 August 2022.

Mkandawire, T. 2001. 'Thinking about developmental states in Africa'. *Cambridge Journal of Economics*, 25, 289–313.

Mkandawire, T. 2011. 'Institutional monocropping and monotasking Africa', in Akbar, N., Botchwey, K., Stein, H. and Stiglitz, J. (eds.) *Good Growth and Governance in Africa: Rethinking development strategies*. Oxford: Oxford Scholarship Online, 80–113.

Moody's Investors Service. 29 July 2019. 'Development Bank of Southern Africa: Update to credit analysis'. *Credit Opinion,* https://www.dbsa.org/sites/default/files/media/documents/2021-03/Moody%27s%20-%202019%20July.pdf, accessed 20 August 2022.

Mosala, S. 2015. 'The national democratic revolution as a basis for public policy formulation in South Africa: Economic policy and transformation, 1994–2013'. Potchefstroom: North-West University.

Mosala, S., Venter, J. and Bain, E. 2017. 'South Africa's economic transformation since 1994: What influence has the National Democratic Revolution (NDR) had?' *The Review of Black Political Economy,* 44 (3), 327–40.

National Planning Commission (NPC). 2020. 'Infrastructure SOEs contribution to NDP Vision 2030'. Pretoria: The Presidency, https://www.gtac.gov.za/Publications/Infrastructure SOEs contribution to NDP Vision 2030.pdf, accessed 8 March 2022.

Nattrass, N. 1994. 'Economic restructuring in South Africa, the debate continues'. *Journal of Southern African Studies,* 20 (4), 517–531.

Nem Singh, J. and Chen, G. C. 2018. 'State-owned enterprises and the political economy of state–state relations in the developing world'. *Third World Quarterly*, 39 (6), 1077–1097.

Noman, A., Botshwey, K., Stein, H. and Stiglitz, J. E. 2011. *Good Growth and Governance in Africa: Rethinking development strategies*. Oxford: Oxford Scholarship Online.

Ocampo, J. A. and Ortega, V. 2022. 'The global development banks architecture'. *Review of Political Economy*, 34 (2), 224–248.

Onis, Z. 1991. 'The logic of the developmental state'. *Comparative Politics*, 24 (1), 109–126.

Ovadia, J. and Wolf, C. 2018. 'Studying the developmental state: Theory and method in research on industrial policy and state-led development in Africa'. *Third World Quarterly*, 39 (6), 1056–1076.

Padayachee, V. and Van Niekerk, R. 2019. *Shadow of Liberation: Contestation and compromise in the economic and social policy of the African National Congress (ANC), 1943–1996*. Johannesburg: Wits University Press.

Pitcher, A. 2012. 'Was privatisation necessary and did it work? The case of South Africa'. *Review of African Political Economy*, 39 (132), 243–260.

Roberts, S. and Rustomjee, V. 2009. 'Industrial policy under democracy: Apartheid's grown-up infant industries? Iscor and Sasol'. *Transformation,* 71, 50–75.

Schneider, G. 2018. 'The post-apartheid development debacle in South Africa: How mainstream economics and the vested interests preserved apartheid economic structures'. *Journal of Economic Issues,* 52 (2), 306–22.

Sguazzin, A. 23 November 2021. 'Government pension fund sees problems in converting its Eskom debt into equity to help the utility'. *Fin24*, https://www.news24.com/fin24/economy/eskom/government-pension-fund-sees-problems-in-converting-its-eskom-debt-into-equity-at-the-utility-20211123, accessed 20 August 2022.

Shadow World Investigations. 22 June 2021. 'Money laundering networks deployed by the Gupta enterprise in relation to funds paid by SOEs for the ultimate benefit of the Gupta enterprise'. Report submission to Commission of inquiry into allegations of state capture: Day 414.

Smith, A. 2010. 'Civil society in sustainable energy transitions', in Verbong, G. and Loorbach, D. (eds.) *Governing the Energy Transition: Reality, illusion, or necessity*. New York: Routledge, 180–202.

Southall, R. 2006. 'Introduction: Can South Africa be a developmental state?', in Buhlungu, S., Daniel, J., Southall, R. and Lutchman, J. (eds.) *State of the Nation: South Africa 2005–2006*. Cape Town: HSRC Press, xvii–xlv.

Suttner, R. 2014. 'Twenty years of democracy and the question of popular participation'. *Grace & Truth*, 1, 6–18.

Swilling, M. 1999. 'Changing conceptions of governance'. *Africanus*, 29.

Swilling, M. 2008. 'Tracking South Africa's elusive developmental state'. *Administratio Publico*, 16 (1), 1–29.

Swilling, M. and Callaghan, N. 2021. 'State-owned enterprises in South Africa', in Valodia, I. (ed.) *Handbook of the South African Economy*. Oxford: Oxford University Press, 576–598.

Swilling, M., Musango, J. and Wakeford, J. 2015. 'Developmental states and sustainability transitions: Prospects of a just transition in South Africa'. *Journal of Environmental Policy and Planning*, 5 (5), 1–23.

The Presidency. 2007. 'ASGISA Annual Report 2007'. Pretoria: The Presidency, http://www.thepresidency.gov.za/reporttype/jipsa, accessed 17 March 2022.

The Presidency. 2008. 'ASGISA annual report 2008'. Pretoria: The Presidency, https://www.gov.za/sites/default/files/gcis_document/201409/asgisa2008.pdf, accessed 15 March 2022.

The Presidency. 2021. 'Deputy President David Mabuza: Reply to questions in National Council of Provinces 18 November'. Pretoria: The Presidency, website: https://www.gov.za/speeches/deputy-president-david-mabuza-reply-questions-national-council-provinces-18-nov-18-nov-2021, accessed 5 March 2022.

Tregenna, F. 2011. 'A new growth path for South Africa?' *Review of African Political Economy*, 38 (130), 627–635.

Van Niekerk, B., Msutu, T., Reiersgord, N., Msomi, A. and Graham, N. 2022. 'Development impact and the current state of infrastructure in democratic South Africa, 1994–2019'. Development Bank of Southern Africa Working Paper Series WP/2022/01.

Von Holdt, K. 2010. 'Nationalism, bureaucracy, and the developmental state: The South African case'. *South African Review of Sociology*, 41 (1), 4–27.

Whitfield, L., Therkildsen, O., Buur, L. and Kjaer, A. 2015. *The Politics of African Industrial Policy*. Cambridge: Cambridge University Press.

Zalk, N. 2017. 'Industrial policy in a harsh climate: The case of South Africa'. *Transforming Economics*, 327–354.

Zenawi, M. 2011. 'States and markets: Neoliberal limitations and the case for the developmental state', in Norman, A., Botshwey, K., Stein, H. and Stiglitz, J. (eds.) *Good Growth and Governance in Africa: Rethinking development strategies*. Oxford: Oxford Scholarship Online, 140–174.

EIGHTEEN

Conclusion: Getting to inclusive growth and sustainable development

AMUZWENI NGOMA, SEERAJ MOHAMED AND BASANI BALOYI

INTRODUCTION

South Africa faces a raft of longstanding socioeconomic problems which have been worsened by an economic structure in unguided drift. Yet the country clearly has the potential to transform and benefit from more robust and inclusive economic architecture and systems. The purpose of this book is to present the views of a cross-section of experts on the structural transformation of the South African economy over time and how the country can pursue a more sustainable development path in the years ahead.

The chapters in this volume all offer strategic reflections that help to deepen our understanding of the evolution and workings of the South African economy. Special attention is given to the weaknesses in the country's economic infrastructure, the role of the state, the power relationships between the state and non-state actors, the dynamics in the labour market, structural changes within the sectoral and spatial contexts, the accumulation and social reproduction of capital, investment trends, the disruptive nature of technology and the changing nature of work.

In this concluding chapter, we set out to do two things: first, to highlight the points of convergence and tensions between and within the different contributions; and second, to suggest a set of strategic imperatives that, if acted upon by the relevant actors, will help to drive more inclusive growth and sustainable development in South Africa.

THE STATE OF KNOWLEDGE OF THE ECONOMY

As Levy et al. (2021) argue, ideas and institutions fuel economic growth. South Africa boasts a respectable body of post-apartheid scholarship on the structure and performance of the economy. Discussions therein are vigorous. But, as with many other sites of knowledge, the discourse is disjointed and prone to 'fetishistic' descriptions, as Ashman asserts in Chapter 3. Arguably, two types of debate typically characterise South Africa's economic literature. The first is the longstanding debate on *how* to characterise the South African economy (see Freund, 2017; Illife, 1999). The second is the debate on the character, drivers and outcomes of post-apartheid economic policy choices.

Freund (2017), more than Illife (1999), offers a combined review of apartheid and post-apartheid economic literature in terms of what it taught us about the South African economy. But Illife (1999), more than Freund (2017), seems to capture the essence of the literature in a way that foreshadowed what would become the hyper-fragmentation of South African economic thought, which has ultimately contributed to largely uncoordinated (and sometimes incoherent) policy postures, incomplete implementation and weak outcomes.

Illife (1999) compresses the early post-apartheid debates on the nature of the 20th-century South African economy into three propositional categories. Under proposition one, the analyses acknowledged that, by the mid-1970s, the South African economy had entered a structural crisis period. Seemingly mirroring contemporary analyses (including those contained in this volume), South Africa's structural crisis was seen to be characterised by a limited internal market, stagnant manufacturing output, high inflation, weak exports, a weak currency, low reserves and savings, and high unemployment (Illife, 1999).

Under proposition two, the analyses recognised the above-mentioned drivers of the structural crisis, but they framed their explanation thereof within 'the dominant "minerals–energy complex"', which, 'especially since its amalgamation with the financial institutions, was not committed to industrial modernisation' (Illife, 1999: 99), thus foregrounding a financialised minerals–energy complex perspective.

Under proposition three, from which Illife (1999) argues post-apartheid economic policy appears to have emerged, the analyses suggested that 'nothing was fundamentally wrong with the structure of South Africa's economy' and that economic growth had instead been retarded by 'apartheid' and 'was only deepened in the late 1970s by international depression, and in the 1980s by sanctions' (1999: 99). This set of arguments did not entertain the idea of a structural crisis; rather, South Africa's economic crisis and low growth rates were the result of political isolation, militarisation, high taxation, low savings and the pursuit of monetarist policies without any accompanying budgetary restraint. Perhaps even more important was the conclusion that these analyses arrived at: there was nothing about the structure of the South African economy that 'could be changed quickly without even worse effects in stimulating inflation or deterring investment' (Illife, 1999: 99).

For almost three decades, these three propositions – supported by added theoretical texture and empirical depth – have characterised the rigorous debates on the South African economy. As this book shows, in the post-global financial crisis (GFC) and post-COVID-19 periods, analysts have been hard-pressed to deny a structural crisis – which thus represents a discontinuity with proposition three.

Of course there are discontinuities, as many people do not openly or forcefully deny the dysfunctionality of the country's economic structure. As the analyses in this book show, how the South African economy is understood fundamentally affects economic (and other) policies and day-to-day outcomes. The fact that the economy continues to be hampered by low growth poses a severe risk to the goals of inclusivity, higher levels of employment, better jobs and workers, and a reduction in poverty and inequality. Various combinations of, or different points of emphasis in, the three propositions as well as new views have flourished, reflecting greater incorporation of global ideas and ideologies. But these debates are marred by contestation over their orientation and content, which is exacerbated by the strength of the personalities, institutions and sponsorships of their various proponents.

In contextualising the evolution of South Africa's economic structure, this book accents the contributions of different economic sectors, their linkages and their relationship with value chains. Above all, the book argues for societal resilience, household reproduction and wellbeing as central aspects of structural transformation. It also stresses the need for a shake-up and changes in the current structure of power relationships in the economy and in the relationship between the state and vested (corporate) interests.

SOUTH AFRICA'S STRUCTURAL FAULTLINES

The chapters in this volume suggest that efforts to understand the structure of the South African economy require more than 'the search for take-off points and single-factor explanations' (Illife, 1999: 88) for the relative contributions of different sectors in terms of gross domestic product (GDP), employment, investment and capital stock over time. It also requires more than a consideration of the relative levels of export success and integration into global value chains. Rather, we contend that an understanding of structural transformation ought to include theoretical and empirical insights into societal resilience, household reproduction and wellbeing.

Such a broad interpretation of structural transformation is a break from neoliberal market supremacy. Indeed, this book explains the limitations of neoliberal ideology. Despite post-GFC and fleeting COVID-19 reflections on the flaws of neoliberal ideology (see MISTRA, 2016, and Chapter 3 in this volume), neoliberal ideology remains hegemonic. Unlike the COVID-19 period, the post-GFC period was characterised by a far more enduring global critique of neoliberal orthodoxy. Notably, this discourse was also the subject of *The Great Recession and Its Implications for Human Values: Lessons for Africa* (MISTRA, 2016).

Yet, as the contributions in this book reveal, neoliberal hegemony has manifested unevenly. Having become fractionalised and characterised by different points of emphasis over time, it is the result of intersecting, colliding and contradictory sets of political economies. Even in the face of such unevenness and plurality, this book arrives at the unifying conclusion that South Africa's post-apartheid macroeconomic dispensation continues to undermine meaningful structural transformation.

South Africa's general adherence to its particular economic principles over the past few decades (especially macroeconomic principles), even when such adherence has been inadequate, has undermined and eroded transformation and development. The first part of this book responds to the discourse on the neoliberal hollowing out of development by envisioning local economies as national systems of accumulation within a global context. It provides a specific entry point for framing the structure of sectoral and value chain analyses in the second part of the book. Moreover, the book portrays the minerals–energy complex/minerals–energy–finance complex (MEC/MEFC) as a system of accumulation, which is evident from a political economy analysis of global and domestic events. This political economy approach rejects the neoliberal limitations that constrain the development discourse and policies.

The analyses in this book emphasise the interrelationship between extraordinarily high and rising levels of inequality in South African society and the dysfunctional economic structure that has taken shape. We therefore propose that economic policy and programmes adopt an approach to development that integrates economic, ecological and social dynamics so that we can understand the evolution of the economic structure and, importantly, efforts to transform that structure.

The South African economy requires large-scale structural transformation to address the serious, persistent problems of unemployment, poverty and inequality as well as the serious, interrelated risks posed by climate change, geopolitical conflicts, and possible future pandemics and financial and economic crises.[1] In Chapter 8, Das Nair and Bell assert that post-1994 structural transformation has been inadequate, characterised by a limited amount of transformation which has occurred in only a few sectors in the economy.

There is literature on industrial development and policies that deal with South Africa's failure to transform the economy, demonstrating that the economy has not evolved from its low-productivity state, with low value-added and less sophisticated activities, to a higher-productivity state, with high value-added and more sophisticated activities. The iterative and path-dependent process of 'learning on the job' has been curtailed across the economy. If allowed to flourish, it would have been evident in upgraded economic activities, supported by investments in new technologies, new forms of machinery and equipment, and wide-ranging skills development. The economy has not developed the logistics and other productive and high value-added services that go hand in hand with the production of high value-added products and services. Nor have government institutions and business entities – which typically grow and develop when there is widespread structural transformation at the sectoral level – evolved adequately.

There is also literature that considers the social structures of accumulation within the broader context of international political economy developments (see Chapter 2 by Fine and Mohamed and Chapter 3 by Ashman). While there is a large overlap between how economic development and economic transformation (or the lack thereof) are perceived or understood, economic transformation generally focuses less on the reporting of activities and details of different sectors in the economy (even though the details of the different sectors inform the analyses). Its institutional focus is on the powerful economic actors, such as large corporations (including state-owned enterprises/SOEs) and the state; it also takes into account the role of organised labour and the impact of class relations. Moreover, it provides historically and institutionally grounded insights into the persistence of high levels of unemployment and poor levels of accumulation in society.

Both approaches to structural transformation (i.e., economic development and economic transformation) recognise the importance of relevant historical developments in the economy and the role played by institutions, over time, in analysing structural economic transformation. The overlap between the two approaches is well illustrated in Chapter 6 by Vilakazi and Bosiu who look through a system-of-accumulation lens to analyse the evolving structure of the South African economy. They elucidate how the system-of-accumulation approach requires one to engage with linkages and agency in industrial sectors and value creation. The ability to analyse these linkages requires an understanding of the interactions between powerful economic actors and the processes of the state.

Using this approach to analyse the economic transformation of the South African economy helps one to move beyond simplistic analyses that blame either the state or the market for the failure to transform the economy. It recognises that the private sector is not homogeneous and that SOEs are major actors in the economy. It examines the interactions (both conflicting and cooperative) and linkages between firms in an economy where a small number of corporations have an extremely high degree of ownership and market control. It also examines the interactions and linkages between business and the state. This approach takes seriously the major impact that neoliberal policies and financialisation have had on important global economic outcomes, such as inequality, investment, corporate restructuring and global value chains (to name a few), and the specific influences that these have had on domestic economic outcomes, including structural economic transformation (or the lack thereof).

Previous works by Mazzucato (see, for example, Mazzucato, 2015, 2018, 2021) and Chapter 16 in this volume by Ngoma and Ngcaweni offer further insights that dispel simplistic views based on the state and market dichotomy. Instead, such works recognise the entrepreneurial and broader developmental and innovative leadership role that the state can play, in partnership with business and other parts of civil society, to transform the economy. The authors of Chapter 16 argue that the role of the state is not just to fix markets but is also key to the creation of value and the shaping and co-creation of markets. Workers across the public sector therefore play important roles in shaping current and potential future economic outcomes. Chapter 17 by Swilling, Callaghan and McCallum, on SOEs and development finance institutions (DFIs), further contributes to this nuanced perspective by focusing on political settlements and the actions of economic actors within the norms and boundaries of existing, evolving institutions in the economy.

In short, the general context of the chapters in this volume is that economic perspectives on transformation which make an artificial distinction between the social, environmental and economic aspects of society (while also ignoring global influences) cannot provide appropriate solutions either to the multiple crises facing South Africa or to several serious, interrelated global risks. The message conveyed is that the economy and what is produced, even in a capitalist society,[2] must be influenced and even directed by all members of society, possibly through political settlements and agreements, and that the state has a key role to play in managing the economy and market formation. In fact, today – more than ever – the state must play a developmental role to ensure both environmental and economic sustainability and a just and equitable transformation of the economy.

The chapters in this book show that a major component of a transformation strategy is the deliberate implementation of developmental economic policies to address the extremely high levels of unemployment, poverty and inequality in the country and to build resilience in the economy. Solutions include industrial and other policies and measures to transform the sectoral structure of the economy. These are catalysed and shaped by growth in domestic aggregate demand in relation to the provision of social security, services and welfare sectors, public infrastructure development, and a stronger role for SOEs and DFIs.

The intersection between macroeconomic policy and financialisation – outcomes and new possibilities

An important theme that permeates this book is the effects of South Africa's macroeconomic policy choices and implementation on the structure of the economy and on employment, poverty and inequality outcomes. The various chapters show that at a macrosocial level, there is not only a debilitating separation of the social, ecological and economic aspects of society, but also a disarticulation in the way the state directs and manages the economy, evidenced by the character and content of the policies it pursues.

In Chapter 2, Fine and Mohamed highlight that neoliberal accumulation underpins the financialisation of the economy and that such accumulation hinders socioeconomic development. This is an important finding because it challenges the ideological premise regarding how this system is propagated. The authors assert that appropriate policymaking cannot be achieved by taking the conventional neoliberal route. Instead, they call for a bold rereading and reframing of domestic macroeconomic policies within the global financial architecture, with the state acting as the central driver.

Adelzadeh (Chapter 4) and Rakabe (Chapter 5) concur with the above argument, both analytically and practically. They detail South Africa's macroeconomic policy outcomes from 1994 to the present, highlighting various vulnerabilities that have emerged both at a structural level and a micro level. Importantly, too, Ashman (Chapter 3) illustrates the shift from the minerals–energy complex (MEC) to the minerals–energy–finance complex (MEFC), facilitated by the post-1994 macroeconomic policy dispensation. In Chapter 8, Das Nair and Bell highlight the impact of South Africa's conflicting macroeconomic policy landscape on stability. This macroeconomic approach has debilitated structural transformation and the performance of the manufacturing sector, once a critical source of employment in the country.

Adelzadeh (Chapter 4) proposes a six-pillar macroeconomic model, designed to alter the direction of the economy and generate more inclusive growth, with greater benefits accruing to the poor. Rakabe (Chapter 5) suggests that South Africa's macroeconomic predicament calls for the adoption of a credible fiscal rebalancing plan. Adelzadeh's six-pillar macroeconomic model offers this. The key elements of the six-pillar model are economic growth, socioeconomic development and high employment. To address the causes of macroeconomic vulnerability and instability, Adelzadeh and Rakabe propose a wider macroeconomic framework that takes into account not only macroeconomic outcomes and risks associated with monetary and fiscal variables (the focus of neoliberal macroeconomics) but also aggregate demand, unemployment, poverty and inequality.

Structure of the economy, sectoral and value chain changes

Fine and Mohamed (Chapter 2) explain that greater financial regulation and direct state intervention in the allocation of finance towards industrialisation are required – similar to the experience of the Asian Tigers. Ashman (Chapter 3) and Vilakazi and Bosiu (Chapter 6) emphasise the potent role that finance has played in the economy and the extent to which non-financial corporations and other parts of the economy have become financialised. These developments, supported by the government's neoliberal approach to macroeconomic policy and financial regulation, have influenced investment, employment, ownership, concentration and the structural composition of the South African economy.

Chapters 2, 3 and 6 contend that the post-apartheid economy's failure to diversify out of the mining–energy core has (re)produced socioeconomic and ecological crises. The economy remains driven by the same corporate groups and subsidiaries that grew under, and benefited from the systems and structures erected by, colonialism and apartheid. As argued by Das Nair and Bell in Chapter 8, the growth of finance and services, media and telecoms and e-commerce has been combined with deindustrialisation, deagrarianisation and rising household debt.

Das Nair and Bell (Chapter 8) argue that while South Africa has managed to transform certain sectors and industries, its record is uneven and discontinuous. As a result, the country has experienced limited industrial structural transformation evidenced by the continued dependence on lower-productivity and energy-intensive, resource-based activities, amongst other things. The authors trace the evolution of the manufacturing sub-sectors of automotives and agro-processing as well as the grocery retail sector. Their analysis considers policies that have liberalised South Africa's trade regime and facilitated the country's integration into global trade and financial markets. Persistently high concentration characterises the food value chain, particularly at the agro-processing and retail levels. The authors argue that power imbalances have shaped the evolution of these sectors and that state institutions, such as the Competition Commission, have attempted to address these imbalances. Furthermore, policy responses have been directed at leveraging the power of large lead firms to facilitate the upgrading of small and medium enterprises (SMEs) in their supply chains. The authors recommend that policymaking should also focus on the regional dynamics prompted by large South African multinational corporations (MNCs) operating in the Southern African Development Community (SADC) region.

Ashman (Chapter 3) states that although the MEC has fragmented, the state no longer drives the country's industrialisation strategy. The South African economy now exhibits neoliberal and financialised patterns of accumulation. Ashman states that 'apartheid's state-led MEC has morphed into a neoliberal and financialised one following the patterns of global accumulation – with a strong role played by the state in these processes'. Ashman makes the case for radical economic policy shifts in a push for reindustrialisation.

Altering the policymaking posture and outlook

The state should reorient the regulation of financial markets so as to reverse the prevailing economic outcomes. Vilakazi and Bosiu (Chapter 6) characterise these outcomes as: low demand, low growth, concentration and oligopolisation of most sectors, low investment and/or short-term speculative investments, and the retention of high profits and dividend payouts. These outcomes, which are shaped by attitudes that reinforce financial exclusion, perpetuate the legacy of racial and gender exclusion in all aspects of the economy. State support and incentives for investment in productive sectors have not adequately taken into account the extent of financial and other forms of exclusion that persist in the economy.

Such exclusion is demonstrated in a case study by Cawe in Chapter 7. He discusses the lost opportunities associated with state support and market formation in the relatively new South African renewable energy sector, which has led to weak integration and participation of black industrialists in that sector. Preceding this, Das Nair and Bell (Chapter

8) argue that sectoral policy in the retail sector has not supported small retailers and spaza shop owners (rural, urban or peri-urban). Instead, the policy framework has allowed large, established retail groups to cherry-pick the best locations in townships and rural areas, thus displacing small, locally owned black retailers. Cawe (Chapter 7) recommends various policy and regulatory actions that could influence the distributional and industrial outcomes of the Renewable Energy Independent Power Producer Procurement Programme (REIPPPP). He asserts that the government should adjust its policies and regulations to increase the participation of black industrialists and other black-owned businesses in the renewable energy sector.

Economic inclusion, social reproduction and labour

In Chapter 14, Sefalafala, Castel-Branco and Malabela indicate that declining investments in the productive sector, together with outsourcing and automation, have contributed to higher levels of unemployment. While reindustrialisation through the manufacturing and mining sectors requires high-level skills, the authors point out that the South African workforce has been adversely affected by deskilling. They conclude by urging the trade union movement to arrive at a deeper understanding of the outcomes of technology adoption and how these shape labour-market outcomes, including employment rates and skills development successes.

In Chapter 11, Netshitenzhe makes a policy recommendation in connection with the parallel streams of lived economic experiences within the South African economy. He distils various trends and recommends the expansion of special economic zones (SEZs) and the further development both of the agricultural sector and small, medium and micro enterprises (SMMEs) as mechanisms to drive higher employment, greater economic inclusion and reduced duality in the economy. These proposed measures could lead to improved alignment of policies with the National Development Plan (NDP) goals, which could in turn support structural economic transformation and improve market access for small and informal enterprises, including micro enterprises such as spaza shops, in South Africa's spatial value chains.

Regional integration, compacts and political settlements

South Africa's engagement with the rest of the African continent is critical for the structural transformation of the country and the region, as Hirsch asserts in Chapter 12. From his assessment of patterns of engagement and levels of trade and investment, he concludes that the potential for deeper regional integration has been weakened by product protectionism which affects imports in some African countries. Regional integration has been further hampered by slow progress in building regional value chains and ultra-cautious attitudes about allowing Africans to move freely across borders on the continent. Hirsch contends that facilitating greater regional integration requires the development of both public-sector and private-sector capacities and the education of citizens on the advantages of African integration. The state, sector leaders and domestic and multinational enterprises must thus craft a new political settlement that also stabilises the social compact, as argued by Abba Omar in Chapter 15 and Swilling, Callaghan and McCallum in Chapter 17.

In Chapter 16, Ngoma and Ngcaweni trace the evolution of the state and the roles of senior bureaucrats in driving economic growth. The macro organisation of the state has affected its ability to coordinate and drive economic development policies and programmes. In assessing the capacity of the state to bring about economic restructuring, Swilling, Callaghan and McCallum (Chapter 17) explore the granular micro dynamics of intra-state relations. They suggest that intra-state relations can enable the rebuilding of SOEs within the wider context of state capacity development for the purpose of post-state capture and post-pandemic economic reconstruction. They also introduce the political settlements debate to frame the analysis of state capacity, focusing specifically on SOEs and DFIs, with more than R47.6 billion having been syphoned off the SOEs and one DFI. This amount, of course, excludes the opportunity and social costs associated with the loss. As such, the authors argue that the development of state capacity and effective institutions depends on the ability to insulate institutions from corruption. Practically, they suggest that this involves extending political protection to strategic and operational areas, which includes protecting competent people to initiate, lead and operationalise purposeful and impactful mandates.

New forms of political settlement are required in areas that would drive economic growth, particularly infrastructure development aimed at satisfying basic needs. A point emerging from Chapters 15, 16 and 17 is that these political settlements must be applied to sectors aligned to the Economic Reconstruction and Recovery Plan (ERRP). The just energy transition, the digital transition, sustainable water infrastructure, and bulk freight and transport systems must be targeted, which would include ensuring that the localisation imperative is not overlooked.

Abba Omar (Chapter 15) outlines South Africa's experience in compacting. He uses the recent ERRP compacting process to reflect on the relationship between a developmental state, on the one hand, and the achievement of economic growth, increased employment, and reduced poverty and inequality, on the other. Several lessons emerge from this assessment. First, the author points to the ability of social partners to cohere around a mission that addresses a crisis. Second, this ability is truncated by the collective inability to drive consistent and measurable implementation. The state's lack of capacity to coordinate and drive this function and to operationalise the ERRP with concrete targets is identified as a key weakness. Abba Omar concludes that social compacting as a strategy for economic and employment growth and reduced poverty and inequality is hindered by low investment. Consequently, an elite pact is necessary, possibly aimed at increasing private-sector investment in the economy.

CONCLUSION

We live in a time of ongoing, intense domestic and global crises. It is a time when several serious, interrelated risks threaten domestic political, social and economic stability. Such risks include future pandemics, coups d'état and political instability on the African continent, threats to democracy around the world, and increased geopolitical schisms, evidenced by Russia's war in Ukraine and tensions between Western powers and China over Taiwan, which in turn are deeply intertwined with risks of financial meltdowns and economic recessions.

All these risks affect and often reverse developmental progress. The erosion occurs slowly over years and decades and is periodically punctuated by sudden and extremely damaging or disastrous shocks. The impacts of these disruptive events and trends are often cumulative, with countries' ability to recover from disasters and crises often limited by the prevalence of other, even more severe crises or disasters. Over the past few years, the world has lived through several of these crises and disasters, which have cumulatively weakened the resilience of households, businesses and public finances to withstand future crises. Unemployment, poverty and inequality have worsened around the world – albeit in varying degrees – since the global financial crisis of 2008, the subsequent widespread pursuit of austerity-led fiscal policies and the COVID-19 pandemic. Regarding the latter, the disruptions to energy, food, freight, and global and regional supply chains have contributed to rising inflation and the current cost-of-living crisis. Of course, a large proportion of the population in developing countries, including South Africa, have long been struggling with poverty, deprivation and cost-of-living crises. Therefore, the COVID-19 pandemic simply exacerbated already-high fuel and other prices and dealt another blow to struggling households.

The social unrest in KwaZulu-Natal and Gauteng in July 2021 provided a stark warning regarding the social tensions in South African society, which have been seriously exacerbated by the corrosive effects of the COVID-19 pandemic. These events demonstrated how a combination of political tensions and rising unemployment, poverty and inequality can trigger sudden, devastating loss of life and livelihood and billions of rands worth of damage to property and infrastructure. Another important lesson, emerging from the 2022 floods in KwaZulu-Natal, was the need for policies aimed at economic transformation to build in safeguards against the risk of unexpected natural disasters which can cause extensive damage, particularly at the household level. The weak coordination (across national, provincial and local governments) in the allocation of disaster response funds in the aftermath of the floods provides a poignant example of the shortcomings of the state, including an inability to provide basic services and social benefits in an efficient and effective manner, and the detachment of the economy from environmental concerns.

By the beginning of 2023, the world was facing a new bout of uncertainty and instability due to increased inflation and a shift away from quantitative easing towards quantitative tightening by the US Federal Reserve (US Fed) and the European Central Bank (ECB). This shift from a prolonged period of very low interest rates to high interest rates is set to create further global instability and uncertainty, including the possibility of contagion from financial and economic problems elsewhere, and exacerbate the risk of recession and sovereign debt defaults across the globe. These problems add to the socioeconomic disruptions caused by international challenges such as the COVID-19 pandemic, climate change and geopolitical conflicts as well as domestic problems relating to structural unemployment, poverty, inequality and the resultant erosion of the social fabric.

Consequently, there is even more urgency for broad-based economic transformation in South Africa aimed not only at transforming the economic sectors and their respective contributions but also the financialised MEC system of accumulation. Alongside the deindustrialisation and financialisation of the economy, South African households feel the negative effects of inadequate basic services and social transfers, lacklustre attempts at structural transformation and diversification, and the demobilisation of civil society and trade unions, exacerbated by the hyper-casualisation and informalisation of work.

Such interrelated state and private (corporate) weaknesses in a highly unequal and concentrated economy serve to deepen *and* perpetuate the accumulation crisis, persistently low economic growth rates, high levels of poverty, inequality and unemployment, as well as an expanding population of the working poor. Critically, too, they threaten the democratic social compact. These weaknesses have manifested within the context of an evolving political settlement and a conflicting macroeconomic policy landscape that, while emphasising stability and structural reforms, has, in fact, hindered the performance of South Africa's manufacturing sector (Bell et al., 2018).

REFERENCES

Bell, J., Goga, S., Mondliwa, P. and Roberts, S. 2018. 'Structural Transformation in South Africa: Moving Towards a Smart, Open Economy for All'. CCRED Working Paper No. 9/2018, https://ssrn.com/abstract=3269732, accessed 4 April 2022.

Freund, B. 2017. 'The significance of the minerals–energy complex in the light of South African economic historiography'. *Transformation,* 71 (1), 3–25.

Illife, J. 1999. 'The South African Economy: 1652–1997'. *Economic History Review,* 52 (1), 87–103.

Levy, B., Hirsch, A., Naidoo, V. and Nxele, M. 2021. 'South Africa: When Strong Institutions and Massive Inequalities Collide'. Carnegie Endowment for International Peace, https://carnegieendowment.org/2021/03/18/south-africa-when-strong-institutions-and-massive-inequalities-collide-pub-84063, accessed 4 April 2022.

Mazzucato, M. 2015. *The entrepreneurial state: Debunking public vs. private sector myths.* New York, NY: PublicAffairs.

Mazzucato, M. 2018. *The value of everything: Making and taking in the global economy.* New York, NY: PublicAffairs.

Mazzucato, M. 2021. *Mission Economy: A Moonshot Guide to Changing Capitalism.* New York, NY: Harper Business.

Mapungubwe Institute for Strategic Reflection (MISTRA). 2016. *The Great Recession and Its Implications for Human Values: Lessons for Africa.* Johannesburg: Mapungubwe Institute for Strategic Reflection.

Wolff, M. 2022. 'How to think about policy in a polycrisis'. *Financial Times,* 29 November 2022. https://www.ft.com/content/a1918fec-2c8f-4051-ad78-c300b0fc9adb, accessed 1 December 2022.

NOTES

1 The term 'polycrisis' has become popular recently. See, for example, Martin Wolff, *Financial Times* columnist, on 'How to think about policy in a polycrisis' (Wolff, 2022).

2 In fact, a form of capitalism should be developed in South Africa that delivers the type of economic transformation needed to build an egalitarian, resilient and democratic society.

INDEX

J

N

T

www.ingramcontent.com/pod-product-compliance
Lightning Source LLC
LaVergne TN
LVHW052014200926
848481LV00005B/1486
* 9 7 8 1 9 2 0 6 9 0 3 9 7 *